Assault from the Sea

ASSAULT FROM THE SEA

Essays on the History of Amphibious Warfare

EDITED BY LIEUTENANT COLONEL MERRILL L. BARTLETT, USMC (RET.)

Naval Institute Press
Annapolis, Maryland

Third printing, 1989

Library of Congress Cataloging in Publication Data
Main entry under title:

Assault from the sea.

Bibliography: p.
Includes index.
1. Amphibious warfare—History.   I. Bartlett,
Merrill L.
U261.A87   1983   359.8'3   83–2178
ISBN 0–87021–088–2

Printed in the United States of America

To the memory of my father
Lewis (Mickey) Bartlett
1904–82

Contents

Foreword

Ever since the days of the Phoenicians, the ability to land on defended shores has been a source of strength for those who possess it and a source of concern for those who must oppose it. Many people from many nations have grappled with the problem, both in theory and in practice. This anthology charts, most successfully, a wide range of amphibious thought and experience. As such, this effort by Lieutenant Colonel Merrill L. Bart-lett will have significant value both for the historian and for the futurist. In improving our national amphibious capability, we must merge an understanding of the lessons of the past with the promise of technology.

Robert H. Barrow
General, U.S. Marine Corps
Commandant of the Marine Corps

Prefatory Note

Far too many casual students of military history, both in and out of uniform, have relegated the art of amphibious warfare to a World War Two niche. Little serious thought has been given to the utility of amphibious forces either before or after that relatively short period.

To be sure, those war years saw such developments and refinements in the art of amphibious warfare that they constituted (in the view of Liddel-Hart, for one) probably the greatest tactical innovation of that period. In the Pacific, especially, the emerging tactical capability was matched to a clear-cut strategy, whose advance wargaming was so complete that the Pacific campaign held few if any surprises until the appearance of the *kamikaze* late in the war. In the European theater, the Allied amphibious capability also provided the means to regain the strategic initiative. The persuasive and steadily growing Allied amphibious threat imposed a strategic distraction upon Hitler that forced him to withhold a significant portion of his reserve instead of employing it on the eastern front where German manpower was desperately needed by the time of the Normandy invasion.

The advent of nuclear weapons followed by precision-guided weaponry has greatly thinned the ranks of true believers in major amphibious assaults against even moderately well-armed and emplaced defenders. In response to the challenge, new flexibility has been built into the air components of amphibious task forces and landing forces. Ever mindful of their role as practitioners of the art of the possible, amphibious forces continued to serve as workhorses in times of crisis.

Since the end of World War Two, most of the nonroutine deployments of U.S. forces have been amphibious. They have ranged from the division-sized assault at Inchon in the 1950s, to more individual-sized responsibilities of the *Mayaquez* variety in the 1970s, to the peace-keeping missions of the landings in Lebanon in 1982. Since 1945, in fact, nonroutine deployments of battalion-sized or larger amphibious forces have averaged about two per year.

Yet despite their demonstrated use over the years, amphibious forces still tend to be thought of as a ponderous relic of World War Two—haunted, in a sense, by widespread recollections of the Golden Age of Amphibious Warfare, which was in fact complex, deliberate, noisy, and usually lethal to great numbers of both attackers and defenders.

But things have been changing, albeit fitfully. New developments in amphibious ships and assault-landing craft are breaking the shackles of the 20-knot limit on speed of advance and the 8- to 10-knot limit on ship-to-shore movement. Progress is being made in overcoming other traditional amphibious limitations such as beach gradient and trafficability. New flexibility in combined surface and air attack capabilities may even solve a longstanding problem of amphibious warfare: how to initiate an assault from the sea (zero combat power at the water's edge). Instead of the bloody frontal assault, modern strategy would enable the traditional amphibious force to assume early localized tactical defensive postures by widening the amphibious-threat envelope. Defense at the high water mark would become impossible, and the defender would have to rely on counterattack after an unopposed landing. The ancient Chinese philosopher Sun Tzu recognized this combination of strategic offense and tactical defense as the best of both military worlds.

The conceptual framework for the introduction of late-developing surface technology must look well beyond the lessons of World War Two to see how technology can best be applied in amphibious operations.

John G. Miller
Colonel, U.S. Marine Corps
G3, III Marine Amphibious Force

Acknowledgments

The idea for this collection of essays had its genesis during a review of a Navy Reserve Officers Training Course entitled "The History of Amphibious Warfare." As designed, the course was more a history of the U.S. Marine Corps. While the marines are certainly deserving of their splendid reputation and particularly their role in the development of modern amphibious doctrine, I suggested to the review committee that the history of the Marine Corps could not be fairly equated to the history of amphibious warfare.

The committee agreed; other historical examples of amphibious warfare—successful and unsuccessful, tried and untried—need to be included in any course with such an encompassing title. But published works covering the broad spectrum of this subject are few. This anthology, drawing together published and unpublished essays, is the collective effort of numerous individuals to fill this void. I am indebted to the original committee associated with the revision of "The History of Amphibious Warfare": LtCol. John B. Fretwell, University of Florida; Maj. Maxwell D. Johnson, University of Virginia; Maj. John J. O'Leary, Auburn University; and Maj. Larry S. Schmidt, Headquarters Marine Corps. Support for our revision was ably provided by Mr. Norman E. Thrash and Maj. Donald L. Rosenberg, both of the staff of the Chief of Naval Education and Training.

The compilation and editing of this volume took place at the U.S. Naval Academy.

Support was wholehearted and generous; two superintendents, Vice Admiral William P. Lawrence and Vice Admiral Edward C. Waller III, and the Academic Dean, Dr. Bruce M. Davidson, were supportive. Three directors of the Division of English and History, Colonel Frank Zimolzak, Colonel James A. McGinn, and Colonel C.E. McDaniel, and two chairmen of the Department of History, Professor Larry V. Thompson and Professor Philip W. Warken, gave their wholehearted approval to my involvement in this project. All of my colleagues in the Department of History were helpful; I would especially like to thank Professor Paolo E. Coletta, Assoc. Professor Phyllis Culham, Assoc. Professor Craig L. Symonds, Assoc. Professor James P. Thomas, and Asst. Professor Jack Sweetman for suggestions as to content and coverage. Worthwhile ideas as to substance and scope were provided by Mr. Clayton Barrow, editor, the U.S. Naval Institute *Proceedings* and by Colonel John E. Greenwood, USMC (Ret.), editor, the *Marine Corps Gazette*.

The staff of Nimitz Library at the Academy did yeomen service in the search for elusive essays, many of which were published abroad. Mrs. Donna R. Hurley completed an exhaustive search of the literature with the aid of the computer. Assistance with interlibrary loans was cheerfully undertaken by Ms. Cathie K. Hall, Ms. Rosamond H. Rice, Mr. Adam M. Mecinski, Mr. William P. McQuade, Mrs. Gloria N. Perdue, and Mrs. Lucille S. Porter. The very best administrative support made this work possible; I am indebted to Miss Dana Cook, Mrs. Sue Miller, Mrs. Barbara Rutledge, Mrs. Bettie Sheridan, and Ms. Judy Waltz for their able assistance. Mrs. Agnes I. Hoover, Naval Historical Center (Photographic Section), Washington, D.C., and Mr. Clayton Barrow, editor, U.S. Naval Institute *Proceedings*, provided most of the photographs.

If the following pages suggest any skill on the part of the editor, then I am indebted to Professor Alvin D. Coox, San Diego State University, and Professor Stuart B. Kaufman and Professor Keith Olson, both of the University of Maryland.

The staff of the U.S. Naval Institute has been most supportive and understanding. Mr. Richard Hobbs, acquisition editor, assisted immeasurably with the administrative tasks associated with the preparation of this volume. Ms. Cynthia Barry edited each essay painstakingly. If readers are pleased with the easy readability of this anthology, then they are indebted to her.

Finally, my family has had to endure more than their share of dialogue on the subject of amphibious warfare. Additionally, my wife "volunteered" to compile the index. For their forbearance, I thank my wife, Blythe, and my children, Blythe and Brendan.

Introduction

For most American naval historians, the history of amphibious warfare follows a familiar outline. Discussions usually begin with an examination of the failure of the Gallipoli campaign during World War One. After more than a year of war, the opposing armies had reached an impasse on the western front; British offensives preceded by massive artillery barrages resulted in little besides horrendous casualties, and the front lines hardly moved. The conflict would not be ended by costly frontal assaults or, to use Winston Churchill's pungent phrase, by "sending our armies to chew barbed wire in Flanders."[1] Yet the disaster at Gallipoli convinced naval and military strategists that large-scale amphibious operations were impractical for modern warfare. The analysis of that campaign by the U.S. Marine Corps and the application of this study to the formulation of a modern and ultimately successful amphibious doctrine is well known to students of naval history.

The traditonal explanation of the role of amphibious warfare begins with Gallipoli and then traces the development of amphibious doctrine by the U.S. Marine Corps during the 1930s, mostly in anticipation of the island war against Japan, and largely on the basis of intelligence reports of Marine Corps Lieutenant Colonel Earl "Pete" Ellis. An early luminary on the subject of amphibious warfare, Ellis predicted supposedly the requirement for naval forces to wrest the mandated islands in the Pacific from the Japanese. As

one of the essays in this anthology reveals, Ellis did in fact journey to the Pacific in the early 1920s to see for himself, and he died there, apparently of alcohol abuse. The myth surrounding Ellis suggests that he submitted reports concerning the Japanese fortification of the islands in the Central Pacific, and these accounts served as the basis for preparations for the amphibious operations conducted by the Marine Corps in the Pacific during World War Two. An interesting tale, but it is only fancy and legend; the reasons for the employment of the U.S. Marine Corps in the Pacific during World War Two are found elsewhere.

In a series of costly but effective amphibious operations, island after island fell to U.S. Marine Corps and Army forces from 1942 to 1945. The efficacy of such naval warfare seemed hardly questionable, even though the high casualty figures stunned some observers. Yet in the immediate postwar years when the United States began a drastic alteration of its armed forces, the future of amphibious forces seemed in doubt. In 1949, General of the Army Omar Bradley remarked during congressional hearings: "I am wondering if we shall ever have another large-scale amphibious operation. Frankly, the atomic bomb, properly delivered, about precludes such a possibility."[2]

Less than two years later, a major amphibious operation was conducted during the

[1]Raymond Callahan, "What About the Dardanelles?" *American Historical Review* 78 (September 1978): 641–48.

[2]House Armed Services Hearings, October 1949, p. 525, quoted in BGen. Edwin H. Simmons, USMC (Ret.), "The Marines: Survival and Accommodation," a paper delivered at the George C. Marshall Foundation Conference, Lexington, VA, 25–26 May 1977.

Korean Conflict. Operation Chromite witnessed the landing of two divisions—U.S. Marine Corps and U.S. Army—at Inchon behind the lines of the invading North Korean Army. The brainchild of the indefatigable General of the Army Douglas MacArthur, the amphibious force was the "anvil" for the United Nations troops driving north from Pusan; the North Korean invasion of South Korea was broken. The worth of amphibious operations seemed to be proved by the success of the Inchon landing, while the military failures of the Korean Conflict served to discredit the emphasis on American airpower and the ability of manned bombers to isolate the battlefield.

The possibilities of amphibious warfare garnered little appreciation after the Korean Conflict. Subsequent naval campaigns were of limited scope. Confrontations of greater magnitude, such as the Cuban Missile Crisis of 1962, were settled without shots being fired even though major amphibious forces were deployed. Some observers of naval warfare found solace in the belief that amphibious warfare had become an anachronism, and their conclusions were buttressed by the limited impact of amphibious warfare on the Indochina Conflict.

Clearly, such a terse and parochial interpretation of the history of amphibious warfare is historically inaccurate. While the important role of the U.S. Marine Corps in the development of amphibious doctrine cannot be ignored, to suggest that the U.S. Marine Corps was the only contributor of important examples of successful amphibious operations is inaccurate historically. This anthology therefore begins with a discussion of a naval campaign conducted during the days of galley warfare, the invasion of Marathon in 490 B.C. The founder of the Naval War College, Rear Admiral Stephen B. Luce, was one of the first naval strategists to draw attention to the use of "naval infantry" or "marines" as an adjunct to naval warfare before the age of sail.[3] Subsequent early examples

of amphibious warfare are discussed in *Landing Operations* and *Amphibious Operations*, two early studies of amphibious warfare, long out of print.[4]

For the era encompassing the competition for empire, from the sixteenth to eighteenth centuries, numerous examples of amphibious warfare—successful and unsuccessful—abound. Naval planners began to see the existence of naval infantry trained and suited for amphibious operations as a permanent and important part of existing naval forces. From the decline of Spain as a great sea power in the sixteenth century through naval engagements in colonial North America a century later, the importance of amphibious operations was illustrated repeatedly. During the Napoleonic Wars, British forces were faced again and again with the requirement to conduct amphibious operations. Early perceptions of amphibious warfare in both the European and American littorals are discussed in thoughtful and well-researched essays in this anthology.

In the nineteenth century, from the end of the Napoleonic era to the advent of the Age of Mahan, several examples of amphibious operations demonstrated both an increased need for this type of seaborne warfare and the growing complexity of this adjunct to naval campaigns. A recently published study of British naval operations in the Persian Gulf toward the end of the Napoleonic era underscores the importance of amphibious warfare as an adjunct to the naval support necessary to maintain an empire during the age of sail.[5] The war between the United States and Mexico witnessed a relatively new thrust in amphibious warfare. Aggressive American navy commanders, disappointed because Mexico had no real navy with which to deal, devised a series of small amphibious operations—more correctly termed "amphibious raids." The forces for these forays came from a pool-

---

[3]M. Almy Aldrich, *History of the United States Marine Corps* (Boston: Henry Sheperd, 1875), ch. 2, pt. 1.

[4]Dr. Alfred Vagts, *Landing Operations* (Harrisburg, PA: Military Service Publishing, 1946), and Arch Whitehouse, *Amphibious Operations* (Garden City, NY: Doubleday, 1963).

[5]Edward Ingram, "A Scare of Seaborne Invasion: The Royal Navy at the Strait Hormuz, 1807–08," *Military Affairs* 46 (April 1982): 64–68.

ing of the marine guards aboard the various U.S. naval vessels on station off Mexico and California. Examples of amphibious warfare from mid-century to the age of Mahan can also be found in Asian waters: in Foote's punitive action against the Chinese in 1856, and in attempts by European powers to supplant local power in Vietnam.

Marine forces used typically in the small-scale amphibious operations characteristic of the age of sail had, by the middle of the nineteenth century, absorbed two important functions: that of playing a part in small amphibious units and that of maintaining order and discipline among the foreign-born enlisted force, usually obstreperous and prone to alcohol abuse. The latter assignment seemed at times more important than the former. But the exigencies of the age of Mahan and the emergence of powerful, coal-driven navies would change this perception.

The new navies of the Age of Mahan needed coaling stations, and amphibious forces stood ready to protect these supply points, usually small islands or prominent seacoast positions near potential areas of naval and military strife. This obvious requirement spawned a generation of acrimony between the U.S. Navy and Marine Corps, in which the latter interpreted the former's reformist attempts as sub-rosa machinations to have the Corps disbanded. Happily, the acrimony subsided and the advance base concept, as the new requirement was called, was tried first in 1913–14 and appeared successful. Large-scale amphibious operations occurred in Asian waters as well: the Japanese invaded Korea in 1894 as part of a small war with China; a conflict erupted between Russia and Japan in 1904–05, and the Japanese invaded Port Arthur in Manchuria with amphibious forces.

After World War One, military strategists debated the potential of manned aircraft and navalists argued endlessly over the relative merit of the battleship vs. the aircraft carrier.[6] Very little attention was paid to the possibilities of amphibious warfare. The doctrine thus developed by the U.S. Navy and Marine Corps would be used over and over again in the central Pacific, but not for the reasons imagined.

Marine Corps forces were used during the war with Japan, not because the landings were rehearsed in the 1930s in a scenario involving Japan, but because of interservice rivalry. Global strategy during the war was influenced greatly by the forceful and irascible chief of naval operations, Fleet Admiral Ernest J. King. King's interests were in the Pacific, and he left the conduct of the war in the Atlantic largely to his U.S. Army and British counterparts. U.S. Marine Corps forces were employed in the Pacific because they came under King's powerful hand, stretching from Washington, D.C., to Fleet Admiral Chester A. Nimitz' Pacific Fleet Headquarters in Hawaii.

The conduct of these various campaigns in the Pacific has received considerable study; each island invasion has been the subject of at least one lengthy monograph. Several works exist which discuss the entire range of amphibious operations in the Pacific; however, a fresh new generation of historians is at work examining these naval campaigns with a less sanguine view and at times appearing to be iconoclastic.[7] More important to the selection of the essays for this anthology, most studies of amphibious operations conducted during World War Two tend to ignore the role of the U.S. Army in amphibious warfare and of naval campaigns conducted by European forces, especially the Soviets. This anthology contains several essays to overcome this bias.

With President John F. Kennedy's enchantment with the possibilities of U.S. intervention to prevent the expansion of Marxist-inspired governments, amphibious forces seemed especially well-suited for the conduct of such military operations. Although not sent ashore, elements of at least two Marine Corps divisions were at sea during the

[6]Allan Moorehead, *Gallipoli* (New York: Harper and Row, 1956; reprint edition, Annapolis: The Nautical and Aviation Publishing Co., 1982).

[7]See, for example, Harry A. Gailey, *Peleliu* (Annapolis: The Nautical and Aviation Publishing Co., forthcoming).

Cuban Missile Crisis of 1962. On the continent of Asia, the Second Indochina Conflict erupted with increased communist insurgency in the early 1960s. The landing of American marines in the spring of 1965 seemed to underscore the continued efficacy of amphibious operations; however, U.S. Marines conducted few such forays after 1965 and those were of little importance to the overall outcome of the conflict. The South Vietnamese marines did conduct several important amphibious operations in this tragic conflict and one such campaign is the subject of an essay in this anthology. Riverine warfare, an aspect of amphibous warfare, received attention in the conflict; unfortunately, the U.S. Marine Corps—the logical practitioners of this form of amphibious warfare—was occupied otherwise in the northern privinces. Thus, the conduct of riverine warfare fell to U.S. Army and Vietnamese forces.

Since the tragic conclusion to America's commitment in Southeast Asia, the possibilities of major amphibious operations have seemed less attractive to most strategists, except in Marine Corps councils. The numbers of amphibious ships have declined steadily, and U.S. Navy planners are relying more and more on support from the merchant marine community. A recent position paper originating from the Office of the Chief of Naval Operations, in which priorities for 1983 are listed, contains no mention of increasing capabilities to support the conduct of amphibious warfare.[8]

The efficacy of amphibious operations has recently been brought under close scrutiny, this time by the British invasion of the Falkland Islands. In April 1982, Argentine forces took control of the Malvinas (as they renamed the British colony) and prepared to defend what they considered their lawful territory. Predictably to all but the Argentine government, the British mounted a considerable military and naval effort to retake the islands. In the following months, airborne and marine forces joined infantrymen from elite British units to retake the islands in a complicated and costly amphibious campaign. Faced with critical shortages of amphibious shipping, the admiralty was forced to put the luxury liners *Canberra* and *Queen Elizabeth II* into service as troop transports. In the following weeks, British losses were heavy: the destroyers *Sheffield* and *Coventry* were sunk, as well as the frigates *Ardent* and *Antelope*. Other vessels were added to the casualty list along with the loss of twenty-three aircraft.[9] Even though British naval and amphibious forces were eventually victorious in retaking the islands, critics questioned the feasibility of amphibious operations in the modern age.

Questions surrounding the feasibility of amphibious operations will no doubt continue to arise given the awesome potential of modern weapons technology. The essays selected for this anthology were meant to apply an historical solace by offering the lessons of the past. Serious students of the history of naval warfare may question the inclusion of a certain essay or the absence of a work on a known amphibious operation. The editor has been obviously constrained by the availability of scholarly material suitable for this volume and by the necessity to keep the length of the anthology within reasonable size. On balance, these historical analyses, and others similar in nature, continue to support the thesis that the projection of sea power ashore—an "assault from the sea"—remains a reasonable option of naval warfare.

Merrill L. Bartlett
Lieutenant Colonel, USMC (Ret.)
Annapolis, Maryland

---

[8]CNO position paper (undated [1982]), copy in possession of the author.

[9]"Falkland War Losses," *Washington Post*, 16 June 1982.

Assault from the Sea

AGE OF SAIL

Marathon, 490 B.C.

BY WILLIAM L. RODGERS

The great war between the Greeks and Persians in 480 and 479 B.C. had its origin a generation or more earlier, after Darius had reunited the Persian Empire established by Cyrus. The center of the Persian might lay in Persia and Media between the Caspian Sea and the Persian Gulf. Since the middle of the sixth century B.C., Cyrus and his son, Cambyses, had extended their power toward India on the east, and to the west they had conquered Syria, Egypt, and Asia Minor. In the latter region were included the Greek settlements which fringed its coasts and were particularly strong along its western shores bordering on the Aegean Sea.

After Darius had established himself as master of the empire, he extended its eastern limits as far as the Indus River and in about 512 B.C. he crossed the Bosphorus and invaded Thrace. He seems to have gone as far north as the mouth of the Danube, but his movement in this direction does not seem to have been successful. Nevertheless, he held all the southern part of Thrace, although his hold on the warlike inhabitants was not secure. On the whole, the Persian prestige was not raised by the expedition.

It is not entirely clear to modern historians what was the inducement for Darius to wish to extend his domains into Europe. It seems probable, however, that the free Thracians in Europe were in sympathy with their blood kindred in northwestern Asia Minor, as the Greeks of Europe were in sympathy with those

Greek and Roman Naval Warfare (Annapolis: U.S. Naval Institute, 1964), pp. 13–28. Reprinted by permission.

living on the eastern side of the Aegean. It is well known that the political subjugation of part of a district inhabited by a single race does not make for a quiet border. It might well have seemed to Darius that it was necessary for him to rule in the Balkan peninsula for the sake of preserving peace in western Asia Minor.

A few years after the somewhat insecure Thracian conquest, difficulties between Athens and Sparta caused the former to turn to the Persian governor of Lydia bordering on the Aegean Sea and to ask his aid. It is unnecessary to trace the relations between Athens and Persia. The result was that Athens became convinced that it must be prepared for open enmity with Persia, but hostilities were postponed by the outbreak in 499 B.C. of an Ionian revolt among the Greek colonies along the eastern shores of the Aegean, which had not long been subject to the Persians. In the first year of the insurrection, the Athenians and Eretrians aided in it, but then withdrew, although for a time the Ionians held their own. The revolt was not finally ended until 494 when the king's fleet destroyed that of the Ionians in the Battle of Lade, a position on the west coast of Asia Minor, about thirty miles south of Ephesus. The advance of the coastline upon the sea has now made the scene of the fight an inland position. The Persian fleet proceeded to gather the fruits of its victory by reducing the island states of the Aegean Sea. Macedonia and Thrace had taken advantage of the revolt to throw off Persian rule but had not taken part in hostilities, so the fleet next went to the

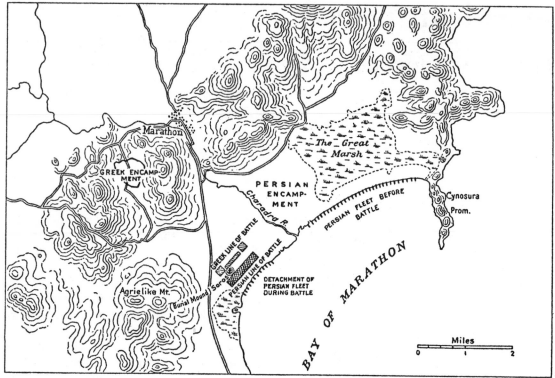

Battle of Marathon.

farther shores of the Propontis which it subdued.

In 492 the king was once more ready to push into Europe. Large Persian reinforcements were sent west from Susa, the Persian capital, and Mardonius, the son-in-law of King Darius, took command of all the forces ashore and afloat. He was successful in establishing his authority in Macedonia and southern Thrace, but, after this conquest, the fleet was greatly damaged by a gale it met in passing the promontory of Mount Athos and did not advance further. Nevertheless, the king by no means renounced his purpose of punishing Athens and Eretria for their aid to the Ionian revolt, while on the other hand these cities had abundant warning.

Persian Plan of Campaign against Athens in 490 B.C.

The experience gained in overcoming the Ionian insurrection combined with the further difficulties met by Mardonius seems to have caused the king to decide that the difficulty of moving a combined fleet and army through and beyond Macedonia for the conquest of Greece was such that, while he would not renounce his purpose, he would change his method. He determined that the obstacles to cooperation between army and navy on the long coast route from the Hellespont to Greece made a movement advisable by the short sea route directly across the Aegean from Samos to Euboea (Negropont) by the chain of islands. That line of travel forbade a great expedition, as the ships of those days were unequal to the transportation of the whole military strength of the great empire, and successive trips would be needed. It was the practice for rowing men-of-war to carry very few supplies on board in order to be light and speedy on the day of battle. They were therefore under the necessity of renewing stores at brief intervals. In particular, little drinking water was carried, and to the last days of rowing ships they were constantly hindered in the execution of their plans by the need to break off to renew their water.

Consequently, Darius decided to limit his objectives. He announced that he proceeded against the Athenians and Eretrians only, who had aided at the outbreak of the Ionian revolt. But it is probable that beyond the acknowledged purpose, the king wished to seize a secure base in the Attic peninsula whence he might afterwards advance to conquer all Greece.

The Persian fleet and army assembled in the summer of 490 in Cilicia on the south coast of Asia Minor, under the command of Datis, a Mede, who replaced Mardonius because of the latter's failure in 492. Herodotus does not tell us the number of men in the force, but says there were six hundred trieres which carried the infantry in addition to their crews, and there were horse transports. As has been previously mentioned, these early trieres were smaller than those of a generation or two later. Estimating their normal crews at one hundred twenty men, we may assume that the carriage of army stores would reduce the men on board to one hundred men each. Allowing fifty rowers, ten mariners and officers, and ten soldiers as the reduced crew of each, we have left room for not more than thirty soldiers as passengers.

When Herodotus says that the trieres numbered six hundred, his statement may mean that the horse transports were altered from trieres and were included in the six hundred. In ancient statistics of this sort, it is better to accept minimum figures. Let us suppose that three hundred trieres were fitted to carry horses at the usual rate of one horse as the equivalent of five men. Then each horse ship would take five horses with their riders. The ships' crews would then come to six thousand officers and mariners, thirty thousand rowers, and six thousand ship soldiers (epibatœ). To these we add as passengers fifteen hundred cavalry, seventy-five hundred infantry, and fifteen hundred noncombatants, a total of fifty-two thousand five hundred men with a combatant landing force, including the ships' soldiers, of fifteen thousand men as a maximum. (Some modern commentators put the Persian host present at the battle as low as four thousand.) This calculation merely serves to show that even on Herodotus's statement the expedition was not a very large one.

The Persian Army

As for the organization of the Persian army, the empire was divided into some twenty satrapies in each of which a state or group of states was allowed a considerable measure of local self-government, under the control of an imperial satrap, who was civil ruler and levied a provincial tax, payable to the king. Local security and order were imposed by a royal garrison in each satrapy, composed mainly of Medes and Persians, under a commander appointed by the king, directly responsible to him and independent of the satrap. When a great war made it necessary, provincial levies were made in addition to the regular army.

The Persian army took over much of its organization and armament from that of the Assyrian Empire which it overcame. There was cavalry, at first mounted archers and later lancers, but always skirmishers rather than shock troops. The infantry were divided into light and heavy archers, the latter having helmet and armor and frequently an attendant with a shield. There were also slingers who wore armor and took their places with the infantry of the line. From Spaulding's *Ancient Warfare*:

> The Assyrian tactics . . . depended upon fire power, open order, and free maneuver. The Medes, naturally a race of mounted archers, grafted the Assyrian infantry system upon their own, and adopted their wicker shields and short spears. Being horsemen, they continued to emphasize the cavalry, and being mountaineers, they neglected the chariot. The Persians copied the Medes; their native institutions being presumably very similar. They made the bow their principal weapon, and their infantry armament and equipment were not well adapted to the phalanx and shock tactics. The spear was short; the shield small and rounded, or else copied from the Assyrian type and used primarily to cover an archer while firing. . . .

No great changes had taken place between Cyrus and Darius. A comparison of accounts of both earlier and later dates would indicate a steady increase in weight of cavalry armor, a gradual substitution of the javelin for the bow in the mounted service, and an increase in the use of slingers. But these modifications did not affect the essential character of the army. It still made cavalry its principal arm and fire (meaning missile discharge) its principal mode of action. The heavy infantry formed the center of the line; having come to bowshot, it halted and opened fire from behind its wicker shields. The slingers and light infantry undoubtedly acted as skirmishers, retiring behind the line when they were "squeezed out," and possibly using overhead fire, although the opportunity for this must have been very scant, for the heavy troops themselves were formed with considerable depth. The infantry made no effort to close with the enemy; the fire must have been in the nature of a holding attack. The decisive charge was given by the cavalry on the wings.

The Greek Soldier

Unlike the Persian, the Greek relied on shock tactics rather than on missiles.

The Greek military system was based on universal military service. . . . Organization and tactics were based on heavy infantry and shock. . . . The typical Greek warrior was the *hoplite* or armored pikeman. As auxiliary arms there were cavalry, and light infantry including archers, slingers, and *peltasts* or javelin men, protected chiefly by the small shield which gave them their name. The universal formation was the phalanx—a heavy line of armored pikemen. . . . Eight ranks was a very common depth. . . . Of course, only the front ranks could engage, the others replaced losses and kept up the forward pressure. . . . The fire power of the phalanx was zero. Its auxiliaries remedied this defect only in part, for if used in front as skirmishers, they had to be drawn off to the flanks some time before contact, and their weapons being of short range, overhead fire could not be very effective. The charge of the phalanx, however, was almost irresistible, its defense almost unbreakable. In either case, its weakness was the flank, for its maneuvering ability was very small, and it was difficult to change front or refuse a flank. . . .

Here was where it most needed its auxiliary arms. But these auxiliaries dared not attack decisively, even in flank; they might annoy the (hostile) phalanx, check the momentum of its charge, or weaken its defense; but only another phalanx could break it.

Although the decisive battles, both by sea and land, were fought in the second Persian expedition under Xerxes, yet the first in Darius's reign with Datis as commander was most important to both sides in giving them knowledge of each other's strength, armament, and practices.

Campaign of Marathon

This account of the campaign of Marathon follows generally as to times and geography the comments of Grundy on Herodotus as given in his work *Great Persian War*. The fleet, with the army on board, left Cilicia in the summer, probably in the latter part of July 490 B.C., and proceeded to Samos in Ionia.

From Samos the fleet steered west southwest to Naxos which had resisted the Persians in 499. This time the Persians had a partial success, but most of the inhabitants escaped to the hills. After burning the city, the expedition moved through the islands toward Eretria, collecting troops and hostages from each. (There could not have been many additional men embarked, for lack of room.) Eretria, the first objective of the expedition, is in the island of Euboea on the Strait of Euripus which separates Euboea from Attica. The city had heard of the coming expedition and sent to Athens for help. Athens could spare little aid, but did what she could. On arrival at Eretria the Persians met resistance and for six days they were withstood until treachery gave them possession. They pillaged the city and enslaved the inhabitants.

After a short delay the Persians crossed the water to Marathon, a point on the Attic coast about 25 miles from Eretria and 26 miles by road and 60 miles by sea from Athens. Hippias, an exiled Athenian tyrant and renegade, had advised this place for disembarkation, as it was suitable ground for a cavalry camp. The site of the landing was a beach more than 5 miles long, running northeast and southwest, protected from the northeast by the rocky promontory of Cynosura or Kynossema, extending out as a breakwater for more than a mile. A plain reaches inland from the beach for a distance varying from 1½ to 2 miles. A large marsh fills most of the northeast part of the plain and a smaller marsh terminates it on the southwest, and the bed of the torrent Charadra cuts across the middle of the plain. Behind are rocky hills. The total area of the plain is about 10 square miles, but of this the marsh cuts off one-half and the torrent bed forms an obstacle running through the other half. Two roads lead to Athens. The more direct one, running back into the hills, leaves the plain by two branches which soon join and lead to Athens over a difficult path impracticable to cavalry, which was the most valued arm of the Persians. The other road leaves the plain along the line of the beach and later turns inland to Athens. This was a very good route for cavalry.

The reason for landing at Marathon as given by Herodotus is not very convincing, for the Athenian plain itself and the neighboring one on the Bay of Eleusis were better for cavalry than that of Marathon, although, because of proximity to the city, more exposed to counterattack during disembarkation. The political situation in Athens gives an adequate explanation of the landing at Marathon. The party divisions were very high in the city. Hippias, who was with the Persians, had his party in Athens, and they were expected to aid in giving possession to the enemy. Herodotus tells of a helio-message by a flashing shield within the city, which was believed to have guided the Persian movement, although no one could be discovered with whom to connect it. The Aristocratic party in Athens, headed by Miltiades, was anti-Persian; the Democratic party was willing to have Hippias restored to the control of the city by the help of the Persians. The probable object of the Persians in landing at Marathon was not to seek a battle there but to draw the Athenian garrison away from Athens. At Marathon the Persians could afford to wait while treachery should have time to work, and if the garrison should come to Marathon, there would be more opportunity for the conspiracy to grow in the city. Then, either with or without a battle at Marathon, a part of the Persian force might embark with the fleet and proceed with the fleet to Athens (about 60 sea miles) while the remainder of the Persians at Marathon could contain the Athenian field army there.

In readiness for the campaign, the Athenians had an understanding with the Spartans, who were to come to the aid of the former when summoned. Accordingly, on the news of the fall of Eretria, the Athenians sent a runner to the Spartans to call them out. He is said to have finished the trip of 140 miles on the second day, which was the ninth day of the third (lunar) month (about 2 September). He returned immediately with the announcement that the Spartans would come, but that religion required them to wait until after the full moon. They started on the fifteenth and arrived at Athens on the seventeenth (of the third month).

Herodotus does not tell us on what day the Athenians heard of the Persian landing at Marathon, but a comparison of other dates makes it appear to have been about the tenth of the month. The Athenian field force then departed to meet the enemy, under Callimachus, the polemarch (commander-in-chief), and ten generals, each commanding one of the ten tribal regiments which made up the army. Of these leaders, Miltiades was the most prominent politically and the council of war and the polemarch seem to have deferred very much to his views as to the conduct of the campaign. It is probable that his ascendency in the decisions affecting the actions of the army was largely due to the powers of the army council whose majority was led by Miltiades. It may be that when Callimachus and the council had decided on the general plan, they left Miltiades with a free hand to carry it out, or Miltiades may have been the author of the plan which the council adopted.

Herodotus does not give the size of the Greek army which went to Marathon, but later classical authors estimate it at from nine to ten thousand Athenians and one thousand allied Plataeans. Grundy points out that as the Athenian numbers at Plataea in 479 B.C. were eight thousand heavy-armed and as

many light-armed troops, and that many citizens were serving at the same time in the
fleet at Mycale, we should think that ten
thousand at Marathon is an underestimate,
although not a large one. In spite of the large
party in the city hostile to the government,
Grundy believes that no considerable garrison was left in the city. On the other hand,
if we start with an estimate of the Persian
forces based on six hundred ships carrying
fifteen hundred cavalry and thirteen thousand five hundred infantry, of which six
thousand properly belonged to the ships'
crews, and suppose that half of the ship soldiers were landed at Marathon, we have only
ten thousand infantry available for the battle
and we know that the Greeks were less, so
we may suppose their numbers to have been
only seven to eight thousand, leaving a considerable garrison in the city.

When the Athenians marched out over the
upper road on the tenth, they were under the
impression that they would meet the Persians on the way. The Persians, however, had
not moved since landing on the spot, and the
Athenians camped in the hills, about a mile
from where the road forks as it goes down to
the plain. This was a strong position, as the
Persians could not effectively attack in the
hills, and were they to march by the beach
road on Athens or begin embarkation to move
there by sea, they could be attacked at a disadvantage. Here the enemies lay for several
days, the Persians encamped on the plain with
their ships anchored close to the beach, probably with their sterns aground for easy communication. The Greeks held their strong
position in the hills. There must have been
some communication between the Persians
and their partisans in the city, so that they
learned that the Spartans were to start out
on the fifteenth after the full moon. As time
passed and the expected uprising in the city
did not take place, it must have become apparent to the Persians that they would have
to take decisive action before the arrival of
the Spartans or the campaign would fail. In
consequence, it seems probable, although
Herodotus's account is not informative, that
the Persians embarked a part of the army,
including all the cavalry, to move directly on
the city, while the other half remained in
position to hold the Athenian army away from
the city.

It is probable that the Persian camp was
northeast of the torrent bed, between it and
the marsh, with the ships nearer Cynosura.
The position gave room enough for both infantry and horses and the nearer the ships
were to Cynosura the better shelter they had
from the usual north and northeast winds.
Moreover, there was only a narrow stretch
of beach between the marsh and the sea, so
that it was possible for a very small force at
the end of the beach to cover the embarkation of the entire expedition. If the ships had
their sterns resting on the beach as previously suggested, the embarkation could be
readily carried out, even in the presence of
the enemy. Although the Persian camp was
on the northern side of the Charadra torrent
bed, it was from the southwestern end of the
plain that the best road led to Athens. Therefore, the part of the Persian army which was
to contain the Greeks moved to a position
on the right bank of the Charadra in order to
be able to take the road itself and at the same
time close it to the enemy. This decision of
the Persians seems to have taken effect on
the sixteenth of the month (9 September).

Upon the arrival at Marathon, the Athenian generals held a council of war, at which
Callimachus, strongly urged by Miltiades,
decided in favor of battle. But there was no
need for haste. The longer the Persians remained inactive, the better chance there was
that the Spartans would arrive before the battle. The conduct of the battle was left by
consent of the council to Miltiades. He was
the leader of his party and a distinguished
ruler and soldier, and Callimachus was willing to be guided by him, although in the battle he did not relinquish the position of honor
on the right flank which was his as commander-in-chief and occupying which he lost
his life in pursuit of the enemy. The center
of the field of battle is no doubt indicated by
the great mound (soros) heaped up over the
graves of those who lost their lives in the
fight. It is a mile and a quarter south of the

Charadra and half a mile from the shore, and about the same distance from the Little Marsh.

As the Persian fleet with the cavalry and right wing on shipboard stood off for Athens the remaining left wing drew up nearly parallel to the beach and offered battle between the road and the beach with the necessary detachment of ships against the beach in the rear ready to take the soldiers off when their object had been accomplished. As was said, the usual Persian tactics were to stand and open a missile fire with their main body, while the flanking cavalry enveloped the enemy and attacked his rear. On this occasion there was no cavalry, for that had started for Athens on shipboard, but the idea of envelopment was an essential part of the missile fight for which the Persians were armed. We must give their intelligence service credit for having ascertained the number opposed to them, and, consequently, it would have been prudent for Datis, the Persian commander, to have retained enough with him to form a line longer than that which he might expect the Greeks to occupy in confronting them. Probably he did so. But this superiority in length of the battle line would not be excessive, for his available strength was not overwhelming, and he had to take Athens and possibly meet the Spartans before completing the work. On the side of the Greeks, their strength was in the frontal charge and the close spear-fight, and their weak point was in the flank, where a serious attack was disastrous.

If we take the grave mound as being near the center of the battleground, and note the remark of Pausanias in his geography that part of the Persian army was driven into one of the marshes, it then seems probable that the Persian line faced northwest with the left resting near or even across the beach road to Athens, with the marsh nearly in its rear, and the right wing extending nearly parallel to the beach. Its length did not exceed a mile and was probably less. It was Miltiades's solution of the problem of preventing Persian envelopment to which our European civilization is indebted for victory and which gave

him enduring fame. The council and Callimachus consented to his spreading the somewhat scanty Greek numbers over the entire frontage of the enemy so as to deprive him of the opportunity of envelopment except by weakening his main front. The light-armed Greeks no doubt were stationed so as to give what protection they could to the flanks of the phalanx.

But the mere extension of the Greek line was not the principal feature of Miltiades's plan. Not only did he make the phalanx cover the whole Persian front, but he still further reduced the number of ranks in the center in order to increase them in the two wings. This strengthening of the flanks at the expense of the center gave the Greeks the best chance of success where it would be most profitable to obtain it and where the enemy was accustomed to make his victorious effort.

The sight of the Persians embarking half their army while the other wing formed to close the beach road was clearly the opportunity for which Miltiades was waiting. The Greek army descended from its hill camp and formed opposite, and about a mile away from, the Persians who, as Herodotus says, were surprised to see so small a body venture to attack without either archers or cavalry. It is not necessary to believe that this means that there were no light-armed Greeks at all, merely that the Persians were not looking to have a close fight thrust upon them. Herodotus says that the Greeks formed their line and then advanced on the Persians at a run. It is impossible, however, that heavily armed men could have run a mile and still have strength remaining for a fight with unwearied foes. All through the history of warfare, both ashore and afloat, every prudent commander husbands the strength of his men to bring them fresh to the great physical exertions and exhausting emotions of battle. What is probable is that the attacking Greeks advanced slowly until they approached archers' range. There, just outside of range of, say, 200 yards, they waited to rest and restore alignment, and when ready and the sacrifices were reported as favorable, they moved at speed through the fire zone and attacked with the spear in close formation.

The battle is described as long and obstinate. The weak Greek center was not strong enough to overcome the opposing archers, who were Persians by race and the best troops and who were armed also with short swords for in-fighting. On the contrary, the Persian center was able to break through the thin hostile line and pursue it toward the hills. But the heavy Athenian wings, secure from envelopment, were successful and the two victorious wings both turned on the Persian center. In this new situation the Greeks must have been nearer to the beach than the enemy, if, indeed, they did not actually interpose. This second phase of the action became completely favorable to the Athenians. They destroyed the Persian center also and pursued it to the beach and laid hold of the ships to which the fugitives were escaping. They called for fire to destroy them and succeeded in capturing seven. When we think of the physical difficulty in wading out to take possession of ships manned by seamen and rowers who had not been engaged and were waiting only to rescue their comrades, it is evident that the defeat of the Persians must have been overwhelming to permit as many as seven prizes. The Greek effort at the water's edge must have been the supreme one, for here fell the commander-in-chief as well as another of the ten generals, besides many others of note.

The Persians at Athens

The escaping ships with the defeated army went to Aegileia Island, about 8 miles away from Marathon, where they had confined their Eretrian captives and, embarking them and the booty, followed the other division around Cape Sunium to the Bay of Phalerum off Athens. While the battle was in progress, the first division of the Persian force was on its way to the anchorage off Athens. It is not likely that it could have made the passage in less than thirty hours. The speed of such a great number of ships, laden with troops and spoil, must have been less than usual, not more than 2 knots. Thus, the victorious

Greeks did not delay for rejoicings but hastened back to Athens (only 26 miles away) and were able to camp outside the city on the hills above the port before the enemy had arrived. At Marathon they had camped on the ground of a temple to Hercules, so here they chose the precincts of another temple to the same deity who had brought them good fortune the day before.

The Spartans started from home at the full moon and made the 140-mile march to Athens in three days. They arrived before they were expected, on the seventeenth, and only a few hours after the Athenian army returned. No doubt their presence still further discouraged the Persians, who made a brief stay at Phalerum for a junction with the second division of the fleet bringing the Eretrian captives, after which all departed for Asia.

Review of Campaign

The Athenian tradition magnified this great victory, and Creasy, in his *Fifteen Decisive Battles of the World*, includes it in his series. Such a place it scarcely deserves, for Darius's defeat merely provoked him to put forth the utmost might of Persia to overcome this petty people whence encouragement had come to his revolted subjects in 499 and who had now defeated and driven off his punitive expedition. He was resolved on an ethnic frontier like so many other great rulers and for such as Europe has recently striven without success. But Darius did not live long enough to complete his preparations and left the accomplishment of the task to his son and successor, Xerxes. The decisive battles came ten years later in the sea battle of Salamis and still a year later on shore at Plataea, when European superiority in battle over Asiatics was established in that part of the world, the region of the Aegean, till the Turks came fifteen hundred years later.

In reviewing the campaign, whose tactics set the precedent for the conduct of later maritime effort, we must first note the supreme strategic and tactical skill shown by Miltiades. Although not the commander-in-chief, his hegemonic control over the council of tribal leaders was such that he did with the army as he pleased. No doubt when the Athenians hastened from Athens toward the landing place of the enemy, they expected or thought it probable that the encounter would take place in the hills. But as they marched, successive runners must have told them that the enemy was inactive on the beach. When the Athenians arrived and recognized that they held the entrance to the hills and were nearer to Athens by that route than the enemy was by the beach road, Miltiades had the strategic insight to perceive that he could choose the place and time of battle. For him, delay was advantageous, for the Spartans were coming, although late. He therefore did nothing till the Persians showed their hand, confident that then he could fight them to advantage either in the hills, if they made a frontal attack on his camp, or as they embarked, if they took ship. If they took the beach road he could forestall them before Athens.

As for the tactical features, Miltiades so managed it that there was no opportunity for the Persians to use the maneuver for which they were armed and trained, namely, the enveloping archers' fight. In their charge the heavy-armed Greeks were under fire scarcely more than a minute and a half, and in that time a good bowman could get off no more than seven or eight arrows. The total losses of the Greeks were 192 killed against 6,400 Persians, and the most severe fighting was in the close action when attempting to seize the ships. It is plain that the admirable thing above all was Miltiades's decision to attack the army of the great empire and abide by the result. We can now see that the victory had to go to the spear and the panoply but it was to Miltiades's credit that he was the first of European Greeks to venture and win. He showed the way to many others.

The land fight at Marathon is discussed here for two reasons: first, because naval warfare in early times was largely an affair of landing and raiding for booty, as in this case; and, second, because the tactics of land fighting developed before their principles were applied in fleet battles. The tactics of Marathon became the norm of naval battle for the next generation, after which tactical novelties found a basis in improved ships handled by skillful seamen who were also thorough drill masters. Marathon taught the Greeks that successful land battle against Asiatics would be through the spear fight against missiles and the refusal of envelopment. This idea developed as naval warfare progressed.

Inconclusive Victory at Marathon

The captives Datis brought back from Eretria were well treated by Darius who settled them on lands he gave them near Susa, his capital. But the capture of Eretria was a small accomplishment for the great king. In spite of the final suppression of the Ionian revolt after years of effort, the campaign of Marathon must have greatly shaken Persian prestige, for the king's authority was based on his Medes and Persians by race who held in subjection a great number of unrelated and unsympathetic tribes and nations. The royal garrisons everywhere imposed peace and order under which labor and industry were remunerative to all the vast population of workers. If the king's armies failed for long to grant his subjects peace, his empire would pass away like those of his predecessors, the Assyrians and the Babylonians.

A new attempt against Greece was therefore indispensable, and the king had been shown that he could establish a foothold in European Greece only by a force large enough to meet a formidable combination among the Greek states. This would require much time, for the organization of the empire was such that it was a prolonged affair to call out the tribal levies to supplement the standing army of Persians by race. Not only the men but the munitions required time to provide. Besides, Darius was now growing old and it is very probable that his personal weakness was felt in the outlying provinces. However this may be, in 486 Egypt revolted and the next year the old king died. It was not until 484 that his successor, Xerxes, recovered Egypt and was able to prepare for an European campaign.

Hastings, 1066

BY BRIGADIER C. N. BARCLAY, CBE, DSO, BRITISH ARMY (RET.)

The publication of this number of *The Army Quarterly and Defence Journal* coincides almost exactly with the 900th anniversary of the Battle of Hastings—14 October 1066.

Information about the Norman Conquest is meager. The remarkable pictorial record—the Bayeux Tapestry—and nearly all the old chronicles, were inspired by Normans, have a Norman bias, and are otherwise not entirely reliable. This account is the result of several years research and a number of visits to the battlefield. It is based on known facts, supplemented by reasoned probability. Where uncertainty exists it has been indicated.

Very few events in history compare in importance with this battle. It lasted only a few hours and only a few thousand men took part, but it completely changed the story of England and subsequently many other parts of the world.

On 5 January 1066 the childless king of England—Edward the Confessor—died, after a reign of twenty-four years. He had been a scholar rather than a man of action: the son of a Saxon father and a Norman mother, he had spent most of his life in Normandy and was French-speaking. The Confessor has been aptly described as "a French monk rather than an English king," and indeed he is best known as the founder of Westminster Abbey and for his introduction of Normans into the leading appointments of church and state. This Norman "fifth-column" was to prove very useful to William during the invasion period.

The Army Quarterly and Defence Journal, "England's Last Invasion: the Battle of Hastings—1066," 93 (October 1966): 41–46. Reprinted by permission.

On Edward's death he was succeeded by Harold, the son of the great Earl Godwin. Although Harold's claim on hereditary grounds was a poor one, he was a true Saxon, the late king's brother-in-law, and a man of sterling character. Here it must be emphasized that the English Crown had never been strictly hereditary. Nomination by the Witan (or Council of Leaders) was the main factor and Harold had received that nomination—unanimously it is believed.

Nevertheless, on hearing the news of Harold's accession, Duke William of Normandy immediately denounced him as a usurper and perjurer, on the grounds that Edward and Harold had both, some years previously, acknowledged him as the rightful heir. The duke promptly followed words with deeds and started preparations for the invasion of England. The struggle between the forty-four-year-old Saxon Harold and the thirty-eight-year-old William of Normandy had begun.

The Norman Invasion and the Battle of Hastings

Duke William's first actions were for the security of his own realm during the period he would be away on the English adventure. He obtained the early approval of Pope Alexander II, who sent him a special banner and a ring said to contain a lock of St. Peter's hair. It is likely that William also obtained some form of guarantee from the French king that he would not attack Normandy during his absence.

His next step was to plan the collection and building of sufficient shipping to convey

Detail of the Bayeux Tapestry showing the Normans arriving in England, 28 September 1066. Courtesy of Photo Zodiaque.

his force of men and horses, together with their supplies, across the English Channel.

Lastly he had to assemble a force of the right kind, and sufficient strength, for the enterprise. This force was not entirely Norman: it contained a number of adventurers from other parts of Europe—Bretons, Frenchmen, and Flemings—attracted by promises of grants of land and other "loot," if the invasion succeeded. By the middle of August all was ready, but the expedition was not to sail for another six weeks—supposedly owing to contrary winds.

We can now take a peep at what was happening in England. Harold received early warning of the duke's intentions and, with the English fleet based on south coast ports and army contingents at strategic places, prepared to give the Normans a hot reception. By mid-September the expected invasion had not taken place and it was then that a series of circumstances arose which completely upset Harold's plans. He was compelled to discontinue his naval patrols and send the fleet to London to revictual. At the same time he had to disband most of the levies (or *fyrd*) of the southern counties who had been guarding the coast. By custom these levies were limited to forty days service a year.

That was not the end of Harold's troubles. Early in September there came a threat of invasion in the North, from Harald Hardrada, the warrior king of Norway in collusion with Tostig, the English Harold's estranged brother. The Norwegians landed on the northeast coast in mid-September, defeated an English force under earls Edwin and Morcar on 20 September, and then set up camp at Stamford Bridge about 5 miles from York. Harold, on receipt of this news, hurried north with his housecarls (the elite English household troops) and, raising the northern levies, surprised and completely defeated the Norwegians at Stamford Bridge on 25 September. Hardrada and Tostig were both killed.

Meanwhile conditions in the English Channel had become more favorable for William, and the Norman duke set sail and landed unopposed near Pevensey, on the Sussex coast, on 28 September. The story goes that Harold received word of this new invasion while in York celebrating his victory over the Norwegians. Instantly he took steps to meet the new situation by starting out with his housecarls on a 195-mile march to London, at the same time sending word for the midland, eastern, and southern levies to assemble in the capital. By about the 6 October the king was in London awaiting the men coming in from nearby shires.

Almost immediately after landing William moved his army a few miles to a prominent hill overlooking the port of Hastings. There he constructed a fortified camp, sent out foraging parties to collect supplies, and terrorized the neighboring countryside.

Historians differ as to the original plans of the two leaders; but it seems likely that Harold, who had a reputation for impetuosity, intended to deliver a surprise attack on William's camp in the same way as he had dealt with Hardrada of Norway. William, although a resolute leader in battle, was more cautious in his preliminary arrangements. It appears probable that he intended to remain in his fortified camp, let the English attack and batter themselves against his defenses, and then give the coup de grâce by a counterattack with his powerful force of mounted knights. As we shall see, circumstances were to arise which resulted in the reversal of these plans: William was to do the attacking and Harold's English assume the defensive.

Before describing the actual battle it will be as well to give a brief description of the armaments, organization, strengths, and methods of fighting of the opposing forces.

The English army consisted of two distinct elements—the housecarls, or regular household troops, and the shire levies or *fyrd*. The housecarls were mounted, but they always fought on foot, using their horses for mobility. The levies were a part-time militia who could be called out for forty days per annum in an emergency. They had no means of movement except on their feet and consequently were rarely employed far from their own homes. The English weapons were the bill (a long-handled form of battleaxe) and the spear. Some men carried slings and it is thought there may have been some archers, but only a few. A good many of the levies were armed only with farm implements. All the housecarls and many of the levies carried a shield, some being round, but most of them kite-shaped. These shields were used to form the famous "shield wall" of Saxon sagas and

poems, behind which they fought when on the defensive. The English soldiers of the eleventh century had little tactical skill, relying for success on tough hand-to-hand fighting. The strength of the English army at Hastings has been grossly exaggerated by some writers. It is impossible to give a precise figure, but at the beginning of the battle it was probably about six thousand (including about twelve hundred housecarls), with reinforcements coming in piecemeal throughout the day.

The Norman army consisted of about seventy-five hundred infantry similar to the English levies, but probably much better trained and equipped. There were also about thirty-six hundred mounted knights, who differed from the housecarls by fighting mounted—a form of action unknown to the English. These estimates of the Norman strength have been worked out from the number of ships believed to have been available—namely about seven hundred—and are thought to be approximately correct. The numbers engaged in the actual battle were certainly less, owing to sickness and the fact that a garrison is believed to have been left at the fortified camp at Hastings. The knights carried a battleaxe, a spear (or lance), and usually a sword, and were also equipped with a kite-shaped shield. William's foot-soldiers carried a battleaxe or lance and a shield. The Normans also had a considerable force of archers, probably about one thousand. These were not equipped with the powerful longbow of a later period, but with a much smaller type with a range of probably little more than 100 yards. As will be seen from the account of the battle which follows, the Normans had developed an efficient system of fire and movement between archers and knights.

By about 9 or 10 October we find Harold in London assembling and organizing his army. Some of his advisors are thought to have urged delay, in order to give time to assemble an overwhelming force, but the king by nature favored a bold policy. He was also probably influenced by the fear of Norman reinforcements arriving and by a desire to spare southern England from the ravages of William's patrols. In the Norman camp there were signs of impatience at what some leaders regarded as the duke's overcautious strategy. They would have preferred a rapid march on London.

We can skip the next few days and turn our thoughts to the situation on the evening of 13 October. By then Harold had made up his mind, and his leading troops were in the process of taking up a position on Senlac Hill, some 7 miles northwest of Hastings. In all probability this was intended to be a covering position for the assembling of his army, preparatory to an attack on the Norman camp at Hastings. Some time that day Duke William became aware of the king's intentions and decided to advance and attack him on Senlac Hill. On receipt of news of the Norman advance Harold decided to convert his covering position into the main one for a defensive battle.

Senlac Hill is a low ridge facing south on which the town of Battle and Battle Abbey now stand. About a mile to the south was Telham Hill, a feature of some prominence, but with gentle slopes. In between these two hills was a valley along which ran the Sandlake Stream, at that time probably not a serious obstacle to man or horse, but making the surrounding ground soft and marshy. The whole area was open country, devoid of houses and with some, but not very many, trees. About a mile to the north of Senlac Hill was the southern edge of a dense forest—the Weald—which stretched nearly all the way to London, more than 50 miles distant. A single track connected London and Hastings and ran through the center of what was to become the battlefield.

The early morning of the fateful day—14 October 1066—found the English army in position on Senlac Hill on a frontage of about 1,000 yards with their flanks protected by what the old chroniclers described as "ravines." William's army was in process of deploying on the lower northern slopes of Telham Hill. By about 9:00 A.M. the two armies were facing each other—in my estimation about 700 yards apart—in full battle array. The Normans were in three divisions:

Right: French and Flemings, with Eustace of Boulogne and the Norman Roger of Montgomery in command.
Center: Normans, under the duke.
Left: Mainly Bretons, with the Breton Count Alan Fergant in command.

Each division had three echelons. The archers were in front, behind them were the men-at-arms (or infantry) and in rear the mounted, lightly armored knights. The tactical plan was for the whole army to advance: on getting within effective range, probably about 80 yards, the archers would open fire. The infantry would then advance and attempt to make gaps in the defenders' line through which the mounted knights could penetrate and create havoc in rear of the position.

The Norman duke's strategy had given him a considerable initial advantage. He had brought his men to the battlefield well organized and fresh; whereas Harold's army, hastily assembled in London and having just completed a long and tiring march, was forced to fight defensively instead of attacking and was incomplete when the battle started. His men continued to arrive in driblets throughout the day.

It is probable that the battle started at about 9:00 A.M., or perhaps a little later, when the Norman army began its first attack. This attack was a definite failure, although it had an important sequel. Everywhere the duke's men were repulsed. On their right and in the center the withdrawal was orderly, but on the left the Bretons poured down the hill in headlong flight. This proved too much for some of the English on that flank who, contrary to Harold's orders, broke ranks and rushed down the hill in pursuit. The duke reacted quickly: collecting a body of mounted men from his center division he charged the pursuing English in flank. Very few escaped. This was a substantial local success for the Normans, but the English position remained intact.

There followed a pause in which William reorganized his force for another assault, and

Harold repaired his disorganized right flank. This pause is thought to have lasted at least an hour, probably considerably more.

The second attack took much the same form as the first, but was more successful in inflicting casualties on the English. For a second time some of William's troops retreated in disorder, being closely followed by over-eager English, and once again the duke managed to inflict heavy casualties on the pursuers by charging them in flank with his mounted knights. Exactly where this took place remains in doubt but probably in the center or possibly on the right. This incident has led to the legend of a feigned retreat by the Normans in order to entice the English from their defensive position. It is an attractive story, but I am not convinced that it *was* feigned. Although the Saxon position was still unbroken it had been seriously weakened by heavy casualties, particularly aong the leaders and the housecarls who formed the front line and had borne the brunt of the fighting. There is evidence that at this stage the line was considerably contracted, thereby forfeiting the protection of the "ravines" on the flanks.

There followed another long pause. Sunset on this day was about 5:00 P.M. and by now it was well on in the afternoon. The duke must have realized that the hours of daylight permitted only one more assault, but he had good reasons for believing that English resistance was seriously weakened.

The final attack began in the late afternoon, and slightly different tactics were employed. The archers were ordered to use high angle fire and concentrate on the area oc-cupied by Harold—conspicuously marked by his two standards, the Royal Standard of Wessex and his personal one, The Fighting Man. It is also probable that strong detachments of mounted knights were directed against the now open flanks of the English position. At an early stage the king was wounded by an arrow—shot in the eye it is believed—and this may be said to have been the beginning of the end. His two brothers, Gurth and Leofwine, and most of the other leaders, had fallen. The English army began to disintegrate, taking refuge in the thick forest to the north. Only the survivors of the gallant housecarls continued to fight on round the wounded Harold. Finally a small body of knights broke through the ring and killed the last of the Saxon kings.

There was little further resistance. Duke William of Normandy was left master of the field and, as it turned out, had won the Crown and Realm of England by a single battle, lasting no more than seven hours.

Epilogue

William was crowned King of England in Westminster Abbey on Christmas Day, 1066. Resistance after the battle had been short-lived. Most of the leaders of southern England had been killed at Hastings and there was insufficient national feeling to continue the struggle. By 1071 the Conquest may be said to have been complete: thereafter William and his successors were more concerned with rebellions and intrigues among their own Norman nobility than among their Saxon subjects.

Mongol Attempts
to Invade Japan, 1274, 1281

BY ARTHUR J. MARDER

Yoritomo, head of the Minamoto clan, set up a feudal government at Kamakura in 1192, with himself as shogun. Although a ship-administrator (*funa-bugyō*) was appointed to supervise the shogunal fleet, and the more powerful feudal lords along the coast established naval bases in their own domains and trained seamen, Japanese sea power was in a state of decay at the time of the Mongol invasions—the Bunei and Kōan campaigns of 1274 and 1281, respectively.[1]

In 1274, the Mongol emperor, Kublai Khan, set out to conquer Japan with a force of about thirty thousand Mongols, Chinese, and Koreans, including sixty-seven hundred Korean and Mongol rowers and helmsmen. His fleet consisted of nine hundred ships of which three hundred were large 100-ton warships (transports), three hundred were landing craft, and three hundred were water supply boats. The armada left Aiura (Happ'o), Korea (modern Masampo [Masan]), on 2 November. The Japanese fleet was so much weaker than the vast Mongol fleet that it made no attempt to intercept the expeditionary force at sea. The Mongols had uncontested command of the sea in the Korea and Tsushima straits, that is, the waters between southern Korea and Japan. One immediate result was that the Japanese island outposts of Tsushima and Iki were quickly overrun and the small garrisons exterminated. The armada then swept on Hakata Bay (modern Fukuoka Bay) in Chikuzen Province, northwestern Kyushu. On

18 November a landing was effected at Momomichibara at the western edge of Hakata Bay. The topography of the shore at this point was suitable for simultaneous debarkation from transports drawn up in a row, but as the landing operations were extremely primitive and were harassed by furious attacks of the Japanese defenders, it was not possible to land at will. Nevertheless, the Mongols were able to land as many as six thousand troops, plus horses. On the nineteenth other landings were carried out on the coast west of Hakata. Desperate fighting raged in the Hakata, Hakozaki, and Akasaka areas as the invaders tried to push on to Dazaifu, the military headquarters of Kyushu, situated in the interior of Chikuzen.

The number of the Japanese defenders is not clear, but there were probably no more than three thousand to four thousand in all. The Japanese had evolved an individual style of fighting, and all accounts of the battles pay tribute to the courage and morale of the officers and men. However, the Mongol advantages of fighting in well-ordered formation and of possessing hand-operated mortars, which hurled a kind of incendiary bomb, proved too much for the Japanese. In the late afternoon the Japanese defenders were forced to retreat behind the once formidable but now dilapidated fortifications which the Emperor Tenchi had built after Hakuson-kō. Behind this defense line of embankments with moats, the Japanese waited for reinforcements from Shikoku and western Honshu and worried about the next day's operations. "We lamented all through the night," records the

American Historical Review 51 (October 1946): 1–34.
Reprinted by permission.

Hachiman Gūdoki, "thinking that we were doomed and would be destroyed to the last man and that no 'seeds' would be left to fill the nine provinces." But unknown to the Japanese the Mongols had withdrawn that evening to their ships. The reasons appear to have been these: the unexpected stubbornness of the Japanese, exhaustion of arrows (the Mongols were prepared only for the swiftest kind of blitzkrieg), anticipation of a storm by the pilots, and perhaps also fear by the Mongols of a Japanese night attack, when their primitive tactics might have been deadly. In retreating, the Mongols set fire to several of the villages on the coast of the bay, maltreating the children and old people who had not been able to flee.

That night, 19–20 November, a violent gale suddenly blew up. "The violent waves of Hakata Bay reached almost to heaven." Over half of the Mongol fleet sank as ship after ship crashed into the rocky shores of the bay. Nearly half of the Mongol force, more than thirteen thousand men, was lost. The panicky remnants returned to Korea. From the scant evidence the gale was not anything like the hurricane of the second invasion in 1281. But thanks to this "divine blessing," the first invasion had been frustrated before it had developed into a great crisis. Japanese historians, however, stress the fact that the enemy had decided to beat a retreat to their ships before the gale sprang up, and that, even had there been no gale, the Mongols would have withdrawn from Japanese waters because of the "state of their arrow supply and other inadequacies in their preparations."[2]

Because the Mongols might return sometime, the Japanese took precautions, constructing a stone wall on the Kyushu coast in the Hakata Bay area. It may have been as long as 25 miles and was at least 13 feet high. Horses could be ridden up the inside sloping wall, while the side that fronted the bay dropped sharply like a precipice.

Kublai Khan tried again in 1281 after completing his conquest of China. This time he used all his military resources. The second armada consisted of two sections. The "Eastern Route" force, composed of nine hundred ships and forty-two thousand men (fifteen thousand Chinese and Mongol soldiers, ten thousand Korean soldiers, and seventeen thousand Korean rowers and helmsmen), concentrated at Aiura, Korea. The "South of the Yangtze" force, comprising a Chinese army of one hundred thousand men, sixty thousand or more rowers and helmsmen, and thirty-five hundred ships, assembled in what is now Kiangsu Province. It was arranged that the two forces should meet by 2 July at Iki, then attack Kyushu and advance on Dazaifu.

On 22 May 1281, the Eastern Route army left Aiura, invaded Tsushima on 9 June and proceeded on the 14th to Iki and occupied that island, too. In both places the defenders were, as in the first campaign, vastly outnumbered. Instead of waiting at Iki for the Yangtze army, the Eastern Route army tried to steal a march on it by advancing ahead of schedule. On 21 June, Japanese lookouts on the northern Kyushu shore made out the "tasseled prows and fluted sails" of the invaders' fleet. It was a detachment of about three hundred ships, which passed off Munekata on the northern coast of Chikuzen and arrived at Nagato Bay, from which position it commanded Shimonoseki Strait. The object of this move was to divert relief troops from Honshu from the main battle that was about to develop in the Hakata region.

The main Eastern Route force advanced on Shigashima (Shiga Spit), a land extension of the entrance to Hakata Bay. The fleet anchored off the spit and determined efforts were made to land troops. During several days of continuous fighting the Mongols were able to land only one unit in the face of savage Japanese resistance. The Japanese were not content with passive defense, but put out small but swift and highly maneuverable boats (ten to twelve men per boat) from the vicinity of Hakata and harassed the much larger and more numerous enemy ships with night hit-and-run attacks. Fanatical Japanese would close with an enemy ship, knock down their own mast, use it as a bridge to board the enemy ship, engage in hand-to-hand fighting and sword play, set the ship on fire, and return. On one occasion thirty Japanese swam out to the Mongol fleet, boarded a warship, and lopped off the heads of the crew. The most daring exploit was carried out in broad daylight when Kusano Jirō and a picked crew rowed out to an enemy ship and, despite a hail of darts, one of which slashed off one of Kusano's arms, managed to board, set the ship on fire, and carry off twenty-one heads. Another Japanese hero, Kōno Michiari, put out with two boatloads of men, all apparently unarmed. The Mongols looked on, supposing that the Japanese were coming to surrender. Coming close, the Japanese boarded one of the ships, exercised their two-handed swords, captured the commanding officer, burned the ship, and returned safely. Matters reached the point where the Mongols were compelled to spread out nets, and to tie portions of their fleet together by ropes so as to ensure that the ships would be within easy supporting distance of each other. The courageous "naval" exploits of men like the two Kōno (Michiari and Michitoki, respectively nephew and uncle), the Ōgano brothers (Taneyasu and Tanemura), and Kusano Jirō are part of Japan's national heritage.

There is nothing to explain why the Japanese boats used in the campaign were so much less formidable than those of a century earlier at Dan-no-ura. As regards weapons, the raiders wielded the bow and arrow, sword, and *kumade* or rake, generally of bamboo, which was used for boarding an enemy ship. They also had shields for protection against arrows.

Frustrated at Shigashima, the Mongols retreated to Takashima Island on 30 June at the entrance to Imari Gulf, Hizen Province (south of Chikuzen). The dates and details from this point on become hazy. Landings appear to have been attempted on the northern coast of Hizen with the purpose of outflanking the Japanese defenses in Hakata Bay. They were not successful. Difficulties multiplied for the Mongols. Forced to remain on board their cramped ships, with scarcely enough breathing space in the scorching heat, three thousand men were carried off by an epidemic. The ships themselves began to rot. Moreover, the Yangtze army had not ap-

peared. Under these conditions it was decided to wait for the Yangtze army and then try to settle the campaign with one decisive blow, meanwhile being as cautious as possible in order to husband strength. In this, the Takashima stage of the campaign, the Japanese "caused the enemy's liver to become cold" (that is, frightened the Mongols) by repeating the hit-and-run attacks at sea. However, because their losses were heavy, the Japanese, too, became cautious. A stalemate resulted on land and sea.

The center of action shifted to Iki in mid-July. The main Yangtze army had finally left Ningpo in south China on 5 July, and reached Hirado Island, Hizen, below the entrance to Imari Gulf, at the end of July or the early part of August. Meanwhile, on 16 July, an advance squadron of three hundred ships had joined the Eastern Route army at Iki. As soon as the Japanese learned that the Mongols had concentrated at Iki, they once more made daring attacks on the Mongol ships in the waters adjacent to Iki. On 12 August the combined Eastern Route and Yangtze forces concentrated at Takashima, preparatory to making a supreme effort to crush Japanese resistance and march on Dazaifu.

As the climax of the campaign approached, the Japanese seem to have realized that individual valor would not be enough to stave off defeat. "It is abundantly plain," says Murdoch, "that the whole nation, from the ex-emperor downwards, passed most of their time during the great crisis on its knees before the gods imploring them for the overthrow of the invader." The ex-emperor Kameyama sent a proxy to the Ise Shrine to petition the imperial ancestor, the Sun Goddess, for divine help. Japanese records relate that as the sacred envoy arrived at the shrine and offered the imperial prayer, a cloud appeared in the clear sky. It spread quickly and developed into a hurricane of terrific force on the night of 15–16 August. The Mongol ships were helpless in the face of it. Most of them sank through collisions, others were driven on the rocks, and others were simply blown over. "The sea looked as if divining rods had been scattered." Those who drowned were "numberless," according to the Japanese sources. When the Japanese saw what had happened, they immediately followed up their advantage by sending an amphibious expedition of hundreds of war vessels under Shōni Kagesuke to wipe out the scatered enemy troops on Takashima. About three thousand prisoners were taken. Exaggerated Chinese records (*Yüan-shih*) tell us that only three of Kublai Khan's fighting men were able to reach China. In actual fact, somewhere between thirty and thirty-five thousand of the original force returned alive, along with about two hundred of the ships. It was unquestionably one of the worst defeats in military history.

So ended the only serious invasion attempts ever made on the main islands of Japan. The outcome was the undisputed command of the sea between Japan and the continent for three centuries. The Japanese later built a 71-foot high monument on the shore of Chikuzen Province to commemorate the Mongol defeat of 1281. Under the bronze statue of the Emperor Kameyama is engraved the inscription: "The enemy capitulated" (*Tekikoku Kofuku*). This might suggest that the Japanese were under the illusion that they had defeated the Mongols by force of arms. Actually, it became a universally accepted fact in Japan that the hurricane had been sent by heaven, since it had coincided with the climax of the national prayers for the dispersal of the Mongols. For this reason the wind of 15–16 August is called the "Divine Wind of Ise" (*Ise no Kami-kaze*) in Japanese history. It was thereafter the traditional belief that Japan was a divinely protected nation and therefore could never be successfully invaded by any enemy. "So strongly are the people imbued with this faith," Professor Kuno has written, "that there is absolute national confidence in the ultimate success and justification of all her causes and claims in any dealings with foreign nations."[3] A contemporary Japanese historian observes: "From that time the word *Kamikaze* (Divine Wind) has come to symbolize the faith of the Japanese people in the belief that Providence is constantly with them in

times of national adversity."[4] It was, therefore, not by accident that the Ise Shrine became the center of national worship and that Japan felt herself to be the *Shinkoku* or "Divine Nation." When nearly six hundred years later Perry came to pay his respects, in the words of a native annalist, "Orders were sent by the imperial court to the Shinto priests at Ise to offer up prayers for the sweeping away of the barbarians."[5]

It would, however, be a serious mistake to think that all the Japanese of today have placed their sole reliance on divine protection. Japanese historians of this generation are critical of the prevalent national belief that it was the Divine Wind above all else which saved Japan in 1281.[6] While acknowledging the usefulness of the Wind, they have minimized its importance by intimating that it did no more than give the coup-de-grâce to the enemy and by asserting that even without it the Japanese would still have stood a good chance of defeating the Mongols. These writers stress the heroism, the hard fighting, and the offensive spirit displayed by the officers and men from start to finish and the fact that, although the battle was finally decided by the Divine Wind, for over two months the Kyushu troops alone had held the enemy at bay. Had not the Wind intervened to end the battle, so runs the argument, the defenders, reinforced by the first-class Kantō troops from northeastern Honshu, would have had nothing to fear. The point is also made that the Yangtze army consisted mainly of subjected Chinese from south China who were despised by the Mongols as *bantsu* (barbarians) and were poor fighting men of inferior physique.

Japanese historians have drawn a large lesson from the Mongol campaigns—that the nation must not rely on divine winds in future wars with powerful enemies and that national security could best be achieved by the possession of a strong navy.

Notes

[1] Japanese primary source literature on the invasions is very scanty. The principal sources are the *Hachiman Gūdoki* (Personal Notes Regarding

the Hachiman Temple), a chronicle of the Mongol invasions written in the Kamakura period; Takezaki Suenaga's famous Mongol Scroll, and *Nichiren Shonen Chugasen* (Illustrated Biographical Sketch of Nichiren), which is Vol. 220 of the *Zokugunshorniju* (A Collection of Representative Texts of Old Japan), compiled in the nineteenth century. The most important Chinese source is the *Genshi* (Chinese: *Yuan-shih*) (History of the Mongol Dynasty), one of the twenty-five dynastic histories of China. The most important section on the invasions is the *Nipponden*, or section on Japan. Often quoted, too, is the *Togoku Tsugan* (A General History of the East), a Korean work of the sixteenth century.

Japanese writings consulted on the invasion include Omori, *Dai Nippon Zenshi* 2:302–16; *Dai Nipponshi Koza* 3:242–48; Ogasawara, pp. 48–54; Omori, *Nippon Chuseishi Ronko*, pp. 193–214; Takayanagi 1:258–66, 280–95; *Nippon Kaijo Shiron*, 149–65; Izu Sachio and Matsushita Yoshio, *Nippon Gunji Hattatsushi* (The History of Japanese Military Development) (Tokyo: 1938), pp. 58–59; Naganuma Kenkai, *Shinsetsu* (New Views on Japanese History) (Tokyo: 1930), 2:125–26; Uzūzankaku (publishing house), ed., *Isetsu Nipponshi* (A New Interpretation of Japanese History)

(Tokyo: 1932) 1:300–45, *passim*; Ikeuchi Hiroshi, *Genko no Shinkenkyu* (A New Study on the Mongol Invasions) (Tokyo: 1931) 1:117–52, 307–16 (Vol. 2 consists of reproductions of the Mongol Scroll). The best account in English is Murdoch 1:507–25.

[2] There is no evidence that the Japanese fleet played any role in the campaign. I can find no references to the Japanese naval attack on the Mongol ships on the night of the nineteenth, which is described in Nakaba Yamada, *Ghenko: The Mongol Invasion of Japan* (New York: 1916), pp. 143–46.

[3] Yoshi S. Kuno, *Japanese Expansion on the Asiatic Continent*, 2 vols. (Berkeley: 1937, 1940) 1:51.

[4] Akiyama Kenzo, *The History of Nippon* (Tokyo: 1941), p. 161.

[5] Cited in William S. Griffin, *The Mikado's Empire* (New York: 1890), p. 179.

[6] *Dai Nipponshi Koza* 3:255; Omori, *Dai Nippon Zenshi* 2:316; *Nippon Kaijo Shiron*, p. 163; Omori, *Nippon Chuseishi Ronko*, pp. 203–04, and Takayanagi Koju, ed. *Dai Nippon Senshei* (A Military History of Japan) (Tokyo: 1937) 1:289, 296–97.

Spain as an Amphibious Power, 1538–94

BY ALFRED VAGTS

The fall of Constantinople could not fail to affect the dominion of the sea in the Mediterranean. The Arab saying that "God has given the earth to the Musulmans and the sea to the Christians" was perhaps true through the greater part of Muslim history but at times certain Muslims like Kair-ed-Din or Barbarossa would arise to be proclaimed Beylerbey of the Sea.

A corsair of Albanian blood, Barbarossa was one of those outsiders, if not renegades, whom the Turks admitted to their armies and navies as a matter of course and who were indispensable for the maintenance of their dominion. He established Turkish rule in North Africa where Spain had acquired Mers-el-Kebir (1505), Oran (1509), Bougie and Tripoli (1510), the latter being handed over to the Knights of St. John by Charles V in 1530, after they had been expelled from Rhodes in 1522. Barbarossa drove the Spanish from Algiers in 1529 and in 1534 seized Tunis, where they had supported local rulers. In the same year he appeared off the Italian coast, destroying shipyards, taking castellos, raiding the countryside, and dragging inhabitants into slavery.

Panic was great in southern Italy, which had not known such invasion for some four hundred years. Yet another Carthage seemed to have arisen from the ruins and the Holy Roman Emperor Charles V thought it a worthy Christian and necessary Spanish enter-

Landing Operations (Harrisburg, PA: Military Services Publishing Co., 1952), pp. 201–19. Reprinted by permission.

prise to dislodge the Turks, in whose attacks his enemy Francis I of France had connived. Francis confided to the Pope that he intended to instigate such forays rather than merely resist them. Charles prepared an armada in Spain and Italy, which included some belated Crusaders who found themselves at loose ends and many more mercenaries. The two columns met off the Sardinian coast near Cagliari from where they sailed to Tunis in June 1535, landing on the shores of the Gulf of Tunis without encountering opposition.

Goletta, Barbarossa's castle, was besieged from both the harbor and the land. After it had been taken by storm, the Spanish found some of the guns marked with the French lily. Tunis fell likewise, and old Christian prophecies were recalled of an emperor who would subdue the whole world and would decree that every man on pain of death was to adore the cross, whereupon this ruler would receive the crown from an angel of God in Jerusalem and depart this life.

Charles seemed appointed for this role. But the disunion of Christendom more than ever stood in the way of realizing such dreams. Barbarossa hit back at the Spanish in the following year by raiding the Balearic Islands with the remnants of his fleet and Francis I renewed the war against Charles. The Antichrist ally of the Most Christian King, Sultan Soliman, sent over from Avlona (Valona) into Apulia eight thousand light horse under the leadership of a pasha and an Italian renegade who wasted the land and carried thousands away into slavery. These bands withdrew when a French invasion planned in northern

Destruction of the Spanish Armada, July 1588. Courtesy of the Beverly R. Robinson Collection, U.S. Naval Academy Museum.

Italy did not come off, and Spanish and Venetian squadrons threatened to converge on their communication lines (July-August 1537). Soliman settled down before the Venetian fortress of Corfu for some three weeks but, fearing to be cut off from the mainland by the Christian fleet, retired after some fierce assaults on the place which continued to remain Venetian almost as long as the power of Venice lasted. But about this time Venice lost her hold on the Aegean islands—Scyros, Patmos, Aegina, Paros, Naxos.

The Failure of the Venetian-Spanish Alliance

Venice and Spain, the two foremost Christian sea powers engaged together against the Turk, might have achieved more had the two partners trusted one another more. But Christianity once more proved no reliable basis for coalition warfare where diversity of state interests interfered. Andrea Doria, the emperor's grand admiral, holding Barbarossa at bay late in the war season of 1538, took Castel Nuovo from the Turks with a landing force after having battered the place from his ships, an enterprise which as yet did not seem forbidden by theories about the superiority of land-based guns. When this place, situated

within the traditional sphere of influence of the Venetians, was not handed over to them, they retired from the struggle against the Turk for some thirty years and made a peace at Constantinople which saved them their last island possessions, Zante and Cyprus, Crete and Corfu.

Not until 1541 could Charles think of returning to the corsair-infested African coast where Algiers and Tunis continued to be thorns in the maritime flank of his empire. Too late in that year to be favored by weather he assembled Italian, German, and Spanish forces off Algiers, which juncture provided the last successful feature of that Christian enterprise. Algiers would not surrender when summoned on 25 October, as only part of the Spanish force had landed and the commandant said that he had not only brave men inside his fortress but a wild sea as an outside ally. Of the latter, Doria, the Pope, and others had vainly warned Charles. The next day the bad season began with heavy rain and hail. A three-day storm smashed the ships against one another or piled them on shore. Provisions and ammunition were lost or spoiled. Meanwhile Moorish cavalry appeared in the field.

With his cold and unfed troops panicky by

now, Charles was forced back to Cape Matafas, 15 miles away, where the continuous bad weather conditions—similar to those which hampered the Allied forces in this region during the winter of 1942–43—convinced him that he must return to Spain. Although recognizing this failure as an "act of God," he would seem to have essayed to excuse Providence by complaining that if time had been allowed him to complete his landing before the weather broke, Algiers would have fallen. Some in his entourage were bold enough to tell him that if the Moorish troops had only been a little stronger, no man of his forces would have escaped.

They might also have added, had they known it, that the devastating storms had kept at a safe distance the fleet of Barbarossa whom the sultan had dispatched from Constantinople at the news of Charles's expedition. The return voyage, which was made by the Spanish forces at the winds' will, was also full of peril. In Bugia (Bougie) where Charles paused, solemn processions were held, the emperor himself participating, to pray for a safe departure from these fatal shores. Not until 1 December was Charles back in Cartagena. Of their holdings in North Africa the Spanish lost all except Mers-el-Kebir and Oran.

A small yet important part of the Christian claim to dominion in the Mediterranean was preempted by the Knights of St. John, those seagoing cavaliers of the postfeudal age. They had for a long time been headed by Jehan Pariset de la Valette, who had shared in the siege of Rhodes and in many raids and sea fights and had even for a time been a galley slave until ransomed, an experience as mortifyingly unknightlike as can be imagined. After they had lost Rhodes and become homeless, Charles V, to enable the Order "to use its strength against the pagan enemies of the Christian Commonwealth," conferred on it the islands of Malta and Gozzo and Tripoli in Africa (1530). From these places the Order offered one of the few constant checks on the depredations of the corsairs.

Only spasmodically would the Latin sea powers unite against this threat, as in the enterprise against Dragut, a successor to Barbarossa, who in certain ways occupied the same relationship to the sultan as the grand master of the knights did to the emperor. In the attack on his stronghold, Mehdia, the Spanish-Italian ships combined with those of the Pope, Tuscany, and the Maltese knights. An historical reminiscence, a quotation from Appian about ancient siegecraft, is said to have inspired the viceroy of Sicily with the idea of placing siege artillery on a number of galleys immovably anchored together in the harbor and thus smash the town's sea walls. Knowledge that these were usually the weakest part of the defenses of a coastal fortress might also have encouraged the enterprise.

The Siege of Malta by the Turks

Sultan Soliman II was unwilling to suffer tamely this setback in Africa and sent out a large fleet to clear away the giaours and their most active fighting force, the Maltese knights. Malta itself was then found too well fortified and defensively organized to be taken. The landing force was repulsed by cavalry but Tripoli was surrendered by the knights. In 1564 the sultan, intending to crown his vast successes on land by a land-and-sea enterprise, sent out a large force estimated at from thirty thousand to forty thousand men against Malta which was held by between six thousand and nine thousand men, assembled around a nucleus of some five hundred knights. The season for the siege, which began in May, was well chosen, but some of the other points involved in the combined operations for this famous investment were not well managed. The failure of the siege together with the battle of Lepanto, definitely checked Turkish sea power. The sultan was unfortunate in his timing, for the Maltese knights, headed for eight years by la Valette, had fortified Malta against the long-awaited assault. In fact, their masons were still employed when the Turks arrived.

If the Turks were the foremost military power of the time, their Malta enterprise illustrated the difficulties of combined operations. The sultan, whether for political or other reasons, had left the question of the supreme command over all his forces in Malta unsettled, putting the land troops under the command of Mustafa Pasha, his vizier and a veteran commander, and the fleet under that of Piali, the capitan-pasha, a young scion of his own house. The sultan instructed them to wait for the arrival of Dragut from Africa and settle together with the latter the final plans for the siege. In a council of war, however, the naval commander persuaded the others that the first action must be the assault on St. Elmo, the fort blocking the entrance to Marsamuscetto harbor, in order to obtain an all-weather safe anchorage for his fleet.

To reduce this fort alone took the Turks, who had landed without immediate opposition, no less than five weeks; it cost them seven thousand killed, including Dragut, and as many wounded, as against losses among the defenders of one hundred thirty knights and twelve hundred others. During these weeks, until 24 June, the Turks neglected all other objects in the island such as Citta Notabile, where most of the civilians were sheltered behind medieval walls and towers. Not until 7 September did the Turks turn their furious energies toward reducing the other Maltese forts, putting them under concentric fire from the land side and from across the Great Harbor, making more than a dozen attempts at storming them, including one undertaken from galley and rowboats against the sea walls and slopes of the forts.

Christian Victory

By September the stores of food and ammunition inside the fortress began to run low. And still there was no sign from the Spanish viceroy in Sicily, a tardy if not cowardly leader of a relieving force which seven hundred impatient knights and soldiers had quit in order to join the besieged. Learning of the viceroy's ever-increasing armada but not of his vacillations, the Turks determined to deliver one more assault before abandoning the island. This was urged by the capitan-pasha whose crews had been severely depleted and who dreaded the coming of the equinox. The final

attack took place on 1 September and was repulsed, with great losses to the Turks. Prodded into action at last by his council of war, the viceroy had left Sicily on 20 August with some ten thousand men, nearly equal to that left to the Turks. The fleet was dispersed, however, and finally got off from Trapani only on 3 September, reaching Gozzo on the 5th. On the following day six to eight thousand men disembarked at the northwest corner of Malta. They soon joined the weak Christian forces holding out in the Citta Notabile, while the fleet sailed around to the harbor to salute and inspire the besieged. Before they had hardly been more than menaced by the armada, the Turks began a hasty reembarkation, leaving stores and disabled or unmanned ships behind. They had not gone far when Mustafa, because of the lack of molestation by the relieving force and because he heard reassuring reports about its size, decided to land once more in the north of the island. A skirmish with the Spanish showed him that the latter were by far the stronger, and the Turks retired in confusion to their ships, losing another one thousand men, with disgrace awaiting them on their return to Constantinople.

The siege of Malta, for the attacked a successful maritime Thermopylae, ended the Turkish endeavor to extend their naval dominion to the western Mediterranean where they still maintained mere outposts in the haunts of the corsairs of the Barbary coasts. These pirates, who eventually emancipated themselves from the Porte, were too weak to threaten seriously the holder of sea dominion in the western sector, although thanks to Christian commercial competition and jealousies they were allowed to prey upon shipping for nearly three hundred years more. In the eastern sea the Turks drove Venice, which had stood selfishly aside in the earlier sea struggle against the infidels, from Cyprus (1570–71), for the relief of which the Christian sea victory at Lepanto under Don Juan of Austria occurred too late by two months.

Malta, perhaps the strongest sea fortress of the sixteenth and seventeenth centuries, was an impressive symbol of Christian unity at sea, although it never saw another siege until the one from the air in 1942. But after Lepanto, this unity was not easily maintained. Even in the year following Lepanto a force of Spaniards and Venetians, much smaller and less cohesive, failed in combined operations around Modon, the site of ancient Pylos and Sphacteria. Into this bay, a narrow harbor with the entrance secured by the fortified town of Navarino and batteries on the opposite headland, the Spanish-Venetian fleet had driven the hastily rebuilt Turkish fleet. Don Juan d'Austria, the Spanish naval commander, declined to face these land guns and tried to put his ships into the bay of Modon.

Landing troops, led by Prince Alexander Farnese, later one of the best Spanish commanders in the Netherlands, were repulsed before Navarino by Turkish troop sent overland. Although the Turkish fleet was rapidly disintegrating—their ships were leaking, munitions were low, and epidemics were spreading among the crews—the Christians failed to seize the advantage. The season was advanced; it was October now, for politics had postponed the meeting of the squadrons until September, and Don Juan felt he had to abandon the enterprise. The Turks were allowed to straggle back to Constantinople.

The Vulnerability of the Invincible Armada of 1588

The Mediterranean was the lesser theater for Spanish overseas activities, most of which were directed across the Atlantic. In this case, weather conditions and longer distances called for different fighting equipment, and war fleets under sail evolved. In the Mediterranean the sailing orlog ship had as yet only occasionally appeared, and war fleets were composed almost entirely of galleys propelled by oars. The man-of-war under sail, however, called for battle tactics very different from those commands which directed galleys on sea or battles on land. War fleets under sail were definitely *sui generis*.

The largest single overseas enterprise of Spanish land and sea power, and its greatest failure down to the time of Napoleon, was the abortive Invincible Armada of 1588.

Planning for this invasion marked an important step in the history of war preparation; it was an early postfeudal bureaucratic attempt at organization and control on a gigantic scale, but the procrastinations of Philip II fatally hampered it. The project in its inception went back almost to the time of the Spanish conquest of Portugal (1580), which had given Spain considerably more of an Atlantic seafront. The conqueror of that country, the famous Duque de Alba, was originally chosen to head the Armada against England. Before his death in 1582 he had submitted plans far more detailed than many others by which wars had been waged in that age. He included estimates of the time required for preparation—eight months, the duke thought—and an outline of the necessary ships, military forces, and cost.

According to Alba's plans, a fleet of sailing ships was to be raised, in large part chartered in the harbors from Italy to the Elbe, consisting of 150 large ships with an aggregate tonnage of 77,250; 40 *urcas*, round-bottom freighters, of 200 tons each; and 320 small vessels of altogether 25,500 tons. A fleet of 46 galleys, each with a crew of 80 *hombres de cabo* (noncommissioned officers and soldiers) and 200 rowers was also include in the plans. The large ships were to take aboard 20 Italian *fragatas* (a frigate was originally a small oar-propelled vessel) and 20 *falucas*, small coasting vessels with oars and sometimes lateen sails, to be used in the immediate landing operations, together with 200 flat *barcas*, or barges of a type that had been found useful in the Spanish conquest of the Portuguese Azores. This specialization of landing craft also provided an indication, if only a subordinated one, that military thought and practice of the Middle Ages was relegated largely to the past.

Alba's plans also called for fifty-five thousand foot soldiers (twenty-eight thousand Spaniards, eleven thousand Italians, and sixteen thousand Germans), of whom forty five thousand would be actually available, allowing for ten thousand sick, deserters, and so forth. Of the forty-five thousand, the landing force would require thirty-five thousand, while ten thousand would serve on the vessels. In addition, the estimates demanded twelve hundred men and the same number of horses for cavalry, three hundred thirty-four field artillerymen, three thousand engineers (gestadores), seven hundred men for train personnel, and fourteen hundred mules as draught animals. Altogether, Alba's strength was to be some eighty-seven thousand men, perhaps the largest military overseas expedition up to then—on paper. The cost was enormous, even after deducting current army and navy expenditures which would have to be met in any case. The cost of feeding the men was not included.

The whole plan was based on a flourishing shipping industry and a still-solvent economy, as well as on the experiences of an able military leader. But Alba, who had lost favor with Philip, died in 1582 and a new leader was chosen in 1583. The Marquis of Santa Cruz was an energetic veteran naval commander who had taken part in the battle of Lepanto and had, as admiral of the ocean, won for Spain the Portuguese island possessions in the Atlantic. He had urged the expedition against England, as he considered that country Spain's most dangerous enemy.

Paper Strength of Armada

The plans of the marquis were only a little less elaborate than those of Alba, but the king put off their implementation and whittled away at the costs. Thus the size of the armada was made much more modest. On paper its strength consisted of only 132 vessels of all sorts, amounting to nearly 60,000 tons with 2,431 guns, carrying 21,621 soldiers and 8,066 sailors; the military personnel comprised 16,973 Spaniards; 2,000 Portuguese; 581 adventureros, or volunteers, from the younger needy nobility; and 78 gunners. Some 180 chaplains (one for every 155 persons) were allowed for, but only 85 surgeons, doctors, and medical assistants.

The Pope and his prelates blessed the Armada in its new crusade across the seas, which gave rise to a quip, after 1588, that after all heretics made far better sailors. Philip speculated on receiving armed support from the

still-strong Catholic element in England, which, however, did not stir in his behalf. The larger part of the Armada took to sea from Lisbon on 29 May 1588. It was already behind a schedule that had envisaged the conquest of England during the good season, and the delays were still not over. Off Coruna (the Groyne) where the main fleet was to be joined by the ships from Biscay, Castile, and Guipuzcoa, the Armada was the target of severe squalls, and another six weeks were spent in repairs and revictualling. Stores had been bad from the outset, because of rascally contractors, and had deteriorated, causing much sickness. However, the weather was not quite as bad as the admiral reported to King Philip, finding it "the more strange since we are on the business of the Lord and some reason there must be for what has befallen us."

The leader of the Armada, as far as it was not directed by the king himself who functioned with true Spanish-Austrian autocracy as director of war from the court, was not a man to cope with these difficulties. The seventh Duke of Medina Sidonia had replaced Santa Cruz, who had died early in 1588. The new leader possessed no military or naval experience except in connection with the defeat he had suffered at the hands of Drake in the defense of Cadiz, and he lacked an inborn capacity for leadership. He complained that he was always sick at sea. He was master of one of the greatest fortunes in Europe, and Philip may have chosen him as a symbol of the legitimacy bestowed by wealth and religion. On the other hand, the king may have been merely demonstrating his sway over even the highest and proudest grandees in Spain, for the duke accepted the office against his will and solely at the insistence of the king. The case of Medina Sidonia would tend to confirm the thesis of military and social history—that the owners of great fortunes, such as Nicias, Crassus, and Soubise, have seldom proved to be competent leaders in war and that such bold enterprises as overseas expeditions would be better served by less well-born or opulent commanders. William of Normandy and Don Juan of Austria are two examples of outstanding commanders who were born, in fact, illegitimate. Medina Sidonia was merely cringing in his applications to the king's munificence; an admiral of the ocean who hardly even showed personal courage in the combats between the English and the Armada.

From the Groyne the Armada proceeded on 12 July, taking course for Plymouth where the larger part of the English fleet was assembled. Smaller English detachments in conjunction with the Dutch fleet were blockading the Flemish ports in order to prevent the Spanish commander, Prince Alexander Farnese, from joining Medina Sidonia for the descent on England. This possibility had been envisaged by Philip in his sealed orders for the Armada which were opened when the English coast was sighted on 20 July. They instructed the commander to sail for Dunkirk, avoiding the English fleet, and there to wait until Parma with his army of some thirty-four thousand men would sail in the direction of the Thames and London, under protection of the Armada, a conception somewhat resembling Napoleon's last plans for the Channel crossing in 1805. Adhering to these orders, the Armada—much encumbered by its transports and harassed by the swifter sailing, better shooting, and lighter craft of the British—sailed for Calais, thus missing the opportunity to beat the English main fleet, win control of the Channel, and possibly land on the Isle of Wight.

Beginning of the End

When they cast anchor at Calais on 26 July, Medina Sidonia sent messengers to Parma, who replied that he would not be ready for another fortnight, that the landing craft which he had built by royal order could not fight at sea, and that in order to enable his troops to leave port the Armada must drive off or destroy the Anglo-Dutch squadron blockading Dunkirk and Nieuport. Before the Spanish could break the blockade, the English sent fire ships among them while they rode at anchor on the night of 28 July, to their confusion, fear, and loss. Terror was heightened by the memory of many Spanish soldiers of the effect witnessed by them of the infernal

engines drifting against Farnese's Scheldt bridge during the Antwerp siege of 1584–85.

The Armada scattered and several ships were lost, although not a great number. In the general discouragement a council of war decided that it was imperative to save as much of the fleet as possible and that they were now too weak to attempt a landing in England. The less timorous proposed to sail for Hamburg and refit there, but the more pusillanimous majority had no thought beyond fleeing back to Spain. They plotted a course around the north of England, because the winds in the Channel remained consistently adverse to the taking of a direct course over the Atlantic. With only fifty-three ships, Medina Sidonia finally arrived in home ports, far more of his vessels falling victim to the exceptionally severe gales of the summer of 1588 than to the guns and fire ships of the English.

Great historical events such as the failure of the Armada are not always of an equally great military significance. The inherent weaknesses of the Armada did far more to ensure its collapse than the offensive action of the English fleet. Nevertheless the latter did more to ward off the Spanish invasion threat than could probably have been effected by land forces had the Spanish won beachheads in England. A possibly deservedly low opinion was held of the quality of Elizabethan defense organization. Some of the sixteenth-century Italian diplomats in England, who in the absence of military attaches might be said to have exercised that function, thought the military strength of England so low that ten to twelve thousand Spanish or Italian infantry, plus two thousand cavalry, would suffice to restore Catholicism as the state religion beyond the Channel. In their opinion, which to a certain degree was the product of wishful thinking, "if a foreign prince were only able to land an army on English soil, and win the first battle, he would encounter no further difficulties since, owing to the inability of the people to endure fatigue, and their nature, they would no longer oppose him." True, as one diplomat admitted, landing was not without risk,

"All similar attempts since 1066 had failed and William only succeeded on account of the weakness of the opposing army." But he insisted that "although the English showed great aptitude for sport, and readiness in times of danger, it could not be said that they cared much for arms. Their only opportunity to make use of them was in war, and once that was over they forgot all about them."

While the Armada is generally regarded as the most serious invasion threat between 1066 and the time of Napoleon, it was not the last contemplated, even in Philip II's day. There was a small-scale Spanish descent on Cornwall in 1595 and still another was feared for 1596, when an armada being assembled at Cadiz was partly destroyed by the English in a preventive naval action off that port. Among the Catholics in England and Ireland there were always abundant and active fifth column elements useful to invaders, even if Papist plots were never quite as serious as they were painted. English military unreadiness provided a constant temptation to such projects. England generally defended itself by means of its ships, which in this case cruised against and raided Spain. Nevertheless, the English feared, and its enemies hoped, that this mobile wall formed by the superior number and capability of the ships might not suffice for effective combat. In this was rooted both temptation and hope for the invader and apprehension among the English that their people would fall prey to invasion panic.

Preparing for the Future

In moments of national alarm it would so clearly appear that sea power alone was not enough to prevent a landing that measures would be set in motion to stiffen English land power. The militia would be reorganized and the standing army strengthened "in hope we should be better provided hereafter not to be thus taken *tarde* on the sodain," or suddenly out on a limb, as an Elizabethan letter writer, hearing news of yet another Spanish armada, expressed it. A week after this had been written

came news [yet false] that the Spaniardes were landed in the yle of Wight, which bred such a

feare & consternation in this towne [London] as I would little have looked for, with such a crie of women, chaining of streets and shutting off the gates as though the ennemie had ben at Blackewall [on the Thames below Greenwich]. I am sorry and ashamed that this weakness and nakedness of ours on all sides shold shew yt self so apparently as to be carried far & neere to our disgrace both with friends and foes. Great provision is made for horse as being the best advantage we are like to have yf the ennemie come.

In a speech from the throne after 1588, Elizabeth scolded and threatened her subjects: "Some upon the sea coast forsook their towns, fled up higher into the country, and left all naked and exposed to his [Philip's] entrance. . . . If I knew these persons, or may know of any that shall do so hereafter, I will make them feel what it is to be fearful in so urgent a cause." However justified such reproof of the panicky elements might have been, the fact should not be overlooked that at nearly the same time the handling, or even the instigating of invasion panics became, and remained, one of the standard tricks of governments. Governments early in the modern era found out that an invasion panic may be a powerful force which they might otherwise oppose. Invasion scares were, in modern language, strong shots in the arm of the body politic and were so employed by the Elizabethans.

Sir Francis Bacon tells how England was again alarmed in the autumn of 1599 by rumors of an approaching Spanish fleet, so that an army was hastily raised in defense of the kingdom. "But there was no such thing" and the discovery of the falsity of the moves provoked only cynicism. In fact the preparations were made with regard to treasonable moves, later brought out into the open, of Essex in Ireland. As Bacon, who was well acquainted with the workings of Elizabethan government, wrote:

And it is probable that the Queen had some secret intimation of this design. For just at that time there grew up rumors [such as are commonly spread when the sovereign is willing they should circulate] and went abroad all over the land, that a mighty and well appointed Spanish fleet was at hand. . . . And yet these devices of the Queen were even by the common people suspected and taken in bad part; in so much that they forbore not from scoffs, saying that in the year '88 Spain had sent an Invincible Armada against us and now she had sent an Invisible Armada; and muttering that if the council had celebrated this kind of Maygame in the beginning of May, it might have been more suitable, but to call the people away from the harvest for it [for it was now full autumn] was too serious a jest.

More often, however, panics spontaneously originated among the English people, even if the various governments did not share them. One of the sundry-suspected "dark invaders" who preoccupied the English mind was Count Gondomar, the Spanish ambassador in the 1610s and 1620s. While he was always on the best terms with James I, the people were persuaded that he was making surveys and other preparations for a Spanish invasion. Pamphlets were sold in which Gondomar was represented "in the likenesse of Matchiauell" and "his treacherous and subtile practices to the ruine as well of England as the Netherlandes" (1620) uncovered. He was the Dark Knight in a political play by Thomas Middleton, "A Game at Chesse," in which Loyola himself, the founder of the Jesuit Order, speaks the prologue, proclaiming his wicked designs concerning England. The anti-Spanish and Puritan element may have been particularly incensed at Gondomar, not only because he had been instrumental in bringing Walter Raleigh to the block but also because he had been active and successful in his native land in warding off several English and Dutch raids at an earlier time. Another "dark invader" coming more directly from Rome, was Archbishop Rinucci, sent as nuncio to Ireland in the later stages of the Civil War, landing there with arms and money in October 1645. For three and a half years he made the confusion of that war more confounded. This, like any intervention in Irish affairs from Rome or elsewhere, only increased the ferociousness of the English toward the Irish.

Less Protestant and more Renaissance in style was the "invocation of the Druids to the gods of Britain, on the invasion of Caesar" in a play of 1633, *The True Trojans*, by an unknown author. The "Trojans" were of course the Britons. It called on the ancient deities to

Help us, oppressed with sorrow,
And fight for us tomorrow.
Let fire consume the foeman,
Let air infect the Roman;
Let sea entomb their fury,
Let gaping earth them bury;
Let fire and air and water
And earth combine their slaughter!

The Moon Goddess, "commandress of the deep," was implored:

Drive back these proud usurpers from this
isle . . .
Protract both night and winter in a storm,
That Romans lose their way, and sooner
land
At sad Avernus' than at Albion's strand . . . .
Shed light on us, but lightning on our foe.

The martial strength of Elizabethan England lay in its navy rather than its military forces and in its aggressive, rather than its home, defense. Whereas the Spanish, even with the Armada, sought close combat, trusting to the known superiority of their infantry on board these ships, English naval tactics, as if in continuation of insular tendency towards keeping the enemy at arms' length, adhered to a policy of distant combat, *Fernkampf*, relying on superior gunnery and sailing. With such various tactical tendencies, it is understandable that in England army and navy grew unevenly and apart, little inclined toward cooperation in time of war.

Drake Repulsed at Lisbon

Lack of military and naval cooperation was amply demonstrated by the failure of the expedition of Drake and Norris to Lisbon in 1589. While the Cadiz expedition of 1596 under Lord Howard of Effingham, Raleigh, and Essex succeeded in defeating a Spanish fleet and taking and looting Cadiz, Elizabeth was still dissatisfied that the enterprise had not been pushed to a more conclusive end instead of being allowed to terminate abruptly. Effingham as lord high admiral had from the outset wanted to restrict the expedition to naval operations, and it was Essex who insisted on landing as part of the venture, which would deprive the fleet of the opportunity of profiting materially by taking further prizes. Realizing this sympathetically, the council of war decided against further land operations and voted to return home.

The often excessive individualism of Elizabethan land and sea commanders was not conducive to the success of combined operations in which every one of the participants must know and fill his place. Such operations, in particular landings, were more apt to be successful when undertaken by sailors with aid from armed men—more or less forerunners of marines. One is almost tempted to say that the most successful of the Elizabethan wars were unofficial actions like those of Drake in 1572–73 against Nombre de Dios and on the Isthmus of Panama, or against various Spanish places during his circumnavigation of the globe (1577–80) although Drake took and burned several Spanish strong points in the more official war of 1585, including St. Augustine in Florida. In appraising the importance of these victories it must not be forgotten that most of them were gained against small and poorly fortified places.

Operations at Pernambuco

One of the best detailed landing operations undertaken in private *régie* during these English raids on the Spanish Main was that which occurred in "the well governed and prosperous voyage of Mr. James Lancaster, began with three ships and a galley-frigat from London in October, 1594, and intended for Fernambuck in Brazil." The leader, later Sir James Lancaster, commander of the first fleet sent out by the English East India Company in 1601 and one of the chief directors of that company, had in earlier years combined fighting and trading in Portugal and now resumed this mixture of "commerce, priva-

teering and war, triune, inseparable," as Goethe calls it.

As admiral of the enterprise of 1594, which was financed by several aldermen and "others of worship in the city of London," Lancaster led an original force consisting of three ships of altogether 470 tons and 275 men and boys. The frame and other timbers for a galley was carried on board "of purpose to land men in the country of Brazil." This landing craft, with fourteen banks, mast and sail, in her prow, "a good sacar and two murdering pieces," was put together in a friendly harbor not far from Pernambuco. After this place had been reached, Lancaster with some eighty men embarked in the galley which at daylight was to go in ahead of the rest and obtain control of the harbor. But when the sun arose the ships had drifted away from the entrance and were now forced to work back, thereby losing the advantage of surprise. After an exchange of shots with the fort at the entrance, with neither party doing any harm, Lancaster got ready to row in with his galley. Three great Hollanders anchored in the harbor mouth obligingly moving out of his way, ridding the admiral of what he considered the chief obstacle to the progress of his invading craft.

While the English were still waiting outside the harbor for the flood tide, the governor of Pernambuco sent a messenger to inquire their intentions. Lancaster answered that "he wanted the caracks' goods, and for them he came, and them he would have, and that he should shortly see." The inhabitants, organized in three or four troops of about six hundred men, manned the fort at the harbor entrance to repel the English whom they now "perceived to be enemies." As soon as the flood set in, the latter attempted to land with their galley and several boats which had orders to be run "with such violence against the shore, that they should all be cast away without recovery, and not one man to stay in them, whereby our men might have no manner of retreat to trust unto, but only to God and their weapons." Although the fort began to play on galley and boats and guns carried away a piece of the galley's ensign, the English kept on moving in and ran galley and boats ashore right under the fort's walls with such speed and shock that they broke up and sank at once.

At our arrivall, those in the fort had laden all their ordinance, being seven pieces of brasse, to discharge them upon us at our landing; which indeed they did: for our admirall leaping into the water, all the rest following him, off came these pieces of ordinance: but almighty God be praised, they in the fort, with feare to see us land in their faces, had piked their ordinance so steepe downewards with their mouthes, that they shot all their shot in the sand, although it was not above a coits [quoit's] cast at the most betweene the place wee landed & the face of the fort, so that they only shot off one of our mens arms, without doing any more harm; which was to us a great blessing of God: for if those ordinances had bene well levelled, a great number of us had lost our lives at that instant. Our admirall seeing this, cried out, incouraging his men, Upon them, upon them; all (by Gods helpe) is ours: and they therewith ran to the fort with all violence.

The garrison of the fort then retired inland and the admiral signaled to the ships in the roadstead to come into the harbor. He had the fort's ordinance directed against the high town from whence the most danger of a counterattack threatened and, leaving a small garrison in the fort, marched the rest of the men toward the low-lying part of the town where the warehouses containing all the desirable goods were situated. These taken and the beachhead sufficiently well secured for the purpose of the expedition to collect and transport away the riches in the storehouses, the lading of these goods was begun. Some prisoners were employed to haul the carts to the harbor, "which was to us a very great

ease. For the countrey is very hote and ill for our nation to take any great travell in."

His foresight, which seems to have been as good in the military as in the commercial field, caused the admiral to take measures against fire ships, lest the Portuguese might send them down the river flowing into the harbor to his damage. Such alarming contraptions need not be dreaded by the wary, as our relation puts it: "When it cometh upon the sudden and unlooked for, and unprovided for, it bringeth men into a great amazement & at their wits ende. And therefore let all men riding in rivers in their enemies countrey be sure to looke to be provided before hand, for against fire there is no resistance without preparation."

Lancaster seems in all respects to have been a very rational person, by his indication of what perhaps might have been done regarding rationalizing the economy of war if business acumen and practice had been more generally applied to it. After a stay of a month he decided that he had accomplished all that he came to do and had all the more valuable loot aboard his ships and that the resistance of the Portuguese might cause him trouble. So telling his band, as became a later East India Company director, "that it was but folly to seeke warres since we had no neede to doe it," he prepared to depart. Some of the more militant among his young bloods wanted to go inland after enemy troops that had shown an inclination, although ineffectual, to prevent their departure. Sallying far beyond reach of support from the beachhead, many "by their forwardness came all to perish." After this final sacrifice to Mars by an expedition that rather was dedicated to the god of trade, Lancaster turned his craft toward England and reached home safely with his plunder.

Beachhead, 1715

BY VICE ADMIRAL FREDERICH RUGE,
FEDERAL GERMAN NAVY (RET.)

Sweden's Charles XII began the Great Nordic War (1700–21) when he was but eighteen years old. After a successful attack on Denmark, which concluded with the signing of the Treaty of Travendal, he next defeated the Russians under Peter (later the Great) at Narva but failed to exploit this victory. For almost a hundred years, Sweden had dominated the Baltic with a strong navy which had prevented all attacks on the homeland and supported the well-trained Swedish armies in the conquest of vast areas on the opposite shores. In this way a country of less than a million inhabitants exerted a significant influence on the history of Central Europe.

In contrast to his predecessors, Charles XII did not understand sea power. While he fought the king of Saxony and Poland (probably for personal reasons), he allowed Peter to regain access to the Baltic in the Gulf of Finland and to found St. Petersburg (now Leningrad) with the naval base of Cronstadt. Although it was no more than 50 miles distant from the nearest Swedish base at Viborg, Charles did not attack here when he reopened the war against Peter but marched deep into southern Russia, overextending his communications and overstraining his forces, as Napoleon and Hitler did many years later. As a consequence, he suffered a shattering defeat at Poltava in the Ukraine and lost his entire army. Escaping into Turkey, he succeeded in inducing the Sultan to attack and defeat the Russians. The two countries, how-

ever, soon made peace and Charles was forced to leave Turkey. He rode across Europe back to Stralsund in Pomerania, where he arrived late in 1714.

During his absence, most of the Swedish possessions south of the Baltic had been lost; only part of Pomerania was still in Swedish hands. Although Charles had no more than seventeen thousand men, he attacked several Prussian outposts west of the Oder River early in 1715. Prussia mobilized and concluded treaties with Saxony, Poland, Russia, and Denmark, with the aim to drive the Swedes from German soil. Stralsund, their well-fortified main base, had been beleaguered several times but taken only once—in 1678 by Friedrich Wilhelm, the great elector of Brandenburg, who landed an army on the island of Rügen and cut Stralsund off from the sea. (Albrecht von Wallenstein, the emperor's general in the Thirty Years War (1618–48)—nominated "General of the Baltic and Oceanic Seas"—in vain had sworn that he would take Stralsund "if it were forged to the sky with iron chains." The beginnings of his fleet were destroyed by the Swedes, however, and Stralsund, supplied from the sea, could not be taken by his army.)

After lively diplomatic activity, the Allies agreed quickly on the following plan of operations against Rügen: the Prussians and Saxons were to advance on Stralsund from the southeast, the Danes from the southwest; any attempts of Swedish forces to break through were to be prevented under any circumstances; and Stralsund was to be cut off from the sea and taken.

U.S. Naval Institute *Proceedings* 92 (December 1966): 50–57. Reprinted by permission.

The respect for Charles XII as a resourceful and bold general was considerable. Nevertheless, the land campaign could be expected to develop without undue difficulties, for the Allied forces numbered around sixty thousand men. At the beginning of July 1715, the main armies began their march into Swedish-occupied Pomerania. After two weeks of slow but well-coordinated operations commanded by the king of Prussia, they joined hands before Stralsund. At the same time, the Danes invested the small port of Wismar. The roads proved too bad for the siege trains. The methodical attack on the outer fortifications of Stralsund had to be postponed until the heavy guns could be transported by water.

The naval operations were far more intricate. It was necessary to win sea power in the central Baltic, at least temporarily, in order to convoy a special shallow draft squadron to the fortified entrances of the Greifswalder Bodden, a diminutive enclosed sea, held by a squadron of small Swedish ships. Simultaneously, a large transport fleet had to be collected and escorted to Greifswald after the special squadron had forced its way into the Bodden and put the Swedish ships out of action. Then the troops and the horses were to be carried in merchant ships to Rügen and put ashore by means of ships and fishermen's boats.

Of the three Allies, only the Danes had a navy. It consisted of twenty-four ships-of-the-line (four of them given as "repairable" in the carefully kept lists) with fifty to ninety guns, sixty on an average, which were mostly 24-pounders, a few 36-pounders; twenty-one frigates, a few with 18-pounders, the others with 12-pounders or smaller calibers; ten brigs; ten two-masted special craft with one large mortar each; and six heavily gunned flat boats specially built for shallow water. It proved difficult to find the money and the men to commission the bulk of this fleet. About 40 percent of the crews were Norwegians, 30 percent North Germans.

With about thirty ships-of-the-line, the Swedish navy was distinctly superior. In the spring of 1715, two fleets were commissioned: one of nineteen ships-of-the-line, twelve frigates, twelve galleys, and other shallow-draft vessels against Russia; another of five ships-of-the-line and two frigates for the western Baltic. Four more ships-of-the-line were to defend the fairways leading up to Stockholm, the capital and naval base. The disposition of the Swedish fleets was evidently influenced by the Russian naval development. Peter the Great had started on a large shipbuilding program immediately after Poltava, his main fleet had reached a strength of thirteen ships-of-the-line and ten frigates. In July 1714, a Russian galley fleet had defeated a numerically inferior Swedish force at Hango-Udd (in Russia, *Gangut*) in the Finnish skerries. That is why only a small Swedish squadron operated against Denmark. At first, its four ships-of-the-line (the fifth was not yet ready) under Rear Admiral Count Wachtmeister took up a watching position south of the Sound, not far from their own bases in southern Sweden, where they could retire if a superior Danish fleet appeared.

However, Charles XII overrode this sensible arrangement of his Admiralty by sending orders directly to Count Wachtmeister telling him to proceed westward into the waters off Lübeck, to make prizes and "to fight." Fight he did but on a lee shore against overwhelming odds, eight ships-of-the-line and a frigate under Rear Admiral Gabel, which the Danes sent after him when he started making prizes of their merchant ships. On 24 April 1715, after a battle near Fehmarn Island, in which the Swedes suffered heavily, they ran their ships aground just outside Kiel (the present German naval base). One only was burnt, the others could be refloated and were taken to Copenhagen. Some hundreds of the prisoners took service with the Danes, others were allowed to join the armed forces of Venice.

As a result of the bad strategy of Charles XII the two fleets were now equal. For various reasons it took both sides a long time to get them to sea. On 15 July, the Danes under Admiral Raben sailed from Copenhagen. He had sixteen ships-of-the-line only, because some had to be left behind for lack of men. On the following day, north of Rügen, this fleet was joined by the special shallow-draft flotilla under Vice Admiral Sehestedt which was to be escorted down the east coast of Rügen. At night they anchored. On 18 July, after a council of war, Sehestedt carried on whereas Raben turned back. He was afraid that he would be cut off by a superior Swedish force. Actually, the Swedish fleet, twenty-one ships-of-the-line under Admiral Sparre, had put to sea on 16 July, also destined for Rügen and also with a convoy which carried mainly supplies and some ten thousand muskets among other urgently needed material.

Raben's best cruiser captain, Peter Wessel, later ennobled as Tordenskiold, sighted and reported the Swedish fleet on time. Although Sparre had the weather gage and intended to fight (his ships hoisted the "blood flag") Raben succeeded in slipping away under a press of sail. The Danish Admiralty congratulated Raben upon the *habilité* with which he had conserved the fleet. Allied Headquarters (before Stralsund) were of a different opinion. According to the Prussian war diary, the two kings (Frederick IV of Denmark and Friedrich Wilhelm I of Prussia) felt grave apprehensions for Sehestedt's flotilla, which now seemed to be at the mercy of the Swedish fleet.

Sehestedt had nearly thirty vessels, none drawing more than 8 feet, and three armed with 18-pounders. On 20 July, he tried to force his way into the Bodden via the East Deep (minimum depth about 10 feet). He had to desist, however, because the wind was contrary and the fire from nine 24-pounders on Ruden Island too heavy. On the following day, the Swedish fleet appeared and found Sehestedt well prepared. He had anchored off the north end of Usedom Island as closely in-shore as possible. With a draft of 24 feet at least, the Swedish battleships could not get into effective range (600 yards, with a highest range of 2,000 yards for 24-pounders). The Swedish frigates were repeatedly forced to retreat because they had 12-pounders only. Sehestedt asked his king for the intervention of the Danish main fleet but added that he

could hold out for several weeks even with Usedom in Swedish hands.

At first, he obtained water from the island; then, Swedish cavalry stopped that, and field artillery harassed his ships. He moved a mile to the north, out of their range, and had his cooks prepare the food with salt water. On 25 July, the Prussian war diary noted that Sehestedt's flotilla was considered as lost, and that Stralsund could not be taken in this campaign. At the same time, however, the Prussian king took energetic steps to improve the situation. During the night of 30–31 July, two thousand Prussian infantrymen and eight hundred cavalry crossed the Swine (the main arm of the Oder River) from Wollin to Usedom in fishing boats. After suffering heavy losses, the Swedish garrison of Usedom fled to the mainland. Sehestedt's flotilla could be supplied with water, food, and ammunition again. According to the diary of a Saxon general, the two kings first celebrated this success rather abundantly and only then visited the flotilla.

Raben now received the strict royal order to attack the Swedish fleet. The Danish Admiralty admonished him to apply "conduite and seamanship" and to avoid too great risks. At the same time they found more crews for him. On 5 August, he put to sea with twenty-one ships-of-the-line (1,325 guns) and six frigates. On 8 August, he sighted the Swedish fleet (twenty ships with 1,300 guns and six light vessels) at anchor about 10 miles north of Sehestedt. There was a good breeze from the northwest, both fleets formed line ahead on a northeasterly course. Fire was opened at 1:00 P.M. and kept up till in the evening the battle ended for lack of ammunition. Neither side had made any attempt at tactical maneuvers or to close in. Contrary to custom and order, Wessel's frigate had taken the place of a battleship which had been damaged and had left the line temporarily.

The Danes fired two hundred rounds per gun on the engaged side using up 133,000 cannon balls and 30,000 hundredweight of powder. They had 127 dead and 485 injured, the Swedes 145 and 333. The Danes obtained approximately 3 percent hits (Battle of Jutland: The British 2.7 percent, the Germans 3.2 percent). Neither side claimed to have won the battle. On the whole, the Swedish fleet seems to have suffered more. In any case, it went back to the naval base at Karlskrona and was not ready for sea again before the end of September. Raben now anchored in sight of Sehestedt as proof of his strategical success.

Some of the shallow-draft vessels entered the Stettiner Haff, another diminutive enclosed sea, via the Swine, in order to destroy the Swedish ships there. These fought stubbornly and eventually succeeded in escaping through the Peene River past Wolgast (already in Prussian hands) to the Greifswalder Bodden. Now, supplies and especially the heavy siege guns could be transported by water from the Prussian arsenal at Stettin on the Oder River to Wolgast at least. To open the inland waterway to Greifswald, the Prussian king gave orders to storm the strong Swedish fortification at Peenemünde (Mouth of the Peene). After a short bombardment, 1,065 Prussians and Saxons succeeded in overwhelming the defenses, with a loss of 608 killed and wounded. This operation made quite a stir because it was customary to reduce fortifications by slow methodical attack.

Sehestedt's flotilla was reinforced by three Norwegian galleys and *Hjaelperen*, a kind of sailing monitor with sixteen 24-pounders, drawing only 8 feet forward and 7 aft. But Ruden island was too heavily fortified even for *Hjaelperen*, and the New Deep was selected for the attack. The Swedes had scuttled several ships there. Against adverse winds, fire from Swedish ships, and the hazards of navigation, it took Sehestedt from 16 to 25 September to work his way through. Once the Danes were inside the Bodden, the game was up for the lightly armed Swedish ships. Most of them found shelter in small ports on the Bodden where they were blockaded by the Danes. Sehestedt was promoted to (four star) admiral "with full pay."

During the naval and military operations for the mastery of the central Baltic and the enclosed seas Bodden and Haff, energetic steps were taken to collect a large transport fleet. Prussia had agreed to contribute vessels for carrying five thousand men, but actually furnished more than half of the total number of transports (181 of 337) and about two-thirds of the entire carrying capacity. The Prussian vessels came from at least fifteen ports up to Königsberg (at present Kaliningrad) in East Prussia. They sailed singly or in small convoys to the Swine and, after the Peene had been opened, to Greifswald. The Danish transport fleet, lured in Denmark, Norway, and northwest Germany, also went to the Swine, in one large convoy, protected by Raben. All the transports were rather small because none drew more than 10 feet. The Danes paid a fixed amount according to the size of the ship, the Prussians paid for the upkeep of the crews only on the grounds that they could not earn money anyhow as long as there were Swedish ships at sea. For rapid disembarking, at least three hundred small barges and boats were collected from the vicinity of Greifswald. The transport fleet was ready there about the middle of October, rather late in the year. There were suggestions to postpone the "great enterprise" to the following year, but with great energy Friedrich Wilhelm I (who was twenty-seven years old) saw to it that the preparations were continued. He was in supreme command, with Field Marshal Prince Leopold von Dessau commanding on land and Admiral Sehestedt on the water. Evidently, this arrangement worked well. In all the voluminous correspondence, official and private, there is not the slightest hint of any difficulties in the command setup and the cooperation.

Table 1 shows the composition of the landing force. In full strength, this would have

Table 1. Composition of Landing Force

	Battalions Infantry	Squadrons Cavalry
Danes	10	18
Prussians	10	15
Saxons	4	2
Total	24	35

been 14,000 men infantry and 6,000 horses. Actually, there took part 12,245 infantry (staff included), 4,974 cavalry, 26 guns, 26 ammunition wagons, and 5,183 horses. The whole force was formed into five brigades infantry and four brigades cavalry. These brigades were also the transport units. A naval officer was detailed to each as transport officer.

On 1 November, the embarkation was begun by putting water, provisions, and fodder aboard. There is no report on the details of embarking and disembarking, but in the considerable number of war diaries, log books, orders, and "press" reports available, enough facts are mentioned to give a fairly complete picture. According to the Prussian war diary, getting the troops on the ships took longer than expected. Now Greifswald is a small port which definitely had not room enough for more than three hundred transport vessels from 5 to 60 last. A *last* is the measure of carrying capacity used at that time. It may be compared with a net register ton but is somewhat larger and means room and buoyancy for at least 2.4 tons weight. On the Rügen operation, a ship of 8 last carried seventy infantrymen, one of 15 last, one hundred twenty men. The artillery was put on seventeen ships "from Stettin and Kolberg" (that is, the largest ports), evidently of strong construction. The vessels for the horses had been specially prepared and were capable of transporting from ten to sixty horses each.

The cavalry started going on board on 3 November. From the fact that a gale interrupted this part of the preparations, it is evident that the horses had to be ferried over to the transports. Some reports mention specially designed flat-bottomed barges for carrying horses. An etching of a landing in 1712 in the same area shows a wooden pontoon at right angles to the beach with a ramp on the landside and some small boats with oars and sails alongside the other end. Some mounted cavalrymen are on the ramp and on the pontoon, which obviously could serve as a link between shore and ship or could be towed away.

On the night of 7 November, all the cavalry were safely loaded. How it was done with the horses is nowhere mentioned. It seems to have been taken for granted that the merchant sailors could handle cargoes and horses in a competent way whether with block and tackle or via ramps. In view of the rapid disembarkation, ramps are more probable for the horses. Hardly any seaway was to be expected, for the landing area was a shallow and well-sheltered bay. Moreover, in the middle of November, the water of the Baltic is not much above the freezing point, and the nights are damp and cold. Letting the horses swim ashore would not have been very healthful for them.

The infantry went aboard in the following two days, the kings and generals on 10 November. On 11 November, a council of war was held in the *Kronen*, the Royal Danish yacht. Orders and a signal book, printed in Danish and German, were issued. In the afternoon, anchors were weighed, but the wind increased, and the fleet soon anchored again.

On 12 November at 6:00 A.M. the transport fleet eventually put to sea, well protected by Sehestedt's flotilla, which kept a close watch on all Swedish ships. It was two days after the full moon, and there was a good breeze from the west. Sehestedt planned to disembark by moonlight. When this was begun on 13 November at 3:00 A.M., the wind backed to the south-southeast and increased. A considerable confusion ensued, a boat was rammed and sank (the men saved, however), and Sehestedt called the operation off. For two days, the wind was too strong. When it abated and veered to the west again in the forenoon of 15 November, Sehestedt and Prince Leopold proposed to change the plans and to sail at once to Gross-Stresow in order to disembark there. The kings agreed. At 11:00 A.M. the cavalry brigades began to move, followed by the others at short intervals. At 11:45 the entire fleet was under way. At 2:30 P.M. the *Kronen* dropped anchor off Gross-Stresow.

The transports with a draft of less than 5 feet had orders to run aground. On the approach "the men were to be chased back to the helm," as an order has it. All the warships and most of the transports seem to have anchored, however. At 3:30 P.M. the men of the first wave went into the shallow-draft means of disembarkation attached to each transport. They were of very differing types. One battalion (620 men) was taken ashore by a galley (220 men), two barges from the Oder River (160 men), and two galiots (240 men). Another battalion of 530 men was landed by one large barge (or pontoon) (182 men), three Oder barges (260 men), and six rowing boats (98 men). A third battalion was put ashore by eighty-three boats. To each battalion, a large cutter from one of the Danish ships-of-the-line was attached for towing and general assistance.

On the whole, the men were evidently expected to get on land not exactly dry-shod but with little difficulty and without getting very wet. Special care was taken to ensure that they kept their cartridges (which were not waterproof) high and dry.

Prince Leopold went ashore with the first wave in order to reconnoiter the situation personally, for he expected a Swedish counterattack. He was followed by some of the generals and by Colonel Wutchenau. The weather had turned fine and calm, no difficulties were encountered because, according to all reports, everything had been planned with meticulous care. This paid off now. At 5:30 P.M. all the infantry were ashore. The guns followed. Disembarking the cavalry began at 10:00 P.M. when the moon had risen. After three hours, it was interrupted by a heavy Swedish attack.

A troop of Swedish cavalry had observed the landing and reported to Charles XII, who at once set out with one thousand infantrymen, twenty-five hundred horses, and eight field guns. Because of bad roads he had not been able to gain Gross-Stresow earlier. Prince Leopold had arranged his men in battle order, making good use of the terrain, and had put *chevaux de frise,* carried from Greifswald, in front. Charles XII concentrated his force

against a narrow sector where unfortunately for him there were two rows of obstacles. His men were not able to penetrate them at the first attempt. They came under a heavy cross fire and were attacked in their left flank by cavalry. Charles XII was seriously wounded; his force lost four hundred dead, two hundred prisoners, and all the guns.

On 16 November, at 1:00 P.M., twenty-three hours after the first anchor had been dropped, the whole multinational force marched off in the direction of Stralsund. Two days after, Altefähr, its bridgehead on Rügen, surrendered. Stralsund held out, the Allies began the methodical attack. On 22 December, Charles XII left the town for Sweden and on 28 December, it capitulated. The campaign was ended, Sweden had—for the time being—lost her last possession south of the Baltic.

In the last two hundred fifty years, technical progress in warfare has been immense. And yet, that almost forgotten campaign of 1715 had problems which seem strangely modern to us. There was the decisive importance of being master of the sea. There was the dictator as we might call him, feared as a military leader, who tried to use his sea forces like divisions on land and who did not know when to stop. There was the problem of rapidly disembarking troops with no sea experience whatsoever. Obviously, the military commanders willingly accepted the advice of the naval experts although these were inferior in rank and probably in social standing, too.

Last, but not least, there was an alliance of sovereign countries with differing interests. They had one common and dangerous enemy, who was a threat to each of them. Therefore, their leading men came together and worked closely together, far more in the spirit of their treaty than in the letter only. Much was done to foster mutual trust and confidence. In this way, the main problems of any alliance—inner cohesion and consistent action—were satisfactorily solved, and the common aim was reached.

Parliament and the Marine Regiments, 1739

BY ALFRED J. MARINI

"Of the Marines it is impossible to speak too highly; they are as fine, as efficient, and as well disciplined a body as any that the State has at its disposal." A little over a century before Hans Busk made this statement, Britain's marine forces were neither fine, nor efficient, nor well disciplined; and the "State" certainly did not consider them any great addition to the national arsenal. Indeed, at the beginning of the Spanish War in 1739, Britain had no marine forces save four "invalid companies" carried on the army list since the Treaty of Utrecht.

Regular seagoing regiments had been introduced into the British navy in the days of Cromwell when the Lord Protector sent some of his most zealous "redcoats" to serve with the fleet in the First Dutch War. Following the Restoration, the Duke of York and Albany's Maritime Regiment of Foot was raised by Order in Council on 28 October 1664. It is from that organization that the present Corps of Royal Marines date their inception. Following the Glorious Revolution, the "Duke's Regiment" was placed under the command of Prince George of Denmark. The regiment was divided into the "First and Second Marines" in 1690 and at the Treaty of Ryswick it was disbanded.

Six "Marine Regiments" were raised in 1702, and like the old "Duke's Regiment" after 1688, were under the command of the Lord High Admiral, Prince George of Denmark. It was these marines who, by their

Mariner's Mirror 62 (February 1976): 55–65. Reprinted by permission of the Society for Nautical Research.

suffering and tenacity, gave the present corps the singular battle honor carried on its Colours: "Gibraltar." Like their predecessors, "Queen Anne's Marines" were disbanded in 1713, and by 1739 the only vestige of them was four "invalid companies" which did not exist.

The preceding historical sketch of the marine forces prior to 1739 is illustrative of the ad hoc quality of the seagoing regiments. Raised in times of national emergency, they were disbanded as quickly as possible upon peace. Any number of reasons can account for this: expense, fear of an increment to the standing army, and others, all viable. However, this "on again-off again" nature of marine service had several very harmful effects. Frequent raisings and disbandings prohibited continuity and regimental pride as seen in bodies like the Royal Scots Greys and the 3rd Carabiniers, which could trace their history, consecutively, to their raisings in 1685 and 1678 respectively. This in itself is ironic as the "Duke's Regiment" anticipates both of those organizations by more than fifteen years.

Another disadvantage concerned the officers. Again, continuity was a problem. Officers, particularly in the War of the Spanish Succession, saw plentiful action and were beginning to develop theories on "marine service" when the war ended. When the marine regiments were disbanded these officers either went on half-pay or transferred to the Line, of which the marines were technically a part. With no trained marine officers available in the interim from 1713 to 1739, the budding theories of "marine service" were left to wither and die. And this points to the third and most serious problem: doctrine.

James Donovan once remarked, "One of the more common human failings is the tendency to react to new phenomena with old reflexes." This seems particularly true in the area of weapons and doctrine. Whenever a new weapon or weapons system is introduced into a nation's arsenal, the military planners have to decide what to do with that weapon, or weapons system, *after* it arrives. Many are of the opinion (this author among them) that a great many problems could be avoided if doctrine was developed before, or at least concurrently with, the weapons system. This problem has persisted throughout military history and is well illustrated by the introduction of the Fast Carrier Task Force and Fleet Marine Forces into the United States Pacific Fleet in 1943–44. Both weapons systems were revolutionary, but until sufficient commanders and doctrine were developed for them, *in the field*, they exerted no great influence. After the doctrine was forged, they became irresistible.

The focus of this article will be upon the dual problems of doctrine and ambiguity. For two days, in November of 1739, the House of Commons was brought face to face with those questions. And though they did not realize it, or for that matter intend to do it, the Commons lifted much of the ambiguity which had surrounded the marine forces since 1664. For most writers these debates are lost in the much larger issue of the Spanish War and, admittedly, for one not interested in marine history they are tendentious specimens of Augustan prose. However, this writer sees in them something crucial in the development of the corps during the century that followed the debates.

As mentioned previously, prior to 1739 there was no clearly understood definition of the term *marine*. Was a marine a soldier serving aboard ship, or was he an apprentice sailor serving time as a soldier? Did the marines come under the jurisdiction of the army or of the navy? The marine establishment had always been an anomaly; raised and mus-

tered like the Line, they spent the majority of their time at sea. Pay proved a very difficult problem because army regulations specified that before a regiment could be paid it had to be mustered. And this could prove a problem when one marine regiment might be split up aboard half a dozen of the king's ships. Their officers purchased their commissions from the War Office, yet at sea all marines—officers and men alike—took orders from the sea officers. Theoretically, at sea a midshipman could, and did, issue commands to a captain of marines. These were nagging and persistent questions which, in November of 1739, had no answers.

When war with Spain had become inevitable, George II had summoned his Parliament into session early. The reasons were readily apparent. Because of its geography as an island nation, Britain always had the time to learn how to fight a war *after* it had become involved. As a result, it had traditionally tended in peacetime to deny its armed services the equipment, training, and thought required to keep them ready for battle. In November 1739, Great Britain found itself in an even worse state than usual: the army was negligible; the navy was "built by the mile and cut off as needed," and the Walpole government was unwilling and inexperienced to prosecute a major conflict. In short, the nation, embarked on what was assumed to be a small and easy struggle, lacked the capacity to win it. Against this backdrop, Parliament was called to order on 15 November 1739.

From his throne, the king informed Parliament of the events which had so recently culminated in the declaration of war against Spain, calling the conflict "a just and necessary war" which the Spanish atrocities in the Caribbean had "rendered unavoidable." The sovereign went on to say that he had augmented his forces both by land and by sea "pursuant to the power given me by Parliament" and that he trusted in Parliament to grant supplies for "any further augmentation" he might deem necessary. The king wasted no time in informing Parliament of the further augmentation he desired. "In the prosecution of this war a number of soldiers to serve on board the Fleet may be requisite, and I have judged it proper that a body of Marines be raised." Concluding, the king said, "And I cannot doubt, from your devotion to my Person and Government . . . but you will grant effectual supplies . . . and enable me to carry on the war with vigour."

The king's proposal to raise a body of marines was roundly supported in the House of Commons, but a question soon arose as to how the marines ought to be raised. Robert Walpole and the king favored raising six new marine regiments which would be trained and equipped solely as "amphibious" forces, functioning on land as well as at sea. The opposition, particularly William Pulteney, wanted to draw the six marine regiments from the Line. Taken at face value, there seems nothing so profound about this difference of opinion; certainly it was something on which a compromise could be reached (as indeed it was). The important thing, however, was that during the ensuing debate the Commons was forced to delineate just what did and, more important, did not constitute "marine service."

Though they hardly realized it, Walpole and George II, in maintaining the position they did, were laying many of the guidelines for the permanent organization of the Marine Corps which would come in 1755. Had they acquiesced to drawing the marines from the Line, there would have been no marines at all. Rather, there would have been only those vague and ill-defined entities known as "regiments raised for sea service" which had proven so troublesome and useless in previous wars.

Twelve days after George II had asked Parliament to grant supplies for the raising of six marine regiments a bill was introduced in the House by Samuel Sandys calling for the raising of the regiments "in the most frugal manner, and upon the least expensive establishment." This introductory motion calls for careful scrutiny. The "nursery of seamen" concept, which saw the marine as a sailor in training, was still adhered to by many, Sandys apparently among them. He noted that at the beginning of nearly every war Britain became involved in, it found itself short of skilled seamen. The natural consequence of this shortage was the "hot press," so feared throughout the eighteenth and first quarter of the nineteenth centuries. According to Sandys, this hot press resulted in "an entire stop to our trade, which ought never to be done, but in the case of imminent danger from invasion."

Elaborating on the prospects of an invasion, he said that Britain's undue fear of a cross-channel incursion had always resulted in the maintenance of a large army at home. Rather than press the valuable merchant seamen, Sandys reasoned, put "land men or land soldiers" on board the fleet as marines, freeing Britain of an added expense and the merchant seaman from the press.

The Sandys motion does have one interesting observation in it concerning the marines as useful "for making invasions and incursions of the enemy on land [better] than the most expert seamen, very few of whom are bred to that sort of discipline." If the marines were to be used in that capacity then, according to Sandys, they should be veteran soldiers rather "than a body of raw, ill-disciplined men, newly raised for that purpose." Sandys went so far as to say that the marines should have been on board the fleet prior to the declaration of war: "It was time enough to declare war when they were arrived there [America] and ready to attack the enemy."

Briefly summarized, Samuel Sandys's motion incorporated several theories concerning marine service. One saw the marine as a neophyte seaman, learning his trade while serving as a soldier. When he had become a competent seaman he would serve in the fleet, freeing the government from the necessity of pressing the merchant seamen. Then there was the conception of the marine simply as a soldier carried aboard ship. Finally, there was the amalgamation of the two, which saw the marine knowledgeable enough to work the ship if necessary but trained also as a land soldier. Sandys mentioned all three, but endorsed none in particular. He was adamant only on the point that the marines should come from the Line and not be newly raised.

The "nursery of seamen" concept had proven a fallacy since the days of the "Duke's Regiment." Merchant seamen would always be pressed in time of war until the practice of impressment was abolished. It took a good deal more to make a marine than a soldier immune to seasickness. The defense of a warship's decks in action called for discipline and split-second timing; keeping up sustained small-arms fire, boarding, and repulsing boarders could not be learned overnight. Clearly the "soldier and sailor too" concept was the most valid. The marine should be acquainted with the techniques of sailing a man-of-war, yet he also had to be a soldier, functioning as those marines had at Gibraltar. If passed, the Sandys motion would create marines in name only. Being army troops they would find it difficult to adjust to life at sea and probably be counterproductive.

The Sandys motion was seconded by Philip Gybbon who, like Sandys, felt that the war should be brought "to the doors of the enemy," but he felt it should be carried there by Britain's old regiments which had proven themselves. Sir William Yonge favored raising new regiments, but only because he felt drawing the marines from the home forces would weaken England's ability to repel an invasion, which he felt was sure to come. Indeed, Yonge exhibited a tremendous naivety concerning the duties of marines aboard ship:

> In fighting a ship there are no marches, or counter marches: there is no part of the land discipline required, but that of loading or firing a musket; and a country fellow from the plough, may, in three days, be taught to do this adroitly as the most expert soldier in the army.

Yonge's remarks illustrate the almost total ignorance of many members of Parliament (M.P.) concerning the specialized training required for marines. The idea that a farmer could be made into a soldier overnight was one which persisted far too long in Britain. An ordinary soldier could not be well trained in a short time; and a marine, who had to learn both the land and sea disciplines, certainly could not.

George Lyttleton spoke after Yonge and said that, unlike his colleague, he appreciated and understood the extensive training the marines would require. In peacetime he would vote for newly raised regiments, but this was war. Given the present situation the newly raised men could receive only a modicum of training. To raise six new regiments rather than embarking six veteran regiments would be like "exchanging six good horses for six new, but untried, horses before embarking upon a journey." That these six new regiments would be a dangerous increment to the standing army was given voice by Joseph Danvers: "I wish there was not a red coat to be seen within the kingdom. . . . A standing army in all countries is an evil." Then showing he appreciated the gravity of the situation concluded ". . . but it is an evil we must submit to."

Whether the Sandys motion passed was to be decided by the two antagonists of the war debate, William Pulteney and Robert Walpole. For Pulteney this was yet another chance to embarrass Walpole. Had not the king asked for speedy action on the marine regiments? Had not the Commons responded? Was not Walpole, the king's minister, delaying that speedy action because he differed on some "minor" point? Pulteney's pointed questions were a skillful and nearly successful attempt to represent Walpole as unfaithful to the king and even unpatriotic.

Pulteney began his speech by deriding Spain's ability to resist British might. And while it was true that Spain was in a state of decline, subsequent events in America were to prove that it was not yet ready to roll over and die. What was the good of keeping the best regiments at home in time of war, Pulteney asked. Do you send raw, untrained men overseas because "they cannot so handsomely dance through their exercises at a raree show?" Common sense alone dictated that the best troops should go into action first if a speedy victory was to be won.

Pulteney certainly had a point, but the reason for keeping the best troops at home was rooted deep in the British military tradition. British generals and strategists still adhered, in 1739, to the "German war." America might have its moments, but real glory and honor were won in Europe. When war with France came, and most were sure it would, the flowers of the English and French armies would meet in Europe in the tradition of Bouvines, Agincourt, and Blenheim.

Pulteney buttressed his argument by saying that the marine regiments were expensive to maintain. The marines had always required specialized equipment, and in the pandemonium of a sea battle much of this equipment was lost or destroyed. On this point Pulteney could not be refuted. Of all the speakers favoring the Sandys motion, Pulteney best understood the nature of marine service. "I know that the marines ought to be men bred to land as well as sea discipline," he said. There existed, he contended, a misconception about the type of land service they ought to be trained for: "If marines were to serve a whole campaign at land, and to be made part of the regular land army, I shall grant, that they ought to be formed into regiments." Pulteney viewed the marines rather as a support force of shock troops which could be used in assaults upon fortified positions. If such were the case they should be divided into companies with a total not to exceed three thousand men as opposed to the six thousand requested by the king.

Pulteney's argument shows that of all the speakers so far he had the best conception of what marine service was, but there were some flaws in his case. When he advocated the marines as a support assault force, they were to support the seamen. Seamen were not the proper forces for assaulting fortified positions; this task had devolved upon them long before there were marine forces. A successful assault required strict discipline, something not evidenced by most seamen. The tragic incident at Gibraltar in 1704, where some two hundred seamen were killed when, in their enthusiasm, they carried torches into a captured powder magazine, illustrates this.

As warfare became more specialized it would require even more training and discipline to execute an amphibious assault. And the seamen, for all their courage, were not suited for this.

Thus far the debates had enumerated certain *specific* qualities pertaining to marine service. First, the marine ought to be familiar, to some extent, with the sailor's art. Second, he must have a measure of training in land warfare. Third, the marines should be divided, either by regiment or by company, into a special unit for "incursions" against enemy territory. Slowly the cloud of ambiguity was beginning to lift.

Following Pulteney, Robert Walpole addressed the House. No, he was not obstructing the king's wishes; no, he was not unpatriotic. Parliament had rushed pell-mell into the war and here they were, doing the same thing with the marines. Had any of his colleagues examined the Marine Establishment of 1702? Might this not have been useful? He *had* examined the 1702 Establishment. Sandys and Pulteney had advocated "small and inexpensive" companies of seventy men each. Under the 1702 Establishment the highest number of men per company was sixty. So the small companies advocated by his opponents were not so small as they thought.

If the marines were drawn from the standing army would that save the nation money? No, Walpole said, because new men would have to be raised and trained to fill the vacancies left by the marine draft. Marine service offered bounty and a share of prize money for captured ships; no such bounty was offered in the land regiments. As a result, bounties would have to be offered to induce men to enlist in the infantry. In one pocket out of the other; no loss, no gain.

If the regiments were newly raised, would they be as poorly trained as Sandys and Pulteney feared? In America, the best time to campaign was in the winter, when the troops would not be susceptible to the various tropical diseases. Walpole said that no adequate forces could be ready for transport to America for at least eight months. In that eight-month interim the new marines could receive considerable training and be ready for action by the autumn of 1740.

Walpole then turned to the "nursery of seamen" idea. Was it a valid concept, he asked?

> A great many fellows that called themselves seamen, have been rejected or turned out of our men of war, because they were not found to be expert seamen, nor in any way fit for their business. These men . . . will make good marines though they could not be accepted as good seamen.

A marine did not have to be an expert seaman, if he were, then he would not be a marine. However, a man with some knowledge of seamanship could make a good marine. Should he be called upon to function as a sailor he could; but there was no reason, in Walpole's opinion, to insist that every marine be a potential able-bodied seaman.

Pulteney had advocated the company, rather than the regiment, as the basic marine unit. Marine companies might be fine, Walpole said, if they were to be used only in small attacks or skirmishes, but where the contending forces numbered in the thousands, the regiment was necessary. The Sandys motion had called also for a very small number of officers. What would happen, Walpole asked the opposition, when the marines were engaged in land action and a number of their officers killed or wounded? Who would command if a large number of officers should be incapacitated?

In his summation Walpole urged his colleagues to give a little more thought to the Sandys motion. Point by point, he had shown its many flaws. It would not be inexpensive and provide small companies, as its proponents said it would. It was not true that newly raised regiments would be embarked poorly trained. Lastly, the Commons had the chance to look at the Establishment of 1702 rather than going into the issue blind, as they were doing.

The choice was theirs. They could pass the Sandys motion and have a marine force in name only, or they could do some investigating of the 1702 Establishment and go a long way to create a real marine force. Walpole's appeal to reason was strong enough to defeat the Sandys motion by a vote of 177 to 95. When Parliament adjourned for the day, the M.P.s must have been more confused than ever, but through their efforts the nature of marine service was becoming less confusing.

The following day, 28 November, Lord Polwarth introduced a motion calling for the examination of the 1702 Establishment so that the House ". . . could clear up that point, and put the House upon a method of rendering our marine forces as serviceable as it is possible." At this point Walpole interjected that while it was good to look at the old establishment, the new one should not be modeled on the lines of one formulated thirty-five years before: "that can have no effect but . . . to disappoint his [the king's] royal endeavours for the service of the nation."

Samuel Sandys, who had introduced the original motion, then made a startling admission, which illustrates the whole point of this essay:

> This motion [to see the Establishment of 1702] becomes very necessary; for unless the establishment be produced, the House can have no regular information as to what a marine is.

Samuel Sandys, who had sponsored a bill which would have raised three thousand marines, now admitted that he did not know what a marine was. Admitting his misunderstanding, he said that he assumed all that was wanted was a body of soldiers who would serve as replacements for seamen. Obviously he was mistaken since the House now wanted to establish a "body of marines in the true sense of the word." What had begun as a minor debate along party lines was now becoming a bipartisan attempt to formulate doctrine.

Lord Polwarth, upon examination of the 1702 Establishment, noted that the marines were classed as army troops and as such represented an increment to the standing forces. Since they spent most of their time at sea, he reasoned, it might not be a bad idea to put the marines under the jurisdiction of the Admiralty. Unfortunately the wisdom in Polwarth's idea was not grasped, for it was not until 1747, after much mismanagement and suffering, that Admiral George Anson got the marines placed under the jurisdiction of the Admiralty.

A week later, after the Establishment of 1702 had been thoroughly examined, a compromise was achieved. The six marine regiments were to be newly raised, but five men from each regiment of the Line were to be appointed sergeants and corporals. The bulk of the men were to be newly enlisted and trained specifically as marines. Parliament appropriated £118,000 for the six regiments which numbered 4,890 officers and men. In January 1740, four additional regiments were raised bringing the total marine strength to ten regiments consisting of 8,000 men.

What was the net effect of the 27–28 November debates? In retrospect, these debates constitute what must be reckoned one of the most influential legislative acts in the history of the Marine Corps. More than a victory for Walpole, more than a defeat for his opposition, this debate saved the marines from relegation to a seaborne infantry. Walpole had insisted, and made his opponents realize, that marines were not simply land forces carried aboard men-of-war. That the earlier marines had been trained for both land and sea was an important part of his argument. If all that was desired were "regiments for sea service," then raise them. Do not, Walpole charged, raise such bodies and call them "marines."

During the course of the debate a word had been used by several M.P.s which would take on greater meaning in years to come. The word was *amphibious*. "The marines service is amphibious; they must know how to behave by sea as well as by land." When Sir William Yonge said that, he probably had no idea that the term *amphibious* was to become synonymous with the marines of all

nations. This was what separated the marine from both the soldier and sailor. He was part of each, but neither totally. Marines were attached to the fleet; they might make landings like the army; they might form garrisons like the army. Yet when the time came they were replaced by the army and went back to the fleet. All of the above duties were *marine* duties, not the duties of regiments for sea service.

If the debates of 27–28 November 1739 had done little else, they had gone a long way in defining what was and what was not a marine. The unhappy experiences of the forthcoming war would answer still more questions. The importance of this cannot be overestimated when looking toward the future. In 1755, when war again was imminent, there was no such debate in Parliament as to how the marines ought to be established. In 1747 they had been brought under the control of the Admiralty and in 1755 an Act of Parliament ratified that action. Since then they have been an adjunct of the Royal Navy.

For seventy-six years the marine forces had been shrouded with uncertainty and ambiguity. What were they? Who were they? What did they do? What did they not do? Why were there even marines at all? In two days, the House of Commons answered many of these questions, but others persisted for a long time. At any rate, this was the first recorded attempt by Parliament to deal with a question of doctrine, and in this writer's opinion, they did well by themselves.

One of Rudyard Kipling's lesser known poems deals with the Royal Marines and it seems to lend itself well for conclusion. Kipling's hero, Tommy Atkins, is aboard a troopship in the Suez Canal and he sees a man chipping paint aboard a battleship. The man is dressed in what appears to be an army uniform and Tommy asks, " 'Oo are you?' Sez 'e 'I'm a Jolly-'Er Majesty's Jolly-Soldier an' Sailor too!' " Soldier and sailor too.

Amphibious Operations in Colonial North America

BY COLONEL BROOKE NIHART, USMC (RET.)

The idea of marines as an adjunct naval service complementary to the navy went back beyond British custom all the way to the Greeks and Romans. But the colonists, in their battle for independence from Britain, did not have to rely on merely second-hand knowledge of amphibious operations from the mother country; they had their own amphibious experiences in the New World. The colonists were littoral and maritime. Trade was mainly by water—inland by rivers, and by sea between coastal colonies and Britain and its Caribbean and African colonies. War, also, was conducted on water.

As early as 1654 an amphibious force sailed from Boston to Port Royal in Nova Scotia where the Massachusetts colonists landed to neutralize the base from which the French had been harassing shipping and fishing. By the time Massachusetts Governor William Phips prepared to launch an attack in the summer of 1690, there had been five expeditions to Port Royal. In August of that year, Phips headed up the Saint Lawrence toward Quebec. Phips's naval gunfire was inadequate against Quebec's citadel, his landing force ill-trained, and cooperation between fleet and landing force lacking. After a week, he raised the siege and returned to Boston, losing a few ships on the way.

The Americans launched abortive amphibious assaults on Port Royal in 1704 and 1707 but were successful in 1710 when a British-led expedition with twelve hundred

New England troops and six hundred British marines seized the French base. The success of a professionally led operation spearheaded by regular marines, in contrast to earlier amphibious failures with hastily raised militia landing forces, doubtlessly remained in colonial memories for a couple of generations.

To the south, Britain and Spain by 1739 were contending over the Florida boundary and Caribbean commerce. Georgia's Governor Oglethorpe provided the southern colonies with an amphibious experience by leading Georgia and Carolina troops successfully in seaborne attacks against Spanish forts on the San Juan River. He failed, however, against Saint Augustine in 1741 and 1743.

The conflict with Spain, known as the War of Jenkins' Ear for the *cause célèbre* English merchant captain mutilated by the Spanish, centered on British attempts to take Spanish Caribbean colonies. In an address to Parliament, the king argued that the war would require "a number of soldiers to serve on board the fleet" and "that a body of marines should be raised." Parliament gave him six regiments of marines a month later and soon after an additional three marine regiments to be organized in the colonies. The regiments were raised in all colonies except New Hampshire and the three southernmost colonies that were engaged on the Florida coast.

Admiral Vernon, commanding the Caribbean squadron, before his departure from England, wrote requesting a company of marines for each of his ships, "which would have strengthened us in numbers, as well as had their expertness in handling their arms,

Marine Corps Gazette, "Our Pre-Colonial Experience," 60 (July 1976): 29–34. Reprinted by permission.

Quebec, 13 September 1759. Courtesy of the Beverley R. Robinson Collection, U.S. Naval Academy Museum.

to have incited our seamen with the imitation of them." Vernon thus voiced one of the earliest rationales for marines as an elite force.

Vernon got his marines the following year in transports from England and America. While the British marines were generally well trained, the Americans were neither trained nor disciplined and in addition were poorly equipped. Bad command relationships between the amphibious and landing force commanders, heavy casualties from both the Spanish and tropical disease, and mutinies among the Americans doomed the attack against Cartagena in 1741.

George Washington's half brother, Lawrence, was senior company commander of the Americans. Upon his return and shortly before he died of disease contracted on the expedition, he named his estate on the Potomac *Mount Vernon* as a tribute to the admiral whom he greatly admired. The Cartagena expedition, although a disaster, served to keep alive the amphibious idea among the few American survivors.

In 1713 France began building a mighty fortress at Louisbourg on the far northeasterly tip of Nova Scotia. From this vantage, the French reasoned, they could control the approaches to the Saint Lawrence, New England's trade with the homeland, and the Grand Banks fisheries. By 1744, and after huge construction cost overruns that taxed Louis XV's treasury, the fortress-base was complete and France joined the war of the Austrian Succession. Repulsed at Port Royal—now called Annapolis Royal—the French from Louisbourg settled for seizing a New England fishing base at Canso, some 50 miles west of Louisbourg.

Despite the recent disaster at Cartagena and with British regulars pinned down in Europe, Governor Shirley of Massachusetts and the other New England colonies resolved to rid themselves of the menace. William Pepperell, a Maine merchant and militia colonel, was to lead the expedition of ninety transports and more than four thousand colonial troops. A British squadron of warships from

The landing at New Providence, 1776. Painting by V. Zveg. Courtesy of the U.S. Navy Historical Center.

the West Indies was to convoy the transports and support the landing. On 5 April 1745 the expedition retook Canso without the help of the West Indies squadron, which had not yet arrived. Three weeks were spent exercising the troops at Canso while waiting for the squadron and reconnoitering Louisbourg. With the squadron's arrival the landing was made and siege laid to the fortress. The colonists' determination, their skills as artisans and woodsmen, the presence of experienced militia artillerymen among them, plus a bit of luck and enemy ineptitude resulted in a French capitulation after two months of siege. For the first time American amphibious experience had been reinforced by a wholly domestic success.

The return of Louisbourg by the British to France by the Peace Treaty of Aix-la-Chapelle in 1748 was a great disappointment to New England and furthered the growing movement toward colonial unity. This movement led to the Albany Conference of 1754 and eventually to the Revolution.

French and British expansionist policies in North America clashed again in the French and Indian War, which began in 1754. Louis-bourg had to be retaken before the Saint Lawrence could be entered and Quebec seized. In 1758 an expedition was mounted with a landing force of nine thousand British regulars and five hundred New England rangers under James Wolfe, who had been at Cartagena with Vernon. The British landed under covering naval gunfire over beaches defended by French in field fortifications and laid siege to the fortress, which capitulated after another two-month siege.

Quebec was seized the following year and then all of Canada. Louisbourg was leveled in 1760 and thus was ended French power in North America. The final act of the French and Indian War, however, involved Spain, lured into an injudicious alliance with France in mid-1761.

England declared war on Spain in January 1762 and quickly organized an overseas expedition against Cuba. About 25 percent of the expeditionary force, or four thousand men, were to be raised in the colonies of New York, New Jersey, Connecticut, and Rhode Island. By 6 June the English task force arrived off Havana. A feint landing west of the harbor drew away defenders from the preferred landing beaches east of the city and the main landing was made virtually unopposed. A two-month siege of the powerful harbor forts followed with the Spanish capitulating soon after the fall of Morro on 30 July. The Americans arrived in time for the final mop up and garrison duties. Although colonial participation in the seaborne assault phases of the Louisbourg and Havana campaigns had been negligible, further experience in overseas expeditions had been gained and the amphibious tradition in the colonies firmly implanted

Not only was this tradition ingrained in colonial military thought with participants of Cartagena, the two Louisbourgs, and Havana expeditions still living and indeed with some serving in the Continental forces, but it was codified in the literature of war available in the personal military libraries of most colonial gentlemen of the day. There were at least three amphibious textbooks published in the few years before the Revolution.[1]

With a century of experience in amphibious operations and with available "how-to" books for reference, it is little wonder that the Continental Congress authorized the raising of two battalions of marines but three weeks after deciding on a navy. Indeed, marines had first been mentioned in Congress a month earlier in connection with a possible attack on two British brigs loaded with arms and ammunition on their way to Quebec. Their capture would secure badly needed munitions for Washington's army besieging Boston. Congress resolved on 5 October that two armed ships be sent out by Massachusetts with the help of Rhode Island and Connecticut to intercept the arms ships. The resolve enjoined the ship captains appointed to encourage the enlistment of seamen and *marines.* Clearly, the Congress considered marines as essential and integral to any naval undertaking—reciprocal and interdependent as powder and shot, musket and bayonet.

By 13 October, Congress backed up its resolve of the 5th by voting to fit out the two armed ships to intercept the Quebec-bound munitions ships. A naval committee was appointed to settle on the details. It shared a

partially overlapping membership with another committee, that on Nova Scotia. Silas Deane of Connecticut, John Langdon of New Hampshire, Stephen Hopkins of Rhode Island, and John Adams of Massachusetts served on both.

The Nova Scotia Committee was considering the petition of some of that colony's inhabitants to join in rebellion the colonies to the south. This prospect was sweetened in the minds of the committeemen by the possibility of capturing a large stock of military stores located at Halifax at the same time.

The committee solution was an amphibious expedition to Nova Scotia and on 10 November 1775 its proposal to the Congress was passed as a resolve to raise two battalions of marines, each of ten fifty-man companies. This organization was selected as suitable for land or sea with one company just right as a detachment for a small brig-size warship and two companies right for the largest frigate.

During the siege of Boston the summer of 1775, Washington fitted out several small ships for naval tasks along the Massachusetts coast. They were manned by Marblehead fishermen of Colonel Glover's regiment with the crews divided, logically, into seamen and marines.

Washington was tasked with fitting out the two ships authorized by the 13 October action of Congress. Again they were manned by Glover. Although ordered to intercept the two Quebec munitions ships, they contented themselves with raiding the Nova Scotia and Prince Edward Island coasts and returned with loot but no munitions ships, to Washington's severe reprove.

In early November, Congress authorized four more ships and found them on the Delaware River. They were merchantmen and two were converted to small frigates and two to brigs. Two sloops and two schooners from New England joined the small squadron in Philadelphia where they began conversion, arming and fitting out in November and December.

Also on 10 November, Congress passed another resolution leaving the Nova Scotia expedition and raising of the marines to Washington, still besieging Boston. Washington did send spies to Nova Scotia but expressed reservations on the expedition and to raising the marines from his small army. He was in the midst of reorganizing and reforming his army and he gave as his reason against raising marines from it the same valid excuse every general gives when asked to organize an elite corps from his forces—it would disrupt his already shaky organization and his best officers and men would be removed from him.

Congress relieved Washington of the responsibility for raising marines on 30 November and indeed, on the 28th, had taken steps to raise the marines itself by commissioning Samuel Nicholas as the first marine officer. Recruiting and training followed in December and the marines, 234 of them, reported aboard six of the eight ships at Philadelphia.

The little amphibious task force, stuck in Delaware River ice during January and February, continued to fit out and exercise at guns and rigging with the marines making forays ashore to round up and return deserters.

Esek Hopkins, brother of committeeman Stephen Hopkins, had been named "commander-in-chief of the fleet" and while stuck in the ice had received a series of operations orders. The final and inspired order was to send the commodore and his little amphibious squadron to New Providence in the Bahamas to seize British guns, powder, and shot stored there in Fort Montagu. This he did after a 3 March unopposed landing two miles east of the fort, and the fledgling navy and Marine Corps were off to an auspicious beginning.

The story of the New Providence landing and of subsequent adventures of the Continental Marines has been detailed elsewhere.[2] Suffice it to state, however, that their service encompassed every type of action ever contemplated for marines and was a complete precursor to their next two hundred years.

Even on their return from New Providence they participated in a sea fight and throughout the Revolution fought from gun decks and fighting tops and in small landing parties. A marine battalion fought as part of Washington's army at Princeton in 1777, sharing a key role in the victory. In 1778 they returned to New Providence, and the marines made another major amphibious landing in Maine on Penobscot in 1779. Marines operated on inland waterways in a variety of roles and the end of hostilities found them escorting the national treasury from Boston to New York.

All but two of the states had navies—small ships for local coastal and riverine defense. Most of the state navies included marines on their ships. Massachusetts's navy sailed beyond mere coastal defense, participating in the Penobscot expedition along with its state marines. Several hundred privateers, armed merchant ships sent out to raid enemy sealanes, included marines in their complements as they scoured West Indian and European waters.

Some one hundred thirty officers and two thousand men served in the Continental Marines with several times that number in states and privateer marines. Conceived in the experiences of colonial and European wars and reinforced by theoretical considerations, marines in the Revolution fully justified congressional, state, and privateer captain's decisions to raise them.

Writing more than fifty years later, James Fenimore Cooper, in his *History of the Navy*, made this evaluation:

> At no period of the naval history of the world, is it probable that marines were more important than during the war of the Revolution.

Notes

[1] Thomas More Molyneux, *Conjunct Operations; or Expeditions That Have Been Carried on Jointly by the Fleet and the Army, with a Commentary on Littoral War* (London, 1759); John MacIntire, *A Military Treatise on the Discipline of the Marine Forces when at Sea together with short instructions for Detachments Sent to Attack on Shore* (London, 1763); and Lieutenant Terence O'Loghlen, *The Marine Volunteer* (London, 1766).

[2] Charles R. Smith, *Marines in the Revolution* (Washington, D.C.: Government Printing Office, 1975).

British Amphibious Operations during the Seven Years and American Wars

BY DAVID SYRETT

The cooperation and support of a strong navy was one of the greatest advantages enjoyed by the British army during the last half of the eighteenth century. To exploit this advantage and to meet the strategic requirements of the Seven Years War and the American War, the British armed forces set about developing and mastering the complex skills and techniques of amphibious warfare.[1] A highly sophisticated scheme for conducting amphibious landings emerged as a result, one which enabled the British to exploit militarily the advantages of naval power. The campaigns against Louisbourg, Quebec, Guadeloupe, Belle Isle, Martinique, and Havana during the Seven Years War owe their success to Britain's skill in transporting her armies across seas and landing them on hostile shores. And clearly such campaigns of the American War as the invasions of New York, Rhode Island, Pennsylvania, Saint Lucia, and South Carolina would have been impossible without a knowledge of the techniques of amphibious warfare.

An amphibious assault is one of the most difficult of military operations. Detailed planning and considerable skill are required to transfer an army from ship to shore in battle formation. During this period the British learned that preparations had to be made long before the expedition sailed for or reached its destination. Troops and equipment had to be embarked, arranged, and controlled

while at sea in such a way that the order, discipline, and organization of the army was maintained.[2] Special command procedures and equipment had to be developed to transfer the troops in proper battle order from the ships to the shore. And finally, plans had to be made for the navy to support the army once it was ashore.

To maintain the organization of the army while at sea, once the troops were embarked and arranged on board ship, every British transport, victualler, and storeship engaged in an amphibious operation raised a distinguishing flag indicating its cargo or the army unit it carried. For instance, in the fleet carrying the British force to invade Saint Lucia in 1778, all ordnance transports flew blue vanes from their mainmasts, while the four transports carrying the 28th Regiment flew white flags with two red balls from their foremasts.[3] Ships with the commanding officers of army units and such officers as the adjutant-general were further distinguished by "a Swallow-tail in their vanes."[4] The army's chain of command and communications were maintained at sea by a special set of signals which the commander-in-chief of the army used to summon to his ship such key officers as brigade majors, adjutants, and general officers.[5] These signals and the identifying flags enabled the commander-in-chief of the army to exercise control over his troops while on board ship.

The navy commander-in-chief commanded all the ships, vessels, and small craft used in the operation.[6] The transports, storeships, and victuallers were divided into groups

Mariner's Mirror 58 (August 1972): 269–280. Reprinted by permission of the Society for Nautical Research and of the author.

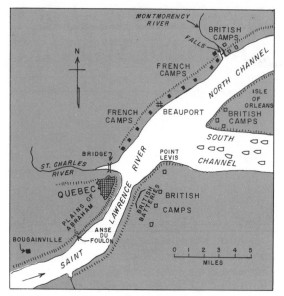

British amphibious operations on the Saint Lawrence River during the Seven Years War.

Safely transporting the army to its intended landing site was the responsibility of the navy, but when should the navy's responsibility end and the army's begin? A clear division of command responsibilities between the army and the navy is essential in an amphibious operation, hence it must be decided in advance at precisely what point in the course of a landing the command of the operation passes from the navy to the army. The failure of the raid at Rochefort in 1757 can be attributed in part to the fact that the question of command responsibilities had not been settled before the operation. When General Sir John Mordaunt was courtmartialed in 1758 as a result of Rochefort, Admiral Sir Edward Hawke stated that he

always looked upon it to be his Duty, as Admiral, to convoy the Troops to the Road of *Basque*, and there, if possible, to find out a Landing-place for them, and, in case of their landing to give them all the Assistance in his Power for that Purpose; but with respect to the Question, "Whether they should land, or not" . . . he consequently thought, it was the Part of the Generals to determine that Question by themselves . . . he thought it was a Matter of Judgement which merely related to them, and that the Sea had nothing to do with it, farther than telling them [the Generals], they had found out a Landing place, and were ready to land the Troops, if they thought proper, and to give them all the Assistance in their Power.[12]

The problem, however, is not as simple as Hawke would have it, for the proceedings of the Mordaunt courtmartial clearly reveal that the decision not to land at Rochefort was largely the result of advice tendered by captains in the navy who were to conduct the operation.[13] Apparently much was learned from Rochefort, for confusion concerning command responsibilities is not evident in subsequent amphibious campaigns of the Seven Years War. Thereafter the commanders of the army and navy in consultation selected the landing place, and then "the whole Command of them is given to a Sea Officer, who conducts them to the place of landing; . . . the Marine Officer has little to do till the men are out of the Boats for then is the Time

and placed under the command of navy officers known as agents for transports, who issued orders to the individual ship masters;[7] however, at times the army did not trust the masters of transports to obey these orders and directed that an army officer on each transport enforce them.[8] Before sailing, the master of each transport was issued sealed orders to be opened in case of separation,[9] and the naval commander-in-chief issued an "order of sailing" assigning each of the transports, victuallers, storeships, and the naval escorts their stations for the voyage.[10] If the invasion fleet had to traverse a body of shoal water or pass through a narrow channel, navy officers in small craft would be sent ahead to make soundings and to mark the channel. James Cook, for example, surveyed and mapped the Saint Lawrence River in advance of the British fleet proceeding to attack Quebec.[11] The above measures—assigning agents for transports to command divisions of transports, issuing sailing orders and rendezvous, and reconnoitering the intended route of the invasion fleet—were taken by the navy to ensure that the army arrived safely at its objective.

for him to show his Judgement."[14] Thus, it was decided that the army assumed command not upon arrival off the landing site but when the troops left the boats.

Once off the intended landing site, measures were taken for the protection of the transports. Warships were stationed around the anchorage and patrols of guard boats set up.[15] Simultaneously preparations were begun for the landing and orders for the conduct of the operation were issued. It was the task of the commanders-in-chief of the army and navy to formulate the tactical plan for the assault, for, as General Sir John Ligonier noted in 1757

> There is a Chance in the best concerted Military Enterprizes, which every Man of long Service must have experienced; what Share then must be left to Fortune in an Expedition, where neither the Country, nor the Number of Troops, you are to act against, is known with any Precision.
>
> The Capacity of the Generals may supply this Want of Intelligence, but to give them any positive Plan or Rule of Action under such Circumstances, I apprehend would be absurd.[16]

Thus, beaches had to be scouted, and sometimes small parties of men were landed to reconnoiter the region behind the intended landing place. On the night before the landing on the Isle of Orleans in the Saint Lawrence River, for instance, General James Wolfe sent forty rangers to reconnoiter the island. Staff conferences were also held at which the forthcoming operation would be explained to junior officers. In 1758 Admiral Edward Boscawen assembled the navy officers who were to conduct the landing at Louisbourg and gave them "strict charges to be diligent in the execution of those orders."[17] While seemingly nothing more than common sense, such measures as guarding the transport anchorage, reconnoitering the landing place, and explaining the operation to subordinate officers were in fact extremely vital owing to the complex and dangerous nature of an amphibious assault.

Preparations had to be made as well by the troops on board the transports. In 1779 a group of Scots on board the transport *Apollo* pre-

pared for an assault landing by spending the preceding night sharpening broadswords and donning Highland costume.[18] More conventional preparations entailed having the soldiers parade on the deck of the transport several hours before disembarking to have their arms and equipment inspected.[19] Usually each man was issued sixty rounds of ammunition,[20] two flints,[21] several days' rations,[22] and his canteen was filled with a mixture of rum and water.[23] In order to reduce the amount of equipment each soldier had to carry, most of the bedding and equipage was left on the transports.[24] Sometimes pieces of cloth or leather were issued to the troops to cover the locks of their muskets to keep them dry. The muskets, depending on the nature of the operation, were generally loaded and, just before disembarking, slung barrel upwards over the shoulder to prevent the shot from dropping out. Bayonet and cartridge belts were also slung over the shoulders to keep them from getting wet.[25]

While the troops were getting ready to disembark, the officers of the navy were preparing to convey them to the shore. In most major amphibious assaults, the navy commander-in-chief appointed either a commodore or a senior captain to command the operation. At Quebec Admiral Sir Charles Saunders appointed Captain James Chads to conduct the landing at Wolfe's Cove, and Admiral Sir George Pocock charged Commodore Augustus Keppel with the conduct of the landing at Havana.[26] In 1776 Admiral Lord Howe appointed Commodore William Hotham to conduct the landing on Long Island, and in 1780 Vice Admiral Marriot Arbuthnot directed that Captain Keith Elphinstone command the assault landing at Charleston.[27] However, at the landing at Cancale Bay near Saint Malo in 1758, Commodore Lord Howe, the naval commander-in-chief, conducted the landing himself; and in the American War Commodore Sir George Collier, during a series of coastal raids on Virginia and Connecticut in 1779, personally took charge of the disembarkation and landing of the troops.[28] It was the task of the navy officer charged with the conduct of an amphibious landing, with the assistance of other naval officers, to disembark the troops from transports into small craft, to form these craft into assault waves, and then to convey the force to shore in combat formation.

Whenever possible, the first waves of assault troops were rowed ashore in flat-bottomed boats. According to Robert Beatson, flat-bottomed boats were developed after Rochefort, for the need for a proper landing craft was among the many lessons learned by the British from that abortive raid.[29] Two different sizes of flat-bottomed boats were developed. The larger type was 36 feet long, 10 feet 2 inches in breadth, 2 feet 11 inches in depth amidships between keel and gunwale and was equipped with tholepins and thwarts for twenty oarsmen. The smaller type of flat-bottomed boat was 30 feet long, 9 feet 9 inches wide, 2 feet 11 inches deep amidships and was fitted for sixteen oarsmen. Except for size and number of oarsmen, both types were essentially alike: flat-bottomed, clinker-built, with bluff bows, and steered by a detachable rudder and tiller. Two ring bolts were mounted on the keel inside each craft in order to hoist the boat in and out of the water.[30] Each flat-bottomed boat was equipped with the requisite number of oars, a 40-pound grapnel, a mast, a yard, a lugsail, and all the necessary sheets, lines, and halyards.[31] Individual commanders sometimes added to the equipment of flat-bottomed boats. Commodore Sir George Collier, for instance, took a flat-bottomed boat which he used on cutting-out expeditions on the Maine coast in 1777 and mounted a coehorn on the bow and barricaded the gunwale with rolled-up hammocks to protect the occupants from small-arms fire.[32]

At various times small craft other than flat-bottomed boats were specially constructed for amphibious operations. In 1776 at Staten Island the army built a number of craft capable of carrying one hundred soldiers and of having ramps mounted on their bows for unloading cannon;[33] and General Benedict Arnold (in British service) had a number of special boats made which mounted cannon and carried about a hundred men for use on the rivers in Virginia.[34] Longboats, cutters, and barges belonging to transports and warships were occasionally employed as well,[35] however, flat-bottomed boats were much preferred for amphibious operations. Wolfe complained of the shortage of flat-bottomed boats at Quebec; General Howe, in a letter to his brother, stated that the shore-to-shore assault preceding the battle of Bunker Hill suffered from a lack of flat-bottomed boats; and, in the first months of the American War, both Major-General Thomas Gage and Vice-Admiral Samuel Graves lamented the shortage of flat-bottomed boats.[36]

Flat-bottomed boats were carried to the scene of an amphibious landing on the decks of transports and warships.[37] Special booms and other tackle were sometimes fitted to the transports to enable them to hoist the flat-bottomed boats in and out of the water.[38] On the command of the navy commander-in-chief, the flat-bottomed boats, each under the command of a navy lieutenant or petty officer, would be launched and manned by experienced boatmen drawn from among the seamen aboard the warships and transports,[39] although on occasion soldiers were used to man them.[40] Upon receipt of a signal from the officer commanding the landing, the boats would pull to the transports to begin to embark troops. Each transport disembarking troops raised a distinguishing flag which was lowered again as soon as the soldiers were in the boats.[41]

Depending upon their size, the flat-bottomed boats carried forty to sixty soldiers drawn from the same rank and file, thereby enabling them quickly to form up in combat formation upon landing. The soldiers were seated facing each other on two thwarts which ran lengthwise down the center of the boat, and their commanding officers and sergeants were stationed in the stern-sheets and bows.[42] While in the boats, the troops were under orders to remain seated and silent and not to fire their muskets.[43] When all the troops had been embarked, the flat-bottomed boats proceeded, upon receipt of a signal from the flagship, to an assembly point to be placed in formation for the landing.[44]

At the assembly point, the navy officers in charge of the landing arranged the flat-bottomed boats into a formation which resembled as closely as possible the army's order of battle.[45] First the boats were grouped together in echelons, then the boats within each echelon were formed into two or three parallel lines, the placing of each boat being determined by the troops on board. To simplify the task of arranging the boats in the correct order, each flat-bottomed boat had a number painted on its bow and flew a small flag indicating what unit it carried.[46]

The troops were generally landed in echelons, the size of each echelon depending upon the number of boats available and the nature of the landing site. The landing had to be planned, and the boats arranged, in a manner which would ensure that as soon as one echelon landed another would reach the shore. The first troops to land had to be promptly reinforced by successive echelons. One of the main reasons a landing was not attempted at Rochefort on the night of 28 September 1757 was the inability to reinforce quickly the first echelon to land.[47]

The first echelon was usually composed of elite assault troops, with the bulk of the landing force following in the succeeding echelons. For example, when General Howe's army landed on the shores of the Elk River in 1777, the first echelon was made up of light infantry, grenadiers, and German *jägers*; the second of two British infantry regiments, British guards, Hessian grenadiers, and the Queens Rangers; and the third, fourth, and fifth echelons of twenty regiments of British and German infantry. The artillery, cavalry, and equipment for Howe's army were landed after the infantry was ashore.[48]

When the navy officers finished arranging the flat-bottomed boats, warships were stationed in front of and on the flanks of the formation to guide and escort the small craft to the landing site. When Howe landed on the shores of the Elk River, for instance, the first echelon of flat-bottomed boats was led toward the landing place by warships in the formation shown in Figure 1.[49]

The movement of the formation of warships and flat-bottomed boats was controlled by the navy officer in command of the operation by signals such as those employed by Commodore Sir George Collier in a raid on Virginia during the American War. As Collier preceded the first line of flat-bottomed boats, "Signals were occasionally made . . . to *advance*, or to *Halt*, by the display of small *Red* or *Blue* Flags, and had there been a necessity of Retreat *a White one* was to have been shown."[50] Establishing a system of signals to control the movement of both boats and warships helped to maintain the carefully planned formation and thereby ensure that the troops arrived on the beach in as close an approximation of their order of battle as possible.

While the flat-bottomed boats and their escorts were assembling, other warships were deployed to cover and support the landing. Sometimes warships would be deployed to stage diversions in an attempt to draw the attention of the enemy away from the actual site of the landing.[51] The main task of warships during an amphibious assault, however, was to destroy the defenses of the enemy and to isolate and dominate the landing area with naval gunfire. In the abortive Rochefort raid, the transports' longboats were fitted with 6-pounder brass cannon in order to "scour the beach of any forces the enemy might bring down to oppose the desent."[52] But it was evident that the gunfire from ship's boats was inadequate to support a major landing, and thereafter heavy warships were generally used. During the landing at Cancale Bay in 1758, Commodore Howe deployed H.M.S. *Rose*, H.M.S. *Flamborough*, and H.M.S. *Diligence* "to cover the landing of the troops, clear the beach, and silence the battery." The landing at Havana in 1762 was

Figure 1. Flat-bottomed boats with the first debarkation.

	Vigilant	
Swift		Senegal
Sphinx		Apollo
	Roebuck	

supported by the guns of fourteen warships.[53] During the American War, the landing at Gravesend on Long Island in 1776 was covered by the guns of H.M.S. *Rainbow*, which was stationed in such a way as to be able to fire directly at the beach, at the only building in the area, and at the same time enfilade the Brooklyn Village-Gravesend Road.[54] One of the most spectacular, and perhaps most effective, uses of naval gunfire to cover a landing in the American War was during the shore-to-shore assault at Kipps Bay on Manhattan. On the night before the landing, five heavy frigates were stationed broadside to and within fifty yards of the American shore defenses. As the first wave of flat-bottomed boats left the shelter of Newtown Creek on the Brooklyn shore, these warships opened a rapid and heavy fire on the American beach defenses. In fifty-five minutes of firing, H.M.S. *Orpheus* expended 5,376 pounds of gunpowder. The violent bombardment leveled the enemy field fortifications and drove the American defenders from the landing area in confusion.[55] By the completion of the New York campaign of 1776, the British had become so impressed with the effectiveness of naval gunfire against shore targets that they specially rebuilt and strengthened a merchant ship to carry sixteen 24-pounders for the sole purpose of conducting shore bombardments.[56] Because of the great number of heavy cannon they could bring to bear on a target, warships were extremely effective in overpowering enemy beach defenses, and the British used naval gunfire whenever possible in support of amphibious operations.

As the first wave of flat-bottomed boats neared the beach, the naval bombardment ceased and the soldiers unslung their muskets and removed the lock covers. Just before the boats entered the surf, a grapnel was thrown over the stern to act as a kedge, and when they reached the surf, seamen jumped into the water to hold the crafts' bows steady. The troops then scrambled over the sides of the boats and into the water, waded ashore, and assembled on the beach in combat formation, ready to advance inland to cover the landing of the rest of the army. The moment the troops reached the beach, the flat-bottomed boats withdrew from the shore and rowed to those transports flying flags signifying that they had troops still on board.[57] And so it went, until all the troops were ashore.

After the initial landing was made, the navy continued to support and assist operations on shore. As Ligonier noted in 1757, the landing force was logistically dependent on the navy and "A safe and well secured Communication between the Camp and Sea, from whence you are to receive your Supplies of all Kinds, is absolutely necessary; the whole depends upon it."[58] The army's supplies and stores were landed by the navy, and in campaigns such as the sieges of Havana and Charleston, the military effort was totally dependent upon the navy and its small craft to ferry the army's supplies from the fleet to the battlefield.[59] Naval vessels and small craft also gave the British army great tactical mobility after a landing. Wolfe could never have scoured the shores of the Saint Lawrence River above the city of Quebec without the assistance of the Royal Navy, and during the American War the complex troop movements executed during the campaign around New York City in 1776 would have been impossible without waterborne transport. And on numerous occasions, such as at Quebec, Belle Isle, and Havana during the Seven Years War, and at New York and Charleston during the American War, parties of seamen were landed to support the operations of the army.[60] The conveying of stores and equipment from ship to shore and the use of naval craft to carry out tactical troop movements, and of other measures such as deploying parties of seamen on shore in support of the army were all undertaken by the Royal Navy to further ensure the success of an amphibious operation.

The British gained much from the exploitation of naval power through amphibious warfare during the Seven Years War and the American War. Mastery of the planning and skills needed to transport troops across seas and land them on hostile shores gave the British army great strategic mobility. Sir

Charles Middleton, the comptroller of the navy during the American War, went so far as to maintain that a small amphibious force based in England would pose a strategic threat to the entire North Atlantic basin.[61] There can be no doubt, however, that naval power and the ability to conduct amphibious operations conferred upon the British army during the last half of the eighteenth century a strategic importance and striking power far greater than the mere size of the force alone warranted.

Notes

[1] Thomas Moore Molyneux, *Conjunct Expeditions; or the Expeditions that Have Been Carried on Jointly By the Fleet and Army. With a Commentary on a Littoral War* (London, 1759).

[2] For an account of living conditions of troops and the methods employed to maintain discipline while on board transports, see David Syrett, *Shipping and the American War: A Study of British Transport Organization, 1775–83* (London, 1970), pp. 182–92. See also Piers Mackesy, "Regulations in Troopships: Home Popham and the Russian Expedition of 1799," *The Mariner's Mirror* 56 (May 1970): 229–30.

[3] D. Bonner-Smith, ed., *The Barrington Papers* (Navy Records Society, vol. 81, 1941) 2: 97–8. For other examples, see Ipswich and East Suffolk Record Office, Albemarle Archives, HA 67: 461/109, Distinguishing vanes of transports; *Major Andre's Journal* (Tarrytown, NY: 1930), pp. 101–7 (hereafter cited as *Andre's Journal*); *Diary of Frederick Mackenzie: Giving a Daily Narrative of His Military Service as an Officer of the Regiment of Royal Welch Fusiliers During the Years 1775–1781 in Massachusetts, Rhode Island, and New York* (Cambridge, MA: 1930) 1: 115.

[4] *Andre's Journal*, p. 35.

[5] Albermarle Archives, HA 67:461/109, Signals to be Made From a Ship of War to Call on Board the Officers of the Army; *The Barrington Papers* 2:300; *The Kemble Papers, Collections of the New York Historical Society for the Year 1883* (New York, 1884) 1: 472, 474.

[6] Public Record Office, ADM 1/4131, p. 55.

[7] *Diary of Frederick Mackenzie* 1: 120; Bernhard A. Uhlendorf, trans. and ed., *Revolution in America: Confidential Letters and Journals, 1776–1784, of Adjutant General Major, Baurmeister of the Hessian Forces* (New Brunswick, N.J., 1957), pp. 93, 97–98. For an account of the duties of agents for transports, see Syrett, *Shipping and the American War*, pp. 37–66. See also Mary Ellen Condon, "The Administration of the Transport System During the War Against Revolutionary France, 1793–1802," (dissertation, University of London, 1968), pp. 27–29.

[8] *Kemble Papers* 1: 328, 380.

[9] *The Montresor Journals, Collections of the New York Historical Society for the Year 1881* (New York, 1882), p. 196; and *Diary of Frederick Mackenzie* 1: 118.

[10] David Syrett, ed., *The Siege and Capture of Havana, 1762* (Navy Records Society, 1970), 104: pp. 59, 138–39; *The Barrington Papers* 2: 302; Henry Parry, ed., *Minutes of the Proceedings at a Court Martial Assembled for the Trial of Capt. John Moutray, of His Majesty's Ship the Ramilles* . . . (London, 1781), p. 148. See also H. W. Richmond, ed., *The Spencer Papers, 1794–1801* (Navy Records Society, vol. 58, 1924) 3: 164.

[11] One of Cook's charts of the Saint Lawrence River is in the National Maritime Museum. See also Syrett, *Siege and Capture of Havana*, pp. 92–93, 237; *The Montresor Journals*, pp. 205–6, 441; *Andre's Journal*, p. 107; Harry Miller Lydenberg, ed., *Archibald Robertson, Lieutenant General Royal Engineers, His Diaries and Sketches in America, 1762–1780* (New York, 1930), p. 142; *Diary of Frederick Mackenzie* 1: 84–5; John Knox Laughton, ed., *The Naval Miscellany* (Naval Records Society, vol. 20, 1901) 1: 148; and William Hugh Moomaw, "The Naval Career of Captain Hamond, 1775–1779," (dissertation, University of Virginia, 1955), p. 336.

[12] The Proceedings of a General Court-Martial . . . Upon the Trial of Lieutenant-General Sir John Mordaunt, by Virtue of His Majesty's Warrent. . . . (London, 1758), pp. 114–15 (hereafter *Mordaunt Court-Martial*).

[13] Ibid., pp. 58, 63–64, 90–91.

[14] Ibid., p. 74; General Orders by His Excellancy the Honorable William Howe from 30th June Ending October 1776, 21 August 1776; and John MacIntire, *A Military Treatise on the Discipline of the Marine Forces, when at Sea: Together with Short Instruction for Detachments Sent to Attack on Shore* (London, 1763), p. 225; and *General Wolfe's Instructions to Young Officers*. . . . (Philadelphia, 1778), pp. 103–04.

[15] *Commodore Lord Howe's Regulations respecting the guard of the transports whilst upon the Enemies coast, 20 June 1758* (Massachusetts Historical Society).

[16] *Mordaunt Court-Martial*, p. 73.

[17] Beckles Willson, *The Life and Letters of James Wolfe* (New York, 1909), pp. 436–37; Robert Beatson, *Naval and Military Memoirs of Great Britain from 1727 to 1783* (London, 1804), 2: 72, 129, 168; John Entick, *The General History of the Late War* . . . (London, 1763), 3: 225; Lydenberg, *Naval Miscellany* 1: 122, 148; and Edward H. Tarum, Jr., *The American Journal of Ambrose Serle, Secre-*

tary to Lord Howe, 1776–1778 (San Marino, CA., 1940), p. 71.

[18] James J. Graham, ed., *Memoir of General Graham with Notices of the Campaign in which he was engaged from 1779–1801* (Edinburgh, 1862), pp. 13–14.

[19] MacIntire, *Military Treatise on the Discipline of the Marine Forces,* pp. 224–25.

[20] *The Montresor Journals,* p. 442; General Orders by Howe, 30 June 1776, Morristown National Historical Park Manuscript Collection. The troops which landed at Wolfe's Cove were issued with seventy rounds of ammunition, Willson, *Life and Letters of James Wolfe,* p. 489. However, some authorities during the Seven Years War thought only about forty rounds of ammunition per man should be issued before an amphibious assault. See MacIntire, *Military Treatise on the Discipline of the Marine Forces,* pp. 224–25; *General Wolfe's Instructions,* p. 70. In 1782, Admiral Rodney directed that each marine sent ashore should be issued with "besides what his cartouch box contains, twenty-six full musket cartridges . . ." Julian S. Corbett, ed., *Signals and Instructions, 1776–1794* (Navy Records Society, 1908) 35: 314. Sixty rounds, however, appears to have become the standard issue in the British army. See C. W. C. Oman, *Wellington's Army, 1809–1814* (London, 1968), p. 301.

[21] *Kemble Papers* 1: 369.

[22] The troops landed at Wolfe's Cove carried two days' rations, while marines preparing to land at Belle Isle were issued three days' rations. During the American War, the soldiers who went ashore at Gravesend on Long Island carried three days' rations, while those landed several weeks later at Kipps Bay had two days' rations. Willson, *Life and Letters of James Wolfe,* p. 480; *Barrington Papers* 1: 298, and General Orders by Lord Admiral Howe, 20 August-14 September 1776.

[23] Willson, *Life and Letters of James Wolfe,* p. 480; and *Kemble Papers* 1: 473.

[24] Willson, *Life and Letters of James Wolfe,* p. 480; *Kemble Papers* 1: 312, 373–74, 475–76; *Andre's Journal,* p. 37; General Orders by Lord Admiral Howe, 30 June 1776. During the Seven Years War and the American War, the average infantryman carried 63 pounds, 3 ounces, of arms and equipment. See G. Tylden, "The Accoutrements of the British Infantryman, 1640–1940," *Journal of the Army Historical Research* 48 (Spring 1969): 8–9.

[25] MacIntire, *Military Treatise on the Discipline of the Marine Forces,* pp. 224–25; Edward Everett Hale, ed., *General Sir William Howe's Orderly Book at Charlestown, Boston, and Halifax 17 June 1775 to 26 May 1776* (London, 1890), p. 225.

[26] Willson, *Life and Letters of James Wolfe,* p. 480; and Syrett, *Siege and Capture of Havana,*

p. 158. For another example, see *Barrington Papers* 1: 301.

[27] Public Record Office, ADM 1/487, pp. 60–63; W. G. Perrin, ed., *The Keith Papers* (Navy Records Society, vol. 62, 1927) 1: 145–52. For another example, see Hist. MSS. Comm., Hastings MSS 3: 182.

[28] Beatson, *Naval and Military Memoirs of Great Britain,* 2: 167; and National Maritime Museum, HIS/7, pp. 122–24, 139–40.

[29] Beatson, *Naval and Military Memoirs of Great Britain,* 2: 167. It is also alleged that Commodore Lord Howe designed the flat-bottomed boat. See Frederick Kielmansegge, *Diary of a Journey to England in the Years 1761–1762,* trans. Countess Kielmansegge (London, 1902), p. 257.

[30] Draft of the landing boats built in May 1758, Draft Room, National Maritime Museums. Models of flat-bottomed boats can be found at the National Maritime Museum and the Science Museum.

[31] Public Record Office, ADM 95/95, p. 159. I wish to thank Mr. R. J. B. Knight for this information.

[32] National Maritime Museum, HIS/7, pp. 49–50, 91. For other examples of barricading boats, see Public Record Office, ADM 106/207, 7 February 1762; William Bell Clark, ed., *Naval Documents of the American Revolution* (Washington, D.C.: 1964), 1: 718, 836–37.

[33] Add. Mss. 21680, p. 136, British Museum.

[34] Graham, *Memoir of General Graham,* p. 33.

[35] Willson, *Life and Letters of James Wolfe,* pp. 479–80; and *Keith Papers* 1: 153.

[36] Willson, *Life and Letters of James Wolfe,* p. 474; Hist. MSS. Comm., Sackville-Stopford MSS 2:4; Public Record Office, ADM 1/485, p. 393; and John Fortescue, ed., *The Correspondence of George the Third from 1760 to December 1783* (London, 1928) 3: no. 1662.

[37] Beatson, *Naval and Military Memoirs of Great Britain,* 2: 167; National Maritime Museum, ADM B/191, 30 April 1776. See also *Spencer Papers* 2: 339.

[38] Richard Middleton, "The Administration of Newcastle and Pitt: the Departments of State and the Conduct of the War, 1754–1760, with Particular Reference to the Campaigns in North America" (dissertation, University of Exeter, 1968), p. 161.

[39] Howe's abstract of instructions to be observed by each particular officer commanding a flat-bottomed boat, 8 June 1758, Massachusetts Historical Society; *Barrington Papers* 1: 300, 305, and 2: 303; Syrett, *Siege and Capture of Havana,* p. 158; *Keith Papers* 1: 145–46; National Maritime Museums, MSS 67/073 (uncat.); CAL/110 4 May 1776. During the American War, the seamen belonging to the transports, being civilians, received sixpence per day for manning flat-bot-

tomed boats. Public Record Office, ADM 1488, pp. 523–24.

[40] *Mordaunt Court-Martial*, p. 58; *Kemble Papers* 1: 320–21.

[41] Howe's instructions respecting the disposition of the flat boats on the disembarkation of the troops, 8 June 1758; *Barrington Papers* 1: 301, 2: 303; 305; Syrett, *Siege and Capture of Havana*, p. 159.

[42] Thomas Simes, *The Military Guide for Young Officers Containing a system of the art of war . . .* (London, 1776), pp. 62–63; Clark, *Naval Documents of the American Revolution* 1: 251; and Howe's instructions, 8 June 1758.

[43] *Kemble Papers* 1: 473; MacIntire, *Military Treatise on the Discipline of the Marine Forces*, p. 226. These orders were not always obeyed: during the landing at Kipps Bay in 1776, the German troops sang hymns and British shouted profanities while enroute to the beach. Hist. MSS. Comm., Hastings MSS 2: 183–84.

[44] Howe's instructions; Syrett, *Siege and Capture of Havana*, p. 159; and *Barrington Papers* 2: 303.

[45] Simes, *Military Guide for Young Officers*, pp. 62–63; *Barrington Papers* 1: 300, 305, 2: 303–05; and Syrett, *Siege and Capture of Havana*, p. 159.

[46] *Barrington Papers* 1: 301, 305, 2: 305; and Syrett, *Siege and Capture of Havana*, p. 159.

[47] *Mordaunt Court-Martial*, pp. 58, 90–91.

[48] *Andre's Journal*, p. 36.

[49] General Disposition Preparative to the Landing of the Army, 24 August 1777, Simcoe Papers, William L. Clements Library. For other examples, see Syrett, *Siege and Capture of Havana*, p. 165; National Maritime Museum, HIS/7, pp. 122–24; Lydenberg, *Robertson Diaries*, pp. 142–43. For later examples see *Spencer Papers* 3: 349; and C. Northcote Parkinson, *War in The Eastern Seas 1793–1815* (London, 1954), p. 401.

[50] National Maritime Museum, HIS/7, pp. 122–24; *Barrington Papers* 2: 304; Syrett, *Siege and Capture of Havana*, p. 159; Corbett, *Signals and Instructions*, p. 363; and Hale, *Howe's Orderly Book*, p. 2.

[51] *Barrington Papers* 1: 304; Syrett, *Siege and Capture of Havana*, pp. 163, 167. See also *Spencer Papers* 2: 341.

[52] Beatson, *Naval and Military Memoirs of Great Britain*, 2: 68.

[53] Ibid., 2: 168.

[54] National Maritime Museum, JOD/9, 26 August 1776; HIS/7, pp. 11–12.

[55] G. D. Scull, ed., *Memoir and Letters of Captain W. Glenville Evelyn of the 4th Regiment ("King's Own"), From North America 1774–1776* (Oxford, 1879), p. 84; Lydenberg, *Robertson Diaries*, pp. 97–98; J. K. Laughton and J. Y. F. Sullivan, eds., *The Journal of Rear-Admiral Bartholomew James, 1752–1828* (Navy Records Society) 6: 31; and Hist. MSS. Comm., Hastings MSS 3: 183–84.

[56] Moomaw, "The Naval Career of Captain Hammond, 1775–1779," pp. 315–16.

[57] McIntire, *Military Treatise on the Discipline of the Marine Forces*, pp. 225–26; *Naval Miscellany* 1: 123, 149; Syrett, *Siege and Capture of Havana*, p. 174; Public Record Office, ADM 49/2, p. 216; CO 5/263, p. 14; and *Keith Papers* 1: 145–76.

[58] *Mordaunt Court-Martial*, p. 75.

[59] Syrett, *Siege and Capture of Havana*, pp. 168–292; *Keith Papers* 1: 145–76.

[60] Willson, *Life and Letters of James Wolfe*, p. 445; *Barrington Papers*, p. 306; Syrett, *Siege and Capture of Havana*, p. 174; Public Record Office, ADM 49/2, p. 216; CO 5/263, p. 14; *Keith Papers* 1: 145–46.

[61] John Knox Laughton, ed., *Letter and Papers of Charles, Lord Barbham* (Navy Records Society, vol. 38, 1910) 2: 45–47.

Problems of an Amphibious Power: Britain against France, 1793–1815

BY PIERS MACKESY

"He that commands the sea is at great liberty, and may take as much or as little of the war as he will." The writer was the Elizabethan Sir Francis Bacon; the source, Sir Julian Corbett's *Some Principles of Maritime Strategy*, published in 1911 as England prepared for a titanic naval struggle with Germany. Corbett was trying to read the lessons of the past in order to discover the future, and his eye fell inevitably on the previous great British maritime wars a century earlier against the French Revolution and Napoleon. To these wars he applied Bacon's aphorism. He observed that England had failed to match French strength in Western Europe, yet had fought a successful land war backed by maritime communications at the extremity of Europe in Portugal. From this he concluded that the tendency of British warfare was to take the limited form. Instead of engaging in continental warfare with all its resources, Britain had stood off from the European heartland. It had threatened the coastline with movable amphibious forces, mopped up French colonies which seapower prevented the enemy from reinforcing, and waged campaigns "limited by contingent" at the extremities of Europe. The lesson for the future seemed clear, and he preached it just five years before Britain launched vast armies into the battle of the Somme.

Who was wrong? Was it the Asquith government of 1914–16, which allowed Britain's military resources to be sucked into France?

Naval War College Review 30 (Spring 1978): 16–25. Reprinted by permission.

Or had Corbett misunderstood the past? Could it be that Britain's policy in the Revolutionary and Napoleonic wars was not one of deliberate strategic limitation, but a second-best imposed by conditions which had reduced it to near paralysis? The latter is nearer the truth.

Britain's political aims fluctuated somewhat with the fortunes of the war, but through the greater part of the twenty-two-year struggle its aim was virtually total: the overthrow of the enemy's regime by the armies of the continental powers, and its replacement by a government acceptable to the allies. The reason for this was not really ideological but pragmatic. The successive revolutionary governments of France had shown themselves to be incapable of negotiating or maintaining a stable peace settlement because of their own domestic instability. It was believed that only the restoration of the monarchy could give France that internal stability on which the future peace of Europe must rest. For a short time the advent of Bonaparte appeared to offer a stable basis for a settlement, and the Peace of Amiens of 1802 was an experiment to discover whether Napoleonic France could provide a secure foundation for European stability. The answer was soon apparent: it could not. The Napoleonic regime was indeed there to stay, but the personality of the ruler himself, incapable of defining or limiting his aims, was a permanent threat to the balance of power in Europe and the security of Britain and its colonies.

The two things—the European balance of power and Britain's maritime security—were inextricably tied to each other. Without a balance of power on the continent, England was unsafe. If a single power, whether Spain or France or a united Germany, dominated Europe, it would soon obtain the naval resources to challenge Britain's maritime security and overseas possessions. To maintain the European balance, Britain had to pay whatever price was necessary. At times, indeed, it required only the limited intervention which Corbett extolled: perhaps to reassure or manipulate an ally by supplying an auxiliary force, as was done to support Austria in the First Coalition of 1793–95; or to save an ally, as when Britain protected the flank of the hard-pressed Frederick the Great in the Seven Years War by maintaining an army in Hanover; or to protect an area of particular interest such as the Low Countries or Portugal. But there were times when the balance of power required a massive intervention.

It is easy to be deceived by the scale of the British military contribution into supposing that it was deliberately limited as an act of policy, for Britain's manpower resources were slender. With perhaps half the effective manpower of France, it had to begin by manning its huge navy, which absorbed one hundred forty thousand men at the height of the Napoleonic Wars. Of the army, as much as two-thirds were locked up in the defense of colonies and overseas bases such as Gibraltar. Ireland required a large garrison for internal security as well as to prevent invasion. And to expand the army to meet other needs was difficult, as conscription was ruled out for reasons historical, political, ideological, and economic. All these considerations meant that England could not put into the field an army on the scale of the continental powers. It ranked as a great power not because of its army but because of its wealth, which it used to keep the armies of other powers in the war. It did this in two ways: by direct subsidies to its allies, Austria, Prussia, and Russia, to help them to pay the costs of their armies; and by paying for auxiliary troops from the lesser powers to fight alongside the British army and augment its numbers. The

"Hessians" of the American War of Independence were the heirs and predecessors of generations of German auxiliaries.

Britain's intervention in the wars of the French Revolution began in 1793 in the conventional way, with British strategy striking a balance between its continental and colonial interests. Expeditions were mounted against the French islands in the Caribbean, while an Anglo-German contingent fought alongside the Austrians and Dutch in Belgium. But in 1795 the collapse of the coalition totally and permanently altered Britain's strategic prospects. The French overran Belgium and Holland, and the Prussians declared a zone of neutrality in North Germany which included King George's electorate of Hanover. Suddenly the bases from which the British army had intervened in Europe were closed to it, and with the exception of Portugal the whole Western European coastline from Gibraltar to the Danish border was occupied by enemies.

Thus the British army was reduced to amphibious warfare. It had no secure bases in Europe where it could land and organize for operations; no prearranged supply system; no friendly army to fight alongside it. Intervention on the continent now meant landing across open beaches in country occupied by the enemy.

Was this such a disaster? Napoleon has been quoted by Corbett and others to show that it was not. "With thirty thousand troops in transports in the Downs," wrote the emperor in 1810, "the English can paralyse three hundred thousand of my army." But Napoleon wrote, as he spoke, in hyperbole. He was not interested in the truth of his words, but in their effect; and he had recently been disconcerted by how close the British expedition to Walcheren had come to destroying his naval base at Antwerp. He was not stating a truth, but gingering the minister responsible for his coastal fortifications. His words were very far from the whole truth. If he believed them, he knew little of the limitations of amphibious warfare.

Amphibious operations as we know them are a product of twentieth-century technology. Airpower, specialized landing and support crafts, and shipping which does not depend on a fair wind to bring it to its assault stations and keep it there: these, by the middle of the Second World War, had transformed amphibious warfare. In the Napoleonic period everything was different. Amphibious operations moved in a fog of uncertainty, beset by every conceivable difficulty and limitation.

Perhaps it is right to start with tactics before making grand generalizations about strategy. The fire support available to an assault force preparing to land cannot be compared even relatively with what can be achieved today. The broadside of a warship, it is true, was tremendous, and the batteries of a ship-of-the-line were equivalent to the artillery of an army. But a ship was a large target and very vulnerable to fire and explosion. Its guns fired with the roll of the ship, and military targets on shore were small compared with the hull of a warship. The embrasures of a shore battery were narrow, and unlike a ship's broadside its guns fired from a stable platform. With these advantages, a single cannon in a tower could beat off an 80-gun ship-of-the-line with severe damage and casualties. Nor could the naval cannon of the day employ indirect fire. They could engage only visible targets: enemy troops sheltering behind a crest were invulnerable.

The only assault craft of the day was the flat-bottomed boat, powered by sixteen or twenty naval oarsmen and an auxiliary sail. It carried forty or sixty infantrymen. By convention the loading and marshalling of the assault craft was the business of the naval commander, who saw his sole concern as being to dump the soldiers on the beach. The confusion this caused was enormous. Sometimes parts of battalions were landed and parts left in the ships. Companies, battalions, and even brigades were intermixed on the beach at the mercy of a swift attack. Eventually the confusion proved intolerable, and through the initiative of Sir Ralph Abercromby the military commanders took a hand in the organization of the landing. The loading of the

boats was tactically planned, and techniques were worked out to help the assault craft to keep their direction and station in the line. The landing at Aboukir Bay in 1801 was a model operation.

But an orderly landing was only the first of the military commander's problems. He did not have a balanced force of all arms; he had only infantry. An hour or two after the first landing he could expect some cannon, brought ashore in pieces and assembled on the beach with block and tackle. But he had no horses to move them, only the muscle of seamen borrowed from the fleet who dragged the guns over dune and field to engage the mobile artillery of the enemy. Nor had he cavalry to reconnoiter or pursue. To transfer horses from the transports to the beach was slow and difficult even in the calmest weather. When Abercromby made his assault landing in Holland in 1799 he had only one squadron of cavalry, 1.6 percent of his force rather than the 20 percent recommended by the contemporary Clausewitz. But even that single squadron could not be landed in the surf, and it was only after four days that a port was captured and the horses were landed at a quay.

The slow landing of the force could sacrifice the advantage of strategic surprise. An unopposed landing in the Baltic in 1807 took a week to complete; and a year later Wellesley's unopposed landing in Portugal required five days for the landing of nine thousand men with such horses and vehicles as he had been able to ship. Even then he had scarcely any cavalry when he advanced from the beachhead, for of his two hundred dragoons only sixty had horses. He met the French under Marshal Junot at Vimiero and defeated them, but he could not pursue. "We only wanted a few hundred more cavalry to annihilate the French army," he lamented. The consequence of this lack of cavalry was the Convention of Cintra which threatened to blight his career. That was the price he paid for an amphibious landing.

The same troubles hampered the supply system. It was difficult to ship enough wagons and horses, so the commander had to rely on organizing local resources after the landing. But instead of arriving in a friendly country with an organized base, he landed in enemy-held territory, and if the French cavalry knew their business they had swept it clear of horses, vehicles, and cattle. It might be possible to use the shipping as a floating base, as Wellesley did in 1808 when he advanced on Lisbon, but to do that confined the army to the coast road. Even then there was no guarantee of supplies. In the autumn of 1799 when the British army in Holland outran its overland communications, the bad weather which had destroyed the roads meant that no ship could drop an anchor off the coast. The advance ground to a halt, and the army had to retreat to shorten its communications.

So it was in every landing. If the commander made good his foothold, he lacked the tactical mobility to exploit it; he lacked mobile artillery, cavalry, transportation. The harvest of the initial surprise could not be reaped, and the enemy was free to make his strategic concentration at leisure after the landing force had been committed. This was the story of the one great enterprise in Western Europe during those years, the Anglo-Russian invasion of Holland in 1799.

There were other problems, such as the difficulty of collecting intelligence and the uncertainties of inshore navigation among shifting tidal sands. But the hardest task which the planners faced was to find the shipping. One should look hard at the shipping requirements for the force of thirty thousand troops which Napoleon postulated in transports in the Downs.

For the troops themselves, a short voyage from England to Western Europe required 1¼ tons per man, or just under 40,000 tons of transport shipping. But that was only the beginning. They needed victualling ships, storeships, hospital ships, and above all, horse transports, which I believe to have been the greatest limiting factor in British strategy. A few horses could be carried in the largest transports: for the Walcheren expedition of 1809, twenty-one were fitted into *Caesar*, a first-rate ship-of-the-line temporarily converted to a troopship. But the ideal horse

transports were single-decked vessels with their decks scuttled for ventilation, and the only ones available in any numbers were the coalships of the north of England. These colliers, crammed with the bulky forage and water the horses needed, could each carry about thirty horses, about enough to service a pair of cannons. The statesman Henry Dundas calculated that to ship a single cavalry regiment of six hundred men to Portugal with their horses would require 20,000 tons of shipping. This would dislocate the coal trade of England and disrupt the fuel supplies of London. To hire the shipping would cost a fifth of the annual subsidy which kept the Russian army in the field. And even at this price one horse in four would die on the voyage, and the survivors would be unfit for operations for some weeks after they were landed.

With that point of reference one can examine the reality of Napoleon's notion of thirty thousand British troops poised in their transports off the coast of Kent. The shipping tonnage in British ownership around 1800 was about 1½ million. For the expedition to Holland in 1799 the Transport Board had to hire 90,000 tons of shipping for a force of about thirty thousand men, and with that tonnage the force had to be shuttled across the North Sea in successive echelons, dependent on the right succession of winds. The availability of shipping was seasonal—it was difficult to hire in the spring and summer, which was the season for amphibious expeditions—and it was cyclical, when trade was booming, shipping was scarce. There was a desperate shortage of seamen even for the navy, and press-gangs were scouring the ports and taking men off incoming merchant convoys for the fleet. The economic dislocation of permanently tying up about six hundred merchant ships with their crews in the Downs would have been severe. And the monthly hiring cost would have been of the order of £150,000 a month, more than the total sum which Pitt reckoned could be spared to subsidize the great continental armies of the Second Coalition. Was the price worth it for the sake of a mere thirty thousand troops whose striking power would be so hampered by the limitations of amphibious warfare?

So when Napoleon tossed off his aphorism about thirty thousand troops in the Downs he was as usual writing not to establish the truth but to create an effect. He wrote with a disregard for maritime complexities which was wholly characteristic. A British naval officer who knew him in exile in Elba wrote of him thus: "Napoleon has no idea of the hazard incident to movements upon a coast, nor of the difficulties occasioned by winds and tides, but judges of changes of position in the case of ships as he would with the regard to troops upon land."

It suited Napoleon's purposes to ignore not only the cost in shipping of maintaining an amphibious force, but the complexities of planning and organization required to launch an amphibious invasion from sailing ships. With the communications and economic resources of the day, to bring together the troops, the troopships, victuallers and storeships, the stores, the horses, the forage and fuel, the naval escort, and the landing craft was a tremendous feat of planning which involved many departments and required a succession of fortunate winds. One of Napoleon's generals came much closer to reality than his master. General Mathieu Dumas wrote an account of the British expedition to Holland in 1799, an operation which historians have usually dismissed as a chaotic muddle. But Dumas judged differently: "Those who have executed or followed the details of the embarkation of an army with its artillery, hospitals, baggage and ammunition may be astounded at the speed of the British preparations."

It is worth dwelling on the operational and administrative problems of an amphibious invasion because grand strategy ultimately is based on minor tactics—and on logistics. The exclusion of Britain from the continent after 1795 produced tactical and logistic problems which dominated strategy for thirteen years until the opening of the Peninsula War, in spite of the conviction of certain British statesmen that what was politically and strategically desirable must be technically feasible.

What sort of war was it possible for Britain to fight? How were political ends related to military means? Was it realistic to try to fight a total war for the overthrow of the enemy's political system with means so limited? Sir Julian Corbett's answer was to pull out Francis Bacon's dictum quoted at the beginning: that the power which commands the sea may take as much or as little of the war as it pleases.

But if Napoleon's dictum is nonsense, Bacon's is at best a half-truth. The British could usually take as *little* of the war as they would, because they commanded the sea and were immune from invasion; but they could not take as *much* as they wanted. Their political object was unlimited: decisive victory and the overthrow of the enemy government. But they actually fought a limited war, imposed on them not by political choice but by the straitjacket of amphibious operations. Yet from these extraordinary circumstances, when Britain was excluded from access to an existing war front in Europe, Corbett extrapolated his doctrine that Britain's natural way of war was limited warfare waged from the sea.

The whole of the rest of English history shows that the country has been inescapably tied to the balance of power on the continent and has had to pay whatever price was necessary to maintain it, even if this meant fighting a full-scale war in Europe. Such was the case in the Napoleonic Wars. The British did believe that they were fighting for political survival as a great power and for social survival against the doctrines of the French Revolution. They paid immense sums to continental allies, and they put all the soldiers they could spare into continental warfare. But they were limited by the bottleneck of shipping and the lack of an organized war front in Western Europe into which they could feed their army.

It follows from this that no major landing in Western Europe could ever be contemplated unless there was an active war front in the east to hold down the major forces of the French. In the absence of an existing western front for the British to reinforce, they had to create a "second front" by landing from the sea. This meant that one of the two German great powers, Prussia or Austria, had to be in the war to form an eastern front, as without one of the German powers the Russian army had no access to France.

This need imposed a cyclical pattern on British strategy. When Austria or Prussia was fighting, the British committed an army to Europe. When the eastern front collapsed, the British army was forced to evacuate its continental bridgehead, and revert to maritime and colonial warfare; and this not from design but from necessity. Three times in successive coalitions the British army was committed to the heartland of Western Europe: in the first coalition of 1793–95 in Belgium, in the second in 1799 in Holland, in the third in 1805 in Hanover. In each case the continental allies collapsed, and the British army was forced to withdraw.

When that happened Britain stood isolated and alone and was reduced to a defensive maritime strategy with limited offensives. This happened in 1795, in 1800, briefly in 1806 after Austerlitz, and decisively in 1807 after the Peace of Tilsit. The characteristic pattern of this withdrawal to the defensive was in three phases. The first consisted of emergency operations to weaken the enemy's battle fleets and remove neutral fleets from his grasp, and thus to secure the command of the sea on which any future strategy depended. These operations consisted either of amphibious attacks on enemy fleets in harbor, as was attempted at Ferrol and Cadiz in 1800 and contemplated against Port Mahon in 1808, or of measures to keep neutral fleets out of French hands, such as the strike against Copenhagen and the removal of the Portuguese fleet from the Tagus in 1807. The second phase of the offensive was to secure overseas naval bases—the Cape of Good Hope, Ceylon, Malta, Madeira—and deny them to the French. There is a striking parallel between these phases and events after the fall of France in 1940: the moves to secure French naval forces at Oran and Dakar and the occupation of the Faroes and Iceland.

Once these essential measures had been taken to safeguard the command of the sea, British warfare moved on to its third phase, which consisted of limited offensives against enemy colonies and forces overseas. The purposes of these offensives were to secure British colonies by pinching out enemy threats; to open new markets for British trade in order to replace the European markets from which it was now excluded, and thus to finance the continuing war; and to strengthen Britain's bargaining position in case she were forced to negotiate a compromise peace as she did at Amiens in 1802.

The most striking example of these limited offensives is General Abercromby's expedition to Egypt in 1801, designed to secure the long-term safety of British India and to aid the negotiations at Amiens. After the Peace of Tilsit in 1807 expeditions were mounted against the Spanish colonies in America, though these were diverted at the last moment to Spain and Portugal. All these, however, were survival measures. They could not lead to victory and might in the long run trickle into defeat. British ministries always recognized that only coalition warfare could lead to decisive victory. Their diplomatic efforts were always directed at Russia to bring one or both of the German powers into an alliance and open an eastern front.

When that happened, and other powers took the field against France, it became imperative that the British army should make its contribution to the whittling down and destruction of French military power. But where, and how? One choice favored by historians is the Mediterranean. But, in fact, the British never undertook a serious offensive there, and for good reasons. An expedition to the Mediterranean would tie up immense shipping resources. It would bottle up troops who could not be recalled to meet an emergency at home. The force's logistics would be dependent on Austrian resources, and Austria had shown that she could not be relied on for wholehearted military cooperation. When troops were sent to the Mediterranean, therefore, their purpose was defensive: to dislodge the French from key positions in the narrows of the central Mediterranean—Malta, Sicily and Naples—on which the defense of the Levant and India depended and to secure bases from which the British fleet could command the inland sea. The Mediterranean was a defensive theater, not an offensive one.

In Western Europe the most alluring point of attack was France itself. The British might count on local aid from insurgents in the Vendée, and the attack could be an effective diversion in favor of the eastern front. But the risks were great, for the enemy's reaction would be powerful and determined. When an invasion of France was planned for the spring of 1800, William Pitt remarked that it could either win or lose the war at a single stroke. The scale of the invasion would have to be vast, and Pitt's secretary of state for war, Henry Dundas, came to the conclusion that it would be utterly beyond England's resources in manpower and shipping to undertake it. The plan was abandoned, and the invasion of France from the seas was never contemplated again.

Raiding was another matter, but the thirty thousand men postulated by Napoleon were too few to take on a major objective like the naval base at Brest, and the previous history of raids on minor ports did not show that they could achieve results in proportion to the risks. Raiding would not create an adequate diversion in favor of the eastern front.

If the invasion of France were rejected, any serious attack on the heartland of Western Europe had to be mounted at some point further away from the center of French military strength. This meant to the northward, in the Low Countries, Hanover, or the Baltic. In these areas diplomatic considerations complicated the purely military ones. Britain's continental war aims made it desirable to be in military position when the war ended to influence the future arrangements for Belgium and Holland. A British landing could also be used to influence the conduct of the German powers: to influence Austria's attitude toward its former possessions in Belgium, and to encourage Prussia to enter the war, which was by far the most effective indirect blow which the British army could achieve against the French. In the Baltic the use of Stralsund in Swedish Pomerania depended on the cooperation of Sweden.

Balancing these political considerations were two military ones. The landing must be far enough from the center of French military power to allow a foothold to be consolidated before a counteroffensive could develop. But still more important, in the absence of an organized allied army to cooperate in the landing area, the British army needed insurgent help to consolidate a major landing. Insurgent aid was the great hope of those who urged a landing in France; it would, William Windham promised at the end of 1799, "give you more men than you would know what to do with." Similar hopes had lured Lord Grenville into the Dutch expedition of 1799; hopes which proved to be totally delusive, for the Dutch lacked sufficient ideological conviction or economic inducements to risk their skins before the British proved that they were there to stay. The landing in Hanover in the autumn of 1805 counted on the men of the old Hanoverian army to rally but had no time to test the will of the population, though it brought away a large reinforcement for the King's German Legion.

All the British landings in the heartland of Europe came to untimely ends; not so much because the hopes of insurgent aid were disappointed, as because their limited scale made them totally dependent on an active eastern front to tie down the French army. They were frustrated by two strategic principles. The French enjoyed interior communications between the British and their eastern allies. And Napoleon was the supreme practitioner of what Clausewitz was later to formalize as a theory; that the great victory carries the decision everywhere. To obtain that victory he was prepared to strip other areas to the bone. In spite of his later hyperbole about the British seaborne threat from the Downs, he consistently refused to be diverted by threats from the sea. In 1800 he stripped Western

Europe of troops to form his Army of Reserve, and the great victory at Marengo restored his authority. In 1805 he evacuated southern Italy and Hanover, and the British landed in both areas: Austerlitz made their beachheads untenable. In 1809 he abandoned Dalmatia, and his victory at Wagram restored the rule of Marshal Marmont. What did it matter if a handful of British troops landed at Cuxhaven or Naples without cavalry or wagons? He would deal with them when he had won his victory on the eastern front.

With Napoleon actions counted far more than words. When he wrote about those thirty thousand British troops in the Downs, he was stirring up countermeasures in the wake of the Walcheren expedition. But the answer to a raid on a naval base was fortifications, as he well knew. The answer to an invasion by a British field army was to screen it with whatever was at hand while he sought his major decision elsewhere. In 1807 when his Grand Army was deeply engaged with the Russians in Poland, he did not withdraw a man of it to face a possible British landing, but organized a covering force which consisted mainly of Dutch and Spanish troops, a disaffected and unreliable combination. The payoff came with the battle of Friedland and the negotiations on the raft at Tilsit. The Clausewitzian *Hauptschlacht* had decided all the peripheral issues. So it had always been. When Masséna had defeated the Russians at Zurich in 1799, or Napoleon the Austrians at Ulm and Austerlitz in 1805, there had been not the remotest possibility that the British army could maintain itself on the continent against the counteroffensive which the French were then free to organize.

The battle of Friedland and the peace of Tilsit in 1807 marked the end of twelve years of British amphibious efforts and amphibious impotence. The continent was now totally dominated by Napoleon with the collusion of Russia. England withdrew into strategic and diplomatic isolation. It looked to its moat, seized neutral fleets, and prepared to launch new colonial offensives. Then in the following year the revolt of Spain re-

solved its strategic dilemma. It had proved to be incapable of maintaining a second front in the heartland of Europe. But far out at the extremity it found all that it had needed but had been unable to find between the Pyrenees and the Baltic. It obtained a secure foothold in Portugal, a country with a defensible frontier and a port at Lisbon which could be made impregnable. Portugal took over the role which Holland and Hanover had filled in the eighteenth centry, an established base whose resources and communications could be developed and used by the British army. In the Portuguese army the British found troops of high potential who could be trained to fill the role which Hessian and other German troops had supplied as auxiliaries in earlier wars. British communications by sea and river were far superior in speed and security to the overland lines of communication of the French, who were no longer favored by an interior position as they had been in France and the Low Countries. In Spain there was already in-being an insurgent movement of a hard-living and fanatical people who provided the determined and sustained aid which had not been forthcoming from the Dutch and Germans. At the extremities of the Peninsula, Spanish regular armies survived to complicate the operations and command structure of the French.

The Peninsula provided England with a solution for its strategic problems. In times of isolation it could hold on there. And when other great powers took the field, as Austria did in 1809 and Russia in 1812, Wellington could sally forth from behind the protective barrier of the Portuguese frontier and take the offensive in Spain.

But this happened a long way from the center of Napoleon's power, and it was not amphibious warfare. After the initial landing and the capture of Lisbon in 1808 the British army was operating from an established base as it had done in Western Europe in the eighteenth century, with a friendly country and local allies.

Bacon and Napoleon have been quoted on the power of an amphibious nation. One might balance them with a late nineteenth-century

German, Colmar von der Goltz, who pointed out some of the limitations of amphibious warfare in his day—the limited number of troops that could be deployed; the small proportion of cavalry, artillery, and transportation; the consequent difficulty of gaining elbowroom; and the dependence on a popular uprising or the intervention of a neutral force. All these indeed were problems which the British had experienced in the wars against revolutionary France and Napoleon. And von der Goltz concluded baldly with these words: "In a highly civilized and thickly populated country, landings never have any prospect of great success." This had been true of the Napoleonic era, and it remained true until the middle of World War Two.

Aboukir Bay, 1801

BY CAPTAIN BRENDAN P. RYAN, USMC

Most historical studies on amphibious warfare focus on British operations at Gallipoli in World War One as an example of the first modern assault against a defended beach. The studies include earlier operations (such as Vera Cruz) as part of the historical development of joint operations. Unfortunately, too often the criteria for labeling an operation modern have rested on the time of the event or the sophistication of weapons used rather than the level of planning and complexity of the landing plan. Often the assault on Tinian in 1944 is cited as the most brilliant and successful of modern joint operations. Yet 143 years earlier, in 1801, a British army conducted an assault against a defended beach with remarkable efficiency and success, using most if not all of the modern amphibious assault techniques.

When General Sir Ralph Abercromby reached Gibraltar in October 1800, he found dispatches from London awaiting him. General Abercromby had come from an operation off Cadiz where a lack of hard intelligence and cooperation between army and navy commands had resulted in a fiasco. It was merely the most recent in a series of operations remarkable for poor performance and planning. At Cadiz, as on several other occasions, John Moore was a subordinate commander under Abercromby. These two men were among a small number of liberal and

Marine Corps Gazette, "Amphibious Warfare, 1801 Style," 63 (July 1979): 47–51. Reprinted by permission. See also Richard A. Cahill, "The Significance of Aboukir Bay," U.S. Naval Institute *Proceedings* 92 (July 1967): 79–89.

modern-thinking officers in the moribund senior ranks of the British army at that time. The disgrace the army suffered because of the ridiculous operations of the past five years was unbearable to them, and they resolved to work out methods to ensure future success.

The dispatches awaiting Abercromby came from Henry Dundas, secretary of state for war, a man of considerable ignorance and of a notable lack of talent and abilities. As the commander-in-chief of British troops in the Mediterranean, Abercromby was to be involved in several offensive operations carried out in response to the changing diplomatic climate of Europe. Specifically, British bumbling had succeeded in completely alienating Tsar Paul and driving Russia into a favorable stance with France. With this development approximately twenty-five thousand French troops in Egypt became a greater menace than before. These remnants of Bonaparte's Oriental adventure in 1798 had been stranded in the "Land of the Pharoahs" by the destruction of the French fleet at the Nile by Nelson and Bonaparte's subsequent solo return to Europe.

British fears over the remaining French forces were spurred by the growing amity between France and Russia and the recent defeat of Austria at Hohenlinden. Should France succeed in forming a coalition, Britain might be forced to withdraw from the Mediterranean. Bonaparte would not miss such a chance to reinforce his Egyptian command and revive his ambition against India. Britain also was concerned about Russian interest in India. A Russo-French understanding and French troops in Egypt added a new dimension to the situation. Yet another consideration arguing against the loss of British power in the Mediterranean was the wisdom of allowing so large a group of veterans to return to France's muster roll.

Thus there were strong military and diplomatic reasons for the British to consider eliminating the French threat in Egypt. Coupled with these was the more subtle need of the administration in London, and Henry Dundas in particular, for a successful operation. The Royal Navy, in capturing several French ships between Alexandria and Toulon, intercepted many letters from French officers painting a picture of extremely low morale and discipline among the French forces. In Dundas's reasoning, Abercromby should have little trouble defeating the French in the field and saving the administration from a completely black reputation.

Henry Dundas directed Abercromby to assemble fifteen thousand men with the intent to clear Egypt of French forces. He was to cooperate with a fleet and army provided by the Ottoman Turks. Marmorice Bay, northeast of the island of Rhodes, would be a resupply stop for the British expedition and a coordinating point for the two allies. Minorca and Malta were planned as staging areas for British forces and resupply points. Abercromby was to be supported by the Mediterranean Fleet under Admiral Lord Keith. Keith had considerable experience in joint operations, having commanded a marine battalion during the seizure of Charleston in 1780 and served at Toulon in 1793 as the officer responsible for the reembarkation of Lord Howe's forces during the withdrawal. Nevertheless he was an uninspiring leader and a temporizing colleague. Abercromby's patience resulted, however, in the highest degree of cooperation between the services seen in years. Serving as a brigade commander would be John Moore, thus reuniting the successful and determined team. Abercromby was to rely heavily on this brilliant and innovative officer.

Preparation for the campaign by the min-istry in London was reprehensible. The Royal Navy was directed to support Abercromby, but no specific instructions were given. Because there was no overall commander, all actions were dependent on a spirit of cooperation. The transports provided were in horrendous condition, contributing significantly to the army's sick lists. There were no transports suitable for horses, and no provision was made for water resupply, fodder, or accurate intelligence. It was typical of Dundas and his ministry not to hesitate in throwing fifteen thousand British troops into a tropical climate against an enemy of unknown position or strength without adequate provision for water beyond what was normally carried aboard ships of a necessarily selfish navy, with little or no chance of resupply until a city should fall. It never occurred to him that should the fleet be forced to sea by enemy or weather, the army would die of thirst. In his desire for a politically redeeming victory, Dundas created the conditions for yet another disaster. Abercromby knew British ministers too well to be dismayed and carried on as best he could, commenting, "There are risks in a British warfare unknown in any other service."

Moore was sent ahead to talk with the Turks. Abercromby, not willing to rely on the vague and shallow intelligence supplied by London, gathered together all the Royal Navy officers who had been near Egypt to learn something worthwhile. From the meeting, Aboukir Bay, 18 miles east of Alexandria, was chosen as the landing area, because of the excellent shelter it provided the fleet. But as to the sort of beach or hinterland the army might encounter, there was no word. With all preparations completed as best could be expected, the expedition departed Gibraltar in two squadrons, the first leaving in the beginning of October.

On 29 and 30 December the fleet dropped anchor in Marmorice Bay. There Abercromby learned for the first time of the complete failure of the Turks to fulfill their commitment. There were neither supplies nor the desperately needed horses. At first Abercromby had been willing to abandon his plan to land at Aboukir in favor of an administrative debarkation at Damietta, thereby joining the Turks for a combined invasion of Egypt. But the lack of support at Marmorice laid the seeds of distrust and doubt. Then Moore returned to report that the Turkish army was "a wild ungovernable mob incapable of being directed to any useful purpose." Abercromby was then left to carry on alone, attempting to effect some semblance of resupply and procure horses for his artillery and eleven hundred dismounted cavalry. A further delay in the expedition resulted.

While delayed in Marmorice Bay, Abercromby and Moore continued planning. They sent several Royal Engineers to reconnoiter the beach. Both generals were determined to prevent the confusion and chaos that marked previous operations. The plan drawn up was practiced for several weeks. This extent of rehearsals had not been seen since 1596 in the preparations for the Earl of Essex's expedition against Cadiz.

Abercromby and his staff conceived a plan calling for three parallel lines to advance simultaneously on the beach in the first wave. The first line would consist of flatboats carrying infantry spaced at 50-foot intervals. Following in a second line were cutters from the fleet also carrying infantry. Finally came a line of cutters towing launches, which were loaded with the artillery pieces and their crews. The dress of the lines was to be carefully kept, so that each line landed together. The interval between flatboats was vital in order to allow the following cutters to reach the beach. This procedure was practiced to perfection at Marmorice. The flatboats carrying the grenadier company (or that company which held the right of each battalion's line) would carry the colors for distinction. Thus the remaining companies of the line could form up immediately on the grenadiers as though on parade. The boats of the wave were serialized and loaded, so the troops landed in the order in which they would form to fight.

The ability of the army to land prepared for battle was considered essential. Abercromby could land six thousand men at a time, but believed he would face as many as ten thousand French troops. The landing force could have no heavy preassault bombardment, because shallow water would prevent the fleet from approaching any closer than five miles to the objective.

Planning also had to account for post-assault movement, because Abercromby still had few horses for transport. Nevertheless on 22 February 1801, he sailed for the objective area, but not without trepidations. "I never went on any service entertaining greater doubts of success," he said, "at the same time with more determination to conquer difficulties."

The fleet arrived at Alexandria on 1 March where, for no apparent reason, Lord Keith approached close to the harbor, thereby warning the French of the British presence. The following morning he dropped anchor in Aboukir Bay. Then he discovered that the Royal Engineers sent on reconnaissance had been captured. Abercromby and Moore set off themselves in a cutter for a personal appraisal of the landing area.

The beach at Aboukir rimmed a crescent-shaped bay for approximately 2 miles. At the northern end of the horn was Aboukir Castle mounting several heavy pieces that had the beach in enfilade for up to 1,800 yards. At the southern end was a blockhouse with at least one modern gun. In the center of the objective area rose a high sand hill flat on top. To its south lay a confusion of lower sand dunes rising in tiers from the beach. Although the French had excellent natural cover and concealment, the two British generals could perceive no entrenchments of any sort. The enemy's presence was confirmed only by highly visible local security on the beach and the skyline.

Because of the guns at the castle, Abercromby and Moore decided not to land any farther north than the central sand hill, with the hill itself as the objective of the British right. This would limit the assault to the one-mile sector of beach to the south. The blockhouse would be neutralized by a gunboat. When he returned to the fleet, Abercromby gave orders for the landing to go the next day, but a fierce gale swept in and made debarkation impossible for four days. Thus the French were given four additional days to prepare.

General Menou, the overall commander in Egypt, failed to concentrate his forces, preferring to reinforce his scattered dispositions. Only sixteen hundred infantry and two hundred cavalry with fifteen guns under General Friant were at Aboukir.

The British order of battle was:

- Guards Brigade: Major General Ludlow—1/Coldstreams, 1/3rd Guards
- 1st Brigade: Major General Coote—2/1st, 54th (2 battalions), 92nd
- 2nd Brigade: Major General Craddock—8th, 13th, 18th, 90th
- 3rd Brigade: Major General Lord Cavan—50th, 79th
- 4th Brigade: Brigadier General Doyle—2nd, 30th, 44th, 89th
- 5th Brigade: Brigadier General John Stuart—Minorca Regt., De Roll's and Dillans Regiments
- Reserve: Major General John Moore, Brigadier General Oakes—23rd, 28th, 42nd, 58th, 4 companies/40th, Corsican Rangers
- Cavalry: Brigadier General Finch—1 troop 11th Light Dragoons, 12th, 26th, Hompesch Light Dragoons
- Artillery: twenty-four 6-pounders, sixteen 12-pounders, six 5.5-inch howitzers, seventy-six siege pieces

On 7 March the gale abated. The landing was set for the next day. That evening two boats were moored close inshore to mark the points between which the flatboats were to form line. The troops of the second wave, to be brought ashore after the beach was secured, were transferred to lighter draft vessels so as to be closer to the beach. At 0200, a rocket rose from the flagship. The landing began. All boats went to their loading points. By 0330 all were loaded and moving silently across the 10,000 meters to the rendezvous.

By daylight most had reached the line of departure, but much time was spent ensuring that the proper order was established. The first line consisted of fifty-eight flatboats each carrying fifty troops loaded with three days'

rations and sixty rounds of ball ammunition. To their rear was the second line of eighty-four cutters and the third line of fifty-one launches and fourteen field guns. On each flank there was a bomb vessel (mortar ship) and two gunboats. A little before 0900 the gunboats opened fire, and the lines began to advance. In order, from the position of honor on the right, to the left flank the force would be landed in the following order: 40th (Somersetshire Regiment); 23rd (Royal Welsh Fusiliers); 42nd (Black Watch); 58th (Northhamptons); Corsican Rangers; 1/Coldstream; 1/3rd Guards (Scots); 2/1st Regiment (The Royal); 54th (Dorsetshire).

From Aboukir Castle, the sand hills and farther south, the French guns opened fire with round shot. Several boats were hit. As the British closed the range, grape and landgridge were added to the fusilade churning the water white around the boats. The center of the line, especially the Coldstream Guards, suffered the worst. Musketry and canister were soon sweeping into the British lines, but the advance continued steadily. The fire reached a crescendo as the boats grounded in the surf, but the assault force sprang ashore and formed up. General Moore, taking the 40th, 23rd, and the 28th into line without pausing to load their weapons, charged directly against the central sand hill and carried the position with the bayonet. This assault dispersed the major portion of the French forces, consisting of the 61st Demibrigade, and captured four guns.

To Moore's left, Brigadier Oakes with the remainder of the reserve landed only moments behind Moore. As Oakes came ashore, his force was charged by the French cavalry while the British were still in the surf. The 42nd (Black Watch) formed up in the knee-deep water and calmy drove them off with volley fire. The Highlanders then advanced vigorously, driving the enemy out of the sand hills to their front with cold steel and taking three guns.

To Oakes's left, the Guards Brigade ran into trouble. Having lost two boats and been thrown ashore out of order, they were confused. The French cavalry, having reformed, then tried a second charge, but with the help of the 58th, Brigadier Ludlow threw them back again, set his battalions in order, and advanced inland to his place in line. Brigadier Cavan and his brigade landed in time, dispersed a body of French infantry trying to outflank the Guards and advanced.

With the initial force ashore, the boats returned to the fleet for the second wave. Meanwhile the forces on Moore's left continued to advance inland, clearing the sand dunes and taking eight guns in the process. Within two hours the beach was cleared. The French were driven onto the open plains to their rear with the loss of fifteen guns.

The battle essentially had been won in the first twenty minutes when Moore seized the central sand hill. However the finest performance was undoubtedly given by the 42nd as they formed in the surf to repel a cavalry assault. This battalion lost 21 killed and 156 wounded, including 8 officers. Next seriously hurt was the Coldstreams with 97 casualties. Altogether the army lost 31 officers and 621 other ranks. The navy boat crews suffered 97 casualties, attesting to the ferocity of the defenders' fire. The estimated French loss was between 300 and 400.

By nightfall Abercromby's army was united several miles inshore. The French successfully united their forces, forcing Abercromby to fight two more engagements. The second action was decisive in the campaign, but in this on 21 March, Abercromby was mortally wounded. He died aboard ship on the 28th. Upon his death, his old friend and commander, The Duke of York, remarked:

> His steady observance of discipline, his ever watchful attention to the health and wants of his troops, the persevering and unconquerable spirit which marked his military career, the splendor of his actions in the field, and the heroism of his death are worthy of the imitation of all who desire, like him, a life of honour and a death of glory.

The operation was eminently successful and highly applauded, even by the French.

Abercromby has been overshadowed, however, by his brilliant comrade Moore and later, of course, by the Duke of Wellington. Nevertheless this officer deserves a high place of honor among British military greats.

Despite the obvious lessons to be learned from the success of the operation, British military minds continued to operate in ignorance. The landings at Walcheren Island in 1809 were in the more familiar pattern of fiasco that had marked earlier operations.

Notes on Sources

The standard reference for any campaign of a British force is Sir John Fortescue's *History of the British Army*, 13 vol., upon which this essay is largely based. Other useful materials include:

Burgoyne, LtCol. Sir John M., *A Short History of the Naval and Military Operations in Egypt from 1798 to 1802* (London: Sampson, Low, 1885).

Burbury, Sir Henry, *Narratives of Some Passages in the Great War With France* (London: Peter Davies, 1927).

Dunfermline, Lord James, *Lieutenant General Sir Ralph Abercromby, KB: 1793–1801* (Edinburgh: Edmonston and Douglas, 1861).

Gleig, The Reverend G. R., *Lives of the Most Eminent British Military Commanders*, vol. 3 (London: Longmans, 1832).

Marshall-Cornwell, James, "The First British Expeditionary Force to Egypt, 1801," *Journal of the Royal United Services Institute* 122 (September 1977): 52–55.

Paine, J., "Sir Ralph Abercromby: The Bicentenary of a Famous Soldier," *Journal of the Royal United Services Institute* 79 (August 1934): 574–80.

Wheeler, LtCmdr. D., RN, "Abercromby's Egyptian Campaign of 1801," *Journal of the Royal United Services Institute* 103 (February 1958): 89–93.

The majority of primary documents on the expedition are official reports and correspondence held by the Public Records Offices in London and Edinburgh, and private papers in various repositories throughout the United Kingdom. Some primary material is available in published form, of which the two most valuable are:

Walsh, Captain Thomas, *Journal of the Late Campaign in Egypt* (1803).

Wilson, LtCol. Robert, *History of the British Expedition to Egypt* (1803).

Vera Cruz, 1847

BY COLONEL JOHN FLEMING POLK, USA (RET.)

Major General Winfield Scott, senior officer of the U.S. Army, submitted a plan for the further conduct of the war against Mexico to Secretary of War William L. Marcy on 29 September 1846. The plan envisaged ending the war with a decisive stroke. An amphibious expedition would be mounted and the port of Vera Cruz seized, followed by a march to the final vital objective: Mexico City. The army element would consist of approximately ten thousand troops drawn from General Zachary Taylor's expeditionary forces in northern Mexico and directly from the United States. General Taylor's force would maintain a passive defense in the vicinity of Monterey, because despite victories, no decisive action could result in northern Mexico. The Home Squadron of the U.S. Navy, under Commodore David Connor, which was performing blockade duty in the Gulf of Mexico, would support the expedition. The operation was scheduled to take place in early 1847 in order to avoid the annual yellow fever plague at Vera Cruz. The sudden gales, or "northerners," prevalent in the early part of the year, would have to be hazarded. A troop list and material requirements accompanied the plan. Secretary Marcy accepted the plan and placed it before the president at a cabinet meeting.

After several cabinet meetings, President Polk ordered Scott's plan to be put into effect, with refinements. Secretary of the Navy

John Y. Mason was ordered to reinforce the Home Squadron by diverting the ship-of-the-line *Ohio* and sloops *Germantown*, *Saratoga*, and *Decatur* to Commodore Connor. In addition, the navy would purchase five coastal schooners, or barks, then man and equip four of them to serve as shallow-draft gunboats; the fifth would be reserved for supplies. The army was responsible for chartering transports and for procuring surf boats. The question of who would command the Army Expeditionary Forces and the Navy Home Squadron was not resolved immediately.

Although Secretary Mason had doubts as to Commodore Connor's physical fitness, and had written him several times urging more aggressiveness, he did not relieve him of command. Instead, he created the rank of vice commodore and dispatched Captain Matthew C. Perry to the Home Squadron to serve in this capacity until Connor's normal tour of duty was completed, at which time Perry would take command. Secretary Marcy strongly recommended General Scott to President Polk as the most capable officer to command the expedition. The president did not doubt the military qualifications of "Old Fuss Feathers," but he did doubt, with some justification, Scott's loyalty to the Democratic administration. He held a private interview with Scott on 19 November, at which he spoke quite candidly to Scott about loyalty and cooperation. Scott's replies apparently satisfied the president because at the end of the interview he appointed Scott commander of the expedition.

Marine Corps Gazette, "Vera Cruz 1847: A Lesson in Command," 63 (September 1979): 61–67. Reprinted by permission.

The battle of Vera Cruz, 1847. Drawing by H. Billings; engraved by D. G. Thompson, 1863. Courtesy of the U.S. Navy Historical Center.

Implementation of the plans had progressed fairly well by the time the questions of command were resolved. The army had started procurement of its surf boats. These were designed by a naval officer and came in three sizes so they could be stacked for transportation. Each carried approximately forty men. The crew consisted of eight men: a commander, a coxswain, and six oarsmen. Each boat was equipped with a kedge and line for reentry into the surf and to prevent broaching. Scott prepared a final memorandum to the secretary redefining troops and materiel requirements. The secretary then held a final interview with General Scott on 23 November and gave him the following letter of instruction:

War Department, Washington
November 23, 1846

Sir——The President, several days since, communicated in person to you his orders to repair to Mexico, to take command of the forces there assembled, and particularly to organize and to set on foot an expedition to operate on the Gulf coast, if, on arriving in the theater of action, you shall deem it to be practical. It is not proposed to control your operations by definite and positive instructions, but you are left to prosecute them as your judgment, under a full view of all circumstance, shall dictate. Your work is before you, and the means provided, or to be provided, for accomplishing it, are committed to you, in the full confidence that you will use them to the best advantage.

The objects which it is desirable to obtain have been indicated, and it is hoped that you will have the requisite force to accomplish them.

Of this you must be the judge, when preparations are made, and the time for action arrived.

Very respectfully,
Your Obedient Servant

W. L. Marcy
Secretary of War

TO: General Winfield Scott

Commodore Connor, with the Home Squadron in the Gulf, was having his problems. Blockading the Mexican Gulf Coast was an arduous, drudging task. He lacked sufficient light-draft vessels to cross the bars of the Mexican ports, and he was plagued with shortages of men and supplies. The nearest naval base was at Pensacola, one thousand miles away, and repair facilities there were limited. Coal and water were always a problem. His requests for tenders went unheeded, necessitating extra work in the transfer of supplies from ship to shore and shore to ship. Nevertheless, the blockade was effective.

General Scott and Commodore Connor wrote each other early. Scott requested information and recommendations. Connor made reconnaissances, developed intelligence sources, and met Scott's requests. Between the two of them, they evolved a plan and settled on their mutual responsibilities. Scott accepted Connor's recommendations as to rendezvous areas, landing beach, fire support plan, and control of shipping. Timing was stated in general terms to allow for contingencies.

Commencing on 25 February, approximately sixty transports began rendezvousing off the Isle de Lobos. These transports carried twelve thousand troops, consisting of two regular divisions, one volunteer division, a siege train, a regiment of cavalry, and necessary supplies. The transports came from six different ports and all did not close until 1 March. They were met by the *Massachusetts*. All captains were called aboard, briefed, and given sailing orders. On 2 March, the *Massachusetts* led the convoy toward an anchorage at Anton Lazardo. Despite a small gale, the transports arrived at San Lazardo on 5 March and were directed into anchorage by sloops from the Home Squadron. Commodore Connor and General Scott conferred immediately. Because they were concerned about the possibility of new gales, they decided on a prompt reconnaissance, followed by a landing. On 6 March aboard the screw ship *Perita*, Commodore Connor and General Scott with his senior commanders and personal staff, among whom were captains Robert E.

Lee and Joseph E. Johnson and lieutenants P. T. G. Beauregard and George Gordon Meade, observed the landing area and the City of Vera Cruz.

Commodore Connor had selected Callado Beach as the landing area. This beach was out of range of the guns of Vera Cruz and Castle San Juan de Ulna, and was also protected from the Gulf surf by Sacrificious Island. The island did limit, however, the number of ships that could be employed in the landing area. The seaborne reconnaissance was deliberate and close to the shore and fortifications. The junior officers were most concerned with the complacency of their seniors as the *Perita* was bracketed with fire from the castle. However the two commanders settled on a firm plan.

On the morning of 9 March, the soldiers debarked from the civilian transports into the surf boats crewed by the U.S. Navy sailors. The troops then were carried to the navy vessels and reembarked. With the surf boats in tow, the navy ships proceeded to the lee side of Sacrificious Island where the troops debarked again into the surf boats. They deployed into a formation of ten boats wide and six deep. Aboard were the veteran troops of General Worth's division and the marine detachments from the Home Squadron. The formation was flanked by the light draft gunboats of the Home Squadron which stood close into shore. Aboard the *Massachusetts* General Scott ordered the specially agreed-upon joint army-navy signal hoisted. The boats commenced to run in for Callado Beach. The gunboats fired a volley that dispersed the Mexican cavalry observed on the beach, and the troops landed unopposed. In five hours the three divisions, consisting of more than eight thousand men, had been shuttled ashore with no casualties. The attack on Vera Cruz had begun. The plan was simple. Vera Cruz, now surrounded by land and sea, would be bombarded and starved into submission. Scott and Connor hoped that no costly direct assault would be necessary. The unloading of siege guns and supplies began on the 10th. Commodore Connor designated Commander Sands as officer in charge of unloading. Sands called up the supply ships from the anchorage to the landing area according to the availability of space and surf boats. As the ships finished unloading, they were dispatched individually back to the United States. A northerner lasting from 12 to 17 March hampered unloading.

By the 21st, the army siege batteries were in position south and west of Vera Cruz but lacked ammunition. On the 22nd, the navy brought ashore three 32-pounders and three 8-inch shell guns, together with double crews and ammunition. Two hundred men were required to manhandle the guns into positions prepared to the left of the army batteries by Captain Lee. Little firing was done ashore on the 23rd because of the lack of ammunition. However the Home Squadron kept the Mexicans under pressure with a bombardment by a flotilla under Commander Josiah Tattnall. The tempo was raised on the 24th and 25th. The navy guns fired more than one thousand rounds, destroying the enemy batteries at Fort Santa Barbara. On 26 March, General Jose Juantandero requested a truce and firing ceased. The only American casualties had been to army and navy gun crews. The infantry had remained safely in defilade behind the sand dunes. The formal surrender occurred on 27 March.

The joyous, triumphant occasion was not witnessed by Commodore Connor. On 20 March he received a letter from Secretary Mason directing him to turn over his command to Commodore Perry. He departed for home aboard the *Princeton* the next day. Commodore Connor never saw the reinforcements to the Home Squadron ordered by President Polk. They arrived after the battle.

The amphibious expeditions to Vera Cruz were the first major overseas operations conducted jointly by the U.S. Army and the U.S. Navy. Despite the lack of knowledge or experience on the part of the civilian leaders and military commanders directing the operations, the action was successful. Compared with later operations in the Civil War, Spanish-American War, and early World War II, the Vera Cruz expedition was a huge suc-

cess. The conduct of the civilian leaders and the military bears examination.

President Polk made the major decisions, but only after due deliberations with his full Cabinet. (Some of the Cabinet thought the operation might be costly or even disastrous.) He gave positive instructions to his secretaries of war and navy. He also gave attention to the selection of the major commanders, then did not interfere with the operation once it was started, even though he had some private doubts and did criticize his service secretaries.

Secretary of War Marcy demonstrated a clear concept of his functions and responsibilities. He recommended the army commander to the president and faithfully backed his recommendation. He ascertained the requirements and used initiative and zeal in acquiring them. His letter to General Scott delineated clearly the line of authority between the civilians and the military. (The letter should be required reading for new secretaries of defense and officers of the war colleges.)

Secretary of the Navy Mason apparently did not understand his duties or was incapable of performing them. Reinforcements directed by the President did not reach the theater of action on time. Requests from Commodore Connor were handled in a routine manner. There was no anticipation of requirements or impetus to send supplies forward. Mason created an awkward situation by having his commander (Connor) and that officer's relief (Perry) aboard together for some months. Finally, he relieved his commander in the middle of a successful operation.

General Scott demonstrated foresight in preparing for the expedition. He considered all aspects of the operation, including weather and disease. He made his requirements known early. As one result, the first specially built American landing craft (surf boats) were obtained. The assembly of the transports in rendezvous on schedule from numerous ports could have been accomplished only through superb staff planning. Most of all, Scott established an early rapport with his navy opposite, Commodore Connor. Scott apparently recognized Connor's professional qualities and accepted his recommendations. Scott fully trusted him with all movements at sea and from ship to shore.

Commodore Connor performed remarkably well under adversity. He received little support from the Navy Department and knew he was in ill grace with the secretary. His selection of transport areas and landing beach proved sound. His seamanship and executive ability were amazing. Landing twelve thousand soldiers from sixty civilian transports, together with supplies, in adverse weather in tricky waters without the loss of a ship or a man is a record without parallel. Finally, his placing ashore of guns and of crews to aid the army demonstrated a will to accomplish the major mission. Scott and Connor made a remarkable team. They anticipated joint amphibious doctrine by one hundred years. Further they used techniques of amphibious warfare that allegedly were developed only as late as World War Two.

British Invasion of the Crimea, 1854

BY JOHN SWEETMAN

"They lay like a vast field of poppies, men convulsed with cholera, groaning with dysentery, rigid from fever or heatstroke and clusters of wild-eyed stragglers, strewing blankets, greatcoats, shakos, even ration bags in their wake, tumbling along after the main body." The march of the allied armies, from their landing beaches on the west coast of the Crimea, toward Sevastopol was under way. Agonies such as these, however, were totally unimagined when, on 28 March 1854, the *London Gazette* published an official "Declaration of War" against Russia.

Since Peter the Great, Russia had sought to dominate the Bosphorus Straits, so securing unrestricted passage into the Mediterranean, and, as the leading nation of the Eastern Orthodox Church, to establish a religious protectorship over Turkey's fourteen million Christian subjects. To safeguard her Indian trade routes, Britain had resisted these ambitions.

In 1852 a religious quarrel over guardianship of certain holy places in Jerusalem (then Turkish) broke out, which Russia used to pursue her aims. A period of intense diplomatic activity followed. Then, on 8 June 1853 Vice Admiral Dundas and the British Mediterranean fleet sailed from Malta to "the neighbourhood of the Dardanelles . . . for the protection of Turkey against an unprovoked attack and in defence of her independence." Shortly afterwards, Russia decided to occupy Moldavia and Wallachia (modern Rumania,

Army Quarterly 93 (October 1966): 99–110. Reprinted by permission.

then two provinces under Turkish suzerainty) to obtain "by force, but without war" her "just demands." On 2 July Prince Gortschakoff led Russian troops over the Pruth, as "various arbitrary acts of the Porte have infringed the rights (of the Orthodox Church) . . . to the defence of the Orthodox religion." "To all our faithful subjects" within Russia, the tsar had launched a holy war. To other powers, his aims appeared more secular and political.

Russia ignored a Turkish ultimatum of 4 October to withdraw from the two provinces and on 23 October the sultan declared war. One day earlier, the British and French fleets, respectively under Dundas and Admiral Hamelin, had entered the Dardanelles. But there was no immediate prospect of British military intervention, for strong Turkish military defenses along the Danube had not yet been forced.

On 30 November public opinion changed dramatically, although the military situation was not appreciably altered. Six Russian warships utterly destroyed a Turkish naval force in Sinope harbor, 300 miles east of Constantinople, killing four thousand Turks. News of the disaster reached Britain twelve days later. Enraged citizens, openly blaming the British government's inaction, held vigorous pro-Turkish meetings and several newspapers were blatantly truculent: *The Morning Advertiser* claimed Britain and France had interfered only "to betray unfortunate Turkey" and urged military action against Russia. Attacking Lord Aberdeen's coalition government as "the imbecile men,

Bombardment of Odessa, Russia, 22 April 1854. Courtesy of the U.S. Navy Historical Center.

the minions of Russia," it queried: "Has justice ceased to occupy her throne in the English heart? Has the national honour lost its hold on the minds of the people of these realms?" *The Westminster Review* put forward economic arguments for direct interference: "Our passage to India . . . (and) our commerce with all free nations depends upon it . . . our merchants will rue their blind folly in declining to stop him [the tsar]." *Reynolds News* meanwhile attacked the prince consort, known to favor peace.

Aberdeen still hoped for peace and, as late as 12 February 1854 wrote to Lord Clarendon, his foreign secretary: "I still say war is not inevitable." But by now *The Times* was proclaiming that "an aggressive posture was not only moral, Christian and patriotic, but self-evidently judicious, businesslike, progressive and manly." When a Russian steamer on the Pruth fired two Turkish villages with heated roundshot, press reports, hard upon the "Massacre of Sinope," treated the action as a devilish atrocity. As more papers emphasized the threat to India, *The Times* intimated that "this war may shake the world" and people in the streets cried, "Avenge Sinope!" Nicholas I was described as "that fiend in human form" and *Punch* published a cartoon showing Aberdeen blacking the tsar's boots.

On 4 January 1854, the combined British and French fleets entered the Black Sea, with orders to take action if Russian ships refused to return to port. On 27 February Clarendon dispatched the crucial ultimatum to St. Petersburg, requesting that Russia undertake within six days to clear Moldavia and Wallachia by 30 April. "Refusal or silence . . . (would be) equivalent to a declaration of war." The tsar disdained to reply, thus Britain entered "The Crimean War."

On 10 April a formal treaty of alliance was concluded between Britain and France (to which Turkey acceded on the 15th) and next day Nicholas I declared war, protesting that "Russia fights not for the things of this world, but the Faith." The press might be enthusiastic over this, but Charles Greville, clerk to the Privy Council, prophetically noted in his diary: "Before many months are over, people will be heartily sick of it, as they are now hot upon it." Commenting upon war fever in 1854, eight years after John Bright said: "When people are inflamed in that way, they are no better than 'mad dogs.'"

Already on the Black Sea, Dundas commanded a formidable British naval force of eighteen warships and thirty-nine frigates. It was this force which undertook Britain's first hostile action. On 13 April HMS *Furious*, dispatched under a flag of truce to evacuate the British and French consuls from Odessa, was fired upon by Russian shore batteries.

Next day, seven British vessels bombarded the city and, on 16 April, seventeen British warships discharged a 900-gun broadside to signal the commencement of a massive bombardment. When truce proposals were rejected, this continued intermittently until 6:00 P.M. on 22 April. Squadrons also bombarded Sevastopol, blockaded the Danube, and reconnoitered the eastern Black Sea.

Elsewhere, the Admiralty was also active. On 11 March Sir Charles Napier in the 131-gun *Duke of Wellington* led fifteen vessels out of Portsmouth harbor amid scenes of wild enthusiasm. "Ship after ship shook out its vast sails with marvellous rapidity . . . hundreds of signal flags were spread on the quarter-deck [of *Duke of Wellington*], causing the space to appear like a variegated flower-bed." To add to the splendor of the occasion, Queen Victoria, in the Royal Yacht *Fairy*, accompanied the armada to Spithead. It was all very emotional and visibly splendid. Seeing Napier depart, Tennyson wrote part of "Maude": "It is better to fight for the good than rail at the ill." But the purpose of this expedition to the Baltic was vague and, in fact, it achieved little.

Meanwhile preparations were under way to collect an expeditionary force from an army which had fought only minor colonial conflicts since Waterloo. Not required to face an actual enemy, colonels had determined to create sartorially impressive regiments and troops passed endless hours in perfecting complicated parade-ground movements. When, in 1853, large-scale maneuvers were organized at Chobham, efficiency in the art of war was not so evident. Bewildered officers and puzzled men frequently lost contact during exercises and several officers felt "the whole damn'd thing . . . a waste of time." Thus on 9 July, *The Times* could only discover a sports day to cover at Chobham. Well might an artillery officer remark: "The army is a shambles." Lord Raglan, a Peninsula veteran of sixty-four, was chosen to lead the expeditionary force. Undoubtedly brave and industrious, he nevertheless caused frequent alarums by referring to the French as "the enemy" and the Turks, his other allies, as "bandits."

In February 1854, before Clarendon's ultimatum expired, Sir John Burgoyne, an experienced engineer, traveled to Constantinople to study Turkey's defenses. At the same time, British troops were leaving England in a curious collection of chartered liners and merchantmen—low paddle-steamers with leaning stovepipe stacks belching filthy smoke amidships contrasting unfavorably with the higher, broader sailing ships, magnificent under full sail.

On 22 February battalions of the Grenadier and Coldstream Guards sailed from Southampton, the first detachments of the expeditionary force to leave. Three days later the Second Battalion, the Rifle Brigade, sailed from Portsmouth. A young private's wife, disguised as a soldier, was discovered embarking with the troops. In keeping with the sentimental enthusiasm of the occasion, a sympathetic commanding officer let her go aboard. On 28 February the Scots Guards left Birdcage Walk for Portsmouth. Marching past Buckingham Palace in the morning sun, guardsmen saw Queen Victoria and her children waving from the balcony and, as they marched down the Mall toward Waterloo Station, a milling throng crowded the roadside. Deafening applause greeted bands playing, "Cheer, boys, cheer," "The girl I left behind me," and "We are going far away." A solid mass of enthusiastic Londoners waved the trains away and at Portsmouth the reception was no less delirious.

Throughout spring and early summer, troop sailings were regular, but, as the novelty of colorful departures wore off, scenes of wild enthusiasm gradually disappeared. When the 8th Hussars left Plymouth at dusk on 25 April, there were neither fluttering handkerchiefs nor military bands. Nevertheless, with splendid disregard for security, *The Times* published details of troop movements. Sergeant Timothy Gowling of the Royal Fusiliers might observe the troops "were going out to defend a rotten cause, a race that almost every Christian despises," but few would have agreed with him in that summer of 1854.

Once aboard the troopships, conditions for men, women, and horses were distinctly unpleasant. The horses were accommodated below, often in dim light, insufficient ventilation, and stifling heat. Two ranks of horses, each supported round the belly and shoulders by a canvas sling suspended from above, faced one another, with a line of wooden mangers between them. Thoroughly panic-stricken, the wretched beasts thrashed helplessly in their slings until their shoulders and bellies were raw and their bodies a mass of dripping sweat and blood. Courageous soldiers dodged swinging lanterns, lashing hooves, and slithering, unsecured mangers to wash the horses' nostrils with vinegar. But before long many animals hung pitifully exhausted and, in *The Shooting Star* alone, four died during the Biscay crossing. The troops were also below "in the midst of darkness and confusion, but such a torrent of grumbling and blasphemy," in beds three tiers high, between which were slung hammocks. Several troopships, despite their steam engines, experienced rough crossings of the Bay of Biscay and were unable to make much headway against powerful winds. Men and women, battened below and "weakened almost to delirium by sickness and nerves," went through agonies in an atmosphere thick with the sweat of sickness and fear, amid continuous moans from the injured and suffering.

After a week, the ships found temporary shelter under the forbidding rock of Gibraltar. Whitewashed houses, dominated by grim batteries hewn out of the rock, overlooked the bay. Once ashore, the soldiers climbed narrow streets with central gutters, passing (or gleefully entering) numerous winehouses. Through Main Street, whose shops had no signs to indicate their stock but a sample of their wares (sugar, soap, tobacco, pipes, blacking, and so forth) suspended on a string outside the door, they went to the busy market. There picturesque Moors in flowing robes, tawny Spaniards, and rugged Gibraltese noisily offered their wares.

Soon the ships sailed on the three-day journey to Malta. In the more placid Mediterranean, conditions aboard improved, but some horses, maddened by the oppressive heat, had to be shot. At Malta, the troops enjoyed a longer and more relaxed stay, even if the lo-

cal, thin wine was blamed for outbreaks of dysentery and diarrhea. The high harbor walls and dominating forts of Valetta were romantically likened to an Arabian Nights setting. Officers and their wives gaily thronged the Union Club and generally a holiday atmosphere prevailed.

On 30 March the first contingent left Malta for the Dardanelles, arriving at Gallipoli on 8 April. The narrow, pebbled streets, without pavements and lined with "overhanging houses, rickety, dirty and dilapidated," fascinated the troops, in spite of the "abominable collection of stagnant filth reeking with unbearable odours" and the motley assembly of "Jews, Turks, heretics, squabbling children and myriads of hungry dogs." Bearded, robed men, veiled women, and the slippered, smoking stallkeepers contributed to an air of Eastern mysticism. At first conditions were fairly reasonable, even if neither beer nor porter were available. But the British were essentially disorganized. They bargained with "Bono Johnny," whilst the French laid down a fixed scale of charges, rapidly erected signs and restaurants, and demolished inconvenient buildings.

Amid British confusion, Lord Raglan arrived unannounced. Dressed in a blue frock coat, he unobtrusively strolled through the town. His arrival contrasted sharply with that of Prince Napoleon, the emperor's cousin, but only a divisional commander. Wearing a splendid, gold-laced uniform and plumed hat, he was greeted by a resplendent guard of honor and an Imperial salute from French warships. Raglan, who had traveled via Paris for military conversations, only stayed one day in Gallipoli before moving to Constantinople. By the end of May, eighteen thousand British and twenty-two thousand French troops were at Gallipoli. As conditions in the town were fast deteriorating, most of the British force followed their commander north.

At first sight Constantinople, from the clear blue waters of the Golden Horn dotted with curious, light caiques, seemed attractive. On closer inspection, it proved little better than Gallipoli. "Of all the villainous holes that I have ever been in, this is, I think, the worst," wrote one disillusioned Briton. The city consisted of ancient archways, constricted alleys (lined both sides with open shops and booths, offering everything from treacle to Bibles), and countless mounds of rancid dirt—all overlooked by a maze of minarets and mosques. Bored and disappointed the army resorted to alcohol: one night alone, twenty-four hundred British drunks were reported. Above all, the weather became uncomfortably hot.

Across the strait at Scutari, conditions were no better: As the ships neared the town, the white tents and scarlet uniforms of the early arrivals attracted the attention of eager eyes. The sights within Scutari harbor were less exciting. Bloated animal carcasses, stinking offal, and rotting vegetables floated on the greasy water, which slopped against a single, rickety, wooden jetty. Swinging the horses on to its trembling planks was extremely hazardous. Once ashore, the soldiers were besieged by dirty beggars, wretched urchins, and growling dogs. The Turkish barracks, allotted to British troops, were infested with fleas, rats, and other vermin which fearlessly attacked humans on sight. Officers and men were forced into tents rather than endure this. Mercifully, the stay at Scutari was not prolonged.

Small British detachments were left at Gallipoli, Scutari, and Constantinople, the remainder moved into the cooler temperatures and summer mists of the Black Sea, to disembark at Varna during June and July. From the harbor the small, white houses of the town seemed to confirm this was "a very healthy spot." On the newly constructed piers and jetties, red uniforms, splashed with white belts and gold braid, bustled among piles of ammunition boxes, fifes, drums, shot, and shell. But once ashore, surrounded by persistent flies, the town assumed a familiar Turkish character. Two-story wooden buildings with red-tiled roofs, but mostly windowless, lined confined, pot-holed streets, angled towards a central drain almost invariably overflowing with putrid filth. Inevitably too disorganization was soon apparent. Cavalry horses had to be loaded, kicking and

squealing, into rowing-boats to be ferried ashore: many a hussar courted ruination of his uniform, by plunging into the bay to swim to land, rather than risk a flying hoof. In the town itself, the French, unlike the British, posted their own street names, clearly indicated their officers' residences, organized shops and restaurants, and established a post office.

British regiments were dispersed within reach of Varna and conditions at first were by no means unpleasant. Grapes, melons, wild strawberries, and other edible berries were in abundance and "beautiful orioles, gawdy woodpeckers, jays and grosbeaks shriek and chatter among the bushes, while the nightingale pours forth a flood of plaintive melody." Shooting parties hunted buffalo and wild deer, men swam and fished. Soon, however, the days became unbearably hot, the lakes were found to contain slugs, leeches, and snakes, and a daily hot wind from the west covered everything with a layer of choking limestone dust infested by countless stubborn flies. On 2 July a six-hour hurricane struck. "The sound of coughing and retching was heard throughout the lines and everything was coated in white powder, stinking of horse manure."

Worse was to come. On 19 July cholera was confirmed in two blotchy, twisted bodies in the French lines; three days later it reached the British. Within a fortnight the disease claimed six hundred British victims. It rapidly spread, where "teeming soil and stagnant lakes sent up volumes of poisonous miasma beneath the scorching sun," unwanted offal decomposed openly, and no proper drainage or sanitation existed. "So offensive were the exhalations from the camps" that nearby villagers voluntarily deserted their homes. A belief arose that a diet of melons, cucumbers, and 3s. 6d. bottles of coarse, strong brandy would provide immunity. By mid-August hundreds lolled in drunken stupors, as infected flies crawled over their prostrate forms. But the disease still flourished. The hospital at Varna, ill-organized and badly equipped, became a veritable graveyard. "Corpses stretched in blankets (were) rushed to holes on the camp outskirts almost every hour." There were the macabre gaping pits "into which the disfigured corpses were dropped pell-mell by the drunken pensioners of the ambulance corps." In an attempt to reduce infection, tents were hurriedly struck and regiments more widely dispersed.

Meanwhile the military situation had changed considerably and unexpectedly. On 26 June the Russians retreated from the siege of Silistria on the Danube and by 2 August had all recrossed the Pruth, vacating Moldavia and Wallachia. With no enemy at hand, British and French forces now seemed superfluous, but there was no question of going home. Public and press opinion was still militant. Greville observed, "the people are wild about the war," and Queen Victoria said it was "popular beyond belief." In Parliament, Lord Lynhurst, referring to the great calamity if this "barbarous race" (the Russians) should establish itself in Europe, said: "In no event, except of extreme necessity, ought we to make peace."

On 16 July Raglan received a Cabinet dispatch: "Unless, with the information in your possession, but at present unknown in this country, you should be decidedly of the opinion that it could not be undertaken with a reasonable prospect of success ... the fortress (Sevastopol) must be reduced and the fleet taken or destroyed: nothing but insuperable impediments ... should be allowed to prevent the early decision to undertake these operations." Three days later Raglan wrote to the secretary of state for war, the Duke of Newcastle, agreeing to the invasion of the Crimean peninsula, but emphasizing that his information was sparse and that government pressure had forced this action upon him.

Rather half-hearted attempts were made to deceive the tsar. Rumors of an overland advance over the Danube were spread and naval squadrons demonstrated before Odessa. But maritime and siege preparations around Varna were all too evident; British officers were scouring the Levant for small boats; troops were busy constructing fascines, scaling ladders, and gabions; and, in any case,

the British press had been advocating the attack upon Sevastopol for six months. On 10 August a serious fire in Varna destroyed valuable stores and one day later cholera struck the fleets. Attempting to reduce its severity, the admirals put to sea, but *Britannia* alone lost 139 out of 985, before the disease suddenly subsided in the vessels on 20 August. It was not until late August, therefore, that the army was ordered back to Varna.

On 28 July HMS *Fury*, with Sir George Brown, the French General Canrobet, and artillery and engineer experts from both armies, had reconnoitered the west Crimean coast. In accordance with Raglan's instructions, they chose a landing place at the mouth of the Katcha river, 7 miles north of Sevastopol. Dominated from overlooking cliffs by Russian artillery and possessing, in any case, only a narrow beach, it was later declared utterly unsuitable. Allied knowledge of Russian strength was not any more satisfactory. The Foreign Office estimated forty-five thousand (including seventeen thousand sailors) on the peninsula. French sources thought seventy thousand, but Dundas hazarded one hundred twenty thousand. In reality, the only reliable intelligence was that concerning the Russian fleet, obtained by a naval reconnaissance squadron.

A conference on 20 August, the day cholera left the fleets, fixed 2 September for the departure. On 24 August British embarkation began under Admiral Lyons. New stone jetties had been specially built and small boats carried the troops out to "a perfect forest of shipping of every kind," but bad weather postponed departure. Then on 4 September, Admiral Hamelin informed Dundas that French steamers were unable to tow all their sailing vessels and that, moreover, two thousand additional troops must be transported aboard each naval vessel, making it impossible for them to clear for action. This meant that only Dundas's force remained to protect the steam and sail armada, which would disperse widely once under way. Moreover, when Raglan arrived at Balchik on 5 September, he found that the French commander, Marshal St. Arnaud, impatient with the delay, had already sailed off toward Crimea in *Ville de Paris*.

At 4:45 A.M. on 7 September, Dundas signaled the departure. Smoke from straining steamers (each towing two crowded transports) temporarily obscured the five British columns of thirty vessels, followed by warships in single line ahead. The sailing ships, each with a regimental number painted on its side, distinguishing flag and divisional lantern for display at night, were a mass of green, blue and red figures, interspersed with the off-white uniforms, black kerchiefs, and flat hats of the sailors. The Bulgarian hills receded as bands played "Rule Britannia" and the British, French, and Turkish national anthems. Flags flew proudly overhead and massive shore batteries thundered salutes.

After Balchik Bay, the armada was to rendezvous off the Danube estuary. On 8 September Raglan came up with *Ville de Paris*, which, fearful of missing the fleets, had put back 20 leagues northeast of Balchik. In the afternoon, St. Arnaud, who was sick, asked Raglan on *Caradoc* to visit him. Owing to rough seas, Raglan did not go, but sent Colonel Steele, his military secretary, and Dundas to represent him. On board *Ville de Paris* a paper, prepared by certain French generals, was read by Colonel Trochu. Objecting to a landing on the west coast, north of Sevastopol, it recommended the east coast port of Kaffa, some hundred miles from Sevastopol. This, St. Arnaud accepted, would mean postponement of any assault on Sevastopol until spring 1855. He agreed, however, to abide by Raglan's decision. The remainder of the assembly now adjourned to *Caradoc*, where Raglan brushed aside the general's plan.

On 9 September the armada, less some sailing ships still straggling over the horizon, reached the rendezvous. At 4:00 A.M. the next day, General Canrobet joined Raglan, Brown, Lyons, and Sir John Burgoyne for a more detailed examination of the Crimean coast. Rounding Cape Chersoneous, *Caradoc* sighted two old Genoese forts dominating the entrance to Balaclava harbor, then turned north along the west coast of the peninsula, past Sevastopol. Such a large, iron vessel with

noisy engines attracted considerable attention and a Russian flag was run up to lull suspicions. The mouths of various rivers (including Brown's choice, the Katcha) were rejected as possible landing beaches. Near the small town of Eupatoria, 30 miles north of Sevastopol, Raglan discovered Calamita Bay, with a 4-mile stretch of sand, which seemed to answer their need for a large beach that was shallow enough for artillery rafts to be towed ashore and compact enough for the armies to keep in touch. Two salt lakes prevented attack from the landward side, cliffs to the south and low hills a mile inland could be covered by naval guns, and the narrowness of both flanks made defense of the beachhead comparatively easy. An old ruined fort a half a mile inland offered a readymade marker. Without serious discussion, Raglan decided upon this as the landing beach.

The next day the armada moved eastwards and at noon Eupatoria was summoned to surrender. In accordance with local health regulations, the mayor solemnly fumigated the summons before reading it, then gravely informed the allies they might land but must consider themselves in strict quarantine. British troops promptly occupied the town and the allies sailed 8 miles south to anchor that evening off the Old Fort.

The stretch of beach immediately before the southern salt lake had been chosen for the landing on 14 September. In theory, this allowed Lake Kamishlu, the northern salt lake, to act as additional natural cover for the left flank. The French were to place a marker buoy in the bay, opposite the selected beach: they and the Turks would land to its right, the British to the left. Patrolling at first light, Lyons saw this buoy had been positioned too far to the left causing considerable confusion. Rather than waste more time, Raglan ordered the whole British force north to the beach before Lake Kamishlu. Had the Russians determinedly opposed the landing, this separation of the two armies and the exposure of both flanks of each could have proved seriously embarrassing.

Although the first French were ashore at

7:00 A.M., the British were considerably delayed through the misplaced buoy. At length all was ready. *Agamemnon* ran up signal flags and the various ships' boats took up position a mile from shore, facing their allotted transports, in a long line. With raised oars they bobbed gently awaiting the gun to start operations. The impression was of a peaceful regatta. At 9:00 A.M. the signal boomed. Oars flashed and backs heaved as sailors raced to the transports and threw rope ladders to eager hands on deck. Troops in full battle order scrambled down and the boats pulled away amid fanfare. Ashore sergeants shouted and cursed the ranks into some sort of order, as painted posts with colored flags were staked for individual regiments and divisions and the rowers sweated back and forth to the transports, bringing an endless supply of reinforcements. The boats could not all run ashore, so sailors, their broad trousers rolled to the knee, leapt into the water and passed laden soldiers from hand to hand, to avoid soaking their equipment.

For some time the landing continued in an air of banter and good humor—kilted Highlanders being invited to "come along, girls" and timorous "landlubbers" chaffed by hardy sailors. Suddenly excited fingers pointed to a rocky headland to the south. There stood a small party of Cossacks on shaggy ponies, with tiny pennants fluttering on their short lances. Their officer, calmly surveying the activity below, occasionally made notes in a book he balanced on his saddle. So astonished were the allies that no serious attempt was made to dislodge these hostile watchers.

By noon, however, excitement had begun to wane, as ominous black clouds drifted across the sun and white-topped waves began to lap the beaches. Soon a steady drizzle set in. Already, too, sickness had appeared ashore. During the late afternoon, an increasingly heavy swell hampered the landings, but by nightfall twenty thousand Britons, including all the infantry, had landed. As darkness fell, a lashing, howling storm hit the exposed beaches, and the Britons had no tents. Huddled together under soaking blankets, depressed, shivering soldiers consumed a supper of cold pork and a sip of rum. It was a shelterless, harsh initiation to the Crimea.

By mid-day on 15 September the storm had abated, but for several hours the sea was still too rough to recommence the landings. During the closing hours of daylight on the 15th and throughout the 16th, the cavalry disembarked. All horses should have been transported by raft and boat, but in an attempt to speed up the disembarkation several, fully saddled and strapped with field equipment, were put overboard and made to swim ashore. Terrified and confused, some died of heart failure, others made for the open sea and drowned. On 17 September the artillery landed and, for the first time, Raglan ordered tents ashore. By evening on 18 September, all the British had disembarked.

Ashore, lack of transport, water, and supplies caused serious problems. British engineers sank a solitary, brackish well, while initiative by resourceful individuals amassed the paltry total of 350 wagons, 67 camels, 253 horses, 45 cartloads of farm supplies, and 1,000 head of cattle. On 15 September a group of long-robed Tartar headsmen conferred with Raglan, but friendly and cooperative as these small, impoverished farmers were, they had few fresh supplies to offer a large army.

On 18 September Raglan and St. Arnaud agreed that the armies would march south next day. Reveille sounded at 3:00 A.M.: the French and Turks were quickly ready, frequently banging their drums and blowing their bugles to draw attention to the fact. The British were neither ready nor organized. Swarming over the pale beach, dark, jostling figures carried abandoned stores to waiting boats, dug graves, or transported burdened stretchers. Unable to cook, troops ate a raw breakfast of salt pork and, with no time to fill canteens, prepared to march with parched throats. By 9:00 A.M. the whole column was ready.

Headed by trumpeting bands, the armies marched. Casually watched by enemy scouts, discreetly out of range, the French and Turks advanced on the right, the British on the exposed left flank. Troops sang heartily, as they crushed stiff grass and fragrant herbs underfoot. "The finest army that has ever left these shores" was on the move. The invasion of the Crimea was, it seemed, gloriously underway.

Within an hour, however, stifled by tight jackets, doubled with leaden packs, under the scorching sun men tore off straps, haversacks, and clothing, threw aside mess tins, and staggered dizzily to fall face-downwards in the dust. "Our men dropped like stones," wrote Colonel Bell of the Scots Guards, and Lord George Paget's 4th Dragoon rearguard had difficulty in forcing a path through the maze of crumpled forms, weakly calling for water, of which there was none. Lady Erroll, wife of the Rifle Brigade's commanding officer, accompanied the troops on a mule. Soon she was practically hidden under a solid mass of weapons, handed up by laboring men. Thirty hours hence, 362 British dead and 1,640 wounded would lie on the banks of the Alma river. Russian shells, a bitter Crimean winter, and the disorganized filth of allied hos-pitals were to claim 22,000 British victims before Sevastopol was finally captured.

Queen Victoria expected "the exertions of her brave and loyal subjects" to triumph, Newcastle wrote to Raglan: "I will not believe that in any case British arms can fail." The British commander-in-chief himself, watching a military review in Varna, declared that the tsar "cannot be mad enough to fight against troops like these." Despite the appalling privations on the battlefield, too, there were many to echo Gunner Whitehead's sentiments:

Grim war does summon me hence
And I deem it my duty to fight,
Tis an honour to stand in proud England's defence
When once she is proved in the right.

Perhaps, Charles Greville's remark is more appropriate: "It seems to me privately I have hardly seen a madder business."

Burnside's Amphibious Division, 1862

BY ROBERT W. DALY

It is difficult to say exactly who originated the concept of an amphibious division for the Union army. Defending his war record in 1864, General McClellan claimed that he had proposed on 6 September 1861 to organize a small division of two brigades totaling ten regiments of New England men "adapted to coast service." On the other hand, General Burnside stated that while recuperating from the debacle of Bull Run he wrote to Mc-Clellan in October 1861 strongly urging the organization of a division of twelve to fifteen thousand men from the "states bordering on the Northern seacoast." Such a division should have "a fleet of light-draught steamers, sailing vessels, and barges, large enough to transport the division, its armaments and supplies, so that it could be rapidly thrown from point to point on the coast with a view to establishing lodgements on the Southern coast, landing troops, and penetrating into the interior." By holding possession of the inland waters, Burnside pointed out, this division would more than justify its expense by threatening the lines of communication in the rear of the Confederate army being concentrated in Virginia.

Apart from prior service together in the military, McClellan and Burnside had been friends in business, both being officials of the Illinois Central Railroad when the war began. It is conceivable that the imminence of war had led the former army officers and West Point graduates to discuss ways and means

of defeating the Confederacy. With more than thirty-five hundred miles of vulnerable coastline in the South, the advantages of a special force of offensive-minded, heavily equipped, web-footed troops was obvious. Regardless of who thought of an amphibious division, McClellan was in command of the Army of the Potomac and in a position to activate such a force. The secretary of war was easily won over, and Burnside was a natural choice for the command of the division.

Shortly after the gestation period of Burnside's novel division, Flag Officer Louis M. Goldsborough, commanding the North Atlantic Blockading Squadron based upon Fortress Monroe, wrote in November 1861 to the secretary of the navy about a way to simplify the problem of blockading Norfolk:

> It strikes me that we should command the waters of Pamlico Sound, and this may, I think, be easily accomplished if I can be given a few suitable vessels in addition to those already at Hatteras Inlet. The enemy now has seven or eight small but well-armed steamers on those waters, and these I propose to attack and subdue. . . . This done, something further may be attempted in the way of driving the enemy away from Roanoke Island by a combined attack on the part of the Army and Navy, ascending Albemarle Sound, destroying the lock or locks thereabouts of the canal between it and Norfolk, and thus effectually cutting off all inland communication by vessels between the two places.

Thus, when Secretary Welles enthusiastically endorsed the suggestion by Goldsborough, Burnside's division was presented a

Marine Corps Gazette 35 (December 1951): 30–37. Reprinted by permission.

physical objective which would ensure hearty cooperation by the navy. Since the navy had suggested Roanoke Island, the army accepted Roanoke as the testing ground for Burnside and gave him fifteen regiments and unlimited funds for his equipment. The first major U.S. amphibious force was born. Like most infants, it had ailments. While his three brigades were being raised and shipped to camps at Annapolis, Burnside labored in New York to secure his transport. In this he was compelled to compete with a navy hungry to buy the ships needed to carry out the duty of blockading one hundred eighty coastal points. Burnside did not get exactly what he wanted and had to settle for a hodge-podge assortment of 125 vessels. This activity absorbed most of his energy before the campaign against Roanoke, and his concern with logistics left him very little time to develop a tactical doctrine.

Today, because of Burnside's experiences and those of his successors, it is clear that the logistics problem should be placed in the hands of experts. Burnside, however, set his sights on complete self-sufficiency to the point of buying steam gunboats to form a fighting squadron manned by army personnel. Navy or no navy, Burnside intended to have a force which could carry itself to the objective area in its own forty-five steam-and-sail transports, engage enemy naval units with its own nine gunboats, lay down support fires from its own five floating batteries, and draw replenishment from its own supply train of schooners.

With gunboats improvised from pleasure steamers, floating batteries from old canal barges, and transports from anything that could carry troops, Burnside's division was not serviced by elements of an integrated organization. His vessels had few of the virtues and most of the deficiencies of improvisation. The most damaging defect was the wide range of drafts found in such an ill-assorted group. This became agonizingly apparent as his vessels attempted to pass the Hatteras bulkhead into the shallows off North Carolina. The admixture of steam and sail meant irregular rates of advance, and this, in turn, affected station-keeping and tactical dispositions. The unreliability of sail was proved in the division's first week at Hatteras, as Burnside had it gallingly pointed out to him that he wasn't at all self-sufficient when supplies had to come by vessels like schooners which couldn't buck headwinds to keep a schedule. Six water schooners were delayed by high winds, and Goldsborough's steamers had to make water for Burnside's men.

The maintenance and repair of the machinery in heterogeneous sidewheelers and propellers was sufficiently vexing, and the conversion for war of the vessels had adversely affected their stability. The troops were far from comfortable, but as time aboard ship was only about four weeks, the problem of morale never grew as serious as it could have.

All in all, the experiences of Hatteras proved that the efforts of the zealous amateur cannot be compared favorably with the work of a conscientious professional. A week before the operation against Roanoke finally began, Goldsborough wrote to Assistant Secretary of the Navy Gustavous V. Fox: "In case of another joint expedition, everything concerning *all* the vessels should be arranged exclusively by the Navy, & kept under Naval control. *Duality*, I assure you, will not answer, & were you here to witness things with your own eyes you would not differ with me in opinion."

Burnside attempted to substitute foresight for knowledge. Like a good commander, he endeavored to increase his freedom of action in the field by prior solution of situations. Unfortunately, he occupied himself primarily with logistics. Should he need a bridge, he carried two.

Burnside was apparently interested only in carrying his force to the objective area, after which nature would presumably take its course. His only noteworthy bow in the direction of tactics was to work out a system of fleet security. Gunboats acted as scouts and flankers protecting the transports of the brigades, which were in three columns in the order of line of march. At night, the gunboats became outposts. To attain a semblance of uniformity in advance, he put a strain upon the machinery of his steamers by having them tow all of the sailing vessels.

Burnside's logistical work was creditable, but his tactical success in the field was due to his overwhelming numbers and the Confederates' slipshod defenses. In tactics, Burnside planned very little. His three brigades had eight to fourteen weeks at Annapolis while Burnside did a quartermaster's job in New York. During this period, the enthusiastic but raw regiments sweated through basic training that ultimately led to brigade maneuvers. Colonels stressed the manual of arms and close order drill as though their men were to be part of the Army of the Potomac instead of a unique force. Although such drill may have served to make soldiers of the men quickly, it should have been recognized that these new troops would be meeting equally inexperienced fighters, and some time given over to such an elementary procedure as simulating a landing would have been useful. The winter at Annapolis was unusually cold, however, and perhaps the brigadier generals and colonels reasoned that it was ridiculous to risk pneumonia by going through the motions of such a simple process as landing on an enemy beach.

The embarkation in January 1862 should have been a danger signal. As the twelve regiments that were deemed ready for service out of the fifteen in the division were put aboard their transports, the movement got out of hand. Some regiments had to huddle in their overcoats in the Naval Academy yard overnight, separated from their blankets and gear, as Burnside's timetable broke down. The embarkation was far from being a smooth, auspicious beginning. In a way, this was surprising. It wasn't as though whole divisions hadn't been moved before. The Crimean War was a recent example of successful transport of many divisions many times the distances confronting Burnside. Furthermore, Burnside's good friend McClellan had written an excellent report of his observations on the art of war in Europe and was one of the few men in America capable of giving sound advice, as his personal acquaintance with the

British and French effort in the Crimea was extensive.

In addition, a foul-up in Burnside's logistics gave his troops an enforced three weeks of idleness at Hatteras, which should have been used to develop some skill in debarkation. The troops who went ashore, however, did so only to stretch their legs. If the Confederates had the resources to develop a proper defense for Roanoke Island, such a casual attitude toward fundamentals would have meant blood. As it was, Burnside's amphibious force was destined to receive its training under bloodless circumstances.

Battered by storms, Burnside's motley fleet gathered slowly at Hatteras, where the diversity in drafts dragged out the assembly period as ships had to be lightened and worried by brute force across the bulkhead of the inlet. Goldsborough, whose own twenty vessels had been carried through the inlet with ease by 15 January, fumed impatiently during the delay. Finally, on 5 February 1862 Burnside was ready, and operations against Roanoke could begin.

The collection of the expedition had been undertaken in a secrecy unusual at a time when newspapers freely and fully reported information that modern intelligence services would sacrifice lives to obtain. In this instance, the press was strictly curbed. As Goldsborough put the case, "If the enemy should get wind of our intentions he may give us trouble enough to render a demonstration upon Norfolk itself desirable, in order to create a diversion, & thus prevent him from reinforcing Roanoke Island with thousands of men via the canal." Fortunately for the success of the venture, the Confederacy was still organizing for war and had not attained its subsequent grim competence.

The Confederates understood the strategic significance of Roanoke, but they could not agree on how defenses should be made or on the garrison required. As the war broke out, General Huger, commanding at Norfolk, felt a twinge of anxiety about Albemarle Sound in his rear and put a small regiment on the island. He did not think, however, in terms of amphibious attack when he later was requested by Brigadier General Wise to send reinforcements, because Huger was content to believe that the Yankees couldn't march an army up the sandspit to Norfolk.

Huger's men had already begun construction of the final fortifications, and while Commodore Lynch and D. H. Hill agreed that the principal defenses should have been built at the marshes at the foot of the island, Hill realistically accepted what had been done and bent his efforts toward throwing a line of entrenchments across the middle of the island. Hill was relieved on 26 November before this could be done, and his successor was the zealous amateur soldier Henry A. Wise, formerly governor of Virginia.

Wise was staggered by the importance of his post and the inadequacy of the means allotted it. He began in December a relentless barrage of correspondence which later exonerated him of any guilt when the Confederate Congress investigated the loss of Roanoke and fixed responsibility upon the secretary of war and Huger. Wise's estimate was then officially accepted:

> It ought to have been defended by all the means in the power of the Government. It was the key to all the rear defenses of Norfolk. It unlocked two sounds . . . eight rivers . . . four canals . . . and two railroads. . . . It guarded more than four-fifths of all Norfolk's supplies of corn, pork, and forage, and it cut the command of Gen Huber off from all of its most efficient transportation. . . . It should have been defended at the expense of 20,000 men and of many millions of dollars.

Instead, Wise found himself with two undermanned North Carolina regiments and three companies of a third regiment for gun crews. He could not expedite the transfer to him of his own battle-trained legion, which might be considered an ancestor of the regimental combat team. It included the three branches of infantry, cavalry, and artillery, numbered about three thousand men, and was designed by Wise to be an integrated force. He had come from fighting with his legion in West Virginia to arrive in command of Roanoke on 8 January 1862, exactly one month before its fall.

The fortifications of Roanoke consisted of Fort Bartow, built of turfed sand, with six long and obsolete 32-pounders in embrasure and three more en barbette firing over a curtain to the south; Fort Blanchard, built also of turfed sand, 2½ miles north of Bartow, with four 32-pounders en barbette; and Fort Huger, also of turfed sand, closed in the rear by a breastwork, mounting eight 32-pounders in embrasure and four en barbette. On the other side of the island, a two-gun battery at Ballast Point protected the communication line into Shallowbag Bay. In the middle of the island, a redoubt 80 feet long sat athwart the causeway road through a dense swamp and was flanked by breastworks. Across on the mainland, Fort Forrest, mounting seven 32-pounders, had been built on two barges rammed into the swampy shore. Croatan Sound was obstructed by a double line of sixteen sunken vessels and a system of pilings still being put down when the attack developed.

For mobile defenses, the 8th and 31st North Carolina Infantry Regiments did not inspire Wise. During the winter, heavy, constant rains had brought onslaughts of pneumonia, typhoid fever, and measles which put 25 percent of the effective strength sick in the twelve large barracks or three much-needed hospitals. Uniforms were inadequate—whatever a man could manage. Blankets were made out of brightly colored carpeting, and coarse duck substituted for leather in such items as equipment slings and haversacks. Pork and grain were plentiful, but not adequate as a diet, and tobacco and coffee were scarce. Weapons were as varied as their owners' garb, and ranged from shotguns through superb sporting rifles to gigantic knives. Field artillery consisted of three guns, a 6-pounder, a 24-pounder navy howitzer, and an 18-pounder. For this last gun, only 12-pounder ammunition was available. As seventeen companies of his legion drifted in driblets to Nags Head, it was no wonder that Wise was buoyed up by their excellent equipment and morale.

Then, eight days before the attack, Wise was incapacitated by an attack of pleurisy, so that active command on Roanoke rested upon the shoulders of Colonel H. M. Shaw.

Shaw was forty-five years old, slight in figure and medium of height, and had the misfortune to have been born in Rhode Island. His reputation did not survive his doomed fight.

As the expedition at last got under way on 5 February, Burnside had some thirteen thousand men in his transports and was protected by his gunboats and nineteen naval vessels. McClellan's orders to Burnside contained the essence of a battle plan: "It is presumed that the Navy can reduce the batteries on the marshes and cover the landing of your troops on the main island, by which, in connection with a rapid movement of the gunboats to the northern extremity as soon as the marsh battery is reduced, it may be hoped to capture the entire garrison of the place."

Goldsborough was thus assigned a clear mission and his orders to subordinates primarily dealt with the artillery requirements for reducing batteries. On his own initiative, however, he sought to take advantage of the division of Confederate forces by ordering the *Chippewa* up from Beaufort to bombard Nags Head from the Atlantic side in support, and later to harass the Confederate retreat up the sandspit. The *Chippewa*, however, had gone to Fortress Monroe to coal, not aware of the supply at Hatteras, and so was not available.

The expedition anchored before sunset 10 miles south of Roanoke, while Lieutenant Jeffers went ashore to get a Unionist who might be able to improve Burnside's knowledge. As it was, Union intelligence was accurate enough with respect to the batteries, except for those that Goldsborough anticipated at the marshes. With respect to forces, however, information was erroneous. The Confederates did not have 2,300 men on the island and 5,000 in reserve. They had only an effective force of 1,435 on the island, a reserve of seventeen companies totaling about 800 men at Nags Head, and an ill-fated battalion of 500 men from the 2nd North Carolina Infantry who landed from Norfolk in time to be captured.

February 6th opened with rain that settled into thick fog by noon, postponing all operations after an optimistic signal by Burnside to prepare to land. About 1015, the *Ceres* and

Putnam dashed into Croatan Sound, ran up about four miles, and returned to report that they had seen fifteen steamers and ten sailing vessels at anchor. Flag Officer Lynch's eight gunboats were thereby counted almost accurately in with the sixteen miscellaneous vessels sunk to block the channel. This erroneous information caused Burnside to strip five of his gunboats of their troops in order to supplement Goldsborough's fighting line.

The long-awaited appearance of the Yankees fired Wise with energy, but not enough for him to find the strength to lead his troops into the field. He had to dictate his orders to Shaw. Assuming that the four forts, Lynch's gunboats, and the line of obstructions were sufficient to protect the northern portion of the island, Wise correctly saw only two possible landing places on the low, swampy, wooded shores. One was Ashby Harbor, about midway on the island, and the other was Pugh's Landing, some four miles to the south. His orders were explicit:

> . . . You will move the whole of your infantry, except what is ample for the batteries, stationing one-third at Pugh's, one-third at Ashby's, and the remaining third at the breastworks called Suple's Hill. If the enemy attempt to land at Pugh's the force will re-enforce that at Pugh's and fight every inch of ground at the water's edge as long as prudence will permit.

In case Burnside landed at Ashby, the force at Pugh's was to speed north to the area. The precious field guns were to be protected at all costs for the final stand to be made at the central breastworks. If the Yankees broke through the barriers and Lynch's gunboats and rounded the island before attempting to land, Wise considered Roanoke lost and promised Shaw that every effort would be made to give him transport across Roanoke Sound.

Considering the inadequate resources which the Confederates had, this plan, if coupled with a determination to fight hard, would have given the Union's amphibious force some trouble. Instead, Shaw modified the orders to suit himself. He stationed Colonel Jordan with two hundred men at Ashby and Captain Whitson with a company at

Pugh's. The remainder of the available infantry were under arms at the camps or at the breastworks. Shaw himself went to Fort Bartow to observe.

By 1000, 7 February 1862, the expedition was under way. Burnside and Goldsborough had conflicting information about the defenses, and both were concerned about the unknown hazards at the landing area. Ashby Harbor had been selected as the only practicable beachhead for more than ten thousand men, but a glance at the map showed that Sand Point took the area in flank. Next to the failure to throw up batteries at the entrance to Croatan Sound and to have concentrated the effort of driving piles and sinking obstructions across a narrow channel not one hundred yards across, Goldsborough was most surprised by the Confederate failure to place a battery at Sand Point. Steaming ahead of the fleet, the *Underwriter* signaled this welcome news at 1125, and Goldsborough was thoroughly relieved. "The omission to guard this point was favorable to the arrangement of landing the troops at Ashby's Harbor," he reported. "Had it been protected, our difficulties would have been materially increased." And then he had further welcome news. The array of gunboats originally and erroneously reported by the *Ceres* turned out to be Lynch's eight. With better than two to one superiority alone, Goldsborough moved to the attack with the continued help of the five army gunboats.

Goldsborough engaged Lynch and immediately demonstrated the weakness of the Confederate battery positions. Only Fort Bartow was within effective range, and of the nine guns there, Goldsborough nullified the six in embrasures by hugging close to the shore below the fort. Only Bartow's three en barbette guns were really in the fight; all the others were useless even as a threat.

Well out of even ricochet range, Burnside's transports anchored and prepared to disembark their troops. To obtain more precise information, now that everything was going so well, Burnside sent his topographical officer, Lieutenant W. S. Andrews, at noon in a small boat into Ashby Harbor. Jordan's men were screened in the dense undergrowth and trees behind the landing, and Andrews coolly made soundings, surveyed the approaches, and actually set foot ashore before Jordan bestirred himself to send a detail to capture Andrews. Andrews made good his escape, and rowed back out to Burnside with one of his six men wounded in the jaw. His cool competence earned him special commendation in the general's report.

Convinced that there was sufficient water available for the approach, Burnside ordered his brigadiers to prepare to land. The first phase of the ship-to-shore movement had been carefully worked out so far as getting the men to the beach had been concerned. An unknown element, like Jordan and his two guns, however, remained both unknown and unprovided for. In light marching order, with overcoats to serve as blankets, forty rounds of ball cartridges per man, the troops entered their surfboats and milled about until they were in precise order to present a brigade front immediately upon being put ashore.

To the north, lost in the haze of black powder smoke and the water cascading up from shells, the detachment of five army gunboats happily banged away at the Confederate squadron. They hadn't been recalled when Lynch's actual strength was verified. The five floating batteries were busy in the exercise of disgorging their troops. Thus, Burnside's first wave was going to their beachhead without either preliminary bombardment of the surrounding area or provision for on-call fire.

The mysteries lurking in the tall grass and tangled woods did not apparently concern any of Burnside's commanders or staff. All eyes were on the boats being lashed in trains of twenty or more. As each brigade was ready, a light-draft steamer took it in tow and, at about 1500, all was ready. The steamers charged for the beach under a full head of steam.

Commander Rowan, captain of the *Delaware* and Goldsborough's second-in-command, looked away from Fort Bartow in time to see the steamers head for the beach. Having witnessed the reception of Andrews, Rowan quickly got under way and ran down to precede Foster's steamer *Pilot Boy*. As Rowan hastily flung nine-inch shrapnel into the woods occupied by the faintly visible figures of Jordan's two companies, Captain Hazard, the naval officer assigned by Welles to Burnside's staff and in command of the army gunboat *Picket,* broke off action with Lynch and joined Rowan. Spontaneously, then, the landing force had its preliminary bombardment. The *Delaware* and *Picket* pumped huge shells and shrapnel at Jordan, who quickly forgot his orders from Wise and Shaw except to remember that his guns had to be saved at all costs. Without firing even a musket shot, Jordan retired. The four thousand men jammed into some sixty-five boats were thus enabled to glide in unopposed.

No one would seriously argue that Jordan could have prevented the landing, but he obviously threw away an opportunity to teach a sharp lesson. Had Jordan been Stuart's resolute John Pelham, this first wave of Burnside's would have found the landing interesting. Pelham doubtless would have considered the two hundred to three hundred yard barrier of knee-deep mud in front of his position an adequate barrier to provide him the time to shoot and get away.

With two guns, the results would have been punishing rather than disastrous. Assuming three shells per gun per minute, eighteen shells could have been hurled before the first boat cast off its towline, if the steamers had a speed of 15 knots, placing the boats within effective range for three minutes. With the federal troops helplessly huddled together, the gamble of firing double-shotted spherical case or canister during the last minute could have alone produced as many as three hundred casualties.

Having complied with the spirit and letter of Wise's orders, Jordan had ample time as soon as the first Yankees reached shore to have one company man the sling to drag off the field guns while the other company deployed as skirmishers to check pursuit. As it was, pursuit might not have been too serious. The Union regiments formed properly on the beach, taking their time, and then disintegrated into comparative disorder negotiating the swamp and had to stop for reforming upon reaching dry ground. There was no resistance. Roanoke Island inflicted its own casualties in the shape of bruised and scraped shins and twisted ankles.

With respect to the landing, Burnside said, "I never witnessed a more beautiful sight . . . As the steamers approached the shore at a rapid speed each surfboat was 'let go,' and with their acquired velocity and by direction of the steersman reached the shore in line." Thanks to Jordan's caution, the first wave landed without trouble, and the dangers of presenting a stout-hearted artilleryman with a target of men squeezed into a single line of fire was not made apparent.

After this first wave, however, Burnside's organizational work had apparently ended. The recall of boats and reformation of groups must have been left to improvisation, because while twenty minutes sufficed to land four thousand men and Midshipmen Porter's six-gun howitzer battery, the remainder of Burnside's men weren't ashore until midnight.

The battle itself was an anticlimax. In brief, eleven fully equipped regiments totaling eleven thousand men fought two regiments and elements of two others, poorly armed, sickly, and low in morale. Even the pitiful support of the fourteen companies Wise promptly stripped from the seventeen of his legion the instant he heard the sound of the guns could only swell the bag of prisoners. The Confederates had relied upon the impassability of the swampy woods flanking the central marsh, but the Union forces stoutly plunged ahead, avoiding the *chevaux de frise* made before the battery and breastworks of felled trees with axe-sharpened branches. Actually, only seven companies of the Confederates had room on the firing line, and Jordan commanded the reserve, which never came into action. In summary, the operations against Roanoke Island were considered eminently successful by the Union authorities. Practice had been attained in making an amphibious landing on a division scale, and lessons were available for review and improvement.

The Fort Fisher Campaigns, 1864–65

BY CAPTAIN JOSEPH E. KING, USA (RET.)

It is universally acknowledged that the landing of troops on a hostile coast in the face of active resistance is the most delicate and precarious operation in warfare. In the modern era, at least, it involves cooperation and coordination of a high degree among two or three separate branches of the military establishment. Of essential importance in this respect are the details connected with command, intelligence, and communications, before, during, and after the waterborne assault. Once a beachhead has been wrested from the foe, it remains to meet him on his own terrain and crush him, and this phase of an amphibious attack is the most important one of all, for it is here that the objective is won or lost.

The study of any amphibious attack, successful or not, will clarify these elements and their respective importance. Unfortunately, the military scientist cannot recreate a battle under laboratory conditions, but occasionally two campaigns are so similar that they lend themselves almost perfectly to study. Ideal, when viewed from this angle, are the two attacks made by the Union forces on the Confederate stronghold of Fort Fisher, North Carolina, in late 1864 and early 1865, since herein were involved the same terrain and the same objective, and very nearly the same personnel and weather conditions. Yet, for some reason, only passing attention has been paid by military historians to these campaigns, and their accounts usually stress the

strategic importance of the assaults and dismiss briefly the tactical ramifications.[1]

It is the purpose of this essay to subject the attacks on Fort Fisher to a careful analysis, and for that reason, its scope will be substantially narrowed.[2] The various phases of command, intelligence, and communications will be investigated and analyzed as they existed in each operation, and a comparison between the two operations will enable certain basic principles to be enunciated. The question, too, of the value of earlier operations to the military scientist will be discussed and a judgment rendered on it.

When the American Civil War broke out in 1861, the seceding states were almost entirely without industrial resources. That section of the United States was primarily agricultural and it furnished the spinning mills of England with 95 percent of their raw cotton. In undertaking a war against the North, the Confederates counted heavily on cotton as a medium of exchange for the sinews of battle. The Federal navy, however, threw a blockade about the long Southern coastline, and, as the war progressed, the leading harbors were captured or obstructed. By the latter part of 1864, only Wilmington, North Carolina, remained as a port of entry for the blockade runners.

This port lay 16 miles up the Cape Fear River and was linked to the hinterland by three railway lines. At the mouth of the river stood a large island, creating by its position two inlets, each of which required careful guarding by the blockade ships. The north bank of the river formed a narrow peninsula,

U.S. Naval Institute *Proceedings* 77 (August 1951): 843–55. Reprinted by permission.

Bombardment of Fort Fisher, 15 January 1865. Engraving from the original painting by Chappel, published by Johnson, Fry & Co., New York. Courtesy of the U.S. Navy Historical Center.

known as Federal Point—Confederate Point to the Southerners—and on this low sandy spit, the Confederates had erected Fort Fisher, the mightiest coastal defense work in America. It was constructed of sand, sodded and revetted with marsh grass, and had two sides: one facing the sea, over a mile in length; the other facing north, running across a neck of land nearly a half mile.[3] Forty-four of the heaviest modern guns were mounted between traverses on the high parapets, and land mines were scattered along the approaches to the place. On the island, and on the southern bank of the river, there were several smaller forts, dependencies of Fort Fisher. Submarine torpedoes that could be detonated from the forts were laid in the river channel. The system was virtually impregnable, and as long as the Confederates held Fisher, no Federal ship ever passed up the Cape Fear River.

Wilmington shipped and received the supplies that enabled the Confederacy to carry on the war. The blockade runners were occasionally captured, but generally the speedy little vessels were protected by the cover of night. The hostile governments were each keenly aware of the importance of Wilmington and its defenses. Blockade running had become a fine art, and northern authorities were agreed that it could only be ended by the capture of Fort Fisher. As early as 1862 the Navy Department contemplated a blow

at the Cape Fear defenses, but the army was unable to spare any troops. It was not until the fall of Atlanta, in September 1864, that Lieutenant General U. S. Grant turned his attention to Fort Fisher.

Assured now of the support of the army, Secretary of the Navy Welles selected Rear Admiral David D. Porter, an officer recommended by his abilities and by his close friendship with Grant. On 12 October 1864, Porter hoisted his flag in the *Malvern* at Hampton Roads and assumed command of the North Atlantic Blockading Squadron.

The arrival of a new admiral on the Atlantic and the unwonted number of ships observed reporting at eastern naval bases attracted so much notice and gave birth to so many rumors that Grant suspended all activity on the thing for a time.[4] Finally, in mid-November, he appointed Major General Godfrey Weitzel to command the contingent of soldiers.[5] Unfortunately this command was not settled as easily as that of the navy. Weitzel happened to be a subordinate of Major General Benjamin F. Butler, and the punctilious Grant carried on all correspondence with him through the latter. Butler had heard of a tremendous accidental explosion which blasted apart some buildings near London the previous month, and it occurred to him that this type of power, if harnessed, could be used against the foe.[6] He wanted an old hulk, loaded with two or three hundred tons of gunpow-

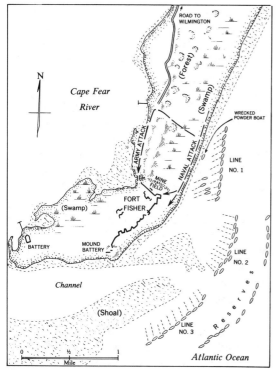

The Fort Fisher Campaign, 1865.

But the powder boat, the violent gales, and the necessity for frequent recoaling conspired to delay the expedition until mid-December. To the surprise and annoyance of Grant and Porter, Butler decided to command the land forces in person. Everything was now ready, and Butler, with sixty-five hundred troops, steamed boldly off Cape Fear, thereby hazarding the last remnant of secrecy.[10] Porter, with the great naval force, arrived two days later, to the disgust of Butler.[11] By now, the general found it necessary to haul off, and he returned to Beaufort, North Carolina, to restock his ships. Then the weather turned stormy and locked him in the harbor, and while he was still there, Porter drove the *Louisiana* under the guns of Fisher and exploded her about 1:30 on the morning of 24 December.[12] Twelve hours later he commenced a fierce bombardment of the place, and while this was going on, Butler's transports reappeared from the northeast.[13] On Christmas Day, after another sharp cannonade, about two thousand infantrymen were put ashore. They made the landing without opposition several miles north of the fort and moved down the peninsula, capturing three hundred enemy troops on the way. They reached a point less than 50 yards from the palisade and commenced sniping at the gun crews.

Whatever the attitude of the defenders might have been later, it was not overly sanguine on Christmas Day.[14] Major General W. H. C. Whiting, the former commander of the district, had been superseded by General Braxton Bragg, a man who apparently inspired little but despair.[15] The former had not been transferred, and at this time was acting commander, during the absence of his superior, then detailed to detached service in Georgia, but his urgent requests for more resources were ignored. He had been completely informed as to the Federal plans, but on the day of the landing he was still desperately engaged in shifting troops to patch together some kind of a force adequate for the test.[16] The explosion of the powder boat had affected neither the fort nor its garrison in the least,[17] and as the Union sharpshoot-

der, towed to Federal Point and run aground under Fort Fisher. When this infernal machine was detonated, Butler foresaw a Confederate garrison so overcome that the troops could go ashore without opposition. The bizarre scheme evoked varied reaction. Grant had no confidence in it, but he did nothing to oppose it.[7] The army and navy ordnance experts were careful and rendered verdicts more equivocal than unfavorable.[8] At first, Porter probably saw in the idea a way to obtain the active cooperation of the army, but as time went on, he became thoroughly convinced of its efficacy.[9] Butler and his soldier boys were, of course, fervent supporters of it all.

The *Louisiana*, an old and worthless ship, was finally loaded with 235 tons of powder. During early December Grant importuned and expostulated without avail, urging Butler to get on his way, with or without the *Louisiana*, and to fall upon Wilmington while its garrisons were temporarily on duty in Georgia against General Sherman.

ers before the works opened up their fire, they received a spirited reply of cannister.

The Confederates received their real shock a few hours after the landing, as they watched the men in blue withdraw and reembark. Butler had consulted with Weitzel, who had been ashore and who feared an attack in the rear from Hoke's Division, which had just been sent down to the Wilmington District from Virginia. Weitzel reported that the fort had hardly been damaged by the naval gunfire, and thereupon the order was issued to abandon the beachhead on Federal Point, in utter violation of Grant's written instructions.[18] When all but about seven hundred troops had been returned to the transports, the commanding general sailed north.[19] The remaining Union soldiers and their prisoners were taken off during the afternoon of 27 December.

While reembarking on 27 December, a soldier was drowned; this was the only fatality suffered by the northern army. Porter was beside himself and begged the general to try again, a request that Butler ignored. Grant was completely disgusted with his surbordinate's antics and with his willful disobedience. He ventured the opinion that Butler went merely to watch the explosion.[20] Washington was in a turmoil, and Butler became the butt of every critic. As might be expected, Secretary Welles blamed the general, while his colleague in the War Department, with fine impartiality, held both Butler and Porter at fault. The president wired Grant for the particulars and received the following reply:

> The Wilmington expedition has proven a gross and culpable failure. Many of the troops are now back here. Delays and free talk of the object of the expedition enabled the enemy to move troops to Wilmington to defeat it. After the expedition sailed from Fort Monroe three days of fine weather were squandered, during which time the enemy was without a force to protect himself. Who is to blame I hope will be known.

The answer was not far nor long to seek. On 7 January 1865, Butler was relieved and ordered to report to his home. He issued a pompous address of farewell to his Army of the James: "I have refused to order the useless sacrifice of the lives of such soldiers, and I am relieved from your command. The wasted blood of my men does not stain my garments." Butler's successor withheld the publication of this melodramatic appeal, but Grant recognized that its very asininity made it innocuous and allowed it to be distributed. The first amphibious attack on Fort Fisher was as innocuous and as bombastic as these words of General Butler.

The second assault on the fort was born in the very death throes of the first. That Grant would ever yield because of the loss of only one soldier, and that because of drowning, is beyond consideration. Even as Porter moved north, he was planning a return, for at his order the ships simulated damage: Some of them were towed away. Weitzel was relieved of the command he had neither exercised nor of which he had been aware,[21] and Major General Alfred H. Terry was appointed to make the second attempt.[22] The same troops were held at the embarkation point and a picked brigade was added. It is quite evident, in perusing the orders and correspondence relative to the taking of Fort Fisher, that all concerned had profited from the abortive attempt. On 2 January 1865, Grant personally gave his orders to Terry. They were similar to those issued to Weitzel but were more explicit. Only if it were impossible to gain a beachhead was Terry to return to Beaufort, there to await further instructions. Once a landing was effected, Fort Fisher was to be attacked, and a siege train was available at Fortress Monroe, if Terry felt it were needed. If the fort fell, the troops were to be marched on Wilmington, and in no event were any operations on Federal Point to be suspended, except on Grant's order. Secrecy was stressed, for the confirmation of these verbal orders was sealed and was not to be opened until the transports had passed Cape Hatteras. Finally, Grant laid complete emphasis on cooperation with the navy: "It is exceedingly desirable that the most complete understanding should exist between yourself and the naval commander. I suggest, therefore, that you consult with Admiral Porter freely, ... defer to him as much as is consistent with your own responsibilities."

Terry went to his task immediately, and by evening, 5 January, the transports were assembled at Hampton Roads. The troops, who had been told that they were on their way to Savannah, were now informed of their real destination. Stormy seas did not delay Terry for any length of time; on 8 January the troop carriers reached their first rendezvous, 25 miles off Beaufort. The general's ships proceeded into the harbor, and there he met the admiral. This first meeting was not an auspicious one. Porter said that a fierce gale was about to strike and he advised Terry to bring in his transports. The latter, aware no doubt that information raced south from Beaufort, coldly refused the advice and let his landsmen suffer nausea for the sake of security. On Thursday, 12 January, the storm subsided and the army and navy moved to the attack. Thirty years later the gallant commander of Fort Fisher recalled with a thrill how he stood on the great bastion and watched the lights of the Union Fleet climb over the northern horizon; on 12 January 1865 his feeling was closer to deep foreboding. Neither Colonel Lamb nor General Whiting had been misled when Porter limped away with his squadrons a couple of weeks before. On New Year's Day, Whiting had penned an urgent plea to the secretary of war in Richmond relative to an obstruction being placed in the river channel, to forestall any federal movement up toward Wilmington. He also observed that there was a strong possibility that troops would land on the coast just north of the great fort, especially since it was known that the garrison was very weak. Whiting concluded: "I know they were aware of this [weakness] from the same source which so correctly gave me the news of the movement." This important correspondence aroused no action in a moribund government—on 14 January, when troops were preparing for the final assault on the fort, President Jefferson Davis wrote that "... the proposition within might be advantageously referred to General Bragg." Five days later, a clerk in the capital filed it away with this endorsement: "No further disposition required, Fort Fisher having fallen." Whiting wrote, but he also acted, and, finally, at the eleventh hour, Hoke's Division again came down from Northern Virginia and filed into bivouac at Sugar Loaf, about 5 miles up the river from the fort.[23] Whiting hoped to use these veterans from Lee's army as a mobile force to drive back any landing on either side of the peninsula. Having made what dispositions he could, he retired to Fort Fisher in a fit of disgust at his slow-moving superiors.[24]

The ill feeling between Porter and Terry was left behind at Beaufort and the attack on the fort was marked by complete unity of purpose. On Friday morning, 13 January at 7:30 A.M., the U.S. Fleet commenced a terrific bombardment, and a short time later, two hundred small boats, manned by sailors, started landing the troops. Actual surprise was, of course, out of the question, but Terry did achieve a distinct tactical advantage in his choice of a beachhead.[25] He chose the narrow sandy spit, 5 miles from Fort Fisher, just north of the head of Myrtle Sound. Any Confederate infantry attempting to drive the Union forces into the sea would be required to wade a quarter of a mile across the shallow sound. Despite a choppy sea, eight thousand northern soldiers were on the beach by 3:00 P.M., each with nine days rations and almost one hundred rounds of ammunition.

Terry, who unlike his predecessor did his commanding on the shore, ordered a defensive line thrown across Federal Point to the Cape Fear River. At 9:00 P.M. this was done, but shortly thereafter the line was pulled south a mile to firmer ground, and by 8:00 A.M. on Saturday, an impressive set of breastworks faced north and effectively isolated the fort from any land communication with Bragg or Hoke.[26] For some reason, early contacts between Union outposts and Confederate skirmishers convinced both southern generals that the line was impregnable and they made no real attempt to break through.

Terry noticed that the western end of his defensive line was beyond the range of the fleet and was vulnerable to any Confederate gunboats in the river. Accordingly he ordered his field artillery brought ashore and sent across the Point to bolster this weak spot. In the meantime, on Saturday, as his men filed down toward the fort, the general made a personal reconnaissance of what he had to overcome. After studying the situation, he gave orders for a general assault on the northern rampart at 3:00 P.M. the next day, and then he hastened out the *Malvern* to consult with the admiral. Terry reported that the naval barrage, which had been carried on incessantly for over thirty-six hours, had done considerable damage to the great guns on land. He had observed at the edge of the escarpment, before the northern face of Fort Fisher, a palisade, and he asked the admiral to pulverize it just before his troops stormed the position. Porter agreed and added that he would neutralize the torpedoes and, when the assault began, would move his fire wherever Terry signified he wanted it; in addition he offered to send a naval brigade to aid in the attack.[27]

All through the night the crash and glare of shells tortured the weary garrison of Fort Fisher.[28] At 8:00 A.M., 15 January, the whole fleet brought the beleaguered stronghold under a murderous fire, more intense than ever, which Terry described as "magnificent alike for its power and accuracy." At 2:00 P.M. the first preparation for the land attack commenced—one hundred sharpshooters crawled down to a line only 175 yards from the parapet and entrenched themselves. Their covering fire kept down the garrison and enabled Terry to move the rest of his troops up behind them. Shortly after 3:00 P.M., at a signal, naval fire bearing on the escarpment ceased, and volunteers went forward with axes and explosives to clear a way through the wreck of the palisade. But the navy had destroyed the torpedoes and the palisade completely, and a few strokes of the axes opened the way. At 3:25 P.M. Terry signaled Porter to stop shelling the bastions and the parapet and he ordered his men to charge. More than five thousand soldiers, on a half-mile front, moved toward the fort. The Union right crashed

through the rubble and mess on the escarpment and the men swarmed up the half-bastion that anchored the western end of the fort. Then a soldier's battle erupted, and all afternoon and for hours into the night, they tore at each other across each traverse until they were down to clubbed muskets and cold steel. Things did not go as well as with the left end of the Federal line and with the naval brigade. Hot, plunging fire from the northern bastion pinned the infantry to the ground, while the sailors, ordered "to board the fort on the run in a seamanlike way" were deserted by the marines, who, for once, failed to fight their country's battles.[29] Caught full in a withering fire and confused by the heavy pall of smoke, the sailors, too, broke ranks and fled. They had created a diversion, however, and the land forces were able at last to gain the parapet.

General Bragg proved too cautious and too slow. Even as Terry flung his defensive line across the Point, his opponent would not bestir himself because he could not envision any danger to the great fort, still able to communicate with his headquarters by water, and because he felt that the ramparts would never fall "if boldly defended by a vigilant garrison." Whiting's entreaties for help were finally answered on 14 January. Bragg sent eleven hundred troops to the embattled post, but only five hundred arrived there because one of the steamers went aground while transporting them. He also sent Hoke's veterans to smash the Union line and relieve the fort, but the smash turned out to be a gentle pat, for after a half-hearted, spiritless effort, the troops fell back and were returned to Sugar Loaf by 5:00 P.M. Saturday.[30]

As the federal infantrymen clawed from traverse to traverse, first Whiting, then Lamb, were caught in the rain of musketry, but their last desperate messages to Bragg actually heartened him, for at least he was sure that the Stars and Bars still waved over the fort, even if its commanders were down.[31] He did the proper thing: he sent down a brigadier general to assume command. Brigadier General Colquitt, with three aides-de-camp, reached Battery Buchanan, at the extreme tip of Federal Point, after 9:00 P.M. He found there a frenzied mass of drunken men, milling about in a panic. He was told that the fort had just fallen and that the conquerors were on the way to take this last bit of ground. None of the men before him were armed, except a sotted Confederate marine, who nearly shot one of the aides. There was nothing to do. The general left and raced to his boat as the first Union skirmishers swept by, only 30 feet away. About 10:00 P.M. General Blackman, commanding the 27th United States Colored Troops, accepted the surrender of the fort. During the next two days the other forts of the system were abandoned and blown up by the Confederates, and the control of the Cape Fear River passed to the United States. Porter and Terry received the thanks of Congress and the latter was awarded a commission in the Regular Army; Whiting and Lamb might have received the thanks of the Confederate Congress for their gallantry, but more pressing business caused the motion to be tabled; that was not unusual in affairs concerning Fort Fisher.

The bitter wrath that enveloped Benjamin Butler tended to obscure the principles demonstrated during the assaults on Fort Fisher.[32] And this gold mine of tactical information has been left almost completely unworked, for when the *argumenta ad* Butler finally subsided, the war was over and men looked only with contempt on the old-fashioned past. It must be borne in mind that there were at Fort Fisher, as on every field of battle, certain imponderables, which belong more to military art than to military science. Observation of the other elements of war may be essayed with more precision, and the results utilized to guide a commander. The three elements selected for scrutiny here are so closely related that the second and third can be reckoned as corollaries of the first. For the sake of clarity, the first, the element of command, will be viewed in its narrow sense. The other two, intelligence and communications, will each be examined in turn.

The matter of command leads to the enunciation of a principle that is not too evident at first. The obvious conclusion, of course, is

drawn from the December foray against Fort Fisher, is that command of an expedition involving two or more services must devolve upon one individual. That principle is valid and immutable, but a glance at the second expedition seems to refute it completely. In this case there were two commanders and the success they achieved was almost perfect. Yet an examination of the facts only serves to strengthen the principle of unity of command. Of essential importance is the outlook of the two leaders, Porter and Terry. After a bit of friction, there existed nothing but wholehearted cooperation.[33] While each officer remained within his particular sphere, each offered everything at his disposal to the other to use as he might wish. There were no spurts of gratuitous advice on military affairs by the admiral or on naval affairs by the general. Terry's artillery covered the river beyond the range of Porter's guns, and the Naval Brigade performed an important military function when it stormed the rugged parapet just behind the high bastion of the fort. The deceptive thing was the presence of two commanders, which could create the impression that unity of command did not exist. In fact, the exceptional thing was that unity of command did exist, as close analysis of the second attack reveals. By happy chance, Terry's commands conformed to what the admiral, in view of his experiences off Federal Point, believed to be proper. Such fortuitous concurrence is not to be relied upon, being too dependent on the human ingredient. The command situation in the later attack, then, comes to fortify even more the principle so obviously unapplied in the first attack.

The second element of interest here is military intelligence. On the strategic level, the gathering of information was adequate. This was not due to a skilled group of operatives, but rather to the nearly total neglect of security measures. Richmond newspapers were carefully scanned to ascertain the moves and intents of the southern leaders, for example, and great reliance was put on the data culled therefrom by the Union generals. A similar situation obtained in the Confederate capital. Northern officials were driven to desperation by the blatant headlines in newspapers, announcing to the South information which today would be highly classified. The troops discussed, without any reserve, their destination prior to embarking for the first assault and even speculated about the worth of the powder boat as a destructive force.[34] General Whiting's informant was aware of federal plans and he knew what information federal officials had garnered about the southern countermoves.

These things perturbed General Grant to such an extent that in October 1864 he postponed the first expedition. When plans were being formulated for the second attempt, he took great care to keep them secret. This time, as has been noted, the soldiers were told that they were going to join General Sherman, and the transports were about to sail before the true object of the attack was disclosed. Notwithstanding, General Lee knew their destination, even as the troops were embarking along the James River. Despite Terry's order, which kept the loaded transports wallowing in a miserable sea, beyond the sight of land, his adjutant, who was sent ashore at Beaufort, North Carolina, found that everyone in the town knew about the expedition to Fisher.[35] Grant endeavored to utilize the strategic intelligence that had been collected, but he was hampered by constant delays, some unavoidable, in the execution of his orders. Such security measures as he tried to enforce were simply futile. The expeditions, therefore, offer no positive lessons regarding intelligence at the strategic level.

In the area of combat intelligence, however, there is some instruction available. The reduction of the fort had long been contemplated by the Navy Department, and there was a systematic effort to gather information about the terrain, the fortifications, and the garrison. When the army joined in the project, General Weitzel was taken down the coast to look over the lay of the land, although, to the annoyance of Rear Admiral Lee, he refused to go ashore for more minute examination of the Point. But the ease with which the beachheads were secured is testimony

that the intelligence was quite effective. During each assault, the army commander on the shore made a close reconnaissance. Confederate prisoners were subjected to interrogation. In the December expedition these two sources brought forth information which was largely responsible for the hasty withdrawal of the troops.[36] In the successful attack, three weeks later, Terry's inspection of the fort determined him to storm it, and when he conveyed the facts to Porter, the result was the brilliantly executed barrage that made almost easy the last few yards of attack. Terry assessed faultlessly the information he had obtained; Butler and Weitzel completely misinterpreted it. The lesson which has been learned now, from other examples, is that there must be a corps of intelligence officers, specialists at evaluating each and every item presented to them and able to render competent advice upon which the commander may act. The scientific method of sifting and extracting the facts is now practiced by the intelligence sections in all naval, military, and air units. Again the case of Terry must be looked on as exceptional, and that of Butler and Weitzel as nearer to the average, for which safeguards must be built.

The third facet concerns communications. The December expedition saw very little use of any high-speed transmission of information. The written dispatch, conveyed by boat, was the wholly inadequate means upon which the commanders relied. It is difficult to say exactly how much the lack of effective and rapid communications contributed to the failure. Using the second operation as a measuring stick, however, it appears that it was a fairly substantial factor. Terry and Porter had devised a system of signaling for use during the second attack, and this method was taught to the fleet by an officer of the Army Signal Corps. Between the two commanders, at least, the speed of communication compared favorably with that of a two-way radio, and certainly they took fuller advantage of it than many modern commanders have made of the means at their disposal. The benefits which accrued to Terry were enormous—at his very fingertips stood the tremendous firepower of the United States Fleet, which he was able to manipulate almost as easily as a single battery of light artillery. This advantage made possible by the rapid communication was exploited to its farthest limit, and, in turn, emphasized the actual unity achieved in the function of command. The principle to be derived from this is quite evident: whenever cooperation between two or more branches is envisioned—even though there be a single overall commander—communications must be quick and direct, unimpeded by the usual and especially traditional channels.

These principles of war are universally accepted now, but this was not always so. Much blood and treasure could have been spared had the military and naval student utilized to the hilt the voluminous accounts of these and other more important American battle experiences. Naturally, it is impossible to obliterate the knowledge obtained from campaigns conducted during World War Two, and probably principles noted in this paper have been, to some extent, influenced by these modern actions. Notwithstanding, it seems to me that this paper, in its essential points, could have been written eighty years ago. Official records, it is true, had not been edited, but they were available for the serious and painstaking student. Instead of relying on written memoirs, which are often colored by subsequent events, the important happenings could have been covered in minute detail with the very men who acted them out. There is no doubt that a careful use of hindsight will sharpen foresight. The ultimate purpose of this essay, then, is to demonstrate how the military and naval past, and American battle history in particular, may be used to determine more finely and exactly the eternal principles of warfare on which Mahan expended his scholarship.

Notes

[1] Alfred Vaghts, *Landing Operations* (Harrisburg, PA: Military Service Publishing, 1946), p. 421; and Allan Westcott, ed., *American Sea Power Since 1775* (Chicago: Lippincott, 1947), p. 173.

[2] Fox to Grant, 5 October 1864, *Official Record of the Union and Confederate Navies in the War of the Rebellion*, 30 vol. (Washington, D.C.: GPO, 1894–1922) 10:525.

[3] William Lamb, "Defence of Fort Fisher, North Carolina," *Papers of the Military Historical Society of Massachusetts* 9 (1912): 350–54, 376. See also Richard A. Yates, "Governor Vance and the End of the War in North Carolina," *The North Carolina Historical Review* 18 (1941): 316–18.

[4] Grant to Stanton, 22 July 1865, *Army Records* 46:41 (part 1). See also Fairly to Baker, 12 November 1864, in ibid., p. 1212 (part 3).

[5] Turner to Weitzel, 6 December 1864, in ibid., p. 837; see also Lee to Welles, 27 September 1865, *Navy Records* 10:488 (part 1).

[6] Porter, *Naval History*, p. 692, notes that Butler got the idea from a magazine explosion near London. An account of this explosion may be seen in *The Times* (London), 3 October 1864.

[7] Ulysses S. Grant, *Memoirs* (New York: Webster, 1885–6) 2:390. See also Grant to Butler, 6 December 1864, *Army Records* 42:835 (part 3).

[8] Delafield to Dana, 18 November 1864, *Army Records* 42:639–44 (part 3); and Jeffers to Wise, 23 November 1864, *Navy Records* 11:215 (part 1).

[9] Admiral David Dixon Porter, *Incidents and Anecdotes of the Civil War* (New York: Appleton, 1891), pp. 269–70. See also Porter to Rhind, 17 December 1864, *Navy Records* 11:222 (part 1).

[10] Butler to Grant, 20 December 1864, *Army Records* 42:1049 (part 1).

[11] Ibid., "The admiral arrived on 18 December from Beaufort, having been detained there from 14 December for reasons presumed to be satisfactory."

[12] Rhind to Porter, 26 December 1864, *Navy Records* 11:226–27.

[13] As Butler came upon the scene, he offered some advice to the admiral: "It would seem to be best that the naval attack should be continued with spirit and effect upon the fort, and endeavor to silence it and keep it silenced." *Army Records* 42:1072 (part 3).

[14] Thirty years later Colonel Lamb asserted that his post was nowhere near surrender. Lamb, "Defence of Fisher," p. 368; the outlook was a little different at the time, as General Whiting's deposition reveals, "Fort Fisher Expedition," *Report of Committee on the Conduct of the War*, 38th Cong., 2nd sess. (part 6).

[15] Lamb, "Defence of Fort Fisher, North Carolina," p. 357.

[16] Whiting to Lee, 29 November 1864, *Army Records* 42:1201 and 42:1233 (part 3).

[17] Lamb's diary entry, 24 December 1864.

[18] Butler to Porter, 25 December 1864, *Navy Records* 11:251 (part 1).

[19] Butler to Grant, 27 December 1864, *Army Records* 42:1086 (part 3). There is a dispute over the number of soldiers left behind. Butler says

there were only three hundred, but he had reason to keep the figure down. The navy's estimate, more plausible, in view of the circumstances, was seven hundred. Glisson to Porter, 1 January 1865, *Navy Records* 11:333 (part 1).

[20] Grant to Stanton, 22 July 1865, *Army Records* 46:42 (part 1).

[21] Butler to Weitzel, 30 January 1865, *Correspondence of Butler* 5:514; and Grant to Butler, 2 January 1865, *Army Records* 46:15 (part 2).

[22] Terry to Rawlins, 25 January 1865, *Army Records* 46:394 (part 1).

[23] Bragg to Taylor, 20 January 1865, *Army Records* 46:431 (part 1).

[24] Whiting to Lee, 18 January 1865, *Army Records* 46:440 (part 1). Lamb recalled the following cheerful conversation on 13 January 1865 when Whiting arrived: "Lamb, my boy, I have come to share your fate. You and your garrison are to be sacrificed." Lamb, "Defence of Fort Fisher, North Carolina," p. 371.

[25] Bragg to Taylor, 20 January 1865, and Terry to Rawlins, 25 January 1865, *Army Records* 46:396–97, 432 (part 1).

[26] Bragg to Taylor, 20 January 1865, and Bragg to Lee, 14 January 1865, *Army Records* 46:432, 1053 (part 1).

[27] Porter to Welles, 17 January 1865, *Navy Records* 11:439 (part 1).

[28] Whiting to Lee, 19 February 1865, *Army Records* 46:441 (part 1).

[29] Lieutenant John C. Soley, USN, "The Naval Brigade," *Papers of the Military Historical Society of Massachusetts* 12 (1902): 254. To make the whole thing really sailor-like, the men were each issued a revolver and a cutlass; *Navy Records* 11:439 (part 1). See also *Army Records* 46:434 (part 1).

[30] Bragg to Taylor, 20 January 1865, *Army Records* 46:432–33 (part 1) and Whiting to Lee, 19 February 1865, *Army Records* 46:442 (part 1).

[31] Bragg to Taylor, 20 January 1865, *Army Records* 46:434. See also Whiting to Bragg, 15 January 1865, *Army Records* 46:1064 (part 2).

[32] Anonymous to Butler, 31 January 1865, ". . . you are at heart a vagabond . . . you are a coward, a poltroon, a jackass, a viper, a brazen, impudent bag of wind, etc., etc., etc."

[33] Porter to Grant, 14 January 1865, and Porter to Welles, 15 January 1865, *Navy Records* 11:432–34 (part 1); see also Terry to Rawlins, 25 January 1865, *Army Records* 46:399 (part 1) and Stanton to Lincoln, 17 January 1865, *Army Records* 46:156 (part 2).

[34] Porter, *Incidents of the War*, p. 271. See also Butler to Mrs. Butler, 23 December 1864, *Correspondence of Butler* 5:434.

[35] Comstock to Rawlins, 9 January 1865, *Army Records* 46:79 (part 1).

[36] Butler to Grant, 3 January 1865, *Correspondence of Butler* 5:463.

AGE OF MAHAN

U.S. Marines in Panama, 1885

BY JACK SHULIMSON

A revolution in the spring of 1885 on the Isthmus of Panama, then belonging to Colombia, threatened American business interests and resulted in the burning of the city of Colon and the seizing of the U.S. consul as a hostage. In the relatively simple decade of the 1880s, the U.S. response was both direct and swift. Invoking the provisions of its 1846 treaty with Colombia to guarantee the freedom of passage across the Isthmus, the American government ordered the deployment to Panama of a naval expeditionary force: two marine infantry battalions supported by a navy artillery battalion, together with ships of the U.S. North Atlantic Station. For nearly two months, marines and sailors kept the peace on the Isthmus. Yet this large-scale intervention, which seemed to foreshadow the amphibious and expeditionary missions of the twentieth-century Marine Corps, had little impact on the organization, strength, and mission of the late nineteenth-century corps.

The Marine Corps of 1885 was a largely unstructured force of 82 officers and 1,880 enlisted men, divided almost evenly between sea and shore duties. Marines were sentries at navy yards or guards on board ship. In this latter capacity, they enforced shipboard discipline, performed various ceremonial duties, helped man the guns, and made up part of hastily organized landing parties. Marines seldom operated in detachments of more than one hundred men at sea or of more than three hundred at even the largest navy

Reprinted by permission of the author.

yards. No unit organization, except what might be improvised in an emergency, existed. The colonel commandant in Washington and his small staff—a paymaster, quartermaster, and adjutant and inspector—handled the small amount of central administration required.[1]

The officer corps was an inbred group, composed mostly of sons of military and naval officers, with some scions from prominent political families. Although there had been some modest leavening during the Civil War, all marines officers until 1883 received their appointments directly from civilian life after passing a perfunctory examination administered by a board of officers. Legend has it that the acronym USMC spelled out "Useless Sons Made Comfortable."[2]

Through the 1870s and early 1880s, nevertheless, there existed a spark of reform, nurtured partially by personal ambition. In 1873 one marine officer in a report to the secretary of the navy of his visit to European military organizations recommended a battalion and regimental organization for the corps and more professional standards for its officers. Two years later, a coterie of progressive officers met at Norfolk and made similar proposals, one of the more outspoken calling either for a resuscitation or a funeral for the corps. Despite such rhetoric and various proposals in Congress, very little changed in the makeup of the officer corps until 1883. A law passed in August of the previous year restricted the number of commissions in the navy to actual openings, but for the first time permitted Naval Academy graduates to opt

A landing force from the *Tennessee* going ashore, Panama, 1885. Courtesy of the U.S. Navy Historical Center.

for the Marine Corps. Sixteen passed midshipmen of the class of 1881 became marine second lieutenants. This reform, however, would not have its full effect until several years later.[3]

While the small group of reformers in the corps focused on the issues of professional conduct and organizational structure, few questioned the traditional missions of the Marine Corps. If they foresaw any new role for the corps, it was as coastal artillerymen and more extensive use of marines as gunners on the navy's ships. Very little thought, if any, was given to amphibious operations on a large scale.[4]

Several navy officers, on the other hand, perhaps inspired by their joint operations with the army during the Civil War, paid a great deal of attention to the formation and development of a naval landing force. Articles appeared during the 1870s and 1880s in both professional journals and official reports concerning the importance of the organization, landing, and deployment of a naval brigade. One of the foremost advocates of this emphasis on joint sea-and-land operations was the founder of the Naval War College, Rear Admiral Stephen B. Luce.[5]

Although mentioned only incidentally in the literature about the naval brigade, the marines were the logical core of any naval landing force. Since the Civil War, marine

detachments had participated in several landings on foreign shores, including Korea in 1871, Panama in 1873, and Egypt in 1882. Moreover, during the war scare with Spain in late 1873-early 1874 over the *Virginius* Affair, marines had hastily mobilized a battalion of more than two hundred forty men and officers. Despite the lack of a permanent amphibious force, the Marine Corps constituted the nucleus for such an organization, as the events in Panama would demonstrate.[6]

The trouble on the Isthmus arose out of disputed elections in both Colombia and Panama during the summer of 1884. Although revolution broke out elsewhere in Colombia, the Isthmus remained relatively quiet, if tense. By early 1885, it even looked as if the Panamanians were about to resolve their internal disputes. Their Assembly had selected a nonpolitical Colombian general as the president of the state, but in March the new president left Panama to lead a military expedition to help suppress a revolt in the Colombian state of Bolivar.[7]

With the serious depletion of Colombian military strength, Panamanian nationalists took over Panama City. In a confusing succession of events, the government forces reoccupied Panama City, but a motley group led by Pedro Prestan, a Haitian-born lawyer, entered the undefended city of Colon on the

Caribbean side of the Isthmus, took several hostages on 30 March, including the U.S. consul at Colon, and then marched out of the city to engage a Colombian force sent from Panama City. The Colombians easily routed the rebel forces, which fell back into Colon, where, on the morning of 1 April, the government troops pushed through the final rebel defenses. During the confusion, the hostages escaped. Prestan ordered the city burned and then slipped away into the jungle with the remnants of his force. A hundred men from the U.S. warship *Galena*, which had arrived in the port earlier in the month, were able to protect the railroad and steamship property but were unable to prevent the torching of the rest of the city.

Compounding the chaotic state of affairs on the Isthmus, Rafael Aizpuru, a veteran Panamanian politician who had led the earlier uprising in Panama City, reentered the city with an estimated three hundred to eight hundred men and forced the surrender of the understrength garrison, thus reversing the situation. The loyalists now controlled the ruined city of Colon, while the rebels held the Pacific terminus of the transit. The railroad and all commerce came to a complete standstill.

These events presented a dilemma to the newly inaugurated Grover Cleveland, the first democrat to be elected president since before the Civil War. In contrast to the Arthur administration, Cleveland and Secretary of State Thomas F. Bayard had little relish for intervention in Central America. One of Cleveland's first acts as president had been to withdraw from the Senate the recently negotiated treaty with Nicaragua that would have allowed the United States to build its own interoceanic canal in that country. Yet the administration could not ignore its treaty obligations with Colombia to keep the Panama transit open nor the danger to American citizens and property.[8]

On the evening of 1 April, the president met with Bayard, Attorney General Augustus H. Gaylord, and Secretary of the Navy William H. Whitney, the former New York financier and lawyer. According to one contemporary newspaper account, the three feared that the United States would be intervening in a "purely domestic broil" but believed they had no choice given the circumstances.[9]

Upon leaving the conference, Secretary Whitney alerted Rear Admiral James E. Jouett, the commander of the North Atlantic Station, embarked in his flagship, the *Tennessee*, at New Orleans. Whitney informed Jouett that a naval landing force would probably be organized for service in the Isthmus and ordered Jouett to send one of his ships, the *Swatara*, to Colon where it would join the *Galena* and the *Alliance*, which had left the day before. The secretary then telegraphed James B. Houston, president of the Pacific Mail Company, that the government had decided to keep the transit in Panama open and asked if Houston could delay the departure of one of his steamers so that it could take an armed expedition.[10]

During the morning of 2 April, the Navy Department was the scene of unusual activity as Whitney consulted with his advisors about the composition of the force that would go to the Isthmus. The relatively inexperienced secretary relied heavily on the various senior bureau chiefs, especially Commodore John G. Walker of the powerful Bureau of Navigation, a skillful bureaucratic politician. According to his recent biographer, Walker had used his position to forge a power base within the department and saw the Panama affair as a "perfect opportunity . . . to strengthen the Navy and to promote an active foreign policy." He selected one of his proteges, Commander Bowman H. McCalla, to head the expedition. Several years later, McCalla recalled that Walker entered his office at 11:00 A.M. that day and told him, "Get ready to go to Colon in command of an expedition to protect the transit." McCalla took the 4:00 P.M. train to New York that afternoon.[11]

In the meantime, Houston, of the Pacific Mail Company, had informed Secretary Whitney that the steamer *City of Para* could depart New York at noon on the third, carrying about two hundred men. Another vessel would sail three days later and could carry another six hundred troops. Houston offered to take the expedition at a cost of $25.00 per man, but Whitney thought that it was unfair for the company to make a profit since the U.S. forces would in part be protecting the property of the steamship company. He made a counteroffer of $10.00 per man, which Houston readily accepted.[12]

By this time, Whitney had taken the first steps to get the expedition organized. After some initial hesitation, he finally ordered the commandants of the navy yards in Philadelphia, Portsmouth, New Hampshire, and Boston to send sizable marine detachments to the New York Navy Yard where a marine battalion was to be formed. He then directed Admiral Jouett to dispatch the *Tennessee* to Pensacola to pick up the marine detachment there of two officers and thirty-six enlisted men, and thence to steam directly for Colon.[13]

About noon on the 2nd, Whitney asked the colonel commandant of the Marine Corps, Charles G. McCawley, to superintend the details relating to the organization and supply of the marine battalion. Somewhat of a martinet, known for his short temper and feuds with subordinate officers, McCawley was, nevertheless, an efficient administrator. He immediately arranged with the Bureau of Provisions and Clothing for sufficient mess kits and cooking kettles to be delivered to the marine battalion and he advised the secretary to ask the War Department to make up a shortfall in tents from the Army Quartermaster Depot in New York.[14]

As the largest component of the marine battalion was to come from the New York Navy Yard, it was only fitting for McCawley to select the commander of the barracks, Major and Brevet Lieutenant Colonel Charles Heywood, to command the battalion. Known as the "boy colonel," Heywood—who at forty-five was thirteen years younger than McCawley—had a reputation as a capable officer and was often referred to as the next commandant. McCawley wired Heywood that the latter would command a force of twenty officers and five hundred men. Stating that

Heywood would receive more detailed "instructions by mail," McCawley advised him to "take all the captains you need" and to make known "what you need for service on shore." The commandant then declared that he had already asked the department for tents, provisions, mess outfits, and medical officers.[15]

In his formal order to Heywood, McCawley stated that the battalion would be attached to the North Atlantic Station. He then wrote, "In giving you these orders I rely upon your zeal, and energy to organize and fully equip your command as quickly as possible in the best manner." Heywood, upon his arrival at Colon, was to place himself under orders of the senior officer present. In a later addendum to the instructions, McCawley informed Heywood that the initial force would be two hundred instead of five hundred and would leave on the third in the *City of Para.* The additional men would follow in a later steamer.[16]

By the morning of the third, all the marine detachments, with the exception of Boston's, whose steamer had been delayed by fog, had arrived at New York. According to a reporter, the marines at the long breakfast tables in the enlisted barracks "were as merry as crickets." There was an air of excitement and expectation throughout the yard for both officers and men. Major Heywood was exuberant as he gave an interview to the press: "I can safely say that there is no better equipped organization in the world than our marines."[17]

About 9:30 A.M. the white-helmeted marines mustered on the parade ground near the barracks, wearing overcoats and capes and carrying knapsacks and rifles. They formed into four companies and then paraded down Flushing Avenue to a cheering crowd. At noon the battalion reformed and marched to the "Long Dock" where the troops boarded the yard tug *Catalpa.* An eyewitness wrote: "A party of ladies waved farewell to Colonel Heywood, the crowd cheered, the soldiers responded, the band played the 'Star Spangled Banner,' and the boat steamed out . . . The sun shone brightly above and all was life and animation around as the *Catalpa* moved slowly down the river" to the *City of Para*. About 5:00 P.M. the transport steamed for Colon with 11 marine officers and 202 enlisted men. Heywood wrote that night to Colonel McCawley: "I have received your instructions and will do everything in my power to carry out your wishes, and hope the fine battalion which I have the honor to command will reflect credit on the Marine Corps."[18]

With the sailing of the *City of Para*, Whitney telegraphed Rear Admiral Jouett his instructions and defined the mission of the U.S. expeditionary force in the most limited terms, telling that the latter must display "great discretion" and that his "sole duty is confined to seeing that a free and uninterrupted transit across the Isthmus is restored . . . and that the lives and property of American citizens are protected." Whitney cautioned Jouett not to interfere "with the constituted authorities" and that he had "no part to perform in the political or social disorders of Colombia, and it will be your duty to see that no irritation or unfriendliness shall arise from your presence at the Isthmus."[19]

On 4 April Jouett arrived at Pensacola, acknowledged the receipt of his instructions, and wired Whitney: "I interpret my duty as requiring me to preserve the free transit of the Isthmus unembarrassed using armed force if necessary to accomplish this object." A private tug carried the marine detachment from the Pensacola Navy Yard to the *Tennessee* and that afternoon the ship departed for Panama.[20]

In Washington, the administration was beginning to have second thoughts about the size of the U.S. expedition to the Isthmus. This was caused in part by the reaction of the Colombian minister to the United States, who in his formal conversations with Secretary of State Bayard waxed and waned from one day to the next in his support of the American intervention. Moreover, Whitney had received conflicting reports from the U.S. consul general in Panama City and the navy commander of the *Galena* at Colon. The former believed that the force on the way was

sufficient, while the latter suggested that another "500 men will be necessary."[21]

Whitney then met again with his senior bureau chiefs and asked for their advice. After the meeting broke up, Whitney told reporters that he believed that the present forces going to the Isthmus would be capable of keeping the transit open. He declared, however, that additional troops could be sent and even referred to a possibility of fifteen hundred marines in Panama, reinforced by navy bluejackets. The secretary then stated that Commodore Walker would be responsible for the deployment of any more men.[22]

Although Commodore Walker had already informed Commander McCalla that it was unlikely that a second contingent would go to Panama, he told McCalla to remain in New York City and continue with his preparations. As Major Heywood had nearly completed arrangements for the first battalion, McCalla concentrated his efforts on putting together and equipping the second contingent.[23]

Both marines and sailors were still arriving or scheduled to arrive from the various East Coast navy yards, with the largest group expected from Norfolk on board the steamer *Despatch:* 121 marines and their officers, together with 65 bluejackets. About 4:30 A.M. on 5 April, the *Despatch* passed Sandy Hook, where it anchored in heavy seas. A marine lieutenant on board the ship remembered that it was "touch and go for a while . . . [until] a tug dropped down and picked us up and soon we joined forces with the others at New York."[24]

On 5 April, Whitney decided to go ahead with the deployment of the additional forces to the Isthmus. He arranged with the steamship company to have the transport *Acapulco* ready to carry the reinforcements, then he informed both the commandant and McCalla that a second battalion of marines was to depart reinforced by a six-gun battery. In his instructions to McCalla, the secretary told the navy commander that he was to assume command of the entire force sent from New York, "subject to the orders of the admiral commanding the North Atlantic

Squadron." Whitney, thus, established a clear chain of command and, moreover, limited the U.S. expedition to keeping the transit open and protecting American lives.[25]

Commodore Walker, however, probably without the concurrence of Secretary Whitney, sent McCalla a second set of instructions that altered considerably the clear lines of command established by the first. Emphasizing the importance of the expedition and "that we should keep the country with us in the matter," Walker directed McCalla to report directly back to Washington, in effect, bypassing Admiral Jouett. The commodore advised McCalla to "keep the Department informed of what occurs, how things are progressing and how they look to you; explain the political situation, go into the whole subject of isthmus troubles as far as you can, and do not spare the telegraph in sending us information." Walker then advised McCalla that the letter was confidential and "There will be no record of it in the Navy Department, but you may consider it as an order to be carefully carried out."[26]

The reasons behind Walker's extraordinary letter can only be a matter of conjecture. The evidence, however, would indicate that while the administration may have been concerned with the immediate troubles on the Isthmus and the implementation of its international legal obligations to keep the transit open, part of the naval bureaucracy, centered around Walker, was taking a longer view of the situation. Most naval officers agreed on the economic and strategic importance to the United States of an Isthmian canal and continued to be suspicious of the activities of the European countries in the Caribbean and especially of the French-owned Panama Canal Company on the Isthmus. Indeed, a newspaper interview with Admiral Jouett, which he later repudiated, stated that the admiral believed that French interests were behind both the revolt in Panama and the difficulties at the time between Guatemala and its neighbors Nicaragua and El Salvador. Walker did not mention any French collusion in his letter, but one could argue that he was thinking in terms of a permanent

amphibious force that would be able to project U.S. power into Central America.[27]

Although he later acknowledged that the two sets of orders placed him in an awkward position, McCalla energetically went about assembling as large a force as he thought he could take with him. He pressed Secretary Whitney to send with him two six-gun batteries composed of two hundred forty bluejackets, instead of the one battery ordered by the secretary. At this point, Whitney balked, writing in longhand on the telegram, "No, one is enough."[28]

By this time, the second battalion of marines of two hundred fifty men and their officers had assembled at New York. Colonel McCawley selected Captain John H. Higbee, the commander of the marine barracks in the Washington Navy Yard, to take command of the battalion and report to Commander McCalla. This battalion, like the first, was a composite force taken from the various East Coast establishments, including Annapolis, New York, Philadelphia, Boston, and Norfolk, as well as detachments from various navy training and receiving ships. On 7 April, in a scene reminiscent of the departure of the first contingent, McCalla's force, consisting of the marine battalion reinforced by one hundred forty bluejackets, departed on the *Acapulco* for Panama.[29]

Upon the departure of the second battalion, Colonel McCawley wrote to Major Heywood and informed him of the pending new command relationships. He stated that Heywood would report directly to Commander McCalla upon the latter's arrival. McCawley declared, however, that Heywood could organize the two marine battalions as he saw fit, unless otherwise directed by McCalla. The commandant then concluded: "I have sent experienced officers to command the companies, and I trust that you will leave nothing undone to reflect credit upon the Corps to which we have the honor to belong."[30]

On 8 April, Colonel McCawley reported to Secretary Whitney the successful completion of the deployment of the two marine battalions. He observed that the Atlantic Coast shore stations had been depleted of half their marine enlisted strength and only eleven marine officers of all grades remained at the eastern posts. McCawley then declared: "It is with pride that I call the attention of the Department to the prompt and cheerful manner in which its orders were obeyed by the officers and men, and to the extraordinary dispatch with which these troops were sent to their destination at such short notice." He then cited the case of one officer, who left a dying mother, rather than be excused.[31]

While the naval expeditionary force deployed from New York, the situation on the Isthmus remained at an impasse. Until 6 April, the only U.S. military presence was the *Galena*, whose one hundred twenty marines and bluejackets ashore protected, as best they could, American property and some three thousand refugees. On the 6th, a second U.S. warship, the *Shenandoah* from the Pacific Station arrived at Panama City. After consulting with the American consul, and over the protest of Aizpuru, the ship's captain, on the 8th, landed a one hundred forty-man force of marines and sailors to protect the Panama Railroad Company property on the northern outskirts of the city.[32]

Other U.S. reinforcements continued to arrive. On the 8th, the *Alliance* joined the *Galena* at Colon. Two days later, both the *Swatara* and the *Tennessee* steamed into the Caribbean port, followed the next day by the *City of Para*. Upon his arrival, Admiral Jouett wrote to the Colombian commander at Colon and asked permission to land the American forces, although "fully aware as I suppose he was that if he refused permission, his refusal would not be allowed to delay the landing." The Colombian officer gave his consent. After meeting with the American consul and the superintendent of the Panama Railroad Company, Jouett cabled Whitney: "All well. I shall open transit tomorrow and keep it open. Everything quiet here, but trouble feared at Panama."[33]

With the arrival early on the 11th of the *City of Para*, Major Heywood reported to Admiral Jouett on board the *Tennessee*. The admiral ordered Heywood to take his battalion

to Panama City later that afternoon to prevent any attempt to destroy the city. Heywood's force was to travel upon an especially prepared train with two attached flat cars, "each carrying one Gatling gun, one Hotchkiss revolving cannon, and one 12 pounder L.B. Howitzer, manned by 30 men, and protected by a shield of boiler iron about four feet high, extending all around the car."[34]

At 1:00 P.M., Heywood's battalion debarked from its transport "in heavy march order," with each man carrying forty rounds in addition to his pack and rifle. With their equipment and supplies, the marines boarded the "armored" train and departed Colon at 2:00 P.M. As planned, the train dropped off the detachment from Pensacola at Matachin and proceeded slowly to Panama City, reaching there about 6:00 P.M. During the night, the battalion occupied an unfinished warehouse belonging to the Panama Railroad Company.[35]

By the night of the 11th, Jouett had placed sizable U.S. forces at strategic points on the Isthmus. At Panama City, not including the landing force from the *Shenandoah*, Heywood had a mixed force of sailors and marines, totaling two hundred sixty officers and men, under his command. A similar force of ninety men was at Matachin, while one hundred seventy-five sailors and marines from the fleet occupied Colon. Approximately one hundred men, fairly evenly divided between marines and sailors, served as train guards. Jouett cabled Whitney: "I have opened the Isthmus transit and trains will run regularly heretoafter."[36]

During the next few days, the U.S. forces continued to consolidate their strength in Panama City and across the Isthmus. On the 12th, Major Heywood moved his men into a larger railroad warehouse and, except for the marines and the artillery, relieved the force from the *Shenandoah*. Heywood's battalion then assumed responsibility for the wharves and the railroad station complex. On the 14th, Admiral Jouett traveled across the Isthmus and inspected the garrisons at both Matachin and Panama City. Pleased with the appearance of the troops, he remarked: "The facility with which they have settled down to camp life is most creditable to all the men and officers."[37]

On 15 April, the *Acapulco* arrived at Colon with the remainder of the naval expedition from New York. After consulting with Admiral Jouett, Commander McCalla landed the troops from the transport the following morning and the men set up a temporary camp at Colon. McCalla, together with a few of his staff officers and a newspaper correspondent from the *New York Herald*, who had accompanied the expedition from New York, took the train to Panama City to inspect Heywood's marines. Heywood accepted McCalla's assumption of command with outward good grace, but at least one officer observed that the marine major was "disgusted at being superseded" by an officer many years his junior in length of service. McCalla returned to Colon that night and decided to remain there; he believed that Heywood had adequate forces and resources to keep the peace in Panama City.[38]

After receiving his official instructions from Jouett, on the 17th, McCalla issued his own orders to his subordinate commanders and made further disposition of his units. He posted most of Captain Higbee's battalion, together with the bluejackets who had arrived on the *Acapulco*, at various defensive positions in and around Colon. One company from the second battalion, supported by navy-manned gatlings and field pieces, relieved the Pensacola company at Matachin; the later unit joined Heywood's battalion in Panama City. McCalla also reinforced the train guards with another company from Higbee's battalion and additional seamen. By the 19th, McCalla had under his command and in place on the Isthmus 796 officers and men: 304 at Colon, 107 at Matachin, and 385 in Panama City.[39]

Commander McCalla further refined his command relations. He gave Heywood command "of the Brigade of U.S. Marines," which included the two marine battalions and the attached navy artillery. Captain Robert L. Meade, the former commander of the Pensacola detachment, assumed command of the 1st Battalion while Higbee retained command of the 2d Battalion. McCalla explained: "This is the best organization of the Marines and the one that will enable me to use that force to the best advantage."[40]

Jouett and McCalla saw the state of affairs on the Isthmus in different lights. After his visit to Panama City, McCalla described the situation as chaotic and warned Commodore Walker that the expedition would have to remain for some time if the transit were to be kept open. He asked the Navy Department for additional gatling guns and three hundred rockets and expressed the fear that the burning of Colon would "be a precedent for the disaffected for some time." Admiral Jouett, on the other hand, was more optimistic and suggested that the political stalemate would be settled in about a week and that the U.S. forces could be withdrawn. He even stated that the sending of the last battalion in the *Acapulco* was unnecessary but observed that "our display of a large force on the Isthmus has had an excellent moral effect and that it would be unwise on account of the reaction in public feeling which would take place here to withdraw our men abruptly."[41]

Despite their different perspectives, both men realized that the crisis for the Americans would occur when the Colombians attempted to reassert federal authority in Panama City. Reports from Bogota indicated that the federal government there was about to send eight hundred Colombian troops to the Isthmus. Fearing that the Aizpuru forces in desperation might attempt to burn the city, McCalla, on the 21st, moved his headquarters to Panama City. At the same time, he transferred two companies of Higbee's battalion and artillery from Colon to reinforce the U.S. forces in Panama City. The following day, the expedition commander issued a detailed plan for the stabilization of the city. Upon order, the marines in three converging columns, supported by artillery and gatling guns, were to advance into the city center and occupy such strategic points as the U.S. consulate, the telegraph office, and the offices of the Pacific Mail Company. If the troops met any resistance, McCalla explicitly directed "commanding officers to overcome it; shoot all who may be found firing or attempting to fire or blow up buildings." He ordered Heywood to have the troops drawn up for his inspection by 5:45 that evening.[42]

On the next day, the 23d, Jouett, apparently unaware of McCalla's plans, informed the latter that he should send two fifty-man marine detachments to occupy the consulate and the telegraph company. Jouett reasoned: "This will show our intention of protecting American interest and should Aizpuru and his men desire to bring on a conflict, let them do it. We would then know what we have to face, and could punish them accordingly."[43]

On the morning of the 24th, the U.S. consul called on McCalla and informed him that Aizpuru had begun erecting barricades in the streets that would cut off the marine brigade from the rest of the city. The naval commander said that he would occupy the city in a half-hour, but since it was fairly close to noon, he decided to delay the operation so that "the men might have their dinner comfortably." Reinforced by a landing party from the *Shenandoah* which remained in reserve, the marine brigade of 446 men then moved into the city. According to one eyewitness account: "2:30 this afternoon the United States forces appeared on the scene as if by magic, three taps of the drum being the signal by which they started. Three columns entered the city and had full possession in about 10 minutes." Upon the advance of the marines, Aizpuru's troops immediately withdrew to their barracks. McCalla had the rebel leader and two of his ministers arrested and confined under marine guard at the Grand Central Hotel. The only incident occurred in the plaza near the cathedral where a large crowd had gathered. A gatling gun manned by some sailors under a navy officer opened fire, but fortunately the weapon had been elevated so that the bullets cleared the tops of surrounding houses and fell harmlessly outside of the city. The plaza was immediately emptied. McCalla wrote several years later that he "did not then investigate the case of the firing too closely, because the

effect of it had been good." He later learned, however, that the officer in charge of the gun had been drinking, and that it was fortuitous that no one had been hurt.[44]

By evening, McCalla had established his headquarters in the Grand Central Hotel and Major Heywood had set up his command post in the American consulate. McCalla had reinforced the troops in Panama City with the remaining companies of the battalion from Colon and also a battalion of marines formed from the ships' detachments of the North Atlantic Squadron. That night, McCalla had 482 men within the city, 154 in reserve at the railroad depot, and a picket line of 188 men outside the city limits. He cabled Washington: "I hold Aizpuru and shall police the city tonight. My lines will prevent any force from entering the city. . . . I shall hold the city until further orders."[45]

In Washington, Whitney, who several times in previous cables to Jouett had expressed his concern over the size of the American expeditionary force and its becoming involved in the internal affairs of the Isthmus, was obviously upset by McCalla's actions. He fired off cables to both Jouett and McCalla, in one asking Jouett to confer with McCalla in Panama City so that the latter understood the limitations of his mission and in the other to McCalla mentioning that he regretted that the commander had found it necessary to interfere "with local control of Panama." Whitney ended his message with the admonition that the only interest of the U.S. government was the protection of the transit and directed McCalla to withdraw at the "earliest moment [after] stable government is reestablished." The following day, Whitney, apparently somewhat mollified by the course of events, sent another cable to McCalla stating that the latter must be the judge when to employ military force, "always keeping in mind that the necessity is regretted here."[46]

Although insisting on the necessity for the initial occupation of the city, McCalla, on the 25th, negotiated an agreement with Aizpuru. Under the terms of this pact, McCalla agreed to withdraw his forces to the vicinity of the railroad station while Aizpuru would guarantee the lives and property of U.S. citizens and other foreigners in Panama City. Moreover, Aizpuru promised not to erect barricades nor to permit any fighting within the city limits. On the 26th, the marines withdrew to the station and the rebel forces were again in control of the city. Aizpuru, however, kept his part of the bargain.[47]

On 28 April, the Colombian relief expedition arrived in the bay and asked permission of the Americans to land at the wharves north of the city, which were within the marine lines. During extended negotiations with Aizpuru as to whether the Colombian troops would be permitted to land and where, Admiral Jouett convinced him to surrender the city to the Colombians. On the morning of the 30th, the Colombian military force landed at the railroad wharf and at a specified time moved undisturbed into the city. Two companies of marines, drawn up along the road, presented arms as the Colombian soldiers marched by, and when the "national flag was hoisted on the citadel and over Government House," the U.S. forces responded with a 21-gun salute.[48]

Although the immediate crisis was over, the personal relationship between Jouett and McCalla had begun to degenerate. Jouett, who at first supported the U.S. occupation of Panama City, later declared he had not been aware of the extent of McCalla's interference in local affairs until he received the secretary's message. Jouett stated that he had seen the occupation only "in a military sense," and that McCalla had "far exceeded his orders, and interfered with local matters to such an extent as to excite the indignation of the whole community and made his position in the city untenable."[49]

In May, Jouett became infuriated at McCalla. The admiral had received several U.S. newspapers and "was astonished to learn" that McCalla had been in direct communication with the department and that several of his dispatches were "directly contradictory to my official telegraphic reports." Jouett directed McCalla to give him a copy of the messages that the latter had sent to

Washington. At the same time, Admiral Jouett also asked Major Heywood to forward a copy of all orders that the marine commander had received from McCalla. On 7 May, Jouett wrote to Whitney and repeated his complaints about McCalla's irregularities. He said that McCalla, by telegraphing directly to the department and bypassing the usual chain of command, "placed his whole command in a most critical position without the slightest necessity for doing so." Although observing that McCalla violated the customs of the naval service, Jouett allowed that his subordinate had the units under him well organized, efficient, "and ready for any service." McCalla defended his conduct on the ground that he was operating under secret orders of the department to report events as he saw them and that he was the commander on the scene and did what he had to do.[50]

With the establishment of government control over Panama City, the American authorities began discussing the withdrawal of the U.S. forces. On 30 April, Jouett wrote to Whitney and suggested that most of the U.S. forces could depart. He recommended leaving one ship at Colon and another at Panama City, and a force of one hundred marines to provide security on the trains. Secretary of State Bayard also advised that at least half the troops return. On 5 May, the commander of the Colombian expedition told Jouett there was no need for more than four hundred men of the U.S. force to remain while he "completed the pacification" of the Isthmus. Finally, Whitney cabled Jouett on the same day: "Send home one-half Marine force if you think it prudent."[51]

There were other factors behind the decision to reduce the American forces, including the fear of disease and a growing restiveness in the command now that the crisis was over. On 28 April, a sentry mistook a marine trying to sneak a bottle of whiskey into the compound as a prowler and shot him. This incident was followed by another the next day in which a marine killed a sailor in a drunken brawl. Despite strict orders forbidding alcohol among the troops, one marine company commander noted in his diary,

"Much drunkenness in command." The greatest concern, however, was the spread of yellow fever as the hot season approached. By the beginning of May, one sailor had died of the disease. Eventually four marines also died of yellow fever, and several took sick before the U.S. forces left the Isthmus.[52]

On 7 May, Commander McCalla, the marine 2nd Battalion, and the bluejackets, who had arrived with him, departed Colon on a Pacific Mail steamer. Little more than two weeks later, Major Heywood and the 1st Battalion boarded the *Acapulco* for the return trip to New York. The following day, 26 May, the Colombian commander officially relieved Jouett of the responsibility for the protection of the transit and all U.S. forces returned to their ships. In Panama, the Colombian authorities quickly reasserted their authority; Preston was captured and publicly hanged and Aizpuru, after his surrender, was tried and sentenced to ten years of exile. A marine second lieutenant, probably expressing the sentiments of most of his comrades about the expedition, commented that "my delight on leaving New York was more than exceeded by my joy on returning."[53]

The press and public generally heaped praise on the conduct and readiness of the Marine Corps. Secretary Whitney, on 12 June, added his congratulations to Commandant McCawley, remarking on "the promptness which is in keeping with the excellent reputation the Marine Corps has enjoyed since its organization."[54]

After basking for a time in the public and official approbation, the Marine Corps soon found itself under attack from an unexpected quarter. In an extended report on the Isthmus expedition to the secretary of the navy, Commander McCalla, while describing the corps "as highly efficient and admirably disciplined," criticized the marines for using the tactics "of a bygone day." He suggested that marine officers needed advanced professional schooling and training in the employment of artillery and machine guns. Moreover, McCalla argued that the marines wasted too much time on shore in barracks and rec-

ommended summer maneuvers for the entire shore establishment in conjunction with the fleet and the army. McCalla criticized the navy, proposing that the department purchase its own transports to carry future naval brigades and that the fleet should practice more realistic landing operations. In effect, McCalla was recommending the establishment of a naval expeditionary force, with a definable role in such an organization for the Marine Corps.[55]

Commandant McCawley angrily responded to McCalla's report. In a lengthy letter to the secretary, the commandant answered in turn each of McCalla's criticisms. Referring to the comments on marine tactics, McCawley replied that the Marine Corps used the same tactics as the army and if these were wrong, "it is singular that it is left to a naval officer to discover this." He then declared that the marines did not waste time in barracks since they were faced with constant guard duty in the navy yards. The commandant rejected the idea of a summer maneuver, stating that it was his experience after serving thirty-eight years of service that he "never found the least trouble in having every duty as well performed in camp as in garrison after a few day's experience." Throughout his letter to the secretary, McCawley emphasized the limited number of officers and men that were available to him. He defined the main missions of the Marine Corps in the traditional terms of ships' detachments and sentry duty at the navy yards. He made no reference to any future expeditionary role for the marines. McCawley ended his letter with the hope that his reply would receive the same publicity as McCalla's report.[56]

The furor over the McCalla report soon died. The Navy Department published the report and Secretary Whitney released Colonel McCawley's letter to the press and there the matter ended. Although the naval expedition to the Isthmus consisted of six ships of the North Atlantic Squadron reinforced by two ships from the Pacific Squadron and well over twelve hundred men, including the troops sent from New York and the crews of the ships, the immediate effect on both the marines and navy was relatively slight. Despite their machinations, neither Walker nor McCalla obtained the permanent landing force they sought. Apparently Secretary Whitney never realized, despite Jouett's continuing protests, the extent of McCalla's independent actions while on the Isthmus.[57]

Heywood, who succeeded McCawley as commandant in 1891, throughout the next decade attempted to define the marine mission in terms of manning the secondary batteries of the new steel navy. A group of progressive young navy officers, however, not only resisted this effort on the part of the commandant but worked, albeit unsuccessfully, to remove marines from warships altogether and into transports for the seizure of advanced bases for the fleet. Although not specifically opposed to the advance base role, the marines merely viewed it as a secondary mission of getting aboard ship and going to the scene of action. By 1898, events had come full circle. During the Spanish-American War, Commander Bowman H. McCalla, in the cruiser *Marblehead*, commanded a naval expedition, which included the transport *Panther* and a six hundred-man marine battalion that seized Guantanamo as an advance base for the fleet blockading Santiago de Cuba.[58] As one historian has suggested, the Panama expedition of 1885 may have been a dress rehearsal for a later decade.[59]

Notes

[1] Commandant of the Marine Corps, "Annual Report, 1885," in *Annual Report of the Secretary of the Navy, 1885*, 2 vols. (Washington, D.C.: 1885), 1:180–81 (hereafter cited as *CMC Annual Report, 1885*).

[2] For discussion of the Marine Corps officer corps of this period, see: *Army and Navy Journal* (9 January 1875): 344; (17 July 1875): 783; (11 April 1883): 841. See also "Social Marines," [*Philadelphia*] *Times*, 7 January 1882, Clipping Book, 1880–89, Record Group (RG) 127, Records of the U.S. Marine Corps, National Archives (hereafter cited as Clipping Book, RG 127). Allan R. Millett has a valuable discussion of the makeup of the officer corps in his forthcoming history of the Marine Corps to be published by The Free Press. For an example of instructions to a marine officer examining board, see, CMC to Maj. A. S. Nicholson,

Capt. R. W. Huntington, 1st Lt. George C. Reid, June 1875, vol. 21, p. 564, Letter Books, Letters Sent, RG 127 (hereafter cited as LBLS, RG 127).

[3] Capt. James Forney report to the secretary of the navy, 15 September 1873, Subject File VR (Marine Corps), RG 45, Naval Records Collection of the Office of Naval Records and Library, National Archives; Capt. Henry Clay Cochrane, "A Resuscitation or a Funeral," pamphlet, 1 October 1875, Henry Clay Cochrane Papers, Personal Papers Collection, History and Museums Division, Headquarters, Marine Corps (hereafter cited as Cochrane Papers, Hist. & Mus. Div.); 22 *U.S. Stat.* 391; *CMC Annual Report, 1885*.

[4] For example, see Capt. Richard S. Collum to Henry Clay Cochrane, 14 April 1877, Folder 22, Cochrane Papers, Hist. & Mus. Div.

[5] S. B. Luce, "United States Naval War College," *United Service*, 12 (1885): 79–90; Foxhall A. Parker, "Our Fleet Maneuvers in the Bay of Florida and the Navy of the Future," *Proceedings of the United States Naval Institute* (PUSNI), 1 (1874): 163–78; John C. Soley, "The Naval Brigade," *PUSNI*, 6 (1880): 271–94; Carlos G. Calkins, "How May the Sphere of Usefulness be Extended in Time of Peace," *PUSNI*, 9 (1883): 155–94; William Brainbridge-Hoff, "Examples, Conclusions, and Maxims of Modern Naval Tactics," in Office of Naval Intelligence (ONI), *Information from Abroad, General Information Series*, III (Washington, D.C.: 1884): 136–38; "The Landing of the Naval Brigade on Gardiner's Island," in ONI, *Papers on Naval Operations during the Year ending July 1885, Information from Abroad, General Information Series*, IV (Washington, D.C.: 1885): 101–10 (hereafter cited as *General Information Series*, IV, 1885).

[6] Capt. Harry A. Ellsworth, *One Hundred Eighty Landings of United States Marines, 1800–1934* (Washington, D.C.: 1974). See also Millett, op. cit. For the activities of the marine battalion formed during the Virginius Affair, see Parker, "Our Fleet Maneuvers," and *Annual Report of the Secretary of the Navy, 1874* (Washington, D.C.: 1875): 11–13.

[7] For general accounts of the revolution in Panama see, E. Taylor Parks, *Colombia and the United States, 1765–1934* (Durham, N.C.: 1935), pp. 202–28; Kenneth Hagan, *American Gunboat Diplomacy and the Old Navy* (Westport, CT.: 1973), pp. 160–87; Gerstle Mack, *The Land Divided: A History of the Panama Canal and Other Isthmian Canal Projects* (New York: 1944), pp. 350–54; Richard S. Collum, *History of the United States Marine Corps*, rev. ed. (New York: 1903), pp. 234–53; Clyde Metcalf, "The Naval Expedition to the Isthmus of Panama," MS, Geographic Files, Historical Reference Section, Hist. & Mus. Div. HQMC (hereafter cited as Geog. Files, HRS, Hist. & Mus. Div.); Daniel H. Wicks, "Dress Rehearsal:

United States Intervention on the Isthmus of Panama, 1885," *Pacific Historical Review*, in press; Bowman H. McCalla, "The U.S. Naval Brigade on the Isthmus of Panama," *General Information Series*, IV (Washington, D.C.: 1885): 41–100.

[8] Wicks, "Dress Rehearsal," p. 10. See also Hagan, *Gunboat Diplomacy*, pp. 158–61; Milton Plesur, *America's Outward Thrust, Approaches to Foreign Affairs, 1865–1890* (Dekalb, IL.: 1971), pp. 176–78; David M. Pletcher, *The Awkward Years: American Foreign Relations under Garfield and Arthur* (Columbia, MO.: 1962), pp. 332–33, 347.

[9] *New York Times*, 2 April 1885, as quoted in Wicks, "Dress Rehearsal," p. 9. See also Mark D. Hirsch, *William C. Whitney, Modern Warwick* (New York: 1948), p. 270.

[10] Secretary of the Navy to Jouett, 1 April 1885, Letters to Officers, vol. 8, pp. 510–11, Entry 16, RG 45; Secretary of the Navy to J. B. Houston, 1 April 1885, Letters from Officers Commanding Expeditions, Naval Expedition to the Isthmus of Panama, McCalla, February-May 1885, Entry 25, Subseries 13, RG 45 (hereafter cited as Expedition to Panama, Entry 25, Subseries 13, RG 45).

[11] Wicks, "Dress Rehearsal," p. 10; Bowman H. McCalla, "Memoirs of a Naval Career," MS, Navy Library, Navy Historical Center, Ch. 14, p. 2. See also Secretary of the Navy to Chandler, 2 April 1885, Expedition to Panama, Entry 25, Subseries 13, RG 45.

[12] See exchange of telegrams between Whitney and Houston, 2 April 1885, Expedition to Panama, Entry 25, Subseries 13, RG 45.

[13] Whitney to Ramsay, Badger, Yates, and Jouett, 2 April 1885, in Ibid.

[14] Collum, *Marine Corps*, p. 237; Commandant of the Marine Corps to Secretary of the Navy, 2 April 1885, Expedition to Panama, Entry 25, Subseries 13, RG 45.

[15] Commandant of the Marine Corps to Major Charles Heywood, 2 April 1885, vol. 30, p. 229, LBLS, RG 127.

[16] Ibid., pp. 233–35.

[17] Clipping from *New York Herald*, 3 April 1885, Clipping Book, RG 127.

[18] Clippings from *New York Herald* and *New York Times*, 4 April 1885, in Ibid. Major Charles Heywood to Commandant of the Marine Corps, 3 April 1885, Letters Received, "H," Box 146, RG 127.

[19] Secretary of the Navy to Jouett, 3 April 1885, Letters to Officers, vol. 8, pp. 513–14, Entry 16, RG 45.

[20] Jouette to Secretary of the Navy, 4 April 1885, Letters Received from Officers Commanding Squadrons, Microcopy 89, Roll 296, RG 45 (hereafter cited as Squadron Letters, M-89, RG 45).

[21] Becerra to Bayard, 2 April and 4 April 1885, 58th Cong., 2d sess., 1904, S. Doc. 143, *Use by United States of Military Force in Internal Affairs of Colombia* (Serial 4589), pp. 58–64; Becerra to Bayard, 3 April 1885, Letters Received from the President and Executive Agencies, Microcopy 517, Roll 49, RG 45; Hagan, *Gunboat Diplomacy*, pp. 144–45; Adamson to the Secretary of State, 4 April 1885, and Kane to Secretary of the Navy, 4 April 1885, Expedition to Panama, Entry 25, Subseries 13, RG 45.

[22] Clipping from *Philadelphia Times*, 6 April 1885, Clipping Book, RG 127.

[23] Walker to McCalla, 4 April 1885, Expedition to Panama, Entry 25, Series 13, RG 45; McCalla, "Memoirs," pp. 2–3.

[24] Mayo to Secretary of the Navy, 3 April 1885, and Manager, Marine Dept. to Secretary of the Navy, 5 April 1885, Expedition to Panama, Entry 25, Subseries 13, RG 45; H. C. Reisinger, "On the Isthmus, 1885," *Marine Corps Gazette* 13 (December 1928): 220–37.

[25] See exchange of telegrams between Whitney and Houston, 5 April 1885, Expedition to Panama, Entry 25, Subseries 13, RG 45; Secretary of the Navy to Commandant of the Marine Corps, 5 April 1885, Letters to Officers, vol. 1, pp. 468–69, Entry 18, RG 45.

[26] J. G. Walker to B. H. McCalla, 6 April 1885, General Letterbook, 1885–89, Container 1, John G. Walker Papers, Library of Congress.

[27] See Hagan, *Gunboat Diplomacy*, pp. 148–49 and Wicks, "Dress Rehearsal," p. 15. For Jouett interview with the press, see Wicks, "Dress Rehearsal," pp. 15–16. For Jouett's repudiation of his interview see his letter to Secretary of the Navy, 1 May 1885, Squadron Letters, M-89, Roll 296, RG 45.

[28] McCalla, "Memoirs," pp. 3–4; McCalla to Whitney, 6 April 1885, Expedition to Panama, Entry 25, Subseries 13, RG 45.

[29] A. S. Nicholson, "Detail of the 2d Battalion for the Isthmus of Panama," n.d., Letters Received, "N," Box 247, RG 127; "Assignment of Marines for Duty in Panama, April 1885," Geog. Files, HRS, Hist. & Mus. Div.; For the sailing of the second battalion, see clipping from *New York Times*, 8 April 1885, Clipping Book, RG 127.

[30] Commandant of the Marine Corps to Heywood, 6 April 1885, vol. 30, pp. 252a–252b, LBLS, RG 127.

[31] Commandant of the Marine Corps to Secretary of the Navy, 8 April 1885, vol. 1, pp. 155–58, Letters Sent, Secretary of the Navy, RG 127, hereafter LSSN, RG 127.

[32] C. S. Norton to Secretary of the Navy, 15 April 1885, Letters from Captains, Microcopy-125, Roll 43, RG 45.

[33] Jouett to Secretary of the Navy, 23 November 1885, Squadron Letters, M-89, Roll 296, RG 45. See also Jouett to Secretary of the Navy, 11 and

17 April 1885, Expedition to Panama, Entry 25, Subseries 13, RG 45.

[34] Jouett to Secretary of the Navy, 17 April 1885, Expedition to Panama, Entry 25, Subseries 13, RG 45, hereafter Jouett, 17 April 1885.

[35] Ibid. See also Heywood to Commandant of the Marine Corps, 18 April 1885, Letters Received, "H," Box 147, RG 127, hereafter Heywood, 18 April 1885.

[36] Jouett to Secretary of the Navy, 11 April 1885, Expedition to Panama, Entry 25, Subseries 13, RG 45.

[37] Heywood, 18 April 1885, and Jouett, 17 April 1885.

[38] Henry Clay Cochrane Diary, 16 April 1885, Cochrane Papers, Hist. & Mus. Div. See also *Army and Navy Journal* 9 (May 1885): 823; McCalla, "The U.S. Naval Brigade," *General Information Series*, pp. 51–52.

[39] Collum, *Marine Corps*, pp. 252–53.

[40] McCalla to Secretary of the Navy, 18 April 1885, Expedition to Panama, Entry 25, Subseries 13, RG 45.

[41] McCalla to Walker, 17 April 1885, Ibid.; Jouett to Secretary of the Navy, 18 April 1885, Squadron Letters, M-89, Roll 296, RG 45; Addendum, 18 April 1885 to Jouett, 17 April 1885.

[42] Jouett to Secretary of the Navy, 20 April 1885, Squadron Letters, M-89, Roll 296, RG 45; McCalla, "The U.S. Naval Brigade," *General Information Series*, pp. 52–54; McCalla to Heywood, 22 April 1885, reprinted in Ibid., pp. 76–77.

[43] Jouett to McCalla, 23 April 1885, Squadron Letters, M-89, Roll 296, RG 45.

[44] McCalla, "The U.S. Naval Brigade," *General Information Series*, pp. 53, 55; McCalla, "Memoirs," pp. 16–17; Clipping from *Philadelphia Press*, 25 April 1885, Clipping Book, RG 127.

[45] "Force employed during the occupation of Panama, April 24, 1885," reprinted in McCalla, "The U.S. Naval Brigade," *General Information Series*, p. 81; McCalla to Secretary of the Navy, 24 April 1885, Expedition to Panama, Entry 25, Subseries 13, RG 45.

[46] Whitney to Jouett, 24 April 1885, Expedition to Panama, Entry 25, Subseries 13, RG 45; Secretary of the Navy to McCalla, 24 April 1885 in Ibid.; Secretary of the Navy to McCalla, 25 April 1885, Letters to Officers, vol. 1, pp. 464–65, Entry 18, RG 45.

[47] Agreement between R. Aizpuru and B. H. McCalla, 25 April 1885, reprinted in McCalla, "The U.S. Naval Brigade," *General Information Series*, pp. 56–57.

[48] Jouett to Secretary of the Navy, 29 April and 30 April 1885, Squadron Letters, M-89, Roll 296, RG 45; Collum, *Marine Corps*, p. 250.

[49] Jouett to Secretary of the Navy, 29 April and 7 May 1885, Squadron Letters, M-89, Roll 296, RG 45.

[50] Jouett to Secretary of the Navy, 7 May 1885 in Ibid.; Henry Clay Cochrane Diary, 5 May 1885, Cochrane Papers, Hist. & Mus. Div.; McCalla, "Memoirs," pp. 9–10.

[51] Jouett to Secretary of the Navy, 30 April 1885, Squadron Letters, M-89, Roll 296, RG 45; Secretary of State to Secretary of the Navy, 30 April 1885, Letters Received from the President and Executive Agencies, Microcopy 517, Roll 49, RG 45; Rafael Reyes, Commanding National Forces, to Jouett, 5 [May] 1885, Squadron Letters, M-89, Roll 296, RG 45; Secretary of the Navy to Jouett, 5 May 1885, Letters to Officers, vol. 8, p. 518, Entry 16, RG 45.

[52] McCalla, "The U.S. Naval Brigade," *General Information Series*, pp. 65 and 87; Henry Clay Cochrane Diary, 4 May 1885, Cochrane Papers, Hist. & Mus. Div.; Jouett to Secretary of the Navy, 25 May 1885, Squadron Letters, M-89, Roll 296, RG 45; Major Charles Heywood to Commandant of the Marine Corps, 7 May and 3 June 1885, Letters Received, "H," Box 147, RG 127; Commandant of the Marine Corps to Secretary of the Navy, 13 July 1885, vol. 1, pp. 193–204, LSSN, RG 127.

[53] Jouett to Secretary of the Navy, 1 June 1885, Squadron Letters, M-89, Roll 295, RG 45; David G. McCullough, *The Path Between the Seas: The Creation of the Panama Canal, 1870–1914* (New York: 1977), pp. 178–79; Frank E. Sutton, 2 Nov. 1885, reprinted in *Second Annual Report of the Class of '81*, U.S. Naval Academy (Butler, PA.: 1886), p. 38.

[54] *Army and Navy Journal* (6 June 1885): 918, and (13 June 1885): 935; Secretary of the Navy to Commandant of the Marine Corps, 12 June 1885, Letters Received, "N," Box 247, RG 127.

[55] McCalla, "The U.S. Naval Brigade," *General Information Series*, p. 61.

[56] Commandant of the Marine Corps to Secretary of the Navy, 13 July 1885, vol. 1, pp. 193–204, LSSN, RG 127.

[57] Secretary of the Navy to Commandant of the Marine Corps, 27 July 1885, Letters Received, "N," Box 247, RG 127.

[58] Graham A. Cosmas and Jack Shulimson, "Continuity and Consensus: The Marine Corps and the Advance Base Mission, 1900–1920," in David H. White and John W. Gordon, eds., *Proceedings of the Citadel Conference on War and Diplomacy, 1977* (Charleston, S.C.: 1979), pp. 31–36. See also Paolo E. Coletta, *Bowman Hendry McCalla, A Fighting Sailor* (Washington, D.C.: 1979), pp. 33, 90, 92.

[59] Wicks, "Dress Rehearsal."

I wish to thank Dr. Allan R. Millett and Dr. Daniel H. Wicks for permitting me to examine their manuscripts and for their research leads. I am also in the debt of Dr. Kenneth J. Hagan for his assistance in the preliminary research stage.

The Culebra Maneuver and the Formation of the U.S. Marine Corps's Advance Base Force, 1913–14

BY GRAHAM A. COSMAS AND JACK SHULIMSON

In January 1914, a marine brigade of 1,723 officers and men defended the tiny Caribbean island of Culebra against a simulated attack by units of the U.S. Atlantic Fleet. Conducted during the fleet's annual winter maneuvers, this exercise was for the Marine Corps a crucial test of its ability to perform the advance base mission which was becoming increasingly the principal rationale for the corps' existence.[1]

The United States Navy, in the efficiency-minded Progressive Era, was trying to orient its permanent peacetime organization, training, equipment, and deployments toward its expected wartime strategy. Influenced by the doctrines of Alfred Thayer Mahan, naval leaders directed their shipbuilding programs and training activities toward creation of a battlefleet able to take command of the sea, at least in the Western Hemisphere. As part of the navy, the Marine Corps also had to find a specific role toward which it could direct its own organization and training. The corps's traditional missions of providing ships' policemen and sharpshooters for the fighting tops had been largely eliminated or made superfluous by modern warship technology. Fortunately for the marines, the technological limitations of those same warships opened the way for a new mission.

This mission was occupation and defense of an advance base for the fleet. Modern battleships, in contrast to the old sailing ships-

of-the-line, required frequent refuelling, maintenance, and replenishment of stores and ammunition. Therefore, if the fleet were to operate any distance from its home ports, it had to have either permanent bases in potential overseas theaters of operations or an extensive train of supply and repair vessels. Since the United States had only a few overseas possessions, the large train was the only feasible solution for the American navy. In any naval campaign, the fleet would have to secure a temporary advance base at which to leave the train while the fighting ships sought the enemy. The fleet, then, required an accompanying land force to seize, fortify, and defend such a base. Further, in defensive operations, for example against a European power invading the Caribbean, land forces would be needed to deny such advance bases to the enemy.

Already part of the naval establishment, the Marine Corps was the logical organization to perform the advance base mission for the navy and, indeed, any landing mission in connection with fleet operations. Traditionally, the marines had provided ships' landing parties and guarded navy shore installations. Moreover, during the Spanish-American War, a marine battalion, deployed with the fleet on board its own transport, had secured Guantanamo Bay as a coaling station for the vessels blockading Santiago de Cuba, in effect establishing an advance base, although it was not called so by name. From its establishment in 1900 as a strategic planning and advisory staff for the secretary of the navy, the General Board assigned the advance base

Robert W. Love, Jr., ed. *Changing Interpretations and New Sources in Naval History* (New York and London: Garland, 1980), pp. 293–308. Reprinted by permission.

Landing party from the *Florida*, Culebra, 1914. Courtesy of the U.S. Navy Historical Center.

mission to the Marine Corps. On 22 November 1900, Brigadier General Charles Heywood, then commandant, formally accepted the mission and pledged that the Marine Corps would cooperate gladly in carrying it out, although he warned that the effort "will necessitate very careful consideration and considerable time will be necessary for accomplishing it."[2]

In 1900, the General Board visualized the advance base force as consisting of a permanently-organized, four hundred-man marine battalion trained in field fortification, the landing and emplacement of heavy guns, the installation and operation of mine fields, and other coast defense activities. This battalion was to form the nucleus of a wartime expeditionary force of one thousand men capable of seizing and holding an advance base. From 1900 through 1912, the General Board, the Navy War College, and the Marine Advance Base School refined and elaborated on the theoretical structure of the advance base force. By 1912, the navy and marines had adopted for planning purposes an advance base brigade divided into two thirteen hundred-man regiments and capable of withstanding an attack by light cruisers and an accompanying landing force. One of these regiments,

the fixed defense regiment, would consist of artillery, engineer, signal, searchlight, and mining companies and would have as its main armament large-caliber warship guns in temporary shore emplacements, supplemented by harbor-defense mines. The second, or mobile defense, regiment, composed of infantry reinforced by field gun and machine gun units, would repulse enemy landing forces. Both regiments, particularly the fixed defense regiment, were supposed to be kept fully organized, equipped, and trained, ready to embark on their own transports and sail with the fleet in the first days of war.

Despite the elaboration of advance base theory and doctrine during these years, practical obstacles prevented the formation of a permanent advance base force ready for deployment with the fleet. Congress never appropriated funds specifically for equipping the force, which meant that it had to compete for dollars with other programs in the rapidly expanding navy. The semi-independent Navy Department bureaus, especially the bureau of ordnance, gave the advance base force consistently low priority. As a result, in 1912 only a partial advance base outfit had been assembled, and most of the equipment composing it was obsolete.

Even if the equipment had been available, the Marine Corps would have had difficulty in providing men to use it. Although the corps nearly doubled in size between 1900 and 1912, from five thousand men to nearly ten thousand, most of these additional marines were required for ships' detachments and guarding navy yards, missions which expanded as the navy did. During most of this period, the marines maintained a one thousand-man brigade in the Philippines, theoretically an advance base force but in fact little more than a colonial garrison. What manpower the marines could spare from these missions was committed most of the time to the various Caribbean expeditions and interventions of the era of the "Big Stick" and "Dollar Diplomacy."

The warship detachments, which included about twenty-five hundred marines, were a bone of contention between the Marine Corps and a group of progressive-minded navy officers led by Captain William F. Fullam. Fullam and his adherents, who were strong supporters of the advance base mission, argued that the marines would have enough men to form a permanent advance base force if they would only remove what the Fullam group considered the obsolete and useless warship detachments. Marine Corps leaders, reluctant to surrender any mission, insisted that service on shipboard maintained the naval identity of the corps as well as providing marines with many of the skills required for advance base operations. The marines advocated further enlargements of the corps so that it could meet all of its responsibilities. This issue came to a head in 1908, when Fullam and his cohorts persuaded President Theodore Roosevelt to issue an executive order withdrawing the marines from battleships and cruisers and redefining the marine mission in terms of naval base defense and expeditionary duty. After a vigorous lobbying campaign by the Marine Corps, Congress forced Roosevelt in 1909 to put the marines back on shipboard. The Navy Department subsequently disavowed its initial support for removing the ships' detachments out of fear that taking the marines off warships would open the way for transfer of the entire corps to the army. For the next four years, the problem of marine manpower distribution remained unresolved.

Although hampered by lack of equipment and conflicting missions, the Marine Corps gradually had begun harnessing its resources to carry out the advance base function. As early as 1901, the corps temporarily established a small advance base school at Newport, Rhode Island. During the winter of 1902–03, a marine battalion of five hundred men landed on Culebra island and emplaced some guns during the annual fleet maneuvers. In 1904 and again in 1907, the brigade in the Philippines conducted similar advance base drills. Prodded by the General Board, the marines and the Navy Department in 1910 renewed and intensified the advance base effort. The marines reestablished their advance base school at Newport and moved it the following year to Philadelphia. Although interrupted periodically by deployment of its staff and students on expeditions, the school developed a systematic curriculum and increasingly focused the professional training and thought of marine officers on the advance base problem. During 1911 and part of 1912, a marine battalion of three hundred officers and men was stationed at Philadelphia in connection with the school, constituting the nucleus of an Atlantic Coast advance base force. Furthermore, the Navy Department began collecting all the available advance base material on the East Coast, which had been scattered among a number of navy yards, at Philadelphia and in 1912 allotted $50,000 to the bureau of ordnance for advance base accessories.

In this same period, the Marine Corps began consolidating its shore-based establishment for greater efficiency and expeditionary effectiveness. Taft's secretary of the navy, George von L. Meyer, in 1910 set forth as a major objective the concentration of most marines at one principal station on each coast, that for the Atlantic Coast being Philadelphia. During the following year, the Marine Corps centralized recruit training at four depots and organized marines stationed at the larger navy yards into permanent one hundred-man expeditionary companies. The closing of six minor navy yards and naval stations during 1911 allowed some enlargement of the marine detachments at the remaining yards. In 1911 and 1912, the marines began routinely forming provisional brigades of up to two thousand men and regiments of seven hundred to one thousand men, from navy yard companies and ships' detachments, for service in Cuba, Nicaragua, and the Dominican Republic. While these expeditions diverted men from advance base training, they provided marines with invaluable experience in organizing and maneuvering what were for the Marine Corps unprecedentedly large troop formations.

By the end of 1912, all of the elements for the creation of a permanent advance base force were there to be put together. Despite the continuing diversion of marine manpower to the Caribbean and the persistent shortages of equipment, the marines and navy had perfected advance base doctrine and had conducted much theoretical and some practical training, to the point where it could be put to the test.

In early 1913, the General Board decided that the time had come to conduct an actual advance base maneuver. During January, the board, after informal consultations with Marine Major General Commandant William P. Biddle, Lieutenant Colonel Lewis C. Lucas, the commandant of the advance base school, and other marine officers, drew up a proposal to the secretary of the navy for an advance base exercise. On 5 February, Admiral of the Navy George Dewey, president of the board, emphasized in a letter to Secretary of the Navy Meyer that the advance base force "is an adjunct of the fleet . . . and its location, as well as its state of preparedness should be such as to enable it to go with the fleet upon short notice." It was time, he declared, to go beyond the "spasmodic efforts during the past 10 years" to organize and equip an advance base force. Dewey recommended that the assemblage of advance base equipment at Philadelphia be completed "without delay" and that an advance base brigade be organized

and make an actual landing, emplace guns, and conduct target practice during the Atlantic Fleet's 1913–14 winter maneuvers. Secretary Meyer on the same day, 5 February, approved Dewey's proposal and instructed Biddle to make the necessary arrangements for the maneuver.[3]

From February through April, the navy and the Marine Corps worked out the size and organization of the marine force that would participate in the maneuver. These deliberations were overshadowed by renewed violence in revolution-wracked Mexico, where General Victoriano Huerta had deposed popular President Francisco Madero. As a precautionary move during February, elements of the fleet entered Mexican waters and the Marine Corps formed a two thousand-man provisional brigade which deployed to Guantanamo for possible later commitment to Mexico. With most of his available men assigned to the Guantanamo brigade, Major General Biddle initially expressed doubts about forming a full-scale advance base brigade for the exercise and recommended instead use of only a fixed regiment of about eight hundred marines. The General Board, supported by Meyer's successor in the new Wilson administration, Josephus Daniels, rejected Biddle's proposal and insisted that both fixed and mobile regiments be employed, at reduced strength if necessary. By early April, the Marine Corps had agreed to assemble a brigade of about sixteen hundred men for the maneuver, with two regiments, each of about eight hundred men. General Biddle also had submitted a detailed statement of his requirements for guns, equipment, and shipping. By this time, the likelihood of American military intervention in Mexico had diminished, and the Marine Corps had completed plans for withdrawing the brigade from Guantanamo, which would free sufficient men for formation of the projected advance base units.[4]

As serious planning for the maneuver began, the marines's old nemesis, Captain William F. Fullam, now aide for inspections, challenged the corps's ability to perform the advance base mission. Fullam used as his point of departure the report of a navy board of officers who had inspected the Philadelphia Navy Yard during March, examining, among other functions of the year, the advance base preparations there. In its report, issued on 19 April, the board found, to no one's surprise, that despite all of the effort since 1900, no effective advance base force yet existed and apportioned the blame for this situation about equally between the Navy Department and the marines. The board's specific recommendations supported many longstanding Marine Corps proposals, including enlargement of the barracks and facilities at Philadelphia, provision of transports for the advance base force, and the securing of a special appropriation from Congress for completing the advance base equipment and organization. Most important, the inspection board echoed the marine refrain that the corps did not have enough men to meet all of its responsibilities.[5]

Beginning on 1 May, Fullam bombarded the secretary of the navy and the General Board with a series of memorandums on the inspection board's findings. He largely ignored those parts of the board report detailing Navy Department shortcomings and instead focused on the Marine Corps failure to maintain permanent advance base battalions. Turning to his favorite hobbyhorse, Fullam argued that the marines would have enough men for this purpose if they withdrew their ships' attachments. Fullam in his memorandums made several forward-looking proposals, including one for the establishment of what amounted to an amphibious task force of warships and transports with an embarked marine battalion. Nevertheless, his principal and most controversial theme remained what he considered the maldistribution of marine manpower, an allegation which the Marine Corps consistently challenged. For every Fullam memorandum, the marines provided, in effect, the same answer: that the Marine Corps would form at least permanent fixed defense battalions if its manpower were increased or its expeditionary responsibilities decreased.[6]

For the most part, the General Board sided with the marines against Fullam. On 21 July, the board in its major comments on Fullam's proposals rejected out of hand any removal of marine ships' detachments, remarking that "this action, if persisted in, may eventually cause the loss of the Marine Corps to the Navy and its absorption by the Army." Like the marines, the General Board pointed to the lack of equipment as the principal obstacle preventing development of an advance base force. Although rejecting Fullam's recommendation that marines be taken off warships, the board agreed that marine manpower was poorly distributed and that the corps could find enough men for the advance base force without any overall increase in numbers. The board proposed that the brigade in the Philippines, which was serving no real advance base purpose, be withdrawn and that other overseas marine garrisons be reduced to free men for advance base units. At the same time, the board expressed its confidence in the capability of the Marine Corps to conduct the advance base mission, a capability that the board believed would be "fully demonstrated by the exercises which have been laid out for the Marines ... this coming winter." The questions raised by Fullam had little impact on the plans and preparations for the forthcoming Caribbean maneuver, but they made the success or failure of that maneuver all the more critical for the Marine Corps. By this time, the Joint Army-Navy Board had decided that the major United States Pacific naval base would be Pearl Harbor and San Diego and that responsibility for garrisoning the Philippines belonged to the army.[7]

With the return of the marine brigade from Guantanamo in April and May, the organization of the units which were to take part in the winter maneuver went rapidly. On 30 June, the commandant informed Secretary Daniels that five of the six companies of the fixed defense regiment had been formed at Philadelphia. These included artillery, mining, engineer, and signal companies, organized according to plans already drawn up by the advance base school. The commandant planned to assemble the sixth company of the fixed regiment on 15 July, using men drawn from the recruit depots. Biddle also declared that the 3-inch landing gun battery for the mobile regiment had been organized and was being trained at the New York Navy Yard, while the same regiment's automatic rifle company was training at the marine barracks in Washington, D.C. The four infantry companies for the mobile regiment, which required no specialized training, would be formed, according to Biddle, "as has heretofore been the case when the Marine Corps has been called on to furnish expeditions; that is, by an equitable reduction in the number of men at the . . . navy yards on the Atlantic coast, utilizing so far as possible the companies already organized, and adding to each organization a small proportion of those men who have nearest completed their fourteen weeks' course of training at the recruit depots."[8]

The assembly of supplies and equipment kept pace with the organization of the brigade. Guided by Commandant Biddle's requests, the bureaus issued materiel to the advance base school, either from their existing stocks or from new purchases. On 23 May, for example, Rear Admiral Nathan C. Twining, chief of the bureau of ordnance, reported that he had already agreed to spend $50,000 for advance base equipment and now "will probably be able to supply for advance base purposes approximately $100,000" from available bureau funds.[9]

In spite of these additional purchases, the marines had to depend heavily on what was on hand, much of which was obsolete, especially for such crucial items as 5-inch and 3-inch naval guns and mines. Only after much difficulty did the marines obtain one high-powered 5-inch 51-caliber naval gun for experimental purposes and prevail on the bureau of ordnance to borrow two 4.7-inch heavy field guns from the army for testing as possible antiship weapons. The fixed regiment's 5-inch battery had four 5-inch 40-caliber guns, which were less effective against ships. The bureaus flatly refused to purchase draft animals for the mobile regiment's field guns, despite marine protests that "it is . . . neither

desirable nor practical to land men from the fleet to take the place of animals for this purpose."[10]

The marines had better fortune securing transports and landing craft. At Biddle's suggestion, the Navy Department refitted the receiving ship *Hancock* at the New York Navy Yard as a marine transport. The marines planned to use the *Hancock*, a 6,000-ton former ocean liner, to carry the fixed regiment and the brigade headquarters, while the existing smaller navy transport, the *Prairie*, would embark the mobile regiment. After jurisdictional wrangling between the bureaus of ordnance and construction and repair, the Navy Department collected or built an odd assortment of landing craft. These included, in addition to the small boats of the transports, two 24-foot cutters, two motor sailing launches, two steam launches, a large steel lighter with a derrick specially constructed for landing heavy guns, and four Lundin lifeboats which could be rigged together in pairs to support rafts.[11]

By mid-summer, most of the equipment and supplies for the fixed regiment had been assembled at Philadelphia and the troops had begun their arduous training. Captain Frederick M. Wise, commander of Company I, the 3-inch naval gun company, recalled:

> The easy days at Philadelphia were over. With drills and four hours a day schooling, we didn't get out of the yard until four-thirty in the afternoon. Then we had to study at night. . . .
>
> Hours every day in the yard we had to haul those three-inch naval guns around. We had to build a portable railroad. We had to dig pits. We had to build gun-platforms. We had to mount the guns. And then, when we had it all done, we had to tear the whole business down and do it all over again.[12]

In September, when the *Hancock* arrived at Philadelphia, the marines added embarkation and disembarkation drills to their training schedule.

By this time, planning for the exercise was well under way. In late July, the General Board and Assistant Secretary Franklin D. Roosevelt selected Culebra, a small island 16 miles east of Puerto Rico, as the advance base site for the maneuver. During the next two months, the General Board worked out the overall schedule and objectives for the problem; Rear Admiral Charles J. Badger, commander-in-chief, Atlantic Fleet, prepared detailed plans for the joint activities of the fleet and the brigade; and the advance base school drew up the plans for the fortification and defense of Culebra.[13]

The resulting scenario and schedule of activities, approved by Secretary Daniels on 20 October, assumed that a European power, designated Red, would declare war on the United States (Blue) on 15 December 1913. The Blue Atlantic Fleet, with its train, would concentrate at Culebra to meet the advancing Red fleet. On 7 January 1914, the Blue fleet would return to the East Coast to counter a sudden threatened attack by a Red detachment. The Blue train would remain at Culebra, and on 8 January the Blue advance base force, the actual marine brigade, would arrive on Culebra and establish its defenses. On 18 January, a presumed Red light cruiser task force, accompanied by a fast transport carrying about one thousand troops, would appear off Culebra, its mission to destroy the Blue advance base and capture the train. From 18 to 23 January, the U.S. Atlantic Fleet, playing the role of the Red aggressor force, would conduct a series of simulated attacks on the advance base brigade, including a landing of sailors and marines. These joint exercises would end on the 23rd and the marines then would remain on the island for target practice and other training, and a possible second attack by the fleet, reembarking for home on 9 February.[14]

Although the aggressor force in this exercise was code-named Red, the scenario was clearly derived from the Navy's Black plan for war with Germany. Since the turn of the century, a long series of Navy War College studies and plans had assumed that in a naval war with Germany, "Culebra is the key to the Western Atlantic and Caribbean regions," either as a concentration point for the U.S. fleet or an advance base for the attacking German fleet. In fact, as is now known, German war plans for naval operations against the United States called for the early seizure of Culebra. For the marines, then, the forthcoming maneuver was a rehearsal for probable wartime operations as well as a test of their organization and capability to carry out the advance base mission.[15]

Marine preliminary activities for the maneuver began on 1 November when Captain Earl H. Ellis, who had recently completed a study of advance base problems at the Navy War College, left for Culebra to reconnoiter the artillery positions and camp sites designated in the advance base school defense plan. Upon his return, Ellis confirmed the feasibility of the planned deployments. While Ellis was still at Culebra, the Navy Department, as a result of renewed diplomatic pressure by the Wilson administration on the Huerta regime in Mexico, pushed forward by a month the formation of the mobile regiment. On 27 November, the regiment, commanded by Lieutenant Colonel John A. Lejeune, sailed from Philadelphia on the *Prairie* for Pensacola. From Pensacola, the regiment could deploy either to Mexico or to Culebra.[16]

At Philadelphia, the fixed regiment, commanded by Lieutenant Colonel Charles G. Long, began loading its equipment on board the *Hancock* on 18 December. This embarkation had many modern features, including the appointment of a single embarkation officer and a fairly sophisticated combat loading plan, which was partially disrupted by the last-minute arrival of some of the supplies. Despite difficulties in moving the heavy equipment from the warehouse to the pier, the regiment had finished embarking all of its men and materiel by noon on 3 January. Besides the six companies and staff of the fixed regiment, the *Hancock* carried the brigade commander, Colonel George Barnett, his staff, and the brigade hospital. Also attached to brigade headquarters and embarked on the *Hancock* was a marine aviation detachment of two officer-pilots and ten enlisted mechanics with two primitive wood and fabric pusher biplanes borrowed from the navy.[17]

At Pensacola, the mobile regiment had

spent a cold, damp December, warmed for some of the younger officers by what Lieutenant Colonel Lejeune characterized as "a very gay time with the girls." On 19 December, Lejeune received orders from Headquarters Marine Corps to embark his men so as to sail on 3 January. In contrast to the fixed regiment with its heavy equipment, the more lightly armed mobile regiment had little difficulty in loading on board the *Prairie*. By 7:00 P.M. on 3 January, Lejeune could report his four infantry companies, automatic rifle company, and landing gun company all embarked.[18]

By 4 January, both the *Hancock* and *Prairie* were steaming toward Culebra. Conditions on both ships were crowded and uncomfortable. The appropriations for refitting the *Hancock* had run out, and the job was only partially completed. Compounding the difficulties, and despite the Marine Corps emphasis on serving on board navy ships, the majority of the fixed regiment had not been to sea before. Most of the men suffered from seasickness. Long remarked, "The carelessness of seasick men resulted in bad odors," but observed that the ship's food was well prepared and served "considering the circumstances." Life on the *Prairie* was, if anything, even worse. Lejeune bluntly stated that the ship "is unfitted for use as a transport." His 2d Battalion commander, Major Wendell C. Neville, compared the marine junior officers' quarters to "a cheap Bowery lodging house."[19]

Except for the creature discomforts, the voyage was uneventful. Most of the higher-ranking officers spent much of their free time speculating on who would be chosen the new commandant. In November, Major General Biddle had announced his intention to retire, and Colonel Barnett and Lieutenant Colonel Lejeune, both of whom had powerful political support, were active candidates for the position. Secretary Daniels had delayed naming Biddle's successor until Congress passed a law limiting the commandant's term in office to four years. As the transports steamed toward Culebra, all marines knew that Daniel's decision was imminent. Most informed observers, including Lejeune, who was aware of his own relatively junior rank, believed Colonel Barnett to be the front-runner. Nevertheless, for both Barnett and Lejeune, successful performance in the Culebra maneuver was all the more imperative.[20]

On 9 January, a day later than scheduled, the *Hancock* and *Prairie* dropped anchor off Culebra. Both regiments began disembarking the following day. Because the *Hancock* was too large to safely enter the principal anchorages of Culebra, the marines of the fixed regiment had to transfer themselves and their equipment onto their landing craft in the open sea. Although hampered by contrary winds and the unsuitability of some of the craft, the regiment by 18 January had managed to move its men and equipment to shore, haul its guns and materiel to the headlands where its batteries were to be located, blast out gun pits, and mount the guns, as well as setting up camp and completing mine firing stations and other installations. The fixed defense regiment was deployed along the southwestern and southern shores of the small, mountainous island, with the 5-inch and 3-inch naval gun batteries and the mine fields positioned to protect Great Harbor, a deep indentation in the southern shore where the hypothetical fleet train was presumed to have taken refuge.

As with the embarkation, the disembarkation of the mobile regiment went more easily. Lejeune positioned one of his infantry battalions on the southeastern tip of Culebra to protect the flank of Great Harbor, with one company located on the offshore islet of Culebrita. The other infantry battalion, supported by the automatic rifle company, deployed along the western and northwestern shores of Culebra, covering the most likely landing beaches. Lejeune placed his 3-inch landing gun company on a 480-foot hill from which it could support the infantry defenses. The marines of the mobile regiment dug trenches commanding the beaches, cleared fields of fire, and cut trails connecting their various defensive positions. They installed barbed wire entanglements, and the automatic rifle company, applying a lesson from the Russo-Japanese War, erected bomb-proof roofs over several of its gun positions. The marines were hampered in their work by the hard rocky soil, the tough tropical vegetation, and inadequate tools. Lejeune complained:

Machetes were of no value, the edges turning after slight use and the handles cracking. The picks were made of soft metal, and the scythes were useless for the same reason. The metal of the drills was too soft, the wire cutters did not cut.[21]

While the two regiments established their positions on shore, Barnett set up brigade headquarters at the abandoned U.S. naval station near the head of Great Harbor. By the eighteenth, the marine defenses were ready. Everyone heaped praise on the way the men had worked. Barnett later recalled:

It was a never-ending joy to be associated with men and officers who worked night and day as loyally, as incessantly under great difficulties and with as much *esprit de corps* as these men did. It was certainly a perfect joy to see them work. They dug and they blasted and pulled and dragged these guns up those mountains in a perfectly phenomenal manner.[22]

On the night of the 18th, ships of the Atlantic Fleet which had arrived off Culebra two days earlier, began the joint exercise. For the next two days and nights, the fleet conducted a series of simulated attacks on the marine defenses. The destroyers made day and night reconnaissances and attempted to sweep the mine fields. Acting the part of enemy light cruisers, the battleships simulated the bombardment of the marine shore batteries. Simultaneously, the marine mining company tracked the enemy ships and pretended to detonate mines under them. During the days, the marine aviators flew reconnaissance and spotting missions over the attacking ships. Marine gunners blazed away with such enthusiasm that Barnett found it necessary to order that:

Owing to the expenditure of the very limited supply of blank ammunition for the Five-Inch

Batteries, . . . those batteries will . . . simulate fire by firing one blank charge as the first round. To simulate succeeding rounds they will fire smoke pots in the afternoon and green stars from Very's pistol at night.[23]

The climax of the joint exercise occurred in the early morning hours of 21 January, when the mixed regiment of twelve hundred sailors and marines from the fleet attempted a landing. For this part of the maneuver, Rear Admiral Badger departed from his general policy for the exercise of not assigning umpires or determining victory or defeat in any particular engagement. Badger appointed Captain William S. Sims of the destroyer flotilla and eight other navy officers umpires for the landing.

Shortly before dawn on the 21st, the assault regiment, supported by the guns of the destroyers of the 6th Division, began its landing at Firewood Bay, on the western side of Culebra. The marines reacted rapidly. They placed heavy rifle, machine gun, and artillery fire on the approaching boatloads of sailors and marines. Observing the action with Lejeune, Sims reported that the landing boats "were plainly visible . . . from all occupied positions, . . . due partly to the moon, which was one-quarter full, to the searchlights of the bombarding vessels playing on the hills above, to a bonfire fired by the defense, and to the fact that all bluejackets were in white uniform." As the boats reached shore, Lejeune reported, the attackers "huddled together in masses along the narrow strip of beach, . . . literally surrounded by a semicircle of fire." The destroyers simulated a heavy bombardment that, in Sim's judgment, would have possibly silenced the marine landing gun battery, which was firing from a dangerously exposed position; but the chief umpire concluded that "it is improbable that the landing force could have effected a successful landing in sufficient numbers to have made any impression on the defense." Nevertheless, as a result of a prior agreement with Barnett, Sims allowed the naval force to continue its attack from the beach. At 0700 he ordered a ceasefire and declared a victory for the defense, which had held its main line of resistance and maneuvered its reserves effectively to contain enemy breakthroughs.[24]

Although the landing and its repulse were the highlights of the maneuver, the marines of the advance base brigade remained on Culebra for two more weeks. The joint exercise with the fleet continued through the 23rd with additional simulated bombardments and mine sweepings. Also on the 23rd, a three hundred fifty-man fleet marine battalion, in a second landing attempt, overran the mobile regiment company on Culebra. After the end of the joint exercise and the departure of the fleet, the fixed regiment conducted target practice and experimental firings of the 5-inch 51-caliber naval gun and the army 4.7-inch field gun. The marines concluded from these tests that both guns deserved further consideration as advance base weapons. The mining company attempted to fire its mines, but only succeeded in detonating one; the connecting cables to most of the mines had leaked and short-circuited the firing mechanism. During the same period, the mobile regiment conducted infantry maneuvers and field artillery target practice. Two special boards of marine and naval officers made studies of alternate advance base sites in the Culebra area and reviewed and elaborated on the existing Culebra defense plan. Early in February, good news arrived for Barnett. At 3:00 one morning, he recalled later, his aide "came running into my room yelling like a wild Indian, telling me I had been appointed Major General Commandant of the Marine Corps." An impromptu celebration parade by pajama-clad officers and men followed in the hot and rainy darkness, concluding with champagne from the *Prairie's* mess.[25]

Even as the target practice and training continued, the marines began dismantling their batteries and moving their heavy equipment back on board the transports. By 9 February, as originally planned, both regiments had completed reembarkation, and the *Hancock* and *Prairie* sailed for the United States. The brigade arrived at Pensacola on 15 February. Barnett then left the brigade to assume his new duties as commandant in Washington, turning over command to Lejeune.

The various elements of the brigade went in different directions from Pensacola, because of the continuing tension with Mexico. Part of the mobile regiment soon sailed on the *Prairie* for Vera Cruz, where, as Lejeune wryly put it, "they will wait for something to happen."[26] The fixed regiment went to Mobile and New Orleans to take part in Mardi Gras festivities. Captain Frederick H. Delano, adjutant of the mobile regiment, looked on these visits as "not good for discipline, but suppose they have to be done to keep the service in the public eye."[27]

For the Marine Corps, the Culebra maneuver was significant in many regards. The maneuver demonstrated that the marines could organize an advance base force on short notice and carry out all the complex steps of an advance base operation. The marines had learned many practical lessons, including the need for expeditionary packaging of supplies and equipment, a more accurate assessment of the proper number and types of landing craft, the importance of adequate ground transportation once on shore, and the value of aircraft for reconnaissance and possibly for bombing enemy ships. Many of the practices employed by the marines in the maneuver, such as combat loading of vessels, would become mainstays of later amphibious doctrine. Participating in the Culebra maneuver, besides commandant-designate Barnett, were two other future commandants of the Marine Corps: Lieutenant Colonel Lejeune, commanding the mobile regiment, and Major Wendell C. Neville, commander of one of Lejeune's battalions. Captain Earl H. Ellis, the brigade intelligence officer, would become one of the Marine Corps's most influential early articulators of amphibious doctrine. Most important, a marine advance base force at last came into being. The two regiments of the brigade, although diverted to expeditionary duty at Vera Cruz and later in Haiti, the Dominican Republic, and Cuba, maintained a continuous existence until replaced by the East Coast Expeditionary Force following World War One. It can be said, then, that the advance base brigade at Culebra was the forerunner of the modern fleet force.

Notes

[1] This paper is based on the following sources: Records of the General Board of the Navy, Operational Archives Branch, Naval Historical Division, Washington, D.C., particularly Files 408 and 432 for the years 1900–1915; Records of the U.S. Marine Corps, RG 127, U.S. National Archives, especially File 1975 for the years 1900–1915; Black War Plan, Ref. No. 5y, War Portfolio No. 1, General Board Records (hereafter *Black War Plan*); General Records of the Navy Department, RG 80, U.S. National Archives; Capt. Earl H. Ellis, Report of a Reconnaissance Made of Culebra Island and Adjacent Cays, 8–23 Nov 1913, with Enclosures, USMC Records, FRC, Suitland, Md. (hereafter Ellis, *Reconnaissance Report*); Biographical and Subject Files, Reference Section, History and Museums Division, Headquarters Marine Corps; George Barnett Papers in Personal Papers Collection, History and Museums Division, Headquarters Marine Corps; John A. Lejeune Papers, William F. Fullam Papers, William S. Sims Papers, and Josephus Daniels Papers, Library of Congress; Annual Published Reports of the Secretary of the Navy and the Commandant of the Marine Corps, 1900–1915; *Army and Navy Journal*, 1900–1915.

The following secondary sources have been consulted: Robert Debs Heinl, Jr., *Soldiers of the Sea* (Annapolis, 1962); Frank O. Hough, Verle E. Ludwig, and Henry I. Shaw, Jr., *Pearl Harbor to Guadalcanal*, Vol. I of *History of U.S. Marine Operations in World War II* (Washington, 1958); Jeter A. Isely and Philip A. Crowl, *The United States Marines, 1775–1975* (New York, 1976); Raymond G. O'Connor, "The U.S. Marines in the Twentieth Century: Amphibious Warfare and Doctrinal Debates," *Military Affairs*, 38 (Oct 1974): 97–103. We are grateful to Dr. Allan R. Millett for permitting us to examine the pertinent draft chapters of his forthcoming history of the U.S. Marine Corps.

[2] President, General Board to Secretary of the Navy, 6 Oct 1900, and BGen Comdt, USMC, to President, General Board, 22 Nov 1900, File 408, GB Records. For general development of the early advance base force, see Graham A. Cosmas and Jack Shulimson, "Continuity and Consensus: the Evolution of the Marine Advance Base Force, 1900–1924" (paper delivered at Citadel Conference on War and Diplomacy, 1977).

[3] Proceedings of the General Board, vol. 5 (1913), pp. 10, 18, 22, 32; President, General Board to Secretary of the Navy, 5 Feb 1913, and Secretary

of the Navy, 1st Endorsement, to MGen Cmdt, 5 Feb 1913, File 1975–10, RG 127.

[4] MGen Cmdt, USMC, to Secretary of the Navy, 24 Feb 1913, File 5503, RG 80; President, General Board to Secretary of the Navy, 8 Mar 1913, File 432, GB Records; MGen Cmdt, USMC, to Secretary of the Navy, 10 Apr 1913, File 1975–10, RG 127.

[5] Report of Inspection of Navy Yard, Philadelphia, conducted 25–28 Mar 1913, from Board of Inspection, Navy Yard, Philadelphia, to Secretary of the Navy, 19 Apr 1913, File 1975–10, RG 127, and Permanent File Binder No. 27, RG 38, Board of Inspection for Shore Stations.

[6] See Aide for Inspections, memos to Secretary of the Navy, 1 May, 23 June, and 28 June 1913, File 432, GB Records; MGen Cmdt, USMC, to Secretary of the Navy, 17 May 1913, File 1975–10, RG 127; MGen Cmdt, to Secretary of the Navy, 7 June 1913, File 432, GB Records.

[7] President, General Board, memo to Secretary of the Navy, 21 July 1913, File 432, GB Records.

[8] MGen Cmdt, USMC, memo to Secretary of the Navy, 30 June 1913, File 408, CB Records.

[9] Chief, Bureau of Ordnance, memo to Navy Department (Materiel), 23 May 1913, File 1975–10, RG 127.

[10] Chief, Bureau of Ordnance, memo to Navy Department (Materiel), 26 May 1913, and HQMC, Memo to Secretary of the Navy (Personnel), 11 July 1913, File 1975–10, RG 127; Senior Member, General Board, to Secretary of the Navy, 26 July 1913, File 408, GB Records.

[11] MGen Cmdt, USMC, memo to Secretary of the Navy, 10 April 1913; Chief, Bureau of Navigation, memo to Council of Aides, 24 April 1913; and Navy Department, memo to Bureau of Ordnance, 21 May 1913; File 1975–10, RG 127. Senior Member Present, General Board, memo to Secretary of the Navy, 26 July 1913, File 432, GB Records; Bureau of Construction and Repair, memo to Navy Department (Materiel), 15 Aug 1913, File 5103, RG 80.

[12] Frederic M. Wise, *A Marine Tells It to You* (New York, 1929), p. 119.

[13] Acting Secretary of the Navy, to President, General Board, 15 July 1913, File 1975–10, RG 127; 2d Senior Member, General Board, to Secretary of the Navy, 26 July 1913, with Navy Department Approval, 29 July 1913, File 432, GB Records; C. E. Vreeland, memo to Secretary of the Navy, 13 Sept 1913, Subj: Comprehensive Plan for Work of Advance Base Expedition from date of Embarkation to Completion of Work, File 1975–80–20, RG 127; Charles G. Long, memo to MGen Cmdt, 5 Oct 1913, forwarding Advance Base School plan for defense of the Island of Culebra, in Ellis, *Reconnaissance Report*; U.S. Atlantic Fleet, memo, 13 Oct 1913, re: Joint Exercise of Fleet and Ad-

vance Base Detachment, Winter 1914, in Ellis, *Reconnaissance Report*, hereafter *Atlantic Fleet Plan*.

[14] *Atlantic Fleet Plan*.

[15] *Black War Plan*, p. 1, and "Studies and Conclusions of Naval War College, 1901–13," App. D, *Black War Plan*. For references to the German plans, see Richard W. Turk, "The United States Navy and the Taking of Panama, 1901–03," *Military Affairs* 38 (October 74): 92–96; and John A. S. Grenville and George Berkeley Young, *Politics, Strategy, and American Diplomacy: Studies in Foreign Policy, 1873–1917* (New Haven, Conn., 1966), pp. 305–07.

[16] Ellis, *Reconnaissance Report* and LtCol John A. Lejeune, Report to Brigade Comdr, Subj: Maneuvers and Operations, 31 Jan 1914, File 1975–80–20, RG 127, hereafter Lejeune, *2d Regiment Report*.

[17] 1st Adv Base Regt, Order No. 1, 17 Dec 1913, File 1975–80–20, RG 127, and LtCol Charles G. Long, Report to Brigade Comdr, Subj: Operations of 1st Regiment from Dec 18, 1913 to Jan 25, 1914, 30 Jan 1914, File 1975–80–20, RG 127, hereafter Long, *1st Regiment Report*.

[18] Lejeune, *2d Regiment Report*; and LtCol John A. Lejeune, to Augustine Lejeune, 30 Dec 1913, Lejeune Papers.

[19] Long, *1st Regiment Report*; Lejeune, *2d Regiment Report*; CO 2d Battalion, 2d Advance Base Regiment, Report to CO, 2d Regiment, Subj: Maneuvers and Operations, 27 Jan 1914, File 1975–80–20, RG 127.

[20] Josephus Daniels, *The Wilson Era: Years of Peace, 1910–1917* (Chapel Hill, N.C., 1944), pp. 322–324; *Army and Navy Journal* 6 (Dec 1913): 437; Folder, "Candidacy for Commandant, 1900–1913," Lejeune Papers.

[21] Lejeune, *2d Regiment Report*.

[22] U.S. Congress, House, Committee on Naval Affairs, *Hearings on Estimates Submitted by the Secretary of the Navy, 1915*, 63d Congress, 1st Session, 7 Dec 1914, p. 446.

[23] 1st Advance Base Brigade, Brigade Order No. 6, 19 Jan 1914, File 1975–80–20, RG 127.

[24] Chief Observer, memo to CinC Atlantic Fleet, Subj: Report of Chief Observer on Landing Operations by the Fleet on 21 January 1914, 23 Jan 1914, File 1975–80–30, RG 127; LtCol John A. Lejeune, Report to Brigade Commander, "Battle of Firewood Bay," 24 Jan 1914, File 1975–80–20, RG 127.

[25] Col George Barnett, memo to CinC Atlantic Fleet, Subj: Report of Maneuvers and Operations from January 3 to January 24, 1914, 3 Feb 1914, File 1975–80–20, RG 127; Lt Col Charles G. Long, Report to Brigade Comdr, Subj: Target and Mine Practice and Reembarkation of 1st Regiment, Jan 24 to Feb 8, 1914, File 1975–80–20, RG 127. Quote is from MGen George Barnett, "Soldier and Sailor Too" (History and Museums Division, HQMC), p. 8.

[26] LtCol John A. Lejeune to Augustine Lejeune, 5 Feb 1914, Lejeune Papers.

[27] Frederick H. Delano to Mrs. Delano, 14 Feb 1914, Frederick H. Delano Papers, Military History Research Collection, Carlisle Barracks, Carlisle, Pa.

Roots of Deployment—Vera Cruz, 1914

BY COLONEL JAMES H. ALEXANDER, USMC

Marines probably remember the 1914 landing in Vera Cruz chiefly for its assembly of legendary figures: Smedley Butler, John Quick, Albertus Catlin, Julian Smith, Logan Feland, "Fritz" Wise, James Breckinridge, Randolph Berkeley, "Hik'em Hiram" Bearss, and four future commandants—Lejeune, Neville, Russell, and Vandegrift. The Vera Cruz military operation itself was unremarkable. Politically, the intervention was a disaster. Yet, as we wrestle today with problems of rapid deployment and strategic mobility, we might well benefit from a revisit to that obscure operation in 1914.

Consider first the issues that currently crowd the agenda of Marine Corps planners: readiness, forward deployment, time-phased force deployment planning, composite force building, strategic lift, joint operations, sustainability, urban warfare, unit integrity, roles/missions, and interservice competition. None of these issues is new. All of them were operative in the Vera Cruz expedition. In fact, the rapid deployment of nearly half the existing Marine Corps and virtually the entire U.S. Atlantic Fleet to Mexico, fully integrated and ready to fight, provides us with a high standard of excellence to match years later. The 1914 Vera Cruz operation, as a deployment model, is worthy of reexamination.

The Vera Cruz crisis evolved from the antagonism of two stubborn men, General Victoriano Huerta of Mexico and President

Marine Corps Gazette (November 1982): 71–79. Reprinted by permission.

Woodrow Wilson of the United States. Both assumed leadership of their respective countries in early 1913—Wilson by national election under a domestic reform platform, Huerta by murdering the revolutionary leader Francisco Madera. Wilson's sensitivities were shocked by Huerta's brutality. "I will not recognize a government of butchers," he declared. The removal of Huerta thus became the cornerstone of Wilson's Mexican policy. Wilson was convinced that Huerta comprised the sole obstacle to the natural ascendency of political democracy in Mexico—a questionable premise. Wilson pursued this objective with all the righteous obsession of a crusade. When months passed and Huerta remained in power, Wilson announced a policy of "watchful waiting." In effect, the president was waiting for an opportunity—a provocation—to justify intervention by force of arms.

Wilson's opportunity occurred on 9 April 1914 when a group of American sailors was detained by federal soldiers in Tampico. Although Mexican officials quickly released the men and offered apologies, Rear Admiral Henry T. Mayo, commanding U.S. forces in the vicinity of Tampico, demanded that the Mexicans hoist an American flag and fire a 21-gun salute. A "contest of protocols and ultimatums" between the two governments followed. Wilson refused to compromise; Huerta, realizing that to fire the salute would be political suicide, refused to go beyond an official apology. Wilson met with his Cabinet on 14 April and directed Secretary of the Navy Josephus Daniels to concentrate most of the Atlantic Fleet in the waters off east Mexico for a show of force and as augmentation of the naval units already on station. Six days later with no resolution to the crisis in sight, Wilson sought congressional approval to employ armed force in Mexico for "affronts and indignities committed against the United States."

At this point the State Department advised the president that the German steamer *Ypiranga*, loaded with arms and ammunition for Huerta's forces, was scheduled to arrive in Vera Cruz on 21 April. This was an unpleasant shock to Wilson, but he moved swiftly. Assured of congressional support, confident that the European powers were too distracted by the Balkan crisis to interfere, and convinced to the end that the Mexican people would welcome American troops as liberators, the president directed Daniels to telegraph orders to Rear Admiral Frank F. Fletcher at Vera Cruz: "Seize customs house. Do not permit war supplies to be delivered to Huerta government or to any other party."

Fletcher complied almost immediately. The landing party, however, was taken under fire by a mixed bag of militia, cadets, and citizens. The ensuing street fighting lasted three days. In the end, nineteen Americans were killed and seventy-five wounded. Hundreds of Mexicans died. President Wilson recoiled in horror at the news of casualties. There were anti-American riots and demonstrations throughout Mexico and, indeed, all of Latin America. And although many Americans clamored for an "on to Mexico City" campaign, Wilson quickly cast about for ways to cut his political losses. He was rescued from his dilemma by an offer for mediation from "the ABC countries": Argentina, Brazil, and Chile. The mediation conference itself accomplished little, but it did extricate Wilson from an unfavorable international position while enabling him to maintain pressure on Huerta by holding Vera Cruz, a major source of revenue and arms for Mexico. Huerta finally resigned in mid-July 1914. American troops evacuated Vera Cruz in November. Mexican-American relations remained tense for years.

Vera Cruz was Wilson's first venture into foreign affairs. His basic mistake was the failure to realize that compulsive modification of political behavior by armed force is a form of diplomacy least likely to produce long-term favorable results. Yet as flawed as Wilson's political objectives in Mexico may have been, there was nothing faulty about the military deployments executed in support of that policy. Troops and ships were moved with commendable dispatch to positions threatening Mexico from three sides. We can learn from this.

The buildup of forces in response to the Mexican crisis occurred in this fashion. Even before the Tampico incident, the president had directed forward deployment of certain forces along the border and off the principal Mexican ports. Army units were assembled on the Rio Grande and in Galveston. Fletcher was off Vera Cruz with the battleships *Florida* and *Utah*. Mayo had the *Connecticut* and *Minnesota* near Tampico. Major Smedley Butler had been ordered to deploy his battalion from Panama to join Rear Admiral Fletcher's force off Verz Cruz as early as January. Neither of the two provisional advance base regiments, which had been formed for fleet maneuvers in the Caribbean and on the island of Culebra in January 1914, returned to Philadelphia after the maneuvers; instead they were directed to Gulf Coast ports to await further orders. "None of us will get very far north until the Mexican question is settled," wrote Captain Frederick Delano to his parents in late January.

Delano was the adjutant for Lieutenant Colonel Wendell C. Neville's 2d Advance Base Regiment at Pensacola. In early March the unit was ordered to divest itself of its advance base equipment and embark four rifle companies aboard the small transport *Prairie* for deployment to Mexico. The *Prairie* arrived off Vera Cruz on 9 March. Lieutenant Colonel Neville and his three hundred riflemen reported to Rear Admiral Fletcher for duty, absorbing Butler's battalion in the process.

Following the Cabinet meeting of 14 April, Secretary Daniels directed Rear Admiral

Charles J. Badger, commanding the Atlantic Fleet, to proceed to Mexico with all available battleships. Badger promptly got underway from Hampton Roads aboard his flagship, USS *Arkansas*, accompanied by *Vermont, New Hampshire,* and *New Jersey. Michigan* left Philadelphia on 15 April; *Louisiana* followed from New York City the next day. *South Carolina* steamed from Santo Domingo in time to join Badger's main body as they rounded Key West. These were heady days for America's new "20th Century Navy," riding the crest of an unprecedented ten-year wave of peacetime shipbuilding and imbued with the nationalistic, expansionist spirit of Alfred Thayer Mahan.

It was a period of transition, too, for the U.S. Marines, although they lacked an articulate prophet like Mahan to illuminate new roles and missions. For years the General Board of the Navy under Admiral George Dewey had been prodding the Corps toward development of an advance base force mission. Time and again, however, the marines had been called out for expeditionary duty ("colonial infantry" some called it) in China, the Philippines, Panama, Cuba, and Nicaragua. Progress in defining a new role was slow. The Corps remained at the crossroads as deployment orders began to be dispatched in mid-April.

Who made the deployment decisions involving marine units in 1914? The Major General Commandant, George Barnett, had been in the job only since 14 February. His staff consisted of three colonels (the adjutant and inspector, the quartermaster, and the paymaster) plus a handful of aides and assistants. Barnett did bring in a "field marine," Lieutenant Colonel Eli K. Cole, to be his assistant commandant, but, overall, it was hardly an operational staff. The commandant was responsible to the secretary of the navy for providing trained and equipped forces in readiness for service with the fleet. Compared with most of his predecessors, Barnett enjoyed fair relations with the navy. He was the first commandant to serve on the General Board and as a member of the "Special Council of Aides" to the secretary of the navy.

And yet it is doubtful that Barnett played too significant a role in the Vera Cruz deployments. More likely, he advised the secretary as to the status and availability of his marines. Most deployment orders during that crisis seem to have originated from Rear Admiral Bradley Fiske, aide for operations, or Rear Admiral Victor Blue, chief of the Bureau of Navigation.

The Navy Department's mobilization directives of 14 April caused more marines to converge on east Mexico. Major Albertus Catlin, as fleet marine officer for Rear Admiral Badger, represented a potential landing force of one thousand marines distributed among the detachments aboard the seven battleships en route from the Atlantic. On 15 April, Colonel Lejeune with his small staff of the Advance Base Force Brigade and Lieutenant Colonel Charles G. Long's 1st Regiment embarked aboard the transport *Hancock* in New Orleans and sailed for Tampico. Actually, "reembarked" is a more appropriate word. Lejeune and Long had just undergone the demoralizing experience of completely offloading *Hancock* per orders to free the ship for use in emergency evacuation of U.S. refugees from Mexico. The debarkation accomplished, there came immediate countermanding orders to reload the marines back aboard, a classic "green-side-out/brown-side-out" drill. There was one significant difference in the reembarkation: the sailing orders directed the marines to deploy "without advance base outfit." In view of similar orders issued to Neville's 2d Regiment when they went aboard the *Prairie* a month earlier, it appears that the pendulum had reversed its course. Regardless of the success of the winter's maneuvers in Culebra, there would be no advance base operations for the marines in Mexico. As Captain Wise remarked, "All the Advance Base business in which we had been drilling and maneuvering for months had been dropped. We were plain infantry now."

At this point in the Mexican crisis the focal point was Tampico. Smedley Butler, ever the opportunist, managed to detach himself from Neville's command to join Rear Admiral Mayo and Lejeune at Tampico. Mayo decided in a council of war that Lejeune would command a combined landing force consisting of Long's 1st Regiment, a naval regiment, and a mixed force under Butler. But it was not to be.

Vera Cruz was the better strategic point. Sandbars at Tampico would prevent most of Mayo's warships from supporting the landing up the river; at Vera Cruz the landing force could go ashore directly into the port, well within range of the guns of Fletcher's fleet. Vera Cruz was also the historical point of forcible entry into Mexico, from John Hawkins and Sir Francis Drake in 1568 to Winfield Scott's tremendously successful assault in 1847. Then there was the matter of the imminent arrival of the German steamer *Ypiranga*, with its cargo of two hundred machine guns and 15 million rounds of ammunition.

Secretary Daniels wired a warning order to Fletcher at Vera Cruz at 0300 on the 21st. He also vectored Badger's Atlantic Fleet battleships to Vera Cruz via Tampico. Mayo was out of telegraphic reach from Washington that night. Fletcher had to relay the change in plans: not only was the Tampico operation off, but Fletcher now needed most of Mayo's warships and all of his marines at Vera Cruz immediately. This was a crushing disappointment for Mayo. The marines, however, didn't wait around. Butler, predictably, was the first to leave, sailing at flank speed on the scout cruiser *Chester*. Lejeune and Long followed on the slower *Hancock*, arriving twelve hours after Butler and missing the hottest part of the action.

Admiral Fletcher did not wait for the augmentation forces from Tampico. Receiving Daniels's execution order at 0600 on 21 April, he launched his assault before noon. The landing party consisted of a naval brigade of marines and bluejackets under command of Captain William Rees Rush, USN, commanding officer of *Florida*. Neville's understrength regiment (more than half of his troops were still in Pensacola at the time) was augmented by a provisional battalion of marines from *Florida* and *Utah* under Major George

C. Reid, the marine officer on Fletcher's staff. Neville's operations order (now displayed in the Marine Corps Museum) was a model of simplicity: "Five hundred Mexican troops with five three-inch field pieces occupy Vera Cruz," it began. Berkeley's battalion was ordered to seize the roundhouse and rail sidings; Reid's battalion, to take the cable office, power plant, and customs warehouses. Most of the marine casualties sustained at Vera Cruz occurred in the ranks of these two battalions. The objectives were seized. At 1800 Fletcher wired Daniels, "About 1,000 Marines and sailors ashore."

Reinforcements arrived throughout the night as Daniels's forward deployment planning began to bear fruit. Butler's battalion arrived aboard *Chester* before midnight and immediately went into the lines near the roundhouse under Neville. Five of Badger's Atlantic Fleet battleships arrived next. Before dawn Major Catlin had formed their marine detachments into a provisional regiment and led them ashore. Neville transferred Reid's battalion to Catlin, and the fleet marines, fighting in a strange city, at dark and in a provisional command, did well. "It was a hot fight while it lasted," recalled Catlin.

The *Hancock* arrived in Vera Cruz before noon on 22 April (D + 1). Lejeune, reporting to Badger and Fletcher for orders, was assigned to command the provisional marine brigade, consisting of the regiments of Neville, Catlin and, now, Long. In his anxiety to get ashore and take command, Lejeune fell overboard while disembarking from the launch and very nearly drowned. It had been a long week for the "Cajun Colonel."

In the meantime, the Wilson Administration's deployment of forces to Mexico had accelerated. The nation, galvanized by the dramatic news from Vera Cruz, was swept by war fever. Crowds jammed the docks and terminals to send off the troops. The press descended on Vera Cruz. Old veterans limped to recruiting stations to offer their services in Mexico. Colonel George W. Goethals, governor of the nearly completed Panama Canal, announced that he could make the waterway usable for U.S. warships up to 20,000 tons, if necessary. The nation was on the move.

The first problem of strategic mobility was to evacuate the thousands of American refugees escaping from irate Mexicans. The immediate crush was handled by foreign warships (there were British, German, French, Spanish, and Japanese men-of-war in Mexican ports when the Vera Cruz landing occurred). On 22 April President Wilson requested Congress to authorize $500,000 for refugee relief. Several steamships were quickly chartered to evacuate the remaining refugees.

The concentration of naval forces off both coasts of Mexico continued. The hospital ship *Solace*, the mine depot ship *San Francisco*, the supply ship *Orion*, and the collier *Cyclops* all reached Vera Cruz within twenty-four hours of the landing. Eight additional battleships arrived in Mexico from various stations within the next two weeks, raising the total to nineteen, including the newly commissioned USS *New York* with its 14-inch guns and the *Mississippi* from Pensacola with the balance of Neville's regiment and six Curtiss "hydroaeroplanes" from the navy's new aeronautic section. On the west coast, Rear Admiral Thomas B. Howard commanded a force of eight cruisers and lesser ships. Colonel Joseph H. Pendleton formed the 4th Regiment of marines from various barracks and stations on the west coast. The regiment sailed aboard the *South Dakota*, *Jupiter*, and *West Virginia* for show-of-force operations off Acapulco, Mazatlan, and Guayamas. *Jupiter* was a collier; nevertheless, Captain Pritchett embarked with his three hundred marines and maintained readiness to conduct landing operations throughout what must have been three gruesomely hot months in the Gulf of California.

The army got off to a slower start. There was nothing particularly wrong with their readiness. Brigadier General Frederic Funston had his brigade well organized and equipped for operations in Mexico. He even had his own mobility assets available. The army transports *Meade*, *Sumner*, *McClellan*, and *Kilpatrick* had been in port in Galveston

for nearly a year in anticipation of orders to deploy Funston's brigade to Mexico. Yet they sat in port throughout the first three days of the fighting in Vera Cruz. President Wilson did not authorize the commitment of army forces until Rear Admiral Badger's request arrived late on 23 April. Why the hesitation? Evidently Wilson had become acutely sensitive to international perceptions during those three days. A landing party of marines and sailors from the fleet might be construed as a temporary intrusion; the occupation of a foreign port by army troops could well be considered an act of war. Nevertheless, Wilson acquiesced to Badger's request and gave Secretary of War Garrison his approval to deploy the brigade.

Brigadier General Funston's frustrations did not end with the long-awaited execution orders. The embarkation in Galveston was ragged. There was not enough room aboard the transports for the artillery. The War Department had to charter, in a hurry, two Mallory Line steamers, *Satilla* and *San Marcos*, to accommodate the shortfall two days after the main body sailed. Funston's force was also delayed en route by "the condition of the transport *Meade*." (Lejeune could have predicted this, based on his experience aboard *Meade* the previous year: "everything appeared to be out of order.") As a result, the army brigade did not disembark in Vera Cruz until 29 April, well after the shooting had ceased.

The marine deployment fared better. There were over three thousand marines ashore in Vera Cruz by the time the army arrived, and more were on the way. In fact, the largest concentration of marines in the history of the Corps, to date, was taking place. It was a credit to the small navy-marine staffs that this was accomplished without recourse to anything like a WWMCCS computer. There was no such thing as a "TIPFIDDLE" (TPFDL: Time-Phased Force Deployment List) in 1914, of course, but the reconstructed list in Table 1 may serve to illustrate the sequence, sources, modes, and timing of the deployment of twelve different marine units to Mexico.

Perhaps the best example of the intricacies

Table 1. Time-Phased Force Deployment List: Marines at Vera Cruz, 1914

Unit	CO	Deployment Date	Port of Embarkation	Ship	Port of Debarkation	Arrival Date	Remarks
Fleet Marines I 1st Battleship Div	Reid	Early 1914	Various	*Florida* *Utah*	Vera Cruz	Jan 1914	Backloaded 30 Apr
2d Regt (-)	Neville	5 Mar	Pensacola	*Prarie*	Vera Cruz	9 Mar	Landed 21 Apr
3d Bn, 2d Regt	Butler	Jan	Panama	*Chester*	Vera Cruz	21-22 Apr	via Tampico
Fleet Marines II Atlantic Fleet	Catlin	15 Apr	Norfolk, etc.	*Arkansas* Other BBs	Vera Cruz	22-23 Apr	Backloaded 30 Apr
1st Regt	Long	15 Apr	New Orleans	*Hancock*	Vera Cruz	22 Apr	incl Col Lejeune
4th Regt	Pendleton	(18 Apr) 22 Apr	(Bremerton) Mare Island	*South Dakota*	"MODLOC" via Acapulco	28 Apr	
2d Regt(-)II	Brown	21 Apr	Pensacola	*Mississippi*	Vera Cruz	24 Apr	2d Increment
4th Regt(-)II	Pritchett	22 Apr	Mare Island	*Jupiter*	"MODLOC" via Mazatlan	27 Apr	2d Increment
3d Regt	Moses	23 Apr	Philadelphia	*Morro Castle*	Vera Cruz	29 Apr	incl Col Mahoney
43d Co	Babb	28 Apr	Philadelphia	*Salem*	Vera Cruz	5 May	D + 14
7th Co., 2d Regt	Beaumont	3 May	Galveston	*Connecticut & Lebanon*	Vera Cruz	7 May	D + 16
4th Regt(-)III	McGill	4 May	Mare Island	*West Virginia*	"MODLOC" via Guayamas	10 May	D + 19

of the buildup of composite marine forces for the Mexican crisis comes from the 3d Regiment. The day after the Vera Cruz landing, a force of 861 marines assembled in Philadelphia. The men were drawn from ten different stations: the marine barracks at Portsmouth, Boston, New York, Washington, Annapolis, Norfolk, Charleston, Port Royal, Philadelphia itself, and the battleship *Ohio*. That evening, the Ward Line steamship *Morro Castle*, just chartered in New York by the Navy Department, arrived at the Philadelphia Naval Yard. In twenty-two hours, the ship was loaded with coal, provisions, 900,000 rounds of rifle ammunition, 1,000 service camp outfits (these from the USMC depot at 1100 South Broad St.) and all 861 marines, including Colonel Franklin J. Moses, commanding. The ship steamed on 23 April and arrived in Vera Cruz on the 29th, just ahead of the army flotilla. *Morro Castle*, incidentally, had been the first private ship impressed as a troop transport by President McKinley in 1898.

Colonel Mahoney was a passenger on *Morro Castle* and relieved Lejeune as brigade commander. On 4 May, Colonel L.W.T. Waller arrived on the battleship *New York* and took

the brigade for the duration; the regiments were thence commanded by Mahoney, Lejeune, and Moses. Waller, the hero/villain of Samar, was then fifty-eight and the senior line colonel in the Corps.

The arrival of Brigadier General Funston and the army touched off a classic debate over control of marine forces that could only be resolved at the presidential level. Some argued that the navy should retain control of the marines and the expedition itself. The army asked for a unified command under Funston. Lejeune sided with the army, with the caveat that the fleet marines should return to their ships. Wilson and Daniels supported this position. On 30 April the bluejackets and fleet marines (under Catlin and Reid) reembarked. The remaining marines under Waller "chopped" to the army.

The flurry of excitement over Vera Cruz subsided quickly once the "On-to-Mexico-City" fervor passed. World War One broke out that summer and eclipsed whatever was memorable about the U.S. deployment. The occupation ran its uneventful course. As a marine sentry in Vera Cruz remarked to war correspondent Jack London, "This is a hell of a war."

What is the relationship of that obscure operation in 1914 to deployment planning today? There seems to be a "continuity of issues" in Marine Corps history. Recalling the list of current agenda items, let's evaluate some potential lessons learned from Vera Cruz.

Readiness. The rapid formation of regiments on both coasts from widely separated stations with little warning was impressive. This was particularly the case of the mount-out of the 3d Regiment, when troops, supplies, and ships converged on Philadelphia from diverse sources and within twenty-four hours were loaded for combat and underway. Muster rolls for the participating units reflect very few stragglers. And the overnight rail connections to get to Philadelphia intact from, say, Charleston, reflected good planning and quick responses. Outstanding readiness, across the board!

Forward Deployment. Early decision making and positioning of forces paid off for the Navy-Marine Corps team. As early as 19 April, two days prior to the landing, Secretary Daniels could boast that there was then "either in Mexican waters, en route there or under orders to proceed, a total of 48 men-of-war, having on board 22,867 officers and men, Navy and Marines." Indeed, the decision to leave the two advance base regiments in the Gulf with their transports after the Culebra maneuvers was a fortuitous one for the Corps; the assault elements of both outfits were ashore and fighting in Vera Cruz within the first twenty-four hours.

Time-Phased Forced Deployment Planning. An accidental convergence? Perhaps, but the results reveal a master's touch somewhere in the planning and execution process. It would be difficult to match the timing today. In effect, the bulk of five regiments of marines (counting Catlin's provisional outfit) were either ashore in Mexico or on station offshore by D + 10. Only Captain McGill's 28th Company on the *West Virginia*, Captain Babb's 43d Expeditionary Company on *Salem*, and Captain Beaumont's 7th Company on *Lebanon* arrived outside the ten-day window. The deployment is even more remarkable considering that more than 5,000 of the 9,991 marines on the muster rolls of the Corps in April 1914 were on the move in support of the Mexican crisis. Major General Commandant Barnett did admit, however, that these massive deployments "depleted the barracks in this country."

Composite Forces. Today, we are concerned about the effectiveness of building combat power by converging MAUs and MABs on a trouble spot to form a composite MAF. In the 1914 Marine Corps everything above company level was a composite outfit—the battalions, regiments, and brigade were as composite a force as could be imagined. But it worked. There was one problem in the rapid turnover of command. The marines ashore at Vera Cruz were commanded during the first two weeks by, sequentially, Neville, Lejeune, Mahoney, and Waller. The marines needed some brigadier generals, and the expedition highlighted the deficiency. Two years later the billets were authorized (Waller, Pendleton, and Lejeune were among the first to benefit).

Strategic Lift. Marines deployed to Mexico aboard two "legitimate" transports, several different battleships and cruisers, a collier, a target ship, and a chartered commercial steamship. The combination worked, but it ruined unit integrity and precluded taking some mission-essential equipment (the advance base gear). It worked largely because of the limited scope of the Vera Cruz operation itself, and because there were enough ships of all descriptions to meet the combined deployment requirements of the army, marines, and naval aviation—and the refugees. It also may have been the last time that there was no real interservice competition for strategic lift. Three years later Barnett had a nasty fight with the secretary of war because the army had priority on use of transports to deploy the initial troops to Europe. Vera Cruz illuminated the need for suitable transports, a lesson that applies today just as it did then.

As a result of recommendations from the General Board beginning in 1910, Congress had authorized new construction of one transport in March 1913. This ship was launched in June 1916, as the USS *Henderson*, 10,000 tons, and became the marines's workhorse, transporting Colonel Doyen's 5th Marines to France in 1917, Lejeune and Butler to the war the next year, and generations of marines to and from China in the 1920s and 1930s. Significantly, of the 182 new ships authorized during the great naval buildup of 1904–15, *Henderson* was the lone transport, and the situation did not change dramatically thereafter. The strategic lift lesson is hard to learn.

Let us also note that the U.S. Merchant Marine fleet was healthier in 1914 than it is today. The Wilson Administration was able to charter commercial steamships with relative ease to meet short-fuse lift requirements for all three services. We would be hard-pressed today to make available two chartered "troopships" on the East Coast in the first three weeks of a nonmobilization crisis deployment.

Joint Operations. Vera Cruz was valuable in giving the marines experience in joint operations with the army. The experience paid dividends in World War One and beyond. Today it is almost impossible to conceive of prolonged single-service operations. Lejeune, with his Army War College background, was the right man on the scene during his brief week in command of the marine brigade. He may have been the first marine to see life beyond the termination of an amphibious operation, a murky area in which we today still are experiencing sharp fights over command relationships.

Sustainability. The Marine Corps may have deployed to Mexico in commendable fashion in 1914, but it certainly was not prepared for an extended employment toward Mexico City should that mission have been ordered. The army was better prepared for that contingency, which undoubtedly explains some of the army's relative problems with embarkation. Lejeune, again, recognized the shortfall and directed the brigade quartermaster to "procure all the carts and animals he could find, as we were without transportation of any kind." Tactical mobility also worried the

commandant. On 26 April he queried the Army Quartermaster's Department whether they would be willing to provide all the land transportation requirements—horses, wagons, harnesses, teamsters—for the marine brigade, including its new artillery battalion.

Medical support has always been a key element of sustainability. In this regard, the role of the hospital ship *Solace* in the Mexican crisis is significant. *Solace* arrived at Vera Cruz on 22 April and was immediately utilized. On 9 May she steamed for New York with forty-five of the seriously ill and wounded from the first two weeks of the operation. Returning to Vera Cruz, she remained on station throughout most of the occupation (Colonel Moses died aboard *Solace* in September). In the ready availability of a hospital ship, the 1914 marines were better off than we are today, as we ponder the merits of resurrecting the USS *Sanctuary* or the SS *United States* while waiting new construction. Even a stopgap "Rapidly Deployable Medical Facility" will not provide the ready services *Solace* did at Vera Cruz.

Urban Warfare. Neville, Butler, and Catlin had to fight through the buildings of Vera Cruz with pick, shovel, and bayonet. The point is significant today because it is a mission we could assign our forward deployed amphibious forces: forcible seizure of an urban port to make it suitably "benign" to accommodate our maritime prepositioned ships. The Mexicans gave the marines hell in this type of fighting in 1914. We can expect similar receptions in other corners.

Unit Integrity. We've discussed the impact of lift constraints on the integrity of Neville's 2d Regiment. We should note also that the advance base organization included an aviation detachment under First Lieutenant Bernard Smith. The aviation unit not only was unable to sail from Pensacola with Neville aboard *Prairie* on 5 March but was also excluded from the Naval Aeronautic Detachment aboard *Mississippi* on 21 April. Smith finally embarked on *Birmingham* and didn't arrive in Vera Cruz until 24 May. While he did fly a few training flights "in country," he was obviously too late to make any tactical contributions to the marine brigade. Sometimes today we still have difficulty in phasing our organic marine fixed-wing air into the objective area in time to coincide with the arrival of the MAGTF.

Roles/Missions and Interservice Rivalry. The press gave favorable coverage to the marines in the initial days of the Vera Cruz operation, especially Smedley Butler's exploits. The army bristled over the marines' claim to be "First to Fight," and smarting over having missed the fighting, took steps in World War One to disprove the claim. The rivalry over who indeed is the most ready to deploy for sustained combat continues today. As for the navy, Vera Cruz marked the beginning of the end of the deployment of large-scale naval landing parties. The sailors fought bravely, but they sustained disproportionate casualties in the street fighting. The ma-rines, after the World War One upheaval, would be well on their way to becoming the navy's power projection force.

The study of the Vera Cruz landing can thus be instructive today. Those 861 marines of the 3d Regiment who deployed from Philadelphia in 1914 aboard the SS *Morro Castle* had to share twelve wash basins, sleep on the deck, and cook their own meals. Their modern day counterparts in the Royal Marines deployed to the Falklands in relative luxury aboard the *Canberra*. The contrast in style is not significant; the important parallel is the readiness of sea soldiers to deploy rapidly to a crisis area aboard whatever mode of strategic lift their government can make available on urgent notice.

Vera Cruz, 1914: operationally insignificant, politically ill-conceived—but an early masterpiece of rapid deployment.

Gallipoli, 1915

BY T. A. GIBSON

"VISTAS were now opening which would have horrified Palmerston—but their very length held a fascination for strategists, amateur alike with professional, that no horizon in France or Flanders could ever match. 'Sideshows?' exclaimed Lloyd George, always an Easterner in outlook, 'the British Empire has done very well out of sideshows!' His history was sound. No one outside of a study recalled the great world war of the eighteenth century (1756–63), or could find the battlefields of Leuthen or Rossbach on a map, but who has not heard of the glorious victories of Plassey and Quebec? In this modern conflict, the course of events once more proved the case for the sideshow, for it was certain that Allenby's ultimate victory at Megiddo, the British entry into Jerusalem, the thunderous collapse of the Ottoman power, were matters of pith and moment not to be compared in the scales of history with the winning of another 1,000 yards of Somme mud." So wrote A. P. Thornton in *The Imperial Idea and Its Enemies*.

It was on 17 March 1915 that those vistas first began to dawn. On that day, when half the globe seemed to be colored a solid Imperial red, and Lenin—who was to promote his own hue of redness—was a revolutionary awaiting safely in Switzerland his long train ride at the behest of the German General Staff, HMS *Phaeton* raced through the Aegean toward Lemnos and its distinguished passenger, the newly appointed commander-in-chief of the Mediterranean Expeditionary Force, noted with characteristic poetical flourish in his diary: "Exquisite, exquisite air; sea like an undulating carpet of blue velvet outspread for Aphrodite." He went on, oblivious of any grim portent: "At noon passed a cruiser taking back Admiral Carden invalided to Malta."

Phaeton's passenger, General Sir Ian Hamilton, had probably seen more active service than any other general officer in the army at the time. He had the unusual distinction of having been recommended for the V.C. twice, at Majuba in 1881 and at Elandslaagte in 1889 and was one of the few commanders who had emerged from the Second Boer War with his reputation enhanced. He had attended the Russo-Japanese War as an observer with the Japanese Army in the field, and had twice been a member of the Army Council, as Quartermaster General and as Adjutant General. If the outbreak of war in 1914 found him a senior general of wide and varied experience, a few months later saw him in a cruiser rushing at thirty knots towards his greatest challenge; past Corfu, his birthplace, with its "thyme-scented breezes."

Hamilton arrived at Lemnos at 3:00 P.M. and promptly hurried over to a cordial meeting on the mighty HMS *Queen Elizabeth* with Vice Admiral de Robeck, now commanding the fleet; also present were their respective chiefs of staff, Major General Braithwaite and Commodore Keyes, Vice Admiral Wemyss, commanding the Mudros base, General

Army Quarterly, "Eyeless in Byzantium: The Tragedy of Ian Hamilton," 91 (October 1965): 82–96. Reprinted by permission. See also Alan Moorehead, *Gallipoli* (New York: Harper and Row, 1956; reprint edition, Annapolis: Nautical and Aviation Publishing, 1982).

Implacable covering the landing at "X" beach, Gallipoli, 1915. *The Times History of the War*, 5:380. Courtesy of the U.S. Navy Historical Center.

d'Amade, commander of the promised two French colonial divisions, and Vice Admiral Guepratte, commanding the French squadron. It was quickly decided that Hamilton should look at the Gallipoli Peninsula the next day from the *Phaeton*.

This reconnaissance by Hamilton on 18 March, peering at the coastline of the Peninsula through fieldglasses from the bridge of a fast-moving warship, assumes great importance as it was to be the main basis of his knowledge of the ground on which to formulate his plan. Its closeness allowed him to be a fascinated spectator of the final stages of the great naval attack of that day. As *Phaeton* rounded Cape Helles into the Straits, a watery inferno unfolded itself: the steam trawlers and minesweepers struggling bravely among the shells from the Turkish concealed mobile guns that lashed the water, the old battleship, *Inflexible*, limping out of the fray with her upper works badly shot about and reporting she had struck a mine; also the French battleship *Gaulois* creeping out towards Tenedos to ground on some rocks. This magnificent spectacle of war affected Ham-

ilton strongly; it was clear to him that the navy had failed gallantly to force the Dardanelles and that the running had passed to the army. He immediately penned to Kitchener: "The *Irresistible*, the *Ocean* and the *Bouvet* are gone! The *Bouvet*, they say, just slithered down like a saucer slithers down in a bath. The *Inflexible* and the *Gaulois* are badly mauled."

In the aftermath of this serious repulse of the navy's power, an important conference took place on the *Queen Elizabeth* and another at 10:00 A.M. on 22 March. According to Hamilton's account, de Robeck admitted "he was now quite clear he could not get through without the help of all my troops." The initiative had now passed emphatically to the army, somewhat to the intense gratification of Hamilton, Birdwood, commanding the Australian and New Zealand Army Corps, and Braithwaite. Before they had gone on board they had agreed to hold their peace and allow the sailors to solve their own dilemma, though "Birdie and my own staff disliked the idea of chancing mines with million pounds ships." A more human

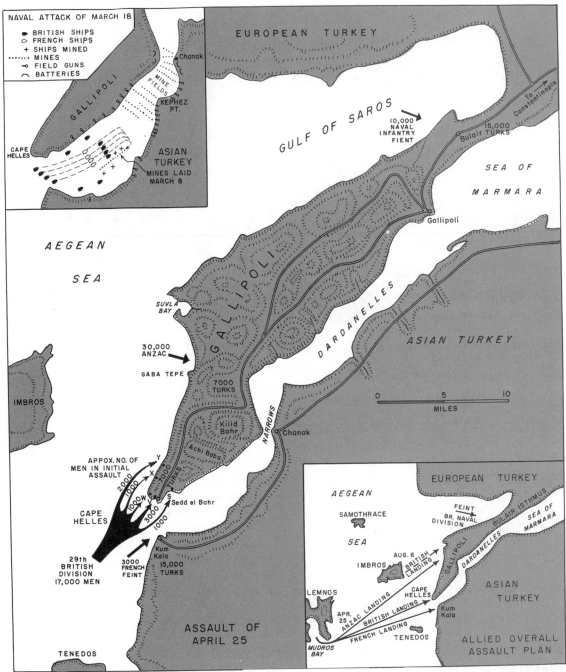

Dardanelles campaign, 1915.

explanation, rather than this pious concern for the other service, is that, not unnaturally, they were now fired with the intoxication of the Dardanelles concept and keen to join in the glory to be won.

But much had to be done before the army could intervene physically. Not only was 29 Division, regarded as the élite of the force, some three weeks away but the transports already assembled in Mudros harbor, particularly those of the Royal Naval Division, were not tactically loaded; guns were in one ship, limbers in another. The transports would have to be emptied and reloaded and though Mudros was an excellent anchorage, it boasted little else. For the wharves and heavy lift equipment, and the accommodation and training facilities for the waiting troops, Alexandria and Egypt were the only solution. Ruefully, Hamilton advised Kitchener that 11 April was the earliest he could mount his amphibious assault.

So the transports sailed away to Egypt and there Hamilton rode about his formations and inspected indefatigably, and tried to weld his polyglot and far from complete staff into a working entity (his A and Q staffs were not to arrive from U.K. until 1 April). Gradually the plan grew into all the multifarious details so necessary in such a complicated operation as an amphibious landing on a defended coastline. But in broad outline, Hamilton's plan of attack remained true to what he gave on 22 March to de Robeck who "is greatly relieved to hear that I have practically made up my mind to go for the South of the Peninsula and to keep in closest touch with the Fleet."

Where to land?—the burning question of an amphibious operation. First, however, it must be made clear that the Asian shore had been ruled out by Kitchener's directive to Hamilton which forbade any landing to be made there. Moreover, the serious limitation of getting wheeled vehicles ashore to support the army if it landed some distance from its objectives inhibited choices on the Asian side, as the two possibilities, Besika Bay and Yukyeri Bay, were some 25 miles from the Narrows. Yet a major landing here had much to commend it: little opposition with no serious artillery support and a rapid march over comparatively easy country could have taken the army up to the rear of the Asian forts whose fixed batteries could only fire seawards.

The Peninsula—how this vital, elongated tongue of crags and wild ravines must have dominated the thoughts of British, Turks, and Germans when the fleet recoiled from the repulse of 18 March and the feverish British military preparations were open knowledge to all. Some 45 miles long and about 12 miles wide at its thickest waist, the Peninsula—it appeared to the British in April 1915—offered only four real possibilities to land a sizeable force: (1) the Bulair area which was served by the Bay of Bakla Liman in the Gulf of Saros; (2) Suvla Bay; (3) the Gabe Tepe area; (4) Cape Helles. Any further intrusion into the Straits for landing places past the Cape was clearly impracticable because of the dominance of the Asian forts.

Hamilton rejected any landing in the Gulf of Saros primarily because he felt that the famous Bulair Lines were too strong—the crow's-nest on *Phaeton* had reported it was bristling with wire in depth—and Bakla Liman Bay was within artillery range of the Lines. Suvla he felt he could not consider further as coastal and topographical data on it was sketchy in the extreme, though it was clear that the plain was overlooked by hills inland and on one flank. He decided to make his main bid on the southernmost tip, Cape Helles, with an equally strong second prong of the attack 13 miles north at Gabe Tepe, striking across the rear of the enemy in Cape Helles and only 6 miles across from the vital Kilid Bahr which dominated the Narrows. Also, a feint was to be made simultaneously at the Gulf of Saros and a diversionary landing at Kum Kale, on the Asian tip, to neutralize the guns that would interfere with the Cape Helles landing.

At Gallipoli in 1915 there was little choice in the method of deployment, owing to the mountainous terrain, the restricted beaches, and the generally improvised nature of the operation. Limited movement of some formations between landing sites was possible and was done, but there could be no shifting internally of the main weight, for most of the rifles ashore were sorely needed to hold the existing ring; the overall tactical picture could only be effected by the entry at a selected point of major reinforcements from outside the theater. And these were by no means readily available but, in the main, three weeks' sailing away and then were grudgingly and belatedly given. It follows that any appraisal of the Gallipoli campaign must therefore look with some discernment at the original plan of attack.

Was Bulair worthy of more than the scant consideration it seems to have got? The Bulair Lines which stretched across the slim neck of the Peninsula were an Anglo-French creation of the Crimean War, but their current reputation rested on the fact that the Turks, in the Balkans War of 1912 when elsewhere their fortunes were at a low ebb, had soundly repulsed the Bulgarians. Since then the lines had been strengthened and reconnaissances in February and March 1915 (by Birdwood) gleaned that it was held in some force. Other objections to it were that it would mean a fight on two fronts if Turkish forces inevitably intervened from Thrace, and even if the neck was effectively closed, the trapped enemy in the Peninsula could always be supplied across the Straits from Asia. Nevertheless, it seemed the perfect strategical place to land; the Turkish forces in the Peninsula would be cut off and bottled up, and even if supply or retreat across the Straits was feasible it was hardly the same as having land communications where numbers and heavy stores and equipment were involved. The lines were easily within the bombarding capability of the great Allied Fleet, the going there was reasonably easy for men and vehicles, though Bakla Liman bay was cramped for the landing of a large force. Major General Sir Charles Callwell, then D.M.O. and also an officer with some knowledge of the problem as he was a member of a planning team that produced a paper in 1906 concluding that the Dardanelles could not be forced by ships alone, stated somewhat cryptically about it: "Strategic and tactical considerations practically vetoed its use, though landing operations could have been carried out at this point on many days when they would have been impracticable at almost any other locality outside the Straits." However, whatever those considerations were, Ian Hamilton's able opponent, Liman von Sanders, certainly thought it was the obvious choice; when landing contacts were made on 25 April, he proceeded personally to Bulair and despite reports of heavy and desperate fighting flooding in from

the south, did not release his 5 and 7 Divisions from there until 9:30 that night, and he himself remained there until next morning. The fact that the bay was entrenched and within artillery range hardly put it in a different category to the other possible landing places.

Suvla, as later knowledge and experience showed, was well suited to a major landing if the hills about the plain were lightly held, but in view of the general ignorance about it in April, Hamilton cannot be criticized for excluding it then. The next site, the extensive beaches immediately north of Gabe Tepe, was an attractive one, especially in view of its convenient striking distance to the Narrows, though the area here was known to be, like Cape Helles, well wired and dug. But when one comes to the Cape Helles area, one wonders what induced Hamilton to land there; it would seem either he felt an obligation to fall in with what he sensed were the navy's wishes or he had sanguine ideas about advancing under cover of the full naval gun support. But this area was the most formidable in defenses and Achi Baba, though only 700 feet, overlooked the whole southern tip. Moreover, it was a frontal and expected approach which threatened some hard slogging to get forward.

Hamilton now did what can only be termed a very un-Montgomery-like action: he called for appreciations from his three senior subordinate commanders, Lieutenant General Birdwood, Major General Hunter-Weston, G.O.C. 29 Division, and Major General Paris, G.O.C. Royal Naval Division. Birdwood, who had formerly been for a landing on the south of the Peninsula but had now changed his ground on learning that the Turkish guns of the Asian shore could command Morto Bay, inclined toward a landing on the Kitchener-forbidden territory of the Asian coast, somewhere south of Tenedos, though it is interesting to find that his Corps Staff were advocates of Bulair. Paris's appreciation seems to have been a chronicle of doom and foreboding and rather tactically naïve: "The enemy is of strength unknown but within striking distance there must be 250,000. . . .

Surprise is impossible. . . . To land would be difficult enough if surprise was possible but hazardous in the extreme under present conditions. . . . Sedd-el-Bahr is the only place where transports could come in close and where the actual landing may be unopposed." But it was Hunter-Weston's "masterly piece of work," written at Malta *en route*, that impressed Hamilton. Hunter-Weston considered that there were only two possible landing areas, about Suvla and about Cape Helles, and of these he favored Helles as "the Fleet can also surround this end of the Peninsula and bring a concentrated fire on any Turks holding it." All these appreciations served to do, not unnaturally, was to depress Hamilton, for masterly though Hunter-Weston's may have been, it certainly ended up with a masterly gloomy conclusion: "but if the views expressed in this paper are sound, there is not in the present circumstances a reasonable hope of success" (though he did qualify this by stating his appreciation was based on information available to him at Malta and that more intelligence might improve his views). Hamilton noted wryly: "The truth is that every one of these fellows agrees in his heart with old von der Goltz, the Berlin experts and the Sultan of Egypt that the landing is impossible."

On 10 April, in his headquarters ship, S.S. *Arcadian*, at Lemnos, Hamilton made a presentation of his plan to de Robeck, Wemyss, and Keyes. He stressed that half the golden opportunity had been sabotaged by the appalling lack of security, especially by the voluble and unmuzzled Egyptian press, and by the delay for reloading at Alexandria and the late sailing of 29 Division. The ideal would be to land his whole force in one great blow but, unfortunately, lack of beach space in any one area close to his objective, Kilid Bahr, and the insufficient small boat lift for a ship-to-shore movement precluded this. His plan was to make his main effort from the beaches of Cape Helles and Sedd-el-Bahr with the Regular 29 Division, with the Anzac Corps landing simultaneously just north of Gabe Tepe to seize "the high backbone of the Peninsula and cut the line of retreat of the

enemy on the Kilid Bahr plateau"; the French were to land temporarily with about a brigade on Kum Kale on the Asian side of the mouth of the Straits to neutralize the guns that could range on to Morto Bay and also to prevent enemy reinforcements moving across from that side, and the naval division would make a demonstration in their transports off Bulair to transfix the enemy there.

It would be interesting to know how much Hamilton was swayed by the appreciations, if at all. As he digested them seriously for the first time on 9 April, sailing to Lemnos from Egypt, and he did his naval briefing on the 10th, it all depends on how much work on the copious and detailed logistic arrangements his staff and their naval equivalents had already done. D-day was now set for the 25th, and probably any alteration at this stage was impossible. Perhaps he looked at the appreciations only to see how other minds sized up the problem.

Meanwhile, on the other side of the hill, the direct result of the great naval attack of 18 March and the fruit of the half-cocked and uncoordinated British handling of the Dardanelles project was more desperate activity to fortify the Peninsula even more formidably for the onslaught they knew quite certainly was coming. On 25 March, Marshal Liman von Sanders, the head of the German Military Mission in Turkey, was appointed to command a 5th Turkish Army, the field force in the Dardanelles, though a German admiral continued to be responsible for the defenses in the Narrows, and the preparations began to feel a much-needed energetic central control. Aided by German officers acting as staff officers, advisors to Turkish divisional commanders and as artillery and engineer commanders, he cancelled the Turkish concept of trying to hold strongly everywhere and by 25 April, with screen forces elsewhere, he had the six divisions of his army withdrawn from the cordon system into three groups: in the north, 5 and 7 Divisions at Bulair; in the south 19 Division in reserve at Maidos and 9 Division at Cape Helles; while across on the Asian side, 3 Division was in the Kum Kale area and 11 Division at Besika Bay. This was hardly an overstrong force for the great task in hand, but on 27 March, von Sanders said to a fellow German: "If only the English will leave me alone for eight days." As it happened, because of the problems Hamilton inherited, he was allowed four weeks. He was acutely conscious of the difficulty of communications in the wild, primitive Peninsula and the labor battalions of non-Muslim subjects—Greeks, Armenians, and Jews—were set to work constructing roads to aid mobility.

At first light 25 April 1915, the great epic of the Gallipoli campaign began. The ultimate loading, assembly, and transport to the battle area of this amphibious force went well. But the Anzac landing, which was meant to be a few hundred yards north of Gabe Tepe, was taken by the current well over a mile to the north, to a little cove locally called Ariburnu and to be named for posterity Anzac Cove. The Anzacs launched into a wild tangle of ravines and scrub, clawing and fighting their way upwards, but the fortunes of war would have it that the commander of 19 Division in reserve at nearby Maidos was a soldier of demonic energy, Mustapha Kemal. Without orders he force-marched his division to the sound of the guns and though some immortals of the Anzac Corps exhaustedly gained the high ground and saw the gleaming waters of the Narrows, Mustapha Kemal's violent, personally led counterattack with his division in support of the reeling 27 Regiment flung the disorganized and tired Anzacs back down their slopes. As they held a precarious bridgehead there, they were raked all day with shrapnel and lost heavily, so much so that Hamilton was awakened at midnight by a message from Birdwood hinting at reembarkation. He replied sturdily that they must "dig, dig, dig."

At Helles, 29 Division was ashore on four of its beaches but lack of a sense of urgency prevailed among those who had had an easy landing. At V Beach, the fifth, however, where the *River Clyde* had driven in on the beach opposite the old fort of Sedd-El-Bahr, a holocaust, with the waters red with blood, developed all day, causing Hamilton grave anxiety until the reprieve of darkness; Sedd-El-Bahr, an excellent landing site under the guns of the fleet, had been thought to be the easiest landing of all. However, the line stabilized and inched forward as follow-up formations from the Royal Naval Division and the French Corps, whose elements had successfully gone firm at Kum Kale by midday 25 April and had reembarked on the night 26/27, came ashore. Hamilton now decided on the first main battle to emerge after the melee of the landings: an attack on the 27th by 29 Division and 1 French Division, supported by the great guns of the fleet, to take Achi Baba. But the assault met fresh Turkish reserves, the whole of 7 Division, part of 11 Division summoned from Asia, and several battalions of 5 Division. It failed, though valuable elbow room for reserves and supply dumps was gained as the line went forward. Achi Baba, despite further great assaults, was to brood over the Allied fortunes until the end of the campaign.

The immediate development after the landings was a race by both sides to build up on the two fronts at Anzac and Helles, with the Turks inevitably winning through their internal communications. The severe casualties Hamilton had sustained now forced Kitchener to reinforce him with 42 East Lancs Division and 29 Indian Brigade from Egypt. After beating off with heavy losses two major Turkish attacks, one each night between 1 and 3 May, Hamilton meanwhile returned to the offensive at Helles; on 6 May, he had two brigades, one Australian and one New Zealand, sail down from Anzac to form a temporary composite division with a brigade from the Naval Division. Again the Allied line went for Achi Baba, but now feeling a grave artillery ammunition shortage, dashed itself. On the night 9/10 May, the usual violent Turkish counterattack came in, and on the 11th the hard-tried and depleted 29 Division was relieved in the line by the now complete 42 Division, and the Anzac brigades went back to their own tortured slopes. Helles now settled down to a struggle of attrition on a line across the tip with 8 Corps, consisting of 29, 42, and the Naval Division under Hunter-

Weston, left, and the French Expeditionary Corps under d'Amade, right. The prerequisites of successful trench warfare—grenades, mortars, and a liberal supply of artillery ammunition—were few and sorely needed, as at Anzac. Also, the spasmodic fire the Allied line was subjected to from enemy batteries on the Asian shore began to have a wearing effect.

Meanwhile, at Anzac, after the first perilous days, succor came on the night 28/29 April in the shape of the dismounted 1 Australian Light Horse Brigade and four battalions of the Naval Division. For 30 April, a general advance was planned but because 1 Australian Division was then at skeleton strength because of battle casualties, it had to be cancelled. A local offensive on the night of 2 May in Monash Gully went well but had to be broken off when a destroyer fired into the leading troops. Apart from local assaults and enemy artillery fire, the ensuing fortnight was quiet, partly because of the departure of the two brigades for Helles but also because of sheer hard work and difficulties of living. All water, ammunition, and supplies had to be man-carried from the beach up tortuous paths under fire. But on 19 May, after a considerable bombardment of the previous day, a massive Turkish attack came in, its estimated strength about thirty thousand, with the determined aim to eradicate the Anzac bridgehead once and for all. The Anzacs knew it was being mounted, from the invaluable air reports of Commander Samson and his gallant RNAS pilots who had sighted a fresh division disembarking at Maidos, and were braced to receive it with the same ardor with which it was delivered. Between 0400 hours and 1200 hours, some three thousand enemy were slaughtered at the expense of five hundred Anzac killed and wounded as the Turks attacked in dense formations. After this disastrous day for the Turks, there was never again any doubt that the Anzac bridgehead was there to stay, and a four-day truce followed to bury the dead whose stench had become unbearable to both friend and foe. The next two months, except for two bloody clashes between 28 and 30 June, saw no fur-

ther major engagements but an ever-present feature of Anzac was the difficulty in procuring water.

On 30 April, Ian Hamilton had transferred from the *Queen Elizabeth* to the *Arcadian* and this was the first time since the landing that his staff had come together. Two very sobering facts were now starkly confronting him and, indeed, all his subordinate commanders: first, that the quality of the Turkish *asker* had been gravely underestimated and, second, the value of the fleet's guns in support of the army ashore, on which so much reliance had been placed, was proving a disappointment.

Of the first, the Turk over the past fifty years had become the funny man and joke of Europe. Seen by the British and French in an indifferent performance during the Crimean War, his record since had been far from impressive, particularly during the very recent Balkans War of 1912. What the critics of 1912 overlooked was the effect of the chaotic supply system which caused some starving Turkish soldiery to eat grass to survive and which failed to provide ammunition replenishment. But although the administration of the Turkish Empire was corrupt and degenerate, its native peasant stock was still sound and stouthearted. Now defending their homeland against an infidel invader, inspired by brave and fanatical mufti and nursed along by efficient Germans who, in the European tradition, were zealous in their man-management, the illiterate but hardy Turkish soldiers were doughty foes. In the great naval attack of 18 March, when the powerful Allied fleet advanced into the Straits exploding their huge shells into the defending battery positions, a Turkish gunner could cry to his fellows: "Comrades, now comes the hour for which our mothers bore us!" One German divisional commander gives two factors that increased the ordinary *asker*'s resistance: the abundance of both rifle ammunition and water. The first gave him the reassuring feeling of being able to defend himself, the second perhaps is even more illuminating: "Finally, the Turk, who is accustomed to drink so much water, is quite impossible as a soldier without this most important element in his life. If we had also been forced to bring out water to Gallipoli in tank ships, and then carry it up on donkeys' backs to the trenches, the bodily resistance of the Turk would have completely broken down."

As for the second, against the excellent, deeply dug Turkish entrenchments, the flat trajectory of the naval guns proved of little avail. Initially the terrifying minor earthquakes had an effect on morale, but once their limited damage became known to the enemy, this wore off, although the Allied soldiers continued to be heartened by the sound of the great guns. It is hard to believe, however, that the fleet went into the campaign able to support the army only with armor-piercing projectiles, and not high explosives, and that the system of target indication and spotting was different in the two services.

On 10 May, Hamilton cabled for two more divisions organized as a corps and on 17 May, he increased this to two corps. A note of perhaps justifiable petulance now crept into his thinking: "The chief puzzle of the problem is that nothing turns out as we were told it would turn out. The landing had been made but the Balkans fold their arms, the Italians show no interest, the Russians do not move an inch to get across the Black Sea." Kitchener replied rather frigidly that one division only, 52 Lowland, was on its way. This division, 25 to 40 percent short of establishment as all T.A. divisions were as they had been milked of their best men for France, arrived at Helles on 5 June, a day after a general attack by 42 Division and the French had started. This gained some 400 yards in the center only as a good advance by 42 Division was checkmated by the French giving ground under heavy Turkish counterattacks. On 21 June, the French Corps redeemed this with a brilliant minor success overrunning enemy trenches on the forward slope of a big spur west of the large reentrant, Kereves Dere. On 28 June, 52 Division was blooded in a successful corps attack with 29 Division which gained possession of a long stretch of a ravine on the other flank, Saghir Dere. This deliberate slogging forward to gain a few

hundred yards induced in turn major enemy attacks to regain the lost ground, and close-quarter trench warfare in all its bloodiness raged. By early June, five more Turkish divisions had reached the Peninsula.

During June, however, Hamilton, who had now moved his headquarters ashore into tents at Imbros, did get some cheering news. On 8 June, the Dardanelles Committee, which was the old War Council and which had not met since mid-May, agreed to send three divisions of the New Army, 10, 11, and 13, and the infantry of two T.A. divisions, 53 Welsh and 54 East Anglian, and these would arrive between early July and early August. Hamilton's command would then be the formidable paper strength of thirteen divisions and five brigades (twenty-nine Indian and four Anzac mounted, serving as infantry), but his existing units were badly understrength and his artillery meager. He now decided to mount on the dark nights early in August his long-desired major offensive to shatter the embrace of the Turkish forces holding the heights about his two bridgeheads and to break through to the Narrows.

But where and how was he to use this new impetus? Hamilton's dilemma can be imagined. For any vital final thrust he would have wished to use his veteran formations from Helles or Anzac rather than the New Army divisions whose underlying caliber was sound but who would come almost straight from their transports unfit and unacclimatized to Gallipoli's searing heat and whose officers were untried. The need for surprise, however, and his own limited resources prohibited any major reliefs and regrouping. As it was, at the end of July, Liman von Sanders, who now had about twelve divisions supported by corps troops, including a powerful artillery, and German special units, realized that something ominous was in the wind and moved 7 and 12 Divisions back to reinforce his old worry, Bulair.

Once again, however, the Gulf of Saros seems to have been brushed aside; de Robeck objected to it because of its greater distance from the concentration area of Imbros and Mudros and its exposure to the submarine menace. The plan devolved, with D-day 6 August, was that the main attack was to be put in from Anzac after last light with the Anzac Division, 13 Division, 29 Brigade of 10 Division, 29 Indian Brigade, and the N.Z. Mounted Brigade, under Major General Sir Alexander Godley, going left flanking in three columns for the dominating ridge of Sari Bair. Just north at Suvla Bay, the other arm of the pincer, the newly arrived IX Corps, was to break new ground altogether. There, under Lieutenant General Sir Frederick Stopford, 10 Division less one brigade and 11 Division were to go ashore, also after last light, and strike inland across the plain. Meanwhile, at Lone Pine on the right or southern flank of Anzac, 1 Australian Brigade was to stage a diversionary attack, and at Helles, VIII Corps also was to hold the enemy reserves opposite it with offensive action.

By 10 August, this great bid by Hamilton had failed after being tantalizingly within reach of success at Sari Bair. The reason was mainly abject incompetence at Suvla Bay and the culmination of a series of tactical misfortunes at Sari Bair but also his own lack of forceful direction. If ever there was a case for a Montgomery-like briefing and "gripping" of all concerned, it was for Hamilton to do so to IX Corps. Instead, this force went ashore at Suvla Bay shrouded in complete bewilderment at unit level as to what was required of it because of the restrictions of secrecy he had imposed. As Major General Fuller says: "Physically and mentally, the operation was a plunge into the dark." When it ultimately dawned on him, condemned to a self-imposed impotence by his remaining based at Imbros during these all-important operations, that complete inertia held sway on the beaches and near environs of Suvla Bay, he did speedily intervene personally on the afternoon of 8 August. Although he did strive to inject urgency and drive into the lassitude and confusion, his mood was more one of burning inward exasperation rather than of breathing fire and brimstone on the incompetent.

Meanwhile, at Anzac, the attack from there had been defeated by the rugged, confusing country which led to night navigation muddles, by some unlucky prior Turkish moves brought on by fright caused by the violent Lone Pine attack, and, as always, dogged defense by the well-dug-in *asker* which allowed von Sanders to hurry reserves to the scene to counterattack and hold the Sari Bair assault and also the Suvla landing. Though juncture was made with the Suvla forces and space gained for the tight Anzac bridgehead, the great design had come to little purpose with heavy casualties. As that gloomy prophet, Ashmead Bartlett of *The Times*, noted, referring to Suvla Bay: "We have landed and dug another graveyard."

Hamilton now moved the veteran 29 Division to Suvla and disembarked there also 54 Division and 2 Mounted Division which had come from Egypt; 53 Division was already there. Within 29 Division and 11 Division under Major General de Lisle, temporarily commanding IX Corps as Stopford had been removed, he mounted a frontal attack on Ismail Oglu Tepe, as the capture of this hill would secure both Suvla Bay and Anzac Cove from artillery fire, but the operation gained little but severe casualties. This attack was in fact the last set-piece major action of the campaign.

On 17 October, the campaign ended for Hamilton; he was recalled to England "on the grounds that he was incapable of advising about evacuation with an open mind." Only the memories remain, and were to remain indelibly through the long years left to him, of the great, near-run struggle. It had been an exhausting, close-quarter type of campaign of bullet-swept beaches and fierce hand-to-hand fighting between tough and brave adversaries amid a burning heat and general pestilence of flies, dysentery, and unburied dead, and the toll of war there had been no respecter of rank and person. Those memories would certainly have included the gallant Major Allanson of 1/6 Ghurkas who strove to the neck between Chunuk Bair and Hill Q on 8 August with some of his own Ghurkas and some men of 6 South Lancs, only to be blasted tragically and irretrievably off it by monitor shells from his own side;

of the two battalions of the Wellington Regiment who reached Chunuk Bair ridge in the same attack; of the resourceful Bavarian, Major Willmer, who so coolly faced the ponderous IX Corps with a weak brigade screen until Turkish divisions force-marched to his aid; of the "diggers" who packed the trenches at Quinn's Post only a few yards away from the enemy, both antagonists bombed up and with bayonets fixed, permanently ready to go into action at any moment; and, finally, that enemy commander of consuming energy, Mustapha Kemal, who later was to become his country's leader.

Ian Hamilton was never employed again. Yet it is hard to think of another general fighting a major campaign of some considerable difficulty who was so badly supported from above and on the flanks. From England he had to contend with half-baked political direction from a muddle-through committee, who trimmed their sails to every breeze, and with a hesitant and lackluster War Office which the overworked Kitchener could not influence. The provision of shells, grenades, and trench mortars to his command was quite parsimonious. And instead of being sent drafts of reinforcements he was invariably sent new, untried units, also under-strength. Though Egypt had been placed rather loosely at his disposal as a support base, his relations with General Sir John Maxwell there, though conducted in his inevitable gentlemanly fashion, were generally unsatisfactory and irritated, mainly over the reinforcement question.

What Hamilton really had to cope with after the checkmating of the initial landings, and which caused his increasing isolation, was the opinion of a powerful faction in England that the Dardanelles was a strategical fantasy and also of the somewhat natural view of general headquarters in France that Gallipoli would drain off valuable resources in men and material otherwise destined for the western front. But striking first at the weaker enemy was a time-honored and profitable British policy that stemmed from the traditional maritime strategy. Was it not Halder, in Hitler's War, who remarked, when the vise

closed about Italy, that "England always strangles the weaker victim"? Of the easterner versus westerner controversy, it is difficult to see how valid westerner views could emerge between 1915 and early 1917, that is, until the proved appearance of the tank.

What of Ian Hamilton's worth as a higher commander executing a vital campaign? Major General J. F. C. Fuller is sharp and to the point: "A soldier of considerable war experience, loyal, chivalrous, imaginative and journalistic, yet a man of little drive and who may be described as an R. B. Cunninghame Graham in uniform."

Perhaps "little drive" is a harsh part of this verdict; overloyal, a lack of a necessary personal ruthlessness, an overtoleration of the other's point of view, is another, if more lenient, appraisal. Any lack of drive doubtlessly arose through his frustration at having to site his army headquarters on the island of Imbros, divorced from the battle atmosphere of the Peninsula. That he felt his divorced existence, away from the scenes of operations, is revealed by the unnecessarily spartan and uncomfortable menage he set up at Imbros. But probably a serious flaw was that he tolerated indifferent subordinates; he was not a bad picker, but he accepted what was thrust on him. The general officers of IX Corps, Stopford, Hammersley of 11 Division, Reed, the B.G.S., Mahon of 10 Division (who at least proved his worth in battle, but whose prickliness about his seniority prevented the appointment of a younger, capable corps commander) are a clear example. Stopford's appointment Hamilton viewed with considerable apprehension, particularly as he had already asked for Byng or Rawlinson, and it is typical of the tragedy of Gallipoli that after the collapse of the great August attacks, Kitchener sent him the efficient commanders he so sorely needed earlier—Byng, Maude, and Fanshawe. Yet he was aware of this weakness and it worried him: "The question that keeps troubling me is, ought I to have resigned sooner than allow generals old and yet inexperienced to be foisted on me?" However, Major General Fuller probably puts his finger on the heart of the matter here:

"As a soldier, Sir Ian Hamilton was a typical product of pre-South African War days, when to the English wars were looked upon as gentlemanly affairs; when the team spirit killed initiative; and [when] soldiership was the equivalent of sportsmanship. On top of this, when after that war a General Staff was created, it was largely modeled on the German. The Moltke idea that the initiative should be surrendered to subordinate commanders once an operation had been launched was accepted."

As an individual, Ian Hamilton may be described as having been born with a military golden spoon in his mouth. The son of a former commanding officer of the Highland regiment he joined and whose nineteenth-century structure was close and distinctly feudal, he seemed predestined to do well, as his early entree into vice-regal circles in India and his admirable personal intrusions into various campaigns confirmed. But even so, his quick advancement had the sound basis of definite high military gifts: his tactical flair, his gallantry in the field, and a professional expertise which is shown by his development of shooting. In his last and greatest campaign, Sir Ian Hamilton was "an unlucky general." This should not detract from the fact that he is a soldier to be admired, for he led a full martial life of much active service in many fields where his courage, professional ability, and chivalry shone.

Of that last campaign, perhaps Sir Philip Magnus has the most cogent comment: "The cardinal cause, nevertheless, of the British defeat was the failure to decide sufficiently soon to give priority to the Dardanelles as the only theatre which held out the prospect of quick and decisive victory in 1915."

Zeebrugge, 1918

BY JOHN MULLEN

In 1918 the Great War had entered a decisive stage. The entry of the United States into the war had provided the Allies with a fresh influx of manpower and resources. At sea the war continued and U-boats were taking a heavy toll on Allied shipping. These U-boats were operating from Germany but they also threatened lines of communication between Britain and the Continent. In 1914 the rapid German advance had captured the Belgian ports of Ostend and Zeebrugge and by rapidly developing the facilities of these ports, particularly Zeebrugge, they soon were in a position to threaten the important communications which supplied the Allied armies in France. These two ports were connected to the city of Brugges by a canal system to which access could be made from the sea. Brugges was connected to the German homeland by a railway. U-boats were transhipped to Brugges in a partially completed state, where they were assembled and then entered the sea by the canals. These canals formed a triangle and inside this the Germans had constructed air strips from which they mounted air raids on Britain. The triangle also formed the heart of the defense system. Heavy and light batteries were installed to defend the coastline. However, the Royal Navy did not present itself and no engagement was fought to decide the superiority of land- over sea-based guns. On 12 May 1917 Zeebrugge was bombarded by the Royal Navy to put the lock system out of action and during this a smoke screen was used to hinder German observation. Though the bombardment itself was not successful, it forced the Germans to adopt stricter defense measures. The effectivity of Ostend as a U-boat or destroyer base diminished as the war progressed. Its proximity to the front line put it in range of the Royal Marine heavy howitzer battery in France and most of its facilities were moved to Zeebrugge.

The Battle of Ypres in 1917 had for one of its objectives the expulsion of the Germans from Flanders and the capture of Ostend and Zeebrugge. In spite of enormous losses no gains were made and the German grip on the ports was as powerful as ever. To expel the Germans from the ports or, if this were not possible, to deny them their use would have to be undertaken from the sea.

The mounting losses of shipping had turned the attention of the Royal Navy to these ports. In November 1916 a suggestion by Admiral Keyes that the ports should be blocked by sinking a ship in the entrance was rejected. In November 1917 it was decided that after all it would be possible to block the ports and if the Allies could not have them, then neither could the Germans. Plans were drawn up and Admiral Keyes was appointed to command the operation. The problem was to devise a means of sinking the ships in a position that would most block the Germans. The position had to be chosen with care to ensure that it would not be possible to circumvent the ships or to dredge around them.

An Cosantoir (June 1968): 184–89. Reprinted by permission.

It was decided to blow the bottoms from them to cause their rapid sinking and to prevent their drifting.

For the ships which were to be sunk in the entrance to Zeebrugge canal to enter the port, some protection would have to be afforded to them from the Mole, which extended in an arc around the entrance to the canal. The Mole was over a mile long and 100 yards wide. On it were storage facilities and hangars for seaplanes. It was connected to the shore by a viaduct which was some 400 yards long and 100 yards wide. A railway connected the Mole to the shore and it was used to service the storage facilities and hangars. In February 1918 a special Royal Marine battalion was formed to eliminate a battery which was situated at the end of the Mole and which would threaten the block ships entering the canal. Lieutenant Colonel F. E. Chichester was appointed to command the battalion but was shortly succeeded by Major B. N. Elliot. The battalion consisted of battalion headquarters, Machine Gun Section; Mortar Section; A, B and C Companies; and Medical Staff. The troops were to be conveyed to Zeebrugge in *Vindictive*, assisted by *Iris* and *Daffodil*, two Mersey ferry boats which had been provided for this operation. Once they had reached Zeebrugge, *Daffodil* was to push *Vindictive* against the Mole until she was secured and then disembark her troops. *Vindictive* was specially prepared for this task. Special ramps had been fitted so that the storming parties could reach the Mole. The *Iris* and *Daffodil* had been fitted with ladders to allow their parties to climb the Mole. *Vindictive* was strengthened for the storm of fire she would have to meet and additional armaments were fitted to give support to the troops once they had reached the Mole.

By the beginning of April 1918, the preparations for the raid had been completed. The men had been trained for their tasks and the material and shipping provided for the operation. Three block ships were to be sunk in the Zeebrugge Canal entrance, The *Thetis*, *Intrepid*, and *Iphigenia*. All that was re-quired now was suitable weather conditions, and on two occasions during the month the force sailed. On 11–12 April it was nearing Zeebrugge when the weather changed, forcing a postponement of the operation. On the eve of St. George's Day, 22 April 1918, the weather was suitable for the raid. The force sailed from various points and a considerable portion of the journey was carried out in daylight. During the passage Admiral Keyes signaled the message: "St. George for England." To which Commander Carpenter of the *Vindictive* replied, "May we give the dragon's tail a damned good twist."

By 11:20 P.M. on 22 April the monitors had opened fire on Zeebrugge. Twenty minutes later the motor launches which were accompanying the force began to make the smoke screen. St. George's Day was one minute old when *Vindictive* arrived alongside the Mole and a few minutes later *Daffodil* arrived to take up her position pressing *Vindictive* against the wall. The fire at this time was intense and the upper works of *Vindictive* were taking a considerable amount of punishment. In the approach to the Mole most of the ramps fitted to *Vindictive* were damaged and only two could be used to allow the storming parties to ascend the Mole. The ladders fitted to *Iris* were damaged against the Mole because of the heavy swell, and her storming parties had to climb the Mole via *Vindictive*. Once they reached the top of the Mole they had to undergo intensive fire from German machine guns in order to reach the battery at the seaward end of the Mole. Though they did not disable the battery, they did in fact prevent it from firing on the incoming block ships. In doing so, they suffered very heavy casualties.

The protection afforded by the storming parties allowed the block ships to approach the canal entrance without too much difficulty. *Thetis* on her way in was hindered when one of her propellers got caught in a net, forcing her to collide with the bank. She had to be sunk while still some distance from her objective. Even though she did not succeed herself, she performed valuable work in directing her other partners in the operation to reach the canal itself. *Intrepid* and *Iphigenia* were able to be sunk in the proper positions, thus blocking the canal. In order to demolish the viaduct two submarines, C1 and C3, were to be rammed into the structure and exploded. Submarine C3 arrived before C1 and succeeded in reaching the viaduct and destroying herself. Her crew were picked up by one of the accompanying motor launches. The crews had been picked up from the block ships after they had been sunk by launches which took great risks in carrying out their tasks but because of their small size they escaped the heavy fire from the German defenses.

At 12:50 A.M. on 23 April the recall was sounded. By 1:00 A.M. all were back aboard their ships. At 1:15 *Vindictive* had cleared the protection of the Mole and was undergoing intensive fire from the Germans. Fortunately she did not suffer any serious damage. Later she was used as a block ship at another raid on Ostend (the one conducted on that port at the same time as this Zeebrugge attack was unsuccessful). The force had been on the Mole for just one hour and in that time had displayed courage and devotion to duty which at such a dark hour of the war gave great encouragement after the great battles in France and elsewhere. They succeeded in blocking the canal and the storming parties had succeeded in their objective of protecting the block ships as they entered the canal. For its gallantry the 4th Battalion Royal Marines was awarded two Victoria Crosses. At Deal on 26 April 1918, a ballot was held in order to determine who should get the awards. Captain Bamford, who received the highest number, and Sergeant Finch, who received the next highest, were awarded the crosses. In order that the gallantry of the battalion be remembered it was decided that no other marine battalion should be named the 4th.

Pete Ellis: Amphibious Warfare Prophet

BY LIEUTENANT COLONEL JOHN J. REBER, USMC (RET.)

At 0620, 21 May 1923, a State Department clerk in Washington logged in the following cable from the American Embassy in Tokyo:

> I am informed by governor general of Japanese south sea islands that R. H. Ellis, representative of Hughes Trading Company, #2 Rector St., New York City, holder of department passport No. 4249, died at Parao, Caroline Islands on May 12th. Remains and effects in possession of government awaiting instructions.
>
> Wilson

A routine follow-up with the Hughes company by a State Department investigator revealed that the president was a retired Marine Corps colonel who appeared uneasy as the questioning began. Finally, the colonel blurted out that Earl H. Ellis was never his employee but was an active-duty Marine Corps lieutenant colonel on an intelligence mission. At the request of Marine Corps authorities, he had permitted his company to be used as a cover for Ellis.

A copy of the State Department cable was passed via Captain Luke McNamee, director of naval intelligence, to the major general commandant of the Marine Corps, John Archer Lejeune. Lejeune had been "Pete" Ellis's friend and patron since they first served together in the Philippines in 1908. At first, Lejeune tried to protect the nation, the Marine Corps, and Ellis by saying nothing. But the story soon leaked and hit front pages all over the country. Reporters demanded to

U.S. Naval Institute *Proceedings* 103 (November 1977): 53–64. Reprinted by permission.

know what a Marine Corps officer was doing in the Japanese islands of Micronesia.

General Lejeune kept silent for as long as possible. Then, at the prodding of Admiral Robert E. Coontz, chief of naval operations, he issued the only statement he ever made on the subject, saying that Ellis was absent without leave. Colonel Ellis, he said, had been a patient at the Naval Hospital, Yokohama, Japan, suffering from nephritis (inflammation of the kidneys) and was last seen on 6 October 1922. He had been on leave touring the Orient. That leave had been revoked before Ellis vanished from the hospital. The official records backed up the general's statement.

The commandant's cold official statement was probably meant only to protect the Marine Corps and the nation from an embarrassing international scandal. His official statement is belied by the warmth with which he corresponded with Ellis's brother Ralph. One year older than Pete, Ralph was the managing editor of the *Kansas City Journal* and the family spokesman. That Pete Ellis himself certainly would have approved of Lejeune's action is evidenced by the contents of an envelope he left with Lejeune. When opened soon after Ellis's death, it contained the colonel's signed but undated letter of resignation from the Marine Corps. Lejeune destroyed it.

The reporters would have had a more startling angle if they had known that two years earlier Ellis had written a secret operation plan for the invasion of Japan's mandated islands. His thirty thousand-word document was entitled *Advanced Base Operations In Micronesia.* It is one of the most amazingly prophetic documents in military history. Approved by General Lejeune on 25 July 1921, it became the keystone of Marine Corps strategic plans for a Pacific war. It formed the basis for the first Orange Plan approved in 1924 by the joint board of the army and navy for offensive operations against Japan in the event of war.

Ellis's predictions as to the general course of a future war against Japan and his recommendations for the prosecution of that war reveal rare insight. "Japan is a World Power," he wrote. "Considering our consistent policy of non-aggression, she will probably initiate the war; which will indicate that . . . she believes that . . . she has sufficient military strength to defeat our fleet." He prophesied the progress of the war in the Pacific and the swift Japanese onslaught. He planned that the U.S. drive should be straight through the Marshalls and Carolines, then northward toward the homeland. This might well have been the actual route in World War Two had not the initial enemy success compelled us to fight in the South and Southwest Pacific, and if General Douglas MacArthur and political considerations had not made recapture of the Philippines obligatory in 1944.

Ellis went even further than strategic operations; he got into the details of new tactical concepts. Night amphibious operations were discouraged, but Ellis concluded that transports with assault troops should approach under cover of darkness and attack in the early morning to have the advantage of the maximum number of daylight hours. He foresaw future requirements such as underwater demolition teams, the shore party organization, naval gunfire spotters with troops, and other special purpose units. "Task forces must be formed before leaving base port," he wrote, "and must be embarked as such. No shifting of troops or material between ships on blue waters is practicable." Foreseeing the requirement for task organization and combat loading, he wrote, "Signal troops, field artillery, demolition experts and other specialists will accompany the first waves of assault." He described the employment of boatheads [beachheads], beach markers with large placards or flags for beach identification and control, aerial bombing support, naval gunfire, feints and the other ABCs of World War Two-type amphibious operations. More realistic than later military planners, he foresaw that we probably would lose the Philippines at the start of the war. Some of his estimates were upheld with amazing accuracy. He listed four thousand assault troops in his tactical plan for Eniwetok in the Marshalls, and this was approximately the number of Army and Marine troops who secured the atoll in 1944.

His document was revolutionary in many respects, but his main theme—which later proved to be the salvation of the Marine Corps and paved the way for victory in the Pacific—was his conviction that the Marines's primary role should be offensive amphibious operations. Many outlying bases would have to be seized from the Japanese. The seizure of such bases naturally would fall on the Marine Corps as the advanced base force of the Navy. This was right on the heels of the failure of the British offensive amphibious operation at Gallipoli during World War One.

Most military leaders of the 1920s, including many senior Marine Corps officers, were still thinking in terms of World War I trench warfare. At best, the Marine Corps's role was thought to be that of advanced base defense, primarily coastal artillery units. But there was no widespread interest in this advanced base defense work even in its pure defensive aspects among officers in the Marine Corps immediately after World War One. And they surely were not thinking about landing against defended shores in the World War Two sense.

In addition to being a master military planner, strategist, and tactician, Pete Ellis was also a very complicated, sick, and neurotic man. Prone to melancholia, he was hospitalized many times for neurasthenia and psychasthenia. He was hyperactive, and his record is replete with accounts of his working around the clock to finish a project, then ending up in a hospital with shattered nerves.

Ellis began his career by enlisting as a private on 3 September 1900 at Chicago. At a time when many enlisted men could neither read nor write, he was a high school graduate. While an enlisted man, he performed guard duty at the Washington Navy Yard. He won a commission on 21 December 1901, two days after his twenty-first birthday. His abilities were recognized early in his career. Consequently, he was given choice assignments usually reserved for more senior officers. General Lejeune had this to say in a letter to Ellis' mother, "He had a brilliant mind and by reason of continued study and application he became one of the best informed officers on military and naval subjects in any branch of the service." A lifelong bachelor, Ellis devoted his life to the Marine Corps.

Young Lieutenant Ellis landed at Cavite in the Philippines on 13 April 1902 for his first duty assignment as an officer. There he came under the influence of such Marine Corps notables as Major Littleton W. T. "Tony" Waller, Marine Captain Smedley D. Butler, and others who helped him form his attitudes and objectives. On 21 January 1903, Lieutenant Ellis reported aboard the USS *Kentucky* (later BB-6), the flagship of the Asiatic Fleet. For the next year and a half, he visited the principal ports of China and Japan. The *Kentucky* frequently stopped at Yokohama, thus providing Ellis an excellent opportunity to begin his study of Japan. A second tour in the Philippines (1907–11) as a first lieutenant and captain found him assigned to such duties as the litigation of land cases at Olongapo, serving as officer in charge of the advanced base material (chiefly guns taken off U.S. warships) and commanding fortifications on Grande Island in the defense of Subic Bay. During this tour in the Philippines, Ellis began his long friendship with Lejeune, then a major, and with Joseph H. Pendleton, then a lieutenant colonel.

It was in the Philippines that the unbalanced side of Ellis's personality first came to the attention of his superiors. The brigade chaplain called on him while he was living in a palm frond house on Grande Island with two marine lieutenants. The chaplain's overly righteous attitude discouraged any kind of rapport. A few drinks and stories before dinner only worsened matters. After the four had eaten in silence and were waiting for the houseboy to remove the plates, Ellis apparently found the situation too oppressive, so he whipped out his revolver and shot the plates off the table.

Such bizarre behavior did not deter his superiors from giving him the most responsible assignments. From the Philippines he was ordered to the Naval War College. There, as a very junior captain between 1911 and 1913, he taught officers who became admirals and generals and later helped set the navy's course for victory in World War Two. On the staff with Ellis was Captain William S. Sims, one of the navy's most brilliant officers and one of Ellis's closest friends. Sims later became president of the War College. While at the college, Ellis wrote a series of papers on advanced base forces and the defense of several Pacific islands, including Guam, Peleliu, and Samoa. He also made numerous converts to his then-radical idea of offensive amphibious operations to seize islands as advanced bases for the navy in time of war. In a 1912 fitness report at the War College he requested that he be assigned "duty in making personal reconnaissances of ports in the Atlantic and Pacific likely to be occupied as advanced bases in time of war."

But the commandant had other plans for him in 1914. Assigned to the staff of the Advanced Base School at the Philadelphia Navy Yard, he made a reconnaissance of Culebra and Vieques islands near Puerto Rico for the 1914 advanced base exercise. Then, the secretary of the navy requested that he be assigned to a joint army and navy board scheduled to convene on Guam in March 1914 to prepare a defense plan for the island. On completion of the plan, he remained as military secretary and aide to Navy Captain William J. Maxwell, governor of Guam.

While on Guam in 1915, Ellis was confined to the hospital for several months, one of the first serious indications of his psychological and hyperactivity problems. His medical record reads, "March 6, 1915 . . . loss of self control and tending to hysteria. . . . Bad effects enhanced by short hours of sleep and long hours at desk work. Advise reduction in work and increase in recreation." A 28 June 1915 entry reads, "Very much depressed and extremely nervous."

During his Guam tour, Ellis had at least one confrontation with the governor and also one with a Japanese policeman on Saipan. The governor noted on his fitness report, "I considered Captain Ellis's manner and tone disrespectful and called him sharply to account for it." While visiting a native friend on Saipan, he expressed his resentment of the inquisitiveness of a Japanese policeman by knocking the man down a flight of stairs. Again, neither of these two incidents nor his frequent hospitalizations swayed his seniors' confidence in him.

On 2 January 1915, Colonel Lejeune was assigned as assistant commandant of the Marine Corps, World War One was six months under way, and the corps was busy with plans for expansion. Lejeune soon found that he needed a small staff to assist him. He immediately had three of the most promising junior officers in the Marine Corps transferred to his office. These were Pete Ellis, Thomas Holcomb, Jr., and Ralph S. Keyser. Holcomb later became the marines's first lieutenant general commandant, serving from 1936 through 1943.

The United States declared war on Germany on 6 April 1917. Three days later, Ellis was promoted to major. In June 1918, Brigadier General Lejeune and Major Ellis sailed together on board the USS *Henderson* for France. Lejeune, soon to be promoted to major general, was assigned command of the 2nd Army-Marine Division. Ellis, promoted to temporary lieutenant colonel, was assigned as adjutant of the 4th Marine Brigade, which along with the Army's 3rd Infantry Brigade comprised Lejeune's 2nd Division.

As part of the French Army, the 2nd Division, at Lejeune's request, was assigned the mission of assaulting Blanc Mont Ridge, a key German strong point on the Hindenburg Line, in early October 1918. Lejeune sent his

aide for Ellis, and the aide reported back that the colonel was indisposed and that the indisposition could be expected to last several hours. Lejeune had the utmost confidence in Ellis—regardless of the indisposition—and wanted his advice on planning the assault. Later, Ellis prepared the plan for an assault which resulted in a penetration of the entire German defensive position forcing them to withdraw 30 kilometers; a Frenchman called it "the greatest single achievement of the 1918 campaign." General Henri Gouraud, whose plan Ellis recommended be discarded, rewarded Ellis with the Croix de Guerre and Palm and the Legion of Honor, grade of Chevalier. Ellis also was awarded the Navy Cross, not on the usual grounds of combat heroism but for excellence in his staff duties. The citation mentioned his imperviousness to fatigue and alertness under strain and sleeplessness, words which indicate that the nervousness and physical disorders diagnosed under headings such as neurasthenia and psychasthenia were becoming much more frequent and serious.

In 1919, Ellis's services were sought by both the navy and Marine Corps, but the routine of peacetime duty failed to supply mental stimulus to an officer of his caliber. From 1918 on, entries of hospitalization and sick leave in his record indicate a rapid nervous and physical decline. He took to drinking with increasing regularity. During 1919 and 1920, his friends noticed a very rapid decline in his physical appearance. In January 1920, navy doctors declared him unfit for active service and prescribed three months' sick leave.

In present times, Ellis might have been assigned to a rehabilitation program. But these were the passive days of the 1920s, so it was not surprising to find him being assigned, at his request, as the intelligence officer of the 2nd Marine Brigade in Santo Domingo. When the brigade commander was queried as to whether he "desired the services of Major Ellis" (he reverted to his permanent rank of major on 20 August 1919), the response was immediate, "Services desired and earnestly requested." When he reported in from sick leave on 17 April 1920, his orders to Santo Domingo were waiting for him. Tropical Santo Domingo was not exactly a health spa in the 1920s. It was the last place Pete Ellis should have gone to recuperate. A dry atmosphere would have been far better.

On 30 June 1920, Major General Lejeune was appointed commandant. Pete Ellis saw in this the opportunity for approval of the request he made in his 1912 fitness report. On 20 August 1920, Ellis sent a letter to General Lejeune:

> 1. In order that the Marine corps may have the necessary information on which to base its plans for further operations in South America and the Pacific Ocean I have to request that I be ordered to those areas for the purpose of making the necessary reconnaissance.
> 2. In the performance of such duties I will undertake to adopt any personal measures (submit undated resignations, travel as civilian, etc.) . . . necessary to ensure that the United States shall not become embarrrassed through my operations.

On 2 August 1920, Admiral Sims requested that Ellis be assigned to the staff of the Naval War College. Lejeune wrote to Sims, expressing regret that he could not comply with the request. Instead, Ellis reported to the commandant on 23 December 1920 and was assigned to the newly created operations and training division to work on his war plan. On 3 February 1921, he checked in at the Naval Hospital, Washington, D.C., where he stated that he had felt his latest breakdown coming on while he was in Santo Domingo. On 7 March, his problem was diagnosed as neurasthenia. On 17 March he began to subsist on the outside and report to the hospital every morning. His subsisting on the outside consisted of working night and day on his war plan in a dingy little office, Room 209, Headquarters, Marine Corps where a "No Admittance" sign was tacked to the door. The midwatch logs invariably showed the entry, "Lights burning in 209. Office occupied."

On 9 April, Ellis requested a three-month leave to visit Belgium, France, Germany, and England. On 12 April, he was released from

the hospital, allowing only a few days to tie up loose ends at headquarters before departing for Micronesia. The three months' leave was a cover for his mission to Micronesia. Before he could get away, he found himself back in the hospital on 18 April with the same old problem, neurasthenia. "Origin on duty . . . nervous and tense, was emotionally unstable . . . coarse tremors of the hands and tongue," said the medical report. "Complained of insomnia, nausea and an irritative cough . . . prescribed hypnotics. . . . Developed what he describes as the 'shakes.' "

On 4 May, Ellis was discharged from the hospital to return to duty; on that same day, Lejeune, in a letter to the secretary of the navy, requested permission for Ellis to leave the United States while on leave to visit Belgium, France, Germany, and England. The next day, 5 May, the letter was returned approved by Franklin Roosevelt, acting secretary of the navy. If a written directive for his mission was ever given to Ellis, it has not survived.

Prior to his departure, Ellis called at the commandant's office to say goodbye. During their farewell conversation, the commandant's secretary noticed Ellis hand Lejeune a sealed envelope which the general took without comment and slipped into his desk drawer. Ellis then departed. It was the last time they ever saw each other.

Looking at the mission in hindsight, the whole thing seems amateurish to a fault. There is no evidence of detailed planning. His cover as a trader was easily seen through by the German traders of Micronesia since he knew little or nothing about the business. The Navy Department apparently never bothered to tell the U.S. naval attache in Tokyo about Ellis, although the attache had primary intelligence responsibility for Micronesia. But with the laissez-faire atmosphere of the 1920s and the amateurish state of U.S. intelligence, permission for such a fishing expedition and the manner in which it was carried out were not so implausible as would be the case nowadays. To reconnoiter an area of such magnitude today might call for the combined resources of the civilian and military intelligence communities. But in May 1921, there was one lone, sick, and neurotic marine. Nevertheless, he was brilliant, courageous, and fired with a deep sense of duty. He was ready to embark on his mission with only the moral support of a pat on the back, a handshake, and wishes for good luck from the few senior officers who were privy to his mission. These included Generals Lejeune, Neville, Haines, and Logan Feland.

Ellis paid a last visit to his family in Pratt, Kansas. He told them he was going to travel for his health, but they would be unable to contact each other. If everything went well, they would hear from him in eight months. But if they did not hear from him, he wanted them to do nothing. There should be no inquiries through Senators Charles Curtis or Arthur Capper or through Congressman Homer Hoch, no publicity, no letters to the Marine Corps. Then he walked out the door of his boyhood home and vanished for almost a year. He was never seen in Europe. When he failed to return at the end of his ninety-day leave, an administrative officer at headquarters sent a brief memo to the adjutant-inspector, Brigadier General Henry Haines, "The leave granted Lieut. Col. Ellis has expired. How shall he be carried on the muster roll?" The memo came back with a note scrawled across the bottom, "Carry on leave," then, as if an afterthought, "until return." was added.

In late March 1922, Colonel Robert H. Dunlap, a close friend and confidant of Ellis on duty at Quantico, Virginia, received the following cablegram from Sydney, Australia:

> Impracticable here. Proceeding Japan. Everything all right cable Club Manila if not agreeable.
>
> Pete

He had just been released from a Sydney hospital where he had been treated for nephritis.

Years later, in 1948, the commandant of the Marine Corps asked General Douglas McArthur to search Japanese files for information on Ellis. Four messages were found, dated October 1921. They were exchanged between the consul general in Sydney, the foreign minister, and the minister of the navy.

Using his cover as a trader for the Hughes Company, Ellis had requested a visa to visit the Marshall and Caroline Islands on business. The minister of the navy said the visa could be granted, but he wanted Ellis's itinerary in advance. Armed with his visa, Ellis tried to reach the Japanese mandated islands from Sydney, but no ships were available. His failure to get passage out of Australia forced him to seek transportation into the islands from Japan, which of course increased the risk.

He booked passage at Sydney on board the *Tango Maru* to Manila. Becoming sick en route, he was placed in a civilian hospital upon arrival at Manila. By chance, a Marine Corps officer recognized him and had him transferred to the naval hospital at Canacao, Cavite, where the admission entry in his medical record reads, "5–17–22. Complains of nervousness . . . very restless, twitching of muscles of face and arms . . . Diagnosis changed to nephritis acute."

On 19 June, Ellis sent the following secret message to Brigadier General Feland at Marine Corps Headquarters:

> It is essential to reach objective by northern route. I have gained complete authority and I do not think there will be any further difficulty. Delayed here while ill but all well now. I desire to continue and if necessary to take six months extension time. I possess necessary funds. Your reply is desired by radio to Navsta Cavite.
>
> Signed Ellis

Neither Ellis's serious illness nor his delay in getting into Micronesia swayed General Lejeune's confidence in him. The reply, signed by the assistant to the commandant, went out "priority" the same day Ellis's message was received:

> Extension granted for period of six months or as much of that time as may be necessary period.
>
> Signed W. C. Neville

Upon being released from the hospital, Ellis stayed at the Delmonico Hotel in the Intramuros (Walled City), Manila. Late in July 1922, he left Manila on board the SS *President Jackson* for Yokohama with a reservation through to San Francisco. The latter action was apparently an attempt to throw the Japanese off his trail. It was one of the last rational, albeit naive, acts of his life.

Early in August 1922, he landed at Yokohama and checked into the Grand Hotel. On 12 August, Commander Ulys R. Webb, Medical Corps, U.S. Navy, commanding officer at the Naval Hospital, Yokohama, received a telephone call from a very excited desk clerk at the Grand Hotel who said that an American guest was quite sick. He asked if a doctor could come quickly. Webb found a man in civilian clothing suffering from nephritis, and there was also evidence that he had been drinking heavily. Determining that immediate hospitalization was necessary, the doctor had the man sent to the Naval Hospital. Upon admission, the patient identified himself as Lieutenant Colonel Earl H. Ellis, U.S. Marine Corps, and said he was touring Japan while on leave. His medical record reads, "August 12, 1922 Diagnosis: #548 Nephritis acute. . . . Probably from condition incident to service in the tropics. Patient also has probably been over indulging in alcoholics. . . . 23 August, to duty much improved, U. R. Webb, Comdr, MC, USN."

A week later, Ellis was admitted again, "9–1–22 #548 Nephritis acute. Readmitted, same symptom, same treatment. 9–14–22 Discharged to duty much improved, at his own request in order to continue his journey. U. R. Webb, Cmdr, MC, USN."

Captain Ellis M. Zacharias, in 1922 a lieutenant commander assigned to the naval attache's office in Tokyo, wrote in his book *Secret Missions* (New York: G. P. Putnam's Sons, 1946):

> The attention of the naval attache [Captain Lyman A. Cotten, USN] was directed to an American who had just arrived in Yokohama and who was seen frequently in rather shabby drinking places and geisha houses . . . As he [Ellis] told it during his lighter moments in Yokohama, he was selected by Washington to go to the mandated islands in the guise of an innocuous traveler "to find out what the hell was going on down there." . . . For several days we maintained our surveillance over the "agent" and watched him toboggan rapidly in Yoko-

hama bars. Every one of his appearances there revealed more data on his proposed trip, not only to us but obviously to Japanese counter-intelligence as well; and we realized that this "secret agent" had outlived his usefulness long before he could embark on his actual mission.

On 20 September, Webb had an ambulance pick up Ellis at the Grand Hotel and admitted him to the hospital. His medical report reads, "Poison, alcohol, acute. . . . Not duty. Due to his own misconduct . . . delirium tremens . . . so shaky cannot feed himself . . . throws everything in his room out of the window. Treated with whiskey, sedatives and food." When Ellis sobered he found himself in a private room attended by Chief Pharmacist Lawrence Zembsch who acted more as jailer than nurse.

Cotten had never been informed of Ellis's mission. If Ellis had been under secret orders from the highest echelon of the government, Cotten would have been in serious trouble for terminating or otherwise disrupting the execution of those orders. Lieutenant Colonel Ellis was obviously in extremely poor physical condition and required immediate medical help which was not available in Japan. So he proposed to have Webb certify him as sick for further transfer to the United States for treatment.

Captain Zacharias said in *Secret Missions*, "Although originally motivated by security considerations, Cotten's concern about the Colonel's physical condition appeared fully justified after Dr. Webb's first examination . . . The Colonel was in no shape even for transportation back home, so we were advised to permit him to regain at least some of his strength in his private ward before sending him on a strenuous journey by transport." Webb prepared the necessary report certifying Ellis as sick and requiring medical treatment in the United States. Upon receipt of Webb's report, General Lejeune revoked Ellis's leave and ordered him to report. But Pete Ellis never received those orders.

Webb gave Ellis his choice of going home by government transportation or buying his own ticket for a commercial liner. He decided instead to turn his back on the security of returning to the United States. On 4 October 1922, Ellis cabled his bank in San Francisco for $1,000. Two days later, he received it. On the night of 6/7 October, he slipped out of the hospital against Webb's specific orders not to leave and departed forever the official custody of the naval service.

Starting at the Grand Hotel in Yokohama where Ellis had been staying, Captain Cotten and his intelligence agents began to make discreet inquiries. They found he had paid his bill at the hotel and ordered an automobile to take some luggage to the Yokohama railway station. Cotten even went to the extent of enlisting the aid of the Japanese missing persons bureau and other local authorities in the search. Both U.S. and Japanese authorities searched Tokyo and Yokohama without success. Ellis probably departed from either Kobe or Moji, using the visa stamped in his passport at Sydney a year earlier as his "ticket" to the mandated islands.

Apparently, he first went to Jaluit in the Marshalls where he stayed about two months. There he became acquainted with Arthur Herrman, a German trader. Herrman was in San Francisco on business on 23 May 1923. There he read about Ellis's death in a newspaper, then called on Major General George Barnett at Headquarters, Department of the Pacific. The following is from General Barnett's 25 May 1923 letter to the Major General Commandant. He reported Herrman said the following:

(a) Stated that he saw Colonel Ellis in Kusaie, Eastern Caroline Islands; and that he also had a brother there who was acquainted with Colonel Ellis.

(b) That he left on the same steamer with Colonel Ellis, and went as far as Palew [Palau] with him in the Western Caroline Islands. This was about April 16, 1923.

(c) That Colonel Ellis at that time was in good health.

(d) That he (Herrman) had known Colonel Ellis for about two months, while at the Marshall Islands. While there Colonel Ellis had heard from the Japanese that there was to be war between the United States and Japan. A great many of the Japanese were drunk, and it was their intention of putting Colonel Ellis in jail.

(e) According to Mr. Herrman, Colonel Ellis was en route from Palew to New Guinea.

(f) That on the steamer between Kusaie and Palew, Colonel Ellis has [sic] eaten some canned eels and had drunk some beer, which made him (Ellis) very ill.

(g) That he (Herrman) saw Colonel Ellis at Jaliut [sic] and was later a patient at the hospital there.

(h) Herrman stated . . . that Colonel Ellis carried a considerable amount of money with him.

(i) . . . Mr. Herrman stated that there was every evidence that the Japanese wanted no foreigners on the islands, and they were very anxious to get rid of Colonel Ellis.

This was the first smattering of information of Ellis's activities since he disappeared from the naval hospital at Yokohama on the night of 6/7 October 1922. Years later, others were to add bits and pieces to the story. In November 1923, Cornelius Vanderbilt III talked with a medical missionary, Miss Jesse Hoppin, when the Japanese allowed his yacht to lie to at Jaluit for repairs after a storm. She said she had known Ellis and had nursed him in her home when he was seriously ill at Kusaie. The Japanese, she recalled, had been furious with him when he entered certain forbidden areas. She had heard threats against his life and felt Ellis had sailed from the Carolines just in time, though she was sure he was under surveillance wherever he went in the Pacific. She gave him a clean bill of health on his departure from Kusaie.

In 1926, Ellis's two sisters had a brief visit with Miss Hoppin between trains at Wichita when Miss Hoppin was returning to Kusaie after a leave to her home in Auburndale, Massachusetts. Miss Hoppin added nothing new during this brief visit. She promised to write to Ellis's sisters, but she never did. In 1933, Miss Hoppin again returned to her home on leave. Now sixty-seven years old, she had spent most of her life in the Marshalls and had lost touch with the United States. Three days after her return home, a Marine Corps officer paid her a visit. Miss Hoppin was more reserved than she had been with Vanderbilt ten years earlier. She refused pointblank to discuss Ellis or his activities. The officer left convinced that the elderly missionary had been warned not to discuss the affairs of the islands to which she intended to return. In 1939, Miss Hoppin went to her home in the United States. The Japanese did not permit her to return to the Marshalls.

In March 1950, the commandant, hoping to learn more about Colonel Ellis's last days, sent Lieutenant Colonel Waite W. Worden to Koror to interview natives who knew Ellis. Colonel Worden's report revealed the following.

Upon arriving at Koror in April 1923, Ellis was met by the chief of native police, Jose Tellei, who checked all incoming passengers. Tellei told Colonel Worden that Ellis's papers showed him as a businessman. He said that neither the Japanese nor anyone else knew Ellis was a marine, but the commissioner of police, who was Japanese, directed that Ellis be followed at all times and further directed that the police wear civilian clothes. The Japanese police thought Ellis was a spy. Ellis stayed at Koror about three days, went to Ponape, then returned to Koror for six weeks. Tellei said everyone called him "Mr. Ellis," indicating that no one knew he was a Marine Corps officer.

When Ellis returned to Koror after his three-day visit to Ponape, he went to live with William Gibbon, a half-caste Englishman, and his native wife, Ngerdako. Gibbon was the only person at Koror who spoke English. After about a week, Ellis asked Gibbon to find him a house in the native area. He said he wanted privacy and didn't want to live in the Japanese community. Gibbon obtained the island chief's house for Ellis. The chief's house was owned by the community, but was unoccupied at the time because the chief then preferred to live in his own private house. Shortly after Ellis moved in, a twenty-five-year-old native woman, Metauie, came to live with him as a concubine. She lived with him until he died.

Metauie said Ellis drank constantly while at Koror. William Gibbon's widow Ngerdako confirmed this at the same time, saying that Ellis drank heavily, sake, beer, whiskey, anything he could get. Once he had no liquor

and he came to Gibbon's house to demand something to drink. When Gibbon told him he had nothing to drink, Ellis, drunk at the time, tried to rip the walls apart with his hands, thinking Gibbon's supply of whiskey was hidden in the wall.

Although Ellis knew he was dying, he continued his daily search, Metauie said. He would leave the house every day saying he was going to take a walk. She didn't know what he was looking for.

Mrs. Gibbons said that he would walk around during the day, looking things over, and was constantly watched by the Japanese. Frequently the Japanese were discovered peeking into his window at night, and loitering on his premises. Ellis went out of the house on several occasions to beat up with his fists such Japanese as were peeking into his quarters.

Jose Tellei also stated that Ellis did a lot of walking around, looking things over, and was shadowed by the Japanese or native police at all times.

Near his end, Ellis must have realized his chances of making any sort of an intelligence find were quite remote. One can only guess at his despair and bitterness of spirit because his search had come to nothing. There was a cruel irony—it was not their strength which the Japanese were trying to conceal. It was their weakness. There were no Singapores, Gibraltars, or Verduns in the mandated islands before World War Two. The Japanese plan was to use these islands as an offensive springboard, not for defense. Much later, the Japanese skill in building improvised defenses, usually from local materials such as coconut logs and coral, was much in evidence. This became especially manifest in the toll of American lives it cost to take such positions. But these were somewhat hastily built after our Makin Island raid in 1942. For example, the elaborate cave system on Peleliu that cost one thousand marine lives was built between March and September 1944.

One morning Ellis went "crazy drunk," according to Ngerdako Gibbon, and by 1700 that day he was dead. She and her husband built a coffin for Ellis, and the next day they buried him in the native cemetery. Metauie, by 1950 a woman of about fifty-three, said she thought Ellis died from "too much sake." It is likely that Colonel Ellis died from the cumulative effects of drinking and his various diseases. There is also at least the possibility that he was poisoned by the Japanese, but the actual cause of death remains unknown.

The day before Ellis died, Captain Cotten was called by the Japanese Navy Ministry to receive news that Colonel Ellis had been located at Koror, but that the doctors there didn't expect him to live much longer. Captain Cotten asked the official at the Navy Ministry to send Colonel Ellis back as soon as possible. The Japanese official replied that details for his return would be arranged within 24 hours, and Colonel Ellis would be brought home at once.

The next morning, a call from the Navy Ministry informed the naval attache that Colonel Ellis had died the night before. Captain Cotten saw in the act of picking up Ellis's remains at Koror a great opportunity to do some on-the-spot intelligence work. "I will send a representative to take charge of the ashes," he informed the Japanese, "This gentleman was an important personality in the United States, and we wish to bury him with the ceremony due his status."

Captain Cotten's request caught the Japanese spokesman off guard, because he was not prepared to handle such a request. After consulting with his superiors, he called Cotten back to say they interposed no objection to sending Chief Pharmacist Zembsch to Koror. After being carefully prepared for the trip in the attache's office, Zembsch sailed from Yokohama on 4 June 1923 to bring back Ellis's remains.

In the 1950 interview, William Gibbon's widow stated that shortly after Ellis died, an American whose name she did not know arrived from Japan. Then she, her husband, and Jose Tellei dug up Ellis's body and cremated it in the open on a pile of rocks. The American placed Ellis's ashes in a small box he had brought with him. He then departed Koror, saying he was going to the states via Japan. She said that he was in civilian clothes, of which he had many kinds, but he "looked like a soldier."

Metauie reported that when the American came, he went to the Koror government to inquire about Ellis. The Koror government called her, William Gibbon, and his wife to point out the burial place. Then the Japanese police, the American and a native working party disinterred the body in the presence of her, William Gibbon, Mrs. Gibbon, and Jose Tellei. Metauie stated further that the American had a small box. When the body was disinterred, it was cremated on some rocks in the open, after which the American placed the ashes in the small box. The American then waited for a Japanese ship, saying he would return to Japan and then go to America. The American was in civilian clothes. The Japanese police took all of Ellis's personal effects and turned them over to the Koror government. When the American picked up the ashes, she saw the box of effects in the government building and thought that the American took this box with him.

Jose Tellei stated that he was present at the time Ellis's body was disinterred, and he witnessed the cremation. He said that the American who picked up the ashes was a Mr. Lorenz (Lawrence Zembsch), whom he knew was a naval officer.

The Japanese kept the naval attache advised of Zembsch's progress and of his arrival at Koror. But then the news abruptly ceased. On 13 August 1923, the Navy Ministry called the attache to say that Zembsch would arrive by ship in Yokohama the next day. Dr. Webb, Lieutenant Commander Zacharias, and several members of the attache staff went down to the pier to meet Zembsch.

After the ship was tied up, they waited a reasonable time for Zembsch to appear, then went aboard to locate him. They were greeted politely by the captain of the ship who personally conducted them to Zembsch's cabin. As they opened the door to the cabin, they saw Zembsch sitting on his bunk. He was unshaven, unkempt, and deranged in mind and physical appearance. Completely unmoved by Dr. Webb's appearance, he did not rise to greet him, but simply stared off into space. Clasped tightly in his arms was the white box used by the Japanese for the ashes of the cremated.

Despite the most attentive medical treatment, Zembsch remained in a catatonic stupor. Webb did not leave his bedside for four days, applying all known methods of mental therapy to get him back to a state of mental coherence. After showing some little improvement, he developed an acute case of amnesia which prevented him from remembering anything of the immediate past. Dr. Webb was convinced that he was heavily drugged. On 28 August, Webb finally got a statement from Zembsch that the Japanese had known Ellis for what he actually was.

Dr. Webb had scheduled another session with Zembsch on the afternoon of 1 September 1923. That morning Zembsch's wife had visited him at the hospital and was getting ready to leave right before noon. At 1142, a devastating earthquake struck the Yoko-

hama area. The hospital was completely destroyed and both Zembsch and his wife perished in the ruins.

After U.S. authorities dug through the debris of the earthquake, the following was received by the American Consul General in Yokohama from the commander-in-chief, Asiatic Fleet:

> Ashes of LtCol Earl H. Ellis, born on 19 December 1880 died Palau, Caroline Islands 12 May 1923; were found in the ruins of receiving vault and identified by Lt. T. P. Riddle, ChC, USN, through a typewritten slip pasted to a strip of wood which had evidently been a part of the outer case of a small casket. Ashes being sent to the United States on instructions of the Department.

The remains were finally laid to rest on Pete Ellis's birthday, 19 December 1923, in his home town of Pratt, Kansas. Today the amphibious training building at the Marine Corps schools, Quantico, Virginia, is named Ellis Hall.

Marines, Aviators, and the Battleship Mentality, 1923–33

BY JOHN P. CAMPBELL

In the United States, with the end of the First World War, reaction against a Wilsonian navy was no less emphatic than reaction against a Wilsonian League. Preoccupied with business and inclined toward isolationism, Americans found the appeal of navalism easily resistible, the Naval Appropriations Act of 1916 and the preachings of Roosevelt and Mahan notwithstanding. Inveterate traditions of antiauthoritarianism, individualism, and suspicion of the military quickly reasserted themselves at the expense of the martial spirit; and the successful presidential candidate in the election of 1920 acclaimed the return not to heroism but to "normalcy," thereby enlarging if hardly enriching the language and setting the tone for the 1920s.

The Washington Conference of 1921–22 to investigate the possibility of limiting naval armaments reflected this fairly predictable national reaction at the end of a victorious war, but also symbolized the ambitions and hopes of societies and organizations devoted to peace and disarmament. The work, indeed, of the predominantly civilian American delegation led by Secretary of State Charles Evans Hughes conformed more faithfully to the suggestions and arguments of, say, the National Council for the Limitation of Armaments than to those of professional naval advisors.

The Five Power Naval Treaty appealed to the public imagination, mainly because the 5:5:3 ratio for the United States, Great Britain, and Japan respectively left the American navy, at least to outward appearances, superior to the Japanese. But this inferiority in a ratio applying only to capital ship tonnage—at best a deceptive measure of naval potential—was accepted by Japan only in return for an American guarantee to refrain thereafter from fortifying bases west of Hawaii. Japan and the United States, consequently, would each be supreme in home waters, an arrangement that nevertheless concealed a major concession on the part of the Americans: for whereas Japan had no claims or possessions to defend in the Eastern Pacific, the United States was heavily committed in the Western Pacific, in the Philippines, Guam, and the Aleutians. Such sweeping and seemingly gratuitous acceptance of strategic disadvantage—in spite of similar British and Japanese guarantees with respect to their bases in the same area—came as an unwelcome surprise to the General Board of the United States Navy. Reduction of tonnage was to be expected at the hands of a parsimonious Congress, treaties or no treaties, but now, in the event of a war against Japan, the Pacific Fleet would certainly find the waters west of Hawaii untenable for want of prepared bases, leaving the Philippines and Guam practically indefensible by naval action. Island bases from which to launch operations against Japan itself would presumably have to be taken by storm.

However surely, in the opinion of the critics of the nonfortification clause, the inad-

Journal of the Royal United Services Institute 109 (February-November 1964): 45–50. Reprinted by permission.

Amphibious Training, *ca.* 1929–30. Courtesy of the Burke Collection, U.S. Navy Historical Center.

equate American garrisons on the Philippines and Guam would succumb for want of naval protection, the problem of attacking mountainous islands or low-lying coral atolls in the Western Pacific might easily have provided an equally good excuse for abject resignation in 1922. The fiasco at Gallipoli in 1915 had convinced military theorists that an attack on a defended beach in daylight would surely be foolhardy and probably suicidal. Technological developments had strengthened defensive might out of all proportion to offensive thrust, even without the additional complication of a vulnerable ship-to-shore maneuver against defenses offering the landing force little or no opportunity for the employment of surprise or tactical ingenuity. One naval authority, writing in 1926, pointed out that "the whole course of history" showed such an operation "to be a desperate undertaking, which has very rarely

succeeded." And as late as 1939 Captain Liddell Hart decided that a landing on an enemy coast would be "almost impossible" in face of determined resistance by the defending air force. By a fortunate coincidence, however, this problem had to be faced in the United States at a time when a small but influential group of Marine Corps officers were attempting a reappraisal and redefinition of the function of the corps—used incongruously as shock troops in the trenches during the First World War.

Actually at least one Marine Corps officer had anticipated as early as 1913 the need to reduce fortified islands before finally launching an attack on Japan itself. The nonfortification clause agreed to at the Washington Conference hardly seems to have altered Major Earl H. Ellis's appreciation of the logistical and tactical difficulties facing American arms within the Japanese sphere of influence—partly, perhaps, because the Japanese went to almost pathological lengths to conceal their activities on islands in the non-fortification area. Before his mysterious death on the Japanese mandate of Palau in the Caroline Islands in 1923, Ellis prepared a war plan of uncanny prescience, including descriptions of the equipment and estimates of the strength of units capable of assaulting strategically important islands, such as Eniwetok atoll. A few of the plans drawn up in the 1920s were later adapted for use during the Second World War, and one that had been discarded with deliberate carelessness misled the Japanese on Guam in 1944. By 1923 some senior officers of the corps, including the commandant, General John A. Lejeune, had reached the conclusion that the most important duty of the marines in peace was, in Lejeune's words, "the maintenance, equipping, and training of its expeditionary force so that it will be in instant readiness to support the fleet in the event of war." In 1927 the Joint Board of the Army and Navy specifically assigned to the marines the task of conducting landing operations.

No amount of acknowledgment of its new role by the corps and no end of injunctions by the Joint Board in any way modified the formidable problems facing such an expeditionary force. The 1920 edition of the *Navy Manual for Ships' Landing Forces* devoted 7 out of 760 pages to the actual landing; these 7 pages were reduced to 5 in the 1927 edition. The corps, moreover, was distracted during the 1920s by irksome interruptions in the shape of a jungle war in Nicaragua and expeditions to China, not to mention its usual peacetime duties of guarding naval installations. Congressional passion for economy was yet another obstacle to the establishment of amphibious operations as a respectable branch of modern military science; like the rest of the American armed forces, the Marine Corps was chronically short of funds and only the personality and contacts of Lejeune kept it up to reasonable strength. In these circumstances what little practical experimentation there was during the 1920s was instructive in a sobering way rather than encouraging.

An exercise at Culebra in the Caribbean in 1924 ended in confusion: the naval bombardment, such as it was, would have left enemy positions unscathed on the reverse side of slopes facing the beach; the solitary transport had been badly loaded, essential items of equipment having been consigned to the bottom of the hold; the small boats could probably have been blown to pieces long before the infantrymen set foot on the beach. Another exercise at Oahu a year later, to demonstrate to critical army officers that the marines could land in greater than brigade strength, served instead to illustrate the deficiencies of the primitive landing craft employed. No more exercises were held before 1932.

There were less obvious reasons than these why the marines failed to make more practical and theoretical progress in amphibious warfare during the 1920s. In the age of Prohibition, the Scopes trial, the Great Crash, and the talkies, public interest in the armed forces, never pronounced at the best of times, all but disappeared. The army and navy attempted to counteract this tendency by advertising the contributions they could make to American society rather than by perfecting their prowess as agents of national defense. The military caste, in fact, had ill-founded hopes during the 1920s that their pariah status in American society, briefly and tantalizingly overlooked during the war, could be permanently suspended by public—and frequently disingenuous—disavowals of professionalism. As Samuel P. Huntington has shown, officers were encouraged by their superiors to be good mixers as well as good fighters, to accept invitations to speak at Rotary meetings, to adjust to the overwhelmingly civilian values of the day. The secretary of the navy boasted in 1921 that the navy "was engaged continuously in useful and humanitarian enterprises" and praised its contributions to scientific and industrial research. A feature of the marines's summer maneuvers were reenactments of Civil War battles, performed at Gettysburg for President Harding and party and, in the summer of 1924, at Antietam for the entertainment and edification of an estimated forty thousand spectators.

Admittedly, amphibious operations—in years when President Coolidge could adjure the Annapolis class of '25 to pay their first attention to the civilian life of the nation and when President Hoover preached disarmament by example—was hardly material for good Marine Corps public relations. A convinced protagonist of amphibious warfare, General Holland K. Smith of the marines, found to his dismay that the main emphasis in courses at the Marine Corps School in 1926 was still on defensive tactics, a feature of the curriculum hardly consonant with his ideas or those of Ellis and Lejeune. Clearly there was a lack of balance and consensus within the corps. And it seems reasonable to conclude that the fondness of many officers for courses and maneuvers more appropriate to the army was the result not only of lack of military gumption on their part but of resentment at the emphasis on professionalism implicit in specialization in such a highly technical branch of military science as amphibious operations.

Addiction to the folly, for whatever reasons, of using a comparatively small military organization of mobile, well-trained troops in a defensive role was a serious hindrance to the adoption of Smith's ideas, but hardly less serious than obtuseness in high ranking minds in the navy, often instinctively and snobbishly suspicious of the Marine Corps and all its works. Smith carried on a campaign throughout the 1920s against what he regarded as supercilious intellectual obstinacy in the higher echelons of the navy. This, in his opinion, prevented many admirals, including Rear Admiral William S. Sims, president of the Naval College at Newport when Smith attended a course there in 1921, from comprehending strategic situations involving naval activity where sea power wielded in the grand manner would not be decisive. According to Smith, Sims was so completely and narrowly naval that his idea of a landing consisted of little more than the appearance offshore of a large naval force whose overwhelming display of might would render the

enemy incapable of resistance, whereupon an improvised gang of bluejackets and marines would emerge from the surf to accept their surrender. More particularly, the admirals, mindful perhaps of the fate of some of the naval units that bombarded the Turkish forts at Gallipoli in 1915, repeatedly offered strenuous objections to the use of naval gunfire in support of landings. Technical objections were not hard to assemble: the high muzzle velocity and low trajectory of naval guns made them poor substitutes for mortars and howitzers; armor-piercing shells were unsuitable for the purposes of bombardment and magazine space aboard a battleship would be seriously restricted if compelled to accommodate high explosive shells as well; and so forth. There were the horrifying possibilities, too, of hostile surface or submarine activity while the bombardment was in progress—all of which, to Smith's chagrin and doubtless alarm, convinced the admirals that bombardments of this kind should be delivered only from maximum range by warships zigzagging at full speed.

Remarkable, then, against this background of insufficient funds, doubting naval orthodoxy, and distractions at home and abroad, was the formation in 1933 of the Fleet Marine Force, committing the bulk of the corps to serving the fleet in war by seizing bases for naval operations; but more remarkable still was the *Tentative Manual for Landing Operations*, drawn up at the Marine Corps School at Quantico shortly afterwards. According to this—worthy of a place among the major documents of modern military theory—a landing on a defended shore should be conducted as a tactical movement in its own right—a tactical movement designed to achieve maximum momentum across the beach—not simply as a ferrying operation. In contrast to the haphazard ideas of Smith's naval antagonists, the concept of the ship-to-shore movement outlined in the *Manual* was of an exceedingly complex military operation, requiring the deployment of considerable forces in the approaches to the beach, precise marksmanship by naval guns, and quantities of the specialized technical paraphernalia of modern war. The *Manual* emphasized, among other things, the importance of loading transports with a view to the priority of requirements of the troops ashore rather than the ideal stability of the ship. Sensible suggestions were made in its pages for well-defined spheres of command for the commander of the invasion fleet and the marine landing force commander, no doubt in an attempt to minimize interservice sniping and to steer clear of an informal junta of the type that had mismanaged Gallipoli.

That it resented the secondary, supporting role assigned to the guns of the fleet by the authors of the *Manual* is at least understandable in the light of the navy's attachment to the battleship. Here was the embodiment of sea power, the floating symbol of national power and prestige. Gunfire had decided all the great naval battles of the past and accordingly the first objective of the fleet should be to bring the big guns of the battleships and battlecruisers to bear on the enemy. The modern all-big-gun capital ship, unsurpassed in speed, fire-power, and endurance, was the ultimate weapon, according to Admiral William D. Leahy in 1941; he and his contemporaries had been trained to think in terms of the set piece gunnery battle between fleets. Nelson himself had said that a ship would be a fool to fight a fort; and his maxim was accepted as equally valid for post-Dreadnoughts as for three-deckers. Battleships, in short, should battle only battleships.

The *Manual* emphasized—and the Second World War was to verify—the importance of air support during an amphibious assault. Aircraft, it was proposed, would spot for the battleships' guns, strafe the reverse sides of slopes protected from the bombardment, and protect the waves of landing craft from enemy air attack. In the vast reaches of the Pacific, air support for landings would almost invariably be carrier-based. Significantly enough, the proponents of naval air power and the daring innovators at Quantico encountered opposition in the same quarter— among the admirals, in Henry Stimson's words, a great "anonymous and continuous" host in the Navy Department who psycho-

logically "frequently seemed to retire from the realm of logic into a dim religious world in which Neptune was God, Mahan his prophet, and the United States Navy the only true Church." And ominously enough, from the point of view of the spiritual leaders of this church, the heresy of air power threatened to produce not merely a flurry of disagreement between rival sects but a thoroughgoing schism, since it was even more threatening in its tendency toward a revision of the authorized version of the doctrine of sea power than the maunderings of Marine Corps generals.

While the *Tentative Manual for Landing Operations* was the result of hard thinking in the form of tactical and strategical reconsiderations within the Marine Corps—so much so, in fact, as to cast doubt on the validity of Mahan's generalization that no armed service can reform itself without pressure from outside—naval aviation was only one aspect of a technological revolution outside the navy. The marines were concerned with the theoretical principles of war, military doctrine. On the other hand, Rear Admiral William Moffett, head of the Bureau of Aeronautics in the Navy Department from its establishment in 1921 until his death in a dirigible crash in 1933, was involved more with dollars than with doctrine. Proposals to purchase expensive equipment with a high rate of obsolescence often provoked bitter internal squabbles in the Navy Department. These frequently echoed a national debate over more general aspects of air power that attracted widespread civilian interest and incited a certain amount of popular commotion. All of this, of course, was in striking contrast to the professional, almost academic, disagreements between the marines and the battleship hierarchy.

Aviation, for some reason, was one of the subjects on which the American public, lacking the inclination to study more significant though less spectacular aspects of national affairs, were self-appointed experts. A pattern of public interest in aviation had been established with the transatlantic flight *via* the Azores of the NC 4 seaplane in 1919, and aviation remained fashionable, a sure source of good newspaper copy. Realizing this, and determined that naval aviation should not perish for want of public interest, Moffett was capable of stealing front page space for a few editions by announcing that an airship (which had still to be built) would fly over the North Pole. Often his cause was helped by the accomplishments of enterprising subordinates; in 1923, for example, the navy won the Schneider air race and held twenty-three out of seventy-eight world records for aeroplanes and twenty-one out of seventy-four for seaplanes. The public was impressed, but hardly Congress, at least when it came down to a question of appropriations, and not at all the admirals, most of whom would have agreed with the comment of Admiral William S. Benson that aviation was "just a lot of noise." The Bureau of Aeronautics, wrote Lieutenant Arthur Radford in a memorandum to Moffett in the spring of 1924, was "in the peculiar position of having sold naval aviation to the public but not to the Navy as a whole."

Within the Navy Department, Moffett was in a position of some delicacy, for public interest in aviation was not always an unmixed blessing, especially when aviation became the subject of a splendid national fuss. This began when Brigadier General Billy Mitchell of the army started a campaign for an independent air force, arguing coincidentally that the navy could no longer fulfill its traditional role as the first line of national defense. Intemperate remarks invited and received intemperate replies, so that something like hysteria quickly distorted the arguments of the contesting proponents of the battleship and the bomber. Wilson's secretary of the navy, Josephus Daniels, defiantly offered to stand at the wheel of a battleship, bare-headed, while Mitchell attacked him from the air, but the public had to be content with a series of compensatory attractions in the shape of bombing tests off the Virginia Capes between 1921 and 1925. The tests, far from settling the dispute, actually made it more acrimonous than before, and inflicted a shock on the admirals from which many of them

never fully recovered. A civilian witness at the first test was startled to observe emotional reactions of unconcealed amazement, horror, and grief among hardened admirals and captains when the *Ostfriesland* heeled over and sank under the onslaught of nothing more than a few bombing planes. "One seemed to be watching the end of an era," he concluded, in a spirit of academic detachment few of the sailors present could have appreciated, "which began when Rome crossed the high seas and smote Carthage."

Aware or not of the end of an era, the admirals were anything but prepared to alter their idea of what in fact was the dominant weapon. Indeed, in the trauma afficting the Navy Department after the bombing tests, Moffett, though himself abhorring the idea of a separate air force and aspiring only to a useful and recognized role for aviation within the navy, was the object of guarded suspicion on the part of his fellow officers. When Mitchell leveled charges of negligence and incompetence against the navy, Moffett retorted, as though to underscore his loyalty to the service, by accusing him of using "the revolutionary methods of the Communists" and of harboring "delusions of grandeur." Nor was Moffett's position helped much when his publicity ventures occasionally misfired; in 1925, a bad year for misfortunes of this kind, the dirigible *Shenandoah*, on a flight to promote public relations, came to grief in an electrical storm over Ohio, while an attempt by three seaplanes to fly from San Francisco to Hawaii flopped only three days later. The secretary of the navy gratefully seized on the latter catastrophe—one seaplane covered the final 450 miles under sail—as conclusive proof that the United States, contrary to Mitchell's prognostications, would be safe from air attack.

The heads of the other administrative bureaus in the Navy Department regarded Moffett as at the very least an upstart and at worst a natural enemy from an alien element. The Bureau of Steam Engineering, by some quaint administrative quirk, was responsible for the purchase of wireless equipment; more than one crisis occurred when it threatened to commission sets for the Bureau of Aeronautics that would be useless in aircraft. A running battle went on between Moffett and successive heads of the Bureau of Navigation over the vexatious problems of personnel and postings. Again, Admiral S. S. Robinson, commander-in-chief of the United States Navy, repeatedly denounced the Bureau of Aeronautics for usurping the functions of the other bureaus and was opposed not only to extra flight pay for aviators but also to having them in command of aircraft carriers and flying schools. Worst of all, during the sittings of the Morrow Board, the most important of many official boards and Congressional committees set up in the mid 1920s to study the best means of using aircraft in national defense, it was revealed that the navy budget officer, Rear Admiral Joseph Straus, was nothing if not skeptical in his attitude toward aviation. Straus, apparently, had made a reduction in the aeronautics budget out of all proportion to the reduction in the budget for the navy as a whole. So, for all the encouraging features of the four volumes of the Morrow Board Report three years earlier, Moffett had to admit in May 1929: "The antagonism to aviation has become so intensely acute that I am more disgusted than ever."

Nothing added to the delicacy of Moffett's position more than his occasional prediction that the aircraft carrier would eventually replace the battleship as the capital ship of the fleet. In 1922 the *Langley*, a converted collier, became the United States Navy's first carrier, serving as a floating center for experimentation in the complicated techniques of handling aircraft on a flight deck and slowing the forward motion of landing aircraft. Two sister carriers, the *Saratoga* and the *Lexington*, with battlecruiser hulls originally scheduled to be scrapped under the terms of the Five Power Treaty of 1922, joined the fleet in 1928—large and vulnerable at 33,000 tons but capable nevertheless of 33 knots. The speed of the *Saratoga* was used to good advantage during the 1929 maneuvers in the Pacific, when the carrier and a fast cruiser escort left the main body of the fleet to make a wide sweep to seaward; while still 200 miles from her objective, the *Saratoga* launched her aircraft to take the Canal Zone defenses completely by surprise. This inventive use of the carrier's offensive potential struck a responsive chord in the mind of a future chief of naval operations, Lieutenant Commander Forrest P. Sherman. As early as 1930, Sherman was thinking in terms of a fleet formation on the lines of the carrier-centered task force of the Second World War. Here were the first glimmerings of a doctrine of war that would raise naval aviation far above the humble level of significance at which the admirals had originally been reluctantly prepared to accept it. Instead of fulfilling an essentially auxiliary role by spotting for the guns of the battleships, carrier-based aircraft, as soon as the intricate skills of dive bombing and launching torpedoes from the air had been developed, could seriously be considered as a replacement for these very guns in delivering the fleet's long-range punch.

Technological and doctrinal innovations by aviators and marines—no less significant than contemporary German innovations later to mature as the *Blitzkrieg*—came, paradoxically, at a time when the navy was being weakened, as it had never been weakened since the years following the Civil War, by decay from within and indifference from without. By 1933 the United States had built up to only 63 percent of her authorized treaty strength; Japan, by comparison, had built to within 5 percent of hers. Efficiency and morale declined as appropriations dwindled. Too often the size of its annual budget determined the Navy's operations rather than analysis of the likely contingencies of a war in the Pacific against Japan. Complacency and the lackluster performance of routine duties, though, hardly in themselves explain the motives of the admirals in their stout resistance to change. Stubbornness of this kind, after all, was not a characteristic of conservative naval opinion solely in the United States Navy in the years from Wilson to the New Deal. To illustrate this, in the Royal Navy before 1914, Admiral Sir Percy Scott had fought a long battle on behalf of the director sight, allegedly against professional jealousy; and, ironically, the American officer who did much to modernize naval marine engineering was to find himself "banished" in 1939, after a campaign accomplished over "the obstacles of blindness, stupidity, selfishness, and even malevolence." The case of the admirals during the 1920s and early 1930s could be matched in other military organizations at other periods in history simply because they were caught up in the central paradox of military thought, one that faces every generation of military leaders; namely, that in few spheres of human activity are change and progress so constant and the need for accommodation and adjustment so unremitting as in the military; yet in few spheres, seemingly, are the ruling minds so rigidly resistant to change.

It would be fatally easy, with the advantages of hindsight, to interpret instances of this paradox in terms of enlightenment and inspiration versus "Blimpism," to use terms like "professional jealousy" and "blind stupidity" with all the venom and intensity of participants. But to do so would require oversimplification verging on willful distortion of fact. The navy's objections to the role of floating artillery to which the admirals felt condemned by the marines, for instance, were not wholly an expression of stupidity, tenacious adherence to senseless tradition, or jealousy. It would, obviously, make no sense to sustain such heavy losses during a bombardment as to cripple the fleet in forthcoming battles to which seizure of island bases was merely a preliminary. Few yet thought of island bases in the context of air rather than sea power. Furthermore, there was often as much honest doubt and confusion on the part of innovators as of conservatives. Admiral Sims, just as outspoken an advocate of air power as Admiral Bradley Fiske—who proposed to defend the Philippines exclusively by air power—went so far as to advise the admirals that the safest place for their battleships in case of an air attack from either ocean would be the upper reaches of the Mississippi, a prophecy of almost blasphemous insolence, from the admirals' viewpoint, that

Sims reserved for the publicity of hearings before a Select Committee of the House in 1925. "Now, as I said before," Sims repeated in 1925, "it is an astonishing thing, the conservatism of the military mind. It is absolutely historical that they never give in. You have to shed their blood before they do it . . . Lots of people that differ with me on these points are old friends of mine that I have known for 40 years. They are men of absolute integrity of character. They believe absoluely what they say. But, by God," he concluded, "you cannot get it out of their heads at all." Strange words indeed from a man whom General Smith regarded as just as hopelessly benighted as the naval mossbacks whose intellectual shortcomings Sims was deploring.

The paradox, therefore, resolves itself into a question of limited identification, comprehensible perhaps only in the language of the social psychologist. As Elting E. Morison has shown, military organizations are societies in microcosm, built around the prevailing weapons systems. Senior naval officers, by instinctively identifying themselves and their professional prospects with a navy dominated by the modern version of the Dreadnought of their youth, unwittingly demonstrated how effectually modern doctrinal and technological change had eclipsed the adaptive powers of the individual and collective mind. Sims was a man of foresight and imagination, far ahead in these qualities of the vast majority of his professional colleagues, a man immune from the battleship mentality, yet even his sphere of identification was not extensive enough to encompass the ideas of Smith and the marines. Hence it is easy to understand why the advocates of the limitation of naval armaments and the congressmen bent on economies found so much readily available evidence to support their cases in the controversial and often contradictory statements of leading navalists.

Eventually unsuccessful in their efforts to alter the public image of the military, American officers during this period were inclined to withdraw into their organizations in face of charges representing them as wasteful and unethical encumbrances on society, obsolete survivors from an unsophisticated age of international violence. Although aviation attracted more attention than the obscure activities of marines on deserted beaches, Moffett nevertheless was involved, had to be involved, in a campaign for funds. How the equipment purchased with these funds was to be put to best use was a question that for the most part had to be relegated to a secondary category while naval aviation was fighting for its very existence. But the accumulation of materiel, however conscientious, can never be the answer to the tactical and strategical demands of national defense. Equipment and techniques can frequently be improvised in time of war but seldom the underlying doctrines governing their application without prohibitively costly practical lessons; for valid doctrines of war, the off-spring of years of careful planning and unambiguous motivation on the part of an expert professional staff, are long in gestation. It follows from this that if war is an extension of policy by other methods, preparation for war should consist of single-minded yet imaginative attempts to anticipate and define the principles of military theory governing those methods, always within the framework of national policy—something usually easier said than done. Precisely this, however, the marines accomplished and naval aviators showed signs of accomplishing during a decade when no need was felt in the United States for defensive, let alone offensive, weapons. The measure of their achievement is the difference between Gallipoli and the massive assaults by sea and air that carried American forces across the beaches of the Second World War.

From Gallipoli to Guadalcanal

BY GUNTHER E. ROTHENBERG

The end of World War One brought a speedy return of the United States to its traditional policy of political isolation and military and naval neglect. By the 1930s the army had become that of a third-rate power; the air corps had plans, but not planes, and even the U.S. Navy, which in the years 1916 to 1920 had been projected as a fleet "second to none," was in steep decline. Moreover, it was a poorly balanced fleet. "American naval policy," one writer observed, "has been guided by considerations of Atlantic and Caribbean strategy . . . very little attempt has been made [to prepare for] war in the Pacific."[1]

And yet, after 1918, the Pacific was the main area of strategic concern. The United States expected no involvement in Europe and expected only minor operations in the Caribbean, but conflicts with Japan were becoming a preoccupation with both popular writers and professional planners.[2] From the early 1920s army and navy planners in Washington prepared a series of war plans, each coded with a specific color, but only the Orange War Plan, war against Japan, was given serious consideration. After considerable debate, the navy, which had hoped to carry out early offensive operations in the western Pacific, accepted the army's contention that there were no forces available to hold the indispensable bases. The final compromise plan, therefore, envisaged a slow reconquest of the western Pacific by way of the Marshall and Gilbert islands.[3]

The necessity to project American sea-

Reprinted by permission of the author.

power across six thousand miles of ocean made it imperative to seize, occupy, and defend advance bases. The disaster of the Gallipoli enterprise in 1915, however, had made amphibious operations against a defended shore anathema to most military and naval officers. The history of the Gallipoli debacle had become a textbook example and had convinced most staff planners that any daylight assault against a defended shore had become impossible.[4] The U.S. Marine Corps, however, realized that here was an opportunity to carve out a new and larger role for itself. From 1921 on the corps devoted itself to developing a "new body of amphibious doctrine that was to lead to one of the most far-reaching tactical innovations of the Second World War."[5]

The marine efforts were spurred by a reoccurrence of intraservice rivalry: the fear that the corps might be reduced to a mere naval police force or that it might be eliminated altogether. As early as the 1880s naval officers had suggested substituting trained sailors for marines.[6] This threat, to be sure, had been defeated. In 1894 Congress assigned to the Marine Corps the mission of providing troops that could establish and defend outlying bases. By 1914 the corps had carried out this mission in Cuba, and had also fought in China, the Philippines, and in a number of small expeditions in the Caribbean. In 1913 the corps activated a permanent Advance Base Force of two regiments, one for fixed, the other for mobile, base defense. At the same time it began an elaborate doctrine for the employment of this force, the theory, if not yet the practice, of "complete tactical responsibility with a unified command." This concept struck a balance between the loose committee system, the combined operations doctrine, used by the British at Gallipoli, where command responsibility was divided between General Hamilton and Admiral de Robeck, and the army-centered marine forces then evolving in Germany and Japan. Progress, in any case, was interrupted by America's entry into World War One. The Marine Corps expanded from some ten thousand to seventy-three thousand men, but most of its strength was employed as line infantry in France, though the Advance Base Force was kept intact at full strength. From 1920 on it was based at Quantico, Virginia, and in 1921 it was redesignated the Marine Corps Expeditionary Force.[7]

Nonetheless, prior to 1921 the Marine Corps was preparing itself for the *defense* of advance bases and *not for offensive landing operations*. No serious thought was given to mounting large-scale attacks against heavily defended shores. In fact, during the early stages of the Orange Plan, naval officers once again advocated that the seizure of the necessary advance bases be accomplished by naval, and not by marine landing forces. In 1921, however, a marine officer, Major Earl H. Ellis, submitted to Major General John A. Lejeune, commandant of the Marine Corps, a set of amphibious plans, which anticipated the problems of a future Pacific war. In these plans Ellis recommended the seizure of a number of fleet bases which would require assault across well-defended beaches in daylight. He also predicted with astonishing accuracy the manpower, training, and equipment required to carry out these operations.[8] Ellis's views gained the immediate support of the commandant and other marine officers. At a critical point in its fortunes, the Marine Corps had found a new mission and from now on, except when diverted to other duties, it concentrated on developing the theory and practice of amphibious assault.

In 1922 and 1924 the corps tested some of the new doctrines in the Panama Canal Zone and at Culebra, an island in the Caribbean.

The exercise at Culebra was an ambitious affair and in addition to standard landing operations and tactical beachhead problems, the marines experimented with pontoon bridging, improvised docks, and even an amphibious tractor model.[9]

Although the marines were diverted to duty in China the following year, and thereafter were kept busy with a number of small expeditions in the Caribbean, the major concepts and the preoccupation with what the corps now conceived as its main mission, were kept alive, though little active work could be done. In 1925, following exercises in the Hawaiian Islands, the Joint Board of the Army and Navy, a body in existence since 1903 to examine common problems, convinced officers of both services that the British amphibious doctrine, which continued to rely on command by committee, would not fit into projected operations against Japan.[10] Instead, the basic marine concepts, especially the doctrine of complete tactical control within a unified command, were accepted. In 1927, convinced by experience as well as by the efforts of Ellis, Lejeune, and other marine officers, the Joint Board recommended that the corps be given special training in the conduct of landing operations, thus establishing the amphibious assault role of the marines as national military policy.[11]

Even so, only after tensions had relaxed in China and in the Caribbean in 1930–31 was the corps able to begin working out the actual details of this new role.[12] In 1933 already, the secretary of the navy had implemented the Joint Board's 1927 recommendation and replaced the old expeditionary force with a Fleet Marine Force operating as an integral part of the fleet. Cooperative efforts by the Marine Corps Schools, Marine Corps Headquarters, and the Naval War College to analyze and study the lessons of Gallipoli began to bear fruit. The main burden was carried by the Marine Corps Schools, where a committee, the Landing Operations Text Board, headed by Major Charles D. Barrett, USMC, completed in 1934 the text for the *Tentative Landing Operations Manual*, published the following year. A modified version of the *Manual,* adopted by the U.S. Navy in 1938 and extensively revised in 1941 and 1942, and also adopted by the U.S. Army in 1941, became a permanent part of U.S. military doctrine during World War Two.[13]

The *Tentative Manual* outlined six major operations as being essential: (1) command relationships; (2) naval gunfire support; (3) aerial support; (4) ship-to-shore movement; (5) securing the beachhead; and (6) logistics. The command doctrine, of course, was cardinal. As used in the manual the term *command relationships* covered both organization and command. An amphibious operation was to be conducted by a naval attack force commanded by a naval flag officer. This task force was to have two main components: the landing force, composed of elements of the Fleet Marine Force, and the naval support force, which would include fire support, air, transport, and screening groups. The landing force commander and the commanders of each naval group were responsible directly to the commander of the attack force. The principal shortcoming of this doctrine was that it did not define when the assault phase of the landing ended and at what point the landing force commander should become free to conduct operations ashore as he saw fit, tactically independent of the naval attack force commander. During the first U.S. landing of the war, Guadalcanal in August 1942, the *Tentative Manual* was followed precisely. As a result, as late as October the landing force commander was still under the control of the attack force commander, though the latter was usually far away. Through the efforts of General Thomas Holcomb, commandant of the Marine Corps, changes were made.[14] In future amphibious operations the landing force commander assumed tactical control of his troops ashore and reported to the next higher echelon, that is, the area commander, as soon as his headquarters were established and operational.

In regard to naval gunfire support, the basic questions were the feasibility of using naval guns as artillery support and shore fire control. Naval guns with their high velocity and flat trajectory had undesirable characteris-

tics when used against land targets. Though this problem was solved at least partially in subsequent exercises that demonstrated the capabilities of naval guns for counterbattery and reverse slope fire, there was criticism as early as the 1937 exercise that naval planners overrated the effectiveness of naval fire and that the softening-up period was too brief to reduce enemy emplacements. This criticism was repeated time and time again by Marine Corps officers during World War Two.[15]

The second critical problem of naval gunfire support was shore fire control, depending on better communications, inexperience of naval gunfire spotters assigned to the shore party, and lack of training for naval gunfire liaison officers. The first, primarily technical, proved minor; the second was resolved by having marine officers act as spotters; the third took more time, and it was not until July 1941 that twelve ensigns completed the first course in naval gunfire support.[16]

The development of close air support was even more difficult. As with gunfire support, the Marine Corps wanted longer periods of preassault bombardment, closer liaison, and more immediate air response. They claimed, especially after Guadalcanal, that the most effective close air support given to their troops was by Marine Corps aviators. At this time, however, marine pilots were not trained for carrier operations and the maintenance of fast and dependable ground-air communications also proved difficult. As a result, really close support for the infantry elements of the landing force did not materialize until late in the war.

Ship-to-shore movement remained another critical area because, until 1939, lack of funds forced the marines to rely upon the underpowered standard V-bottomed ships' boats. Moreover, these boats could not be beached high enough, nor could they back off the beach under their own power. In 1936 Andrew Higgins had designed a shallow draft boat which beached easily and retracted from the beach under its own power. Various versions of his boats, as well as craft developed by the Bureau of Ships, were tested in 1939 and 1940. In the end the Higgins model won out and became the prototype of small landing craft. At the same time, tracked amphibious vehicles (LVTs) were developed and tested by the corps.[17] Until late 1940, however, both the navy and the marines totally neglected the development of landing ships, that is ships capable of crossing a large part of the sea under their own power. This need, however, had been perceived by the British during the Dunkirk evacuation and by 1941 plans and prototypes for copying were available, though not in service.

For securing the beachhead the 1934 *Tentative Manual* recognized that there existed a critical period between full reliance on naval artillery and the employment of the landing force guns. This, in part, was resolved by better communications and by giving special attention to the complex problem of organizing the shallow supply area behind the front line. The *Tentative Manual* prescribed both a beach and a shore party. The beach party was to be commanded by a naval officer, the beachmaster, who controlled both the unloading of supplies and boat movement; the shore party was to see to the movement of supplies and equipment to the front line. Although both parties were to cooperate, the system was unwieldy: there were just not enough men available to handle supplies, and commanders were reluctant to withdraw manpower from the fighting units. In 1941 Major General Holland M. Smith, USMC, recommended that the two parties be combined, with a naval beachmaster as second in command to the shore party commander, and that special labor units be provided for the unloading.[18] These recommendations were adopted and written into the regulations in 1942, too late, however, to be implemented in time for the Guadalcanal landings where "crated equipment, boxed supplies, and drums of gasoline piled up alarmingly," and no clear lines of responsibility existed.[19]

Finally, there was the overall logistical problem of an amphibious landing operation, specifically how to ship the troops and how to load their equipment and supplies. In the first place the navy did not have the right type of transporters available; the troops were loaded on any ship available. During the 1937 exercises the navy even used battleships to carry the landing force. At the same time, the constantly varying ships made proper landing almost impossible. The *Tentative Manual* asserted that each transport should carry one assault battalion with its landing force, and also the battalion's equipment—loaded in order in which the various items would be needed. This concept of combat loading ran counter to usual naval practices. Heavy equipment often had to be stored on deck, lighter equipment in the hold. Moreover, each load was to be autonomous so that the particular combat unit aboard the particular transport would be tactically self-sufficient for the assault and landing and so that the loss of one ship would not be a crippling blow. By 1936 already, the Marine Corps had provided the necessary loading tables, but the first improvised transport ships were assigned to the corps only in 1941. These vessels, converted destroyers, did not prove satisfactory and it was not until the later years of the war that satisfactory vessels became available.[20]

In December 1941 the United States found itself at war with Japan and within a short time disaster after disaster overtook the poorly prepared U.S. and Allied forces. In the summer of 1942, when a Japanese drive threatened the security of the South Pacific area and especially communications with Australia, Admiral Ernest J. King, commander-in-chief, United States Fleet, decided on a limited offensive operation in the Pacific and gained the approval of the president and the Joint Chiefs for such an undertaking. The operation, code-named Watch Tower, was to be mounted against Guadalcanal Island in the Solomon groups.[21]

Although mounted within a short time, without adequate preparations and rehearsals, and nicknamed by some officers Operation Shoestring, the Guadalcanal landings were successfully carried out and, together with Midway, they have been considered the beginning of the end for the Japanese Empire in the Pacific. Yet, these landings also showed that much still remained to be worked out. "Most of the major problems of amphibious warfare," one analysis summarizes, "had been worked out in theory, and valuable practice and experimentation had gone far to refine the doctrine, provide training for a sizeable number of Marine Corps and Navy personnel, and eliminate some of the more critical 'bugs' in the procedure."[22] At the same time, however, it cannot be said that the Marine Corps, or any other branch of the armed services, was, by 1942, fully prepared to carry out its amphibious assault mission. Doctrine had come a long way from Gallipoli to Guadalcanal, but it still needed improvement. Nevertheless, the Guadalcanal landings proved that the doctrine was basically sound.[23] The amphibious doctrines and techniques developed by the Marine Corps made possible the trans-Pacific advance and, in a different context, the invasions of North Africa and Europe.

Notes

I am grateful for the aid provided by BGen. E. H. Simmons, USMC (Ret.), director, Marine Corps History and Museums.

[1] Hector C. Bywater, Sea Power in the Pacific (Boston and New York: Houghton-Mifflin, 1921), pp. 128–29.

[2] See among others, F. McCormick, The Menace of Japan (Boston: Little, Brown, 1917), and Walter B. Pitkin, Must We Fight Japan (New York: The Century Co., 1921).

[3] Maurice Matloff, "The American Approach to War," in Michael Howard, ed., The Theory and Practice of War (Bloomington: Indiana University Press, 1975), pp. 220–21.

[4] Theodore Ropp, War in the Modern World (Durham, N.C.: Duke University Press, 1959), p. 235.

[5] Matloff, "The American Approach to War," p. 222; and Col. Robert H. Dunlap, USMC, "Lessons for Marines From the Gallipoli Campaign," Marine Corps Gazette 6 (September 1921): 237–52.

[6] Peter Karsten, The Naval Aristocracy (New York: Macmillan, Free Press, 1972), pp. 82–83, 91, and 289.

[7] Col. William H. Russell, "Genesis of the FMF Doctrine," Marine Corps Gazette 35 (April 1951): 52–59 and (July 1951): 52–59. U.S. Navy authors on occasion have disputed the Marine Corps's preeminent role in the development of amphibious doctrine. "The Marines," Admiral Richmond

K. Turner wrote, "contributed much . . . so also did the Navy, including Naval Aviation." Cited by VAdm. George P. Dyer, USN (Ret.) Amphibians Came to Conquer. The Story of Admiral Richmond Kelly Turner, 2 Vols. (Washington, D.C.: Government Printing Office, 1972) 1: 202–3. Dyer, however, concedes that prior to 1934 amphibious warfare was neglected by the navy. In the 1934 edition of War Instructions, United States Navy, the subject "amphibious warfare" was not even listed in the index, ibid., p. 223. Therefore, it appears correct to assign the Marine Corps the major role in the development of the doctrine.

[8] Major Earl H. Ellis, USMC, OPlan 712, AdvBOps, 1921. Microfilm rolls, Amphibious Warfare pertinent documents, roll 1, Marine Corps Historical Center, Washington, D.C. (hereinafter cited as Amphib. Warfare Docs.); Jeter A. Isley and Philip A. Crowl, The U.S. Marines and Amphibious War (Princeton: Princeton University Press, 1951), pp. 26–28.

[9] Ibid., pp. 30–32; and Capt. R. Earle, USN, "Landing Operations of the Central Force, November 1921–May 1922," Amphib. Warfare Docs., roll 1.

[10] BGen. Dion Williams, USMC, "Blue Marine Corps Expeditionary Force," Marine Corps Gazette 10 (September 1925): 76–88; USMC, Arch. and Hist. 6rp. MCDEC, Quantico, VA., Hist. Amphib. File, nos. 25–27, "Grand Joint Army and Navy Exercise, Hawaii, 1925."

[11] Isley and Crowl, The U.S. Marines and Amphibious War, p. 28; and Joint Board, Joint Action of Army and Navy (Washington, D.C.: Government Printing Office, 1927), p. 3.

[12] Navy Department GO 241, 8 December 1933.

[13] Tentative Manual for Landing Operation, Navy Department FTP 167; U.S. Army FM 31–5. For revisions, see Dyer, Amphibians Came to Conquer, 1:226–27.

[14] LtCol. Frank O. Hough, USMCR, Maj. Verle E. Ludwig, USMC, and Henry I. Shaw, Jr., History of U.S. Marine Corps Operations in World War II (Washington, D.C.: Government Printing Office, 1959), 1:341–42.

[15] Edward B. Potter and Chester W. Nimitz, Seapower (Englewood Cliffs, N.J.: Prentice-Hall, 1960), pp. 632–33; BGen. Samuel B. Griffith II, USMC (Ret.) The Battle for Guadalcanal (Philadelphia and New York: Lippincott, 1963), pp. 54–55; and "Naval Gunfire Support of Landing Operations," Marine Corps Arch. and Hist. Group, MCDEC, Quantico, VA., Hist. Amphib. File no. 540.

[16] Hough, Ludwig, and Shaw, History of Marine Corps Operations in World War II, 1:15–22.

[17] Ibid., pp. 23–24; Marine Corps Qrtr. and Hist. Group, MCDEC, Quantico, VA., Hist. Amphib. File nos. 37, 112; and 2/LT. Arthur B. Barrows USMC, "A New Departure in Landing Boats," Marine Corps Gazette 23 (September 1939): 39–

40. See also Dyer, *Amphibians Came to Conquer,* 1:204–6.

[18] Hough, Ludwig, and Shaw, *History of Marine Corps Operations in World War II,* 1:21; the autobiography of LtGen. Holland M. Smith, USMC (Ret.) *Coral and Brass* (New York: Scribner's, 1949), passim.

[19] Griffith, *The Battle for Guadalcanal,* pp. 41–42; and Hough, Ludwig, and Shaw, *History of Marine Corps Operations in World War II,* 1:257–58.

[20] Hough, Ludwig, and Shaw, *History of Marine Corps Operations in World War II,* 1:25–35.

[21] Griffith, *The Battle for Guadalcanal,* pp. 25–35.

[22] Isely and Crowl, *The U.S. Marines and Amphibious War,* p. 58.

[23] Ibid., p. 71.

A TWO-OCEAN WAR

The U.S. Marine Corps: Author of Modern Amphibious Warfare

BY COLONEL ROBERT D. HEINL, JR., USMC (RET.)

One of the major military developments of World War Two was the demonstration that amphibious assault against a defended beachhead—one of the prewar "impossibilities"—could succeed despite whatever defense our enemies found it possible to muster. This development, worldwide in its effects, was in large part the outgrowth of the thought and effort devoted to the subject by officers of the United States Marine Corps, stemming in certain respects from concepts which antedated even World War One.

Closely related, both historically and functionally, to the evolution by marine officers of the highly developed science of amphibious operations is the parallel concept of a Fleet Marine Force. Indeed it might truthfully be said that the logical history of modern amphibious technique is in many ways the story of the Fleet Marine Force. The ideas of Marine Corps amphibious thinkers produced the Fleet Marine Force; this unique unit in turn gave body and substance to the doctrinal theories of its creators; and the interaction of the two combined in substantial measure to make possible the victorious beachheads of World War Two.

To be sure, landing operations by marines have been an accepted commonplace throughout their history. Since the U.S. Marines's first landing at Nassau in the Bahamas in 1776, the corps executed as a matter of course some one hundred eighty landing operations between 1800 and 1934, followed

by more than a hundred during the course of the recent war. But there is a great distinction to be drawn between the casual landing of early days and the complex technique of amphibious assault as we understand it today. This development largely spanned the period from the beginning of this century through 1940.

One of the first landings of a modern character was that at Guantanamo Bay in Cuba in 1898. The mission of this expedition was the seizure of a major naval base for fleet operations in the blockade of Santiago, and the instrument employed was a regularly organized battalion of marines (which included marine infantry and field artillery units) rather than the provisional battalion based on ships' detachments which had hitherto been the characteristic American form of organization.

Succeeding years saw increased use of organized battalions and regiments based afloat in transports, but the possible use of the Marine Corps in its present organized form appears not to have received great attention until shortly before World War One when the growth of the U.S. Navy placed the United States among the world's great naval powers.

In any case, shortly thereafter the Advance Base Force, U.S. Marine Corps, a permanent field force, was organized for the occupation and defense of advance naval bases. Even here the idea of defense appears paramount and was probably a corollary of the unexpressed concept that offensive operations were still the function of ships' detachments. However,

U.S. Naval Institute *Proceedings* 73 (November 1977): 1310–23. Reprinted by permission.

Amphibious exercises, Culebra, 1929. Courtesy of the Burke Collection, U.S. Navy Historical Center.

Nicaragua (1912), Vera Cruz (1914), and Haiti (1916) saw these advance base units deployed in offensive operations rather than in base defense. It comes as no surprise to find in the first two issues of *The Marine Corps Gazette* in 1916 leading articles by Major Generals John A. Lejeune and John H. Russell (both of whom subsequently became commandants of the corps) advocating employment of marines in the form of a fleet marine force and pointing out the repercussions and implications of recent reverses at Gallipoli.

The active renaissance of Marine Corps amphibious studies, however, can be very definitely dated from 1921, when the corps established its plan, its forces, and its schools for the express purpose of reducing landing operations to a scientific and technical basis. In that year there was produced at Marine Corps Headquarters a basic war plan which is believed to be one of the most remarkable documents of its kind ever written. It was largely the work of Lieutenant Colonel Earl H. Ellis, U.S. Marine Corps, a brilliant staff officer who was soon to disappear in 1923 while "travelling" in the Japanese Mandates of the Pacific Islands. The "war portfolio" outlined the Pacific war to come, predicted its dimensions, and forecast with remarkable accuracy the part to be played by the Marine Corps in making effective our superior naval power. It foresaw the capabilities and roles of new weapons, including the carrier, submarine, torpedo plane, and long-range bomber,

and noted the need for special amphibious landing craft and fleets of attack transports. Above all, the Marine Corps "war portfolio" foretold the step-by-step base seizure that would be entailed in the effort to advance our sea power westward. Even the detailed assessment of forces required would appear amazingly accurate twenty-three years later; for example, Colonel Ellis stated that a reinforced regiment would be required to seize Eniwetok Atoll. This was the exact force employed for the successful attack in 1944. The full effect of this remarkable blueprint cannot be completely assessed even today, but the steps taken during the same year of 1921 to implement the "war portfolio" indicate that it was received with utmost respect.

The advance base force had passed out of existence in 1917 in response to the practical necessities of World War One, but the idea was not forgotten. It was revived again in 1921 when the East and West Coast Expeditionary Forces were organized for service with the U.S. Fleet. Here the important distinctions to be observed are that the new organizations were offensive landing forces and that they were expressly integrated with the U.S. Fleet as instrumentalities in the application of sea power.

In the same year there was established at Quantico, Virginia, that necessary complement to the field forces, the Marine Corps schools, devoted to the science of amphibious warfare.

Over the ensuing years the reports of fleet landing exercises (the annual large-scale amphibious maneuvers of the fleet and its marine force) and the teachings and writings of the Marine Corps schools are a record of a parallel approach to a common problem. There was recognition that the subject of landing operations needed the same applied study and reduction to technique devoted to other forms of warfare. There were mistakes and false beginnings, but there was also progress. Starting with Gallipoli as the classic object-lesson, and in the entire absence of a source of positive material except the Ellis plan, the problem was dissected into its component parts by segregation and analysis of the major mistakes made in the Dardanelles, followed by a search for methods of correction. The inquiry directed itself quite naturally into these subdivisions:

- failure of command
- lack of means of control
- lack of special material and equipment
- failure of communications
- inadequacy of naval gunfire support
- failure in the field of logistics.

From these analytical beginnings, there were established lines of constructive effort and investigation which, within a few years, gave to the navy and Marine Corps, through its schools, the following:

- philosophy of parallel command relationships
- modern technique of a controlled ship-to-shore movement
- experimental development of landing craft and landing vehicles
- ship-to-shore communications
- doctrine of naval gunfire support
- the fundamentals of embarkation and combat loading of transports
- the fundamentals of shore party organizations.

These matters were well developed and in writing by 1929, when the Marine Corps schools issued a series of tentative landing force doctrines. In little more than one decade later, these doctrines would guide amphibious operations against the Axis powers.

During the 1920s, while the teachers at Marine Corps schools studied and dissected the amphibious operations of the past, the majority of the corps was employed to capacity in major overseas missions. Marine brigades were bringing stable government to Haiti, then under U.S. protectorate; they were quelling savage banditry in Nicaragua; and in China they were helping to protect not only American but all foreign nationals from the hazards of the civil wars and the Japanese aggression which even then menaced the Orient. As a result, the East and West Coast Expeditionary Forces perforce remained largely as paper units.

By 1933, however, the pressure of these duties had measurably slackened, and it became possible to allocate troops to what had long been realized was the primary military raison d'être of the corps: expeditionary forces for service and training as an integral part of the U.S. Fleet.

On 7 December 1933 the secretary of the navy, Claude Swanson, at the urgent recommendation of the major general commandant of the corps, John H. Russell, signed navy department general order 241, a document in which for the first time the title "Fleet Marine Force" was used and in which the concept of this force and its employment was fully expressed. On the next day, General Russell promulgated Marine Corps order 66, which set forth implementing instructions regarding the organization and doctrine of the Fleet Marine Force. As organized in 1933, the Fleet Marine Force (FMF) comprised two brigades of equal strength, one stationed at San Diego, California, for service with Pacific elements of the U.S. Fleet, and the other at Quantico, Virginia, for Atlantic service.

In size perhaps, and in organization certainly, the title "brigade" was, by the accepted military terminology of the day, a misnomer for either of these units. The nearest present-day parallel—a descendant, in fact, of these brigades—is what in amphibious operations we now term the regimental combat team (RCT). Like the RCT, the two marine brigades (the 1st was at Quantico, the 2nd at San Diego) were balanced forces of the combined arms built around an infantry nucleus, a peace-strength rifle regiment. In each brigade the rifle regiment was supported by a battalion of light artillery; service troops; engineers; rather rudimentary antiaircraft; signal communications troops trained in the complex operations of fleet radio and visual communication; and navy medical elements trained and organized for service ashore. As funds and authorized strength permitted, tank and chemical troops were added. Furthermore Marine Air Groups stationed at Quantico and San Diego continued year in and year out to master the essential technique of close air support of troops during landing operations. Knowledge gained in Haiti and in Nicaragua, where marine pilots had perfected the art of dive-bombing and where Marine Corps aviation had provided the first major and continued support to U.S. combat troops, was crucial.

Three predominant aspects marked the FMF of 1933 as novel within the framework of American arms. Virtually all might be styled philosophical attributes of the new marine force, and all found expression in its doctrines of training and potential employment. First is the fact that it was singly and openly organized, equipped, and trained for landing operations incident to naval campaigns. A simple example of this attribute was that its light artillery, rather than being the conventional 75 mm field gun then standard for comparable army units, was instead a pack-howitzer originally designed for mountain use. The howitzer had the advantage of being able to be broken down, manhandled from a ship's motorlaunch and through surf if necessary, and put into the hands of the cannoneers. Transportation was limited, not only by the fiscal stringencies of peacetime, but by dimensions and weights made to conform to what ships' holds, boats, and booms could handle.

Second, the force, small as it was, was never skeletonized or cadred down to the extent that it was not capable of very rapid embarkation in useful combat units and movement by sea. Thus it retained at all times a high degree of readiness and strategic mobility well suited to the policy of a maritime nation whose fleet constituted a first line of defense.

Third, realizing how garrison duty can sap the effective combat training of any tactical unit, the Marine Corps had from the outset made every effort to draw sharp distinction between FMF units and what became known as "post troops"—the units needed for normal garrison, security, maintenance, and similar duties. At each post where FMF troops were stationed, overhead post troops were likewise maintained so that Fleet Marine Force training might proceed unhampered. Individual marines, of course, were rotated between FMF and non-FMF duties so that all members of the corps were fully trained in combat roles.

As an adjunct to the Marine Corps schools which had generated the rationale of the Fleet Marine Force, another agency, primarily concerned with the study of the material problems of amphibious operations, was plainly needed. In 1933, the golden year of the Fleet Marine Force, the Marine Corps Equipment Board was therefore formed. This was the first professional body in the United States to devote its entire time and study to the development of materiel suitable for use of troops in amphibious warfare.

This board, seeking ideas where they were to be found, cooperated with navy and army agencies in the test and development of equipment for the Fleet Marine Force. Its ideas went far toward the early design of suitable landing craft and toward the shaping of heavy materiel specifications to the limits of tonnage and dimensions then obtaining in landing operations. Through the unceasing urge for development of a reef-crossing vehicle so obviously a prime desideratum for the coral-ringed atolls of Colonel Ellis's "war portfolio," the board sponsored and pioneered the now-renowned tracked landing vehicle or *alligator*, the amphibian tractor that carried troops across every beachhead from Tarawa to the Rhine.

Within two years after the organization of the Fleet Marine Force, funds were for the first time available to permit a fulldress amphibious landing exercise employing the Fleet

Marine Force in its role as a part of the fleet. These maneuvers, carried out in January 1935, were executed by the 1st Marine Brigade on the island of Culebra, Puerto Rico, and it was here that the new doctrines and organizations received their first field tests, involving not only the "assault" landing of marines against a "defended" objective, but the establishment of effective ship-shore communications, the logistic support of expeditionary forces ashore by the fleet, and the very elementary beginnings of a practical means of accurately harnessing the immense residual firepower of ships' guns against shore targets.

Repeated annually from 1935 through 1939, these fleet landing exercises (FLEX) grew in scope, provided sure means of discovering the flaws of technique and theory, and enabled materiel to be put to practical test. Equally important, they made certain that the units of the tiny Fleet Marine Force—which even by 1939 included but 4,991 marines—were brought to a keen edge of training for their primary mission and that both officers and men were as much at home aboard assault shipping as in barracks ashore.

Not only as a measure of convenience and economy, but to ensure familiarity by the fleet and Fleet Marine Force with amphibious conditions in both the Atlantic and Pacific, the fleet landing exercises were alternated between the Caribbean, where the Culebra-Vieques area was available adjacent to the Virgin Islands, and the Eastern Pacific, where the Hawaiian Islands and San Clements Island served similar purposes.

By 1940, as a result of thinking at Marine Corps schools and practical field training in the Fleet Marine Force, the following essentials of amphibious technique existed not only on paper but in vigorous being:

- the Fleet Marine Force as a balanced expeditionary component of ground troops and as much an element of the fleet as its submarines or aircraft carriers, ready for overseas operations and trained for amphibious assault
- doctrines for naval gunfire support and close air support during landing operations—the first practical means ever worked out to permit the attacker, even in amphibious assault, to gain without artillery the fire-superiority needed to overbalance the inherent advantages of the defender
- logistic and communications doctrines and troops for the peculiar purpose of bridging wind and water between ship and shore
- specially organized base-defense units designed to possess very high strategic mobility for the rapid occupation and defense development of overseas bases so that the other elements of the Fleet Marine Force need not be dispersed or immobilized in defensive roles.

Needless to say, all these developments in technique and organization had not taken place on an unwritten basis. As early as 1935, the staffs at Marine Corps headquarters and the schools had collaborated in preparation of a *Tentative Landing Operations Manual*, which in 1938 was formally adopted by the U.S. Navy under the title of FTP–167, *Landing Operations Doctrine, U.S. Navy*. Throughout the war this volume, as revised in 1940, served as the basic U.S. doctrine for amphibious operations.

In 1941, the Fleet Marine Force was called upon in two widely differing ways to demonstrate its capabilities. The first and perhaps the more dramatic instance was the occupation of Iceland during July of that year. The second was its assumption of the role of de facto troop training unit for other American units in the amphibious techniques that had been so patiently devised and mastered during the quiet years of peace.

Iceland, garrisoned by British forces including Royal Marines since May 1940, had become critical not only in the Battle of the Atlantic but to the possible defense of the Western Hemisphere. The importance of its remaining adequately secured was fully appreciated by President Roosevelt. For this mission, and with no warning, a provisional marine brigade was organized on 16 June 1941, from available Fleet Marine Force units. Less than a week later, on 22 June, the entire brigade had sailed from Charleston, South Carolina, and on 7 July, more than four thousand marines were disembarking at Reykjavik to reinforce the British garrison and to act as advance party for eventual follow-up movement to Iceland by U.S. Army units as they subsequently became ready and available for this duty.

This oversea movement by a task organization thrown together on short notice for the mission (essentially in support of Atlantic Fleet operations, be it noted) was classic for the Fleet Marine Force and amply demonstrated its capabilities.

Less in the public eye than the Iceland affair, but of considerably greater eventual importance, was the formation almost simultaneously on 6 June 1941 of the Amphibious Corps, Atlantic Fleet, a provisional corps consisting of the 1st Marine Division, the 1st Army Division, marine and army air components, commanded by a Fleet Marine Force staff under Major General Holland M. Smith, U.S. Marine Corps. This corps actually was an embodied means for imparting large-scale amphibious training to army formations, such as the 1st Army Division, which had had no previous indoctrination. Virtually all of 1941 was devoted to bringing the army division to a satisfactory level of proficiency and to accustoming all hands, including the amphibious staffs and units of the Atlantic Fleet, to large-scale operations of this type. During this period, especially noteworthy practical advances were made in shore party and amphibious logistic methods. The results obtained were embodied in FTP–211, *Ship to Shore Movement*, basic in this particular field. Another great field of practical development was the naval shore bombardment exercises carried on under joint sponsorship of marine artillery and navy gunnery experts at Bloodsworth Island in the Chesapeake Bay. These firings constituted the first really large-scale test of the naval gunfire support doctrines embodied in FTP–167 and laid the foundation for the eventual widespread and effective use of naval fire-support not only by marines in the Pacific but by other American forces throughout the world.

The onset of war in December 1941 only heightened the already brisk tempo of training within the Amphibious Corps, Atlantic Fleet, as well as within the shortly-to-be-formed Amphibious Corps, Pacific Fleet, similarly organized from Fleet Marine Force elements and staffs. In addition to preparing marine units for the seizure of Guadalcanal, the two amphibious corps provided the necessarily hasty amphibious training for the 1st, 3rd, and 9th army divisions, together with numerous smaller units. These three divisions were the first units of the army to be so trained and constituted the entire assault landing force of U.S. infantry divisions in the North African operation of 1942.

Over and above the foregoing divisions, before the war had been completed similar amphibious training would be provided by the Marine Corps to the following additional army divisions and other major units: 7th Infantry Division; 81st Infantry Division; 96th Infantry Division; 97th Infantry Division; and Amphibious Training Force 9 (7th Infantry Division plus 184th and 53d Regimental Combat Teams, and the 13th Canadian Brigade), a provisional composite corps for Aleutian operations.

Before we consider the combat operations of the Fleet Marine Force in the Pacific War, we will outline its growth from peace strength so as to provide some idea of the military dimensions of the subject. As we have seen, the peacetime FMF consisted of two so-called brigades (really expanded regimental combat teams each composed of one rifle regiment together with a staff and nucleus of all the combined arms which one finds within a division). By 1941, in the very shadow of hostilities, the 1st Marine Brigade, based at Quantico, Virginia, had already been ordered to Guantanamo Bay, Cuba, for expansion to form the 1st Marine Division. The 2nd Marine Brigade, based at San Diego, California, was also in process of conversion to a division of like numerical designation. Because both "brigades" contained cadres of every specialist element found in the war-strength division, the changeover did not present the difficulties which might have been anticipated.

Before the end of 1942, both divisions had seen action against the Japanese, and the 3rd

Marine Division was forming. Reinforcement of special units, ranging from the hard-working defense battalions to corps artillery battalions and other types of higher-echelon troops, was being organized at a maximum rate. Marine Corps aviation, interchangeable in equipment and training with the navy's carrier-squadrons, was likewise expanding by leaps and bounds. By the end of 1943, the 4th Marine Division had been formed; in 1944, the 5th was in training, and by early 1945, the 6th Marine Division had been organized from an expanded version of a provisional marine brigade which had seen distinguished service in the South Pacific and the Marianas.

In 1944 the Fleet Marine Force was in effect stabilized as a sort of field army consisting of two corps ("amphibious corps" was their complete and correct title), the III and V Amphibious Corps, each consisting of three marine divisions and all supporting troops needed for a corps. In addition, under Fleet Marine Force control, there were maintained all the manifold specialist and service units required to support two corps in amphibious operations. The Fleet Marine Force itself was a type-command, so-called, within the U.S. Pacific Fleet, so that the commanding general of the FMF was as much in control of all marines within the fleet as the commander battleships was in charge of all battleships. At no time was it ever forgotten that the Fleet Marine Force was essentially a fleet element, necessary and indispensable for prosecution of the naval campaign. With the foregoing structure, at a strength of almost two hundred thousand marines, the Fleet Marine Force fought many of its greatest battles, and in this form it concluded the Pacific war. Let us examine the methods and manner in which it fought.

The Fleet Marine Force spearheaded two of the major amphibious campaigns of the Pacific War: the South Pacific campaign and the Central Pacific campaign. These differed radically, not only in terrain and nature of operations, but in strategic concept.

The war in the South Pacific was in some senses a holding attack, an offensive-defensive which only at the last attained the status of a true offensive, and then only for the reduction of outer works in the deep Japanese system of South Sea bases. In the South Pacific, deadly as were the hazards of malaria and merciless jungle, it was almost always possible to "hit 'em where they ain't"—to land against light opposition by choosing a point of attack which the enemy could not defend.

In the Central Pacific the campaign was, from the outset, a true offensive leveled without dissembling at the home islands of Japan. The terrain was entirely different: a series of tiny, isolated, completely and densely fortified atolls or small islands garrisoned to maximum strength. In the attack of such redoubts there could be no tactical surprise, no razzle-dazzle of deception. The entire problem was well understood far in advance, both by the attacker and by the enemy.

Nevertheless, despite every superficial difference between the two campaigns, the battle mission of the Fleet Marine Force, wherever it fought, was to further the naval campaign, and the interdependence of the fleet afloat and the FMF ashore characterized Pacific Fleet operations throughout the war.

Guadalcanal typified not only the South Pacific theater and campaign, but it dramatized to the American public the true meaning and function of their Fleet Marine Force.

In early 1942 it was apparent to the strategic planners in Washington that an operation in Melanesia was required. Guadalcanal-Tulagi suggested itself as a target because of the magnificent harbor at Tulagi and the presence of airbase sites on Guadalcanal. In addition early seizure of Guadalcanal would afford a counterpush for the rapidly developing enemy strength in that area, presumably being massed for futher southward attacks toward the New Hebrides and ultimately the Australia-United States lifeline.

Obviously the operation would have to be amphibious, and obviously it was incident to the naval campaign. Despite prophecies of disaster and recommendations that the assault be delayed (both arising outside the naval service), the 1st Marine Division, FMF, with little more than a month's warning was

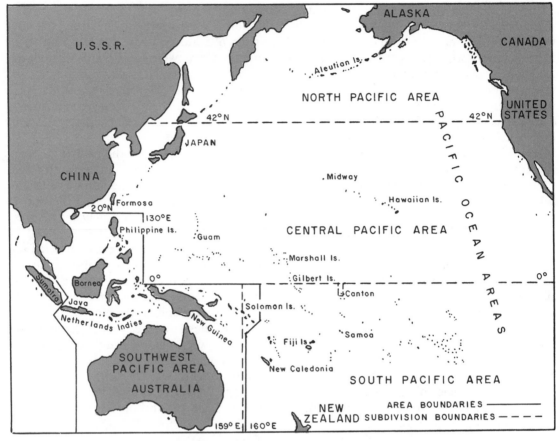

Central and South Pacific campaign areas, World War Two.

committed to the operation by the chief of naval operations, Admiral King. The margin was in some senses never closer during the whole Pacific war. Army units were not available in strength to back up the Fleet Marine Force until some four months after the initial landings in August 1942. Yet by then, Guadalcanal, recognized as a turning point by the Japanese and by the American-British coalition alike, was firmly secured for our use.

To thoughtful students of naval war the prime lesson of Guadalcanal was that, without the Fleet Marine Force, the operation could never have happened. Undertaken as a purely naval venture by fleet units and marines, Guadalcanal, the United States first major offensive, demonstrated the dependence of sea power upon fleet expeditionary troops, as well as the degree to which such troops had been prepared and held in readi-

ness by the FMF. The two dominant attributes of a fleet expeditionary force are its high readiness for employment and its mastery of amphibious techniques. Each is the product of long and specialized training.

Guadalcanal and the subsequent operations of the South Pacific campaign epitomized the former concept, that of readiness. It was Fleet Marine Force readiness which made Guadalcanal possible; which enabled an FMF holding force to secure the New Hebrides in March 1942; and which permitted the offensive to be assumed by August of the same year.

If the battles of the South Pacific proved that the Fleet Marine Force was ready for war, those of the Central Pacific demonstrated its grasp of and virtuosity in amphibious assault. Except for Okinawa—which was really not a part of either the South or Central Pacific campaigns—the entire roll of

Central Pacific battles, from Tarawa to Iwo Jima, was by necessity a series of seaborne frontal assaults against positions fortified and organized with every refinement that Japanese labor and ingenuity could provide. To reduce such strongholds was truly the essence of amphibious warfare—the assaults which the Marine Corps had foreseen and planned for during the decades of peace.

Rather than attempt any survey of all the successive operations between Tarawa, with which the Central Pacific amphibious campaign truly began, and Iwo Jima, which just preceded Okinawa, it would be more enlightening to see how these two amphibious assaults of unsurpassable toughness were executed and to note what improvements in basic technique the Fleet Marine Force had made during the two years between Tarawa and Iwo.

Tarawa and Iwo Jima had many factors in common. Each was a small objective, densely organized into a single major defensive system; each, in its approaches and terrain, precluded any appreciable degree of tactical surprise; and each was correctly estimated in advance to represent a job of the most difficult and desperate character.

In only two major respects did Tarawa and Iwo differ. The first was sheer size. Tarawa was defended by 4,836 Japanese, whereas Iwo's garrison exceeded 22,000, all but about 500 of whom had to be killed. More important than the difference in scale between the two assaults, however, was an intangible—experience. Before Tarawa, although the Fleet Marine Force possessed elite troops and ample doctrinal bases, a frontal amphibious assault against opposition was still theory, not fact. Less than two years later, the FMF had come through not only Tarawa but also the Marshalls, the Marianas, and Peleliu. These bitterly contested assaults prepared the Marine Corps for Iwo Jima, its most harrowing single struggle.

Perhaps the best way to visualize the progress of amphibious assault technique and doctrine between Tarawa and Iwo Jima is to consider with regard to each operation the major components of a successful landing against opposition.

Preliminary preparation of the objective. In each case, "softening up" of the enemy was achieved solely by naval bombardment and preliminary air attacks (carrier- and shore-based). Considering only the nature of the objective, each preliminary preparation was to some extent inadequate, but the contrast in method of preliminary bombardment is startling. Equally remarkable and certainly indicative of experience were the highly accurate forecasts by Fleet Marine Force planners regarding the extent of preliminary bombardment needed for Iwo Jima. An unassailable case was made that the little island would require at least ten days naval gunfire preparation, and although high strategic considerations reduced the actual preliminary bombardment to three days, the outcome confirmed everything that had been postulated by the marine naval gunfire planners for Iwo. The method of Tarawa's preliminary bombardment was that of "saturating" the island by target-areas in expectation that this would reduce all targets of importance. Iwo Jima's method was a precise and methodical reduction, installation by installation, in order of well-determined priorities, of known and tabulated targets— a technique which the experience of Tarawa had proven essential and which the bombardments of the Marshalls (and Guam especially) had proven feasible.

Fires in close support of the landing. At Tarawa, naval gunfire and aviation fires in support of the landing were lifted too far in advance. At Iwo Jima, one of history's heaviest and most closely positioned rolling barrages of naval gunfire preceded the landing.

Logistic support of the landing. One of the major bottlenecks of the Tarawa operation was that of logistic support. Because of enemy resistance and the nonexistence of some elements of now-accepted shore party doctrine, the trickle of supplies onto Betio's beaches was pitiful. On Iwo Jima, troops were well fed and reasonably well supplied, and mail was received several times during the month of battle itself.

Landing craft. The quantity and characteristics of the landing craft available in 1943 for Tarawa were the best available but not the best suited. Perhaps the most notable fact in this connection is that certain navy officers wanted to push the landing in with vehicle and personnel landing craft, whereas the marine planners insisted that only LVTs (amphibian tractors) were suitable to cross the reefs. At Iwo Jima, there was a sufficient number of the correct type of landing craft.

Landing Force Communications. More suitable radio equipment and a generally more complex organization of communication nets, channels, and systems had evolved. At Tarawa much trouble was encountered from wet radio equipment, at Iwo Jima the problem was avoided.

Assault technique and tactics. At Iwo Jima and at Tarawa, the fighting ability of the individual marine came into sharp and bitter focus. On each occasion the battle was one of frontal assault and very close combat against fortified positions. Before Tarawa, although such amphibious assaults had been projected in theory, one had never been executed. Tarawa demonstrated that the doctrines were sound. At Iwo Jima the troops could reap the benefit not only of theory but of tested combat experience. Without Tarawa, the even greater assault of Iwo would not have been possible. For that matter, however, without the years of study, experiment, and development at Quantico, neither Tarawa nor Iwo could have been successful.

By the end of the war, the Fleet Marine Force was poised for invasion of the Japanese homeland. As a result, both the III and V Amphibious Corps were utilized for occupation of conquered or liberated territories in Japan and China. Concurrently, as the situation permitted, their orderly demobilization was carried out, unmarred by indiscipline or untoward incident.

During the past two years, in addition to occupation missions carried on by the Marine Corps, the shaping of the postwar Fleet Marine Force has progressed. In keeping with the now-established U.S. naval concept that every major fleet requires its expeditionary force of marines, the FMF consists of two major forces: Fleet Marine Force Pacific ("FMFPac") and Fleet Marine Force Atlantic ("FMFLant"), for service with the respective fleets.

Each of these Fleet Marine Forces embodies at least one marine division, supporting logistic elements, and marine aviation units for close air support. At present, certain changes in organization are under consideration with the objective of shaping the ultimate organization of Marine Corps tactical formations to meet the prospective demands of modern war so that, regardless of changes in technique or weapons, the FMF may be able to carry out its basic functions, which, of course, are simply stated and remain unchanged.

One possibility along these lines, however, remains relatively unexplored. This is the thought, often informally expressed, that the readiness and mobility of the Fleet Marine Force would lend itself excellently to its employment as the U.S. component of United Nations security forces. Since, in the past, marines have carried out a traditional function, in effect, as "State Department troops"— that is, as expeditionary forces for the projection of U.S. foreign policy abroad in times of peace—it would appear logical that they should carry on this role within the framework of the United Nations.

Regardless of the turn of events, the Marine Corps will continue its studies and will continue to strive for quality, elan, and esprit. Now firmly a part of U.S. sea power, the Fleet Marine Forces will remain in readiness so that the amphibious spearhead of the fleet may never be blunted.

Japanese Landing Operations in World War Two

BY HANS G. VON LEHMANN

TRANSLATED BY PROFESSOR MICHAEL C. HALBIG

No major power looked back on a longer tradition of amphibious warfare than Japan. In his first talks with Adolf Hitler after the surprise attack on Pearl Harbor, the Japanese ambassador in Berlin, Oshima, pointed to this experience: "Japan has practiced amphibious operations for fifty years. For twenty-six hundred years, Japan had no war on its own soil. All wars that Japan was forced to fight were conducted outside the Japanese islands, each time in conjunction with amphibious operations." Japan thus had a major tradition in this area which figured large in the current operations. Methods had been worked out in detail. Oshima suggested the German armed forces incorporate this experience and apply it themselves.

It was primarily the Japanese army which had specialized in amphibious warfare, the navy to a lesser degree. Both forces had to support and supplement one another in amphibious operations, but it was primarily the army which studied and developed the technique of amphibious landings. The basic experience had been gathered by the time of the Sino-Japanese War (1894–95) and, above all, the Russo-Japanese War (1904–05), which was characterized by the "combination of land and sea war." In the following years, army units systematically practiced landings in islands. Experience gathered then was applied for the first time in 1937 during the Sino-Japanese conflict.

Marine Rundschau, "The Techniques of Japanese Landing Operations in World War Two," 68 (September 1971): 527–39. Reprinted by permission.

Based on Oshima's proposals, the German Foreign Office tried to obtain the Japanese landing doctrine. In telegrams number 1230 (20 April 1942) and 1484 (14 May 1942), both countersigned by German Ambassador Ott, in Tokyo, the German military attache, Kretschmar, transmitted the most important Japanese guidelines for landings and technical details regarding special craft developed for amphibious landings. The Japanese guidelines for amphibious warfare were unquestionably the most thoroughly developed from a technical viewpoint and the best tested in practical application. Some fundamental insights could well apply even today and in the future. To be sure, Japan was militarily able to prepare and conduct landing operations as envisioned in the guidelines only up to the Battle of Midway in June 1942, the turning point of the war in the Pacific. The guidelines provide, however, a concrete impression of Japanese amphibious technique, which played only a subordinate role in Germany for reasons of geography and military tradition.

Preconditions for Japanese Amphibious Operations

All amphibious operations were thoroughly planned and thought out. Military planning considered time, location, and technical factors as well as proven weaknesses and strengths of the enemy. Success depended on whether it was possible to develop the amphibious plan in accordance with the guidelines. The disadvantage was obvious: if operations were to take place as planned, it was

A sea battle in the South Pacific. Japanese war art painting by Ishikawa Toraji, 1942. Courtesy of the U.S. Navy Historical Center.

difficult to adapt them to new and unforeseen situations without endangering the entire operational concept. For that reason, planners tried as much as possible to play out in advance the options for action and response available to the enemy.

The time factor played a decisive role. In order to surprise and mislead the enemy, one had to confuse it and hide the operations. Night landings were especially suitable in this regard, and special units spent years practicing them. Night operations hindered enemy intelligence gathering; the Americans at the beginning of the war, for example, expected daytime attacks and were often completely overrun as a result. Equipped with bicycles, small motor-powered vehicles, special boats, optical equipment, radios, and so forth, the landing forces acquired increased mobility and combat capability.

Landings at several spots simultaneously or in rapid sequence generally marked the beginning of a large amphibious operation. They prepared for the operation by establishing beachheads or securing airfields; they served in addition to scatter the enemy's forces and deceive it as to the time and location of the operation. Among the most important preconditions of large amphibious operations were air and sea superiority. Parts of the fleet secured the rear lines of communication. Land-based navy and army pilots generally established air superiority. To the greatest degree possible, the pilots were to surprise the enemy by destroying aircraft still on the ground or by depriving it of its airfields. After the enemy air force had been decisively defeated, the main landing could begin.

At the same time reconnaissance teams determined appropriate sites for the landing, but without making a final selection. Once

Victorious Japanese troops landing on New Ireland, 1942.

the coastal zone for the landing had been determined, it was bombed to interdict enemy batteries.

Arrival of the Transport Fleet

The landing force consisted of army or navy units. All large landings were reserved for the army. In these cases, the navy provided only transportation support and sea and air cover. Together the army and the navy worked out all measures taken during the arrival and landing phase.

The sequence in which the amphibious troops and their materiel were disembarked determined the organization of the transportation fleet. So that certain weapons groups and staffs would not be lost, they were generally spread around among the various transport ships.

Under the protection provided by the navy and its pilots, the transports approached their points of debarkation under cover of darkness. They moved along the coast in one or two columns while reconnaissance units collected information on suitable anchorages and landing sites. As soon as these sites had been determined, anchorages and landing zones were located by fast patrol boats

and studied in detail. Navigational and coastal difficulties during the landing played a subordinate role to weakness or vulnerability of the enemy. Anchorages were supposed to be beyond the range of enemy batteries, and the landing sites were supposed to offer alternates if they became necessary.

The transports were distributed among the anchorages in such a way that they could arrive or depart without disturbing one another. Ideally, their sequencing corresponded to the amphibious battalions' organization. Each battalion had been assigned individual locations within the landing sites. In order to direct the transport fleet, radio channels between all ships needed to be guaranteed.

The Debarkation of the Amphibious Force

In the secondary literature there is the predominant opinion that the navy had the responsibility of manning the invasion force. Friedrich Ruge, for example, writes that, "the naval infantry constituted the first wave of the amphibious force. This simplified the establishment of clear lines of authority. The most senior officer was in command during the crossing and the landing up to the point when the most senior army officer announced that he could hold the beachhead. At that point, he assumed control of the shore command." In reality, the navy only provided coverage for landings by the army. In exceptions, the navy supported the army during the landing with special boats assigned to the first wave.

Once the transports had anchored, the debarkation commandos took over. These special units from the landing force, with years of practice behind them, had the mission of loading the landing craft, moving them to the beach, and returning the empty craft to the transports. There were two kinds of landing craft, developed by the army engineers. One was an armored 3-ton steel boat, 10.2 meters long, 2.4 meters wide, and 1.2 meters high. It had a muffled, 60 hp diesel motor (speed 7.5–8.8 knots) and could be maneuvered using, if necessary, four oars. It could accommodate thirty infantrymen in addition to the five-man crew: a helmsman, a machinist's mate, an anchorman, and two assistants.

A larger, armored steel boat weighed over 9 metric tons, with a length of 14.9 meters, width of 3.3 meters, and height of 1.5 meters. Equipped with the same motor as the smaller boat, it had in addition a landing gate on the bow and two keels each 3 meters long to make the craft sturdier. It was operated by a helmsman, a machinist's mate, an anchorman, a signalman, and three helpers. It could carry seventy fully-equipped infantrymen or ten infantrymen with ten horses, one loaded truck with personnel, or a small armored personnel carrier and crew.

The debarkation commandos used cranes to put the boats in the water. The infantrymen climbed in by means of net ladders. Trucks and horses were loaded with derricks. Luminescent paint in the middle of the loading surface and the landing bridge simplified the loading of cargoes which had to be set down vertically and distributed evenly so that the boats did not capsize. Although the debarkation crews had practiced all aspects of their job for months, there was no way during these operations to avoid the loss of life and equipment, particularly during high seas.

The loaded boats from each transport approached the coast in a single column with a lead boat out in front to provide greater protection against enemy fire. Small stern lights helped orientation. Not until near the beach did the boats assume a position abeam one another; if necessary, the crews opened fire from machine guns and armored personnel carriers. Generally reefs and surf caused greater losses than enemy hits.

The boats were to land in a group, at least within the landing zones assigned to them. As soon as the debarkation crews dropped the stern anchor, the men leaped from the protection of their boats. They used exit rails on the smaller boats and the landing ramp on the larger boats.

After that the motorized vehicles were brought ashore. The horses came ashore last of all. Once a boat had been unloaded, its crew turned around immediately, without

further looking after the landed troops or any damaged or stranded boats. With the help of anchor and poles, the landing commandos pushed the boats back from the beach. Signs with luminescent paint marked the route back to the transports, where a second wave was waiting.

The first landing wave was largely responsible for success or failure of the mission. For that reason every transport, if at all possible, was to take along as many landing craft as necessary to debark virtually all troops at the same time. Armored personnel carriers, light field artillery with forward spotters, army engineers, and communications technicians were also a part of the first wave. Every unit up to platoon size was trained and equipped in such a way that they could fight independently.

The landed troops had the task of taking the first assigned coastal targets immediately, that is, roads, airport, garrison, or town. Much depended on how strong, daring, and quick the units were, whether they had surprised the enemy, and to what extent they faced resistance. The engineers removed any physical obstacles which blocked the route of advance. They also supported to varying degrees the debarkation crews, repaired damaged boats, and were responsible for rescue operations. The advance party operated the light artillery and prepared for the use of artillery pieces arriving with the second wave. The signal corps provided for communication with the transport fleet. After the first assault target had been taken, the troops regrouped to continue their advance or to expand their beachhead.

With the second landing wave, generally at dawn, reserves, horses, weapons, and, above all, artillery and supplies for about ten days were landed. The newly landed troops were to join fighting units immediately. Supported by army engineers, artillery was brought to prepared positions and put to use. If the first wave fell under enemy fire and was pinned down, the second wave was to reinforce them and enable them to continue the attack. In this emergency, the second wave had only the function of a reserve force.

Theory and Practice

The more detailed the landing guidelines, the more difficult it became to hold to them. Despite the decades of experience that might underlie the theory, reality and all of its eventualities still separated theory from actual practice. Bad weather and high winds, high or stormy seas, difficult loading zones (especially surf or reefs) and, last but not least, the enemy's response, could not be predicted or anticipated in the planning stage. Be it a crosswind that blew the landing craft away in the predawn darkness or a radio that suddenly stopped functioning, an unexpected mishap often endangered the success of the entire operation. Thus, it lay in the nature of amphibious warfare that guidelines only recorded what was supposed to take place.

Inherent in the guidelines, unquestionably, was the unfortunate tendency to prejudge military action and thereby to limit freedom of decision. So long as unforeseen difficulties did not occur, the operation ran like clockwork. But once a problem arose, confusion ensued. The goal of deceiving or overpowering the enemy often led to excessively daring plans that overestimated one's own forces and thereby wasted them. If the enemy reacted differently than expected, one's own amphibious force easily fell into difficult straits. At that point, deficiencies in the communications net and in the radio circuit quickly became obvious; the Japanese leadership underestimated their significance. They attempted to overcome any threats to the operation with traditional Japanese military daring—Bushidio (a feudal-military Japanese code valuing honor above life)—and win back the full freedom to act. The guidelines prescribed the continuation of an action despite unanticipated difficulties by adapting the amphibious units to existing circumstances and enduring difficulties until the air force could be brought in. The operation was interrupted only if extremely high losses were already incurred during the approach to the landing zone.

Still, the guidelines allowed for room to act in emergency circumstances, in order to account for the element of uncertainty. The planned reserve landing areas made it possible for the transport fleet to redeploy on short order. If necessary, the focus of an operation could be shifted at the last minute by redirecting the landing craft. If the arrival of the second wave was in danger or not possible, the guidelines gave full freedom to the subcommanders to adjust to existing circumstances. At the moment of fullest danger, of course, there remained only the law of survival.

Such was the Japanese approach to amphibious landings, and they shared their field-tested doctrine with the Germans. Below is the telegram sent from the German Embassy, Tokyo, to the Foreign Office, Berlin, on 21 April 1942, in which the Japanese ideas on amphibious warfare are outlined.

No. 1230, 20 April 1942, for the general staff of the Department of the Army.

The request that the Japanese landing doctrine be made available was to date denied, with the justification that there was no single document, but only partial summaries. From the partial summaries that were made available to me, I have made the following resume:

1. *General.* (a) One needs to distinguish naval landings (Wake, Guam), army landings (Malaya, Luzon) and all large landings. Scholl's conjecture to me in Bangkok—that in the front ranks of every army landing there are other navy amphibious units which take the coastline—was universally denied during a tour of the front and is unappropriate even after a retreat.

(b) Virtually total sea and air superiority is necessary at least for the final, decisive landing. Therefore the purpose of the first landing was often simply to win airfields (Kota Bharu, Apari, Vigan, etc.).

(c) One should seek to surprise the enemy while he is still unprepared. Apart from surprise at the time of the landing, it is important to camouflage the direction of the amphibious transport fleet (certain transports for the Khota Baru landing were disguised as steaming from Bangkok).

(d) Enemy air, naval, and ground forces should be caused to disperse to the greatest degree possible through deceptive maneuvers and through the breadth and comprehensive application of our own forces (Luzon).

(e) Troops should be carefully trained in night landings. Equipped as much as possible with bicycles and motorized vehicles to diminish the number of horses required. Especially important is the training of debarkation commandos, which are to be drawn from the amphibious force itself, and guaranteeing their effective co-operation with the landing force.

2. *Designating the transportation fleet and the landing sites.* (a) The basis for organizing the transportation fleet and the loading of the individual transports derives from the intended organization of the amphibious unit during the landing as well as from the planned sequence of debarkation commandos.

(b) Where an attack by enemy aircraft or enemy ships can be expected, staffs and infantry units should be embarked in such a way that loss of one transport does not mean the complete loss of a single staff or an entire weapons branch (example—the loss of three-quarters of all artillery to be put ashore at Kota Bharu).

(c) The commander of the amphibious force and the commander of the covering naval forces should exchange all planning documents in a timely fashion and should stay in constant radio contact during the approach and landing phases of the operation.

(d) The organization of the transports during the approach phase and while at anchor should be adjusted completely to the landing organization of the unit being transported.

(e) The most favorable time for landing is at night. This means, in particular, that the last hour of the approach phase, the debarkation, and the landing of the first wave takes place by dark.

(f) The transports are to approach their anchorages in groups, one or two columns parallel to the coast.

(g) Landing zones to be selected in such a way that either no enemy resistance, or minimal resistance, can be expected. Anchorages should be out of range of artillery fire. Navigational and geographic difficulties (a steep coast, for example), should therefore be accommodated if necessary.

(h) Always plan for back-up landing zones to which one can divert if changes prove necessary during the approach phase.

(i) The landing zone should be determined early, and should be under constant surveillance from the air. Shortly before the arrival of the transports, the commander of the landing force, if at all possible, should view the landing zone from a fast patrol boat.

(j) Landing zones should be subdivided into landing points (e.g. according to the number of battalions in the first wave).

(k) The transports should be anchored in such a way that arrival and departure are easily possible, and so that the sinking of ships, for example, will not hamper the operation.

(l) The means for transports to communicate among one another is necessary.

(m) Air cover over the anchorage is the task of the navy.

3. *The Japanese landing plan has the following key points.* (a) The landing zone, time, and manner of gathering information about the zone.

(b) Schedule for approach by sea and landing.

(c) Schedule for the initial phase of landing.

(d) Division of landing zone into landing points, which are then assigned to individual units (generally battalions).

(e) Organization of the landing force and their assignment to individual landing points.

(f) Organization of the transportation fleet according to the organization of the landing force.

(g) Action by the transportation fleet (real movement, deceptive movement) and protective measures for the fleet.

(h) Anchorages for the transportation fleet.

(i) Organization of the transportation fleet for anchoring and [determining] the time for anchoring.

(j) Infantry action during the landing.

(k) Participation of navy and air force units in support of the landing.

(l) Air defense in various phases of the landing.

(m) Communication nets during the landing.

(n) Resupply.

(o) Rescue operations.

4. *Debarkation.* (a) After anchoring of the transports, the debarkation crews put the landing craft in the water. The landing force, supported by debarkation commandos, enters the boats.

(b) Together, loaded boats head for the coast after they have gathered in the vicinity of the transports.

(c) Approach to the coast in limited profile, the commander's boat in front. Near the coast, transition to organization in breadth. Enemy fire not to interrupt the approach to the landing.

(d) After the landing of the first wave, the debarkation commandos return to the transports without concerning themselves further with the battle on the coast. The second wave is being prepared on board the transports.

(e) If the scheduled debarkation of the second wave can no longer be expected, as result of boats lost to enemy fire or stranded near the coast or disorientation in trying to locate transport, it is important that all subcommanders can adjust to new circumstances quickly.

(f) Horses go ashore last.

(g) Hope to be able to report technical details on landing craft.

5. *Japanese debarkation plan contains the following details.* (a) Detailing of debarkation commandos.

(b) Preparation, application, and use of landing craft.

(c) Sequence of putting landing craft in water.

(d) Designation of landing zones.

(e) Obstacles to be expected on the beach.

(f) Coordination of operations with special craft.

(g) Any intended camouflaging of the operation with smoke.

(h) Communication nets during debarkation.

(i) Special orders, if any, for regrouping when ashore.

(j) Measures for rescue and assistance: (1) Repair of damaged boats and (2) subsequent resupply of fuel, drinking water, etc.

6. *The navy, including the naval air wing, is responsible for protection from enemy air and naval forces during the approach and landing.* Under certain circumstances, the navy will include light naval forces in the first landing wave to contribute in the attack on the coast.

7. *The attack by the first landing wave.* (a) The basis for successful landings is that the coast is taken as quickly as possible. The first landing wave therefore must be as strong as possible. This leads in turn to inclusion of the largest number of landing craft possible aboard transports. Virtually simultaneous landings at least within the landing points, and if at all possible within the landing zones, is a major goal.

(b) The first landing wave of infantry, with light armored personnel carriers, artillery advance teams, army engineers, and communications corps. The landing infantry are able to fight independently down to platoon level through corresponding outfitting with arms.

(c) For armored personnel carriers incorporated into the first wave, some sharpshooters

to accompany and support the landing craft. Armored personnel carriers must be able to shoot from cannon and machine guns during the approach to the coast.

(d) The first landing wave assumes battle organization when it leaves the boats and approaches assigned targets without losing time through reordering of units. Speed, decisiveness, valor by the first wave determines the success of the landing. Once the first goal has been reached, it should not be too close to the coast—ordering of units and intelligence gathering assumes priority.

(e) Take advantage of any successful surprise using all available means. Once begun, the landing should be continued, even if surprise is not achieved or unexpected developments occur. If the landing force adjusts to circumstances and continues the attack, and the senior force commanders add additional air cover, successful outcome to be expected. With strong air defense, emergency case can develop with the first wave pinned down on the beach awaiting arrival of the second wave.

(f) The first wave cannot count on artillery support for extended period of time. Should therefore apply own weapons immediately. Companies and battalions landing in the first wave need no reserves. The reserves arrive with the newly landed force.

8. *Action by the subsequent landing wave.* (a) Later waves immediately assume contact with force fighting in front of them regardless of previous assignment.

(b) Artillery assumes positions prepared by artillery advance teams or rushes in individual pieces into individual use in the battle zone. Coordination of artillery firing piecemeal as quickly as possible.

(c) Army engineers remove obstacles slowing the landing, both on the beach and in the lanes of approach. Occasionally assistance can be provided them during landing and refloating of the boats and while preparing artillery for fire.

9. *If there is the need to shift focus during landings, regroup as quickly as possible with the aid of landing craft.*

10. *Resupply.* Landing units carry with them sufficient supplies for approximately ten days. Thereafter, resupply by supply ships.

The Japanese Assault on Timor, 1942

BY CAPTAIN R. A. STEWART, USMC

On the morning of 20 February 1942, the Japanese 38th Infantry Group, under the command of Major General Takeo Ito, attacked the Allied garrison on the island of Timor, thereby initiating the first classic combined amphibious assault and vertical envelopment (a paratroop drop) in history. Although not the first instance of combined amphibious and paratroop forces, Timor is a classic case because of the close coordination between the two. The Japanese successfully completed an amphibious landing on undefended beaches while the paratroop forces held up the Australian retreat long enough for the main force to advance and begin an encircling movement.

Earlier examples of paratroopers being used as part of amphibious operations include the April 1941 German paratroop units at British-held Crete, but British control of the sea approaches resulted in destruction of the seaborne force. In January 1942 the Japanese carried out their first airborne operation against the Dutch airfield at Menado on Celebes, which, like the Germans' Crete operation, was captured before the amphibious support forces arrived. A few days before Timor, the Japanese attempted another airborne assault to capture intact the Dutch oil fields at Palembang on Sumatra, but alert British and Dutch forces turned the assault into a fiasco. Unlike these previous operations, Timor represents a well-integrated, mutually supportive example of combined airmobile and amphibious forces. In addition, the Timor operation is similar in many respects to contemporary concepts of amphibious warfare and is worthy of study, not only because the Japanese organization is directly analogous to the modern version of the U.S. Regimental Landing Team but because it is the type of operation marines are trained to undertake.

Japan was one of the first nations to fully recognize the importance of modern amphibious warfare. In the latter part of the nineteenth century, Japan emerged from a long period of self-imposed isolation to embark on a period of rapid modernization. Soon a rising world power, with a modern, well-equipped army and navy, Japan undertook expansionistic plans to extend its influence throughout East Asia. To conduct successful operations on the Asian mainland, Japanese military leaders foresaw the need for a viable amphibious doctrine. Begining with the Sino-Japanese and Russo-Japanese wars at the turn of the century, Japanese military forces devoted major efforts toward improving their amphibious techniques.

By the beginning of World War Two, the Japanese had perfected an effective amphibious doctrine that enabled them to conduct extensive landing operations in the Pacific. Responsibility for amphibious operations lay with the Japanese army which, in the early 1920s, began intensive training in amphibious warfare. A shipping command was organized; its troops manned army transports and were skilled in embarkation and debar-

Marine Corps Gazette 58 (September 1974): 24–30. Reprinted by permission.

kation procedures. The Japanese navy also organized special landing units, trained to operate with the army in an escort and support role. Command of the amphibious force rested with the army. In the wake of the attack on Pearl Harbor, the Japanese undertook a massive amphibious campaign against the weak and scattered Allied garrisons throughout Southeast Asia.

General Ito's 38th Infantry Group, consisting largely of the 228th Infantry Regiment of the 38th Division, had considerable experience in amphibious assault. The 38th Division had conducted its first amphibious operation against the Chinese during the occupation of Canton in 1938. This operation was followed by the assault on the British colony of Hong Kong in December 1941, after which the 228th was refitted for operations in the Dutch East Indies. On 12 January 1942 it boarded transports and sailed to Davao on Mindanao. From Davao, General Ito's force of some fifty-three hundred men, reinforced by six hundred Japanese marines of the Kure First Special Naval Landing Force, aimed to capture Ambon, a major Allied naval base.

Landing on 29 January, the 38th Infantry Group overcame the small Dutch and Australian garrison with relative ease. Timor, however, posed another problem for the Japanese commander for although his convoy would be supported by the Japanese fleet, sizable Allied naval units still operated between Java and Darwin.

The island of Timor lay only 500 miles from the coast of Australia. The harbor of Koepang could provide the Japanese with an excellent base for future operations against the Australian mainland. Timor, 300 miles long and 50 miles wide, is largely mountainous with broad plains surrounding Koepang Bay in the extreme southwest. Timor was unique in that the western half of the island was controlled by the Dutch while the eastern portion belonged to Portugal, a neutral nation.

Hoping to solve the problem of Portugal's neutrality by an agreement similar to that used in Indochina, the Japanese intended to station troops on Portugese territory while Portugal continued to rule the colony. These plans were upset when they received word that a Dutch and Australian force had occupied Portugese Timor, remaining in Dili, the capital, until the arrival of a convoy of Portuguese troops from East Africa. Forced to revise his plans, General Ito would now have to commit one of his three battalions to carry out operations against the main Allied force at Koepang.

Four hundred miles to the south, Lieutenant Colonel Legatt, commander of the Koepang garrison, faced a formidable task in defending Timor. Under his command were some fifteen hundred Australians of the 2/40th Battalion, 2/2 Independent Company, 2/1 Heavy Artillery Battery (two 6-inch guns), 79th Light Antiaircraft Battery, 2/1 Fortress Engineers, an antitank battery (four 2-pounders), and attached signal and medical units. His force also included some six hundred Dutch troops under Colonel van Straaten.

When the Australian force arrived on 12 December 1941, the Allied command had not envisioned a Japanese attack on Timor. The Australians' primary mission was to protect the vital Penfui airfield which was used as a staging base for fighter aircraft flying from Darwin to Java. When the danger to Portuguese Timor became evident, Leggatt was ordered to dispatch troops to defend Dili. The 2/2 Independent Company along with two hundred seventy Dutch troops under Colonel van Straaten were sent into Portuguese Timor, seriously depleting Leggatt's force.

Most of the Koepang garrison was assigned to beach defense along Koepang Bay. A battery of two 6-inch guns was established at Klapalima in the remains of an old Dutch fort. The beach area from Koepang to Usapa-Besar was assigned to Companies "A" and "B." Company "C" was assigned to protect the airfield at Penfui. Company "D" was to be used as a mobile reserve to protect those beach areas east of Usapa-Besar. Lieutenant Colonel Detiger's Dutch troops were assigned the beach area from Koepang west to Tenau. A supply base was established 20 miles up the rear at Champlong, along the probable route of withdrawal. Colonel Legatt set up a forward headquarters at Penfui airfield, a rear headquarters at Tarus, and allotted part of his headquarters force to the village of Babau.

As the Japanese continued their steady advance through the island chain, Leggatt realized that his small force was inadequate for any proper defense of Timor. Hundreds of miles of undefended beaches would make an unopposed landing relatively simple. Unless significant reinforcements arrived in time, his force would defend the Koepang area as long as possible, then withdraw to the interior and conduct guerrilla warfare.

To bolster the defense, a squadron of Royal Australian Air Force Hudson bombers was sent to Penfui. On 26 January, Japanese bombers from Kendari on Celebes attacked Timor, destroying two Hudson automobiles on the ground. As part of the "softening up" process, the Japanese began regular air attacks. Heavy losses in aircraft forced the Australians to withdraw the Hudsons by the middle of February, leaving the garrison without air support or aerial reconnaissance.

On 27 January, the Allied commander on Java, General Wavell, decided that the threat against Timor was great enough to warrant a request for additional troops to defend the island. Seeing Timor as strategic to the defense of northern Australia, the Australian War Cabinet approved the request. Reinforcements that were earmarked for Timor included the 2/4th Australian Pioneer Battalion, the 2/147th American Artillery Battalion, and the 1/148th American Artillery Battalion. The American units had arrived in Darwin during the first week of February aboard the transport *Holbrook*. It had originally been part of the convoy carrying reinforcements to the Philippines but was diverted to Australia when the war began. The Timor defense force was designated as "Sparrow Force" under the command of Brigadier W. C. D. Veale of the Australian Engineers. Arriving in Koepang by plane on 12 February, Brigadier Veale informed Colonel Leggatt of the impending reinforcements. The arrival of the remainder of Sparrow Force would bring

the Timor garrison to nearly brigade strength. The convoy from Portuguese East Africa was expected to arrive at Dili shortly, releasing the Australian and Dutch forces there. The outlook for the defense was definitely improving.

On Ambon, meanwhile, General Ito was completing the final plans and preparations for the Timor landings. The 2/228th Infantry, under the regimental commander, Colonel Doi, was selected to occupy Dili. The main assault force would sail around the western tip of Timor and land near the mouth of the Paha River on the south coast. This force consisted of the 1/228th aboard the *Zenyo Maru*, the 3/228th aboard *Africa Maru*, the 1st Mountain Artillery Battalion aboard *Ryoto Maru*, and the detachment headquarters and supporting units aboard *Miike Maru*. Combat support units for the operation included a light tank company, elements of an antitank battalion, two antiaircraft batteries, two engineer companies, along with signal, transport, and medical units. Naval units supporting the operation included the 2nd Destroyer Squadron, two platoons (118 officers and men) of the Sasebo Combined Special Naval Landing Force, and six hundred paratroops of the Yokosuka Third Special Naval Landing Force.

The Japanese had begun the training of paratroops in 1940 under the direction of German paratroop instructors. The Japanese navy quickly foresaw the usefulness of paratroops in amphibious operations. Such forces would have the ability of seizing airfields and other important objectives before withdrawing enemy troops could destroy them. To meet this need, three classes of six hundred men each were trained by the navy in paratroop techniques and infantry warfare. These specially trained Japanese marines were formed into two battalions, the 1st and 3rd Yokosuka Special Naval Landing Forces. Each battalion had a table of organization of 844 officers and men divided into three infantry companies, a headquarters company, an antitank unit, and a command platoon. These paratroops were trained to jump from the bellies of transports at low altitudes of about three hundred feet and in one second intervals to reduce their dispersion upon landing.

The Japanese marines of the paratroop force assigned to the Timor operation were to land behind the Allied lines near Usau, cut off the main withdrawal route, and capture the Penfui airfield. Operations were scheduled to commence on the morning of 20 February.

On 15 February, the garrison's spirits were lifted when they received news that the convoy carrying the remainder of Sparrow Force, escorted by the American heavy cruiser *Houston*, destroyer *Peary*, and the Australian sloops *Swan* and *Warrego*, had sailed for Timor. A day out of port the convoy was attacked by aircraft from Admiral Ozawa's carriers. The *Houston* took a direct hit which disabled its aft turret. The remainder of the convoy sustained light damage. Alarmed by the attack, Brigadier Wavell ordered the convoy to turn back. Ozawa's planes struck again on 19 February, destroying the harbor of Darwin and sinking the destroyer *Peary* and several other ships. Receiving the news, Veale realized that there would be no relief for Timor.

On the evening of the 19th, an observation post on Semau Island, just west of Timor, reported thirteen warships and transports approaching from the northwest. Leggatt placed the garrison on full alert, then withdrew his headquarters to Tarus while Veale proceeded with his staff to Champlong to organize a defense in that area. Soon after Leggatt received a report that the Japanese were shelling Dili.

Shortly after midnight, the Japanese convoy was nearing the assault beaches. Japanese amphibious doctrine called for predawn landings. This concept, first used in the attack on Shanghai in 1932, gave an element of surprise to the operation, allowed the landing force the cover of darkness and protection from air assault, and placed them in control of the landing beaches by sunrise. Despite the obvious hazards involved in a night landing, this method allowed the Japanese a maximum amount of daylight to consolidate their objectives. Finding the landing beaches undefended, General Ito dispensed with preparatory naval gunfire, which made for additional surprise.

The transports moved as close to the beach as possible before lowering their armored landing barges into the water. By 0200, the first wave of troops were descending down rope ladders into the waiting boats. Once the debarkation was completed, General Ito gave the order for the landing force to begin its ship-to-shore movement. The landing was effected on three widely separated beaches, allowing width as well as depth.

The first wave to secure the beach consisted of the Japanese marines of the Special Landing Force. The remainder of the landing force was divided into three assault units. At 0235, the right assault unit, consisting of the 2nd Company, 1st Battalion and a machine gun section supported by a howitzer, landed half a mile west of the Paha River. Its mission was to advance to Usau, join the paratoops, and prevent an enemy withdrawal. The Center Assault Unit, which included the 3rd Battalion, the headquarters element, and support units, landed just west of Point Mar. One company was to advance and capture the Penfui airfield while the remainder of the unit moved directly on Koepang. By 0315, the left assault unit was ashore five miles west of Point Mar. Two companies of the 1st Battalion, a light tank company, and support troops were to advance along a trail leading to Koepang. Leaving the Naval Landing Force to defend the beach and help with supply operations, the main force began advancing over the roadless, hilly terrain toward their objectives.

Receiving word of the Japanese landing, Leggatt ordered his reserve company, commanded by Captain Trevena, to set up a defense at Upura, blocking the road leading into Koepang from the south. The Sparrow Force Engineers were then instructed to destroy the Penfui airfield. Veale, contacted about the landing, suggested that Leggat withdraw his force to the rear base at Champlong. With the demolitions incomplete, Leggatt delayed on the decision to withdraw. This proved to be a decisive mistake.

Several hundred miles to the north, a flight

of twenty-five Japanese "Topsy" transport aircraft were warming their engines on the airfield at Kendari. As 308 marine paratroops boarded the planes, a flight of bomber and fighter aircraft were winging their way to Timor. Shortly before sunrise the transports were nearing Timor. The command "prepare for jumping" was given and the paratroops began checking their equipment. The planes were only thirty minutes from the drop zone.

As the morning sun began rising above the mountains east of Koepang, the first flight of bombers roared in over Koepang Bay making a beeline for the fort at Klapalima. Within minutes the fort was a shambles. The Japanese had destroyed the battery's communication equipment, mortally wounded the commander, Major Wilson, and strafed Captain Trevena's company several times on the road to Upura.

The buzzers in the transports signaled "standby to jump." Hooking up to the static cable, the troopers began bailing out, descending into a flat, palm-tree clustered drop zone just east of Usau. By 0900, the paratroops had organized on the road to Champlong and begun advancing on the Babau area.

News of the paratroop landing was quickly relayed to Colonel Leggatt, who immediately ordered Captain Trevena's company to Babau. The only men at Babau who could meet the paratroops were rear echelon and headquarters company personnel armed only with rifles. These men, formed into two improvised platoons, offered stiff resistance to the paratroop advance party as it entered Babau. Suffering heavy casualties, the Australians were soon forced to withdraw to Tarus.

With their guns rendered ineffective, the troops in the Klapalima Fort destroyed their equipment and joined the infantry. Leggatt redeployed his force, sending Captain Roff's Company "B" to defend the airfield and Captain Johnston's Company "A" to a prepared position at the Usapa-Besar road junction. A platoon under Lieutenant Sharman was sent to Liliba to contact the enemy while the Dutch force took up positions betwen Upura and Liliba.

By 1020, the left assault force, advancing steadily from the beach, had reached the main trail that led to Koepang. The headquarters and central assault unit reached the main road to Koepang at the village of Baun around 1600 on the afternoon of the 20th. The right assault unit, under Lieutenant Kanbe, continued its advance along a trail leading northeast to Usau.

By the middle of the afternoon, Captain Trevena's company had arrived from Upura. Deploying several hundred yards west of Babau, it commenced an attack on the village. The left platoon, emerging from a maize field, fought its way into the eastern end of the village while the other two platoons attacked the marketplace. Heavy fire from 2-inch mortars and 7.7 machine guns met the Australian advance. The Australians had taken control of most of the village when reinforcements to the embattled paratroops arrived. Receiving heavy machine gun fire and with dusk approaching, Trevena decided to withdraw to a better defensive position at Ubelo.

Advancing rapidly, Major Hayakawa's left assault force had taken Koepang city where they awaited the arrival of the central assault unit and headquarters force.

By evening the situation was deteriorating. Leggatt convened a headquarters conference at Penfui airfield. Realizing that the Japanese paratroops on the road to Champlong were too strong for Trevena's company, he decided to abandon the defense of the airfield and concentrate his forces in an attack on Babau. At 2200, the Australians began concentrating at Tarus. Captain Johnston's company remained in position at the Usapa-Besar road junction until the remaining troops had passed, then withdrew across the Manikan River bridge as sappers prepared demolitions.

Shortly before midnight, Leggatt issued orders for another attack on Babau to commence at 0530 on the 21st. Roff's and Trevena's companies, supported by a section of bren carriers, an armored car, and a mortar attachment, would advance from Ubelo.

Dutch forces began withdrawing from their positions on the Baun road late in the evening of the 20th. Lacking adequate motor transportation, they were slow in reaching the Australian positions near Tarus.

With the road to Koepang clear, Major Nishiyama's central force entered the city early on the 21st. It was joined the following afternoon by the headquarters and support units.

The Australians began their advance at daybreak but movement was very slow, delayed for a time by Japanese snipers. Leggatt's men, without rest for three nights, were near exhaustion. Within an hour, the column was bombed and strafed by the Japanese. Several of the aircraft were downed by gunners of the 79th Antiaircraft Battery.

At 0830, the Australians received word that another paratroop drop had been made near Usua. Three hundred twenty-three more paratroops landed to reinforce their comrades and help in the seizure of the airfield.

Leggatt joined the forward companies to evaluate the situation. Realizing the weary state of his troops, he authorized a short rest before continuing the attack. The advance was resumed at noontime but quickly came under heavy fire. Two platoons of Trevena's company attempted a flanking movement. Suffering heavy losses, they were forced to withdraw. Leggatt had no communication with Roff's company and was unable to ascertain his position. Returning to Ubelo he ordered Captain Burr's reserve company to reinforce the attack. A perimeter of defense was formed at Ubelo by Johnston's company to protect the rear of the force.

Unknown to Leggatt, Roff's company had cleared the paratroops from the maize fields and had taken Babau. Roff and two men entered the building housing the Japanese headquarters, killing the paratroop commander and ten of his men. Establishing a Lewis gun in a nearby building, an Australian corporal killed five Japanese with enfilading fire and drove off several more. Lieutenant William's platoon then rushed forward, driving the remaining Japanese from the village.

Eventually learning of Roff's success, and encouraged by it, Leggatt moved the remainder of his force into Babau that night. By

sunrise on the 22nd, his troops were in place with Roff's company on the forward right, Johnston's to the left, Burr's in the left rear and Trevena's to the right rear.

Sortly after 1400 on the 21st, the 9th Company of Nishiyama's 3rd Battalion captured the airfield. It was soon joined by elements of the paratroop battalion. An hour later Major Hayakawa departed Koepang with three infantry companies, two artillery batteries, and the light tank company in pursuit of the retreating Australians. Two miles east of Klapalima they were joined by the 9th Company arriving from the airfield. The 1st and 9th Companies led the column in the advance on Babau.

The remaining paratroops withdrew to Usau where they were reinforced by the right assault force at 2130 on the 21st. Lieutenant Kanbe quickly began preparing emplacements for his troops, mountain gun, and machine gun section along the length of Usau ridge, astride the road to Champlong.

Out of contact with the Australians, the Dutch commander applied for a truce with the advancing Japanese. Desiring the surrender of the entire force, General Ito declined the truce. Unable to link up with Australians, the Dutch withdrew to the southeast around the Japanese lines, eventually reaching the interior.

Formed into a column, the Australians began advancing toward Usau and Champlong at 0800. Roff's company led the column, followed by Johnston's and Trevena's with Burr's protecting the rear. As the column was forming up, an antiaircraft gun position was attacked by paratroops, who were quickly driven off.

A mile east of Babau, the column encountered a Japanese roadblock at the Ammabi River bridge. Behind the bridge, Lieutenant Kanbe's troops were observed digging in on the ridge. Roff's left platoon suffered heavy casualties as it crossed the river to assault the ridge. Bringing his mortars to bear on the ridge, Roff moved the rest of his company wide around the left. Encountering superior numbers, they were driven back. The Australians discovered that the Japanese were entrenched on both sides of the ridge and at the entrance and flanks of the village.

The remaining mortar units were rushed forward to support Roff. Attacking from the right, across a large open area, Captain Johnston's company met heavy enemy fire and was forced back. A second attack was attempted but it also failed.

Reconnoitering the area, Leggatt decided to consolidate on the main road and prepare for a three company attack. Following preparatory mortar and small arms fire, Johnston's and Burr's companies would attack the ridge from the left of the road supported by fire from Roff's company.

As the three companies prepared to attack, heavy firing was heard from the rear of the column. Several hundred troops of the 1st and 9th companies had encountered the Australian rear guard. Trevena's company, with thirty fortress troops, promptly dispersed the Japanese column. The Japanese reformed quickly and fighting continued throughout the night.

At 1700, the Australians began intense preparatory fires on Usua ridge. With the ridge obscured by smoke and dust, several engineers were able to remove the roadblock. The attack was soon under way. Roff's company encountered heavy fire as it crossed an open area below the ridge, killing both Roff and his executive officer, Lieutenant Gatenby, and taking a heavy toll of platoon commanders and NCOs. With Roff's troops pinned down on the right, Johnston's company quickly took its first objective, a knoll to the left of the road. Burr's company attacked wide from the left, suffering heavy casualties as it approached the village.

Lieutenant Kanbe's troops were decimated by the Australian bombardment and attack. Leggatt and his adjutant, Captain Maddern, moved in behind Johnston's company on the knoll, took over a captured Japanese machine gun and began firing on the Japanese who were pinning down Roff's men. They were soon joined by Company "R" which rushed the ridge from the left and quickly eliminated the remaining Japanese. The single Jap-

anese captured in the attack broke away and jumped into a trench where he opened fire with a machine gun. The Australians quickly reacted and overwhelmed him. The survivors of Roff's company, under the only remaining officer, Lieutenant McLeod, took over the Japanese positions on the forward slope of the ridge as the column moved past.

With the road clear, Colonel Leggatt began to move the column through Usau while Hayakawa's troops continued a contested battle with Trevena's rear guard. With two of the four antitank guns lost in the fighting, the two remaining guns were brought forward to cover the road for the retreating troops. Most of the remaining Australians were loaded on the available vehicles for transport to Champlong.

After several delays the convoy began moving and reached Airkom late on the 22nd. The Japanese force was advancing hard on the heels of the retreating Australians. Some of Hayakawa's troops had begun flanking movements on the column. By early morning, Hayakawa's 1st and 9th companies were joined by the tank company and artillery detachment from Koepang. The tanks began advancing on the rear of the Australian column. Observing a furled white flag above the lead tank, the Australians held their fire only to discover, too late, that it was actually a Japanese battle flag. The tanks had now come too close to the column for the antitank guns to be brought to bear.

Major Hayakawa sent a message to the Australians, warning them that unless a decision to surrender was delivered by 1000, his force would open fire. Leggatt immediately called a meeting of his officers to discuss the situation. They estimated that the Japanese were on both flanks and to their rear in a brigade-size force. The battalion was desperately short of ammunition, water, and rations, and the men were too weary to carry on a prolonged resistance. Leggatt mistakenly believed that Champlong was held by the Japanese paratroop force when it was actually in the hands of rear-echelon troops under Brigadier Veale. Feeling that further fighting would endanger the large number of wounded near the rear of the convoy and result in useless slaughter, the Australians delivered the decision to surrender at 0900 on the morning of 23 February.

Australian casualties in the battle had been heavy—84 killed and 132 wounded. Ito's assault force suffered 67 killed and 56 wounded. Only 78 Japanese paratroops survived the fighting. Ito's victory had placed the Japanese on the doorstep to Australia.

Although the battle for Koepang was over, the battle for Timor had only begun. The Australian and Dutch forces remaining in Dutch Timor joined with those from Portuguese Timor to carry on active guerrilla warfare against the Japanese for almost a year before being withdrawn to Australia in January 1943.

During the assault on Timor, the Australian defense was hindered by lack of communications and artillery support. The Japanese control of the sea and air was decisive. The operation was well-planned and executed, with exemplary coordination among ground, sea, and air units. By its nature, Timor represents an example of amphibious warfare highly relevant to modern concepts of amphibious operations.

Tarawa: The Tide that Failed

BY PATRICK L. McKIERNAN

"Three-fourths of those things upon which action in War must be calculated are hidden more or less in the clouds of great uncertainty." Clausewitz underscores the role chance played in the Battle of Tarawa. A favorable tide was needed to float landing craft over coral reefs surrounding the target area. Would nature cooperate on D-day? On the morning of 20 November 1943, the boated marines learned the answer: "Suddenly the craft jolted and came to a stop. The skipper poured fuel to the engine, but the craft did not move. It was lodged there, solid. He tried to back water, but the craft did not move; the metal of the hull rasped against the barrier. The hammer-blows of the machine-guns rang now with increasing tempo against the plating. . . ."

The principal target at Tarawa was Betio Island. Like so many Gilbert Atolls, Tarawa forms a bow of tiny islets about 30 miles long with a narrow passageway opening westward. In the southwest corner of the atoll is reef-encircled Betio, a low-lying island with a length of about 2 miles and a width of nearly 800 yards near its center. Upon this insignificant speck of Micronesia, the Japanese had hurriedly constructed an airstrip, hacking it out of coconut plantations and surrounding it with an astonishingly formidable fortress of steel, concrete, logs, coral rock, and sand. Many bombproof shelters were covered with 6 feet or more of concrete and armor plate. With at least two hundred major

weapons for a concentrated defense and five hundred pillboxes for protection, the defenders confidently awaited an attack.

Rear Admiral Keiji Shibasaki commanded the island bastion. A huge concrete blockhouse served as his command post from where he issued his definite order "to destroy the enemy at the water's edge." Responsive to his directions was a tough selected corps of vigorously disciplined Imperial Marines. They bowed in respect as Shibasaki boastfully proclaimed that a million Americans could not seize his stronghold. He expected his 4,500 troops to fight to the last marine if necessary; they almost did, for only 146 of them survived the decimation.

One of these survivors, Special Duty Ensign Kiyoshi Ohta recalls the defense planning:

> We expected the American assault at high tide and made the necessary preparation accordingly. We knew the Americans would suffer the least casualties if they landed on high tide and established a foothold.

The long coral reef apron over which the ocean rolls greatly assured Ohta and his comrades that it could serve as an effective barrier against invading forces. To promote impregnability, however, Shibasaki mined the reef shelf in certain areas, covered it with barbed wire fences near the beaches, and erected concrete blocks to force landing craft into presighted lanes of fire.

The coral barrier evoked concern for the Americans planning to seize Betio. How much water passed over the inner shelf at high tide?

U.S. Naval Institute *Proceedings* 88 (February 1962): 38–50. Reprinted by permission.

Tarawa beachhead, 1943.

Enough to float Higgins boats? What possible navigational problems existed? Depth of lagoon passage? Coral heads? With the meager hydrographic data available, these intriguing questions remained unanswerable. A demand for local knowledge became a search for former residents.

U.S. Navy intelligence officers in Australia and New Zealand quietly sought persons who as a result of their nautical experience might be able to assist the amphibious forces. In Melbourne, the officers approached Lieutenant Commander G. H. Heyen, Royal Australian Naval Reserve. He had spent some thirteen years in the Gilberts, during which time he wrote sailing directions, compiled current data for the U.S. Navy Hydrographic Office, and surveyed several of the Gilbert lagoons. His wide acquaintance with local conditions would elevate him to a consequential role in the campaign.

Lieutenant Gordon J. Webster, Royal New Zealand Naval Reserve, soon joined Commander Heyen. Having navigated in the Gilberts from 1939 to 1942, Lieutenant Webster could recall quickly his experiences there:

Throughout the period I remained based at Tarawa, where the anchorage for my type of vessel was about 400 yards off the jetty on Betio Island inside the lagoon. I was, very naturally, constantly ashore in small boats, and often crossed the reef to land either at the District Office, which was situated about 400 yards to the west of the jetty, or at Burns Philp jetty, which lay about the same distance to the east.

This officer's close contact with Betio would serve extensively, for he aided in the planning for the landing and later guided a destroyer into the lagoon on D-day.

Both the Allied officers combed the South Pacific waterfronts for traders, mariners, former islanders—anyone acquainted with the Gilberts. The Burns Philp Company at Sydney, an old trading and shipping establishment, had maintained a business at Tarawa before its seizure, and it was highly probable that it could direct them to mariners familiar with Betio. Fortunately, several of these men were located. Lieutenants S. S. Page and J. Forbes, Royal New Zealand Naval Reserve, responded enthusiastically, along with Captain Karl Tschaun, merchant navy, and Lieutenants E. Harness and Bruno Reymond, Royal Australian Naval Reserve, who had been born in the Gilberts where he sailed in the surrounding waters for many years. They were

Council of war, Gilbert Islands Campaign, 1943. Admiral Chester W. Nimitz is in the center. To his left is LtGen. Ralph C. Richardson, USA. In the foreground, wearing glasses, is MajGen. H. M. ("Howling Mad") Smith, USMC. Courtesy of the U.S. Navy Historical Center.

lifted to Pearl Harbor to begin an experience that for some of them has been misrepresented in several accounts of the Tarawa attack. To consider their contribution is to understand their point of view.

Commander Heyen arrived at Pearl Harbor on 10 September 1943. There he saw the warships of a growing fleet being hoarded for battle. A marked anchorage of new aircraft carriers underlined the strategy of an impending Central Pacific offensive. The Australian naval officer was directed to the man who had been assigned as commander of the Fifth Amphibious Force, Rear Admiral Richmond K. Turner, U.S. Navy.

The amphibious force commander involved himself in the review of hydrographic intelligence. He knew the planned landing at Betio meant that assault craft might have to traverse reefs extending in some places up to 800 yards off shore. An exposed shelf would force the invaders to walk or crawl toward the beaches. If naval and aerial bombardment proved insufficient, those advancing marines could seek no sheltering foxholes. Such speculation led Admiral Turner to follow apprehensively the developing tide predictions.

The critical tidal requirement fostered an intensive search for an accurate assessment of Tarawa's waters. But what was available? In 1841, the Wilkes Expedition had prepared charts of the atoll and these were still being used in 1943 with only slight modifications. There were disturbing notations: "Use these charts with caution," or "This chart should be used with circumspection—the surveys are incomplete." A complex amphibious operation could hardly premise its execution upon such dubious navigational knowledge.

In December 1901, Lieutenant Truscott in HMS *Pylades* surveyed Tarawa and recorded some tidal observations. He did determine the time of the first high water after the moon's passage over the local meridian. Also spring range was recorded at 6 feet. These calculations later served to determine tidal patterns at Tarawa, using Apia in Samoa as a reference.

Lieutenant Commander Heyen's group, dubbed the "Foreign Legion," considered the available data and dismissed some of it as too imprecise for planning purposes. The mariners did not trust predictions based upon Apia, nearly 1,000 miles from Tarawa. Record yielded to recollection. Often these officers had noted tidal behavior in their log books, "Boat work ceased, falling tide—resumed loading (or unloading), rising tide." But these notations were not available. Memory became paramount.

Prediction began with the determination of neap and spring tides. Neap tides occur during the first and third quarter phases of the moon. At these times, tidal range is the smallest of the entire lunar month. Spring tides appear during full and new moon and the waters at these periods manifest maximum range; the highest high tides and the lowest low tides appear. Obviously a spring tide offered the most favorable time for an amphibious attack over Betio's coral reef.

Spring tides had been a significant part of the legion's experiences. Some shallow lagoon entrances restricted navigation to spring periods only. Since there were no drydock facilities at Betio, the mariners would beach their schooners during full or new moon, perform underwater maintenance, and wait for the return of exceptionally high tides.

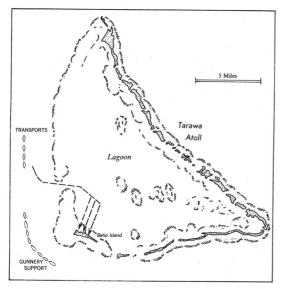

Tarawa, 1943.

troduced various tidal characteristics which the legion endeavored to identify for intelligence officers. Commander Heyen and Captain Tschaun frequently returned to a phenomenon they called a dodging tide. During neap periods, they had experienced, in their judgment, tidal aberrations. The tide seemed to remain steady for hours on end instead of following the usual pattern. Often they had witnessed an unexplainable rise and fall of the water at neaps. Since these irregularities might appear on D-day, the mariners agreed to preface their tide tables with this significant notation:

Neap tides are variable and occasionally ebb and flow several times in 24 hours, but variations from the heights given should not be greater than one foot.

In effect, then, the legion informed Admiral Turner that he could expect as little as four feet of water at the outer edge of the reef during H-hour. This possibility assumed a distressing meaningfulness when the intelligence sections considered the draft of the principal landing craft available, the LCVP or Higgins boat.

An LCVP fully loaded and underway draws 4 feet of water. Thus the appearance of a normal neap tide meant that these boats would cross over the reef's edge with only 12 inches of water to spare. Certainly marines could expect to walk part of the way to shore. A dodging tide at invasion hour signified no passage over the lagoon apron. How might the invaders be brought with greater certainty to the beaches? In a unique proposal, advanced by the marines, the possible answer lay in the use of LVTs.

Metaphorically called "alligators," LVTs were the true amphibians of the Pacific war. Capable of moving over land or water, these tracked vehicles had already been used at Guadalcanal. But their fundamental mission had been to transport supplies and not troops to the beaches. When the navy learned of the proposal to use the alligators tactically, the suggestion led to contentious and decisive language.

Protest came chiefly from Admiral Turner who could offer a cogent and reasonable ar-

The mariners informed Admiral Turner that at the time of the November springs he could expect high tide in the late afternoon or very early morning. To launch an attack for either of these times promised to complicate further an already difficult landing schedule. A late afternoon attack might preclude reinforcements to the beachhead before the sudden tropical darkness hampered logistic operations. A dawn assault might allow little daylight for accurate naval gunfire. These contingencies resolved the question of choice: neither time was suitable for the invasion.

Necessary was a rising tide in the morning, soon after daybreak, to provide for about three hours of naval bombardment. The closest time to this requirement appeared to be 20 November—during a *neap tide* period. This date was selected. How much water could be anticipated?

The legion members predicted 5 feet of water at 1001 on 20 November at the end of a long coconut log and coral pier, which extended at least 500 yards out to the lip of the lagoon reef. Since the coral shelf is an inclined plane, there would be a gradual reduction of water beachward. The mariners therefore promised no dryshod landing.

With seemingly incessant hours of exploratory discussion, numerous conferences in-

gument against the use of LVTs. These vehicles were difficult to control; they just did not steer as well as conventional, screw-driven craft. The angry captain who discovered a hole punched in his ship as the result of an alligator's stubborn steerage would quickly support Admiral Turner's stand on maneuverability. Slow speed and lack of armor made the LVTs highly vulnerable targets. The low freeboard invited further disaster. A stalled alligator frequently swamped because it shipped water readily. Thus Admiral Turner viewed the LVT as unseaworthy for assault purposes. He did not, however, convince one marine officer. Major General Holland M. Smith, commander of all ground troops in the Gilberts campaign, challenged Admiral Turner's stand.

Often referred to as "Howling Mad Smith," the marine commander vigorously pressed the issue. Both men were stubborn, hot-tempered, yet capable leaders who refused to yield to each other's point of view. Admiral Turner insisted that the LVTs would not be carried aboard his ships. General Smith replied, "No LVTs, no operation." This controversy emphasizes the truism that a strong dichotomy of responsibilities often isolates command interests in amphibious operations. Each commander is vitally concerned with possible losses: those afloat and those ashore. This is frequently an inevitable and understandable result of each officer's regard for the consequences of leadership. When General Smith threatened to refer the altercation to higher echelons, Admiral Turner acquiesced and the search for suitable LVTs began.

The hunt proved discouraging. Only seventy-five were available, and these already had gone through the Guadalcanal campaign. The corrosive action of sea water had greatly affected their immersed mechanisms. Many had already been driven beyond their expected operational life. So severe was the shortage that a constant fear of further loss accompanied the rehearsal periods. Through difficult effort fifty new models were obtained, but they did not join the amphibious forces until the ships were off Betio's

hostile shores. These available alligators provided transportation for the first three waves. All other marines had to be boated in LCVPs or the larger LCMs.

Inexperience with coral island fortifications affected the preliminary naval bombardment plans. No prolonged gunfire, typical of later Pacific operations, would precede the landing, since such action served to identify an invader's intentions. To rely upon surprise as much as possible, the gunfire support was to be delivered primarily on D-day. Some optimistic naval officers felt that the preassault bombardment meant the virtual destruction of the defenders.

Could field artillery support also contribute toward this destruction? Adjacent to Betio is Bairiki. Several marine officers advocated the seizure of this island first for the emplacement of field artillery units. Their mission would be to shell Betio prior to the major thrust. But the navy's regard for a quick departure and the shortage of men and ships excluded such action.

As invasion hour approached, final plans began to emerge. Major General Julian C. Smith's 2nd Marine Division in New Zealand had already been assigned to assault Betio. Rear Admiral Harry W. Hill's Task Force 53 would transport these marines to the Gilberts. To the north of Tarawa, American army units from Hawaii were to seize Makin. A complex plan of action, involving nearly 200 ships and 35,200 men, constituted the planned simultaneous attack.

From various Pacific ports, amphibious forces mounted. The 2nd Marine Division, after prolonged training in New Zealand, sailed north on 1 November 1943 for final rehearsals at Efate in the New Hebrides. During one of the frequent critiques held there, staff officers discussed hydrographic data. Major F. L. G. Holland, a member of the legion, introduced a new, if not startling, interpretation of anticipated tidal conditions.

For at least fifteen years, Major Holland, a retired British army officer, had lived at Tarawa. While at Pearl Harbor, he had joined in the assessment of Tarawa's tides to promote the predictions. In fact, documents clearly illustrate that he supported the dodging tide thesis—a possible 4 feet of water at invasion hour. But at Efate he reversed his judgment.

He was astonished to learn of the scheduled neap tide landing. Shaking his fist, the old army officer was nearly in tears as he repeatedly emphasized the strong belief that at landing time there would be no more than 3 feet of water over the reef. Other members of the legion were consulted. They disagreed with Major Holland's evaluation. Since Commander Heyen was participating in the Makin attack, he could not be consulted at this time.

General Julian C. Smith claims that Major Holland's announcement came as no "bombshell" to him. Marines in the various battalions had already been informed of the acute tidal uncertainty. In fact, the possibility of low water had led to the creation of a shuttle system, using the empty LVTs of the initial waves to transfer men from LCVPs to the beaches. Major Holland's estimate could do little to alter plans already in execution. He might be wrong.

From Efate the invasion forces sailed northeastward to the Gilberts where they arrived on 19 November. Into the designated areas warships and transports moved while a quarter moon illuminated Betio. It seemed almost impossible to many of the marines that this tiny island with "its sleepy lagoon in some lullaby-land" would soon erupt into a horrendous scene of fire, blood, and sudden death.

At 0441 on 20 November, the battle of Betio began. The Japanese discharged a red star cluster. Heavy fire from their 8-inch guns followed at 0507. This shelling dramatically introduced the vivid truth that earlier air and sea raids had failed to destroy the enemy's seacoast artillery. It signified the beginning of an unexpected and tough adversity which reduced the assault's momentum nearly to a standstill.

Admiral Hill's flagship *Maryland*, part of the gunnery support group, engaged the enemy in counterbattery fire to silence him. But the battleship proved her age, for she could not serve dually as a command center and a fire support ship. The first salvo from the flagship's 16-inch guns silenced her communication system and left Admiral Hill and General Smith without essential radio contact. In particular, Admiral Hill needed to communicate with carrier planes now due for the scheduled aerial bombardment.

Fear that naval fire might hit carrier aircraft over the target had required the task force commander to discontinue it until the air strike ceased. For a yet unexplainable reason, the planes arrived late, allowing the Japanese to fire with near impunity against cargo and troop transports in the process of unloading. The vessels, amid the splash of shells, moved out of range and, like frightened ducklings, the landing craft followed close behind. Admiral Hill resumed counterbattery fire which continued until 0615 when the carrier planes appeared.

The raid lasted for about ten minutes. It was difficult to see the tiny island, since heavy dust and smoke obscured the beaches. Nevertheless, the pilots dropped their bombs, strafed the landing areas, and withdrew.

Naval shellfire was continued. This planned bombardment constituted the major preliminary fire of the assault. Delivered in a series of phases, the bombardment lasted about two and one-half hours, during which time battleships, cruisers, and destroyers hurled about 3,000 tons of metal into Betio. The spectacular eruptions ashore brought cheers from many boated marines. How could any Japanese survive such a pounding?

From the rendezvous area the first waves of tracked vehicles began the long journey to the line of departure, a good 3½ miles away. The alligators moved more slowly than expected to extend the delay in the landing schedule. Already the essential thrust was not being fully developed.

At 0825 the LVTs left the line of departure and headed for the beaches designated Red One, Two, and Three which were about 6,000 yards away. Smoke from Betio's fires hid them from Admiral Hill's view. Because he had to avoid hitting the alligators as they approached the shoreline, Admiral Hill ordered cease fire at 0854. The first marines to reach the shore were now about twenty minutes from that objective.

Gradually overcoming the bombardment effects, dazed Japanese troops emerged from their extremely strong fortifications. They had time to mass their strength on the lagoon side to await the invaders' approach. Ensign Ohta recalls these opening hours:

> I think that due to the enormous bombardment from the air and the naval vessels the Americans thought that there would be no Japanese; at least, if there were, they would be all wounded or killed soldiers by this time. We took them by surprise and there was a great confusion among the enemy at that time.

Most of the marines in the LVTs reached the beaches safely. As they attempted to move inland, Japanese fire increased with volume and precision. Meanwhile, at the lip of the reef, the unforgettable drama of misfortune and heroism had begun: the landing boats could not traverse the reef. About 3 feet of water covered the coral trap.

Coxswains cursed as their craft ground against the hard coral bottom. Marines disembarked hundreds of yards offshore. Mounting Japanese fire power found it mark. Hundreds of marines fell upon the reef. Shallow water and intense fire reduced the invasion to a crawl toward the beaches. The vital forward thrust had disappeared.

Many of the LVTs after unloading and retiring to the reef's edge sank in deep water as a result of holes from enemy fire. Others developed mechanical difficulties. Some had already been destroyed. Those available engaged in the emergency shuttle system. There were not enough.

Disorganized marines on the beaches maintained a tenuous hold. The overwhelming Japanese fire pinned them to a thin line along the shore behind a coconut log wall. Some marines moved forward. They had begun the perilous process of destroying the enemy hidden in his fantastically fortified positions.

All through the first day of the battle "the issue was in doubt." Attempts were made to send reinforcements, but the tide refused to cooperate. Marines again struggled toward the shore. As darkness approached, the invaders awaited an attack. Miraculously it did not come, and morning brought an intense continuation of the struggle.

The remaining hours of combat show a gradual reduction of Japanese resistance. Marines crossed Betio in the center to divide the enemy. Troops on Red Beach One pushed across the western end of Betio, so that reinforcements could land almost unopposed on these shores. The fresh troops on the second day of battle moved down the airstrip to crowd the Japanese into Betio's tail. After seventy-six hours of hell, the carnage ended. The cost: 1,009 Americans killed and 2,101 wounded.

What was the stateside reaction to Tarawa? How did Americans respond to the losses?

> Americans at home received the news of Tarawa with awe and anger ... the thing that stuck most in the people's minds was the fact that many of the Higgins landing boats piled up on submerged reef, making it necessary for the troops to wade 300 or more yards to shore under murderous fire. ...

"Terrible Tarawa," "Charge of the Light Brigade Tactics," "Tarawa Fiasco"—these criticisms stirred Americans. Even the threat of a congressional investigation appeared, as the nation struggled to absorb the shocking casualty lists.

Secretary of the Navy Knox attempted to explain that ". . . the low tide was caused by the sudden shifting of the wind." Lieutenant General Alexander A. Vandegrift, commandant of the Marine Corps, announced that, "the tides had nothing to do with the losses."

Admiral Hill claims the wind was normal and steady throughout the entire operation. Since he was well aware of the effect of the wind on alligators and landing boats, he frequently checked the weather reports. On target day wind conditions were "light airs from the easterly-southeasterly sections." Aerial photographs taken during the assault support the belief that the wind as revealed by battlesmoke was not strong enough to affect materially the water level.

After the assault, a naval inquiry board convened at Pearl Harbor to investigate the Tarawa action. The tidal question was explored. Available evidence enabled the investigating officers to study the tides with an insight unknown before the attack.

During the first week of December 1943, *Sumner*, a hydrographic ship, arrived at Tarawa, and, amid an occasional Japanese air raid, the crew began to survey tides and lagoon depths. Because the legion had established predictions up to the middle of December, it now became possible to compare actual tide patterns with anticipated ones. Such a comparison was carried out at Pearl Harbor.

At the inquiry, Admiral Turner was called to present his judgment of D-day tides. In his opinion the tidal information prepared before the assault was reasonably correct. He had engaged in a calculated risk that there would be enough water to float the Higgins boat, and he had lost.

Lieutenant Commander Heyen also testified and offered his explanation of tidal behavior during the battle. It centered on the appearance of a dodging tide to upset the landing. Commander Heyen showed the board of inquiry his preassault sketches, illustrating the possible position of landing boats should a dodger appear. According to the Australian naval officer, the tidal characteristics on 20 November were consistent with his group's definition of a dodging tide.

The inquiring officers, upon consulting *Sumner's* records, accepted Heyen's explanation. Tidal irregularities in December 1943 at neaps seemed to support the legion's contention that dodgers do occur at Tarawa. December predictions were fairly accurate.

But the U.S. Coast and Geodetic Survey Office maintains the view that there was no dodging tide on 20 November. Using the hydrographic expression, "harmonic analysis," this office can demonstrate that the condi-

tions necessary to promote a dodger are not present at Tarawa. It supports its stand through a comparison of Tarawa and Port Adelaide, Australia, where dodging tides occur with a known periodicity.

At Port Adelaide the ordinary tidal curve exhibits two highs and two lows in a lunar day. But at neap periods the usual pattern gives way to striking peculiarities. Observations show a tide irregular with respect to time and heights. In fact the recording gauge frequently indicates little or no movement of water. In some instances the level of the water remains almost constant for a whole day while at other times one small tide appears for the same period. These characteristics identify a dodging tide. At Tarawa, however, during neaps the tide remains semidiurnal: two highs and two lows per day.

Why then should the legion have emphasized dodging tides? Certain tidal features at Tarawa no doubt created the mariners' conception of a dodger. Since Lieutenant Commander Heyen as a boy witnessed Port Adelaide's tidal anomalies, his contact with Tarawa's waters were at times reminiscent of his boyhood experiences.

Infrequently at Tarawa the rise of water at neaps is very small. Sometimes the range is less than a foot in six hours, so that there would be less than 4 feet of water over the surrounding reefs. During such a tide the water level has risen and fallen with a duration of several minutes between each undulation. The Tarawa marine superintendent believes this phenomenon is the result of large ocean swells that sweep into the lagoon. A small range would accentuate the appearance of these movements across the reef. It is possible that these tidal manifestations, short-range and ocean swells, promoted the legion's conception of a dodger.

While the U.S. Coast and Geodetic Survey Office disagrees with the dodging tide explanation for the D-day tides, it does nevertheless feel that the legion's predictions for high and low waters were good. This conclusion stems partly from a study made of Tarawa's tides in 1944. Using harmonic constants derived from *Sumner's* survey, a hydrographer "predicted" the past tidal patterns. His investigation shows that on invasion day the high water occurred at 1236 with a depth of 4 feet of water.

The Admiralty Hydrographic Office in London has conducted similar and completely independent research. From December 1948 to May 1949, Tarawa's tides were recorded for the Admiralty. The writer asked the British Hydrographic Office to determine D-day tides. On 20 November, the British reported, the high water appeared between 1200 and 1300 with a height of 4 feet.

These studies support the belief that the hydrographic intelligence was sufficiently accurate for planning and operations. The legion officers predicted a rising tide for mid-morning and when their warning for a dodging tide appearance is considered, they informed the planners of a possible condition that would admit no Higgins boats over the reef. To be sure, their calculations anticipated a tide earlier than the one determined by subsequent analysis. But the time difference is not so serious as it might appear when the small range of a rising tide over a six-hour period is considered. Tidal estimates were not "sadly in error."

The spectacular drama of marines walking or stumbling toward the beaches exaggerated the tidal failure. Had it been possible to inform the American people more thoroughly about the battle, it is conceivable that they might have viewed the event with more discernment and less propensity to attribute so many of the losses to the tide alone.

At Tarawa today the invasion beaches are crowded with dock installations. Natives no longer live on Betio. The landing strip which took the marines to Betio is now hidden by scores of buildings. Some Japanese installations remain. The underground bunkers serve as fuel storage tanks. Shibasaki's command post is now a modern diesel-electric plant. Out of the lagoon shelf, the rusty remains of landing craft prompt the inquisitive mind to explore their presence. Around them swirls the lagoon tide—the tide that failed on 20 November 1943.

The Marianas, 1944

BY LOUIS MORTON

On 20 and 21 March 1967, President Lyndon B. Johnson visited the island of Guam where he conferred with Vietnamese and American officials on the war in South Vietnam. In his arrival remarks, the president noted that Guam had been chosen as the meeting site because of its convenience and for its historical significance. He then said:

> Guam knows war in a way that no other American knows it. It was the only inhabited part of our nation to be occupied by hostile forces during the Second World War.

Just twenty-three years ago this month U.S. forces under Admiral Chester W. Nimitz were bringing the Marianas campaign to a successful conclusion resulting in the return of Guam to U.S. control.

On 12 March 1944, the U.S. Joint Chiefs of Staff directed Admiral Nimitz to seize and occupy three of the major islands in the Marianas: Saipan, Tinian, and Guam. The date set for the invasion was 15 June. With this order, the Joint Chiefs gave the signal for a campaign that took U.S. forces within B-29 bombing range of Tokyo and led to a Cabinet crisis in Japan and to the resignation of Premier Hideki Tojo.

To most Americans then, and to a new generation that has grown up since World War Two, the Marianas meant only a series of small dots somewhere in the middle of a map of the Pacific. The islands lie in the western Pacific, 3,500 miles from Pearl Harbor, and extend in a long arc for about 450 miles. They were discovered by Ferdinand Magellan in 1521 and named by him the Ladrones or Isle of Thieves. Guam, the southernmost island in the group, is 250 miles from the Carolines; Tinian and Saipan, the next lower rungs in the Marianas ladder, are only slightly farther away. To the north is Iwo Jima and the Bonins. Across open waters, 1,100 miles to the west, lie the Philippines—furthermost U.S. possession before World War Two.

U.S. military interest in the Marianas antedates World War Two, and, for the first two years of the war, the islands figured prominently in the emerging strategy for the defeat of Japan. There were at least four excellent reasons for taking the Marianas. The navy hoped by this move to flush out the main body of the Japanese fleet for a decisive engagement. The islands offered favorable sites for forward naval bases. Possession of the Marianas would place the Americans in position to move either southwest into the Carolines, west to the Philippines, northwest to Taiwan, or north through the Bonins directly to Japan. The southern Marianas were ideally suited as airbases for the newly developed B-29, contained good fields, were large enough to accommodate the extensive facilities needed, and were within bombing range of the Japanese home islands. The fact that Guam had been a U.S. possession administered by the navy did nothing to lessen the attractiveness of the choice of targets to the admirals.

Military Review 47 (July 1967): 71–82. Reprinted by permission.

Naval gunfire bombardment, Saipan, 1944. Courtesy of the U.S. Navy Historical Center.

Amphibious Warfare

What distinguished the Pacific from every other theater of operations in World War Two was amphibious warfare. There were amphibious operations elsewhere, but the Pacific was the one theater where assault from the sea was both customary and normal. This meant long lines of communication stretching for thousands of miles across the ocean, and it meant that all operations had to be truly joint with ground, air, and naval forces working in close harmony. The campaign in the Marianas was a prime example of amphibious techniques, as well as one of the most controversial and decisive campaigns of the Pacific war.

By mid-1944, the Americans had fought their way up the Solomons and New Guinea, past the Bismarck barrier, and across the central Pacific as far west as the Marshalls. The southern arm of this two-pronged advance was under General Douglas MacArthur; the other was under Admiral Nimitz. Both received their direction from the Joint Chiefs of Staff and both were joint commands con-

sisting of ground, air, and sea forces. As far as the vast spaces of the Pacific allowed, the general and the admiral were supposed to help each other and coordinate their operations. Although this double-edged strategy represented a dispersion of forces, as General MacArthur and Admiral Nimitz approached each other, each would be able to support the other by air and naval operations. Each would keep the enemy in his area pinned down, uncertain where the next blow would fall and unable to shift his forces.

By timing their blows skillfully and selecting their objectives carefully, the Allies could neutralize the advantages the Japanese possessed in their interior lines of communication while exploiting fully their own advantages. Strategically off balance, the Japanese would have to guard every point in their vast perimeter from the Aleutians to the Indies. The Allies, under no such compulsion, would be free to move their forces and to concentrate at the point of attack.

Under Admiral Nimitz and General MacArthur, the technique of amphibious

Landing craft approach the beaches, Saipan, 1944. Courtesy of the U.S. Navy Historical Center.

warfare reached a high state of efficiency. First, the objective was isolated and its defenses softened by air and naval operations. Simultaneously, other targets were attacked to deceive the enemy as to the true objective. Next came the air-naval bombardment of the target area while the assault force was moving toward the objective. The landing force moved from ship to shore under cover of air and naval gunfire.

The landing itself was usually made in waves or echelons, with rocket-firing landing craft in the lead, followed by amphibian tanks carrying the assault troops directly from the water onto the beaches and then inland. Finally came the landing craft with more infantry, artillery, and supporting troops. Whenever possible, neighboring small islands often were occupied in advance to provide sites for the emplacement of artillery. The advance inland proceeded without pause, air and naval forces providing support when necessary, until the objective was finally secured.

The essential ingredient of success in this type of warfare was the concerted and coordinated action of ground, sea, and air forces under a single commander. In General MacArthur's area, the central fact controlling operations was the range of land-based fighter aircraft. In the central Pacific, where the advances had to be much greater, far beyond the range of land-based fighter cover,

the decisive element was the large aircraft carrier.

If the fast carrier was the essential element of success in Admiral Nimitz's formula for victory, the floating supply base was the key to the operations of the fast carrier force. Consisting of oilers, tenders, repair and salvage ships, and a large variety of miscellaneous vessels, this mobile base was capable of providing the fleet with the supplies and services required for extended operations far from home. In short, it was the logistic equivalent of the fast carrier force.

Vital also to amphibious operations were the landing vehicle, tracked (LVT) and the 2½-ton truck, amphibious (DUKW). The first, more commonly known as the "amtrac" or "alligator," solved one of the chief tactical problems of an amphibious assault—how to get troops across the reefs and onto the beaches. The DUKW solved the problem of getting artillery and critical supplies to the beachhead during the early stages of an assault. Both were truly amphibious weapons of the most modern design, and they rate among the great contributions of World War Two to the art of amphibious warfare.

For the invasion of the Marianas, Admiral Nimitz drew from all the resources in his theater. From the Pacific Fleet he took the bulk of the warships, including the fast carriers; from the Fleet Marine Force, two corps headquarters, three divisions, and a brigade;

U.S. Marines hit the beach, Saipan, 1944. Courtesy of the U.S. Navy Historical Center.

from the army, two more divisions, corps artillery, garrison troops, and the 7th Air Force.

The organization of these forces fell into a pattern that was by now well standardized. Command was single and was lodged in Admiral Raymond A. Spruance who reported directly to Admiral Nimitz. Admiral Spruance commanded everything assigned to the invasion except the submarines on distant missions and the logistic forces afloat. These Admiral Nimitz retained under his own control.

To accomplish his mission of capturing the Marianas, and in the process defeating the enemy fleet, Admiral Spruance organized three major forces—the Joint Expeditionary Force led by Rear Admiral Richmond Kelly Turner; the Fast Carrier Force commanded by Rear Admiral Marc A. Mitscher; and, third, a force consisting of all the army, navy, and marine land-based aircraft assigned to the operation. This last was also commanded by an admiral even though it included the army's 7th Air Force.

Command relationships in this involved organization, where virtually all the higher commanders wore two hats, were quite complex. At the top was Admiral Nimitz who was at one and the same time commander-in-chief, Pacific Ocean Area, a joint command; commander-in-chief, Pacific Fleet, a

naval command; and commander-in-chief, Central Pacific, an area command in which he reported to himself. Below him was Admiral Spruance who was in supreme command of the operation and also commander of the 5th Fleet.

Tactical Command

Tactical command during the amphibious phases of the operation was in the hands of Admiral Turner who simultaneously commanded the entire expeditionary force and its largest component, the northern attack force. Tactical control of the troops ashore was to be exercised by Marine Lieutenant General Holland M. Smith. He was responsible to Admiral Turner until the amphibious phase was ended, and then he would assume command. Like Admiral Turner, General Holland Smith wore two hats, for he exercised tactical control of the troops on Saipan as well as all the troops in the expeditionary force.

Assembling the forces with all their supplies and equipment for an amphibious operation like the Marianas was an enormously complicated job calling for the most detailed planning and split-second timing. Thus, one of the two corps scheduled for the operation was mounted in Hawaii and on the West Coast; the other in Guadalcanal. Ships of the

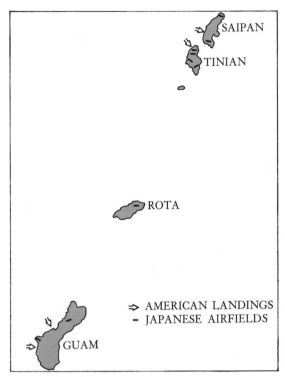

SAIPAN

TINIAN

ROTA

⇨ AMERICAN LANDINGS
– JAPANESE AIRFIELDS

GUAM

Marianas, 1944.

Pacific Fleet that were to participate in the operation were scattered throughout the area.

All these had to assemble in the Marshalls in a specified order at particular times and then move out according to a carefully computed timetable toward the target 1,000 miles away. When finally assembled, the invading force consisted of about one hundred six thousand troops and no less than 535 combatant ships and auxiliaries.

Transporting the troops was the least part of the job; loading the supplies and equipment was the really difficult task. The operation plan provided that assault and garrison forces should be allowed thirty-two days of rations, twenty days of other classes of supply, and seven units of fire. Altogether, a total of about seventy-five thousand tons of cargo representing nearly eight million cubic feet was loaded by the Northern Attack Force alone.

The Saipan invasion force—the 2nd and

4th Marine Divisions—made final preparations for the assault in Hawaii. The journey to the target began on 25 May. On that day, the slower landing ships, tank (LSTs) carrying the LVTs and the assault elements of the two marine divisions sortied from Pearl Harbor. All ships carrying the assault troops rendezvoused on 8 June at Eniwetok where last-minute preparations were completed. The LST left on the ninth, and, by the 11th the last of the attack transports had weighed anchor, and the mighty armada was steaming westward through hostile waters toward still more hostile shores.

Meanwhile, the U.S. bombardment of the Marianas, which had begun early in February in conjunction with the great raid against Truk, continued unabated. In March, land-based aircraft took up the task of pounding Japanese bases within reach of the Marianas. For three months now, they had been bombing the islands steadily, neutralizing Japanese airpower and simultaneously gathering aerial reconnaissance for the invading forces.

While land-based aircraft did their job, submarines on distant reconnaissance reported the assembly of a large Japanese fleet off Tawitawi in the Sulu Archipelago near the Borneo oilfields. This was the 1st Mobile Fleet led by Vice Admiral Jisaburo Ozawa and under orders to seek out and destroy the U.S. Pacific Fleet. The Japanese were as eager as the Americans for a naval showdown and had given Admiral Ozawa the bulk of the fleet and made elaborate preparations for the battle.

In May, as this fleet was assembling, Admiral Ozawa sent a screen of his own submarines south into the Solomons in the mistaken belief that the carriers were there and that Admiral William F. Halsey was getting ready to mount another offensive. It was a natural mistake, for the Southern Attack Force was, indeed, assembling off Guadalcanal, but it was a fatal mistake.

Admiral Halsey, with the escort carriers of the Southern Attack Force, hit the submarines hard. The loss of these underwater craft seriously crippled the reconnaissance capability of Admiral Ozawa's fleet and deprived him of a weapon he could well have used against the invasion force just then beginning to move toward the Marianas. The Allied strategy of a two-pronged advance was paying off.

The ground forces of the enemy on the first target island, Saipan, numbered about thirty thousand troops. Their plan was to stop the Americans at the shoreline, and they had constructed their defenses with this purpose in mind. From positions along the beach, they hoped to knock out most of the landing craft. U.S. troops who, nevertheless, reached the shore were to be destroyed promptly by counterattack.

In keeping with this concept, the Japanese constructed strong points along the shoreline. A similar line was located inland as a base for counterattack. Artillery emplaced in and behind both lines were to fire antiboat missions. All around the island, the Japanese placed navy coast defenses and dual-purpose guns sited to cover the shores, the sea, and most of the sky overhead.

Task Force 58

The first element of the U.S. invasion force to reach the Marianas was Admiral Mitscher's Fast Carrier Force, the famed Task Force 58. On 11 June at 0100, it reached a point 200 miles east of Guam and there launched its first strike. Palau, Yap, Truk, and other islands had been hit during the previous months by the land-based aircraft, but Admiral Mitscher's strike was the big show. For four days the carrier planes smothered the islands, destroying Japanese planes on the ground, knocking out airfields, and hitting everything in sight on Saipan, Tinian, and Guam. Then they moved out to refuel and to hit Iwo Jima to the north.

When the carriers moved out, seven new battleships of the fleet went in to bombard the shore. Firing at ranges of 10,000 to 16,000 yards because they were too valuable to be risked in shallower waters, these giants accomplished little. The next day, old battleships of Admiral Turner's fire support groups arrived and took over. All that day, these old

ships, three of which had been hit at Pearl Harbor, kept up their fire. The results were satisfactory, but still they failed to knock out all the enemy's strong points.

Underwater Teams

While the naval bombardment was in progress, destroyer transports brought in the underwater demolition teams—another amphibious innovation of World War Two. These teams consisted of frogmen trained to map a reef, blow gaps in it, and clear the shoal of underwater obstacles. Under the protective arch of naval gunfire, the frogmen opened the way for the amphibious tractors of the Saipan invasion force.

Following the frogmen came the transport and tractor groups of the Northern Attack Force, circling around the northern tip of Saipan to the west coast where the landing beaches lay. Before sunrise of 15 June, D-day, they had reached the rendezvous point. For the Americans, few of whom had ever seen Saipan, the island lay stretched before them in the clear dawn of a perfect tropical day. In the foreground were the beaches and the town of Charan Kanoa; behind it the low escarpments of the island's mountainous spine; and, farther off, the volcanic cone of Mount Tapotchau.

Aboard the transports, the marines of the 2nd and 4th Divisions breakfasted at 0445. Naval bombardment began at 0530, and, fifteen minutes later, Admiral Turner gave the signal to "Land the landing force." H-hour was 0840. Shortly after 0700, the 34 LSTs carrying the assault battalions moved into position and dropped anchor about a half mile from the line of departure. Bow doors swung open; ramps were lowered; and amphibian tractors and tanks, more than seven hundred of them, crawled into the water and began to circle, awaiting the moment to cross the line of departure, 4,250 yards offshore, and move toward the enemy.

Astern of the assault landing ships lay twelve other LSTs carrying light artillery, most of which would be landed in DUKWs. Still farther seaward lay two dock landing ships embarked with mechanized landing craft that would take ashore the tanks and heavy artillery after the infantry had seized the beaches. About 18,000 yards offshore, the larger troop transports swung at anchor. Aboard were reserve troops headquarters, shore parties, heavy artillery, trucks, tractors, bulldozers, and an assortment of supplies and equipment.

At 0700, naval gunfire lifted to allow a thirty-minute strike by one hundred fifty carrier planes. Then, the close support ships took up the fire again with their heavy guns until the first wave of troops was only 1,000 yards from the shoreline. At that point, the ships switched to 5-inch guns until the troops were within 300 yards offshore.

Landing Plan

The plan for the landing was simple—the two divisions were to go in simultaneously on their respective beaches and advance rapidly inland to the first high ground about 1,500 yards inland, designated the 0–1 line. Once there, the beachhead area would be secured, and the troops could move on—the 2nd Division to the north, the 4th Division across the island to Magicienne Bay on the east coast, capturing Aslito Field on the way. A few days, it was thought, should suffice to capture Saipan. Then, the troops would move on to Tinian and, finally, Guam.

This was the plan, but it did not quite work out that way. Boats bringing in the 2nd Division veered to the left (north) away from Afetna Point and piled up battalions on each other's beaches. The landing plan had provided for a gap between the two divisions at Afetna Point where the enemy was expected to place his heaviest concentration of artillery. But the distance between the two divisions after the landing was more than double that planned. Almost three days would elapse before firm contact between the two divisions was established.

Another failure was the inability of the armored amtracs to get beyond the shoreline and carry the assault elements inland. These vehicles had neither the power to negotiate the rough terrain nor the armament to withstand the Japanese fire. It proved safer for the troops to extricate themselves and take shelter wherever they could find it. Thereafter, they proceeded as best they could on foot or by crawling.

Adding to the confusion of men, tanks, and tractors ashore was the jumble of crates, cartons, boxes, and equipment of all kinds piling up on the beaches. No aspect of an amphibious assault presents more complex problems than that of unloading and distributing supplies; none is more likely to become disorganized and even disorderly. To the casual observer at least, the pileup and congestion of supplies during the first phase of a normal amphibious assault present a picture of complete chaos.

This chaos is more apparent than real in a well-run operation, but even under ideal conditions the problem of ship-to-shore supply is complicated and has no easy solution. At Saipan, it was made more difficult by local problems, such as the strong resistance on the beaches and by unfavorable hydrographic conditions.

Despite the confusion and chaos on the beach and the failure to reach the 0–1 line, it was evident by the end of the first day that the landing was a success. The troops had established a beachhead approximately 10,000 yards in length and over 1,000 yards in depth. Two divisions and their command posts were ashore with almost all their reserves, as were seven battalions of artillery and most of the two tank battalions—altogether about twenty thousand men. Although the beachhead could not yet be considered completely secure or large enough to bring in heavy equipment and logistic support for extended operations, the most critical stage of the ship-to-shore movement was past.

The top commanders of the invasion force were not so sure. Word had come the day before, D-day, from the submarines on distant reconnaissance that Japanese fleet units were approaching the Marianas. They were still in Philippine waters, but trouble was clearly brewing. By the morning of the 16th, Admiral Spruance had rightly concluded that the naval battle he had hoped for was not far away. He canceled the Guam landings optimistically scheduled for 18 June.

For the naval engagement he would need all the warships available, and he took cruisers and destroyers from Admiral Turner's fire support groups to furnish a screen for the fast carrier force. He sent the battleships of these groups westward to cover Saipan against a possible end run by the Japanese carrier fleet. The escort carriers he left with Admiral Turner to furnish close air support for the troops.

The imminence of a full-scale naval battle also required an immediate decision on the Army's 27th Division, the floating reserve still enroute to Saipan. The decision was General Holland Smith's, and he wanted his reserves ashore where he could get at them if necessary. Admirals Spruance and Turner had no objections.

On 16 June, the 27th Division, less one regiment assigned to the Guam invasion, was still about 30 miles away from Saipan. At noon, Major General Ralph C. Smith, the division commander, received orders to land as soon as practicable on the southern beaches of Saipan and there take over the extreme right flank of the line. The troops began to land at dusk of that day.

Japanese Mistakes

While the troops on Saipan were still trying to expand their beachhead, Admiral Spruance prepared to do battle with the approaching enemy fleet. Fortunately for the Americans, the Japanese had made some serious mistakes. First, they had sent their submarines south into the Solomons and lost most of them. Then, when General MacArthur's forces landed at Biak at the end of May, they made another mistake. They sent to western New Guinea almost one-half of the naval land-based aircraft they had so carefully assembled in the Carolines and Palau. These were the planes that Admiral Ozawa, the Japanese commander, was relying on to support his surface forces during the impending naval battle, and he lost them. By the time he learned of the Marianas invasion, it was too late to call back even those few that had survived the attacks of General MacArthur's air force.

When Admiral Spruance arrayed his great force in battle formation west of Tinian on the afternoon of the 18th, he had only fragmentary information of the enemy. Was the Japanese fleet advancing in single formation or in separate groups? This knowledge was vitally important to him, for he had to protect the amphibious forces off Saipan as well as destroy the Japanese fleet. And what if Admiral Ozawa should make an end run? Actually, Admiral Spruance had no cause for worry on this point, for the great Japanese armada, some 400 miles away, was advancing in undivided strength.

But not knowing this, Admiral Spruance's orders to destroy the enemy were qualified with the proviso that Task Force 58 must cover Saipan and the landing force. This was a concern that he could not overlook, and it lay behind many of the decisions he made during the course of the battle. Admiral Ozawa's orders were simpler—strike and destroy the U.S. fleet.

Task Force 58 in battle formation on the eve of the engagement covered an area of 25 by 35 miles and carried 98,618 men in 112 ships. It contained 15 carriers to the Japanese 9 and was superior to the Japanese fleet in every category except heavy cruisers. But Admiral Ozawa counted heavily on fighting the battle in waters of his own choosing, within range of land-based planes on Guam, Rota, and Yap. His carrier planes had a longer range than the Americans', and, with the easterly trade wind, he could launch and recover his planes while approaching, whereas the Americans would have to turn away.

The battle that followed, one of the great naval battles of the war, was essentially an air battle. When the two fleets engaged, they were a hundred miles farther apart than Washington and New York. But the blows that really crippled the Japanese fleet were delivered by submarines on 19 June when Admiral Mitscher's force was on the defensive and steaming away from the enemy. Not until the afternoon of the 20th did the admiral obtain full and useful intelligence of the enemy fleet from search planes. And it was not until evening of that day that anyone on the deck of an enemy ship saw an airplane from the fleet that had dealt it a mortal wound the day before.

Of the three Japanese carriers sunk by the Americans, only one was the victim of Admiral Mitscher's carrier planes; the other two were destroyed by submarines surprised to find such rich targets in their periscope sights. The battle was virtually over by the 21st, and Admiral Ozawa's fleet was in full retreat, with only 35 of its 430 carrier planes still operational.

Difficult Decision

Admiral Spruance now had a hard decision to make. Should he pursue the enemy in the hope of destroying him, or should he return to Saipan? As a naval officer, it was his clear duty to pursue, but, as commander of the invasion, he had other responsibilities he could not evade. He chose the second course and, perhaps, missed the golden opportunity every sailor dreams of—to meet and destroy the main enemy fleet in a single decisive engagement.

For this decision, he has been strongly criticized. But it should be said in his behalf that he dealt the Japanese Navy a mortal wound at little cost to his own fleet. Furthermore, by gaining command of the sea and air in the Marianas, he assured final victory. No matter how bravely and tenaciously the Japanese troops resisted, their doom was sealed. By the afternoon of 23 June, Admiral Spruance was back on station off Saipan.

Much had happened on that war-torn island while the naval battle was in progress. The marine general, Holland Smith had assumed command ashore, and, on 21 June, the supply ships had returned to their interrupted task of nourishing operations ashore. By the 23rd, the three divisions were lined up abreast across the island facing north, the Army's 27th on the right (east) flank. Ahead of them was rugged terrain, Mount Tapotchau, and the surviving Japanese who were determined to die fighting.

On 23 June, General Holland Smith ordered an all-out offensive. The attack got off slowly, and it took the marines and the 27th Division two more weeks of the hardest fighting to reach the northern tip of the island and overcome the final Japanese resistance.

In the Marianas, as everywhere in the Pacific, American soldiers fought two enemies, the Japanese and the terrain. Tough and resolute, the Japanese used the jungle, the thick vegetation, the swamps, and the stony ridges with resourcefulness and skill. Not all the power of modern artillery, armor, and airpower was able to destroy them. In the final analysis, it was the soldier on foot, with rifle, grenade, satchel charge, and flamethrower who had to do the job.

What had the Americans won in the Marianas? To say they captured only three small islands after twenty-four days of strenuous battle is to miss the point. The Marianas invasion force accomplished far more than that. It pierced the first hole in the inner line of island fortifications that the Japanese had constructed to defend their homeland and the empire. The U.S. victory also brought disgrace on the Japanese Cabinet and forced the resignation of Premier Tojo, leader of the military clique in Japan, thus opening the way for the emergence of the peace party and the final surrender a year later.

Of more immediate significance, the seizure of the Marianas gave the United States air and naval supremacy over the central Pacific as far west as the Philippines and northward to the Bonins. With the Carolines neutralized and isolated, the navy now had control of sea communications and bases from which to operate against Japan's vital lines of communications.

Just as important were the airbases for the B-29s. In November 1944, five months after the invasion, the "superfortresses" began bombing Japan, blasting and burning her cities and industries. It was from an airfield on Tinian that a B-29 took off for Hiroshima in the early morning hours of 6 August to drop the first nuclear bomb in history.

Sea Lion: The German Plan to Invade Britain, 1940

BY FRANK DAVIS

For a thousand years following the Norman invasion, the narrow seas separating England from the continent of Europe safeguarded the island. In 1588, Spain's Armada, the largest invasion fleet ever launched against England, was scattered in the Channel by Elizabeth's navy, then wrecked and sunk itself upon the Irish Sea. Thus the title, "Mistress of the Seas," passed to England, a legacy that would keep her invulnerable to all the empires carved upon the mainland. Not until the maturation of aerial warfare during World War Two did the weapon exist with which England could again be threatened with invasion. The 1940 plan, codenamed Seelowe (Sea Lion), would mass German air power against the British Royal Navy. Once the Luftwaffe gained supremacy above the Channel, the Wehrmacht would be put ashore to unleash the blitzkrieg on the British Isles.

Background

Between May 1939, when he disclosed his intention against Poland, and May 1940, when he struck the West, Hitler never contemplated carrying the war across the Channel to England. His plans for the 1940 Western Offensive foresaw no decision in that contest before 1943. The objective of his planned offensive was to secure the seacoasts of Holland, Belgium, and northern France as a base for waging air and naval warfare against England's dependence on overseas supply. Essentially, Hitler wished to implement the

Strategy and Tactics 40 (1973): 20–33. Reprinted by permission.

World War One strategy of severing Britain's lifelines with submarine warfare. The trump card held by the fuehrer in 1940 was the Luftwaffe which could threaten England directly in addition to compensating for German naval weakness vis-à-vis Great Britain.

A month before his triumphant campaign against France, Hitler underwent an unnerving baptism in amphibious warfare. By the fifth day of Operation Weseruebung (the campaign in Norway, April-June 1940), half of Germany's destroyer fleet had gone down off Narvik and helmsman Hitler was succumbing to his first bout with seasickness. Weseruebung was the only German operation of the war which Hitler did not conceive himself. Like the army he dispatched to Norway, Hitler was a thorough landlubber as instinctively uncomfortable directing amphibious operations as he seemed gifted for conducting a land campaign. Getting the fuehrer his sea legs cost the German navy heavily; one heavy and two light cruisers, ten destroyers, and eight submarines were lost off Norway. Later, these stiff losses would return against the German plans with a vengeance, but at the time the cost was overshadowed by a great moral victory. In the face of the Royal Navy, the Germans had put ashore an assault which both overran Norwegian resistance and cast Allied intervention forces back into the sea. Also during Weseruebung, the Luftwaffe demonstrated a surprising effectiveness against the Allied naval forces. Finally, the evidence that the blitzkrieg had become both air and seaborne particularly disturbed the British and enriched the victory that secured the flow of Swedish iron back to Germany.

Operation Yellow (May 1940–June 1940), responsible for overrunning the West in six weeks, marked the zenith of Hitler's warfare. But when Manstein's plan delivered the panzers to the Channel three years in advance of his timetable, Hitler applied the brakes. Confronting the sea again, Hitler and von Rundstedt balked at the Belgian terrain. They insisted on resting the German tanks for the onslaught of southern France, fell on Goring's request to permit the Luftwaffe to contain the B.E.F. (British Expeditionary Force), and so allowed a quarter million British (and half that number French) troops to evacuate Dunkirk between 26 May and 4 June 1940. Although their forced evacuation cost the British heavily in terms of equipment, it delivered two-thirds of the trained British manpower back into the Home Defense in England's bleakest hour. The Luftwaffe's containment of the B.E.F. was supposed to have given Hitler the military leverage he needed to pry England out of the war. Over Dunkirk, however, the Luftwaffe ran afoul of the new British Spitfire fighters, and the German bombs went wasted into dunes and sandbanks. As the British trickled off the beaches, Hitler realized that, after defeating France, he would still have to contend with England. Later in the war Hitler blundered infamously, yet no later decision so damaged his future course than his magnanimity at Dunkirk.

Two weeks after the Dunkirk evacuation, France collapsed and England stood alone across a few flooded miles. Hitler still hoped to negotiate a peace with England. He had no expectation of fighting again in the West. But if there was to be another battle in the West, it would have to be the Battle of Britain.

Problem England

Despite endorsing Hitler's plans to strangle Britain by air and naval siege during the autumn of 1939, both OKH (army) and OKM (navy) began research on the feasibility of invading England. In November, Raeder,

commander-in-chief navy, outlined the expected difficulties. First, the island's terrain favored its defense, and the excellent road and rail net provided for the rapid conveyance of its defenders to any threatened point. Second, the Royal Navy, far superior to what Germany could float, would somehow have to be totally restricted from the approach and landing operations. Third, eastern England between the Tyne and the Thames provided suitable landing beaches, plus good terrain for armored exploitation, and excellent ports the capture of which would be essential to the rapid debarkation of supplies, heavy equipment, and vehicles. Thus, the eastern coastline was preferred over the rugged Channel coast for the landings. An invasion against the east coast, however, entailed a long North Sea crossing from the German Baltic ports during which the fleet would be extremely vulnerable to British air and naval attacks. Aware of his navy's inability to protect such a crossing, and emphasizing the fact that Germany possessed no landing craft and very little transport shipping, Raeder concluded against invasion as an operable form of warfare against England.

The OKH study, code named Northwest, envisaged a landing in East Anglia (east coast) to be conducted by seventeen divisions including two airborne (to capture ports at Yarmouth and Lowestoft), four panzer, and two motorized units. Striking the coast between the Thames and the Wash, with diversionary landings farther north, the expanded bridgehead ("beachhead" had not yet been coined) would serve as the base for a motorized advance on London from the northeast.

Raeder replied in depth to the army plan in January 1940, pointing to the Royal Navy's superiority and their consequent ability to break into the landing zones or to jeopardize the invasion's supply operations. Just having become aware of the Operation Yellow objective, Raeder disclosed the fact that the navy had begun studying the possibility of launching an invasion across the English Channel where the approach path might be able to be secured between barriers of magnetic minefields. Raeder, however, was pessimistic that an invasion fleet could be adequately defended against the Royal Navy even in the narrow Channel waters. Certainly, the German Navy could not defend real or diversionary operations on the North Sea. Finally, Raeder pronounced the OKH plan as impossible in view of the absence of the shipping necessary to lift and maintain such a large-scale assault. He calculated that four hundred steamers would be required to lift the army's seven division assault wave. In all of Europe, fewer than three hundred of the required steamers were available. The navy estimated that the required tonnage in river barges might be assembled and converted for landing operations in no less than six months. Raeder ended his reply by cautioning that a landing could only be attempted during summer and only if continued calm weather were forecasted.

The Luftwaffe staff next received the Northwest plan and concluded that in order to prevent the British air force from irreparably damaging the invasion effort, absolute German air supremacy must be ensured prior to the invasion's launching. Even if air supremacy was ensured, the Luftwaffe still considered an invasion to be a risky affair, only to be attempted as the coup de grace against a previously broken British morale.

Thus the conclusion drawn from these initial inquiries indicated that an invasion could only succeed if air and naval arms were first wrested from Britain. It was reasoned that under those conditions, England would probably cease its resistance and make invasion unnecessary. Furthermore, according to the required time to assemble the barge transport, the order to begin invasion preparations should have been issued immediately if the invasion was to be launched during the summer of 1940. That order would only be issued in July 1940. Like Weseruebung, Operation Sea Lion never appealed to Hitler, nor did it ever become a personal fuehrer project.

Overview

Hitler reacted negatively to the idea of invasion when it was first mentioned to him by Raeder on 21 May, one day after the pan-

zers reached the Channel at Abbeville. Instead, Hitler proposed to intensify the air and naval war against Britain if it continued to fight after France's now apparent defeat. Priority would be reallocated to air and naval armaments over army materiel. As a final resort, Hitler would order the Luftwaffe to strike England as soon as sufficient formations were transferred to bases within easy range of the island.

Hitler believed, however, that the extent of his victory against France would compel the British to accept a negotiated settlement. From the French armistice (25 June 1940), until his Reichstag Speech (19 July 1940—the vehicle of his final peace overture to the British) Hitler consistently endeavored for a political solution to "Problem England." At this point in his winning streak Hitler wanted to cash in his chips and reach an agreement with Britain without further risk or sacrifice. He knew that breaking England by expending German blood would be a senseless and unrewarding task which, even if successful, would impart the spoils of the British Empire, not to Germany, but to the Pacific's antagonists, America and Japan. Hitler himself, long steeped in his scheme of eventually expanding German *lebensraum* into the great land mass of Russia, proposed as early as *Mein Kampf* to marry England to this ambition. Throughout the war Hitler succumbed to both a mild form of Anglophilia and the steadfast belief that Anglo-Saxon England, if not wedded to German anti-Bolshevism, could at least be divorced from the determined opposition to the German cause. Although consistently scorned as Britain's suitor, Hitler continually maintained this personal mythology. This self-imposed deception explains both why he failed to include the invasion of Britain in his Operation Yellow planning, and his subsequent reluctance to deliver that invasion with which he threatened Britain throughout the summer of 1940.

Despite the assurance Raeder received from Hitler ruling out an invasion, the navy continued their invasion planning in order to be prepared should both negotiation and the Luftwaffe fail to stifle Britain's resistance. In late May, the Naval Operations Staff report, *Studie-England,* concluded that a cross-Channel invasion could be more easily mounted and better secured than the North Sea invasion plans of the earlier studies. According to this report a sea lane across the Dover Straits could be protected by the laying of wide mine barriers on both flanks of the approach path. The follow-up work for this report included preliminary arrangements for barge procurement and named several invasion embarkation stations at Calais, Dunkirk, and Boulogne. The navy also produced a twenty-page study of the English Channel coast which detailed suitable troop-landing areas, defense installations, and port and airfield locations in southern England.

On 30 June, Hitler met with Jodl and together they summarized the alternatives for continuing the war against Britain. Negotiation was still uppermost in Hitler's mind and preferable to continuing the war in any way. Thus Hitler and Jodl concentrated on the actions that could be taken to compel Britain to negotiate. A Luftwaffe offensive to destroy the British air force and break the resistance of Britain's civilian populace received top priority. Second priority was given to *Lowe* (Lion), Jodl's own invasion plan which depicted landings on the broad front of England's southern coastline stretching 160 miles from Dover to Bournemouth.

Jodl's plan borrowed army terminology to describe the invasion not as an overseas operation but as a river-crossing in which the navy would perform the bridging tasks, while the Luftwaffe, as at Sedan, would provide artillery support against the far bank—the English beaches. The Luftwaffe offensive which was to cripple Britain from the air was made a prerequisite to the actual invasion which Jodl suggested should be launched sometime in mid-August.

Rechristening the plan as Seelowe (Sea Lion), on 16 July, Hitler ordered preparations for the invasion to proceed under OKW (Jodl's) supervision. Six days later, the British formally rejected the final peace proposal Hitler offered in his Reichstag Speech.

Because of his distaste for amphibious operations, and because invading England could hardly benefit Germany, during the last week of July Hitler reorganized his thinking and reached his Armageddon decision to invade not Britain, but Russia. Britain, to Hitler, had never been more than a detour on the way to Russia. Now, planning counter-clockwise, Hitler would threaten Britain with invasion, keeping Russia off guard, then smash Russia—and in so doing, destroy Britain's last hope for a European ally. From this decision forward Hitler's captaincy of Sea Lion guided that operation not toward actual invasion, but as a cover story to invoke in Britain the greatest terror since Armada days, while the secret invasion plan aimed at Russia simmered in the summer shadows.

Broad vs. Narrow Front

By late July, OKH had been informed of Hitler's decision to invade Russia and found the prospect of that invasion as unalluring as OKM found Operation Sea Lion. During August, while the river prahms (barges) for Sea Lion were being assembled and converted for the cross-Channel invasion, the army and the navy became embroiled over the question of the breadth and timetable for the invasion of Britain. Facing the alternative of invading Russia in the autumn of 1940, the army ultimately turned gung-ho for Sea Lion and reluctantly accepted the navy's piecemeal plan for transporting them to Britain.

The original plan of von Brauchitsch, commander-in-chief, army, formulated around 20 July, called for landings on the southern coast along a 237-mile front stretching from the Thames estuary to Lyme Bay, west of the Isle of Wight. The full invasion force ran to forty divisions consisting of two airborne, three motorized, six armored, and twenty-nine infantry. Von Rundstedt would command the forces in Britain.

Six divisions of 16th Army, embarked at Pas de Calais, would land between Ramsgate and Bexhill. Four divisions of the 9th Army would leave Le Havre for beaches between Brighton and the Isle of Wight. A third landing in Lyme Bay near Weymouth would be conducted by three divisions of the 6th Army to be embarked at Cherbourg. These thirteen divisions, supplemented by airborne forces, formed the initial assault wave. Landings would be made by one regimental combat team per division in the initial assault. This required lift for ninety thousand troops on *S-tag* (D-day). The entire thirteen divisions (two hundred sixty thousand troops) would be put ashore in the first three days of the invasion, after which armored and motorized forces would be force-fed into the bridgehead for the drive to isolate London. In a month, Rundstedt would be in Buckingham Palace. Raeder came down hard against the army plan in several conferences with the fuehrer in late July and August. OKH's demand for dawn landings on an ebbing tide, coupled with the navy's requirement for partial moonlight during transit, restricted the invasion operation to either the period 20–26 August (by which time lift for the initial assault could not be readied) or during the span between 19–26 September, a period of uncertain weather that could prohibit beach landings. Raeder also vetoed the Lyme Bay landings because they would be impossible to protect since the crossing to Weymouth would have to be conducted outside the mine-barriers the navy was planning to lay in the Dover Straits. In any case, the army's plan was beyond the lift capability which the navy was now assembling for a mid-September hop-off. Assuming perfect weather, air supremacy, and no interference from the Royal Navy, Raeder estimated that the thirteen-division assault-wave could be landed in no fewer than ten days.

Hearing Raeder's objections (and seeing flashbacks of Weseruebung), Hitler branded the invasion not Jodl's river-crossing, but a dangerous operation across a sea commanded by a determined and superior enemy navy.

Although the army wished to land in strength on as broad a front as possible, von Brauchitsch, realizing Sea Lion was the only game outside Russia, began budgeting. On 10 August, OKH submitted a scaled-down plan calling for ten divisions to be put ashore in four days. The proposed landings would

now be confined to a much shrunken 100-mile front between Ramsgate and Brighton.

Raeder, less concerned about Russia than he was about the Royal Navy, counterproposed eliminating the Brighton landings, again because they fell wide of the mine barriers, and further retarding the landing schedule to conform with the planned transport capability. By proposing to land six divisions in six days along 60 miles of beach between Folkestone and Eastbourne, Raeder was attempting to sink Sea Lion outright and reprieve the navy from what he considered to be a *Himmelfahrskommando*—a command whose dangers automatically guaranteed a ride to heaven. He didn't succeed. Because Hitler was determined to keep Sea Lion's appearance as menacing as possible, on 26 August he broke the interservice deadlock by coming down firmly behind the naval demands. The next day, a fortnight before Sea Lion was literally to barge its way into Britain, von Brauchitsch was ordered to comply with embarkation and beaching decisions based on the navy's estimate of lift capacity and hazards to crossing.

When Sea Lion was executed, the army and the navy would share the *Himmelfahrskommando*. Halder (army chief of staff) called the Sea Lion plan suicidal. The German assault, initially weak and insufficiently reinforced, would launch a narrow frontal attack against a defended beachhead without even a modicum of surprise. The invasion, according to Halder, would put the army through a sausage machine.

By early September, the launching of Sea Lion ostensibly depended only on the imminent success of the air contest to eliminate the R.A.F., now in its second week. The Luftwaffe Staff indicated that the air force would momentarily become available for its preinvasion tasks which included dispersing the Royal Navy Channel forces and covering the mining and mine-sweeping operations.

On 2 September, the Sea Lion timetable was issued by OKW. The earliest S-tag would fall on 21 September, near the beginning of the acceptable tide and moonlight period. Ten days prior to S-tag, an order confirming the invasion would be issued. This S-10 (11 September) confirmation would initiate the minesweeping and laying operations. The final confirmation would be issued on S-3 when embarkation would begin at several of the loading ports. All planning was subject to cancellation within twenty-four hours of S-hour.

The Naval Mission

Although on 10 September, Raeder assured OKW that sufficient transport would be on hand to meet the launch date, the required initial lift did not become fully available until several days beyond the projected launch date. During the third week of September, the navy filled out the necessary transport which numbered 1,859 prahms (barges), 397 tugs, 68 command boats, 1,000 motor boats, and 100 coastal motor-sailers. In addition the navy had accumulated 159 steamers capable of lifting 700,000 tons—or the equivalent of only two fully-equipped divisions.

Sea Lion would be executed on 26–27 September. The invasion would be conducted by four transport fleets of mixed barge, steamer, tug, trawler, and small-craft composition. Eight hours were allotted for clearing the bomb-damaged and choked embarkation stations. Fifteen or more hours, depending on the point of departure, would be required for the crossing to Britain. The tow-flotillas, each consisting of thirty-three tugs towing two barges apiece, were expected to average only three or four knots against the Channel currents. Off the landing zones, the armada would remain anchored for at least thirty-six hours during which the three-echelon first strike would be ferried ashore in pneumatic river-crossing sturmbootes. Transport Fleet B, departing Rotterdam, Ostend, and Dunkirk, lifted the assault of XIII Corps (16th Army) to the easternmost landing zone designated Beach B which extended between Folkestone and Dungeness. Transport Fleet C, from Pas de Calais, landed the VII Corps (16th Army) on Beach C between Dungeness and Hastings. The three infantry and one mountain divisions of these two corps represented a one hundred ten thousand-man first strike

by 16th Army. Transport Fleets D and E, departing Boulogne and Le Havre, carried the XXXVIII Corps (9th Army) to Beach D running from Bexhill to Beachy Head. The two 16th Army corps, together with this first 9th Army corps, represented the major initial effort which would cross the Channel en masse in the Dover Straits for simultaneous landings at S-hour-dawn 27 September.

In a final compromise to the army's insistence to broaden the landing front, the first echelons of VIII Corps (9th Army) would be separately transported from Le Havre directly across the Channel to a landing zone in Brighton Bay. The first echelons of this corps (approximately twenty-five thousand men) would be reinforced only after the transport of the main effort returned to Boulogne to embark the remaining echelons of the one mountain and two infantry divisions of the VIII Corps. Thus the Brighton landing, although initially simultaneous to the Dover Straits operation, would subsequently lag behind since almost a week would elapse before this three-division assault would be fully put ashore.

The navy saw their main function as one of transporting bodies across the Channel as quickly as practicable. Assuming favorable weather and no British interference, the navy was prepared to deliver six divisions across the Dover Straits to be fully landed by S plus 3, and to fill out the nine landing divisions of the invasion's first wave in about a week. After this, the navy scheduled to deliver two divisions to England every four days. The strong defenses of Dover, and the poor facilities of the other English Channel harbors, caused the Germans to rely almost exclusively on beach landings. Although the barges were ramp-equipped for vehicle discharge, the lack of amphibious training and uncooperative weather was expected to seriously hinder the landing of reinforcements.

As of 10 September, the navy was awaiting air cover to begin laying the cornerstone of the cross-Channel invasion plan which consisted of four successive barrier minefields to cordon off the area of invasion operations. These barriers, although predicted penetrable by the Naval Staff, constituted Sea Lion's primary defense against Royal Navy intervention. A covering force of ten destroyers, twenty-seven U-boats, and about fifty motor torpedo boats, would also be deployed against the expected British response of three or four light cruisers and twenty destroyers assaulting on either flank of the German operations. The Luftwaffe was expected to provide antinaval support in addition to its primary role as the artillery arm against the British beach defenses. Further artillery support both in antinaval and coastal bombardment roles was to come from Hitler's newly emplaced heavy coastal batteries situated near Cap Gris Nez. Thus far, however, the navy-manned Grosser Kurfurst battery with four 28-cm guns, the Friedrich August with three 30.5-cm guns, and the Siegfried battery with four 38-cm guns, had been ineffective in preventing convoy passage through Dover Straits.

The final naval preparations also called for feint maneuvers against the Scottish coast for the purpose of drawing off Royal Navy forces stationed at Scapa Flow. The navy deception would be conducted under the codename Operation Herbstreise (Autumn Journey).

The Landing Force

The German intelligence of late August generously credited the total British defense forces with thirty-nine divisions, half of which were considered full-strength, first-line formations. The British mobile reserve was believed to consist of two armored and several motorized divisions. The Germans correctly assumed that the bulk of the British infantry were deployed in a cordon defense in strengths corresponding to the anticipated threat toward specific sections of the east and southern coastlines. The Germans expected the British counterattack, spearheaded by the mobile reserve stationed near London, to crest within three to five days after S-tag.

Although titularly commanding the landing force, von Runstedt himself remained skeptical that Sea Lion would actually be executed. The field marshal took little interest in the invasion and the bulk of the planning

responsibility was shifted onto the 16th Army commander, General Busch. Busch's 16th Army, together with Strauss's 9th Army, formed Army Group A which constituted the spearhead of the invasion. Busch's operational instructions for Sea Lion defined the initial Group A task as the seizure of a 12- to 18-mile deep continuous beachhead running along the Channel from Folkestone to Worthing. The 80-mile landing front was bisected at St. Leonards, near Hastings; 16th Army to operate east of the center line and 9th Army to the west. The inland limit of 16th Army's initial lodgement ran from Canterbury in the east to Hadlow Down, where it linked up with the 9th Army perimeter which extended the lodgement westward to the South Downs above Worthing. Busch allotted a week to gain this perimeter which would then house the German build-up. The nine divisions of Army Group A would hold this line against the British counterattack, until at least S plus 8, when an additional armored and infantry division were scheduled to arrive behind them. As soon as sufficient motorized forces were on hand, a drive would be unleashed toward the Thames Line, the designated first operational objective skirting south of London along the line Gravesend to Portsmouth. From that line, London would be isolated from the west by motorized forces seeking to attain the second operational objective, marked by the line Maldon-Gloucester. While London succumbed to infantry attack, the motorized units would sweep northward along both coasts and through the industrial centers of the Midlands. Although the army considered the occupation of London as decisive, the assault was planned to carry into northern Britain if it became necessary. Von Reichenau's 6th Army, originally slated for the Lyme Bay landing, would be held in reserve according to the development of the naval situation. OKH still hoped to employ two divisions of 6th Army for the advance on Bristol along the west coast. If the naval situation permitted it, these two divisions would land in Lyme Bay sometime following the main effort in Dover Straits.

Because British resistance was expected to climax during the first week of the assault, the Germans paid significant attention to the problem of securing the initial lodgement. Much reduced from the original OKH plan to land thirteen divisions in three days, the final Sea Lion version landed only six complete divisions during the first three days, although the entire first wave (including the Brighton landing) of nine divisions would be fully ashore within a week of S-tag. The final arrangements therefore allotted two airborne formations, the 7th Fliegerdivision (seven thousand paratroops) and the 22nd Luftlandeddivision (three thousand glider-borne troops), to assist operations on 16th Army's open right flank. The airborne assault behind Beach B (Folkestone-Dungeness) would coincide with the sea-landing of the 17th Infantry Division (16th Army) at S-hour, and would open access routes through the difficult terrain features located immediately behind the beach. These obstacles included Romney Marsh and the Napoleonic Military Canal and Martello Tower line (defenses erected against Napoleon's threatened 1805 invasion). Three submersible tank battalions were delegated for use in this sector where the Germans expected Romney Marsh to be flooded by the British. Once the airborne forces were joined to 16th Army, an overland assault would be conducted to capture strong points at Folkestone, Deal, and the principal southern port at Dover, as rapidly as possible.

The first wave would land not by whole divisions, because of the scarcity of beaching craft, but in three distinct echelons spread over three days during which the bulk of the invasion fleet would remain moored off the landing zones. The first echelon of each division was further divided into an advanced detachment and a follow-up force. The advanced detachments would be the first troops landed. Each consisted of two regimental combat teams (one thousand two hundred fifty men apiece) containing two reinforced rifle companies, combat engineers, assault

light artillery pieces, flame and smoke throwers, gas detectors, communicators, and sailors. The landing echelons numbered about five thousand eight hundred men apiece, or roughly a third of the divisional strength. Hence, the H-hour echelons of the nine landing divisions approximated sixty thousand troops. During the next two days the six divisions, exclusive of the Brighton landings, would be reinforced by their remaining two echelons to bring the total strength ashore by S plus 3 into the neighborhood of one hundred twenty five thousand troops. Elements of the panzer divisions, to be concentrated later when they were fully ashore, would also be landed during the first three days. The 125,000 number, supplemented by the airborne units, and 252 independent submersible tanks, constituted the *first strike* of the invasion. The *first wave* would not be fully ashore until all nine divisions, including the three-division Brighton landing, had their full three echelons landed. This would be accomplished within the first week following S-tag. After this, the second, third, and fourth wave formations would arrive in Britain, hopefully at the rate of two divisions every four days. Following the first wave, priority would be given to introducing motorized units for the advance to the first operational objective. The reinforcements together with the supplies and equipment for sustaining the first wave would be brought ashore at Dover, if available, although the plans assumed that the bulk of material, as well as manpower, would be debarked across the landing beaches.

In summary, the total landing force ran to thirty-five divisions including two airborne, four panzer, two motorized, two mountain, and twenty-five infantry. Also earmarked for the invasion were the two motorized regiments, *Grossdeutchsland* and *SS Liebstandarte Adolf Hitler* (which would operate as part of 16th Army's second-wave formations), and the four amphibious tank battalions to be landed in the first strike.

The German Invasion of Norway, 1940

BY VICE ADMIRAL KURT ASSMANN, FORMER GERMAN NAVY

The German High Command did not embark on the Norwegian campaign in order to improve the military position of Germany by aggressive action. Rather it sought to forestall an occupation of Norway by the enemy. It was in fact nip and tuck as to who would get there first, as subsequent developments revealed. Until the publication of Winston Churchill's memoirs, very few were even aware that there had been a "race for Norway." That both opponents did seek to occupy one and the same objective at about the same time, indeed at almost the same hour, gives this operation a particularly interesting character.

The Norwegian question was broached to Adolf Hitler for the first time on 10 October 1939 by the commander-in-chief navy, Grand Admiral Raeder. According to the War Diary of the Naval Staff and personal notes which the grand admiral made available to the author in January 1944, the former emphasized the great danger for the military position of Germany in the event of an occupation of Norway by Great Britain, as the result of various intelligence indicating British designs on Norway. Second, Raeder called attention to the advantages which would accrue for Germany's own conduct of the war as a result of gaining Norwegian bases. Hitler approved a deliberation of the Norwegian question; there was as yet no mention of a German action against Norway.

Subsequently, further intelligence indi-

U.S. Naval Institute *Proceedings* 78 (April 1952): 401–13. Reprinted by permission.

cated that the British were considering plans to lay hands on Norway and that there were detailed and carefully disguised preparations being made. The thoughts of the Naval Staff now concentrated on the threatening effects for Germany's own conduct of the war, especially in the Baltic Sea area, which would ensue as a result of such a move on the part of Great Britain. The commander-in-chief navy was of the opinion that the loss of Norway to the British, which would also bring Sweden completely under the enemy influence, was synonymous with the loss of the war, particularly since the German war economy was dependent upon the supply of Swedish ore. The fuehrer held the same view, terming the resulting situation as "untenable," and agreed with the commander-in-chief navy that such an eventuality must be anticipated by all means.

Moreover, the question whether and how long Great Britain would respect the territorial waters of Norway—even *without* undertaking an occupation of Norway—was of first importance. How long would they permit the vital and extensive ore transport which moved constantly from Narvik within the protection of such waters to German ports? The Naval Staff took the stand in this regard that such transport was more secure, as long as Great Britain respected Norwegian sovereignty, than it would be if the extensive Norwegian coast line became a war area after a possible German occupation of Norway and the German Wehrmacht then had to assume the protection of such traffic.

The Naval Staff concluded from these con-

A German destroyer taken under fire during the invasion of Norway, 1940. Courtesy of the U.S. Navy Historical Center.

siderations that it was preferable to let the Norwegian question rest until the danger of a British occupation should become acute, or until the British should appear unwilling to respect Norwegian territorial waters. It was considered out of the question that Norway could successfully contest with her own force any British occupation of whatever nature. Moreover, in view of the strong sympathy in Norway for England, it appeared doubtful whether the Norwegians would have the will to resist.

The situation was aggravated by the Russian-Finnish war. The danger appeared very great indeed that the British might get a foothold in Norway as a result of a request on the part of Finland for assistance. On the other hand, the contact with the former minister of war of Norway, Quisling, which had been begun in December 1939, offered some prospect that Norway might be secured by peaceful means against an occupation by Great Britain. Under these circumstances, the fuehrer approved of the proposal of the commander-in-chief navy on 12 December that plans should be made with Quisling for the occupation of Norway by "(a) peaceful

means—i.e. the German Wehrmacht would be called in by Norway—or (b) force." Thereupon the Armed Forces High Command undertook the preparation of "Study North" by a working staff composed of representatives of the three services. "Study North" later received the code name Weseruebung. The participation of the German Wehrmacht would be necessary in any case if Norway were drawn into the German sphere of power, since it was not at all likely that Great Britain would take such action lying down and since Norway was not able to parry the expected British counterblow with its own force.

The commander-in-chief navy was quite aware that the occupation of Norway by Germany would be accompanied with extremely great risk for the navy in view of the heavy superiority of British sea power. Consequently, he too continued to hold that the maintenance of Norway's neutrality was the best solution. However, he emphasized to Hitler once again on 30 December 1939 that under no circumstances must Norway fall into British hands. There was also the danger that British volunteers might accomplish a "cold" occupation of Norway in a disguised

The North Sea, 1940.

form. Serious resistance was not to be expected in Norway, nor, probably, in Sweden.

At the beginning of January the foreign press generally confirmed that active British assistance for Finland was impending: strong British support was necessary, since a defeat of Finland would be dangerous for the Western Powers and northern Norway must not fall into Russian-German hands.

Even though the commander-in-chief navy and his officers in the Naval Staff were in entire agreement that the best solution would be the maintenance of the status quo, nevertheless in January 1940 their mutual views as to the probability and the dangers of British intervention in Norway were not in complete accord. The following extract is taken from the War Diary of the Naval Staff of 13 January:

> The Chief, Naval Staff, is still firmly convinced that *Great Britain intends to occupy Norway in the near future* in order to cut off completely all exports from the Norwegian-Swedish area to Germany, and to paralyze German warfare

on the high seas and in the North Sea; in so doing she will be able to count on Norway's tacit consent or at least that of the Government and large parts of the population because of the Norwegians' anti-German attitude. This opinion is confirmed by special intelligence, which has reached the Chief, Naval Staff. . . .

In partial disagreement with the opinion of the Chief, Naval Staff, the Operations Division of Naval Staff does *not* believe that an early occupation of Norway by Great Britain is probable. Apart from the fact that it is in any case doubtful whether Great Britain is at present capable of mounting the necessary force, the Operations Division, Naval Staff, is of the opinion that such an operation would involve very great risk and prodigious difficulties for Great Britain. The occupation of Norway would bring Great Britain into strong and extremely undesirable opposition to Russia; furthermore, it would immediately call forth powerful countermeasures on the part of Germany. The establishment of British forces in Norwegian bases would directly result in the immediate extension of German operational bases to Denmark and, if necessary, to Sweden; German naval and air forces would thus constitute a highly effective threat to any British activities in the south Norwegian area.

Any British military pressure exerted on *Sweden* through Norway could be rendered ineffective by immediate German action against Sweden, since *German* warfare could achieve substantially greater effect, and much more quickly, than would be the case with British operations undertaken from the Norwegian area.

In the opinion of the Operations Division, Naval Staff, it is very improbable that Great Britain could release such strong forces at home as would be necessary for the occupation of Norway, in order to counter effectively the strong threat by Germany.

We will revert to this very significant strategic estimate of the Naval Staff later on.

On 16 February the Naval Staff was alarmed by the British surprise attack on the German tanker *Altmark* in Joessing Fjord. Even though the ship was under the protection of Norwegian torpedo boats, the British destroyer *Cossack* went alongside and forced her to hand over some three hundred prisoners. This case was a clear warning that henceforth Norwegian territorial waters would not afford such protection for German shipping. On the other hand, the weak attitude which the Norwegian government showed relative to the violation of her sovereignty by Great Britain indicated that Norway would also do no more than enter a formal protest in the event of a German action.

No decision to execute the planned undertaking was made at the conference of Adolf Hitler with the commander-in-chief navy on 20 February. During the first days of March signs pointed increasingly to an imminent British action against Norway. Intelligence recently reported from the latter country that the government had indeed the will to defend its neutrality with all the means at its disposal but that a defense against British military measures by Norway was practically impossible. The armed forces were said to have received orders not to fire on superior forces without permission. Under certain circumstances the Western Powers might be accorded the right of passage by reason of Article XVI of the League of Nations covenant.

It is clearly apparent from the War Diary that concern for the imminent danger now also gained the upper hand in the Operations Division of the Naval Staff over the cool reserve with which it had formerly contemplated the Norwegian question. The same attitude prevailed in the Armed Forces High Command. Any further reserve was dispelled on 4 March when the fuehrer sent out an urgent order, transmitted verbally to the Naval Staff, to make all preparations for Weseruebung with such great dispatch that subsequent to 10 March the fuehrer could direct the execution of the operation on four days' notice. Intelligence pointed increasingly to an impending supporting operation of the Western Powers for Finland, invoking the above-mentioned right of passage. The British radio announced that the Western Powers were determined to give Finland all assistance, if the latter should request them to do so.

Meanwhile peace negotiations between Finland and Russia had gotten under way. It was indicated in a declaration of the Finnish foreign minister that, if the Russian demands should be too high, the Finnish government would request the immediate assistance of the Western Powers. The Finns had been definitely assured of this assistance regardless of the fact that it would necessarily extend the theater of war to the northern area. This was confirmed on 10 March by the official declaration of the British prime minister, Chamberlain.

The Russian-Finnish treaty of peace of 12 March temporarily eased the situation. If Great Britain should now take action notwithstanding, then it could not be in the guise of support for Finland. Under these circumstances, the Naval Staff believed for the moment that intervention of the British was no longer imminent. It assumed that the British government would await a more favorable time.

However, the situation was not relieved for very long. The Naval Staff gained the definite impression from all the intelligence, which it had latterly received from the most varied sources that the Western Powers were determined to lay hands on Norway *under all circumstances*, secondly also on Sweden, for which purpose support for Finland would have been a welcome pretext. This was confirmed by further reliable information which advised that the Western Powers had done all possible to prevent the signing of the peace so that they would not be robbed of this pretext. However, the Naval Staff had no doubt that Great Britain would act regardless, if it considered that the time was ripe. This same view prevailed in fuehrer headquarters.

Subsequently, the Naval Staff was disturbed by the numerous cases in which German merchant ships had been molested within Norwegian territorial waters by British naval and air forces. The Norwegian government endeavored to oppose the British encroachments. As a result of earnest German representations, it made very sharp protest in London on 23 March and directed its forces to open fire on any foreign warship or airplane which should again be guilty of such conduct contrary to international law.

The commander-in-chief navy addressed

the fuehrer in this vein on 26 March. Even though he explained that in his opinion the danger of a British landing in Norway was not acute at the moment, nevertheless, Germany was faced with the problem of executing Weseruebung sooner or later. He took the stand that it should be done soon—if possible, utilizing the new moon (7 April) period. As a result of the presentation of commander-in-chief navy, Adolf Hitler directed on the same day that the operation be accomplished. D-day was not yet set; on 2 April it was ordered for 9 April with the time for landing (*Weserzeit*) at 5:15 A.M.

The fears of the Naval Staff that strong British measures were about to be taken to interrupt German merchant shipping in Norwegian territorial waters were further substantiated by a report from Oslo that the Norwegian Naval Staff was of the opinion the British government would take all measures which it considered necessary in the near future to officially "take over itself the protection of Norwegian territorial waters." It was said that the Norwegian government did not yet know what course it should take in response. Semiofficial press statements from London did not dispute the fact that Great Britain intended to interrupt German merchant shipping in Norwegian waters. This would not, however, be accomplished with force but by means of political pressure on Norway. This served to strengthen the view of the Naval Staff that "in reality just such a British action against Scandinavia is imminent. . . . 'Weseruebung' is beginning to develop into a race between Great Britain and Germany!"

With regard to the date set for Germany's own operation (9 April), the Naval Staff noted in its Diary of 6 April: "Our estimate of the enemy's intention is that he is just about to take action in Norwegian waters or on Norwegian territory. . . . The Naval Staff is of the opinion that *greatest haste* is necessary for the execution of 'Weseruebung.' 9 April appears to be the latest date. It would be desirable to advance this date, but that is no longer possible."—Two days later events substantiated the German Naval Staff's estimate of the enemy situation on 6 April.

On 8 April the British government surprised public opinion with the declaration that British mines had been laid during the past night in three places in Norwegian territorial waters, at Stadtlandet, at Bud and in Vest Fjord, to prevent "ships carrying contraband from making use of the protection of neutral waters." The political effect of the British minelaying was adjudged favorably by the Germans. It was expected that the impending German action would appear justified to neutral countries after this act of the opponent contrary to international law. Militarily, however, the situation appeared to have become considerably more difficult; it now seemed quite certain that in executing our own operation, action would ensue with enemy naval forces standing near the mine fields.

The British mine-laying was the second flagrant violation of international law, after the surprise attack on *Altmark*, which the British had permitted themselves in Norwegian territorial waters. Were these isolated actions or were they links in the chain of further designs which the British government had in mind for Norway?

When the German High Command decided to undertake the Norwegian operations, it knew only that which has been presented above. In the course of the campaign, and a little later on after the occupation of Paris in June 1940, it obtained some very revealing records and other documents, which added up to the following picture.

On the basis of plans which had been prepared in the Allied military discussions of 31 January and 1 February 1940, the Allied Supreme Council in its session of 5 February in Paris had determined to prepare French-British forces in Great Britain for transport to Norway. On 6 February the British foreign minister, Lord Halifax, informed the Norwegian ambassador in London that England wished to have certain bases on the Norwegian coast "in order to interrupt the German ore transport from Narvik." In actual fact, the British intentions went beyond this objective. Acting under British influence, the majority of the Supreme Council had expressed the opinion in the Paris session that

Operation Scandinavia should also be extended to the Swedish ore mines of Gaellivare. In this conference the view was also accepted that the action should not be dependent on an appeal by Finland for aid, but should be executed as a surprise operation in order "to save Finland or at least to seize the Swedish ore and the northern ports." The operation was to be conducted under British command. In mid-February British and French General Staff officers inspected landing places with the consent of Norwegian authorities. The preparation of the British-French expeditionary troops was completed by the beginning of March.

The final decision to undertake the landing operation and to establish bases in Norway was made on 28 March. The fact that peace had meanwhile been concluded between Russia and Finland on 12 March had no effect on this decision. The departure date of the first transports was set for 5 April. This date was postponed at the last minute, with decisive significance for events in Norway. On 5 April the British High Command informed the commander-in-chief of the French navy that the first British convoy could not sail before 8 April, evidently because the British transport preparations had not yet been completed.

In *The Gathering Storm*, Churchill substantiated the picture gleaned from the captured documents. He wrote that the Supreme Council had decided in the Paris session of 5 February to land, in conjunction with the aid-to-Finland project, "in Narvik and/or other Norwegian ports." It was their intention, as he said, to "kill two birds with one stone (i.e., help Finland and cut off the iron ore)." The agreement, and if possible the "cooperation," of Norway and Sweden was to be obtained. Then followed this rather remarkable sentence: "The issue of what to do if Norway and Sweden refused, as seemed probable, was never faced." That this was not a matter of concern can only mean that they were sure that either the Scandinavian states would cause them no difficulty despite formal protest of the action or that they were determined right from the start to break any possible resistance with force. Since the troops

detailed for the expedition were equipped for only an "unopposed landing," the first alternative was probably the appropriate one.

According to Churchill, the British Cabinet decided on 12 March "to revive the plans for military landings at Narvik and Trondheim, to be followed at Stavanger and Bergen. . . ." The date of execution was set for 20 March, but on the same day of this decision (12 March) the Russian-Finnish peace was concluded. Thereupon the execution was postponed.

On 28 March the new French Prime Minister Reynaud attended the session of the Supreme War Council in London, in which it was decided to lay mines in Norwegian territorial waters on 5 April. On 3 April, however, the British Cabinet postponed the operation to 8 April. Churchill wrote in this connection: "As our mining of Norwegian waters might provoke a German retort, it was also agreed that a British brigade and a French contingent should be sent to Narvik to clear the port and to advance to the Swedish frontier. Other forces should be dispatched to Stavanger, Bergen, and Trondheim, in order to deny these bases to the enemy."

According to another British source, the troops were not to land until the Germans had violated Norwegian sovereignty or *"if it seemed certain that they intended to do so."* The similarity to the German attitude is noteworthy.

Meanwhile, on 3 April the British War Cabinet had received certain intelligence that strong German military forces had been concentrated in Mecklenburg and that over 200,000 tons of shipping had been collected in Stettin and Swinemuende. They concluded that Germany had taken these measures "to deliver a counterstroke against a possible attack by us upon Narvik or other Norwegian ports."

As a matter of fact, the British High Command had lost the "race for Norway" when it postponed the date of execution from 5 April to the 8th. German naval forces were then under way for all those places which the Allies had selected for their landings.

The German-Norwegian operation embraced two independent phases: the surprise assault and occupation, and the supply of troop and material reinforcements to extend the positions gained. The following landing places were selected for the blitz occupation: Oslo, Arendal, Kristiansand, Egersund, Stavanger, Bergen, Trondheim, and Narvik. The landings had to be accomplished simultaneously at all places and if possible by surprise. The Germans did not reckon with a unified and determined resistance by the Norwegians—on the condition, to be sure, that the moment of surprise would be utilized by bringing full weight to bear on the day of occupation. Thus the approach was to be made in the fjords during the night, the landings at morning twilight. It was decided that the necessary troop formations were to be transported in warships or—within the range and capacity of the air force—by airplanes. In view of British naval supremacy, the landing units had to be transported by the fastest and surest means and, in order to ensure that the landings were made simultaneously, they had to arrive exactly on time. In the event that the Norwegians should offer resistance, the support of the warships was required not only for the entrance into the fjords but also at the landing of the troops. However, since the loading capacity of the warships was very limited, the heavy weapons, equipment, and ammunition had to be loaded in transports scheduled to arrive simultaneously at the ports of destination. Since the steamers were slower than the warships, it was necessary to sail them ahead of the latter. They had to be disguised as peaceful merchantmen, and if need be they were to be scuttled in time so that the real purpose would not be revealed prematurely in case of Norwegian control measures or British interception.

In Grand Admiral Raeder's presentation to Hitler on 9 March, he emphasized once again the great risk which the navy had to accept in this action in view of British naval superiority. "Nevertheless, given complete surprise, I believe that our troops can and will be successfully *transported to Norway*," he continued. "On many occasions in the history of war those very operations have been successful which went against all the rules of warfare, provided they were carried out by surprise." The grand admiral considered that the most difficult part of the operation for the ships would be the return voyage which would entail breaking through the alerted British naval forces. This had to be accomplished as quickly as possible and with all available support by the air force, particularly for the ships dispatched to the distant northern ports. This requirement ran counter to the interest of the army, since the landed troops naturally laid great store in holding as long as possible the effective support which the warships offered. Hitler determined that the troops at Narvik would have to do without the continued support of naval forces, while two torpedo boats were to remain at Trondheim.

Adolf Hitler decided that Denmark should also be drawn into the German sphere of power in order to safeguard the lines of supply. This was essentially a task for the army; its first move in this connection was the occupation of Jutland. Copenhagen, the important bridge over the Little Belt at Middelfart, and the ferry facilities between Korsor and Nyborg were to be taken by naval operations. The air force was to seize the landing fields.

In the interest of the whole operation, plans were made for a simultaneous advance of the two battleships *Scharnhorst* and *Gneisenau* into the Arctic Ocean and the disposition of twenty-eight U-boats along the Norwegian coast and in the area of the Shetland and Orkney Islands.

The navy had organized the following task groups for the landing:

- Group 1. (Narvik); battleships *Scharnhorst, Gneisenau* and ten destroyers, the latter with two thousand landing troops.
- Group 2. (Trondheim); cruiser *Hipper* and four destroyers with seventeen hundred landing troops.
- Group 3. (Bergen); cruisers *Koeln, Koenigsberg, Bremse*, two torpedo boats and Torpedo Motorboat Flotilla I, with nineteen hundred landing troops.
- Group 4. (Kristiansand); cruiser *Karlsruhe*,

three torpedo boats and Torpedo Motor-boat Flotilla II, with eleven hundred landing troops.

- Group 5. (Oslo); cruisers *Bluecher, Luetzow, Emden,* and three torpedo boats, with two thousand landing troops.
- Group 6. (Egersund); four minesweepers with one hundred fifty landing troops.

In addition there were groups 7 to 9: battleship *Schleswig-Holstein* with a number of auxiliary ships and craft carrying a total of thirty-four hundred landing troops for the tasks in Denmark. The occupation of Denmark was accomplished without friction and without resistance, apart from minor incidents, and led to a peaceful understanding with the Danish government.

All preparations for the extremely daring operation had to be most carefully disguised since the factor of surprise was considered of decisive importance. This was relatively easy for the warship groups but very much more difficult in the assemblage and outfitting of the transport groups composed of merchant ships and in the loading of the mass of army troops and their equipment. The following were prepared for these tasks:

- The so-called "Transport Group," comprising seven steamers of 48,692 tons from Hamburg for Narvik, Trondheim and Stavanger.
- Three "Naval Transport Squadrons," with a total of thirty-eight steamers of 198,999 tons.

The steamers of the "Transport Group" carried the weapons, equipment, and so forth for the landing troops embarked in the warships. They were to steam disguised as ordinary merchant ships and were to arrive in the ports of occupation even *before* the warships. A foolish myth—unfortunately also repeated by Churchill in his memoirs—has it that the Germans had secretly sent arms and supplies to Narvik, hidden in ore ships even before the occupation. There is not a word of truth in this story.

The arrival date for Naval Transport Squadron I, whose ports of destination were Copenhagen, Oslo, Kristiansand, Stavanger, and Bergen, was the landing day (9 April), for

Naval Transport Squadrons II and III, destined for Oslo, the 2nd and 6th days respectively after the landing. About eighteen thousand men and their equipment were embarked in these three squadrons. A further reinforcement of about forty thousand men was to be transported later on in a shuttle service with the steamers of Squadrons II and III.

Since the naval forces assigned to Narvik and Trondheim would have to refuel there in order to make a fast turnaround, the Naval Staff dispatched the tankers *Kattegat* and *Skagerrak* from Wilhelmshaven to Narvik and Trondheim respectively and the tanker *Jan Wellem* from Base North to Narvik. The Armed Forces High Command had issued strict orders to all participating ships that they must not depart from the staging bases earlier than six days before the time of landing. This restriction was also effective for the naval tankers. It will be seen later on that this order allowed the steamers too little time for the voyage and had serious consequences.

Since the Norwegian undertaking was the first combined operation of all three services, for which there were available no lessons of the past, the Armed Forces High Command made very careful preparations for the command organization. General von Falkenhorst was designated as the chief of the Working and Operations Staff Weseruebung; simultaneously he was designated to be later the commander-in-chief army, Norway. Air Force General Geisler with his reinforced Air Corps X was assigned to the command of the air arm. "Corps Area Command XXXII," under Air Force General Kaupisch, was formed for the occupation of Denmark.

The navy was assigned command afloat for the duration of the operation. The Naval Staff assigned the Naval Group Command East, Admiral Carls, to the command of the operation in the Baltic Sea area, inclusive of the *Kallegat* and *Skagerrak*, and the Naval Group Command West, Admiral Saalwaechter, to the command in the North Sea.

The conduct of the landing and the command ashore at the individual landing places was to be assumed by the senior army officer.

The command of the air transport was in the hands of the air force until the execution of the landing. A local "Armed Forces Commander"—army or navy—was to be appointed after the landing at the individual places. The commander-in-chief army, Norway, General von Falkenhorst, was assigned overall command as "Armed Forces Commander, Norway," for the further course of the Norwegian campaign.

Shortly before midnight, 6 April, Groups 1 and 2 (Narvik, Trondheim) under the command of the deputy fleet commander, Vice Admiral Luetjens, left their North Sea ports immediately after embarking their troops and joined forces outside of the river mouths at 3:00 A.M. for the joint advance to the north. On 3 and 5 April the seven steamers of the Transport Group and part of Naval Transport Squadron I had departed from their fitting-out ports, Hamburg and Stettin; the rest of the latter followed on 7 April. The German-Norwegian operation had started.

At 9:48 A.M., 7 April, the force was first reported, even though only in part, by British air reconnaissance in 55°30′ N, 6°37′ E. The British plane reported one cruiser, six destroyers, and eight planes. The report was also read by the Germans. At 2:25 P.M. British air reconnaissance reported a large ship, possibly *Scharnhorst* class, two cruisers, and ten destroyers in 56°48′ N, 6°10′ E. At this time the German force was unsuccessfully attacked by British Wellington bombers; twelve planes were counted. The greater part of the bombers sent out by the Royal Air Force evidently did not make contact. After the visibility of noon, conditions had become worse, which was very welcome to the Germans. To be sure, as a result of the change in weather, German air reconnaissance also had to be discontinued on about the line Stavanger-Peterhead.

The British High Command had recognized from the air reconnaissance reports that a German naval operation to the northward was in progress; they could not as yet deduce the purpose and objective of the undertaking from these reports. The Admiralty had, however, received an intelligence report from Co-penhagen—evidently occasioned by the lively ship traffic to the northward in the Baltic Sea entrances in connection with the operation—that a German expedition of ten ships carrying one division of troops was under way to make a landing at Narvik. In passing on the report to the British Fleet Commander, Admiral Sir Charles Forbes, on 7 April, the Admiralty had described it as "doubtful."

The news that the German fleet was at sea caused the Admiralty to make certain important decisions. Britain's own landing operation was abandoned, the troops then on board were disembarked, the forces which had departed to lay mines at Stadtlandet were recalled, and all measures were geared to the interception of the German force. On the evening of the 7th Admiral Forbes put to sea with the main forces of the British Home Fleet; the cruiser force departed on the following day from the Forth.

At 8:20 A.M., 8 April, the first action between German and British naval forces took place north of the line Bergen-Shetland Islands. The sea had meanwhile become quite heavy; the destroyers steaming at high speed were pounding hard and the soldiers embarked in them found it particularly unpleasant. The British destroyer *Glowworm*, which had lost contact with her force—the battle-cruiser *Renown*—ran into the destroyer *Bernd V. Arnim* of the German screen. The German cruiser *Hipper* presently took a hand in the destroyer action which had ensued and sank *Glowworm* with gunfire; thirty-eight survivors were rescued despite the heavy sea. About noon, Group 2, which had been steaming in formation with Group 1 under the command of the Fleet Commander, was released to execute its task at Trondheim.

In the North Sea 8 April was a day of incidents, which so often play a decisive role in naval warfare. Their effect for the German operation were in part unfavorable, but predominantly favorable.

At 2:20 P.M. the former Polish submarine *Orzel* sank the transport *Rio De Janeiro* of Naval Transport Squadron I, bound for Bergen, when east of Kristiansand. The results of this torpedoing were fatal. The landings of the survivors and the dead in *German army uniform* necessarily revealed the German intentions and warned the Norwegians, thus precluding surprise. The British news agency, Reuters, reported at 8:30 that night from Oslo: "German troop transport *Rio De Janeiro* with 300 men on board torpedoed near Kristiansand."

Group 2 arrived off Trondheim Fjord in the early afternoon of the 8th. Since it was too early to enter, they maneuvered at sea on various courses. At 3:00 P.M., just as they happened to be on westerly course, they were sighted by an enemy plane and reported as one battlecruiser, two cruisers, and two destroyers on course west. The intelligence that the German force was steering on course west brought serious confusion into the previously fairly clear estimate of the situation on the part of the enemy. Admiral Whitworth, who had been given the task of guarding the Vest Fjord leading to Narvik, now decided to operate so that he would block the route of the reported opponent in case the latter should make an advance into the Arctic Ocean. He ordered his force to form a scouting line from Skomvaer to the westward for the night, and thus left the entrance to Narvik unguarded. At 9:00 P.M. the German Fleet Commander detached the ten destroyers for the assigned task at Narvik. They entered Vest Fjord without making contact with the enemy.

The operations of the British fleet commander were also influenced unfavorably by the plane report. When it was received he was steaming on a northeasterly course about 120 miles west of Trondheim. The report caused him to change course to 0° (north), later to 340°, which took him farther and farther away from the scene of action.

During 8 April the German attack groups assigned to the southern Norwegian harbors, whose distances were shorter than those of Group 1 and 2, also commenced their advance. Whereas stormy winds had cleared the air in the northern North Sea, it was very foggy in the south in the forenoon of the 8th, which was favorable for the German movements since they were withdrawn from enemy observation. Group 3 destined for Bergen found itself in an extremely dangerous situation at about 5:00 P.M. A far superior British force of two modern cruisers and fifteen destroyers was only 60 miles away, and between the former and its objective. But—and this was the third fortune of war, this time particularly favorable for the Germans—heavy fog had set in since early afternoon and this prevented any scouting by the enemy. The German force was able to gain the entrance of Bergen without being seen, and then, when the danger was over, the weather cleared up so that the passage into the fjord could be made without navigational difficulties.

After the detachment of the Narvik destroyers, the German fleet commander undertook the projected advance into the Arctic Ocean. As dawn was beginning to break on the 9th, he ran into the *Renown* group of Admiral Whitworth, 50 miles west of Skomvaer. A brief but spirited action ensued; *Gneisenau* sustained considerable damage from a hit in the foremast, while *Renown* suffered no major damage despite two hits. Contact was finally lost because of reduced visibility and increasing range. The Germans continued the advance into the Arctic Ocean, and then returned unmolested to Wilhelmshaven on the evening of 12 April.

Meanwhile, significant events had taken place in the early morning hours of 9 April in the designated Norwegian ports. The ten Narvik destroyers encountered no interference until near their destination; then the Norwegian armored coastal ships *Eidsvold* and *Norge* engaged them at short range until both were sunk by torpedo fire. The commander of the landing troops, Major General Dietl, took over the town without resistance from the Norwegian Colonel Sundlo. Only one tanker, *Jan Wellem*, arrived on schedule; the other one was engaged by a Norwegian warship and was scuttled by her own crew. Refueling of the destroyers was thus delayed and the departure had to be postponed. Moreover, none of the three steamers of the "Transport Group" reached Narvik; two were lost en route to enemy action and the third had to be diverted to Bergen.

Group 2 was fired on ineffectually by a land battery while forcing Trondheim Fjord and reached its destination without further incident. The debarkation of the Trondheim troops was accomplished without resistance. The tanker and two steamers of the "Transport Group" for Trondheim were lost at sea; the other transport finally reached that port after three days' delay on 12 April. The departure of *Hipper* was postponed to the evening of the 10th. Two of the destroyers followed a few days later after 800 tons of oil had been scared up in the city; the remaining two destroyers stayed at Trondheim.

The Bergen Group was also fired on by Norwegian coastal batteries while entering; *Koenigsberg* received three hits, *Bremse* one. The debarkation of troops was accomplished without interference, only minor resistance being offered in the city. The ships of Naval Transport Squadron I arrived in Bergen on schedule. *Koeln* and the torpedo boats undertook the return voyage on the evening of the 9th as planned. *Koenigsberg* and *Bremse*, which were not fully ready for sea, were left behind as support for the troops. Shortly before leaving and while standing out, the *Koeln* force was attacked by British planes; no hits were scored on the ships. During the forenoon of the 10th, British planes attacked *Koenigsberg* at Bergen and scored two direct hits. The ship burned out and capsized.

The initial attempts of Group 4 to force the entrance to Kristiansand failed because of fire from a shore battery and intermittent fog. When the visibility had cleared at 11:00 A.M., the force advanced to the attack again, this time leading off with the torpedo boats and torpedo motorboats carrying the troops for the landing; no more shots were fired by the Norwegian batteries. The debarkation of troops was accomplished by 3:00 P.M. with only minor resistance. In the course of the afternoon three steamers of Naval Transport Squadron I arrived in port with troops and equipment. Meanwhile Arendal and the cable station Egersund were occupied, as planned, without resistance. *Karlsruhe* and the torpedo boats were able to depart on their return voyage at 7:00 P.M. After clearing the

entrance and while steaming at 21 knots on zig-zag courses, an enemy submarine scored a torpedo hit on *Karlsruhe*. So much water entered the ship that the cruiser could not be salvaged. The captain transferred the crew to the torpedo boats and then sank the cruiser. The torpedo boats with the crew of *Karlsruhe* reached Kiel without further incident.

In the morning of 9 April Stavanger was occupied by airborne troops as directed. During the occupation the steamer *Roda* of Naval Transport Squadron I was sunk in the harbor by the Norwegian torpedo boat *Sleipner*. Thereafter, German bombers dealt with the latter in like manner.

For the seizure of the Norwegian capital, Group 5 stood off the strongly fortified Droback narrows at the entrance to Oslo Fjord at 4:40 A.M. 9 April. When the van ship, the heavy cruiser *Bluecher*, was only 550 yards away, the coastal batteries opened fire. Within a few moments the cruiser received two 11-inch and at least twenty 5.9-inch hits, which caused heavy damage. Shortly thereafter two heavy explosions rocked the ship; she had been hit by two torpedoes of the torpedo battery Kaholm. Fires within the ship touched off a magazine explosion; she capsized and sank in deep water.

Luctzow, steaming astern of *Bluecher*, also received three hits in the action but the fighting effectiveness of the ship was only temporarily reduced. The attempt to force the narrows was then abandoned; instead the troops were landed outside of it and the capitulation of the fortifications was accomplished in the course of the afternoon by a combined land, sea, and air attack. The German naval force entered Oslo in the forenoon of 10 April.

Meanwhile the situation in the Norwegian capital had developed as follows. The first German planes appeared over the city at 8:00 A.M., 9 April. The Norwegian antiaircraft batteries opened fire on them but could not prevent the seizure of the Oslo-Fornebo airfield by the Germans. At noon six companies of airborne troops landed here and occupied the most important points of the city. The political situation was not at all clear. Quisling attempted to form a new government with German support, but it struck no spark of sympathy amongst the people. The former government leaders did not resign but fled into the interior. A conference of the German ambassador with the king proved fruitless. The latter sharply rejected the suggestion that Quisling take over the government and could not be moved to give in. The German naval attache in Oslo, who knew the country very well, reported that no German action had been expected in Oslo up to the time of the torpedoing of the steamer *Rio De Janeiro.* It was not until the night of 8/9 April that the pregnant decisions were made which unleashed Norwegian resistance.

Since the military situation on 10 April was not yet so well in hand that all the German naval forces which had entered Oslo could be withdrawn, only *Luetzow* departed for the return voyage in the afternoon of the 10th, since she had to be released for other tasks. It was not accomplished without incident. When the cruiser was northeast of Skagen in the night of 10/11, she received a torpedo hit in the after-body at 1:29 A.M. from the British submarine *Spearfish;* it put propellers and rudder out of commission and much water entered the ship. It was only with difficulty that the unmaneuverable ship could be kept afloat and that tugs could bring her into Kiel in the evening of the 13th.

While these events were taking place on 9 April in the landing ports, the British naval forces off the Norwegian west coast were attacked by the German Air Force. German Air Squadrons 26 and 30 with Ju 88s and He 111s were employed in these attacks. Even though the deterrent effect which the German Air Force exercised on the British fleet was great, nevertheless the damage inflicted on this day did not fully come up to German expectations, nor did it agree with the observations made by the airplanes. The latter claimed a great number of hits on battleships, cruisers, and destroyers, and also on a troop transport. The results actually obtained were the sinking of the destroyer *Gurkha,* a hit on the battleship *Rodney,* and light damage to the cruisers *Southampton* and *Glasgow* due to near misses. The British observed numerous other near misses but they inflicted no damage.

The further course of the campaign was largely influenced by the Allied reaction. The latter began in the early morning of 10 April with the first British attack on Narvik. About 5:30 A.M. the Germans were taken completely by surprise when numerous heavy explosions rocked the harbor of Narvik. Five British destroyers had attacked with guns and torpedoes and scored a tactical success. It had its strategic effect too, in that it thwarted the German plan to depart homeward during the night 10/11 April. What was left of the German naval force at Narvik was finished off on the 13th when the British made a renewed attack with the battleship *Warspite* and nine destroyers. The loss of the ten destroyers was a heavy blow for the Germans, but the addition of about twenty-five hundred men of their crews was a most welcome accretion to General Dietl's defenses.

The Allies, utilizing troops and transports earmarked for their own landing plans, moved swiftly to retake Trondheim and Narvik by pincer attacks before the Germans could consolidate their position in central and northern Norway. Late in April the Trondheim forces had to be evacuated before they reached their goal because of the threatening advance of German Army Group XXI from Oslo. On 28 May the Allies captured Narvik, but did not hold it long. Early in June the Allied troops were evacuated in response to more pressing requirements for troops in the west. On 8 June, General Dietl reported that Narvik was again in his hands. On the day following the Norwegian forces also ceased hostilities.

A naval action concluded the Norwegian campaign, in which the German fleet commander, Admiral Marschall, scored a notable victory. In an attempt to relieve the situation at Narvik, the Naval Staff had dispatched a strong German squadron, including the battleships *Scharnhorst* and *Gneisenau,* to the scene of action. The operation resulted in the sinking of the British aircraft carrier *Glorious* (22,500 tons), the auxiliary cruiser *Or-*

ama (19,840 tons) and the tanker *Oil Pioneer* (5,666 tons), while *Scharnhorst* took a torpedo hit from a British destroyer. It proved to be a final thrust at the withdrawing foe.

The German armed forces can be very proud of the way in which they accomplished the Norwegian campaign—the first great combined operation of all three service branches in the history of the war. The success gained was decisive and well deserved. However, the victory was gained at a price—the toll paid to British naval supremacy. The German navy never recovered from the losses which it had suffered in this campaign.

The British-French counterblow was ill-starred from the beginning because it was undertaken with inadequate forces and underestimation of the German operational possibilities in point of numbers as well as equipment. The counterattack could have had prospects of success only if the communications with Germany had been promptly cut after the first German landings in Norway. To be sure, enemy submarines did attack the main stream of reinforcements and supplies on the waters from Germany to Oslo; they did indeed harass but could not disrupt the supply. Only large means could avail in this situation, that is, the extension of British naval supremacy into the Skagerrak and Kattegat.

Was the Norwegian operation a real necessity from the German point of view, or is there perhaps occasion to see things in a somewhat different light as we look back over the general conduct of the war? In this connection the author requests the reader to review the War Diary entry of the Naval Staff,

Operations Division, of 13 January, 1940. Pursuing the thought of this estimate of the situation, it follows that the British would have committed a strategic mistake had they moved into Norway ahead of the Germans because they could not have held Norway for good. The Germans would have had control of the long arm of the lever since German counteraction via Denmark and southern Sweden was to be expected as a matter of course. There would have developed for the Allies an exhausting new theater of war of first order which would have been extremely difficult to supply in view of German air superiority. Moreover, had the Allies gone into Norway of their own initiative, it would have been a matter of national prestige to hold their ground there.

Unfortunately, the brilliantly conducted military campaign into Norway was a complete political failure for the Germans. The association with the former Minister of War Quisling proved to be a fatal error in the occupation. The choice of Terboven as the reich commissioner for Norway was also most unfortunate. It is little known that Adolf Hitler took leave of Reich Commissioner Terboven before the latter assumed his office in Oslo with these words: "Herr Reichskommissar, you can do me no greater favor than if you make these people our friends. . . ." It would have been very difficult to find a personality less suited for this task than Herr Terboven! His ruthless and sharp pressure measures, plus the usually presumptuous and tactless procedure of the German civil administrators, nipped in the bud any small sympathy for Germany amongst the Norwegian people.

The Dieppe Raid, 1942

BY LIEUTENANT COLONEL CHARLES W. SCHRINER, JR., USMC

On the morning of 19 August 1942, more than six thousand troops, most of whom were Canadian, landed by amphibious means on the French coast at Dieppe. When the raiding force withdrew twelve hours later, 60 percent of that force had been killed, wounded, or captured by the German defenders, whose losses were slight. Moreover, almost none of the tactical objectives had been achieved.

The Dieppe raid, when viewed in terms of casualties suffered and its failure to achieve tactical success, was a severe defeat for the Allies. This much cannot be disputed, but the raid's long-range benefits and the degree to which it helped the Allied war effort have been the subject of continuing dispute. What, if any, were the long-range aims of Dieppe? Did it have a place in Anglo-American strategy in 1942? Were there positive results achieved by the raid that made it worth the price in lives? Did it, in fact, contribute significantly to the successful prosecution of the war? Winston Churchill, reflecting on the Dieppe raid, said:

> Looking back, the casualties of this memorable action may seem out of proportion to the results. It would be wrong to judge the episode solely by such a standard. Dieppe occupies a place of its own in the story of the war, and the grim casualty figures must not class it as a failure ... Tactically it was a mine of experience ... Strategically the raid seemed to make the Germans more conscious of danger along the whole coast of Occupied France.[1]

Naval War College Review, "The Dieppe Raid: Its Origin, Aims, and Results," 25 (May-June 1973): 83–97 Reprinted by permission.

Did those words by Churchill evaluate properly the positive effects of the raid, or were they merely uttered after the fact to justify the casualty lists to history?

The Dieppe raid, along with many others, was conceived by a unique British agency called the Combined Operations Headquarters. Because this was the organization that mounted the raid on Dieppe and dealt with the aftermath, an understanding of its function and its relationship to British military command is essential to an analysis of the raid.

Combined Operations Headquarters (COHQ) grew out of a small organization that was formed by Churchill shortly after Dunkirk to conduct raids on enemy-held coasts. As Britain's raiding capability expanded, so did the COHQ, first under the direction of Admiral of the Fleet Sir Roger Keys and, after 27 October 1941, under Commodore (later Vice Admiral) Lord Louis Mountbatten.[2] COHQ, upon the assignment of Mountbatten, was directed to pursue as its primary function "the preparation for the apparatus and plans for the invasion of the Continent."[3] As a secondary function, COHQ was to probe the enemy with raids at every opportunity and was to be the controlling agency for the commandos.

Combined Operations (really amphibious operations) Headquarters was unique in that it was entirely independent of the Admiralty, the War Office, and the Air Ministry. Lord Mountbatten, in order to promote the inter-service nature of COHQ, was given equivalent ranks in the army and Royal Air Force

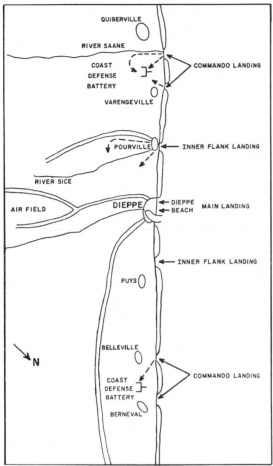

The Dieppe raid. Courtesy of the *Naval War College Review.*

and was elevated to the level of chief of staff, sitting as a member of the Chiefs of Staff Committee on matters of combined operations.[4] His organization became the recognized authority on the conduct of seaborne assault and throughout the remainder of the war contributed significantly to the success of amphibious operations in the European theater.

Raids as an Element of Strategy

On the night of 23 June 1940, the day after Hitler signed an armistice with France, one hundred twenty commandos conducted the first British raid against the coast of occupied France. A small effort, producing no results and memorable only for its amateurism, it marked the start of British raiding policy

which represented one of Churchill's early attempts to take the offense against Germany. After American entry into the war, that raiding policy became an element in the Anglo-American strategy for the defeat of the Axis Powers. The relationship of British raiding policy to Anglo-American strategy is best seen as a function of the British concept of that strategy and of British-American conflict in the development of a mutually acceptable strategic program.

The Allied position during the first half of 1942 consistently teetered on the brink of disaster, reaching its worst point in midsummer. The Japanese appeared unstoppable in the Pacific area and were becoming more and more a threat to India. The Germans repulsed a Russian counteroffensive in the spring, inflicting enormous losses on the Russians and by summer had resumed the attack. By July the Soviet situation appeared desperate, and Stalin was pressing harder for a second front. In Africa, the British surrendered Tobruk in June, and it seemed certain that Rommel would take Egypt. The Battle of the Atlantic was also going Germany's way. During the first half of 1942, sinking of Allied ships exceeded new construction by 3 million tons, and in July the gravity of the situation at sea prompted Churchill to state: "It might be true to say that the issue of war depends on whether Hitler's U-boat attack on Allied tonnage or the increase and application of Allied air power reach their full fruition first."[5] Moreover, bottlenecks in production, supply, and transport severely limited Allied offensive action.

Nevertheless, after Dunkirk, the prime minister had been attempting to mount some sort of offensive operation. His strategic concept of gaining the offensive was to attack the Germans on the periphery, envisaging numerous weak landings in Europe as Britain drew an ever-narrowing ring around the Axis and striking a knockout blow "when the time was ripe."[6] His emphasis on combined operations, his elevation of that command to chiefs of staff level, and his personal support and approval of raids mounted by Combined Operations Headquarters reflected, within the capacity of Britain's resources, his peripheral strategy.

With the entry of the United States into the war, the British concept of defeating Germany came into direct conflict with the U.S. notion of a cross-channel attack at Germany's strength as soon as possible. While it remains beyond the scope of this paper to trace the entire process through which this disagreement was finally resolved, its impact on raiding policy in general and Dieppe in particular merit further discussion. In April of 1942 the War Plans Division of the U.S. War Department developed a plan, known as the Marshall Memorandum, which proposed a large cross-channel attack in the spring or summer of 1943 (later assigned the code name Roundup). Additionally, a minor landing in 1942 was proposed, should it appear that the Russians were about to collapse or that Germany was weak enough to warrant seizing the initiative. The memorandum further advocated smaller raids throughout 1942 along the enemy coastlines, reflecting General Marshall's view that such raids might cause the Germans to redeploy some of their troops from the east and thereby help Russia.[7]

The proposed 1943 landing gained British agreement without difficulty, but a 1942 landing was another matter. While British planners recognized the desirability of assisting Russia through some sort of diversionary operation on the Continent (code-named Sledgehammer), they felt the American notion to harass the Germans into redeploying a portion of their eastern armies along the French coast in 1942 impractical. Instead they proposed a series of medium-sized raids that might tempt the Germans into a major air battle in the west and thereby weaken Nazi air power along the Russian front. To the British in 1942, an Allied beachhead in northwest Europe seemed beyond reality.[8] Despite their best efforts, Marshall and Harry Hopkins were unable to gain British agreement to a 1942 emergency landing and that part of the Marshall Memorandum was tabled. There was, however, full agreement on raids for 1942. The prime minister cabled President Roosevelt that the agreed

program included "more frequent and large scale raids,"[9] and the British chiefs of staff on 18 April approved a memorandum implementing the Anglo-American decisions which, in addressing the agreement on raiding, said: "We have already approved a policy of raids to be undertaken in the summer of 1942 on the largest scale that the available equipment will permit."[10]

Nevertheless, work continued on plans for a more substantial diversionary operation on the Continent. In fact, in a public statement issued on 11 June, on the occasion of Molotov's visit to Washington, the president alluded to a second front in Europe in 1942.[11] But the idea of a substantial landing on the Continent in 1942 was soon killed by Churchill, and by mid-July, the two Allies finally agreed on joint operations in North Africa, with Roundup still a goal for 1943. There was a growing recognition among planners, however, that there would be no invasion of the Continent before 1944. For the time being, the only agreed-upon Anglo-American strategy for carrying the war to the European Continent was the concept of more frequent and large-scale raids.

In summary, the idea of raids was very much a part of the Anglo-American strategy formulated in 1942 and was the one facet of that strategy that was agreed upon throughout. There was a need to do something, in the face of continuing pressure from the Russians and from public opinion for a second European front, and a policy of raiding seemed the only alternative that both Britain and the United States could agree upon in 1942. The landing at Dieppe was one such raid, and while it hardly could be called a major operation, there were no other alternatives at the time.

Origins and Aims of the Dieppe Raid

The plan for a raid on Dieppe was conceived and developed on a level different from that of the Anglo-American debate over grand strategy which occurred in the spring and summer of 1942. While raids in general were a part of the strategic plan for the defeat of Germany, the Dieppe raid itself was not. It was strictly a British project and was initially conceived by Combined Operations Headquarters in early April 1942, before the Marshall Memorandum was presented to the British. The operation was approved by the British chiefs of staff on 13 May 1942 and was set for execution in late June or early July with a code name of Rutter. The initial attempt, on 4 July, was frustrated by bad weather and the operation was canceled. Subsequently revived, the landing was finally conducted on 19 August under the code name Jubilee.

There is little documentation of the higher aims which may have been responsible for initiation of the raid or for its later revival. For security reasons apparently, records were not retained, and no documentation recorded before the raid refers to any political aim and little refers to strategic aims.[12] Lord Mountbatten, in a letter of 11 May 1942 to the Chiefs of Staff Committee requesting approval for a raid on Dieppe, wrote: "Apart from the military objective given in the outline plan, this operation will be of great value as training for operation 'Sledgehammer' or any other major operation as far as the actual assault is concerned."[13] It was also hoped that a major air battle would result in which a substantial part of the German air forces would be engaged and destroyed— thereby alleviating, albeit indirectly, some of the pressure on the Russian front.

Other extremely important higher aims were not mentioned in the plans for Dieppe but were understood to be desired by-products of the raiding policy. There had not been an opposed amphibious landing by the British since Gallipoli in 1915, and the Americans had not conducted an opposed landing since the Civil War. Although there was no lack of modern doctrine, it had not been tested under fire. Problems associated with assaulting and seizing a port had to be explored; techniques for handling a sizable assault fleet had to be tested under actual conditions; new types of assault craft and equipment needed to be tested; and the strength of German defenses should be probed.[14] A summation of these military aims is reflected in General Brooke's conviction that the Dieppe operation was "indispensable to the Allied offensive programme."[15]

Although no political aims were recorded before the fact, there has been considerable speculation since that political considerations played a major role, if not in the conception of the raid, at least in pushing for the execution of Rutter and in the revival of the raid as Jubilee. Churchill's statements and actions concerning the raid, when considered in the broader context of wartime strategy, suggest that Churchill used the Dieppe raid to further his own political ends and to strengthen his position within the coalition.

As mentioned, the decisions resulting in the Dieppe raid were made when the military situation for the Allies was grave. The British and Americans had yet to reconcile their differences in strategy, and it appeared that, without a great deal of help from the West, the Russians might be knocked out of the war—either by defeat or through a separate deal with the Germans. The cry for a second front, repeatedly sounded by Stalin, was taken up in the press and on the streets of London. In his diary entry of 30 March 1942, General Brooke spoke of the "universal cry" to open a second front, stating that public pressure would be hard to contend with.[16] The pressure was to continue into the summer, and in such an atmosphere it would seem impossible to remain idle. Yet British planners were in the process of destroying any chance of action on the Continent that year as they fought the American plan for a landing in 1942.

Events, however, soon persuaded London that some direct action against Nazi-held territory in Europe had to be taken. While the prime minister was visiting Washington in June, attempting to sell a landing in North Africa and to discredit the notion of a lodgement on the Continent in 1942, he received news of the British surrender of Tobruk. This disaster resulted in considerable loss of British prestige in American eyes and reduced Churchill's influence at a time when he was vigorously lobbying for American support of his African project.[17] Furthermore, it left him in a precarious political position at home as he faced a vote of censure in the House of Commons on 26 June. Perhaps in the hope of achieving some sort of success on the battlefield which could shore up his political position with the Americans as well as with the British voters, Mr. Churchill asked General Mountbatten whether he could "guarantee the success of the operation planned on Dieppe."[18]

As further evidence of Churchill's now determined support for immediate raids on German-held territory as opposed to a larger Sledgehammer-type operation, a second Dieppe raid (Jubilee) was launched over the objections of some British officers. After the abortive Rutter operation, General Montgomery, who was then responsible for the army side of the operation as commander, South Eastern Army, considered the affair at an end and wrote to General Paget, commander-in-chief, Home Forces, that for security reasons the raid should be canceled "for all time."[19] He was not alone in that opinion. Troops had been briefed on the objective after embarkation and then released on leave after the operation was canceled. There was ample reason to believe that security had been compromised. Nevertheless, for considerations that are not well documented, the operation was revived. A number of reasons bore on that decision. First, Combined Operations Headquarters considered the failure to execute Rutter a reflection on its competence and pushed for revival. Also, Churchill was prodding the Chiefs of Staff Committee for action, and with his knowledge and concurrence the chiefs of staff approved Jubilee on 12 July.[20] It is significant that only four days before the prime minister stated in a message to President Roosevelt the absolute opposition of the British to Sledgehammer.[21] It must have been at least helpful to the prime minister and his chiefs of staff to have a large-scale raid on the books when Hopkins, Marshall, and King arrived a few days later. None of the decision makers ever suggested that Jubilee would replace Sledgehammer. Nevertheless, the raid may have provided some consolation to the Americans, and it may have served, to some degree, as a partial substitute for Sledgehammer.

The Operation

In addition to about thirty-five hundred naval personnel engaged on combat ships and landing craft, other participants in the Dieppe raid included approximately five thousand Canadian army personnel, twelve hundred British commandos, and sixty U.S. Rangers. Canadian troops made up the largest part of the landing force for several reasons, the paramount being that the Canadians had nothing else to do. Since early 1941 the Canadian prime minister had been insisting that Canadian troops be put into action in some theater of the war; Canadian defense officials suggested employment in the Middle East or on raids to France.[22] Elements of the 1st Canadian Army arrived in Britain in November of 1939, initially to join British forces in France, but after Dunkirk their primary mission was to assist in defending England against German invasion. By the spring of 1942 the Canadian 1st Army had been training for two and one half years without seeing action while forces from the United Kingdom and other parts of the empire fought in Africa and elsewhere. Recruiting and public opinion became problems at home, while morale and discipline became problems for the units in Britain.[23] Employment of Canadians in the Middle East was out of the question as far as Churchill was concerned. Commonwealth troops far outnumbered British troops in that area—a fact which was politically embarassing. The prime minister wrote to General Auchinleck, the Middle East commander, that: "For a long time I have dreaded troubles with the Australians and with world opinion, of appearing to wage all our battles in the Middle East with Dominion troops alone."[24]

The 1st Canadian Corps was under operational control of South Eastern Command, from which troops were to be selected for the raid. General Montgomery, commander, South Eastern Command, offered the mission to the Canadians because he wanted to avoid the problems of a mixed force and because he felt the Canadian troops were best suited for the task. General McNaughton, commanding the Canadian 1st Army, after consultation with his government, accepted the mission. At last the Canadians were going to fight.

The port of Dieppe was selected as a raid target mostly by a process of comparison with other possible objectives. Among those considered by Combined Operations Headquarters were Cherbourg, Caen, Le Havre, Fécamp, Boulogne, and Saint-Malo.[25] Of these, Cherbourg and Le Havre were too large for the size of operation envisaged, Caen and Saint-Malo were too far away for R.A.F. support, Boulogne was considered unapproachable because of its large coast defense batteries, and Fécamp was too small.

Dieppe had a lot to offer. In early 1942 it was generally agreed that when the time came to launch an invasion of Western Europe, a good port, in working order, would have to be seized immediately. Planners for Sledgehammer and Roundup took that approach. This raid would accordingly provide an opportunity to test theoretical doctrine for seizing a port. Dieppe was a good, average-sized port with rail and road connections and an airfield nearby. Additionally, it provided targets worthy to be named as specific objectives of the raid force. German defenses were thought to be strong enough to provide an adequate test but not too strong to be overcome. Finally, it was close enough to England for supporting aircraft to remain on station a reasonable length of time and for the passage of the raiding force to be made from ports in England to Dieppe almost entirely under the cover of darkness.[26]

Nevertheless, Dieppe had its disadvantages as well. The beach before Dieppe is overlooked by high cliffs on either side which provide strong defensive positions. Breaks in the cliffs on either side of the town are small and also well suited to defense. Moreover, German defenses were much better developed than was anticipated. Everything considered, however, Dieppe seemed a reasonable target for the forces assigned and was clearly superior to other possible objectives.

Initially there were two competing plans.

One proposed a flanking attack on Dieppe with troops, supported by tanks, landing at Quiberville as the main effort. That plan was attacked on the grounds that there would be too much delay in seizing Dieppe. Besides, the tanks would be required to cross two rivers, and their ability to accomplish this was doubtful. Furthermore, if the port were not seized quickly, it would not be taken intact and the raid would not be a satisfactory test. The final factor mitigating against the flank attack was the speed with which the Germans would be able to reinforce their defenses. A second plan, calling for a frontal attack across the beaches at Dieppe with tanks and infantry, was therefore adopted.[27]

Two other significant issues, and the decision on each, had a major impact on the operation. Up to the time Rutter was canceled, plans called for a drop of airborne troops, primarily to seize the commanding ground west of Dieppe beach. Since that part of the operation was dependent on the weather, it was eliminated for Jubilee—and the west headland was never taken. The other issue of major importance concerned the debate over the relative value of preliminary bombardment as opposed to surprise. Initially, Dieppe was to be heavily bombed on the night preceding the raid. That was canceled because it was felt by Air Vice Marshal Leigh Mallory, R.A.F. representative for the raid, that the bombing probably would not be very accurate and the element of surprise would be lost. The commanding general, 2nd Canadian Division, General Roberts, approved the cancellation of the bombing attack, but for other reasons. He felt the rubble produced would prevent his tanks from moving through the town of Dieppe. As it turned out, they were never able to enter the town. So the main attack was entirely frontal and without heavy bombardment.

The plan would have commando landings at 0450 at points 6 miles east and 6 miles west of the harbor to seize batteries of 5.9-inch coast defense guns. This phase of the operation was deemed essential because the heaviest guns on supporting destroyers were 4-inch. Also at 0450, Canadian battalions would land 1 mile east and 1 mile west of Dieppe at small beaches to seal off the town, capture the high ground overlooking it, and in the west, capture the airfield. Under cover of fighter attacks and naval bombardment by destroyers, the infantry battalions, supported by tanks, would commence the main attack over the Dieppe beaches at 0520.[28] It is interesting to note that while the aerial bombardment had been canceled to enhance the element of surprise, the timing of the landings was never changed to ensure surprise for the main assault. It was scheduled to take place a full thirty minutes after the initial commando landing—plenty of time for the Germans to come to a full alert.

Specific objectives of the raid were as follows:[29]

• Destroy enemy defenses in vicinity
• Destroy nearby airport
• Destroy radar and power stations, dock and rail facilities, and petrol dumps
• Remove invasion barges stored in Dieppe harbor
• Capture documents
• Capture prisoners.

In the early morning hours of 19 August 1942, a fleet composed of four destroyers, seven landing ship infantry (LSI), twenty-four landing craft tank, and one hundred minor craft approached the French coast carrying the Dieppe raiders.[30] As the leading elements moved toward the beaches, the craft carrying commandos destined for the east flank, landing accidentally, made contact with a small German convoy. A short engagement followed which resulted in confusion among the landing craft, and, although the Germans did not connect the engagement at sea with a landing, it served in varying degrees to alert German defenders along the coast.[31] Of the twenty-three landing craft carrying the commandos, only six reached shore. Five boat teams, immediately engaged in heavy fighting, never got off the beach, and all personnel were either killed or captured. The remaining boat team, landing somewhat apart from the others, managed to reach its objective— a coastal defense gun—and succeeded in preventing it from coming into action for over two hours. The team then withdrew across the beach with all hands. The left flank had

been partially successful, but at enormous cost.[32]

The commando landing on the west flank, with the mission of knocking out a coastal defense battery, was the most successful action of the day. The battery was captured and permanently put out of action, and the commandos reembarked by 0830. Casualties were in an acceptable range—twelve killed, thirteen captured, and twenty-one wounded. The Germans suffered thirty killed and thirty wounded with four captured by the British. The commandos had done their job.[33]

Both inner flank landings failed to accomplish their missions— to seize the headlands overlooking Dieppe and destroy the field battery located on each. On the east the landing at Puys was fifteen minutes late, a significant delay. If the landing had been made as scheduled, at 0450, it would have beaten a German alert, sounded along the coast, by eight minutes. In any event, the German defenders held the assault force on the beach. Poor communications, which were to plague the entire operation, prevented the situation from being reported, and the initial landing was reinforced, adding to the disaster. Of the five hundred plus men who landed at Puys, only sixty were to return unwounded. Nothing was accomplished.

The inner flank landing at Pourville met with some initial success. Although touchdown was thirty minutes late, there were few German defenders waiting, and the assault forces were able to move off the beaches. One battalion moved inland toward the airfield while another advanced on the headland overlooking Dieppe. Both were stopped short of their objectives, and German reinforcements pushed both units back toward the beach. Although plans called for both units to move into Dieppe, aided by tanks coming off the beaches, it became apparent early that they would have to be withdrawn over the Pourville beach. The decision was made at 0900 and evacuation commenced at 1100. Withdrawal was successful, although German fire produced heavy casualties, and the rear guard ultimately surrendered when further evacuation became impossible. Although the depth of penetration at Pourville was the greatest of the operation, its success was problematical in that no major objectives were attained. Canadian casualties included 160 killed.[34]

Scheduling compromised the element of surprise as far as the main landing at Dieppe was concerned. Commenced a full thirty minutes after the flank attacks, the main landing might have been successful if the earlier assaults had accomplished their missions, but as it was, the main attack had to face the undistracted German defenders supported only by fighter aircraft and fire from the 4-inch guns of four destroyers. Air and naval gunfire support went off as scheduled shortly before the landing commenced and bothered the Germans to the extent that the first landing craft were able to touch down without receiving much enemy fire. However, the bombardment lacked sufficient weight and caused the Germans little permanent damage.

The initial landing went off almost exactly on time with two battalions landing abreast. The first tanks, however, were ten to fifteen minutes late arriving, and the infantry was left with that interval between the lifting of the bombardment and the arrival of the tanks without any fire support other than organic weapons. During that interval the first momentum of the assault was lost, never again to be regained.

Between the seawall at the edge of the beach and the town of Dieppe proper is an open promenade, about 100 yards wide, broken only at that time by a casino on the western end. The Canadians were never able, in significant numbers, to penetrate flanking German fire aimed at the promenade and enter the town. Of the twenty-seven tanks that were ultimately landed, only about half crossed the seawall and operated on the promenade. None penetrated into the town because of concrete tank barriers in the streets.[35] The main attack stalled, the troops never could move beyond the beach and were subjected to the concentrated fire of the German defenders until the last man was finally evacuated about 1300. The main landing was a total disaster.

Consistently poor communications with the beaches prevented the naval commander, Captain Hughes-Hallett, and the Troop Commander, Canadian major general Roberts, from ever gaining a clear picture of what was happening. As a result, General Roberts, at one point, committed his reserve battalion to a situation that was already hopelessly lost. Nevertheless, by 0900 it was apparent that the raid had failed, and evacuation was started at 1100 under cover of smoke. At 1250 a destroyer closed the beach for a last look. There was nothing to be seen—the Dieppe raid was over.

Of the specific military objectives assigned the raiders, none were achieved other than the destruction of a coastal battery and the capture of a few prisoners. The cost was extremely high. Of approximately 5,000 Canadians engaged, about 3,300 were killed, wounded, or captured. Only 2,087 returned to England.[36] Additional casualties among commandos, U.S. Rangers, naval personnel, and R.A.F. personnel totaled about 1,200 in all categories.[37] Material losses included 27 tanks (100 percent of those landed), one destroyer, 33 landing craft, and 106 aircraft.[38] The Germans lost about 600 men, 48 aircraft, and one coast defense battery.[39]

Results from a Broad Perspective

Whatever political aims Churchill might have had in mind for the Dieppe raid, the results were few. In England it did quell the cry for a "Second Front Now" among those who wavered over whether an early invasion was possible. The magnitude and difficulty of continental landings were brought home by the events at Dieppe, but among the more fervent advocates of efforts at all costs to aid Russia, Dieppe had little lasting impact. A *London Times* editorial of 27 August 1942 commented that: "Neither the dress rehearsal of Dieppe nor the air offensive directed against the nerve centres of German industry can dispel the impression that the

British war effort is inadequate at a moment when Russia is facing her gravest crisis."[40]

In the face of continuing criticism, Churchill felt compelled to defend the Dieppe raid before the House of Commons on 8 September. In his statement he said that he had personally authorized the raid because he felt it was absolutely necessary to gain information essential to the success of full-scale operations in the future. While this may have been true, no such goal was ever clearly stated in the record before the raid.

If the Dieppe raid eased the American desire for an early invasion of northwest Europe, no one of prominence has said so. The extent of the casualty lists, however, may have made it easier for some American planners and decision makers to accept 1944 over 1943 as the year for the invasion of northwest Europe. If so, the raid, in sort of a negative way, may have eased British-American discord over the future conduct of the war. For Russia, however, the raid may have been a blow to its hopes for an early invasion. Nonetheless, Stalin's persistent demands for a second front continued unabated.

For the Canadians, the first significant bloodying of the Canadian army brought pride to the army and dismay at home. A report by censors of the attitudes expressed in letters written home by soldiers said that: "The morale of all appears very good. Regrets are not shown, but just enthusiasm, satisfaction and pride in achievement, and the Canadians' share in the raid. . . . "[41] The Canadian public, aware only of the losses, tended to blame its own military leadership, but the raid had no measurable impact on the degree of public support for the war.

As has been noted, the R.A.F. had hoped that the Dieppe raid would draw the Luftwaffe into a large battle in which the former would win a significant victory. If enough German aircraft could be destroyed, the Germans, under continuing pressure, would have to draw down their air strength on the Russian Front to replace their losses in the west, thereby easing the burden of the Red army. In terms of size, the battle was enormous.

The British assigned over fifty fighter squadrons to support the raid—more than was available to fight and win the Battle of Britain. Tactically, the effort was a success. The Luftwaffe was not to bother the assault force to any significant degree throughout the day, but strategically the R.A.F. was unable to destroy enough German planes to help the Russians. In his report to the House of Commons on 8 September, Churchill said that the air battle was extremely satisfactory and Fighter Command wished that one like it could be repeated every week.[42] That statement, however, was based on overly optimistic reports that at least 135 German aircraft had been destroyed at a cost of 106 British. More realistic figures disclosed after the war reduced German losses at Dieppe to only 48 aircraft.[43] The British lost twice as many as they destroyed—hardly a successful battle of attrition. The Dieppe raid marked the end of the attempt by the R.A.F. to draw off German air power from the Russian front by that method.

There was an unexpected and long-term strategic advantage gained from the Dieppe raid, one that none of its instigators even considered. Hitler was greatly impressed by the Dieppe raid and referred to it on several occasions as a model that should be used in the development of the Atlantic defenses.[44] Even though it was known positively by the German high command that the Dieppe affair was only intended as a raid of less than a day, Hitler had apparently convinced himself that an actual invasion attempt had been repulsed.[45] From the raid on Dieppe, and the earlier raid on St. Nazaire, Hitler concluded that the eventual Allied invasion attempt would be launched initially against a major port and directed that ports receive a high priority in the construction of defenses and that the lowest priority be assigned to open beaches.[46] The Allies had drawn the opposite conclusion from Dieppe, that it was impractical to open an invasion by initially assaulting a major port.[47]

Although not responsible for its conception, Dieppe also strengthened Hitler's conviction that a string of concrete and steel along the coast of France—the Atlantic Wall—was the best way to defend against invasion and that an invasion could best be stopped on or near beaches. The concept was reflected in the kind of defense the Allies met in Normandy in 1944.

On the day after the raid, Lord Mountbatten, at a meeting of the War Cabinet, stressed in his report the value of the lessons learned at Dieppe and the impact they would have in planning for the invasion of Europe. The lessons were those of tactics, technique, and technology, and while some were simply old lessons learned anew, they focused attention on the many current shortcomings in those areas.

Within a short time after the raid, Combined Operations Headquarters published an extensive report, devoting a great deal of space to lessons learned. According to that report, one of the most important lessons was the "need for overwhelming fire support, including close support, during the initial stages of the attack."[48] Reliance on surprise, to the detriment of fire support, was a mistake. Medium and heavy naval bombardment, as well as continuous air support, was considered essential. Additionally, the development of special close-support naval craft was recommended. Heavy air bombardment, the presence of a capital ship, and close and continuous fire as the troops approached the beaches might have made the difference at Dieppe. The most important lesson, from a strictly naval point of view, the report pointed out, was "the necessity for the formation of permanent naval assault forces with a coherence comparable to that of any other first line fighting formations."[49] Amphibious operations are complex and successful execution requires precise teamwork and constant practice.

Several other requirements were listed, including specially designed tanks to penetrate beach defenses, better protection for demolitions teams employed to destroy emplacements, the need for highly trained beach parties to maintain organization on the beaches,

more reliable ship-to-shore communications, and, to that end, specially designed and equipped command ships.[50]

After Dieppe, Allied planners consistently favored intensive bombardment over reliance on surprise. Similarly, the tactic of seizing a port in the initial assault by frontal attack received little further consideration. The cost of the Dieppe raid had been too high. Thus, earlier planning was significantly revised in light of Dieppe.

The recommendations of the Combined Operations Headquarters moved the British Admiralty to organize a special naval assault force called Force J. In existence through the end of the war, it was used to develop and perfect naval techniques for amphibious assault and as a training vehicle for Allied troops. One product of Force J was the *Force J Fighting Instructions* which promulgated recommended naval techniques for the management of an amphibious assault. It was used not only by the Channel Assault Force, which later invaded France, but also by American Amphibious Forces in the Pacific.[51] Force J was organized and commanded by the former naval commander for the Dieppe raid, Captain Hughes-Hallett.

The lessons of the Dieppe raid must have influenced tactical doctrines for a number of future landings. That they did so for the 1944 Normandy landings there can be no doubt. The official history of the U.S. Army in World War Two makes several references to the Combined Operations report on the Dieppe raid as influencing specific decisions. As an example, the report's conclusion that overwhelming fire support was imperative led to significant additions of naval gunfire support for Overlord as planning progressed.[52]

The recommendations of Combined Operations Headquarters produced ultimately a number of technical innovations that were to prove useful in future landings. Landing craft, already developed to the form in which they were used throughout the remainder of the war, were given armament capable of providing effective close-fire support. Landing craft tanks (LCT) were converted to bombardment vessels by the addition of 4.7-inch guns (LCG), others were made into rocket-firing vessels (LCTR) through the addition of eight hundred to one thousand one hundred 5-inch rocket launchers. These and other similar craft were successfully used in Sicily, Italy, and Normandy.

Specialized tanks, much in evidence at Normandy, resulted from the experience gained at Dieppe under the supervision of Combined Operations Headquarters. At Dieppe the tanks, as well as the engineers whose mission it was to clear the way for them, operated separately and unsuccessfully. By the time of Normandy, innovation had brought the two functions together. Examples included tanks designed especially to scale seawalls, flail tanks used for mine clearing, armored engineer vehicles, tanks designed to carry and place demolitions on concrete fortifications and obstacles, amphibious tanks, and tanks that acted as ramps for other tanks.[53] The list of ideas that were adopted could go on, but the point is simply that the Dieppe raid had lifted the consideration of an invasion of northwest Europe from the theoretical to the practical. The value of negative learning is clear.

Viewed as a model for the future full-scale invasion of Europe, the results of the Dieppe operation were throughly analyzed, widely published, and acted upon. On 10 June 1944, the three American chiefs of staff visited Normandy in company with Churchill, General Brooke, and General Smuts. During their return to London, General Marshall composed the following message to Admiral Mountbatten (by then supreme allied commander, South East Asia) which, at Marshall's suggestion, was sent over the signature of each member of the party.

> Today we visited the British and American armies on the sod of France. We sailed through vast fleets of ships, with landing-craft of many types pouring more and more men, vehicles, and stores ashore. We saw clearly the manoeuvre in process of rapid development. We have shared our secrets in common and helped each other all we could. We wish to tell you at this moment in your arduous campaign that we realize that much of this remarkable technique, and therefore the success of the venture, has its origin in developments effected by you and your staff of Combined Operations
>
> S/Arnold, Brooke, Churchill,
> King, Marshall, Smuts[54]

The raid on Dieppe was the primary source from which the achievements of Combined Operations stemmed.

Looked at from the political and strategic sides, the raid made little sense. Whether it was really conceived in response to the demands of either politics or strategy, or both, remains unclear because no one responsible for Dieppe ever said that the raid was a product of those considerations. If, in the mind of Churchill, it was aimed at calming public clamor for a second front, it seems that the landings in North Africa would have served as well. If he thought it might help his relationship with the Americans, he had no need to do so, for they had already accepted a landing in North Africa. As far as the raid's possible influence on Russian demands, in retrospect, it would appear unlikely that such a relatively small operation of a day's duration could have been conceived by such a man as Churchill as having any impact whatsoever on the Russian front.

If the raid at Dieppe was of dubious political and strategic value, were the losses at Dieppe worth the information the raid produced? Certainly there was a price that had to be paid sometime for that knowledge, and most of the chroniclers of Dieppe have stated positively that the raid was necessary in terms of lessons learned. Perhaps they were moved to do so, at least partially, out of respect for the sacrifices made. Perhaps they are right, but it is a subjective issue that defies proof. How many lives were saved at Normandy as a result of the lessons learned at Dieppe? It is impossible to say. There were many landings in World War Two, and each contributed to the general store of expertise. But in 1942, future landings and their results could not be anticipated. Eventually the Allies would have to land on the Continent, and practical knowledge of how to do so was significantly lacking. If the price had not been paid at Dieppe, a much higher price might have been paid in Italy, for example, to learn the same lessons. The raid on Dieppe was not necessary to the successful prosecution of the war, but it made a valuable contribution. Whether, on balance, more lives were saved later than were lost on the beaches of Dieppe—the only true test of whether the raid was worth the cost—can never really be known. One can only hope that Churchill was right when, speaking of the Dieppe casualties, he said: "Honor to the brave who fell. Their sacrifice was not in vain."[55]

Notes

[1] Winston S. Churchill, *The Hinge of Fate* (Boston: Houghton Mifflin, 1950), p. 511.

[2] Bernard Fergusson, *The Watery Maze, the Story of Combined Operations* (New York: Holt, Rinehart, and Winston, 1961), p. 89.

[3] Terence Robertson, *Dieppe: The Shame and the Glory* (Boston: Little, Brown, 1963), p. 19.

[4] L. F. Ellis, *Victory in the West* (H. M. Stationery Office, 1962), p. 11.

[5] Churchill, *The Hinge of Fate*, p. 887.

[6] Trumbull Higgins, *Winston Churchill and the Second Front* (New York: Oxford University Press, 1957), p. 62.

[7] Gordon A. Harrison, *United States Army in World War II*, vol. 3, part 2, *Cross Channel Attack* (Washington, D.C.: Department of the Army, 1957), p. 16.

[8] Charles P. Stacey, *Official History of the Canadian Army in the Second World War*, vol. 6, *Six Years of War, the Army in Canada, Britain, and the Pacific* (Ottawa: Clautier, 1955), p. 313 (hereinafter *Canadian Army History*).

[9] Churchill, *The Hinge of Fate*, p. 321.

[10] Stacey, *Canadian Army History*, p. 314.

[11] Herbert Feis, *Churchill, Roosevelt, Stalin, the War They Waged and the Places They Fought* (Princeton: Princeton University Press, 1967), p. 69.

[12] Stacey, *Canadian Army History*, p. 326.

[13] Quoted in Ibid.

[14] Christopher Buckley, *Norway, the Commandos Dieppe* (London: H. M. Stationery Office, 1951), p. 230.

[15] Stacey, *Canadian Army History*, p. 337.

[16] Arthur Bryant, *The Turn of the Tide* (London: Collins, 1957), p. 371.

[17] Higgins, *Winston Churchill and the Second Front*, p. 131.

[18] Jacques Mordal, *Dieppe: The Dawn of Decision* (London: Souvenir Press, 1963), p. 68.

[19] Bernard L. Montgomery, *Memoirs* (Cleveland: World, 1958), p. 69.

[20] Robertson, *Dieppe*, p. 134.

[21] Churchill, *The Hinge of Fate*, p. 434.

[22] Robertson, *Dieppe*, p. 17.

[23] Mordal, *Dieppe*, p. 99.

[24] Quoted in Ibid.

[25] Mordal, *Dieppe*, p. 92.

[26] Fergusson, *The Watery Maze*, p. 169.

[27] Eric Maguire, *Dieppe, August 19* (London: Cape, 1963), p. 47.

[28] Fergusson, *The Watery Maze*, p. 174.

[29] Stacey, *Canadian Army History*, p. 330.

[30] L. E. H. Maund, *Assault from the Sea* (London: Methuen, 1949), p. 114.

[31] Stacey, *Canadian Army History*, p. 359.

[32] Mordal, *Dieppe*, pp. 175–84.

[33] Fergusson, *The Watery Maze*, p. 176.

[34] Mordal, *Dieppe*, pp. 191–98.

[35] Fergusson, *The Watery Maze*, p. 171.

[36] Stacey, *Canadian Army History*, p. 389.

[37] Robertson, *Dieppe*, p. 386.

[38] Fergusson, *The Watery Maze*, p. 381.

[39] Robertson, *Dieppe*, p. 388.

[40] Quoted in Mordal, *Dieppe*, p. 256.

[41] Quoted in Stacey, *Canadian Army History*, p. 395.

[42] Robertson, *Dieppe*, p. 389.

[43] Bryant, *The Turn of the Tide*, p. 488.

[44] Hans A. Jacobsen, *Decisive Battles of World War Two—the German View* (New York: Putnam, 1965), p. 228.

[45] Harrison, *United States Army in World War II*, p. 137.

[46] Higgins, *Winston Churchill and the Second Front*, p. 167.

[47] Ibid., p. 166.

[48] Stacey, *Canadian Army History*, p. 399.

[49] Ibid., p. 400.

[50] Fergusson, *The Watery Maze*, p. 182.

[51] Ibid., pp. 184–85.

[52] Harrison, *United States Army in World War II*, p. 193.

[53] Bryant, *The Turn of the Tide*, p. 657.

[54] Winston S. Churchill, *Triumph and Tragedy* (Boston: Houghton Mifflin, 1953), pp. 13–14.

[55] Churchill, *The Hinge of Fate*, p. 511.

The Development of Naval Gunfire Support in World War Two

BY MAJOR GENERAL DONALD M. WELLER, USMC (RET.)

In the summer of 1945 the bloody, grinding struggle for Iwo Jima was nearing its end. Throughout this campaign the marines of the V Amphibious Corps, under generals Smith and Schmidt, had been pitted against the wily commander, Lieutenant General Kuribayashi. With the inevitable end not far off, General Kuribayashi, from his underground command post in the north of the tiny island, broadcast to Tokyo his observations on American tactics and techniques:

> However firm and stout pillboxes you may build at the beach, they will be destroyed by bombardment of main armament of the battleships. Power of the American warships and aircraft makes every landing operation possible to whatever beachhead they like.

Well might the general have made such comments. For over three weeks the tiny island had been surrounded by battleships, cruisers, destroyers, and gunboats, all pouring projectiles into his defenses day and night.

The defenses of Iwo Jima were the most elaborate encountered in the Pacific campaign. The Japanese had literally disappeared from the surface of the earth, their molelike tunneling accelerated by the threat of impending amphibious assault. Blockhouses, with 5-foot walls of reinforced concrete were cleverly emplaced in the volcanic slopes bordering the landing beaches, their apertures flanking the advance of an attacker. Nearly

U.S. Naval Institute *Proceedings,* "Salvo-Splash: The Development of Naval Gunfire Support in World War Two," 80 (August 1954): 839-49; and 80 (September 1954): 1011-21. Reprinted by permission.

one hundred pillboxes, mounting a single weapon, supplemented the blockhouses while seventeen coast defense guns commanded the approaches to the main landing beach. These guns were located in concrete casemates with deep underground magazines and living spaces, resembling a ship's battery in their emplacement and protection. So well were they concealed that only four of these coastal guns had been detected by the photo interpreters.

Nor were the defenses limited to the landing beaches. The island had been divided into a series of defensive positions anchored by blockhouses and other emplacements. Wide fields of fire for artillery, mortars, and rocket launchers were sacrificed in order to provide better protection. The island bristled with antiaircraft ranging from 25 mm to 5.6 inch. Even dual-purpose naval mounts were emplaced. Many defenses were connected by tunnels through the soft sandstone, while a complete system of connecting tunnels circled the base of Mount Suribachi.

The conduct of the defense prohibited the use of the abortive banzai attack (a reckless mass attack), for the Japanese commanders had learned of the failure of these tactics; only small squads were authorized to leave their defenses for suicide attacks against tanks. All Japanese were enjoined to fight from their protected positions to the end and to take ten Americans with them before that end came. Kuribayashi had planned well.

Yet it had been to no avail, unless the twenty thousand marine casualties were reward enough. Kuribayashi had stood help-

Naval gunfire support from the *Nevada*, English Channel, 1944.

lessly by while his antiaircraft batteries were eliminated and while the main batteries of the *Nevada*, *New York*, *Tennessee*, and *California*, from point-blank range, pounded his coast defense into rubble and twisted steel. The blockhouses hidden in the slopes of the beaches were sought out by pointer fire, stripped of their protective camouflage, and blasted apart by the power of the high-capacity projectiles.

If Kuribayashi held any hope during preliminary operations, it must have vanished on D-day when assault elements of two marine divisions landed, supported by ships and aircraft of the fleet. Thousands of rounds had poured onto the beaches and the commanding ground. Even after the troops had landed, the pounding continued. The bombs passed close over the heads of the troops and broke a few hundred yards to their front. Kuribayashi's commanders were hampered at night by their inability to realign their forces, bring up supplies, or even get out orders (all surface telephone lines had long since been blown out) because of the heavy night shellfire de-

livered from the support ships and mortar craft.

While the assault on Iwo Jima was reaching its height, the Japanese on Okinawa were bracing themselves for attack. But the lessons of previous abortive Central Pacific defenses were taken into account. Here the defense was deliberately planned to reduce the efficacy of the American firepower, particularly the naval gun and aircraft.

The commanding general of Okinawa set forth the defense philosophy on 8 March 1945:

The time of opening fire will naturally vary somewhat according to the type of weapons, strength of positions, duties, etc. However, generally speaking, we must make it our basic principle to allow the enemy to land in full. Until he penetrates our positions and loses his freedom of movement inside our most effective system of firepower, and until he can be lured into a position where he cannot receive cover and support from naval gunfire and aerial bombardment, we must patiently and prudently hold our fire. Then, leaping into action, we shall destroy the enemy.

This dramatic reversal of tactics was verified in the assault on Okinawa. When the army and marines of the Tenth Corps went over the Okinawa beaches on 1 April, they were unopposed; it was not until the troops wheeled south that the Japanese exposed their weapons and defenses anchored on the ancient Shuri castle. This new tactic ultimately failed, but the defense was effective enough to prolong the campaign and the full fury of the kamikazi attack was brought to bear on the fleet in a sort of naval banzai. Ashore, the defenders extracted a bloody price. Our own troops crowded the enemy defenses so closely that the naval guns and aircraft could not be used systematically for fear of causing casualties among our own people.

Had such a theory of effectiveness of the naval gun been advanced between World War One and Two, the prophet would have been laughed out of the wardroom and, on the surface, such a conclusion seemed justified by the meager record. The Gallipoli affair appeared to indicate that the naval gunfire support for that operation had failed miserably.

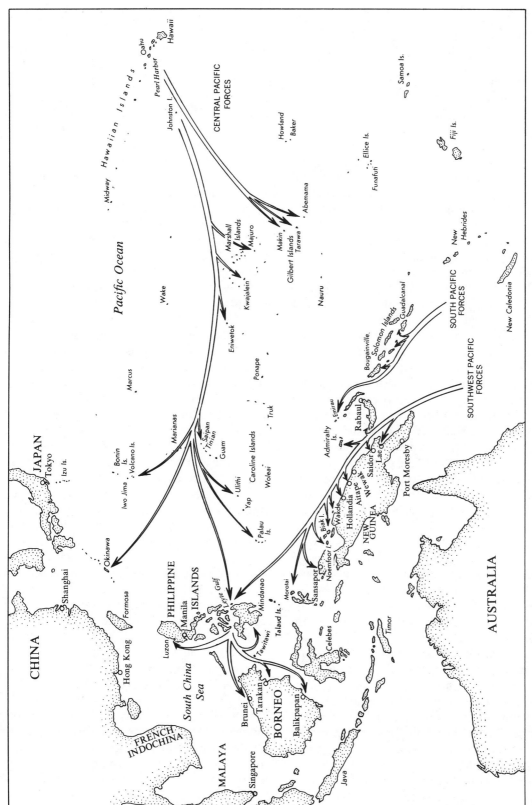

The U.S. amphibious drive across the Pacific in World War Two.

But the popular analyses of Churchill's gambit failed to note that the gunfire delivered on the Turk defenses commanding the main landing beaches of Gallipoli actually drove the defenders to cover; the failure came in not closely integrating this fire with the movement of the pulling boats to the beaches and the debarkation of troops from the collier *River Clyde* which had been grounded close inshore. The fire lifted too soon; the Turks shook off the effects of the bombardment and coolly shot down the Tommies of the 29th Division with a will. (It should be noted that this failure to closely integrate fires with the ship-to-shore movement was to be repeated again in World War Two at Tarawa and Omaha beach.)

The review of the Gallipoli campaign also failed to recognize the contributions made by the guns of the Royal Navy after the landing had been made good. They were responsible in large part for the failure of every Turk attack delivered to drive the British and Anzacs out of their shallow toeholds on the Gallipoli Peninsula; counterattack after counterattack was broken up, chiefly by naval guns. Their climaxing contribution was their support of the daylight withdrawal from the southern beaches of the peninsula. In spite of the most active efforts of the Turks to counterattack and destroy the British force, the fire of the fleet's guns broke up the attack before it could get started, and the losses in the evacuation of the strategic peninsula were limited. But the popular view was that naval gunfire should be tarred with the unsuccessful brush, and the contribution of the big guns passed unnoticed.

After the Gallipoli failure it is quite unlikely that much attention would have been given to amphibious operations in general and naval gunfire in particular had it not been for the growing power of the Japanese Empire; this power drew increasing attention to the problem of countering the threat in the Pacific. Since it was obvious that naval action against the Japanese would require bases from which to project naval operations, it was natural that Marine Corps thinking would reach the conclusion that an important role

would be the seizure and defense of such advance naval bases as would be necessary for such operations. As early as 1923 Major General John A. Lejeune, commandant of the Marine Corps, stated: "The maintenance of an expeditionary force so that it will be in instant readiness to support the fleet, I deem to be the most important duty of the Marine Corps." Further impetus was given to this role by the recognition in joint action, army and navy, that the Marine Corps would be given special preparation in the conduct of landing operations. Although several landing exercises were conducted in the 1920s, no actual naval gunfire exercises were carried out, and little if any progress was made in the employment of the naval gun.

Nevertheless the recognition of the role of the Marine Corps led directly to the organization of the Fleet Marine Force (FMF) in late 1933 with an amphibious mission and, equally important, revision of Marine Corps schools curriculum to include instruction in the seizing of advance naval bases. Out of the school mission came the *Tentative Manual for Landing Operations*, prepared by the instructors of the Marine Corps schools, including the naval officers of the naval section. This manual contained a chapter on naval gunfire support. Thus, theory in the form of a doctrine was developed, while the newly organized FMF was available, together with elements of the fleet, to test the doctrines and techniques evolved in the schools.

Finally, an increased impetus was given to this developmental process by the strides in naval ordnance and gunnery. The threat of hostile aircraft had turned the attention of the Bureau of Ordnance to the design and production of the 5-inch 25 and later the 5-inch 38 antiaircraft gun. This was a most important development in terms of shore bombardment. For the first time there existed a naval gun that fired a projectile with thin walls and a relatively heavy bursting charge and had a combination time and quick-acting percussion fuse. Its explosion in the air or on the surface of the ground released a large number of lethal fragments. Until this combination came along, the only projectile with thin walls and a large bursting radius was the old flatnose, a relic of World War One antisubmarine warfare, and its exterior ballistics left much to be desired. The armor-piercing and common projectiles in the hands of the fleet were not suitable for bombardment. Thick-skinned with fuses designed for the penetration of armor and plates, they dug themselves into the ground when fired against a shore target and then blew, sending a lot of dirt into the air—not too effective.

The trajectory of the new gun was relatively curved as compared with the previous main and broadside batteries, thus permitting firing to penetrate into draws and ravines. The modern rangekeeper coupled with the stabilization of the 5-inch battery rounded out the picture, making indirect fire a practical capability in gunfire support. The 5-inch antiaircraft gun and shell would prove to be the workhorse of fire support during World War Two.

The theory of amphibious operations worked out in the *Tentative Manual* was soon put to practice. A series of fleet landing exercises commenced in 1935, using the little island of Culebra in the Caribbean as the target. Mosquito and Flamingo Bays became familiar to marines and sailors of the scouting forces as the landing force made the run into the beaches in motor launches and whaleboats. In those days, stern anchors were required to hold the blunt sterns of the motor launches to the surf—and more than one young ensign miscalculated the drop point and found himself and his boatload of marines at the end of his tether before the boat had beached; many a zealous marine lieutenant cried "follow me" as he went over the side, only to disappear in a deep spot.

These annual exercises always included gunfire support directed at the rocky terrain of Northwest Peninsula. In those early days it was not uncommon to see admirals and captains clad in white critically examining shell craters produced by the guns of their ships. Unfortunately, most of the firing at Culebra was done with the second team; the old *Arkansas* and *Wyoming* along with *Texas* and *New York*, the cruisers were usually represented by *Omaha* and *Memphis*, and the 1200-tonners did the job in the destroyer class. While the spirit of the gunnery people was high, the obsolete fire-control gear along with the limited range at Culebra circumscribed the practices to direct fire, or indirect fire using an offset aiming point. (No one ever dreamed that direct fire would play a leading role after Tarawa and that the old pointer fire would be back in vogue for pinpoint destruction.)

In the Pacific where the modern ships and the excellent range at Pyramid Cove could have gone a long way in developing shore bombardment know-how, the fleet was preoccupied with surface and antiaircraft gunnery and could spare little time for firing at shore targets. No prophet had arisen to predict the success of the Japanese swoop across the Pacific, and surface action was the principal interest.

Nevertheless, important results in the gunfire support field were realized, some positive and some negative. The inadequacy of the armor-piercing projectile was proved and reproved; this was to lead to the development of the high-capacity shell. The use of air spotters for directing fire on deep targets masked from seaward was shown to be entirely practicable. Sustained bombardment of simulated beach defenses with reasonable safety for attacking troops was demonstrated. Finally, the shore fire control party came in for searching scrutiny from which was derived the basis for its future organization. In those naive days these parties were made up of young and "available" naval officers whose knowledge of the landing force was limited to "extended order" drills on Lawrence Field. These places were reinforced by members of the "radio gang," usually led by a salty chief, whose demeanor indicated extreme displeasure with the whole affair. These parties were particularly welcome to the marines at the observation post, for they were usually buttressed for the ordeal with ample chow.

The somewhat leisurely annual cycle of gunnery exercises at Culebra came to an abrupt end with the appointment of Admiral

Ernest J. King as the new commander of the Atlantic Naval Forces. Teamed with General Holland M. Smith, the commanding general of the 1st Marine Brigade, the two made a potent pair. This fortuitous combination of personalities, although initially striking sparks, soon settled down to a relationship of mutual respect; it may well be that the backing the Fleet Marine Force received in the Central Pacific from the Chief of Naval Operations (CNO) and Commander in Chief, U.S. Fleet (CINCUS) grew out of this relationship.

In any case, gunfire support was caught up along with all the other facets of the amphibious business in a whirlwind of activity. The possibility of landings led to gunfire support, and these plans focused attention on the many unsolved problems in this field. The stage was set for significant progress.

The first and most obvious step to be taken as the result of a half decade of experimentation was the reorganization of the shore fire control party. This little organization was the key to providing gunfire support to the assault troops, before organic weapons of the landing force could be beached and assume their normal role. The shore fire control party (the link between the troops and the firing ship) had to land with the assault, set up their bulky TBX radio equipment, establish radio contact with the firing ship, locate the source of enemy fire interfering with the advance, and spot the fire to the target. This chore had to be accomplished while under fire and in the confusion of the initial attack of a defended beach, so it is not too difficult to visualize their problems.

The practice of furnishing this party from the supporting cruiser or destroyer broke down because of several factors. In the first place, it was much too difficult to place the party with the battalion it was to support. Such transfers had to be largely accomplished in darkness before D-day, and the difficulty of boating the party and finding proper transport under these conditions is obvious. Even if such a transfer could be accomplished, it did not provide sufficient time for the shore fire control party to become acquainted with

the personnel to be supported or their scheme of attack ashore. Finally, maneuvers at Culebra had shown that knowledge of the gunnery capabilities of his ship was not enough; the officer had to know more than the rudiments of the organization, tactics, and techniques of this battalion of riflemen, if he was to fulfill his supporting role. In short, these young officers had to be grounded in both camps, and the duties of a young ensign aboard a combatant ship gave little opportunity for such an education.

When General Smith presented this problem to Admiral King, the admiral recognized the validity of the arguments and gave his approval to the solution proposed—the forming of a "joint task force" at the lowest level. This party consisted of one naval officer, to be drawn from a pool provided for the purpose, and an artillery officer assigned from the artillery organization of the division committed to landing operations; necessary radio personnel and equipment was to come from the artillery. This basic organization, while not wholly satisfactory, was a step in the right direction and served through Tarawa.

As a result, twelve ensigns had their education in the armed guard school abruptly terminated and instead found themselves undergoing instruction at a naval gunfire liaison officer's course at Parris Island. These young men were the vanguard of the naval gunfire liaison officers. They became known throughout the Pacific by their radio call "Oboe." Teamed with their spotter and radio crews, they shared the dangers of D-day with the marines and army they supported. Their voices were heard over radio nets positioning the ship for a more favorable line of fire, obtaining ammunition reports, and when the spotter became a casualty, moving forward and taking over the duties of spotting fire on targets. On occasion they took charge of assault elements that had lost their leaders. Except for the admiration of the Combat Information Center personnel who heard their voices, they got precious little recognition other than the satisfaction of a job well done, but they made gunfire support a reality.

In the school conducted by the gunfire personnel of General Smith's staff, the artillery officers and radio operators joined the naval gunfire liaison officers. Subjects ranged from the capabilities of the naval ordnance installations to tactics of the rifle battalion. Field artillery was used to simulate naval guns in spotting practice. Radio drills in procedure were held. Even the aviators of battleships and cruisers in the Atlantic were caught up in the increased gunfire activity and instruction. They, like the gunfire liaison officers, needed to learn something of the ground tactics of friend and foe in order to be able to recognize a significant target from the air. Aircraft such as the SOC and OS2U operated from fields in Quantico and Fort Bragg as the pilots learned how to spot targets and adjust fire over rolling terrain—later these same aviators were to handle ship's fire in the North Africa, Sicily, and Salerno operations. When the submarine menace prevented the use of the Culebra range, the Fleet Marine Force proposed the use of Bloodsworth Island in the Chesapeake and this mud flat was the scene of shore bombardment exercises in preparation for the assault on North Africa.

The formation of the Amphibious Forces in the Atlantic Fleet, under Admiral Hewitt, with an organic gunnery staff, created a naval agency to take over the naval gunfire training functions of General Holland M. Smith's Fleet Marine Headquarters. The trained naval gunfire liaison officers, maintained as a pool in General Smith's headquarters, were transferred to Admiral Hewitt. Shortly thereafter General Smith moved his headquarters to the West Coast, where in concert with Admiral Rockwell of the Pacific Amphibious Forces, he resumed his amphibious training functions, including those involving naval gunfire.

The War Begins

Admiral Hewitt's first combat assignment was to land General Patton's forces in North Africa, while on the opposite side of the globe Admiral Ghormley had been directd to seize a toehold in the Eastern Solomons, utilizing Admiral Turner's amphibious ships and General Vandegrift's marines of the 1st Division.

Naturally gunfire support would have to be used in both of these landings. The planners were guided by three considerations. The first consideration was the possibility of fleet surface action, which required that a considerable percentage of ammunition be retained to meet it. Thus the amount of ammunition that could be used for gunfire support was limited. Moreover, the preponderance of any ammunition carried aboard combatant ships must be that type best suited for attacking other ships, that is, armor piercing, which, with its low capacity, is not well suited to bombardment tasks.

The second consideration was the assumed vulnerability of combatant ships to air and submarine attack. This would dictate minimum exposure of fire support ships at the objective and would in turn limit the duration of gunfire support to the absolute minimum necessary to establish the troops ashore.

The third was one originally expressed by Lord Nelson, in his phrase: "A ship's a fool to fight a fort." In concrete terms, this meant that a ship could not expect to engage or destroy a coast defense battery without risk of being sunk or seriously damaged. Confronted with this risk, fire support ships must confine themselves to delivering fires from long ranges offshore, while steaming at high speed and maneuvering radically—all of which combined to reduce the accuracy and ability of gunfire to pinpoint important targets.

These considerations, constituting the prevailing concepts of naval gunfire support as World War Two began, added up to this: bombardment of very short duration, delivered by ships firing relatively limited allowances of ammunition often not well suited to the purpose, from long ranges while maneuvering at high speeds. Obviously, the best that could be hoped for as a result would be area neutralization of enemy defenses during troop debarkation and the ship-to-shore movement, followed by a limited amount of support on call.

Even if this concept was accepted by planners, it should be remembered that the experience gained in training had given only partial answers. Up to this time no firing had been delivered over the heads of troops as would be required in order to support operations. Many marines were frankly skeptical, fearing casualties from our own gunfire—others doubted (and continued to doubt until after the Marshalls) that gunfire would take out the beach defenses; nor was the "show me" attitude limited to the troops. Many navy officers were not in sympathy with the mission of supporting troops—after all, ships were built for combat at sea against other ships. But when circumstances required action, there was nothing to do but go ahead, basing required action on the theoretical and practical considerations then known, with the hope that it would all turn out well.

While the attack on Guadalcanal was unopposed at the beaches, nevertheless the ship's gunfire was integrated with the ship-to-shore movement and was fired over the heads of troops in the landing craft for the first time. Shore fire control parties got in some work delivering fire in support of operations at Tulagi.

In the North African operations counterbattery was the major contribution of the supporting ships. *Brooklyn* smothered a four-gun battery of 138.7s while *Savannah* fought it out at Port Lyautey with a battery of the same caliber. Destroyers *Wilkes* and *Bristol* got in the act by knocking out the fire control of a 100 mm battery commanding the approaches to the beach. *Philadelphia* located and fired on a battery of 155 mm field artillery; but the air spotter in his OS2U became impatient with the lack of hits so he went after the battery with depth charges. That did it. *Texas* headed off motorized reserves with her main battery. A young naval gunfire liaison officer earned a name for himself by leading an army unit that had lost its leader in an attack on the Kasbah fort.

The employment of naval gunfire in these two diverse landings was significant. These operations demonstrated the potential of naval gunfire not only to the participants but to navy, marine, and army personnel who would later use it. Thus the effect of the gunfire was of an importance far outweighing the battle result. Had the gunfire caused even a few casualties among our own troops, the employment of naval gunfire in future operations would have suffered immeasurably. It was most fortunate that results were favorable.

As the bitter struggle for Guadalcanal continued, the use of gunfire to extend the attack against the Japanese beyond the range of field artillery came into play. Destroyers which had escorted resupply shipping to Guadalcanal were pressed into service to attack the Japanese troop movements along the coast as well as their supply installations and bivouacs. In the final attack to clear the island, the shore fire control parties teamed with destroyers to shoot up the draws and ravines not open to attack by the weapons of the troops ashore. This contribution was significant.

Tarawa—The Turning Point

Subsequent amphibious operations in the South Pacific were made against light opposition at the beaches—consequently the concept of gunfire support calling for a short intense bombardment for neutralization presumably filled the bill.

But Tarawa was different. Here for the first time, the amphibious operation took on all the features of an assault. This first target in the Central Pacific was a tiny island two and a quarter miles long, by a half mile wide, with a typical fringing coral reef. On this spot of land were about forty-eight hundred Japanese, with the core a naval "Special Landing Force" of Imperial Marines all commanded by Admiral Shibasaki, who boasted that it would take a million Americans one hundred years to capture Tarawa.

The defenses were indeed formidable; Shibasaki had about two hundred coast defense, antiaircraft, antiboat guns and machine guns, and except for the big coast defense guns, all could be used against a landing. The fourteen coast defense guns, including four Vickers 8-inch captured at Singapore supplemented by four twin-mount 4.7s, gave the Japanese a significant antiship capability. All the defenses were so integrated that the attacker would have to subject himself to a heavy crossfire. The marines of the 2nd Division would have to come in organized and ready for immediate combat. To get men ashore where they could fight was the task of the gunfire and aircraft.

Thus the naval gunfire planners were faced with a most difficult problem—a problem so far without precedent. The coast defense organization posed a serious threat to the transports and light-skinned combatant ships, while the lighter weapons could raise havoc with the landing craft, amphibious tractors, and boats carrying the assault waves. Preliminary operations by ship's gunfire, if considered at all, were ruled out since Japanese surface, submarine, and air units based in, or operating from, the Marshalls had the capability of striking our forces in the Gilberts three days after discovery.

The experience of North Africa was at hand to help the planners with the problem of counterbattery. There, however, long-range firing while underway at high speeds was practiced and though not a single hit on amphibious shipping had occurred, the hostile batteries had remained in action a relatively long time. This time could not be afforded at Tarawa, and the planners concluded that the temporary silencing of hostile defenses was not enough. Rather the maximum destruction would have to be achieved in the short time available from first light until H-hour at 0830 and those defenses not destroyed would have to be neutralized during the critical phase of the ship-to-shore movement and the movement of the landing craft from the line of departure to the selected beaches. Thus the planners abandoned two of the three principles that had governed previous gunfire support plans: the concept of neutralization (silencing) was replaced in favor of destruction and, contrary to Lord Nelson's dictum, ships would have to move in to short ranges and fire more deliberately at slow speeds if they were to destroy the enemy.

These decisions were not taken without concern. The Japanese shore batteries posed a significant threat and there was no precedent for dueling with these guns other than at long ranges and at high speeds. Consequently there was a strong likelihood that ships could be severely damaged, while thin-skinned ones could be sunk.

Although preliminary operations by naval gunfire were out, some assistance in this field could be expected from the air. Strikes were planned for Admiral Hoover's land-based air, followed by first carrier attacks beginning on D-2. Primary targets for air were on the coast defense on the tips of the island and the antiaircraft. In spite of this assistance, the gunfire planners had to assume that air would not eliminate these vital targets, and their caution proved wise. Not a single vital target was eliminated by either of these air efforts. Events were to prove that it would be some time before carrier pilots achieved the accuracy necessary to destroy such relatively minuscule targets.

The plan taking shape as a result of these command decisions was divided into three phases. The first was to commence a dawn carrier strike and continue for seventy-five minutes. Three old battleships and five cruisers were to open fire at 15,000 yards and gradually close to within 2000 yards. After an interval to permit taking up final positions to enfilade the beach defenses, firing was to continue for forty-five minutes, until H-5; at which time an air strike was to continue to neutralize the Japanese weapons until shortly before the tractors reached the beaches. After H-hour two destroyers were to continue firing on the opposite side of the island and into the lagoon. During these phases, the entire half-square of the island was to be completely covered, with emphasis on hitting important targets with pinpoint accuracy; fire was to be deliberate to achieve destruction, yet at the same time the gunners were directed to achieve "surprise" by shifting targets at prescribed intervals. The third phase was to cover targets of opportunity after the landing. Short fire control parties with assault battalions were assigned direct-support ships for this purpose. The organization of these parties still followed the pattern established just prior to the war, that is, they were provisional, being made up of artillery officers and radio operators from the 2nd Division artillery, while the liaison officers were navy and supplied in part by General Holland Smith's V Amphibious Corps, and in part from those who had functioned with the 2nd Division on Guadalcanal. All in all the planners felt that that they had done well; there was even some reference to "obliteration" of the island in the final conferences.

At 0441 on the morning of D-day as the transports were taking position, a red flare went up from the Japanese island. Soon after, splashes in the transport area indicated the coast guns were already at it, giving the first indication that the four days bombing by land-based and carrier aircraft had not accomplished the preliminary mission of destruction. But the gunfire plan provided for this contingency. *Colorado* opened up and then reluctantly the *Maryland* with her 16-inch joined. The shore batteries temporarily stopped firing, but they were to continue their efforts until either overrun as in the case of the Singapore 8-inch, or until finally destroyed by a combination of bombing and gunfire.

Smoke and dust rose high on Betio as a result of this counterbattery fire, which in turn interfered with the carrier strike; for this attack was to be primarily directed at pinpoint targets. Instead of a heavy half hour strike, the attack lasted for less than half that period. Phase I of the gunfire plan then went into execution. Meanwhile another hitch in the prearranged plans was developing. A combination of delays in the ship-to-shore movement caused H-hour to be set back fifteen minutes to 0845 and Phase II of the gunfire plan was delayed accordingly. But this delay was insufficient and H-hour had to be

again set back to 0900. Thus Phase II was prolonged for fifteen additional minutes, but this presumably was of advantage. At 0855 (H − 5 minutes) the gunfire ceased except for that by two destroyers.

But the carrier pilots scheduled to deliver the beach strike failed to get the word of the delay of the H-hour. In spite of the fact that the leading wave of amphibians was still at the line of departure four thousand yards from the beach and in spite of the fact that orders emphasized that the strike was to be delivered when the amphibians were about one thousand yards offshore, the planes tipped over into their beach strafing runs. Admiral Hill finally got through and stopped the strike; gunfire again resumed until 0855, at which time the pilots delivered their attack.

But all the delays and hitches in the plan were unknown to the marines in tractors and boats. The fireworks on Betio were impressive. Smoke and dust from the projectiles of the big guns mixed with smoke from burning targets; it appeared that nothing could be kept alive but the delay in H-hour prescribed by Admiral Hill was not sufficient. The tractors were presumed to take forty minutes in the run from the line of the departure to the beach and it was this fact that had led Admiral Hill to reset H-hour at 0900. But either the required speed was not realized or some other delay took place; in any case, the first tractors of the leading wave beached at 0910 and the last elements at 0923. Thus the Japanese, with the exception of those on the eastern beaches, had from fifteen to twenty-eight minutes to shake off their grogginess produced by nearly three hours of bombardment, and, like a boxer saved by the bell, they recovered, manned their defenses, and went to work on the marines.

Even with this period of respite granted to Shibasaki's beach defenders, their fire on the first three waves of amphibians was generally ineffective, particularly on the left beach where two destroyers had continued the fire until just before the touchdown. It was the subsequent waves embarked in boats that had the roughest going. The tide that had been expected to float the boats over the reef had not materialized, and the troops were forced to disembark and wade five hundred to eight hundred yards across the reef. Men were killed instantly or wounded and drowned; the bulk of the thirty-three hundred casualties of the operation came in the movement across the reef; and casualties to supports moving in across the reef continued even into D+1, until the beach defenses were overrun.

Details of the seizure of the island in seventy-six hours, after this dismal beginning, are another story, but contribution of the shore fire control parties and direct-support destroyers needs to be noted. This contribution, while not decisive, was still significant, particularly in view of the lack of artillery on the first day. Even after the bulk of the division artillery was landed, the advance along the long axis of the island made the delivery of flanking fire from destroyer guns of particular effect. While the marines of the 2nd Division had relatively little experience in this type of support, they quickly learned its effectiveness and shore fire control parties were dropping 5-inch shells as close as 50 yards before the operation was twenty-four hours old. For the first time in World War Two, the shore fire control party-destroyer team demonstrated its worth conclusively.

Tarawa was the turning point in gunfire support in the Pacific, not only because of the significant lessons learned but because of the white light of scrutiny that was cast on this operation. The heavy casualties focused attention of navy and marine planners on the shortcomings of every field. Perhaps the most significant lesson learned from this operation was that the Japanese shore battery could be attacked at short range with reasonable impunity; ships could "fight forts," at least Japanese forts. No longer would the concept of gunfire support in the Central Pacific require that ships maneuver at high speeds while firing at long range. Indeed the opposite was recommended by Admiral Hill when he suggested that destroyers operate close enough to the beach to use their 40 mm.

The primary objective of the gunfire plan had been destruction and this objective was thoroughly justified. But close control of the fall of shot through ship and air spotters, as well as ample time, was a requirement for such destruction. Neither of these conditions had been obtained at Tarawa. With up to eight heavy ships firing in an area only a half square mile or less, it was too much to expect spotters to identify their fall of shot, much less spot it to pinpoint targets. To this difficulty of identification of target and own fall of shot was added the necessity of shifting the pattern or fall of shot to attain "surprise." This reduced the possibility of systematic destruction to a matter of chance. In any case it must be remembered that the threat of counterattack restricted the time available for gunfire to the few hours from dawn to H-hour, and regardless of the effect sought there was not sufficient time for destruction. Tarawa, of course, buttressed the argument for destruction as against neutralization in order to reduce casualties. But destruction could only be achieved with slow deliberate fire from short ranges. Thus the requirement for pre-D-day naval gunfire operations was generated.

The failure of the Japanese to mount a significant naval or air counterattack indicated the reasonable possibility of such operations. Part of the failure of the Japanese to react vigorously must have been due to the Bougainville operation which dragged the Japanese fleet from Rabaul to Empress Augusta Bay. Another factor was the heavy strikes made by Admiral Spruance's fast carriers against the staging bases in the Marshalls. Finally, the growing weakness of the Japanese in carrier pilots as a result of the Guadalcanal attrition must have been a factor. In any case, only a few aircraft and submarines got through and, except for the loss of *Liscome Bay*, their effect was negligible. Thus pre-D-day gunfire operations proved not only necessary but feasible and were to feature in the remainder of the Central Pacific amphibious offensive.

Another lesson was the vital necessity of reducing the time lag between the lifting of fires and the touchdown of the leading wave in order to reduce the opportunity for the defender to recover from the shock of the bombardment. Had the fire lifted as planned just five minutes before the beaching of the leading tractors, the assault battalions would have reached the beaches in far better order, with fewer casualties among their leaders and with less mixing of units. This would have unquestionably speeded up the struggle. As a result every attempt would be made in subsequent plans to closely integrate the lifting of fires with the movement of the leading waves. Airplanes with special observers to broadcast the progress of the boats were utilized, while infantry landing craft converted into rocket craft led in the first waves firing their rockets and 40 mm.

Finally the lessons of Tarawa showed the "doubting Thomas" that effective gunfire support required a thorough knowledge of the gunnery problem, thus adding impetus to the use of the Hawaiian shore bombardment range recently acquired in the Hawaiian group. The gunnery lessons were quickly put into effect in the daily practices by the naval gunfire section of General Smith's Corps and the gunnery departments of Cruisers-Destroyers Pacific (CruDesPac).

In short, the concept of gunfire support after Tarawa was a radical departure from the concept which had seemed adequate for the North Africa and South Pacific operations. Instead of a bombardment delivered solely for neutralization, the planners adopted a bombardment for destruction during preliminary operations extending over an adequate period of time and delivered by ships firing deliberately from short ranges. On D-day, gunfire support to ensure neutralization of undamaged defenses and with adequate provision for continued directed support through shore fire control parties became the pattern.

Marshalls—The Classic

Even while the fight for Tarawa was in process, lights burned bright in the Commander-in-Chief, Pacific Fleet headquarters as the Central Pacific counteroffensive started to roll: target—the Marshalls. No atoll group was more shrouded in secrecy than the Marshalls, for the Japanese had posted and en-

forced their "keep off" signs during the period between the wars. In spite of the lack of intelligence, the final plan struck boldly at the western chain. Thus the eastern chain was bypassed in one bold stroke on the conviction that preliminary operations against the Japanese air strength in the Marshalls would neutralize this threat, while the weakened surface and subsurface threat could be held at arm's length by the growing strength of the fast carriers and submarines.

The Kwajalein atoll chosen as the target was an obtuse triangle, with its forty miles inclined in a northwest-southwest direction. At the ends of the base were the objectives consisting of the twin islands of Roi-Namur at the northern extremity and crescent-shaped Kwajalein at the southern end. Characteristic of the atolls, they were limited in size: Roi-Namur to about a half mile square and Kwajalein to about two and one half by one half mile.

By mid-December, as Admiral Hoover's land-based photographic sorties began to fill in the details of the defenses, it gradually became apparent that defense of the twin objectives were neither as numerous nor as formidable as those at Tarawa. Roi-Namur had four coast defense guns of significant caliber, and four large reinforced concrete blockhouses and almost twenty pillboxes housed antiboat and machine guns. There were about thirty antiaircraft guns. These weapons, together with organic equipment manned by the three thousand of the Japanese garrison completed the picture. Kwajalein to the south had about the same density of weapons with over five thousand in its garrison.

The lessons of Tarawa were fresh in the minds of the operational commanders, and these lessons were not learned second-hand, for the team of Spruance, Turner, and Smith continued unbroken. They were determined to reduce the casualties suffered by the landing force at Tarawa. Destruction of the Japanese defenses, as opposed to neutralization, was the goal of fire power. To this end preliminary operations not only by air but also by gunfire ships was laid on and the risk of Japanese counterattack was accepted.

In mid-December the curtain went up on the opening act of the reduction of the Marshalls defenses. Land-based bombers commenced their operations to reduce the Japanese air strength and were supplemented from time to time by fast carrier strikes. In later January the second act began with stepped-up tempo when Admiral Spruance moved in as director. On the 29th and 30th fast carrier groups concentrated their bombs and projectiles on the two objectives, featuring for the first time the use of the high-and-mighty fast battleships in the bombardment role. Six of these went after Roi-Namur and Kwajalein with over two thousand 16-inch and nearly ten thousand 5-inch shells. On the 31st Admiral Conolly made face with the marines and gained his famous nickname, "Close in Conolly," by chivving the old battleships in to 2,000 yards of the target, in this fashion reviving the old pointer fire technique which proved so destructive against Japanese concrete defenses.

The final act opened on 1 February as the marines of the 4th Division and infantrymen of the 7th headed for their objectives. Well-integrated gunfire from the bombardment group, air strikes, artillery of the landing force (emplaced during preliminary operations) and the new rocket ships (LCIGs), which preceded the leading wave of boats, covered the landing. Airplane observers kept the ships and aircraft informed of the progress of the tractors toward the beach and the fires continued until the last minute, precluding a repetition of the premature lifting of the fires at Tarawa. Roi-Namur was in our possession in a day and a half, and Kwajalein in three. The effectiveness of the new concept of fire support was highlighted by the casualty figures. The combined Japanese strength of somewhere between eight and nine thousand was able to kill fewer than three hundred marines and soldiers in action.

Thus the Marshalls was the classic operation—utilizing the Pacific Fleet's new found superiority to isolate the selected objective completely while the targets were pounded before the amphibious assault, leaving landing forces to dispose of the relatively groggy and partially decmated foe. It would never be done so well again.

The Marianas—Lessons are Relearned

It was a bright sunny morning of 14 June 1944, as eight assault rifle battalions of marines from the 2nd and 4th Divisions, veterans of Tarawa and Roi-Namur, moved toward the Saipan beaches in their tractors. This was the biggest amphibious endeavor yet in the Central Pacific—nearly eight thousand men in assault.

The briefings held aboard the attack transports during the long haul from Pearl Harbor had told them how Admiral Mitscher's carriers would strike the Marianas first, to be followed by the fast battleships of Task Force 58 on D−2, and then the old reliables, the old battleships, would move in for a day of destruction preceding the landing. They knew too from a study of the maps and terrain models that this was to be quite a different objective from Tarawa and the Marshalls. Instead of tiny coral atolls measuring only a few square miles, Saipan was thirteen miles long and about five wide. Instead of being flat, it had a mountain named Tapachou with tough rugged approaches—just the type of terrain that the Japanese flair for defensive positions would make very tough to take. They knew that Japan was reinforcing the Marianas as fast as its shipping shortage would permit—so that upwards of twenty thousand Japanese could be in the receiving line.

As the American tractors reached the coral reefline and their tracks bit in to climb the lip, the water was torn with exploding projectiles, interspersed with vicious spurts from the flat trajectories of machine guns. Water cascaded into the air, hiding the leading wave from anxious onlookers to seaward. Reports differ as to the number of landing vehicles lost, but there was no difference of opinion as to the accuracy, density, and continuity of the fire. As each succeeding wave of tractors ground on toward the reef line, it seemed that fire picked it up and escorted it to the beach. Shelling of the beach picked off marines who had disembarked from the tractors.

The tactical plan disintegrated rapidly; instead of the tractors waddling on to the high ground some one thousand yards inland, most of them halted, unable to proceed further. Small cannon and machine gunfire from Agingan Point on the right flank enfiladed the beach and made the advance by the 4th Division slow and hazardous. In the meantime the artillery and mortar fire continued to rain on the narrow beachhead. Casualties mounted.

About two miles inland a long valley running generally parallel to the landing beaches was the scene of feverish Japanese activity. Here about fifty-five pieces of assorted Japanese artillery, including 105 mm, were being loaded and fired as fast as human effort could achieve. Smaller valleys closer to the beach concealed mortars that were adding their explosives to those of the cannon. But the landing force was unaware of their location; not a scrap of intelligence had indicated the presence of these weapons. No ground observer had reached a position to observe these cannon. The landing force was blind. Urgent appeals for the location and silencing of the mortars and artillery went out over all radio channels, command, air, and naval gunfire.

In spite of the urgency, there was considerable delay before aerial observers located the tell-tale flashes and were able to direct gunfire and air strikes onto the target. Actually these weapons were not completely eliminated until the night of D+2; and the Saipan beaches gained the dubious distinction of being the bloodiest in the Central Pacific War—over four thousand were killed and wounded on D-day. Nor were the casualties limited to the riflemen. The shore fire control parties suffered too, losing almost 50 percent of their spotter and liaison personnel as well as having communication equipment knocked out. As a result, direct support by assigned ships was limited until key personnel and equipment could be replaced.

Twenty-three days later those marines fortunate enough to have survived wonderingly watched Japanese soldiers and civilians as they jumped to their death from Marpi Point,

the northernmost point of Saipan. Resistance on Saipan was over.

In the light of the lessons of Tarawa which had been applied with such crushing effectiveness in the Marshalls, it seems strange that the planners for Saipan undertook the seizure of this objective with so inadequate a preparation. They were not strange to the business, for the team of Spruance, Turner, and Smith remained intact. Even the assault divisions were veterans of Tarawa and Roi-Namur. Nevertheless, this island objective of relatively large mass and garrisoned with over five times more Japanese than had defended previous Central Pacific objectives received only two days of pre-D-day bombardment. Nor did the failure end there. The fast battleships were entrusted with the bombardment role in D−2 which they proceeded to execute from long ranges. The air spotters and top spotters were inexperienced in locating targets on a large mass, and the results were far from happy. When the experienced bombardment group of old battleships took up the chore on D−1, there was much shooting to do against the significant coastal battery threat. Little time could be devoted to searching for such targets as artillery and mortars.

In spite of the inadequacy of the preliminary work, the significant casualties were not inflicted by the direct fire weapons emplaced on the beaches, as at Tarawa. The preliminary fires on D-day had simply driven out the Japanese beach defenders as evidenced by the testimony of the intelligence officer of the defense force. When asked about the original intention of defending Saipan from prepared beach defenses, Major Yoshida, the intelligence officer, said that "the naval shelling was just too much for the Japanese to take. Their prepared positions became untenable and they had to retreat in an eastern direction [away from the beaches]."

The major flaw lay in the failure to beat down enemy artillery and mortars during the ship-to-shore movement and after H-hour. It should be remembered, however, that the planners lacked adequate intelligence as the habitual cloud over the Marianas inhibited the gathering of intelligence through air photos. Further, pre-D-day operations failed to uncover these weapons, much less destroy them. In any case, the operation brought home the necessity of scheduling fires on likely artillery and mortar positions even when there was no evidence to prove their location. This lesson was not overlooked in the subsequent operations against Iwo Jima and Okinawa.

The original plan for the seizure of the Marianas included an assault on Guam two days after the Saipan assault, using the III Amphibious Corps under the command of General Geiger. Marine units from the South Pacific including the 3rd Marine Division previously employed in Bougainville and the newly organized 1st Marine Provisional Brigade under General Shepherd made up the III Corps. The attack on Guam had been delayed because of the precarious situation on Saipan and the subsequent committal of the 27th Infantry Division to that island. This deprived the III Corps of a reserve to meet unforeseen contingencies and the landing was delayed until the 77th Infantry Division could be brought out from Pearl Harbor.

The marines of the III Corps would have had no complaint of cramped quarters on the transports had they known that their old friend "Close in Conolly" was opening the holes up front. Admiral Conolly had gone forward from Eniwetok to Guam to take charge of the preliminary operations. The result was the most sustained, systematic, and well-directed bombardment seen in the Central Pacific up to that point. For a period of thirteen days, battleships and cruisers assisted by destroyers and gunboats attacked every known target that could block the way of III Corps. Damage assessment utilizing aerial photos were systematically followed. As new targets were discovered, they were added to the active target list and attacked until destroyed. Altogether more than six thousand rounds of 14- and 16-inch ammunition, almost four thousand rounds of 8-inch, as well as more than twelve thousand rounds of 5- and 6-inch were poured into the Japa-

nese defenses. The same standard of excellence continued with the D-day bombardment. Fires were delivered not only on the landing beaches but also in those areas where mortars and artillery might be located.

The success of this bombardment as compared with that delivered at Saipan makes a striking contrast. Although Guam was defended by about the same number of Japanese and although the terrain was as varied and difficult for the attack, the Japanese never achieved the effectiveness of their brothers-in-arms of Saipan. The bombardment had literally driven the Japanese off the landing beaches, forced them into the hills in disorganized fragments to the extent that after the first week they offered little coordinated resistance.

Considering the fact that Guam and Saipan were defended by almost equal strength, both in troops and defenses, and that the terrain was at least equally difficult, and further that the landing force was substantially equal in each case, the relatively light casualties of seventy-three hundred for Guam as compared with over sixteen thousand for Saipan must be attributed to the unprecedented scope and effectiveness of the naval gunfire support. General Geiger put it better in his official report:

> As a result of the pre-Dog day bombardment most of the enemy installations had been destroyed; his forces had been disorganized and his will to resist had been greatly weakened. The success of this operation with comparatively few losses is largely attributed to this preparation.

The prewar doctrine of naval gunfire support visualized the employment of the ship's gun for only a few hours, just long enough for the attacking troops to establish their own weapons ashore. But the Marianas campaign marked the passage of this last vestige of the prewar concept of support. Gunboats, destroyers, cruisers, and old battleships continued to pour supporting fires by day and night long after D-day.

This change in doctrine, like all changes

in gunfire, was an evolutionary one, brought about by the marked superiority of our own naval forces and because of the increased size of the objectives encountered, combined with the relatively larger and more adequately armed defense forces. In essence, two fleets were available: one built around the fast carrier to isolate and cover the operation from Japanese air and surface forays; the other a bombardment fleet built around the old battleships, with additional cruiser, destroyer, and gunboat types rounding out the formation. Experience gained in ammunition replenishment at the objective now made it possible for ships to refill their magazines at the scene of action, making continued support feasible.

The objectives were no longer tiny atolls limited to a few square miles of flat sand, with a few coconut trees the only vegetation. The Marianas were relatively large with varied terrain and heavy tropical growth—conditions favoring the defense. But even these islands were not so large as to prevent the long-range naval gun from reaching everywhere inland to the flanks and rear of the enemy. On the basis of real estate, the defenders were no longer limited to a small military formation. Division-size units were now encountered, complete with supporting arms of all types, including tanks. Finally, the Japanese code of the Bushido—a feudal-military code valuing honor above life—prevented them from taking advantage of an untenable situation by surrender, as the Germans and Italians had done. Instead death was a Pyrrhic victory, and the United States could win only after virtual extermination. All of these factors combined to argue the necessity for the continued use of the naval gun.

The use of ships in close support had been previously proven for short periods. The month-long campaigns for Saipan and Guam gave the destroyer-shore fire control party combination a real chance to demonstrate its worth. Conventional 5-inch guns united with the organic weapons of the marines in supporting attacks and beating off counter-

attacks. The white phosphorus projectile was brought into the picture when its potentialities for flushing the enemy out of its trenches were realized. Its burning particles rapidly lost velocity and curved into trenches and fighting holes, where conventional high explosive fragments could not reach. Hasty evacuation was the result, giving the small arms of the marines a chance. The 40-mm quads also had their opportunity, often over open sights.

But the most spectacular and popular support of all was the 5-inch star shell which illuminated no man's land with an intense light. The troops loved this support to the point where it was almost impossible to meet their requests. Serious banzai attacks—mass attacks—were broken up by a combination of star shells from 5-inch guns with artillery, mortars, and small arms of the defense. This effectiveness is best illustrated by a counterattack occurring on the night of D + 1, at a time when our forces on Saipan were far from secure. About thirty Japanese tanks, fortified with a battalion of infantry, sortied from Garapan toward the front lines of the 6th Marine Regiment. The noise of the tanks alerted shore fire control parties and calls for continuous illumination went out over the radio circuits to the supporting destroyers. In a matter of minutes the approaching tanks and riflemen were caught as though by daylight. In a short time the tanks were burning and the enemy either cut down or withdrawing—without gaining an inch of ground. Truly the destroyer sailors and marines were a potent combination.

Nor was the support limited to the destroyer. The big ships did the downfield blocking with an assist from the 40 mm and rockets of the gunboats. Old battleships like *California*, *Pennsylvania*, and *New Mexico*, once the backbone of the battle line, went about the systematic destruction of blockhouses, worked over pillboxes, and blew away camouflage with their high capacity projectiles, revealing cleverly hidden defenses, which in turn were reduced to rubble. Key defensive positions selected by the Japanese for use in delaying positions were heavily bombarded, often routing the tenacious Japanese before our troops were forced to come to grips with them, thus saving lives.

On Guam heavy cruisers used air spot and their big guns to make the defenses on Mount Tenjo, a natural citadel, untenable for a significant Japanese force. When the marines of the 9th Regiment scaled the steep approaches, they received no fire, only a few dead and wounded remained as silent witnesses to the effectiveness of the naval guns. Later in the campaign Mount Saint Rosa, in northern Guam, was selected by the Japanese commander as the rallying point and final defensive position to which all remaining Japanese were to repair. Having learned this plan from a prisoner-of-war, General Geiger called on the Bombardment Group to work it over. After five days of heavy attack the Japanese gave it up with hardly a fight. This was the last straw. The remaining soldiers simply melted into the jungles and caves from which they waged an intermittent heckling campaign until death from bullets, dysentery, or starvation or eventual surrender ended their resistance.

The Japanese on the receiving end testified to this continued contribution of the naval gun through the medium of prisoners (although few were taken), diaries, and radio reports from Tokyo. One of General Saito's staff officers somehow found time to write, "I am groggy from intense bombardment and naval shelling—our forces have been continually caught in a concentration of naval gunfire and the dead and wounded continue to increase." Dispatches to Tokyo echoed these sentiments: "The enemy assaulted various strong points with incessant night and day naval gunfire; the enemy is under cover of the warships near the coast; as soon as night attack units go forward the enemy points out targets by using the larger star shells which practically turn night into day—the enemy naval gunfire using mainly a shell with attached instantaneous fuse, has great destructive power. The call fire on land from ships is extremely quick and accurate."

The increased participation of the naval gun in the complete campaign for the Marianas brought problems to light requiring serious study if the new fire support partner was to be fully and effectively utilized. Since the gunnery material had proved itself, these problems were essentially those of training and indoctrination of all elements involved—gunnery people, air spotters, shore fire control parties, and landing force staffs.

The rugged mountainous terrain and larger objective areas made the problem of identification of targets far more difficult for ship and air spotters. No longer did blockhouses, pillboxes, and weapons stand out from the flat platform of the atolls like sore thumbs; now they were artfully emplaced to take full advantage of the natural camouflage and protection offered by the rugged vegetation-covered terrain. The failure to detect the Japanese artillery on Saipan in a valley only a few thousand yards inland from the landing beaches, not only during preliminary operations but also in the early hours of D-day, illustrates this problem of target identification.

This same broken terrain also complicated the problem of spotting the fall of shot to the target once detected. Many an air and top spotter experienced difficulty in adjusting fire when the targets were on ridges or reverse slopes, where a small range change produced a shift in the point of impact fire in excess of the change given. The spotter had simply encountered a target on a ridge and his small change sent the salvo over the ridge and far away, frustrating and time consuming as well as wasteful of ammunition. Effect of terrain on the fall of shot had to be recognized and training was required. Hand in hand with training in target identification was the necessity of indoctrination in the tactics and techniques of the Japanese. This was necessary in order that air spotters could discard unlikely terrain in their search for targets dictated by the pattern of the defense and could recognize a worthwhile target when they saw it. Shore fire control parties shared in this need for increased knowledge. Lack of knowledge of the ship's gunnery installation and the capabilities and limitations of the ship's batteries needlessly complicated the ship's problems in rendering support and reduced effectiveness.

Finally the continued full participation of the naval gun and the airplane, together with the organic artillery and mortars of the landing force, raised problems of coordination. A beginning was made in this area during the Marianas but much remained to be worked out before needless duplication of effort could be eliminated and before all the support could be utilized in the most effective manner. In any case, the naval gun had become a full partner in the landing force effort, beginning with preliminary operations and continuing by night and by day until the objective was secured.

Kahoolawee—School for Bombardment

The island of Kahoolawee in the Hawaiian group has never received much publicity, for this island shares none of the lushness of the rest of the islands. Instead this barren island lying southeast of Pearl attracted little attention other than from those engaged in raising goats until late September 1943. That month, the *Pennsylvania* let go with the first of literally hundreds of thousands of rounds aimed at targets on that bleak island. Before the war ended, over six hundred ship's practices had been fired. An infinite number of gunnery and plotting room officers had gone over instructions and drills with their people, for the course was a tough and rugged workout for the ship's gunnery department. It began at noon and continued until midnight. It ranged from direct fire with forties to indirect fire against a reverse slope target, with a five minute check fire period arbitrarily introduced just to make sure that the set and drift of the current had been figured and applied. The fire support area selected had almost five knots of current and if it wasn't figured and entered in the range-keeper the salvo delivered after the five minute check fire would be off. It included a breakoff of a shore bombardment problem for an air and suicide boat attack, along with a

host of other exercises patterned on some operational experience. The staff of Cruisers-Destroyers Pacific took quite a hard-boiled attitude toward an unsatisfactory performance over this course—and no destroyer went into the forward area without demonstrating proficiency at Kahoolawee.

The shore end of the bombardment range was not fancy, but it was effective. The dugout housing the observation personnel required to conduct and spot the practice received direct hits from 5- and 8-inch shells at one time or another. The organization behind Kahoolawee was a striking demonstration of the teamwork of the navy and marines in the Central Pacific. The marine side of the team was the direct descendant of General Holland M. Smith's naval gunfire setup in the Atlantic. On arrival at Pearl at the head of the newly constituted V Amphibious Corps, General Smith vigorously pressed for the acquisition of a suitable bombardment range. Admiral Reggie Kaufmann of Cruisers-Destroyers Pacific, who had worked closely with marines in gunfire support during the Culebra days, backed the project. The acquisition of Kahoolawee resulted.

Thus began the happy relationship which contributed no small part to the effectiveness of gunfire support in the Pacific. Since General Smith operated a training establishment, as well as a tactical formation, his naval gunfire personnel participated in both training and tactical operations. Tactical lessons resulting from landing force requirements and Japanese defensive techniques could be rapidly integrated into shore bombardment exercises prepared by Cruisers-Destroyers Pacific in collaboration with General Smith's naval gunfire section. Thus the lessons of the Marianas were reflected in the Kahoolawee exercises in a matter of weeks after the end of a campaign.

Immediate steps were taken to remedy deficiencies revealed in the Marianas. Efforts to improve the target identification and spotting ability of float plane pilots of battleships and cruisers had to be limited to replacement pilots awaiting assignment at Pearl Harbor.

However, theoretical instruction together with spotting exercises at Kahoolawee were instituted. Fortunately, a new aircraft formation appeared in the Central Pacific about that time in the form of VOF-1, organized for the specific purpose of spotting naval gunfire and fresh from the Allied landings in southern France. This squadron, flying in Grumman Wildcats, was to make a name for itself in the remaining amphibious operations of the war, at Luzon, Iwo Jima, and Okinawa. The pilots were eager, competent, and versatile and became rapidly adept at seeking out targets, going down on the deck when necessary to literally take a look under Japanese camouflage. Their availability multiplied the effectiveness of gunfire support manyfold and their contribution was significant.

The shore fire control party organization came in for its share of training after the Marianas. This little organization was no longer provisional, for the adoption of the Joint Assault Signal Company in late 1943 had changed all that. This company contained all the elements necessary to act as a link between the troops and the ship, including shore fire control parties for the assignment to rifle battalions, regimental naval gunfire teams for assignment to rifle regiments, and a division team. Each of the shore fire control parties were headed by an ensign or junior grade lieutenant, while the regimental and division teams were headed by a full lieutenant. Communications consisted of TBX portable equipment, and jeep-mounted TCS equipment. Marine Corps officers filled the spotting billets.

The naval gunfire teams which had been badly chewed up in the Marianas were pulled to Pearl harbor, to their great delight. Liberty in the Marianas left much to be desired. The gaps were plugged with replacements provided from General Smith's pool of spotters and liaison officers. Arrangements were made for all naval officers to attend the destroyer gunnery course in order to improve their knowledge of ship's capabilities, while spotters attended a modified version of the same instruction. Practical familiarity with ship's gunnery problems in shore bombardments was ensured by having the liaison officers and spotters ride ships firing at Kahoolawee. Intensive instruction in planning fire support was undertaken, including exercises involving air and artillery staff officers. Thus, by the time the Iwo Jima and Okinawa operations rolled around, the lessons of the Marianas had been thoroughly digested. All hands in the gunfire business were ready.

Gunnery Payoff at Iwo Jima

The atmosphere of Admiral Blandy's cabin on the Estes was tense the night of 17 February 1945, D − 2 for Iwo Jima. The admiral himself was presiding over a conference of his principal staff officers to review what must be done to ensure the landing of marines of the V Corps over the beaches of Iwo Jima. Already the amphibious fleet had sortied from Saipan for the target. There was only one day left.

The two days of preliminary bombardment were disappointing. The photo interpreters could account for the elimination of relatively few beach targets—only three of twenty blockhouses were smashed and only a fraction of the hundred pillboxes had been definitely destroyed. Added to this worry was a new and entirely unexpected threat to the landing.

Early that same afternoon, as the underwater demolition teams (UDTs) were conducting their reconnaissance of the preferred beaches, the twelve gunboats backing up the UDTs were taken under fire. In a matter of minutes the majority had been hit. Even the sick bay of the Estes had many of the wounded from these little ships.

This new threat proved to be thirteen guns in concrete casements; ranging from 120 mm up to 5.6 inch, all sited on a bluff commanding the right flank of the beaches at point-blank range. The intelligence study had said "four possible antitank guns." Of course this was unknown, but there were shell fragments on display in Admiral Blandy's cabin and they could have come from an 8-inch gun!

The conference decided that if D-day was

to be met and the marines were to get ashore, the artillery, mortars, antiaircraft, blockhouses, and pillboxes would have to be destroyed later. The first priority would be to clear the beach defenses and the coast guns commanding the beaches. At first light, the *Tennessee, Nevada, New York, California,* and *Chester* would go in at point-blank range and go to work.

The gunnery tasks of the *Nevada* and *Tennessee* were typical. In *Nevada's* zone were numerous blockhouses and pillboxes. The blockhouses themselves had five feet of reinforced concrete which in itself was no problem to heavy calibers, but the Japanese engineers had dug these forts into the sand and had then graded twenty feet or more of sand on the seaward side of the walls—a practical step, since the embrasures and firing ports were located to deliver flanking fire along the beach. All that the gunnery people on the *Nevada* could see was an ever so slight mound, which they identified as a blockhouse only because the photo interpreter had. The gunnery problem, then, was to strip away twenty feet of sand, expose the concrete, and blow it to rubble.

The gunnery people did not choose to attack this tiny target with main battery salvos, a dramatic but inconclusive method. Rather, they went back to an antiquated method—pointer fire. They laid the director on the target identified, aided by telephone chit-chat between director and pointer just to make sure. An offset aiming point was used out of the line of fire since the character of the target would change with each hit; sights were set for the offset, the cross hairs swung and steadied, then the gun was fired.

If the pointer was steady on, a range and deflection change were applied and another two thousand pound, high-capacity projectile was on its way. Some projectiles ricocheted off, others exploded, blowing the protective sand away from the front of the blockhouse until the concrete face was exposed. It usually took about fifteen minutes and an average of nine rounds to destroy one blockhouse. As the enemy ran from the blockhouse the 40 mm guns would open fire.

In this simple but effective manner, *Nevada* cleared the way for a regiment of marines, who went in standing up and reached their objectives with minor losses.

Tennessee lay to on the extreme left flank of the beach, firing across *Nevada's* and *New York's* line of fire. Her gunnery chore was to blow away the camouflage which hid the troublesome bluff batteries on the right flank of the beaches. By nightfall her 16-inch guns had literally cut many of the concrete casements from the rocky bluff formation, so that they leaned crazily, threatening to slide down to the base of the bluff. Some of the casemate fronts were blown off, exposing the weapons to full view. None of these thirteen guns fired a round on D-day. *New York's* gunnery problems were identical to those of *Nevada,* while *California* from the extreme right finished off a four-gun coast defense battery nestled into the base of Surabachi.

Thirteen hours later, as darkness fell and the big ships retired, the photo interpreters deep in the *Estes* gave their verdict of the day's work: seventeen coast defense guns out, sixteen of twenty blockhouses, and about half of the hundred odd pillboxes in the landing beach area. The heavy ships had opened holes in the line and the marines would get ashore tomorrow. Gunnery had paid off.

D-day was like a spring day as four assault regiments of the 4th and 5th Division headed for the beaches of Iwo Jima. There were no illusions this time. All hands knew that the bulk of the artillery, mortars, and rocket launchers, as well as many inland blockhouses and pillboxes, had not been scratched by the preliminary operations. It would be tough.

The clumsy armored amphibians led the way, passing through the line-of-fire support ships 2,500 out. *Santa Fe* marked the left of the boat lanes, *California* bulked large in the center, while *Vicksburg* kept station on the right. Captain Chandler's destroyer squadron filled the gaps. This was the position of honor; the shore bombardment records of many a destroyer squadron had been combed to select the best. These ships would have to justify the trust, for their firing was more closely integrated with the ship-to-shore movement and the subsequent advance of the marines ashore than any previous amphibious assault. In addition to plastering the landing area thirty-five minutes prior to the landing, these ships would place their 5-inch shells just 400 yards in front of the marines after the landing, lifting ahead on a prearranged time schedule. For adequate clearance of overhead fires, 1,200-foot second powder was to be used. The use of this lower velocity powder imposed an additional burden on the rangekeeper operators, since it would be necessary to introduce gun elevation by hand using tabular values corresponding to the generated range. A mental lapse might place six gun salvos on our own troops. The marines had been warned that the enemy would try to create the illusion of naval gunfire falling short by firing their own artillery and mortars as they had done before.

It was expected that smoke and dust would present a spotting problem, so ships planned on using white phosphorus marker salvos from time to time to check their fall of shot. In addition, all close support ships were assigned an air spotter from the VOF squadron of Grummans operating from an escort carrier, to assist in spotting prearranged fires, as well as to search for targets of opportunity not covered by the prearranged fires. Fortunately the wind on the morning of D-day was long and across the line of fire so that visibility was excellent, control of fall of shot was perfect, and no casualties from our fire occurred.

It was recognized that the marine's advance across a 3,000-yard front could not be uniform nor could it be closely predicted on a time schedule because of varying enemy resistance. There had to be a means, and a positive rapid one at that, to adjust the prearranged schedule to take care of the contingencies. This was the way it was done. In Harry Hill's gunnery control room on the flag bridge level, a gunnery officer wore a split radio head set tuned to two airborne tactical observers of the landing force. The air observers had been carefully briefed on the gunnery plan and the tactical scheme. They watched the progress of the advancing marines with relation to the exploding salvos. When the troops lagged behind the fires, the air observers so reported, making recommendations for the repetition of fires on certain targets—a matter of accurate observation and close judgment. Six times recommendations came over the radio for repetition of fires and six times orders went out to the ships involved to adjust their fires. The system worked.

Special measures had been taken to ensure rapid support on targets of opportunity not covered by the prearranged fires. Because of the high terraces immediately in the rear of the beaches, some parties would not be observed from the beaches themselves. To overcome this lack of observation the naval gunfire liaison officers, with their radio teams, remained offshore in landing craft where they could command the entire slope. The spotter with his radio team landed with the assault and continued inland until he gained the necessary observation. In addition, the air spotter complemented the liaison officer afloat from his aerial spotting station. Between them, effective target of opportunity fire was called down.

Nor were the rear areas containing the one hundred-thirty odd artillery, mortars, and rocket launchers neglected. Heavy ships, including the old *Arkansas* and *Texas* had come halfway around the world from the Normandy beaches to be in on this one with their old 5-inch 51s of another naval day. The new rocket ships with their 5-inch spin-stabilized jobs helped out. But the Japanese curved fire weapons were just too numerous and too well dug in to be quieted for long. By about H-plus one hour, bursting shells on the beaches marked the commencement of a heavy fire which took days to eliminate.

But this fact remains. By the night of D-day the strongest defended objective in amphibious history had been forced. The fact that the D-day casualties were lighter than those sustained for the next seven days bears witness to the effectiveness of the pre-D-day and D-day gunfire.

Defeat of the German Amphibious Landing at Hogland Island, 1944

BY COLONEL V. VASIL'YEV, SOVIET ARMY

TRANSLATED BY PROFESSOR KENDALL E. LAPPIN

In September 1944, Red Banner Baltic Fleet aviation and Finnish coastal defense forces and torpedo boats defeated a German attempt to land amphibious forces on Hogland Island. In the course of this military action, Soviet naval aviation demonstrated its excellent fighting capabilities. We stress the latter circumstance in particular because in the West, and specifically in the published works of the bourgeois historian J. Meister, the facts about this operation are distorted, and there is no mention of the scope and effectiveness of the actions of Soviet aviation.

. . . Alarmed by the Soviet forces' successful offensive which had led to a radical change in the military-political situation in Finland, the Finnish government had been obliged to establish contact with the Soviet Union. On 29 August the Soviet government informed the government of Finland of its willingness to negotiate, on condition that Finland sever relations with Germany and guarantee to expel the German-fascist forces from her territory within two weeks.

Having accepted these preliminary conditions for a truce, the Finnish government on 4 September declared its severance of relations with fascist Germany and demanded the removal of its armed forces from Finnish soil by 15 September 1944. But the German command was in no hurry to remove its troops, and the Finnish government acquiesced to this situation. According to the terms, however, Finland was to be in a state of war with Germany after 15 September. The German forces, once they had provoked armed conflict with their erstwhile "comrades in arms," attempted to seize Hogland Island.[1]

This island, situated in the middle of the Gulf of Finland, on the meridian of Kotka, was the key to communication between the eastern half of the gulf and the Baltic Sea.[2] Since the fascist troops were withdrawing, sea communications had become especially important to them. The enemy wanted to hold onto Hogland as long as possible in order to use it as a naval base and thereby to preserve for themselves a favorable regime for operations in the eastern half of the Gulf of Finland.

On Hitler's personal orders, the fascist command worked out a plan for seizure of the island.[3] Detailed to participate in the operation were a detachment of amphibious vessels (twenty-two landing craft, three minesweepers, several transports and other vessels, and a detachment of screening and support ships—one destroyer, five torpedo boats, eight amphibious gunboats, and twenty minesweeping boats). At airfields in the Rakvere sector were concentrated some forty fighter planes, which were supposed to cover the landing from the air.

The first echelon of the landing force, consisting of two infantry battalions, was supposed to reach the vicinity of Hogland in darkness and to disembark at three points simultaneously: in Suurkyul' Bay, at the

Voenno-Istoricheskiy Zhurnal, "Defeat of the German Landing at Hogland (Suusaari) Island in September 1944," 20 (December 1978): 88–91. Reprinted by permission.

North Hogland lighthouse, and at the midpoint of the island's western coast. The groups in the first echelon were supposed to seize beachheads and hold them until the arrival of the main landing forces, which were to be brought over soon afterward under cover of fighter aircraft.

By 14 September, two attack bomber divisions of the Baltic Fleet's air forces were based at Kotli, Kerstovo, Koporve, and Kummolovo airfields: the 9th Ropshinsk and the 11th Novorossiisk. In addition, one guards fighter regiment of the 1st Guards Vyborg Fighter Division was located at Lavensar' Island (the 3rd Guards Fighter Regiment) and another at Lipovo airfield (the 4th Guards Fighter Regiment), and two reconnaissance squadrons of the 15th Detached Reconnaissance Red Banner Air Regiment were at Goryvaldaye. The Baltic Fleet air forces at that time were preparing to participate in our troops offensive on the Leningrad front, with the mission of liberating the Baltic region.

The Finnish garrison on Hogland numbered 1,712 officers and men; it had fourteen coastal defense guns, four fieldpieces, twenty-four antiaircraft guns, nine mortars, and twenty-four machine guns.[4]

Also on the island at this time were one German communications officer and a platoon of radiomen and radiotelegraphers, who by the terms of the truce were supposed to be evacuated by the end of 14 September. For this reason the German command was well informed on the state of Hogland's defenses.

During the afternoon of 14 September the Finnish commandant received word from the fascist Rear Admiral Bemer that the Germans would be evacuated from the island by a flotilla of minesweepers at 0200 on 15 September. The commandant, without waiting for this flotilla to arrive, ordered the German personnel evacuated on two patrol boats. As they were leaving Suurkyul' at 0015 on 15 September, these boats met the German minesweepers of the amphibious force, and the latter entered the bay soon thereafter.

The commander of the minesweeper flotilla demanded that the Finnish commandant surrender the island without a fight. The latter said he would give his reply in fifteen minutes and reported this demand to his own command. At the same time he alerted the garrison and gave his units their firing assignments.

The fascists, however, succeeded in landing a part of their first echelon, and fighting began. Finnish coastal artillery and infantry got into it. Finnish torpedo boats from Kotka and Klamil came to the aid of the island's garrison. They attacked the German ships and sank two of them. But the Germans managed to seize a beachhead on Suurkyul' Bay and to disembark there, as well as at other points on the eastern and western coasts, some fifteen hundred officers and men, a mortar platoon, and 75 mm cannon.[5] After exhausting most of their ammunition during the night battle and suffering heavy losses, the fascists went on the defensive. The decisive blow in the affair was supposed to be struck by the main landing force, which was scheduled to arrive from the southern shore of the Gulf of Finland. But a force which the enemy had not anticipated intervened in the action—Baltic Fleet aviation.

Beginning on the morning of 14 September, Baltic pilots had reconnoitered the enemy ships in the bays and skerries of the Gulf of Finland, as well as the airfields at Rakvere and Kokhtla. Fighters scrambled to intercept the enemy's reconnaissance aircraft. Baltic Fleet radio and aerial reconnaissance detected the concentration of German ships and craft, the preparations for amphibious landing, and the night battle at Hogland Island.

On the morning of 15 September the Baltic Fleet Military Soviet received instructions from Supreme Command Headquarters to interdict the debarkation of the Germans' main landing force on the island, using naval aviation to repel the landing. This order was passed to the Baltic Fleet Air Force command post, which was located at Goryvaldaye. The commander of Baltic Fleet Aviation, Colonel General of Aviation M. I. Samokhin, was at that time in Panevezhis, to which some torpedo-plane units had been detached for action against the enemy's communications in the central Baltic.

Consequently aircraft operations to interdict the German amphibious landing from disembarking on Hogland Island were directed by the chief of staff of the Baltic Fleet Air Force, Major General of Aviation A. M. Shuginin. He decided to blockade the Rakvere airfield and thereby to destroy the landing ships and craft on the approaches to Hogland by depriving them of air cover. While the battle was in progress, some additional dive-bombing missions against landing craft in Suurkyul', Kharalakht, and Mokhin bays were ordered by the commander of the Baltic Fleet, Admiral V. F. Tributs.

At first light on 15 September, aerial reconnaissance detected on the approaches to Hogland Island three groups of German ships and vessels, comprising some thirty landing craft, two transports, six minesweepers, and about fifteen motor launches, most of the landing craft, including the transports, being at Kharalakht, Kyasmu-lakht, and Mokhin.[6] At Suurkyul', fascist ships were still engaged in a gunnery duel with the Finnish coastal artillery.

Starting at 0730 on 15 September, fighter planes of the 1st Guards Vyborg Fighter Division (Colonel V. G. Koreshkov in command), in groups of sixteen to eighteen, blockaded the Rakvere airfield. Then dive-bombing attacks were made on the trailing ships carrying the main landing force by the 9th Red Banner Ropshinsk Attack Bomber Division (commander, Colonel M. A. Kurochkin) and the 11th Novorossiisk (commander, Colonel D. I. Manzhosov). The Germans attempted, by radio deception, to divert the subsequent strikes of the Baltic Fleet Air Force away from themselves. Using our joint radio frequency and the call letters "Ol'kha" (the call sign of one of our torpedo-plane units then based at Panevezhis which was not taking part in the action of Hogland Island), they gave the order not to attack the ships lying west of the northern part of the island. This order was transmitted by microphone from a very powerful radio station in flawless Russian.[7] The enemy's ruse, however, was soon discovered. By order of the chief of staff of the Baltic Fleet Air Force, a radiogram was sent at once to all airborne aircraft and their units, instructing them to ignore any transmission with the call-sign "Ol'kha" and to continue destroying the ships lying west of the Hogland.

After the sixth dive-bombing attack, delivered at 0845 by twenty-four IL-2 attack planes covered by thirty-two fighters of the 11th Novorossiisk Attack Aviation Division on the third group of landing craft farthest from the island, all three groups began to move away from Hogland. Two landing craft were sunk, two ships damaged, and five fighter planes shot down.[8]

Dive-bombing attacks were delivered on landing craft and German personnel in Suurkyul' Bay. For example, at 1420 hours twenty-four IL-2 attack bombers and twenty-six Yak-9 and LAGG fighters under the command of Hero of the Soviet Union Major F. N. Trugenev delivered a concentrated bombing strike from an altitude of 1200 to 50 meters on the craft in Suurkyul' Bay. After this strike the attack bombers and fighters strafed the enemy on the wharves and beaches of the bay with machine gun fire. As a result of this strike (according to aircrews' visual observation and photographic data) one schooner, two dry-cargo barges, and a tug were sunk. Finally, between 1810 and 1817 hours, sixteen IL-2 attack planes (led by Senior Lieutenant V. S. Tellinskiy) delivered a final bombing strike from 1400 to 400 meters altitude on the landing craft in Kharalakht Bay. In this attack two landing barges were sunk, one was damaged, and five fighter planes were shot down.

In the heat of the action by Soviet aircraft, the island's Finnish garrison mounted a counterattack. The fascists who had been disembarked on the island, deprived of their ships' fire support, were obliged to surrender. At 1845 hours, the last of the landing-force units laid down their arms.[9]

In repelling the fascist amphibious landing on Hogland Island, units of the Baltic Fleet Air Force made 533 aircraft sorties, 183 of them by attack planes. As a result of fifteen bombing strikes, nine landing craft, one transport, one escort vessel, one tug, and one minesweeping boat were sunk, and twelve landing craft were damaged, and in eight air battles, twenty-two enemy aircraft were shot down.[10]

Thus Red Banner Baltic Fleet aviation delivered some shattering blows to fascist ships and disrupted the disembarkation of the main landing force, leading eventually to the failure of the German-fascist operation to seize Hogland. The airmen of the Baltic Fleet Air Force units and divisions displayed strong offensive spirit, courage, and combat expertise.

Notes

[1] *Istoriya Vtoroy Mirovoy Voyay, 1939–1945* [*History of the Second World War*] (Voyenizdat, 1978) 9: 35, 36.

[2] Hogland is 11 kilometers long and 3 km wide at its widest point. Its terrain is hilly. Suurkyul' is its roomiest bay. From the northern tip of the island it is 19 km to the Finnish skerries, 43 km to Kotka, and 45 km to the island of Lavensar', on which were located at that time an advance base for fighter aircraft and the Baltic Fleet's Island Naval Base. The basing area for the two attack aviation divisions of the Baltic Fleet's air forces deployed on the south shore of the Gulf of Finland lay within 125 to 140 km of Hogland.

[3] J. Meister, *Der Seekrieg in Den Osteuropaischen Gewassern, 1941–1945* [*The Sea War in East European Waters, 1941–1945*] (Munich, 1958), p. 95.

[4] Ibid., p. 90.

[5] Soviet Central Naval Archives Branch, f. 200, d. 17531, 1. 108.

[6] Ibid., f. 261, d. 17531, 11.134, 136.

[7] Ibid., f. 122, d. 7744, 1.66.

[8] Ibid.

[9] Soviet Central Naval Archives Branch, f. 260, d. 17531, 1. 193.

[10] Ibid., d. 19105, 1. 319–350.

On Course to Novorossiisk

BY E. EUSTIGNEEV
TRANSLATED AND EDITED BY PROFESSOR JANE E. GOOD AND
PROFESSOR JAMES A. MALLOY, JR.

The army of the northern Caucasus, supported by the Black Sea Fleet and the Azov Military Flotilla, conducted the Novorossiisk—Taman offensive from 9 September to 9 October 1943. During the course of this operation a powerful German army was routed and the entire Taman Peninsula cleared of the enemy. A special place in this campaign belongs to the 18th Army, which together with the Black Sea Fleet carried out the Novorossiisk amphibious operation. The high point of this operation was the liberation of the port and city of Novorossiisk on 16 September. Three weeks later the long struggle with the German invaders of the northern Caucasus was victoriously concluded.

The road to this victory was, however, long and difficult. In Novorossiisk it began on 19 August 1942 with the bitter battles of the 47th Army forces in Novorossiisk against the units of the 17th German Army approaching the city. Although the city itself fell to the fascists, the Soviet military forces and fleet kept the enemy from breaking into the Caucasus along the Black Sea shore. The German divisions were halted at the cement factories in Novorossiisk and in the foothills of the Caucasus. For the next year Soviet soldiers and sailors contained the enemy attacks on this frontier. Their courage and heroism laid the foundation for the ensuing victory over the fascist invaders of the northern Caucasus.

"The battle for Novorossiisk," observes L.

Voenno-Istoricheskiy Zhurnal 20, (1978):120–25. Reprinted by permission.

I. Brezhnev in *Malia Zemlia*, "has entered into the history of past battles as one of the examples of the unbending will of the Soviet people for victory, of their military valour and fearlessness, of their boundless devotion to the Leninist party and to the Socialist motherland."[1]

Of particular significance in the battles for Novorossiisk is the legendary amphibious landing in the region of Stanichki of the naval forces under the command of Major Ts. L. Kunikov on the night of 4 February 1943. The newspaper of the 18th Army, *Znamiia Rodiny*, contained the following description of this amphibious landing:

Among the commanders of this naval campaign it is difficult to single out particular individuals for unusual virtues of military skill, bravery and heroism. Kunikov, however, can be singled out. His name, like lightning, has struck the Germans and will always remain in the memory of a grateful Soviet people. The detachment of sailors under Kunikov's command was entrusted with a crucial task. He spent the entire day with his troops, talking with many of them. That night, utilizing a favorable wind, the detachment crossed the stormy bay and once on the bare, rocky land the sailors grappled with the enemy in battle. Sappers selflessly swept away barbed wire and blew up mine fields. The marines used their bayonets and grenades to dislodge the Germans from their fortifications and dugouts. At daybreak when the Germans saw before them only a handful of marines, they launched a counterattack. From their numerous coastal artillery guns, mortar batteries, and machine gun nests they plastered the land and tore it apart. Every delay threatened the detachment with death. Kunikov, sensing the absolute necessity of advancing, turned to his men: "We must seize the guns that are firing on us." He gave a command; his firm words breathed strength and courage. His men went forward. Dressed in his Red Army uniform, saturated with salt water, the major, with automatic pistol in hand, led the marine regiment into the attack. . . .

Sgt. Romanov, with four Red sailors, had captured a German bunker. That night they mastered the artillery piece and machine gun that they found there. At dawn, when the Germans went on the offensive, Romanov and his men laid down a hurricane of fire. With their well-aimed shots they destroyed half of a company of Hitlerites and scattered the others. Sgt. Bogdanov showered an enemy battery with grenades and killed part of its crew. The Germans who survived the attack fled with shouts of "Seamen! Seamen!" They were afraid of the marines and called them the "Black Death."

This battle lasted several days. Not one man showed cowardice. There was no food or fresh water. The marines, closely united in their bloody circumstance, shared in brotherly fashion whatever food that could be found. The detachment of Major Kunikov fulfilled its duty; it captured and resolutely held a patch of land that was highly advantageous to us from a tactical viewpoint. But victory came at a high price. Lt. Oglotkov and a number of other comrades died in battle. A German shell exploded and mortally wounded Maj. Kunikov. From this incident the marines took a motto: "Fight just like the Kunikovs fight." Kunikov had been killed, but the remaining Kunikovs carried on the battle for which their commander had perished.[2]

Exploiting the success of the Kunikovs, the command of the 47th and then of the 18th Army constantly undertook measures for augmenting the victory of the landing party. In particular they sought to convert the tactical beachhead in the region of Stanichky–Myskhako into a strategical one. The heroic defense of the landing group force at Malia Zemlia attracted the attention of the main forces of the 17th German Army, which strove to throw its defenders from the beachhead into the Black Sea. In close cooperation with the main forces of the 18th Army, which was defending eastern Novorossiisk, the valiant marines ground down the enemy with aggressive raids and concentrated fire on the counterattackers. Eventually the enemies' fire power was destroyed.

In his book *Malia Zemlia*, Brezhnev graphically portrays the skirmishes of the heated battle:

> The Fascists attacked with confidence, believing that in the dense smoke covering Malia Zemlia, nothing could remain alive. But their attacks were met with fierce resistance and they were compelled to fall back. They left behind hundreds and hundreds of dead bodies. Then it began all over. Again there were the heavy batteries, again the dive bombers howled, the attack planes [*stormoviks*] raged . . . the earth burned, the roads smoked, metal melted, concrete fell to the ground. But the men, true to their oath, did not retreat. Companies withstood the charge of battalions. Battalions ground down regiments. Barrels of machine guns became red hot. The wounded continued to fight against tanks with grenades. In hand-to-hand skirmishes they struggled with rifle butts and knives. It appeared that there would be no end to this battle.[3]

The army newspaper *Znamiia Rodiny* presented the following account during these dangerous days for the defenders of Malia Zemlia:

> The day will come again when bunches of grapes will burst with sweet juice. . . . Here gardens again will bloom, here wheat will again grow, and special foods will again be served on the sanitorium decks. But today Malia Zemlia is experiencing battle. It bristles with bunkers and barbed wire and is ringed with mine fields. Thousands of eyes watch for the enemy. Guns, deeply dug in the earth, belch fire. Malia Zemlia is ready to defend itself and to attack. To live at the same time war is being waged on Malia Zemlia is difficult. People are killed here, and in this process are transformed into true soldiers. The Germans have a special label for the forces attacking Malia Zemlia—"double-dipped Communists."[4]

In the battles for Malia Zemlia the Germans suffered a complete defeat despite their preponderance of troops, tanks, artillery, and planes. They also had huge supplies of ammunition and occupied advantageous positions.

From May to August 1943 the marines managed not only to hold the beachhead they had won from the enemy, but also carried out skirmishes to improve their position and reconnaissance to help determine the location of enemy positions. Through this aggressive defense they not only wore out the enemy but also protected their own strength and prepared for a decisive storming of the powerful fascist fortifications. Their ultimate goal, of course, was to liberate Novorossiisk and to drive the enemy from the Taman Peninsula.

The staff of the Soviet High Command in August 1943 gave the forces of the North Caucasus front the task of breaking through the enemy defense at the Golubin line. The goal was to cut and destroy the German forces in a piecemeal fashion. The breaking of the Golubin line at its center would be difficult because of the hills and forests and because the enemy expected an attack along the Golubin line and had concentrated their forces there. Lieutenant General I. E. Petrov, the commander of this front, decided to strike the main blow on the left wing in hopes of breaking the Golubin line in the area of Novorossiisk. The enemy, believing their forces to be impregnable at this point, did not expect an attack here. But Petrov reasoned that an attack here would allow his ground forces to be coordinated more closely with the Black Sea Fleet. Also the seizure of such an important region of defense as Novorossiisk, along with the passes of Neberdzhaevsky and Volchi Gate would weaken the overall German defense of the Golubin line. Finally Petrov believed that if his plan proved successful, the German retreat route to the Kerch Strait would be cut.

The forces of the 18th Army and the Black Sea Fleet were assigned to execute the Novorossiisk operation. The commander of the 18th Army was General K. N. Leselidze. He was aided by General S. E. Kolonin, member of the Military Council, General N. O. Pavolsky, chief of staff, and Colonel L. I. Brezhnev, chief of the political section.

Five divisions of the 5th German Army Corps were deployed against the 18th Army. The Germans had more than five hundred guns and mortars.[5] The enemy had prepared two defensive zones at the approaches to Novorossiisk. The city's houses and apartment buildings were equipped as strong points. The streets were covered by a system of barricades and communication trenches. Throughout the city and on the approaches to it the Germans erected more than five hundred different defenses that consisted of dense wire and mine obstacles. In the port buildings on the docks and breakwaters in Tsemessky Bay the Germans installed machine guns and artillery. The entry into the port from the sea side was covered by boom nets and mines.

The combination of the hilly, forested terrain, the isolation of Soviet forces in Tsemessky Bay, and the disposition of enemy troops permitted the Germans to hold Novorossiisk firmly. The Soviet command needed to prepare thoroughly for this operation if they hoped to be able to effect the bold and swift actions of the 18th Army and Black Sea Fleet.

The plan for the offensive operation of the 18th Army consisted of seizing the city and port of Novorossiisk in a synchronized thrust from three sides. Two thrusts, one from west of Novorossiisk and one from Malia Zemlia east of the city, were to be by land. The third was to be a daring amphibious landing directly in the port. The immediate task was to seize Novorossiisk in close coordination with the landing of the Black Sea Fleet, to unite the army formations which were separated along Tsemessky Bay, and to reach the Medfodievsky line. Furthermore, all the army forces were to develop an attack on the Verhnebakansky Pass of Volchi Gate. The plan called for two shock landing groups. Colonel V. A. Vrutsky was to head the eastern and Commander N. A. Shvarev was in charge of the western. A landing force group was to deliver a simultaneous thrust from the land and sea.

For the debarkation and protection of the landing a special fleet of one hundred fifty fighting ships and auxiliary craft, commanded by Rear Admiral G. N. Kholostyakov, was created. For the artillery to help the amphibious assault there were 800 mortars, ranging in caliber from 76 to 203 mm, 227 mounted rocket artillery, and 150 airplanes from the front line.

Preparation for the operation involved giving misinformation to the enemy and masking the movements of the armed forces and ships. A great deal of effort was directed toward the careful coordination of the units of the 18th Army with the forces of the fleet. Also, much attention was given to party work with the men of the 18th Army and Black Sea Fleet, the goal being to create high morale among the troops so they would be able to overcome the difficulties of the amphibious landing. The party and Komsomol organizations were strengthened among the soldiers and sailors. At the start of the operation communists and Komsomol (Communist Youth Organization) members comprised up to 45 percent of all troops, and 60 to 70 percent of the marines. More than half of the soldiers and sailors in the assault were participants in previous landing operations.

The political workers of the 18th Army, headed by Colonel Brezhnev, conducted fruitful work with the troops. They carefully verified how the preparation for the operation was going and calculated the forces required for it. Brezhnev was always found among the troops. He conversed with them and conducted conferences with the commanders and political commissars, attended party and Komsomol meetings, and signed party cards for those accepted into the ranks of the all-Russian Communist party.

The political administration of the Black Sea Fleet and the Political Department of the 18th Army composed a pamphlet for the marines which concisely outlined how to conduct oneself during the sea passage and disembarkation and on shore. These pamphlets were distributed to all the participants.

Sailor-agitators, who previously had participated in joint army-navy operations, carried out work in the various units. Navy representatives talked about what the disembarkation for the amphibious landing would be like, how to conduct oneself in the landing craft, how to alight into the water,

and and how to overcome the enemies' obstacles on the shore. The army-agitators also passed on their experience to the marines. Those units picked for the assault practiced exercises to prepare for the landing. As a result of these various preparatory exercises, the personnel of the 18th Army and the marines were ready to fulfill the complicated tasks of the operation.

The storming of the enemies' fortifications on the Golubin line began on the night of 10 September with a heavy artillery barrage and aerial bombardment. Torpedo boats under the command of Captain V. T. Protsenko burst at full speed into the port to attack weapon emplacements on the docks, mooring lines, and shore. Assault groups blew up the boom net obstacles. Then the landing began.

Simultaneously, an attack of 18th Army shock troops was launched in the east from Tuapsinsky Road and in the west from the Myskhaksky beachhead. The enemy, recovering from the sudden attack, stubbornly resisted. German reserves were moved into the area the Soviets had targeted for the breakthrough. Heavy street fighting continued throughout the day and night.

On the western shore of the bay the forces of the 255th Naval Rifle Brigade, commanded by Colonel A. S. Potapov, violently fought with this enemy. The 1339th Rifle Regiment under Lieutenant Colonel S. N. Kadanchik boldly attacked the enemy. They won control of the Importny pier, seized the key strong point—the factory "Proletariat," and broadened the beachhead on the eastern shore of the bay. Kadanchik died in this battle and was posthumously awarded the order of Hero of the Soviet Union.

The assault of the 393rd Marine Battalion headed by Lieutenant Captain V. A. Botylev demonstrated extraordinary heroism. They fought a courageous battle in seizing and retaining the port's mooring lines. Airplane pilots M. E. Efimov and F. N. Turgenev, Heroes of the Soviet Union, aided the landing forces with their aerial bombardments.

The German command, on evaluating the danger in the Novorosiisk region, quickly rushed up reserves there, intensified their aerial and artillery bombardments, and organized furious counterattacks. The intensity of the fighting increased hourly.

By the morning of 10 September the success of the military actions of the marines and of the regiments of the eastern group against the fierce counterattacks of the enemy was evident. But more offensive forces were needed. The command of the 18th Army, in order to strengthen the marines's position and to develop the attack of the eastern forces, decided to throw the army's reserves into the battle. A special second echelon landing was therefore launched. The 55th Guard Rifle Division and the 5th Guard Tank Brigade were hurriedly transported to one area of the factory "October," in order to strengthen the second and third landing units near the elevator pier and the cement factory "Proletariat," the 290th Rifle Regiment of the NKVD and the 1337th Rifle Regiment from the recuperating 318th Rifle Division were transported there.

The Military Council of the 18th Army appealed to the fighting forces of the army which were engaged in the offensive struggle for the liberation of Novorossiisk. It stated in its address:

Fighting Comrades! By means of a swift sprint and a crushing blow together with the marines of the Black Sea Fleet you have broken through the defense of the enemy. Your sailor caps are covered with glory. . . . Valiant Knights of the Kunikov type, glorious Potalors, tireless infantrymen like Kadanchik have again covered themselves in glory with their remarkable victory—which marks the beginning of the total destruction and annihilation of the German Guards in Tamana. There will be no end to National happiness. A significant part of beloved Novorossiisk is already in our hands. Glorious successors to the heroic defenders of Odessa, Leningrad, Sevastopol and Stalingrad, you are fulfilling the cherished dream of your fighting comrades, who are struggling at Maj Myskhako to unite Malia Zemlia with Bolshaia.

The Military Council of the army warmly congratulates you for the initial military successes and calls on you to tirelessly and tenaciously advance forward and only forward to the complete liberation of the Tamsky peninsula where our children, wives, mothers, and fathers, worn out under the fascist yoke, await you with outstretched arms. Comrades of the Red Fleet, Red Army, Commanders and Political Workers! Without respite, follow on the heels of the enemy, surround and destroy him. Yet another blow against the enemy, Comrade Fighters, and Novorossiisk will be entirely cleansed of the German-Fascist wretches.[6]

The appeal of the army's Military Council played a big role in further lifting the fighting spirit of the forces and in strengthening their offensive thrust.

The successful landing of units of the second echelon of marines and the entry into the battle of the 55th Guard Regiment and the 5th Guard Tank Brigade proved to be the decisive influences on the subsequent military actions. However, stubborn resistance bombardments by the Germans, frequent counterattacks by the enemy, and massive sudden artillery and mortars slowed the tempo of the offensive. For that reason the main forces of the eastern group attacked along the narrow coastal strip.

All the participants in the fighting offensive showed a fierce character. The forces of the 18th Army revealed a high level of bravery and heroism; with great persistence and courage they forced the enemy out of the dugouts, concrete bunkers, and various shelters.

For five days there continued the storming of the powerful knot of enemy defenses near Novorossiisk. The armed forces and the marines on 16 September chased the enemy from this important Black Sea port and broke through its defenses on the right wing of the Golubin line. The 18th Army continued the attack in the direction of Anapa, creating a threat to the rear of the enemy's principal forces on the Golubin line. The forces of the North Caucasus front had the opportunity to expand the resolute offensive along the whole front. On the night of 9 October the Taman Peninsula was liberated from the fascist invaders. The long and bloody struggle for the Caucasus was concluded. The 17th German Army suffered some nineteen thousand dead and wounded. The Novorossiisk operation is a persuasive example of how in close cooperation the army and navy were able to break through a strong enemy defense from the direction of the sea. It has entered the history of the Great Patriotic War as one of its most illustrious events.

Notes

[1] Leonid I. Brezhnev, *Malia Zemlia* (Moscow: Politizdat., 1978), p. 38.
[2] *Znamiia Rodiny*, 11 April 1973.
[3] Brezhnev, *Malia Zemlia*, pp. 19, 22.
[4] *Znamiia Rodiny*, 30 April 1943.
[5] *Voenno-istoricheskiy zhurnal* No. 2 (1973): 79.
[6] *GTSAMO, SSSR*, p. 371, op. 6386, d. 103, 1.3.

Soviet Amphibious Preassault and Landing Operations in World War Two

BY CAPTAIN (1ST RANK) N. BELOUS, SOVIET NAVY

TRANSLATED BY PROFESSOR KENDALL E. LAPPIN

The defeat of the German fascist forces at Stalingrad created favorable conditions for their expulsion from the northern Caucasus. An important role in offensive operations was assigned to the Black Sea Forces Group, commanded by Lieutenant General I. F. Petrov. On 24 January 1943 he ordered the 47th Army (under Lieutenant General F. V. Kamkov), in cooperation with the Black Sea Fleet (commanded by Vice Admiral F. S. Oktyabr'skiy), to attack the right wing of the German 17th Army in the Novorossiisk sector and by attacking the Taman Peninsula to clear the enemy out of it.

By order of the commander, Transcaucasus Front, the Black Sea Fleet,[1] with aircraft, coastal artillery, and naval gunfire, was ordered to assist in breaking through the enemy's defenses in the vicinity of the cement plants, to make amphibious landings in the enemy's rear in the Yuzhnaya Ozereyka and Stanichka sectors, to divert a part of the fascist forces away from the 47th Army's main offensive thrust, and in collaboration with that army's troops to capture Novorossiisk.[2]

The ground troops' attack, supported by naval aviation and naval gunfire, began on 26 January.[3] But they were unable to penetrate the defense. On 3 February, commander, Black Sea Fleet, ordered the 47th Army troops to make amphibious landings in the Yuzhnaya.

Voenno-Istoricheskiy Zhurnal, "Example of Amphibious Preassault and Handling Operations," 20 (September 1978): 32–38. Reprinted by permission. The author served in the Baltic Fleet naval infantry during World War Two.

Preparation for the landing of amphibious forces in the Novorossiisk area had begun back in November 1942, when General of the Army I. V. Tyulenev, commander, Transcaucasus front, ordered the Black Sea Fleet Military Soviet to be ready for amphibious landings. At first this took the form of preliminary calculations on such matters as making a decision to conduct amphibious landing operations, defining the areas of responsibility of the operation commander and the naval forces commander, planning the landing, organizing the reconnaissance, and ensuring the cooperation of landing forces, ships, and aircraft. Subsequently, such matters as the tactical and operational planning documents and the organization of the forces-control system were made more precise. In addition, the order in which landing craft would approach the beach and the order in which the main and demonstration assault units would disembark were worked out in greater detail, and practice drills were planned for the forces. Steps were taken to provide intelligence, engineering, political, logistic, medical, and navigational-hydrographic support for the operation.

Because the landing forces and ships were assembling and preparing very close to the front lines and under systematic observation by enemy aerial reconnaissance, it was difficult to keep the measures secret. Therefore much attention was devoted to camouflage and to strengthening antiaircraft defense. Another difficulty was that it was not possible to establish at once a precise time for the operation. This was changed several times, depending on the progress of our ground troops' operations. The makeup of the forces and means assigned to it was also changed.

The principal matters requiring special preparation of the men and equipment assigned to the operation were: practice in moving *bolinders*[4] to the beach with the aid of tugs and in getting tanks ashore quickly via their bow ramps; practice in positioning these barges immediately offshore and using them as docks for unloading equipment and cargo; bringing gunboats and minesweepers close inshore to disembark troops via their forward gangways, while simultaneously mooring them to the sides of barges in order to unload equipment and cargo via the latter; towing barges across open water, using ships and disembarking them quickly on unequipped beaches; training landing force troops to size the enemy's strong points and to destroy his firepower and personnel under nighttime conditions; coordinating the movements of the amphibious force ships and reforming them at night into detachments as specified by the operation plan; and maintaining constant coordination within the landing force itself and between the landing force and ships, ground troops, aviation, and coastal artillery.

To work out these and a number of other problems, a special training plan was drawn up and appropriate orders and instructions were printed. The plan provided for commanding officer training, practice drills for landing craft and troops, fire-correction stations, and means of communication. The training began on 14 December and continued right up until the start of the operation.

Since the barges, gunboats, and minesweepers were always busy moving people, equipment, ammunition, and provisions here and there for the Black Sea Forces Group and did not have time for training per se, their practice for the forthcoming operation had to take place mainly during their transport activities. This worked out well because they performed their transport tasks at various times of day, in all kinds of weather, and under frequent harassment by enemy aviation. In addition, they unloaded troops and equipment on unequipped beaches. It was possible, however, to conduct five daytime and four nighttime practice exercises involving barges and tugs: embarking and disembarking troops; onloading and offloading equipment; moving tanks and motor vehicles aboard barges and ashore via special ramps under their own power; distributing people, equipment and cargo on deck and in holds; and tugs towing barges by the bow and broadside on. Taking part in this training were three barges, five tugs, the 142nd Battalion of the 255th Naval Infantry Brigade, and the 563rd Detached Tank Battalion. In addition, to practice rapid embarkation and disembarkation of troops and onloading and offloading of equipment on unequipped beaches, nine nighttime and four daytime practice drills were held for transports and gunboats, and several for minesweepers and patrol boats.

Especially noteworthy were the methods of preparing for demonstration landings. Mock-ups of small craft were built on the beach: the sides of the boats were indicated by curving lines beaten into the ground, their internal spaces by holes, and their superstructures by wooden constructions. Each unit went through four practice drills using these. Subsequent drills were performed with the actual means of debarkation. While the onloading, movement, and reverse offloading of the landing force were being practiced, an exercise and a series of drills were held on the theme, "Fight for a bridgehead, followed by a battle for possession of occupied position," in which the tactical aspects of interlocking and destroying the enemy's firepower and base points were practiced. The men were taught how to jump into the water with their weapons, climb ladders, and throw grenades from uncomfortable positions. They learned how to use captured weapons and throw knives, how to render first aid, how to load the magazines of their automatic weapons blindfolded, and how to determine by sound where enemy fire was coming from.

The participants in this operation got some essential practice, and the staffs were able to make precise calculations for each of the ships taking part in the operation of the time required for loading, over-water movement, and unloading of personnel and equipment. Training of the landing-force units and ships took place under the direct observation and inspection of the overall commander of the amphibious operation, the debarkation force commander, and their staff officers, who were present aboard the ships and with the landing-force units at all times.

The plan called for thirty-minute artillery preparation and for gunfire support of the landing force ashore. This task was assigned to shipborne and coastal artillery. The ships practiced concentrating their fire by areas, correcting it by using data provided by spotter aircraft, determining their own position accurately while firing, and maintaining combat documentation. The following measures were taken to prepare our naval artillery. Ten days before the operation the squadron commander, Vice Admiral L. A. Vladirmirskiy, called a meeting of commanding officers and heads of gunnery and navigation departments, at which all were informed about the mission of artillery in the forthcoming operation (without exact time and place being specified). At this meeting some navigational calculations were made, and methods of firing on shore targets were discussed. Under the direction of the squadron staff, two joint combat exercises were organized, in which all personnel of the gunfire cruisers were deployed to their battle stations just as they were to be in the forthcoming operation. To train communicators and pilots in fire-correction, an actual firing was performed by the destroyer *Besposhchadnyy*, from the Batum roadstead, on a coastal area in the Chorokh River sector. A firing range with dimensions and targets like those in the Ozereyka sector was selected. Two MBR-2 airplanes took part in the spotting. To ensure that the gunboats' fire would be effective, fire-correction teams consisting of a gunnery officer, a chief petty officer and three radiomen were formed. Their preparation consisted of establishing and maintaining communication with ships; they transmitted the firing orders and pertinent gunnery instructions and corrections. Forty

practice drills and exercises were conducted with these teams. All of them took place at night, under conditions similar to those of combat. Among the documents developed, the most substantial were "Scheduled Table of Artillery Fire," "Target Bombardment Plan," and "Instructions for the Employment of Screening Force Ships."

Preparation of coastal artillery for the operation took the form of careful reconnaissance of enemy fire emplacements, adaptation of gunnery procedures to the local topography, and the production of some preliminary ranging fire on enemy command and observation posts and individual gun emplacements. In order to determine the number and location of enemy weapons, extensive use was made of roving batteries, so-called because, when conducting a bombardment, they would constantly change their firing position. The enemy would open fire in reply, at which time our instrument gunnery reconnaissance would locate the enemy batteries by the flashes and sound of their firing. This yielded extremely good results.

In communications, preparation consisted of beefing up the communications equipment of the operation commander's flagship and secondary command posts (FKP and ZKP) and of the command posts of force commanders and ship captains; testing the condition of communications and correcting deficiencies noted; developing documents (communications orders, plans and standing instructions); and actual practice in using the communications facilities, both radio and wire, of ships and fire-correction stations.

Throughout preparation for the landing a great deal of attention was devoted to reconnaissance, which was supposed to determine the nature and condition of the enemy's defensive engineering structures, the number, type and location of his fire emplacements and personnel and so forth. Called upon to perform these tasks were aircraft, submarines, torpedo boats, naval infantry, the lookout and communications service, air warning stations and fire-corrections stations.

On 1 December the Black Sea Fleet staff made specific reconnaissance assignments, on the basis of which detailed reconnaissance plans were set up by the staffs of the Fleet Air Force and the Novorossiisk Naval Base and by the intelligence branch of the Black Sea Fleet staff. Reconnaissance was performed by aerial observation, photography, radiotechnical means, and specially trained reconnaissance teams. Torpedo boats and hunter-killers made twenty-two sorties to put such reconnaissance teams ashore. To maintain constant surveillance of the enemy within the port and city of Novorossiisk, a special observation post was set up in the vicinity of the "Proletariat" cement plant and supplied with radio equipment. All the intelligence information obtained was processed and transmitted to surface-ship and aviation forces and to amphibious units.

During the preassault and landing period, party-political work aimed at successful performance of the combat mission was conducted within landing-force and aviation units and aboard ships. The Black Sea Fleet Military Soviet (member, Rear Admiral N. M. Kulakov) made a special appeal to all personnel, calling upon them to perform honorably the combat tasks confronting them. The Black Sea Fleet Political Administration (Captain 1st Rank G. I. Semin, chief) organized special seminars with political workers and secretaries of primary party units, in which the forms party-political work would take in the forthcoming operation were discussed. On the morning of 3 February, before the landing force was embarked on the ships at Gelendzhik, Captain 1st Rank G. I. Semin held a meeting of all political workers assigned to the operation by the fleet's political administration, plus the political deputies of the debarkation force commander and the commander of landing craft, on the party-political work to be done during embarkation of the landing force, movement by sea, and fighting for the bridgehead.[5]

Specially appointed hydrographic officers conducted briefings of personnel participating in the operation, studying the water area and beach at the landing points. The submarine A-2 was twice sent into the Yuzhnaya Ozereyka sector to conduct observation of the site of the forthcoming landing by periscope. The directorate of the Hydrometeorological Service (UGMS) of the Black Sea Fleet detailed a special group of officers, headed by the Deputy Chief of UGMS. Their principal task was to determine when there would be two to three consecutive days of calm weather and to notify command thereof. This was important because weather conditions in the Novorossiisk area are extremely difficult in the fall and winter season; there is a great deal of stormy weather, and days of calm weather rarely occur.

The main landing force was to be set ashore in the Yuzhnaya Ozereyka sector and a secondary force in the Stanichka sector. For the purpose of disrupting communications and creating confusion in the enemy's rear, it was proposed to make an airborne landing (eighty men) in the Vasil'yevka-Glebovka area, as well as demonstration landings at Zheleznyy Rog Cape and at Anapa, Varvarovka, and other points. Designated to make up the main landing force were two brigades of naval infantry, one rifle brigade, one antitank artillery regiment, one tank battalion, and one machine gun battalion. Detachments of transport vessels, screening ships, disembarkation equipment, and fire-support ships were formed, in order to provide them with transportation, set them ashore, and support them with gunfire.

The secondary landing force comprised one naval infantry battalion, which was commanded by Major Ts. L. Kunikov.

Air support for the operation was entrusted to an air group consisting of 137 aircraft of the Black Sea Fleet Air Force and 30 aircraft of the 5th Air Force. This air group was headed by the commander of the Black Sea Fleet Air Force, Major General of Aviation V. V. Yermachenkov.

In all, more than seventy ships and craft were assigned to the operation. Overall control of the operation to seize Novorossiisk was exercised by Lieutenant General I. Ye. Petrov. Vice Admiral F. S. Oktyabr'skiy was in overall command of the naval aspect of the operation. Immediately subordinate to him were Rear Admiral N. Ye. Basistyy as disembarkation commander, Vice Admiral L. A. Vladirmirskiy as commander of the screening force, Rear Admiral G. N. Kholostyakov as commandant of the Novorossiisk Naval Base, and Major General of Aviation V. V. Yermachenkov as commander of the Black Sea Fleet Air Force.

In accordance with the plan approved by Vice Admiral F. S. Oktyabr'skiy, this fleet proceeded to carry out the amphibious landing operation. Deployment of the ships took place from Batum (screening force), Tuapse (transport force with second wave of landing force and a screening detachment), and Gelendzhik (landing-craft detachment with first wave of landing force and fire-support detachment). The weather was not favorable for the crossing. For this reason the ships were late in reaching their designated positions, and the landing in the Yuzhnaya Ozereyka sector, which was scheduled for 0130 on 4 February, did not begin until somewhat later.

At 0045 on 4 February, in accordance with the operation plan, aviation delivered a bombing strike on Yuzhnaya Ozereyka. Simultaneously the airborne assault was launched in the Vasil'yevka-Glebovka area. At 0345 disembarkation of the first wave of the amphibious landing force began in the Yuzhnaya Ozereyka sector. The fire which had broken out as a result of our air strikes illuminated the landing area very brightly, and the landing encountered strong enemy resistance consisting of intensive artillery, mortar, and machine gun fire.

Fearing attack by enemy aircraft, our command decided at dawn to discontinue the landing operations. Thus our main forces for the principal thrust of the attack did not get ashore. The ones who did, however, with unprecedented courage and tenacity, mounted a decisive attack, quickly seized Yuzhnaya Ozereyka and began to penetrate into the hinterland of the enemy's defense. Soon they were cut off from the beach, and for two days in the Glebovka sector they waged fierce battles with overwhelmingly superior enemy forces. With great difficulty and heavy losses, after expending all their ammunition, our

fighting men broke out of their encirclement and into the Stanichka sector.

Here, at the secondary point of attack, the landing had taken place under more favorable conditions. At 0130 on 4 February, the Novorossiisk Naval Base artillery opened fire on the landing zone, and 10 minutes later, with the approach of the landing detachment to the shore, shifted its fire to the enemy's hinterland defenses. Thanks to the element of surprise, artillery support, and the heroic performance of Major Ts. L. Kunikov's naval infantrymen, this landing was successful. These amphibious troops killed about a thousand Germans and captured some weapons. It is interesting to note that to support the landing from seaward, rockets were successfully fired from the launchers of the minesweeper *Skumbriya*. When Rear Admiral Kholostyakov learned of the rockets' success in this sector, he ordered that this be done for the remaining units of the secondary landing force. By the morning of 4 February some nine hundred men with ammunition and provisions had been landed there.[6]

The success of the landing in the Stanichka sector was due in considerable degree to the high morale and fighting qualities of Major Kunikov's naval infantrymen, who quickly seized the coastal fortifications and began to enlarge the bridgehead in the direction of Stanichka and the Myskhako State Farm. Before the landing began, they had signed a document of solemn promise, which said: "In going into battle, we take an oath to the Homeland that we will act swiftly and boldly, without sparing our own lives, for the sake of victory over the enemy. Our will, our strength and our blood, to the last drop, we dedicate to the cause of our people and to thee, our dearly beloved Homeland. . . . It is and will be our law to move only forward!"[7]

The amphibious warriors kept their promise, with honor. By dawn on 4 February they had captured a small (some 4 kilometers of beach front and 2.5 kilometers in depth) but very important bridgehead. Thus the legendary Little Land (*Malia Zemlia*) was born.

Taking account of the situation which had

come about, the fleet commander on 5 February redirected the landing force's main offensive in the direction of the secondary thrust which had gone off so famously. This was a correct decision. Control of the amphibious effort was turned over to Rear Admiral Kholostyakov. During the night of 6 February two gunboats, four minesweepers, two minesweeping boats, and seven patrol boats landed forty-five hundred men in the Stanichka sector. The following night, because of heavy enemy fire on the beach area, no landings were made. Thereafter, gunboats making night runs to Stanichka did not approach the shore, but transferred their troops to patrol boats, which took them in to the occupied bridgehead. (This transshipment procedure was retained until September 1943.) From 4 to 9 February in the Stanichka sector more than seventeen thousand men, twenty-one cannon, seventy-four mortars, eighty-six machine guns, and four hundred forty tons of ammunition and provisions were delivered.

As the fighting progressed, the troops of the landing force expanded their bridgehead to a distance of 7 kilometers along the shoreline and to three or four kilometers in depth, bringing it out to a line which ran from the southern outskirts of Novorossiisk to Fedorovka to Myskhako; but because of their small numbers, they were not able to develop their success any further. Still, the importance of the landing was very great. These Soviet forces had captured a bridgehead and were diverting substantial enemy strength to oppose them. They had completely denied the use of the port of Novorossiisk to the German command.

The enemy tried everything it could think of to liquidate the Little Land bridgehead. There was even a special operation under the code name Neptune. But the enemy's innumerable attacks were shattered on the iron tenacity of the Soviet fighting men.

Commanding officers and political workers were the very soul of the Little Land defense. Some tremendous organizational and political work was done by the chief of the 18th Army's political branch, Colonel L. I. Brezhnev. He displayed a tireless zeal for the improvement of party-political work, did not tolerate any spirit of routine, and conducted all activities creatively and purposefully. This political-branch chief concerned himself constantly with the fighting men: their food, rest, living conditions, and facilities. He shared with the defenders of the Little Land all the hardships of life at the front. There was not a division, brigade, or regiment on that bridgehead with which Brezhnev did not repeatedly spend time. Very often he would go right into combat formation, into battalions and companies, to talk with the soldiers and officers, he took interest in literally everything—from ammunition deliveries to news from home received by the men. The spiritual state of the fighting man before and during combat was a constant concern of this political-branch chief. The sensitivity and consideration of Brezhnev toward every individual was never forgotten by the defenders of the Little Land.

Thanks to the work of army and navy commanding officers and political workers, these amphibious warriors never for one moment felt themselves cut off from the Big Land (*Bol'shaya Zemlia*); and this gave them strength and inspired them to new feats of heroism.

The combat actions on the Little Land bridgehead have been brilliantly described by L. I. Brezhnev; so we shall not discuss them here. We shall merely quote the words of L. I. Brezhnev in a speech during a ceremony awarding to the hero-city of Novorossiisk the Order of Lenin and the "Gold Star" medal, on 7 September 1974: "Many times I was in the front lines of combat formations in the Little Land. I must confess to you, comrades, that never in all my four years at the front did I see heavier, bloodier fighting than in the Little Land."[8]

Having seized and held the Little Land, our troops, considerably inferior to the enemy in numbers and equipment, held out and created favorable conditions for the defeat of the German army groups in the Novorossiisk area. The defense of the Little Land demonstrated the high moral, political, and fighting qualities of our amphibious warriors; it displayed firm control of both large and small units during the landing itself and in action ashore, exemplary coordination of joint operations involving ground troops, ships, and aircraft, and many examples of courage, heroism and tenacity, fidelity to the military oath, love for our great Homeland, and devotion to the Party and the government.

"The amphibious landing on the Little Land can be looked upon as a model of the military art. The successful landing of the first assault wave, the efficient build-up of strength, the advance of the landing-force troops on a strongly fortified and land-mined beach—all this required precise coordination among infantry, combat engineers, seamen and artillerymen, and it was executed brilliantly."[9]

Notes

[1] At that time, the Black Sea Fleet was under the operational command of the commander, Transcaucasus Front.

[2] Central Naval Archives Branch, f. 12, d. 6091, 11. 20–22, 63–65.

[3] Ibid., f. 10, d. 6042, 1.4.

[4] The *bolinder* is a non-self-propelled landing barge. Before this operation, they were refitted and attached to a gunboat division. Bolinders displace 530 tons, are 45.8 meters long, and 7.2 meters wide. Each one can carry up to ten tanks or a battalion of troops.

[5] Central Naval Archives Branch, f. 109, d. 24015, 1.20.

[6] Ibid., f. 55, d. 7479, 1.41.

[7] Leonid I. Brezhnev, *Leninskim Kursom* [On Lenin's Course], vol. 5 (Moscow: Politizdat, 1976), p. 127.

[8] Ibid., 5:128.

[9] Leonid I. Brezhnev, *Malia Zemlia* [The Little Land] (Moscow: Politizdat, 1978), p. 14.

Landing Operations of the Soviet Naval Fleet during World War Two

BY W. I. ATSCHKASSOW

TRANSLATED BY PROFESSOR MICHAEL C. HALBIG

As is well known, the Great Patriotic War was largely continental in character. The struggle against the fascist conquerors was necessarily conducted largely by land forces. Accordingly, the mission of Soviet naval forces consisted of supporting these forces. Amphibious landings, mostly tactical in nature, constituted a large part of this mission. They served to support coastal units of the Soviet army in both offensive and defensive operations. All told, 113 landing operations were conducted, of which a few were operational. These included particularly the operations of Kerch-Feodossiya, of Kerch-Eltigen, on the Muhu Sound Islands, as well as those of Tuloksa, of Pechenga-Kirkenes, and of Novorossiisk. The number of troops put ashore in these operations totaled three hundred forty thousand men. Approximately two thousand warships, several thousand auxiliaries of the most diverse sort, and about ten thousand aircraft were also involved.[1]

In the official documents from the prewar period on the deployment and operational roles of the Soviet naval forces in battle, amphibious landings were divided according to size and mission into strategic, operational, tactical, and diversionary actions. Amphibious landings had as a goal the creation of a new battlefront through which one attempted to affect the overall course of the war. At least one special corps was designated for this sort of deployment. Operational landings supported the operation of the land forces. The landed troops were then to move into the enemy's rear areas and surround him in the interior. Numerically, these troops could amount to as much as a division, organized along specialized lines. Tactical landings were designed to guarantee the success of one's own naval forces in the coastal region as well as to outflank enemy troops from the water side, and then to attack them in the flanks and in the rear. Tactical landings were usually carried out by a reinforced rifle regiment. The goal of camouflaged, surprise landings by diversionary units was to create distractions in the enemy's rear area. In certain circumstances, amphibious and airborne landings could be conducted simultaneously.

A landing operation consisted of several aspects: planning, embarkation of the troops, crossing to the landing area, the amphibious assault, and completion of the mission in the coastal area. The movement of the landing force proceeded in the sequence: Coast-Transport/Landing-Coast. During the prewar period, relatively large amphibious operations were conducted in military districts with coastal waters as well as by the fleets as a part of their battle training. In the Great Patriotic War, amphibious landings took place particularly in 1941 and 1944. In 1941, the landings were defensive operations. All other landings were offensive, with fleet and amphibious forces working together.

Typical examples of tactical landings from the first part of the war were actions in the vicinity of Sapadnaya Liza Bay. Contributing to the success of these landings was the excellent cooperation with parts of the 52nd

Militargeschichte 16 (1977): 297–306.

Soviet landing craft, World War Two.

Rifle Division, whose defenses were established along the coast, as well as the rapid preparation of the amphibious troops, the speedy crossing to the landing site, the rapid pace of the landing itself, for an attack in the enemy's flank.

Another successful tactical landing was the landing of the 3rd Black Sea Marine Regiment near Grigorievka, east of Odessa, on 25 September 1941. The amphibious force supported the simultaneous attack of the 157th and 421st rifle divisions against the left side of the enemy forces attacking in Odessa. The goal of this operation was to destroy the enemy troops and restore the line of defense in the eastern part of the Odessa defensive sector.

Special features of this landing are that it was launched from warships and that it took place at night. This caused difficulties in naval gunfire support and complicated cooperation with the air force. Poor visibility hampered the conduct of close-in fighting along the coast and the deployment of the landing craft. The night landing did make possible, however, a camouflaged surprise at-

tack in an area where the enemy had air superiority. An additional special feature of this landing was that one part of the amphibious force was landed simultaneously near the village of Schliza. This force interrupted the enemy's lines of communication there and harassed his headquarters. This airborne landing was one of the first of its kind landed during the Great Patriotic War.

Because of the battle site, difficulties developed in deploying the landing craft; as a result, the amphibious force commander, Captain First Rank S. G. Gorshkov, decided to conduct the landing on schedule but chose dinghies instead to land the troops.

The Grigorievka landing was highly regarded both for its concept and its execution. The success of the landing and the actions of the amphibious force on the beach depended in large measure on the decision of Captain First Rank Gorshkov to use dinghies. This assured the simultaneous assaults by the rifle division and the amphibious force.

The largest amphibious landing both in dimensions and in goals during the first part of the war was at Kerch-Feodossiya. This was done by the Caucasian Front and the Black Sea Fleet from 25 December 1941 to 2 January 1942. Its goal was the liberation of the Kerch peninsula and the opening of a new front in Crimea. The intention was to draw enemy forces from their encirclement of Sevastapol and create favorable conditions for the liberation of Crimea.

The operational plan envisioned landings along a broad front, particularly near the community of Ak-Monai on the northern coast of the Kerch peninsula and near Feodossiya, on the south coast, in order to cut off the enemy troops west of Kerch by outflanking them. The main attack was to be at Feodossiya, with smaller forces directed against various points along the opening of the Kerch Straits into the Black Sea (Sea of Asov). In Feodossiya, elements of the 44th Army, with a total strength of forty-four thousand men, were to be put ashore with their weapons and battle gear. In the area of the Kerch Straits, the landing of about thirteen thousand men from the 51st Army was planned. In addition, approximately three thousand men from the 44th Army were to go ashore at Cape Opuk.[2]

The Feodossiya landing was planned to take place directly in the harbor in order to shorten the length of the operation. The first landing wave was transported aboard warships which had to penetrate the harbor area. Special storm troops on smaller boats, in their role as forward units, took control of the piers to secure the arrival of the first landing wave aboard warships.

In order to block the retreat of the enemy's forces on the Kerch peninsula, airborne troops were landed near Arabat by TB-3 aircraft.[3]

The successful completion of the Kerch-Feodossiya operation removed the danger of an enemy advance across the Kerch Straits to the Taman Peninsula and forced the German 11th Army, which had laid siege to Sevastapol, into a defense posture. From this operation, Soviet naval forces collected extremely valuable experience in the preparation and execution of similar such operations, including circumstances when the enemy put up strong coastal resistance and had an extensive air force at its disposal. A completely new aspect for the navy were the troop landings by warship directly in the enemy harbor, a method later designated as Coast-Coast. It was determined in the course of this operation that artillery preparation was inappropriate, because the landing of troops was best done covertly, taking advantage of the element of surprise. In Feodossiya, naval gunfire served the enemy as a kind of warning signal so that the first landing wave in the harbor was subjected to considerable enemy fire. An additional peculiarity of the Kerch-Feodossiya amphibious operation was the fact that it took place without air support of any kind.

The most important action of this kind during the entire Great Patriotic War was conducted by forces of the 18th and 56th Army, the Black Sea Fleet, and the Asov Flotilla, from 31 October to 11 December 1943 at Kerch-Eltigen. This operation was intended to create favorable conditions for the liberation of Crimea by the 4th Ukranian Front and the Northern Caucasian fronts. The operations plan envisioned simultaneous landings along three coastal segments. The amphibious force of the 56th Army was to be put ashore on the spit of land north and east of Kerch and then occupy this area as well as the city of Kerch. The amphibious force of the 18th Army was to land near Eltigen and build a beachhead near Kamysch-Burgun-Cape Takil. The subsequent mission of both amphibious units was to liberate the eastern part of the Kerch peninsula.

The geographic peculiarities of the area for the planned operation and the mining of the Kerch Straits were cause for the landing being conducted with only light amphibious craft and after careful minesweeping. The amphibious force had fire cover from 667 army and fleet guns (77 mm to 203 mm) and from 90 grenade launchers. One air group was deployed in air support. It consisted of about six hundred aircraft from the naval air force of the Black Sea Fleet and from the 4th Air Force.[4]

The amphibious operation at Kerch-Eltigen offers an example of landing large forces against a major, well-prepared amphibious defense, as well as for the comprehensive deployment of ground and coastal artillery in support of the amphibious force. Because of poor weather, the landings could not take place simultaneously along several coastal segments but had to be conducted in stages. As a result, the enemy forces did not have to focus on several battles at once and could direct the main attack against the 18th Army.

The Soviet amphibious forces were still able to repel the enemy's attacks. The iron discipline of the 18th Army had its basis above all in the extensive and multifaceted training carried out by Party and Komsomol (Communist Youth Organization) organizations, the army's entire Party and political apparatus directed by the battle-tested expert L. I. Brezhnev during the preparation and execution of the operation.

In the course of this operation it became clear that the air force's role had grown considerably, both for direct support of the landing and for the landing assault itself. The supreme commander of the 18th Army requested the naval air commander of the Black Sea Fleet to express the infantry's gratitude for its assistance in repelling the thirty-seven enemy infantry and armor attacks during the two and one-half days.[5] Transport aircraft were also used for the first time in such operations to resupply the landing forces with munition and foodstuffs. The aircraft of the Black Sea Fleet and the 4th Air Force flew 4,411 sorties during the Kerch-Eltigen amphibious operation in addition to 17 bomber group sorties.[6]

Among the amphibious operations taking place during the third period of the war, the Tuloksa and Muhu Sound island landings had special significance. The Ladoga Flotilla, the Baltic Red Banner Fleet, and troops of the Leningrad Front were involved. The Tuloksa amphibious operation conducted by the Ladoga Flotilla took place shortly before the landings to free the islands in the Viborg Bay of the Gulf of Finland.

The Karelian Front's offensive along the eastern shore of Lake Ladoga at the end of June 1944 required use of the Ladoga Flotilla. The Karelian Front commander proposed to the commanding officer of the Ladoga Flotilla to put an amphibious force ashore in the tactical rear of the enemy defenses. Because such a measure promised no operational advantages and no complete success, and because the enemy would have been able to transfer its superior forces quickly from the nearby front to repulse the landing force, the flotilla commander, Rear Admiral V. S. Tscherokov, suggested that the landing be made in the operational rear of the enemy defenses, that is, at the mouth of the Tuloksa River into Lake Ladoga, and thereby interdict the enemy's most important lines of communication and reinforcement.[7] The landing was to take place in two stages, four to six hours apart. The commander of the Karelian Front, General K. A. Merezhov, and the commander of the Baltic Red Banner Fleet, Admiral V. F. Tribuz, approved this proposal.

During preparations for the landing operation, the Ladoga Flotilla was supported by the Karelian Front's 7th Army in taking the River Svir. A special feature of this landing operation was the systematic, mission-oriented intelligence gathering during preparations which simplified the landing and the actions of the force once it was ashore. Also essential was the proper organization for use of naval gunnery in support of the landing force: a special artillery group was established for each battalion of the 70th Brigade.

The landing took place on the morning of 23 June 1944. The 23rd Independent Naval Infantry (Marine) Brigade spread out quickly across the beach and began the attack. They disrupted the road and rail connections and destroyed an enemy artillery unit. The enemy ordered reserves into the landing area and began to put up bitter resistance. As a result, once the landing force reached Lake Lindoya and the highway and railroad line, it was forced into defensive posture. The enemy, meanwhile, summoned additional reserves and initiated dogged attacks against the 70th Brigade, which began to run low on ammunition. Towards noon on 24 June, a crisis developed for the landing force when the enemy, in a resolute storm attack, began destroying the beachhead using artillery and mortars. Although the Ladoga Flotilla transferred all its munitions supplies to the amphibious force and increased artillery support as much as possible, the brigade strength was obviously not sufficient to surmount the crisis. The Karelian Front commander therefore ordered the 3rd Marine Brigade to be put ashore. This action completely transformed matters in the landing zone. By the evening of 24 June, the enemy was forced into a defensive stance and finally had to withdraw. In the early morning of 27 June, the amphibious force, having completed its mission, joined the forward units of the 7th Army and took part in the remainder of the offensive.

Contributing to the success of this landing was the thorough planning and preparation. As a result, improvisations such as had been necessary in the first period of the war could be avoided. The landing zone and the individual landing points had been carefully selected. The number of transports and landing craft, and gunfire support ships, the order of march, the landing, and the possibility of repeated use of the landing craft had all been precisely planned and exactly organized.

Despite all these considerations, however, one error emerged in estimating the size of the amphibious force which might have jeopardized the operation. In landing the marine brigade about 35 km behind the front, it had not been taken into consideration that the enemy, in the era of mechanized armies, could redeploy his forces in the landing area within two hours. But the enemy delayed the start of effective measures against the Soviet landing force and did not redeploy its forces into the landing zone until ten hours later. These experiences again confirmed the need for a mobile reserve in the landing force which can be rapidly deployed on land or water.

The amphibious operation on the Muhu Sound islands took place in particular geographic circumstances. As a result of the intensive mining of the Gulf of Finland, it was also impossible to use the large combatants from the Baltic Red Banner Fleet.

The Muhu Sound islands had especial importance for the German Supreme Command because they covered the sea lanes into Riga. They were therefore to be defended at all cost. With this goal in mind, the German troops on the island were reinforced in mid-September by an infantry division. By means of an offensive of the three Baltic Fronts, the Soviet Supreme Command planned to cut off the German Army Group North from East Prussia, liberate Riga, and clear the enemy out of the Kurland peninsula. In the context of this operation, the Leningrad Front, together with the Baltic Red Banner Fleet, was to carry out an amphibious operation to liberate the Muhu Sound islands.

During the initial phase of the amphibious operations, in which a large number of boats of the most diverse sort were employed, naval infantry liberated the island of Vormsi on 27 September 1944. This opened the Vodsi-Kurk narrows for ships' passage and allowed the vessels subsequently to be stationed along the Estonian coast. Later action to liberate the Muhu Sound islands was transferred to the 8th Army, to which the Estonian Rifle Corps belonged. For the landing operation, the Baltic Red Banner Fleet prepared fifty-five fast patrol boats, thirteen coastal patrol boats, thirteen minesweepers, eight armored craft, as well as numerous cutters and tenders. Command of the forces in this operation had not been clearly determined and delineated. Command of the ground forces was with the Supreme Commander of the 8th Army, Lieutenant General F. N. Starikov. Rear Admiral I. G. Suyatov was the commander of the participating fleet forces. Despite much overlapping and disagreement, the outcome was remarkably precise organization and cooperation between naval and ground forces, both during the accelerated preparation and actual execution of the amphibious operation.

The operation plan envisioned capturing the islands one after the other. The first island to be liberated was Muhu, separated from the main landing by a three mile wide narrows. Landings on the Island of Hiiumaa (Dago) and Saaremaa (Osel), both heavily defended, were to follow. In accordance with this decision, the troops from the 8th Army and the naval forces were organized into two groups: the northern group for the liberation of Hiiumaa and the southern group for the landing on Muhu.

The island of Muhu was liberated on 29–30 September by the amphibious force which crossed the narrows on fast torpedo boats and landing craft, while receiving artillery and mortar support fire from the mainland. The enemy had to withdraw to the island of Saaremaa, but in retreat blew up the causeway between the two islands.

The landing on the island of Hiiumaa, which was supposed to take place as quickly as possible for operational and tactical reasons, was delayed until 2 October 1944, because the available landing craft could not be employed during stormy weather. Despite heavy enemy fire, the fast torpedo boats put the first wave ashore at the pier in the Heltermaa Harbor. By holding enemy artillery batteries down, fighter bomber units made victory much easier. After pushing back the enemy's amphibious defenses, the landing force pressed the attack into the island's interior under the cover of bomber and fighter-bomber units. Although the enemy tried to stabilize his resistance effort through surface forces, he had to retreat to the island of Saaremaa during the night of 2–3 October 1944.

Most difficult of all was the liberation of Saaremaa, because the enemy had reinforced his ranks on the island with the 218th Infantry Division and additional troop elements drawn from Muhu and the other islands which had been lost. Lieutenant General Schirmer, commander of the German troops on the Muhu Sound islands, assumed that a Soviet landing on Saaremaa would most likely take place along the island's north and southeastern coasts, and therefore deployed his troops so that they could operate in any possible direction. Defensive works were constructed in areas with the greatest threat.

After the liberation of Muhu and Hiiumaa, the Soviet forces immediately began with the landing on Saaremaa. The Estonian Rifle Corps had meanwhile been concentrated on Muhu, and additional ground forces and amphibious craft stood ready at Rohukula and Virtsu and near the island of Kassaar. The naval forces and air force at the front conducted air intelligence operations over the island and its sea approaches.

Army artillery provided gunfire preparation and support of the landing at the beginning of the assault while the battle was still on the beach or in the vicinity of the coast. The ships used during the landing were not capable of providing fire cover. Moreover, as a result of the geographic conditions, the landings on the neighboring islands closely resembled the taking of water obstacles. One characteristic feature of the actions to liberate Saaremaa was the participation of airplanes, particularly from the naval air wing. They collected intelligence on the landing defenses of the enemy on the island, covered from the air the concentrations of Soviet surface forces in the Gulf of Riga, and provided air cover for the landing force during the assault and in all phases of the amphibious battle; they also flew bombing sorties against the ships and transports of the enemy in his staging areas and transportation centers, as well as against the water approaches to the island of Saaremaa.

The landing of Soviet troops along a broad front tied down all the enemy's troops on Saaremaa. There were thus no troops available to the German commander to initiate a counterattack. Because it proved impossible under these circumstances to organize a stable defense of the central part of the island, the German commander was forced to withdraw his troops en masse back to the Sorve Peninsula and establish a defensive line there. The liberation of Sorve basically represents a new, separate battle action by the Leningrad Front and the Baltic Red Banner Fleet.

The landing to liberate the Muhu Sound islands in the fall of 1944 was the largest battle of this kind conducted by the Baltic Red Banner Fleet during the Great Patriotic War. It contributed to the development of Soviet naval doctrine precisely because of the military-operational peculiarities of the landing zone. The experience gathered from the landing on islands separated from the mainland by narrows is of special value for Soviet naval forces. The close proximity of these islands to one another and to the Estonian coast on the one hand, and the military situation along the land front in the Baltic region in late September 1944, on the other, favored a somewhat unusual type of landing—the direct transfer of forces from coast to coast. The relatively small size of the narrows between the islands even allowed for the crossing to take place quickly, with relatively slow amphibious craft, under cover of darkness. Based on the experience from the battles on Saaremaa on 5 October 1944, one could presume that a timely airborne landing behind the first line of German defenses might have dramatically speeded up all subsequent actions by Soviet troops to free the island and the Sorve peninsula.

In any generalization of Soviet amphibious operation experience from the Great Patriotic War, one needs to take note of the concentration of such operations during both the defensive and offensive phases of the war. During the first period of the war, forty landings took place, or 35 percent of all such actions conducted during the Great Patriotic War. Fifty-seven thousand men took part in these operations.[8] On the average, one landing took place every ten days. As the actual battles demonstrated, the amphibious operations were the most active form of cooperation between naval and ground forces, in addition to being an especially complicated kind of warfare.

The large number of landings by Soviet naval forces was helped along by the peculiarities of the naval combat theaters, the military situation in these theaters and along the coast, the superiority of Soviet naval forces in number of ships compared with the enemy, and the high morale of Soviet officers and men. Amphibious landing doctrine went through a drastic development during the Great Patriotic War. Largely from this development, a Soviet school of thought regarding amphibious operations resulted. Mission goals were achieved in all operational landings and in 80 percent of the tactical landings. Contributing to this success rate were both the energetic penetration of enemy defenses and the rapid, covert preparation of amphibious operations, even though embarkation points and landing zones were generally not far from the front. In this context, the camouflaging of actions assumed special importance; the element of surprise played a role in no fewer than seventy-six amphibious landings. The landings took place not only during different periods of the war, but also during every time of year; for example, the landings of Kerch-Feodossiya and Merekiul (February 1944) were conducted in winter.

Among the most important aspects of Soviet amphibious operations was that they took place over relatively short distances. This meant that in virtually all instances Soviet air cover was available from nearby airfields. Moreover, the bomber force and combat air groups developed into an important element in the landing assault; the bomber forces were brought to bear before the actual landing, while combat air supported the landing itself and the actions of the landing force along the coast. Combat experience confirmed the prewar attitude entirely regarding the usefulness of airborne actions in conjunction with amphibious landings. For most landings, the enemy had superiority in numbers of ground troops. At sea, however, Soviet forces met enemy resistance in only three instances. Short-term preparations were also a mark of Soviet landing operations. Sixty-one of 113 landings were prepared in less than twenty-four hours. The reasons for this were the peculiarities of the operational and strategic situation along the Soviet-German front. During the first period of the war, when the Soviet armed forces did not have the strategic initiative, it proved necessary to meet the rapid advance of enemy forces by landing forces in coastal areas, or by stabilizing lines of defense for naval bases and important coastal regions. In the last two periods of the war, the speed of preparation was determined by the rapid tempo of advancing Soviet forces. During this phase, the Soviet naval forces, using operational and tactical landings, had to react quickly to changes in the military situation in coastal regions. This dynamic activity by landing forces was based on a high level of operational and combat training by staffs and troop units.

The enemy defenses also influenced the development of forms and methods of amphibious landings considerably. The ever-increasing strength and depth of these defenses, and their growing maneuverability forced Soviet forces into maximum reinforcement of amphibious forces and improvement of their maneuverability in order to be able to deploy these forces quickly and attack in the most favorable area. The landings on the Muhu Sound islands and the landing at Stanitschka-Yuzhnaya Ozereyka on the Black Sea are examples of this sort of operation. Rapid development of new mines and their massive use, together with the difficulty of mine defense, required special measures to protect landing forces during water crossing and in the assault area itself. Antisubmarine protection was easy by comparison, because the geographical and navigational conditions in the landing areas, and the use of small ships and large numbers of boats, virtually removed the threat of enemy submarines. Experience demonstrated the need to limit the time for landing and establishing a beachhead, in order to forestall the enemy's deployment of amphibious defenses, particularly his more mobile forces. Even though the extent of various defensive measures was expanded during combat at sea, protection of the amphibious operation in all its phases was particularly important to prevent counterattacks by the enemy even before the landing of the amphibious force.

Surprising the enemy particularly in the most complicated and most significant phase of the operation, the beach assault itself, became more and more difficult as the possibilities for electronic intelligence grew through use of reconnaissance aircraft. During the final phase of the war, these developments led to active countermeasures among the landing forces. The landings then generally took place at night, to guarantee secrecy and the element of surprise. Combined artillery and air raid actions preceding the landings was of course more difficult under these circumstances, and fire to pin down the enemy defenses could not be applied as massively and effectively as would otherwise be the case. Rocket launchers, particularly missile launchers, played a large role in pinning down the enemy's defenses and his counterfire at the end of the war.

In order to speed up the landing, and thus shorten the time during which the landing force was subject to enemy fire, transport and amphibious craft of special design were needed. The lack of these craft negatively influenced the tempo of landings, which in turn forced the use of a great variety of boats. These were maneuverable and mobile enough, but had virtually no means of protecting themselves from enemy fire. Equipping the landing units with modern combat technology and weaponry, particularly tanks and self-propelled vehicles, made large demands on the cargo-carrying abilities of transport and amphibious craft, as well as on the speed in embarking and debarking operations. Trying to penetrate the enemy's rear areas with limited forces using the coastal flank was demonstrated to be of little value. Landing operations especially during the first period of the war showed that the landing forces have to be strong enough to carry out their mission. The unfavorable termination of landing operation and failures by ground forces attacking in the coastal zone frequently led to defeats. Similar errors occurred in February 1943 along the Black Sea coast during the landing at Yuzhnaya Ozereyka and even a year later on the Baltic coast during the landing at Merekiul.

The landing operation on the Muhu Sound islands and the landing at Kerch-Eltigen confirmed the large possibilities for coastal and field artillery in supporting amphibious troops.

The landings conducted by the Baltic Red Banner Fleet advanced the development of forms and methods for similar operations along rocky coasts and island areas.

The landings established the major role of naval infantry in all the theaters of the war.

Naval infantry, as the driving force of the first wave of the amphibious troops, was able to defeat the enemy's landing defenses quickly and penetrate into its interior areas.

The multifaceted and mission-oriented party political work played a large role in the success of the amphibious operations. It was carried out during all phases of combat and by all units of the cooperating forces on a large scale. The members of the Soviet army and the Soviet navy also developed mass heroism during the amphibious operations of the Great Patriotic War and won for themselves undying fame. Commanders such as admirals A. G. Golovko, V. F. Tribuz, F. S. Oktyabr'skiy, L. A. Vladirmirsky, I. S. Yumaschev, S. G. Gorshkov, N. Ye. Basistyy, J. F. Ralli, I. G. Suyatov, and G. N. Kholostyakov had a special part in the successful and daring execution of landing operations.

The experience gathered by Soviet naval forces during the conduct of landing operations continues to hold great significance for the development of naval doctrine, even though changes in weaponry that have taken place in the meantime also have to be taken into consideration.

Notes

[1] Cf. *Der Kamafweg der sowjetischen Seekriegsflotte* (Berlin: 1976), pp. 220, 356ff., 362ff., 389f., 402ff., 429ff.

[2] G. F. Godlevskii, A. M. Grecanjuk, V. M. Kononenko, *Bocbody boevye* (Moscow: 1966), pp. 102f.

[3] G. P. Safonov, *Vozudsoye desanty vo vtoroj mirovoj vojne* (Moscow: 1962), pp. 36ff.

[4] Central'oyi Voenno-Morskii Archiv, f. 24, d. 32 692, 1. 10.

[5] Ibid., f. 6, d. 39 234, 1. 51–55.

[6] Ibid.

[7] Ibid., f. 13, d. 13 198, 1. 4.

[8] Ibid., f. 6, d. 11 242, d. 33 324.

Preparations for the Amphibious Invasion of Normandy, 1944

BY SUSAN H. GODSON

In the Normandy attack, known as Operation Neptune-Overlord, Admiral John Leslie Hall, Jr., had two distinct functions. Both duties were exceedingly complicated and important. As commander of Assault Force "O," he had to plan and execute the landing of half the American ground troops at Normandy. But first, as commander of the Eleventh Amphibious Force, he had to supervise joint training and make sure that ships and craft were ready for the invasion.

In early 1944, when preparations for the Normandy assault began in earnest, the Allies were on the offensive around the world. On the eastern front the Russians shoved back German armies and planned a massive attack to coincide with the Normandy invasion. In Italy Allied armies slowly and painfully inched northward. Another amphibious invasion at Anzio, designed to help the sagging ground war, nearly failed. Vicious German resistance kept the troops on the beachhead for four long months. But with increasing impunity, Royal Air Force and U.S. Eighth Air Force bombers relentlessly sowed destruction in Germany's heartland. On the other side of the globe the Japanese fell back in Burma and India. In the southwest Pacific the Allies continued their advance along New Guinea's coast. In November 1943 the Americans began their drive through the Central Pacific by landing on Tarawa in the Gilbert Islands. Here the naval and landing forces

Viking of Assault: Admiral John Leslie Hall, Jr., and Amphibious Warfare (Washington, D.C.: University Press of America, 1982), pp. 107–27. Reprinted by permission

learned many of the same amphibious lessons discovered by Hall and Hewitt a year earlier in North Africa. Two months later, and seven months after the amphibious turning point at Sicily, the navy put together efficient amphibious attacks at Kwajalein and then Eniwetok, in the Marshalls. The string of island campaigns rolling toward Japan was under way.

The time was ripe for an overwhelming cross-channel invasion that would close the ring around Germany. After gaining a beachhead at Normandy, Allied armies would push through France and into Germany. Final plans for the operation emerged after Eisenhower, the supreme allied commander, arrived in Britain in early 1944. The American and British navies would land Allied armies on a 50-mile front between the Cotentin Peninsula and the Orne River in the Bay of the Seine. D-day would be 5 June. The Germans, fully expecting the onslaught, had plenty of time to fortify the coasts of France. Salerno and Anzio had shown how tough landings could be against well-defended beaches.

Admiral Sir Bertram H. Ramsay, commander-in-chief of the Allied Naval Expeditionary Force (ANCXF), would be responsible for Neptune, the amphibious assault phase of Overlord. Under Ramsay, the Americans and British would have separate naval forces. Rear Admiral Alan G. Kirk's Western Naval Task Force would land Lieutenant General Omar N. Bradley's U.S. First Army on two beaches of the Carentan estuary. Under Kirk, Hall would carry the Fifth Corps to the Omaha beach while Rear Admiral Don P.

Invasion Rehearsals, English Coast, 1944. Observing are (left to right) LtGen. Omar Bradley, USA; RAdm. John Leslie Hall, USN; MajGen. Leonard T. Gerow, USA; and MajGen. Clarence L. Huebner, USA. Courtesy of the U.S. Navy Historical Center.

Moon landed the Seventh Corps on the Utah beach. In the Eastern Naval Task Force, Rear Admiral Sir Philip Vian would lift the British Second Army to three beaches between Arromanches and the Orne River. Normandy would be the supreme test for Allied amphibious capability.

At the end of November 1943 Hall reached Britain and settled into his new command, headquartered at Plymouth. By this time Hall was fifty-two years old, and the responsibilities of the past year had taken their toll. Still ramrod straight, vigorous, and commanding-looking, he had, nevertheless, aged considerably. His hair was snow white, his face deeply lined. He cared deeply about his duties and his men. They were on his mind constantly. He often took a little time from his arduous duties to play a few rounds of golf, following his lifelong habit of seeking physical and mental relaxation in sports.

When Hall began his work, he took over the small Amphibious Forces, Europe, and an organization comprising 235 landing craft and 9 bases. Both units merged into the Eleventh Amphibious Force. Hall had to train thousands of amphibious assault personnel for the most crucial invasion of the European war as well as help the British defend the advanced amphibious bases scattered throughout the United Kingdom. His command would involve his first real taste of combined relations. Hall quickly turned his attention to the best means of training his amphibians. Considering the enormity and importance of the upcoming operation, his responsibilities were mind-boggling. Seasoned by his command of the Eighth Amphibious Force, he now acted with the assurance born of experience. This time there was no gnawing self-doubt about his own capability, although his duties were larger and more complex than ever before. Hall would have to work with the British as well as the American army and navy.

Fortunately Hall had no staff problems in Britain. Realizing he had a good team, he brought most of his staff with him from North Africa. Captain Little became planning officer, and Commander C. H. K. Miller replaced him as head of operations. Commander Melling, Hall's communications star in Morocco, was back on the staff.

Hall and his staff lived on board the *Ancon*,

the first amphibious command ship to arrive in the theater. A Panama Railroad steamship converted to a force flagship, the *Ancon* had been Kirk's command ship at Sicily and Hewitt's at Salerno. She had communications equipment and circuits far exceeding many shore communications centers. At last, Hall felt, he would have no concern about an inadequate flagship.

Hall organized his force along the same lines he had used in the Mediterranean. There were task groups to handle landing craft and bases, transports, gunfire support craft, beach battalions, and escort sweepers. The invasion training center consisted of the joint amphibious schools.

Under the efficient leadership of Rear Admiral John Wilkes, the landing craft and bases group oversaw U.S. naval bases, now increased to sixteen, in the United Kingdom. Wilkes had to make certain that American ships and craft were kept in good running order. So successful was his outfit that an astounding 99.3 percent of the vessels were operational on D-day. Wilkes trained officers and sailors to man the landing craft and boats. The crews received intensive instruction and practice in ship-to-shore movement, landing and retracting, and maneuvering the craft. They learned about beach party operations, beach markings, salvage, and maintenance. After practicing at their bases, the crews took part in joint training exercises. Wilkes trained about eighty-seven thousand men to handle nearly twenty-five hundred ships and craft. With his headquarters at Plymouth, Wilkes often consulted with Hall. Wilkes was a highly competent and skilled commander but was a little abrasive. Hall sometimes had to smooth British feathers that Wilkes had ruffled.

The transport group, under Commodore C. D. Edgar, had four transport divisions. Edgar had effectively handled transports in Hall's three earlier operations. Taking troops aboard his big ships, Edgar taught them landing procedures. To sharpen the amphibious skills of the crews and soldiers, the transports participated in joint training exercises.

Training and experimentation with small craft for close gunfire support fell to Captain Lorenzo S. Sabin. Normandy would be the first operation with all task forces using British shallow-draft gunfire support craft as a preplanned part of fire support. Hall had learned the crafts' value in the northern area at Salerno. Frustrated by late deliveries of British craft, Sabin taught American crews of LCT(R)s (landing craft tank, rocket), LCGs (landing craft gun), and LCFs (landing craft flak), and other small vessels to use their guns and rockets in early support of ground forces.

Beach battalions often combined their training with army engineer special brigades. These men had to keep the beaches clear after the landing. They practiced landing craft salvage and removal of underwater and beach obstacles. Naval combat demolition units worked with army combat engineers in mastering obstacle removal. When Hall learned about sophisticated obstacles on and off the Normandy beaches, he enlarged and strengthened the demolition units. They built replicas of the deadly German obstacles and practiced destroying them.

Hall established joint amphibious schools to provide specialized training. As he had in the Mediterranean, he stressed naval gunfire support. Under the guidance of force gunnery officer, Commander Boatwright, Lieutenant (j.g.) Robert G. Osborne ran the school at the British Naval Academy at Dartmouth. Here army officers and men learned naval gunfire control techniques and communications. Men from joint assault signal companies trained for the first time as spotters. After these men finished at the school, they took part in firing exercises and joint training exercises. They boarded the ships they would be on for Normandy for a week's observation of firing. Gunfire support ships, including British and French, practiced at nearby Slapton Sands. Heavy gunfire ships held firing exercises at Firth of Clyde in Scotland. New SCR-609 FM radios helped contact between shore fire control parties and fire support ships.

After his harrowing experiences in the Mediterranean, Hall bore down hard on combat loading techniques. His transport quartermaster school instructed twelve classes of army officers and enlisted men. They learned how to combat load transports, landing craft, military transports, and cargo ships. These men received early assignments to their transports. The intensive training would pay off during loading for Operation Neptune-Overlord.

Hall's communications officer, Melling, oversaw the joint communications school. He trained army and navy men in classrooms and on board ships. Always complex in any amphibious assault, communications promised to be especially difficult in the massive Normandy operation. There were many radio transmitters, broadcasting stations, and jammers clogging all frequencies in Normandy, which might complicate assault communications.

Practice and still more practice, Hall maintained, would lead to mastery of vital amphibious skills. He kept up his refrain of wanting no more gold star mothers than necessary. His policy of familiarizing soldiers and sailors with their duties and with each other had worked well in the Eighth Amphibious Force, so he continued the same routine. When army and navy groups arrived in Britain, Hall quickly assigned them to their invasion units. As part of "practice" training, troops went on escorts, minesweepers, and destroyers for sea orientation. Soldiers practiced driving vehicles on and off landing craft and operating their equipment during loading, sailing, and unloading. Some sailors learned to use army equipment. Boat crews constantly practiced boat operation, beaching and retracting, and unloading cargo from large ships to smaller craft.

As the training program grew, Hall's force taught army units specific aspects of joint landings. The troops had been through preliminary amphibious training before they left the States. Hall's command gave them intensified practice and training in Britain. Throughout the five-month preparation period, the force provided planning and exercise facilities for infantry and armored regiments, field artillery and gun battalions, regimental and battalion combat teams, cargo

exercise forces and engineer shore and special brigades, and air force and special troop units. A training exercise usually lasted four days. The first day was for loading and sailing, then two days for daylight and nighttime landings, and the last day for returning to base.

While "practice" training continued, Hall's command organized and executed more than two dozen small- and large-scale joint training exercises. Vitally interested in these joint exercises, Hall supervised their planning and often personally commanded them. As naval forces refined their assault techniques, the exercises grew from battalion to reinforced division strength and included assault and follow-up landings. For larger exercises, Hall used naval gunfire and air support—at least air support was part of the plan. The aircraft usually failed to show up because of bad weather or some other reason. American destroyers reached Britain late in the training period, so British ships provided fire support. A weakness of the exercises was beach clearing. The ships were only partially loaded for combat, and beach congestion never simulated a real D-day. For most exercises, troops embarked at ports in southern Britain and landed at Slapton Sands or Tor Bay.

On 3–4 January 1944 the first major exercise, "Duck I," took place at Slapton Sands. Although the new amphibious command had insufficient time to prepare, political expediency dictated the date. Churchill had forced the residents of Slapton Sands to move because the area was to be a gunnery practice range. To justify his action, he then pressured American commanders in London to stage an exercise using live ammunition. More than two dozen high-ranking British and American officers came from London to watch the mock attack. Hall's force landed Major General Charles H. Gerhardt's Twenty-ninth Division, a part of the Fifth Corps. With this first exercise, Hall started "marrying up" naval and army forces in their units for Normandy. They would have plenty of time to train together. Watching from on board an LST, Hall observed the ragged edges of the exercise. There were insufficient ships, overloaded troops and vehicles, and generally poor joint coordination. Bradley also tried firing 105 mm howitzers from LCTs as the assault waves neared the beach. Hall found the process unsatisfactory because the army guns had unstable sights. Why not use gunfire support craft for the same purpose? Later, army, navy, and Royal Navy officers met on board the *Ancon* and then at Fifth Corps headquarters at Taunton to analyze the landings. The frank discussions revealed many correctable errors.

Heading for the meeting at Taunton, Hall's driver got lost. Fearful of a German invasion, the British had removed all road signs. After several passers-by failed to give directions, Hall's chief of staff stopped the next man who came along. In full military uniform, von Heimburg stepped from the car and thundered, "I am Captain von Heimburg. We are lost." The fellow froze in fear and muttered incoherently. "My God, Von, why did you tell the fellow your name?" laughed Hall. "He probably thought the Germans had finally invaded England."

Hall's amphibians had more time to prepare for subsequent exercises. In mid-February "Duck II" landed a regimental combat team at Slapton Sands. Hall watched from an LCI(L). To unload the LSTs, the assault force experimented with the new Rhino ferries. Rhinos were pontoons joined into barges and propelled by outboard motors. Better than "Duck I," the exercise still showed difficulties with joint coordination, traffic control, and handling of landing craft. Before the landing, Hall met with Bradley and other American generals to discuss assault techniques. After "Duck II," they held a joint critique on board the *Ancon*. These "before" and "after" conferences, Hall firmly believed, increased mutual understanding of operational problems.

In March some of Major General Leonard T. Gerow's Fifth Corps took part in a full-scale exercise, "Fox." These forces would actually land on Omaha beach on D-day. The assault force experimented with several new techniques. After DUKWs successfully carried ashore ammunition for emergency use,

Hall included this procedure in his assault plans. The force also tried out different methods of waterproofing vehicles. The exercise attracted many high-ranking officers. Bradley, several British generals, and Admirals Ramsay and Kirk watched from the *Ancon* or an LCI(L). Following Hall's standard custom, commanding officers attended a prelanding orientation and later evaluated the exercise. The landings favorably impressed Ramsay and the British generals.

As D-day drew nearer, Hall's amphibious force held two full-scale rehearsals. Duplicating as closely as possible the actual assault landings, rehearsals were almost as complicated to plan and execute as real invasions. The same process took place. After the army commander devised a scheme of maneuver ashore, the naval commander pointed out maritime difficulties. Both commanders resolved their differences. The naval operations staff drew up a landing attack plan to get the troops ashore on time and in the proper order. Joint staffs then wrote communications, air and naval gunfire support, and combat loading plans. Preparation for a rehearsal or an actual assault was a time-consuming project. It required the closest cooperation among army, navy, and air commanders and their staffs. Joint planning, so tenuous at North Africa and Sicily, had come a long way.

Admiral Moon, slated to land the Seventh Corps on Utah beach, held his rehearsal on 27–28 April. Called "Tiger," the exercise simulated the prospective Normandy attack. Before the assault force got to Slapton Sands, German submarines slipped in and sank two LSTs and damaged another. More than six hundred men were dead or missing. Under this heavy cloud, the landing continued. Using many craft slated for Force "U," Moon put twenty-five thousand troops and twenty seven hundred fifty vehicles ashore. More problems plagued the exercise. The beach engineer organization broke down, and interservice coordination was poor. Reminiscent of the Mediterranean, air support never arrived.

Hall's "Fabius I" dress rehearsal, from 3 to

6 May, landed most of the First Division, scheduled to assault the Omaha beaches. The rehearsal closely followed the landing plan for Normandy. Preceded by air and naval bombardment, twenty-five thousand troops went ashore at Slapton Sands. Engineers removed beach obstacles and mines and opened exits inland from the beach. Remembering his Mediterranean experiences, Hall insisted on complete unloading of ships in both "Tiger" and "Fabius I." Shore parties and beach battalions had thorough practice in dealing with the usual beach pileups. Many high-ranking U.S. Army, Navy, and Royal Navy commanders watched the rehearsal from on board the *Ancon*. Again, Hall held prelanding and follow-up conferences. Army leaders considered "Fabius I" heartening. Hall, striving for perfection, realized there were still rough spots to smooth. "Fabius I" was a great improvement over the Sicily and Salerno rehearsals. To Hall, the expert trainer, must go the credit for recognizing and acting on the need for realistic rehearsals.

As Hall continued to ready the invasion forces, many people in the United States realized that a European invasion was imminent. They could only speculate on when and where it would be. Admiral Harold R. Stark, commander of U.S. naval forces in Europe and of the Twelfth Fleet, sent Hall a young public relations officer to write news releases. Too busy to bother with possible leaks from his top secret command duties, Hall sent the officer back to London. Modest almost to a fault, Hall eschewed publicity. He felt he should fight the war rather than provide newspaper headlines. In later years the admiral regretted his decision. The navy never got sufficient credit, he believed, for its great contributions to European victory. Apparently he had failed to realize that personal and naval publicity were inseparable.

Hall was responsible for technological improvements and innovations that took place in his force. He had little technical ability himself, so he encouraged experts such as Wilkes to experiment. Wilkes's landing craft and bases group worked constantly to improve their vessels. They corrected many deficiencies which Hall had noted at Sicily and Salerno. All LSTs got new equipment for better communications, vehicle loading, casualty evacuation, and mooring the Rhino ferries. Some LSTs became fighter direction tenders or hospital ships while others received rearmament or changes in davits for easier lowering of landing boats. Wilkes improved steering gears and heating equipment in the LCI(L)s. Some craft had new radio and radar installations. Major structural changes strengthened the LCTs. Wilkes's men added bulwark doors for side loading and extended the ramps' length. Wilkes discussed all major changes in the vessels with Hall.

To help land stores on the far shore, naval construction battalions rigged up Rhino ferries, or pontoons lashed together and powered by dual engines. Thirty-seven of these 42×177-foot self-propelled lighters were ready to help unload larger ships. Always unimpressed with anything to do with pontoons, Hall considered Rhinos a waste of time and money. It was better to use the excellent landing craft already available than to fool with these new gadgets, he thought.

Wilkes's command devised another innovation, the mobile radio station. The amphibious base at Exeter built twelve units to ease the gap between the assault and the establishment of permanent communications centers ashore. Made from weapons-personnel carriers and one-ton trailers, the mobile stations housed ample sending and receiving equipment.

Other large-scale experimentation corrected earlier problems. Men at advanced training bases thought of better ways to waterproof vehicles and to land small craft in a surf. They improved unloading coasters (small British coastal vessels used port-to-port) and refloating stranded landing craft.

Aware of the complicated underwater obstacles off the Normandy coasts, Hall pushed his demolition experts to develop new explosive devices. They devised the unique Hagensen pack, which had a plastic explosive, composition C-2. A major innovation, the Hagensen pack became standard equipment in underwater obstacle removal.

Other new schemes were less promising. After arriving in the United Kingdom in late 1943, Hall met with First Sea Lord Sir Andrew Cunningham and Admiral Ramsay. The British officers showed him blueprints for artificial harbors, called Mulberries, that Allied navies would use off the French beaches. Years earlier the British had tried a similar harbor at Gallipoli. The Mulberries would substitute for major ports to unload LSTs early in the invasion. They were extremely complicated engineering projects. Floating steel units would serve as breakwaters. Then thirty-one enormous concrete caissons (phoenixes), towed and sunk in place by the attack forces, would form seawalls of the artificial harbors. Long piers (whales) would run ashore from the phoenixes. As one destroyer sailor to another, Cunningham asked Hall's opinion of the Mulberries. Anyone who had seen the sea toss around the French breakwater of 150-ton concrete blocks at Casablanca would laugh at such a foolish idea, Hall replied. Cunningham agreed. Ramsay, mindful that Roosevelt and Churchill had dreamed up the plan at the Quebec Conference, thought the Mulberries would work. Landing between one hundred fifty and three hundred LSTs on one tide would be far more efficient than unloading only two ships at a time on a Mulberry, Hall argued. His task force would succeed, Hall told Ramsay, in spite of bothering with a useless, fancy dock that would be unable to weather the first severe storm. In contrast to Hall and Cunningham, many American and British naval officers were excited about the artificial harbors' potential. Construction of two Mulberries, one each for the American and British forces, went ahead, at exorbitant expense to the Royal government.

To provide a ready supply of gasoline and oil, Operation Pluto projected pumping fuel through pipes across the English Channel. Hall fumed at what he considered yet another impractical scheme. Did no one realize, he asked, that a pipeline required oil tanks on the far shore for storage? If a beach were clear enough to permit building storage tanks, it was clear enough to send in naval tankers. Ships could pump oil far more quickly than a cross-Channel pipeline.

The Pluto and Mulberry projects, Hall believed, were demonstrations of impractical engineering ideas devised by the well-intentioned Roosevelt and Churchill, acting on the advice of nonmaritime engineers. Including a few amphibious force commanders in planning sessions would have helped the national leaders, Hall thought. Such naval officers could easily point to weaknesses in amphibious landing projects. Ultimately they could have saved money, manpower, and material.

Gooseberries were a more promising idea. Made by sinking old ships' hulks at the three-fathom line, Gooseberries would create a breakwater for ships and craft near the beaches. After the landings, tugs would tow and sink more than eighty ships off the five assault beaches.

Hall heard about still another innovation, DD (dual drive) amphibious tanks. With Admiral Vian, commander of the Eastern Naval Task Force, he watched a training exercise at Portsmouth using DD tanks. The British-designed duplex tanks had twin propellers for swimming and a track drive for going on land. Launched from LCTs, they would float ashore with their inflatable ''bloomers'' and provide immediate artillery support. Hall watched the big thirty-two-ton tanks lumber slowly toward shore, then run parallel to the beach. Within easy range of enemy machine guns, they were sitting ducks. Unimpressed with the latest pontoon gadgetry, Hall was opposed to taking DD tanks in his assault force. Bradley thought he had a winning secret weapon, however. Hall reluctantly agreed to land the tanks in the first wave at Omaha beach.

While training and amphibious experimentation continued, Hall attended many formal social events. Invitations came for Their Majesties' Afternoon Party, and for luncheons and dinners at the British Admiralty and with the Lord Mayor of London. Hall found it far more relaxing to socialize with Lord and Lady Astor, whom he had met when he and Mrs. Hall vacationed in Britain ten years earlier. Lord Astor was the mayor of Plymouth. Lady Astor was a Virginian, and her older sister was a friend of Hall's mother. The Astors could always find a bottle of Scotch for a hard-working sailor.

In addition to training, Hall had to help plan the vast, complex Normandy assault. Such planning required sustained contact and consultation among army, naval, and British commanders. Usually tactful, Hall was similar to Eisenhower in his ability to get along with other military figures. Commanders at Hall's echelon made no major invasion decisions. They had to execute, at the force level, Eisenhower's and Ramsay's orders. In the Mediterranean, Hall had only fleetingly dealt with the British. Combined planning was new to him. Hall's relations with British and American commanders were typical of the unevenness of Anglo-American and army-navy "harmony" and reflected the problems of combined and joint planning, but cooperation had to work.

Admiral Sir Ralph Leatham, commander-in-chief at Plymouth, was Hall's most frequent contact in the British navy. Although Leatham controlled the movement of all ships in his command area, his main duty was to make British facilities and resources available to Americans. At Plymouth the British had built a large underground command post with elaborate communications systems. Shortly after Hall's arrival, Leatham showed him the setup. When Leatham told Hall he could command his Normandy assault from the underground facility, Hall laughed. He could hardly imagine a task force commander holed up in Britain while his ships were fighting the Germans. "I'll be with my men off the Omaha beach," he said quietly. Since the *Ancon* was berthed at Plymouth, Hall saw Leatham often. The two admirals developed a good working relationship and a close friendship. They coped with problems ranging from British control of U.S. ships in the Plymouth command to social and welfare matters. Their genuine spirit of cooperation exemplified sound Anglo-American relations.

Equally amicable but less frequent were Hall's relations with Admiral Vian, commander of the Eastern Naval Task Force. Hall had known Vian in the Mediterranean where both men had taken part in the Sicily and Salerno operations. In Britain they attended conferences and exercises together. A thorough-going fighting man, Vian showed excellent amphibious judgment, Hall thought.

Hall's contacts with Admiral Ramsay were limited. Most top-level information sifted to Hall through Kirk. After Ramsay decided to have two American and three British naval assault forces, in March he ordered Hall to form Forces "O" and "U" as separate units. The order was a mistake, Hall believed. It would make administration, training, and maintenance far more difficult than keeping American naval forces under the unified command of the Eleventh Amphibious Force. In effect, Ramsay's order put the amphibious forces into dual attack organizations months before the invasion.

Distinctly resentful of British operational control of Neptune-Overlord, Hall reacted adversely to Ramsay's memorandum on how to write good orders. American upper-echelon orders contained only the barest essentials and left methods of execution to the good sense of subordinate commanders. In contrast, the British overloaded their orders with minute detail, leaving little to the discretion of lower commanders. Ramsay's memorandum, Hall felt, was silly. He paid no attention to it. The memorandum and the ill will it caused was another example of less-than-harmonious relations between Ramsay and American naval officers. Kirk also found Ramsay a difficult man to work with. Hall had a low opinion of Ramsay's capabilities and believed the Allies could have chosen a more competent man to command the naval forces at Normandy.

Hall tangled with still another Britisher. In February the Allies learned they would receive fewer ships than they had requested for the invasion. Eisenhower sent Hall to General Sir Bernard L. Montgomery's headquarters in London. Montgomery was in charge of all ground forces for Normandy. Hall explained to Major General Sir Francis de Guingand, Montgomery's chief of staff, how the Allies would have to adapt to reduced shipping. Montgomery would never accept such a reduction, de Guingand emphatically stated. Hall was amazed at such arrogance—the American services promptly relieved officers who refused to accept orders. He answered, "I'm not going back and tell the commander-in-chief that you say that your commander will not accept it . . . I'm here to tell him how to do it." If the British used American loading techniques, they would have enough craft. Hall never told Eisenhower what de Guingand had said.

Regardless of the uneven dealings with commanders in the United Kingdom, Britishers coming out of the Mediterranean spoke of Hall with admiration and affection. His achievements won him high honors. By order of King George VI, he received an honorary appointment as Companion of the Most Honourable Order of the Bath for "great skill and devotion to duty" as commander of the Gela force at Sicily. In February he and Kirk, who had won the same award, received their decorations at a colorful ceremony attended by top British naval officials. After reading the citation, the First Lord of the Admiralty hung the medal around Hall's neck.

On the surface, American naval officers displayed a harmonious front, but undercurrents and personality clashes were present. Hall had the closest dealings with Kirk, his boss. Kirk had given Hall a free hand in organizing the Eleventh Amphibious Force. Hall went to London many times to consult with Kirk about the operation plan for Force "O." Hall never thought much of Kirk's ability as a combat commander. Kirk was, Hall said, a showman with an eye for publicity. Kirk had been four classes ahead of Hall at the Naval Academy. Perhaps Hall was disgruntled because Kirk got the top American naval post for Neptune. With the exception of Hewitt, Hall had more amphibious operational experience than any flag officer in the European theater. Hewitt thought Hall was the better qualified man and was unpleasantly surprised when Admiral King selected Kirk. Apparently King quickly regretted the decision, too.

Stark, commander of the naval forces in Europe and of the Twelfth Fleet, was outside the chain of operational command for Normandy. He handled naval logistical and ad-

ministrative needs. Hall always saw Stark during his trips to London, and Stark sometimes visited Hall's flagship. The two men had a warm regard for each other. The gentle and kindly Stark, Hall always thought, had gotten unfairly shunted aside as chief of naval operations after Pearl Harbor. Stark was glad Hall would command a task force at Normandy. Hall provided, Stark wrote, "one of the greatest feelings of security I have . . . under your steady and controlling hand all that can be done will be done towards creating an effective Army-Navy team."

Admiral Moon, slated to command Force "U," arrived at Plymouth in early March. His only amphibious experience had been commanding a destroyer squadron in Torch. Moon was, Hall thought, in over his head in taking on an assault force. Moon worked too hard. He never learned to let others handle less important duties. He fretted about his force, his landing exercise, and the upcoming assault. Unsure of himself, he constantly consulted Hall. Hall liked Moon and felt sorry for him.

Throughout the preparation phase of Overlord, Hall was in frequent contact with the army. Unknown to Hall until many years later, officers at Eisenhower's headquarters in London gave him a nickname suited to his amphibious prowess: the Viking of Assault. The sturdy hulk of a man, with his bronzed, weatherbeaten face and bright blue eyes, did look like a Norseman of a bygone era.

Hall's main army associations were with the corps and division commanders whom he would land at Omaha beach. Hall regularly saw General Gerow, the Fifth Corps commander; General Gerhardt, commander of the Twenty-ninth Division; and, more often, Major General Clarence R. Huebner, First Division commander. Huebner's division would make the initial assault on D-day. The men conferred about training programs and exercises and about plans for Normandy. Their proximity to Hall's headquarters at Plymouth—Gerow was at Taunton, Gerhardt at Tavistock, and Huebner at Blandford—prevented planning difficulties such as those preceding Sicily. Hall considered Huebner a solid, reliable officer. He had risen through the ranks from cook to commanding general and had taken command of the First Division after the Sicily invasion. Gerow, as gentlemanly as Hall and a fellow Virginian, was a graduate of the Virginia Military Institute and became commander of the Fifth Corps in mid-1943. A man of highest integrity, he was always understanding of naval problems. Hall became disillusioned with Gerhardt. He watched the general climb on a stage at Plymouth during a performance of "Arsenic and Old Lace." Speaking extemporaneously, he blabbed nearly all the details of the Normandy attack except the date of D-day. The two men got along well professionally, however. Hall found no army reluctance to rely on naval command during the assault such as he had experienced in the Mediterranean.

Eisenhower got consistently low marks from Hall. Hall considered the supreme allied commander a mere figurehead, while the British made the important strategic and tactical decisions. Feeding into Hall's evaluation were probably the many occasions in the Mediterranean when he felt Eisenhower or his headquarters had mishandled situations. A fighter, Hall was disdainful of deskbound generals and admirals. In later years Hall passed unduly harsh judgment on Eisenhower: "He was one of the most overrated men in military history."

While preparing for Normandy, the army and navy quickly settled possible command difficulties. In December Hall had written Kirk about the vexatious problem. It was always necessary, he explained, "to convince Army commands that the landing and support of the troops is the Naval Commander's responsibility. I hope someday this will be very clearly stated from the highest commands, and will not remain just a unilateral Naval declaration and understanding." Kirk and Bradley had served in earlier joint operations and were aware of potential misunderstandings and confusion. On 23 February they issued a comprehensive agreement clearly defining the responsibilities of each service. Stressing the need for closest coop-

eration, the document spelled out army and navy duties for training, loading, operations, debarkation and unloading, and beach clearing. Most important, the naval task force commander had full control of both services after embarkation until the commanding general was established ashore. The Kirk-Bradley agreement was a milestone in amphibious warfare. Relieved to have common problems solved before they arose, Hall was delighted.

Friendliness also characterized army-navy personal relations with Ninth Air Force commander, Lieutenant General Lewis H. Brereton. As usual, the Army Air Forces remained outside the scheme of joint operations and refused to adopt any unity-of-command doctrine. Air force representatives took part in planning sessions for training exercises and for the Normandy assault. However, aircraft slated for the exercises often failed to appear. Slow in letting the navy know its plans for Neptune, the air force complicated invasion preparation.

The army in the European theater apparently exchanged little amphibious information with its counterpart in the Pacific. The navy followed a different pattern. Hall and Kirk exchanged information, technological advances, plans and orders, and action reports with Hewitt in the Mediterranean and Vice Admiral Richmond Kelly Turner and others in the Pacific. Hall stressed the sharing of amphibious information. "All of us were pioneers, really, in joint operations, right at the start of World War Two, and perhaps even as late as 1944 . . . we learned together . . . we learned the hard way."

Joint and combined working relations had progressed remarkably since those early days before North Africa. However, major conferences sometimes severely strained those fragile ties. The navy had its own share of problems.

A lack of landing craft and gunfire support ships threatened to consign the Normandy assault to the dustbin of failure. In mid-February Hall attended the "Landing Craft Conference" in London. Rear Admiral Charles M. Cooke of King's staff and a member of

General Marshall's staff met with representatives of Eisenhower's staff, Kirk, and Hall. Churchill had complained about the shortage of "some goddamn things called LSTs." To ease the shortage, the men at the conference agreed to transfer landing ships and craft from the Mediterranean and to send more LSTs from the United States. Better loading and servicing would help provide enough lift.

The men then discussed gunfire support ships. The British had earlier agreed to provide gunfire support for Neptune, and King went along with the idea. Hall's assault force would have the aged British battleship *Warspite,* which limped along at ten knots and boasted of one operating turret; the old American battleship *Arkansas;* a few small British destroyers; two French cruisers; and a Dutch gunboat. When Hall heard this, he banged his fist on the table and exclaimed, "It's a crime to send me on the biggest amphibious attack in history with such inadequate gunfire support. Any tiny island invasion in the Pacific can get plenty of gunfire support ships. Why am I not able to get even enough destroyers?" he asked.

"You have no right to talk like that," admonished Cooke.

"Who has a better right?" demanded Hall. "I'm landing the Fifth Corps and the Rangers on a heavily defended beach. I don't want them all killed because we didn't have enough naval guns." Although he knew Cooke could have him relieved of his command, Hall doggedly fought for more support ships. Kirk said nothing during this exchange. Cooke carried Hall's message to Washington. Hall *did* get more American combatant ships— three battleships and two destroyer squadrons, which he trained in April and May. Without Hall's sounding off, the troops never would have made it across the Omaha beaches.

At another high-level conference Hall tried again to reduce his probable casualties. In early May top commanders met at Ramsay's headquarters to decide the exact time of H-hour. Knowing about the treacherous obstacles off the Omaha beach, Hall pleaded to land his forces on the half-falling tide. The

low water would give his demolition teams a chance to remove the obstacles. The other assault commanders wanted to land on a rising tide. Montgomery, who had the final say, was against staggered times for the attacks because the Allies would give up any element of surprise. Sadly, Hall acquiesced. He knew he would lose more men because of the decision. To ease the tension after the disagreement, Hall passed around the front page of that day's newspaper. Ramsay had just been switched from the retired to the active naval list. The banner headline read, "Birth Rate Increases in England." Directly under it another headline proclaimed, "Ramsay Active Again!" The officers had a good laugh.

On 15 May the largest joint and combined meeting took place at St. Paul's School in London. King George VI, Churchill, Eisenhower, Montgomery, Ramsay, Air Chief Marshal Sir Trafford Leigh-Mallory, and all the lesser commanders were there. A well-placed enemy bomb could have wiped out the entire command for the Normandy invasion. After the group heard assault plans for each of the services, Field Marshal Jan Smuts, prime minister of the Union of South Africa, soured the gathering. He doubted the invasion could succeed. The king, however, earnestly expressed his confidence because God was on the Allied side. Churchill gave one of his rousing, optimistic speeches.

While training and the numerous conferences continued, Hall supervised the preparation of his force's assault plan. His plans staff worked closely with the staffs of Gerow, Gerhardt, and Huebner to determine how the navy could meet army requirements. In comparison with Hall's earlier invasions, the planning phase seemed almost leisurely. There was plenty of time. Hall often called the assault group commanders on board the *Ancon* while his own operation order was still being prepared. These officers offered suggestions for Hall's order and became thoroughly familiar with overall attack plans.

When the staff plan was ready, Hall spent long hours poring over its complex details. He rarely left his desk except for meals. The plan was unsatisfactory to him. It focused on operations and movements rather than on accomplishments. An operation plan, Hall felt, should show the completed picture—how you want the enemy to look after you have beaten the devil out of him—rather than dwell on small tactical details. He finally called in Boatwright, his versatile gunnery officer. He told the young officer the things he wanted in the first part of the plan and sent him off to make the changes. Boatwright quickly returned with a perfect opening section of the operation plan. In the finished product, Hall's order described the desired accomplishments of the assault and then went on to detail the actions of the force's components.

After Hall issued his order on 20 May, another problem threatened the security of the operation. Hall learned a trusted member of his staff, who had access to the sensitive order, was a homosexual. At that time such a predilection was a disgrace and grounds for courtmartial. But D-day was near. Calling attention to the officer, Hall feared, might cause him to commit suicide or to reveal secret information to the enemy. Hall handled the matter discreetly. Without mentioning the problem, he let the officer continue his duties until after the Normandy invasion, then quietly sent him back to the United States.

As Hall's ships assembled in scattered ports in the United Kingdom, combat loading began. This time it was completely successful. Determined to avoid the difficulties he had experienced in the Mediterranean, Hall worked closely with the army in overcoming earlier problems. After careful training in

Hall's transport quartermaster school and early assignment to their transports, army officers prevented misunderstandings and mistakes in combat loading. Hall severely restricted the transports' cargo. He allowed only embarked troops and several dozen vehicles on board each one. Stores and equipment could come later. Hall was gratified at army willingness to work with the navy on this important and usually confusing aspect of amphibious warfare.

The well-run preparation stage of Operation Neptune-Overlord contrasted with earlier seaborne assaults. Gone was the uncertainty and hesitancy, the groping for means and methods. Military commanders, many tempered by trial and error experiences in North Africa and the Mediterranean, moved with assurance in preparing for the most complex and hazardous operation to date.

Under Hall's guidance, the Eleventh Amphibious Force became a giant reservoir of ships and trained men for the American assault and follow-up forces. The command expanded from 235 landing craft in November 1943 to 2,493 vessels by June 1944. Hall trained about one hundred twenty thousand naval officers and men and about one hundred thousand army personnel. He established the rigorous training program, supervised joint exercises and rehearsals, encouraged innovations in amphibious equipment, and dealt with British and American commanders. Improvements in amphibious warfare and Hall's growing expertise moved ahead together. Justifiably, he was pleased when his force prepared to sail for Normandy. "We were ready," he smiled.

Amphibious Aspects of the Normandy Invasion

BY HANSON W. BALDWIN

The amphibious operations of the Pacific, which in 1945 will open their greatest chapter, will profit by the lessons learned on the beaches of the Bay of the Seine in the summer of 1944. But in turn the success of the Normandy invasion and the defeat of Germany owe much to the experiences gained and the techniques developed in the earlier campaigns of the Pacific. Germany lost the Battle of Normandy—and, as a result, the war—because the Allies were able to land and supply over open beaches an army that numbered a million men twenty days after D-day, and close to three million within four months. The Germans had based their defense of the West on the defense of ports; they underestimated the Allied amphibious strength and the Allied ability to supply an army over open beaches.

The enemy was bemused with his own lies about the effectiveness of the submarine campaign; many of the German prisoners taken in Normandy were amazed at the Allied armada of ships and craft of all types used in the invasion of Normandy. The capacity of our landing craft and the Allied skill in the general technique of amphibious war were other surprises. One of Hitler's greatest mistakes—and he has made many—was his failure to keep a closer eye on developments in the Pacific, developments which have revolutionized the difficult art of amphibious war. Two other factors, one of them an erroneous German G-2 "estimate of the situation," ensured the success of the invasion of France and the victory in Normandy.

Even before D-day the Germans had expected the Allies to make their main landings in the Pas de Calais area. When our first assault was made against the base of the Cotentin peninsula, the enemy continued to cling to his belief that another landing would be made in the Pas de Calais area. His troop dispositions, his strategy, and captured documents all emphasize this mistaken estimate. The Germans were encouraged in their wrongheadedness. Lieutenant General George Patton's Third American Army, then in England, was concentrated at British east ports on D-day, and climbed into and out of landing boats for the benefit of German reconnaissance planes and German agents. The obvious inference, one which the Germans made, was that an attack against the Pas de Calais-Dunkerque-Belgium area was in the making. At the time that the Bay of the Seine landings were being made, naval demonstrations were made in the Pas de Calais area. Other feints were also made. A small force was concentrated in Scotland to "threaten" Norway, and dummy parachutists were dropped as far south as Rennes in Brittany.

After D-day, careful security, which hid for as long as possible the exact whereabouts of Patton's Third Army, contributed to the German confusion. Lieutenant General Lesley J. McNair, then chief of the Army Ground Forces, was sent to England, and after his death, Lieutenant General John L. DeWitt went, as part of a "cover" plan to convince the Germans that another United States Army

Marine Corps Gazette 28 (December 1944): 34–40. Reprinted by permission.

Unloading British tanks and trucks, Normandy, 6 June 1944. Courtesy of the U.S. Navy Historical Center.

or army group was posed to strike at the Northern French coast. As a result of feint, subterfuge, and secrecy, the enemy was fooled until the Battle of Normandy was won.

The Third Army was concentrated within the Cotentin peninsula, where it massed with the First Army, for the successful breakthrough attempt of July 25.

The Germans stripped the Breton peninsula of most of its troops in order to reinforce the Normandy battlefront. Patton's army, therefore, rampaged across Brittany with little opposition when the breakthrough was finally made. On the other hand, the Nazis, until just a short time before the breakthrough, kept the strength of the Fifteenth Army north of the Seine virtually intact. As a result, the enemy was defeated in detail; the Seventh Army was smashed in Normandy, and the Fifteenth Army was no match for our victorious troops when they crossed the Seine. Had these two German armies been concentrated, the whole campaign in France would have had a different course. Surprise, subterfuge and security are of fundamental importance in war.

The second great factor that made victory sure in the invasion of France was air superiority. It was a superiority so complete that it was virtually air domination. The preparatory bombardments and the close support of ground troops were helpful and extremely useful, but air power's greatest contribution was against enemy communications and supply routes. For a time the supply problem of the enemy was exceedingly difficult, in places almost insoluble. German division commanders spoke in those days of Normandy hedgerow fighting, of seeing only six German planes over their division areas in four weeks. The enemy was forced to move by night, to burrow and hide by day. Reinforcements, replacements, and supplies came up piecemeal. The enemy "build-up" was much slower than our own, in part because Allied planes limited German mobility, slowed down all its combat reactions, and reduced its power to maneuver. Partially because of this slowness in concentration, partially because the Germans retained a large army in the Pas de Calais area, the expected large-scale German counterattack against our beachheads never developed, and victory on Normandy, and France, was won.

Any appraisal of the invasion of Normandy against the background of our Pacific experience must be critical as well as laudatory. In general, the operation was superbly done.

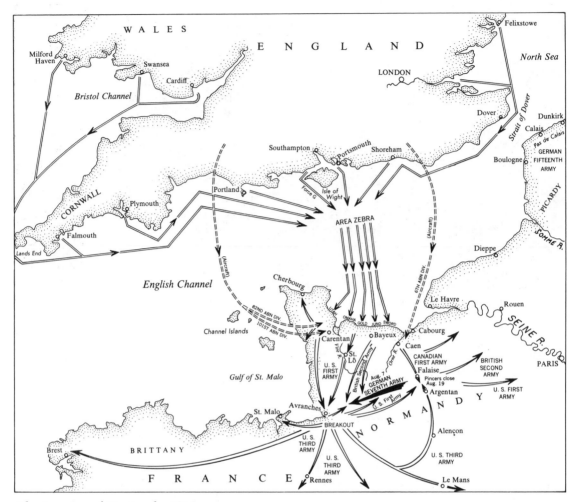

The invasion of Normandy, 1944.

No operation of similar scope or difficulty is recorded in prior military history. It deserves the descriptions it has received—"Wellsian," "Jules Verne," a "modern miracle." In detail, much was magnificent, some was not. This correspondent believes that Pacific amphibious technique is more advanced than that used in the invasion of France, but this statement must at once be qualified by emphasizing that none of our Pacific operations have been of such magnitude as the invasion of France, and in none of the assaults yet made in the Pacific have we invaded continental land masses where our beachheads might be subject to counteroffensive by large strategic reserves.

In both oceans an absolute prerequisite of success has been naval superiority, control of the sea. In the invasion of France that control was very nearly absolute. The few German sea attacks were confined to mine-laying planes; a few isolated torpedo planes; E-boats which succeeded only once, and then without result, in breaking through the outer screen; submarines, which were ineffective; and "gadgets," like "human torpedoes" and explosive-laden, radio-controlled motor boats. But for the sake of the record it should be emphasized that the naval vessels that supported the invasion of France did not constitute, as too often reported, "the greatest fleet in history." Actually, the combat fleet in the Bay of the Seine, and that available in distant support, was far less impressive in numbers and in strength than any one of many task forces which have been utilized in the Pacific. In the days before invasion, this correspondent and many naval officers frankly viewed the naval support available with some concern. It consisted in large measure of older vessels. Not a single new battleship nor a single aircraft carrier was employed. As it happened, the naval support was more than adequate, partly because not as many German coast defense guns were sited within range of the landing beaches as had been feared. But in any military operation, especially one so difficult as an amphibious invasion, it is better to be safe than to be sorry. If the force is available, the naval support should not be the minimum necessary but should be the maximum possible.

In the interests of the future record, it should also be noted that the German coast defenses in the Bay of the Seine area were not as concentrated, and not as strong per yard of sea front, as the Japanese defenses of Tarawa or Kwajalein. At least two army generals who had served in the Pacific—Major General Charles H. Corlett, commander of the XIX Corps in France, and in the Pacific commander of the Seventh Division in the Aleutians and at Kwajalein; and Major General J. Lawton Collins, commander of the VII Corps in France and a veteran of the New Georgia battles in the South Pacific—were able to make comparative judgments about the defenses. This correspondent talked with these observers and many others, and the consensus of opinion was German defenses were weaker than anticipated.

Not until the late Field Marshal Erwin Rommel made his inspection of the coastal defenses of France in the winter of 1943–44 did the enemy commence vigorous and energetic work on the scale expected. At the time of invasion the defenses were formidable but still incomplete. Underwater obstacles had been laid, but all of them were completely exposed at low tide and hence subject to destruction by hand-placed charges. Numerous pillboxes and casemates were still under construction. The minefields were not as extensive as feared. The coastal defense

was a "crust"; there was very little defense in depth. Poles and posts against glider landings, called "Rommel's asparagus," were still being placed in fields. "Omaha" and "Utah" beaches at the base of the Cotentin Peninsula were not, therefore, as difficult beaches to assault as were the beaches at Tarawa and in the Marshalls. But they did present different problems. "Omaha" beach was hemmed in by 90- to 100-foot bluffs, surmounted and seamed with pillboxes which enfiladed the beach and exposed our assault troops to plunging fire. "Utah" beach was backed up by inundated areas which had to be crossed. Each amphibious landing presents a distinct and individual problem; each must have minute planning and careful terrain study.

Other lessons that can be learned from the invasion of France may be summarized according to the following six points. First preinvasion bombing was particularly helpful in destruction of bridges and disruption of railroad freight yards, thus partially isolating the invasion area. Coastal batteries were also destroyed, or had to be reemplaced elsewhere, either in woods or in casemates. The close-support bombing during the invasion was handicapped by weather. Weather so greatly limits and sometimes completely shackles the air arm that victory should never be built upon the assumption of maximum use of that arm. On D-day, in France, the heavy bombers, bombing a few minutes before H-hour, had to bomb blind through overcasts. To avoid hitting our own troops they bombed over rather than short; most of the bombs fell inland and the beach defenses were not affected. The lack of navy and Marine Corps aircraft trained to close support work in amphibious operations was felt. Few of the fighter-bombers or dive-bombers "took out any of the beach pillboxes, for there was very little pinpoint bombing on D-day. Other air weaknesses, since remedied, were lack of American night fighters, very few night "intruders" for harassment of enemy communication lines, and the lack of rocket-equipped planes. P-47s were finally equipped with navy rockets, which Major General "Pete" Quesada, able head of the Ninth Fighter Command, has said he prefers to army rockets, because they are larger and do not use tubes, and hence do not reduce the plane's maneuverability.

Second, shells, like bombs, did not reduce the enemy's beach defenses. Naval gunfire did neutralize or knock out a number of the enemy's coastal batteries, and large shipping suffered no serious loss from the enemy's gunfire. The beach defenses and pillboxes were hurt, but not knocked out, since the preparatory bombardment was far briefer than some of those in the Pacific had been, and the enemy defenses "weathered" it. A great volume of shellfire is necessary to produce morale results.

Third, a rocket barrage from landing craft—the final blow before H-hour—helped to break up the enemy's barbed wire, destroy mines, and stun the enemy but had no appreciable effect on pillboxes. Rockets were widely dispersed and inaccurate but have undoubted morale effect. However, they must be used in great volume.

To sum up the foregoing three points, it might be said that amphibious assaults are best prepared by intense preinvasion bombing. Heavy bombers must concentrate chiefly upon communications centers. Mediums, lights, dive, and fighter-bombers, using bombs, rockets, cannon, machine guns, incendiaries, and phosphorus, must operate against pillboxes, beach defenses, and pinpoint targets in continuous not intermittent operation. At the same time the naval gunfire should be of maximum possible intensity and duration, with AP, or anticoncrete shells used where necessary against concrete works, and common, or high-explosive against field fortifications, barbed wire, and the like. The rocket barrage also depends for effectiveness upon volume, and to some extent upon continuity.

Fourth, amphibious tanks, or the marine "amphtracs" ("alligators" and "water buffaloes") were not used in the invasion of France, except in minor supply roles. One high-ranking army general wanted to use them, but was persuaded that the configuration of the beach made it unnecessary. Nevertheless, they would have been highly useful on D-day. Many of the army's "ducks" swamped in the rough water. The "duck" is not the best of rough-water craft. Many "ducks" in the Bay of the Seine were overloaded by naval officers who were in charge of unloading the assault troops and equipment. Some of the "ducks" had been sandbagged to protect their drivers and passengers against mines, the sandbags were snagged, and when water washed in, the sand was washed down into the bilge pumps, clogging them. The assault wave, instead of being led by amphtracs which could crawl out of the water up on to land, was led by other types of invasion craft. Much of this gear was swamped, and some of it was knocked out by German gunfire. The "doughboys" came ashore in landing craft vehicle personnel (LCVPs), or landing craft tanks (LCTs), or similar standardized landing craft, and many of them had to struggle through thigh-deep water under enemy fire. The marines who were at Tarawa know what that means. Amphtracs, which might have been used but were not, have proved their great utility in war, but we have not yet, by any means, completed the development of amphibious mechanized and armored vehicles. Mechanized warfare is still in its infancy, and every branch of it should be developed to the full. And it is clear that tanks should be landed with the leading assault waves.

Fifth, in the early days of the invasion, optimum use was not made of all the vast fleet of landing craft assembled in the Bay of the Seine. Direction was not always good; too many landing craft lay off the beaches empty with no orders, while the men ashore badly needed supplies and reinforcements. The navy unfortunately broke down the chain of command in the landing craft fleet. Landing craft infantry (LCIs) were detached from their units, squadron and flotilla commanders were bypassed, and there were some hours and days of confusion. On the beaches, the army's special engineer brigades, and the navy's shore battalions did not always work as closely or as intimately as is essential. There was lacking in France some of the smoothness of the best Pacific operations.

Sixth, the build-up phase was, however, expedited by a number of "wrinkles" that the Pacific might well emulate. The artificial harbors erected off the Bay of the Seine were, in some ways, luxuries, and did not greatly increase the capacity of the invasion beaches, but they did ease unloading. Breakwaters of "blockships"—old merchant marine or naval vessels deliberately sunk off the beaches to provide sheltered unloading areas for landing craft—proved of great usefulness during rough weather. The great steel rafts, anchored further offshore and intended to break up the wave action, were a partial failure, though the huge concrete caissons which formed the major part of the permanent breakwaters of the artificial ports, were more successful. Flexible oil pipelines laid at the average rate of about ten miles a day across France were another successful innovation. The American genius is well-adapted to supply and construction work. In the opinion of this correspondent our logistics, including the construction of docks, pipelines, airfields, and the like, are far ahead of those of any other nation—the Germans not excepted.

The greatest lessons the Pacific theater can learn from the invasion of France are two: the closest sort of cooperation is essential between all services, all arms, and all branches in amphibious operations; and in the final analysis, machine power is never enough. It is the man on two feet with hand grenades, rifle, and bayonet—backed up by all that modern science can devise—the man with fear in his stomach but a fighting heart, who must secure beachheads. He it is who wins the glory and pays the price, who changes the course of history. Man is still supreme in a mechanistic war.

Amphibious Assault on South Beveland, 1944

BY BRIGADIER C. N. BARCLAY, CBE, DSO, BRITISH ARMY (RET.)

This article discusses an amphibious operation by a brigade group (U.S. Regimental Combat Team) which took place in 1944. Although it is necessary to give a brief factual account of events, the main emphasis is on those aspects which carry lessons for future guidance. History, military history in particular, has little to commend it unless it teaches us how to avoid the mistakes and improve upon the successes of our predecessors.

The summer of 1944 saw a series of almost unprecedented successes by Allied forces in northwest Europe. The Normandy landings in June had been followed by the break-out from the beachhead and an advance of some 300 miles eastward across France to the Low Countries. But by early October the tempo of operations had slackened. The attempt in September to "jump" the Lower Rhine at Arnhem with airborne troops had failed. It looked as if the battlefront would remain west of the Rhine for the winter and that the war would last well into 1945.

The great port of Antwerp had been occupied on 4 September with its dock facilities only slightly damaged. It could not, however, be used by Allied shipping until the Scheldt Estuary had been made safe. By mid-October the Allies held most of the mainland forming the southern bank of the estuary, but the Germans still held the two Dutch islands of South Beveland and Walcheren to

Marine Corps Gazette, "Assault on South Beveland—1944," 48 (March 1964): 20–24. Reprinted by permission.

the north. Attempts by Canadian troops to force a way up the narrow isthmus joining South Beveland to the mainland had been unsuccessful. By this time it was a matter of urgency for the Allies to use Antwerp for supplies and reinforcements. As winter weather might be expected to start at any time, the decision was made to assault and occupy the Dutch islands before the end of October.

The plan was for the 52nd (Lowland) Division and some commando units to make an assault crossing of the Scheldt. First they were to occupy the island of South Beveland—joining with the Canadian troops who were slowly battling their way up the isthmus. Second, they were to attack the island of Walcheren.

The task of assaulting the south coast of South Beveland was given to the reinforced 156th Infantry Brigade Group of which I was the commander. The two assaulting battalions, the two follow-up battalions, and certain attached units, numbered about four thousand. The enemy garrison of the whole island was correctly estimated at about sixty-five hundred.

Planning

The proposed operation had previously been discussed among the staff of Headquarters II Canadian Corps, and early on 23 October I arrived at Corps Headquarters, accompanied by two staff officers, to begin detailed planning. It was then revealed, for the first time as far as I was concerned, that the assault was scheduled to take place on the morning of the 25th. It did not take long to decide that this timing, if not impossible, would result in hurried planning and slipshod execution. After some forceful discussion it was later decided to postpone the operation until the 26th.

After deciding the time, providing all the information available, and introducing me to the commanders of units who were to cooperate in the operation, the Canadian Corps staff told me to get on with the job. I was given all the help and information I wanted but was left to work out my own detailed plan.

The assault crossing of the Scheldt was to be carried out in "buffaloes" (known earlier as "alligators") or "landing vehicles tracked." These amphibious vehicles of American design and production will be familiar to many readers of this anthology. Those in use at that time could swim at 7 miles per hour and had a good cross-country performance on land. They were bullet- and splinter-proof and could carry twenty-eight fully equipped men, or a light vehicle and eight men, or 4 tons of stores. The units of my brigade, however, had no previous experience with LVTs. Most of us had never heard of them; only a few had ever seen one.

There were three major points to be considered:

• To decide from aerial photographs and intelligence reports which areas were too heavily flooded for active operations, as the Germans had carried out extensive inundations.
• To determine the landing place and the time.
• To determine whether the LVTs could be relied on to surmount the steep and high dike surrounding the island (most of which was several feet below sea level).

It had been assumed that we would land near Ellewoutsdijk which was opposite Terneuzen, the place of embarkation. This seemed to me too obvious and the area too well defended. I decided to land much further east—between Hoedenskerke and Baarland. This also had the advantage of bringing us nearer the Canadians fighting their way up the isthmus. I also came to the conclusion that although parts of this area were flooded, the inundations were not sufficient to seriously hinder operations. They might even increase the element of surprise.

After a short talk with the commander of the 1st Assault Brigade, Royal Engineers, who controlled the craft, I was satisfied that the LVTs could negotiate the dike and transport the first wave of troops to their objectives inland. I was also satisfied that the LVT crews were sufficiently well trained in navigation to carry the operation in the dark.

As a result of these preliminary investigations the following plan was made:

(1) The assaulting units to move forward from the area of Ghent in Belgium, where they were billetted, to Terneuzen on the night of 23/24 and during 24 October, and spend part of the 24th and the 25th loading their LVTs with vehicles and stores and practicing the embarkation and disembarkation of personnel.

(2) The two assaulting battalions to leave Terneuzen at 0330 on the 26th and land south of Hoedenskerke at 0445 hours—the 4/5th Royal Scots Fusiliers on the right with their right flank on, but not in, Hoedenskerke and the 6th Cameronians extending the assault area to the left to include Baarland.

(3) Shortly before the assault craft touched down the supporting artillery—some two hundred heavy, medium, and field guns in positions on the mainland—was to carry out a short but intense bombardment of the beach and dike area. To assist navigation the field artillery was to fire colored "marker" shells on the beaches, and light antiaircraft guns were to mark the flanks with tracer ammunition. In the interests of surprise these aids were not to come into action until twenty minutes before the "touch down."

(4) A deep beachhead was to be formed at once, the LVTs in most cases taking the troops right to their objectives—in some as much as one mile inland. The infantry, however, was to be prepared to disembark instantly, and proceed on foot, should it prove impracticable for the LVTs to take them the full distance. It was hoped that in the dark and

half-light the Germans would mistake the vehicles for tanks, which in fact they did.

(5) As soon as it became clear that the beachhead was established, the leading follow-up battalion, the 7th Cameronians, and a squadron of amphibious tanks, would reinforce the beachhead. Further reinforcements would follow with a view to joining up with the Canadians from the isthmus and occupying the whole island as quickly as possible.

The Plan In Action

In all essentials the operation worked according to plan. The place of landing was a complete surprise and the leading troops were only lightly opposed. The Germans, however, reacted quickly. A rather half-hearted counterattack was staged, but was beaten off. During the night of 26/27 some enemy snipers and saboteurs infiltrated into the beachhead; they caused some inconvenience but were soon rounded up.

Ellewoutsdijk was captured on the 28th and junction with the Canadians was made on the same day. By the 31st the whole of South Beveland had been cleared. Other troops met with similar successes against Walcheren and by 26 November the Scheldt Estuary had been swept of mines and the first of many Allied convoys entered the Port of Antwerp. But all that is another story. This article is concerned only with the establishment of the initial beachhead.

Comment

The operation had gone as smoothly as could be expected. Nevertheless, however successful a venture of this kind may be, there are always some features which give cause for justifiable criticism, and a few which merit notice because they contribute to success. The following are some of these, mostly taken from notes I made a few days after the conclusion of the operation.

Planning

We should, in my view, have been given more time to prepare the operation, especially as the troops were unfamiliar with LVTs. Even with the twenty-four-hour postponement we were very hard-pressed to be ready in time. Actually, the decision to use the 52nd Division in this role was made a week or so earlier, and there was no reason why I should not have been put in contact with II Canadian Corps on 19 or 20 October. In the event, no harm was done by this delay, but I have always felt that we were lucky and were hustled unnecessarily.

In my opinion the distribution of work during planning between the higher headquarters and my brigade was exactly right. I was given every possible assistance, all the information available, and all the additional support and facilities I could reasonably expect. Then I was left to make my own detailed plan and carry it out in my own way.

Value of Surprise

The place of landing was a complete surprise to the Germans. We discovered later that they were aware of our intention to assault South Beveland and expected the operation to take place between 25 and 28 October. They were convinced, however, that we would land at or near Ellewoutsdijk and had made plans for our reception with typical German thoroughness. The actual landing some 5 miles further east, in a partly flooded area remote from any port or harbor facilities, was quite unexpected. Even when the artillery bombardment opened shortly before the first troops went ashore, the German headquarters thought it was a feint and still expected a seaborne assault on Ellewoutsdijk. I would emphasize the immense value of surprise in an operation of this sort.

Tactical Considerations

A study of previous operations of this kind had shown me that it was customary to establish a very small beachhead at first—perhaps no more than 200/300 yards deep—and then to extend it gradually. In face of very heavy opposition this was no doubt necessary; but it had always seemed to be a very cumbersome, time-wasting, and "safety-first" method, to be avoided if possible. It delayed the arrival of reinforcements and heavy equipment and gave the enemy a chance to recover from the initial blow. In this case I considered that we would be justified in going for an initial beachhead a mile or so deep. My decision was, of course, very largely determined by the ability of the LVTs to take the infantry that distance inland, in comparative security, in the dark. This worked out well; only three LVTs failed to deliver their troops at or very near the right place and in these cases the men made their way on foot without very much difficulty.

As a consequence of forming a large initial beachhead, a number of Germans, acting in a guerrilla capacity, remained within our lines. Others infiltrated through the thinly held front before it became properly organized. These were a great nuisance during the first forty-eight hours and caused a number of casualties. They were dealt with by follow-up units, but it would have been better if special troops had been earmarked for the purpose from the start. This is a problem which may often arise when a deep beachhead, or bridgehead in a river crossing, is established by night or in half-light.

It was really the LVTs which enabled us to make the deep initial beachhead so successfully. They got the troops to their objectives quickly with all their equipment (including antitank guns) without fatigue. In the dark the enemy mistook them for tanks and this gave the impression of a much more formidable assault force than was in fact employed.

Two mistakes were made in connection with the amphibious tanks. They swam the long journey up and across the Scheldt well but on arrival found great difficulty in getting over the dike; in consequence only five were used. I blame myself for that. I should have gone more carefully into the matter and arranged for a party of engineers to help them negotiate the dike. The five which were used were almost entirely confined to roads in the early stages, as the flooded ground was too soft for them. Many of the smaller roads and tracks were too narrow and the tank tracks overlapped them.

The operation was more in the nature of a seaborne landing than a river crossing but this had not been fully appreciated during planning. Consequently, there was no beach administrative organization, such as was normally provided for a seaborne assault. We should have had a small improvised "beach group" with signal communications, traffic control personnel, police, supply personnel, a small party of engineers, and other elements. Within a few hours this was provided quite easily from sources within the brigade group, but I accept blame for the fact that it was not done at the beginning.

Our liaison arrangements with the Canadians advancing up the isthmus were not satisfactory. Such arrangements as existed were through Headquarters 52nd (Lowland) Division and Headquarters II Canadian Corps—both of course located on the mainland—and these communications were much too slow. Later this was improved by means of special direct wireless sets and, once the two forces had joined up, by direct contact between local commanders and liaison officers. More care and thought should have been given to the matter in the planning stage.

One can think of many ways in which modern equipment could have been used to advantage at South Beveland, and of these the possibilities for helicopters impress me most. They were not in general use in 1944, but had they been available there were several roles in which they might have been employed: possibly in the initial assault, to bring in reinforcements after the establishment of the beachhead, for supplies, for evacuating wounded, and for liaison purposes. As in many other actions in World War Two, it would make an interesting and profitable exercise to consider how this operation could have been conducted if, say, one hundred helicopters had been available.

Conclusions

There are numerous examples of amphibious assaults by larger forces than this one, against stronger opposition and under tougher conditions. The attack on South Beveland was carried out by a comparatively small force which operated largely in isolation—a condition which was unusual in the large-scale operations in Europe in World War Two. I feel that the lessons and experience of this action may be of some value to those who might be involved in similar conditions of conventional warfare in the 1960s.

Finally, I would point to the paramount importance of a high standard of training for an operation of this kind. The 52nd (Lowland) Division was at that time very well trained. It was lucky enough to have had a long period of tough training in Scotland in a variety of roles; its units had many individual officers with long battle experience; it had not suffered heavy casualties; and its morale was high. With these advantages—which were not enjoyed by some Allied units that had fought continuously, and suffered heavily in earlier battles—its troops were able to carry through a complicated amphibious operation on little more than forty-eight hours notice. Nor must we forget the LVTs designed, produced, and made available by our American Allies, and so ably navigated by their British crews.

Lost Opportunities of Amphibious Warfare in World War Two

BY W. R. SENDALL

Some nine years have now passed since the invasion of Sicily on 10 July 1943 touched off the series of amphibious operations by which the Nazi fortress of Europe was stormed. In the interval, we have had a number of authoritative accounts of these great operations of war from both sides of the battle front. No campaigns in history have ever before been so well documented from the historical point of view. It is now possible to weigh the balance of success and failure, of opportunities taken and missed, with an eye to the future.

In making this assessment there is one important fact that must be taken into account. In the entire period from the Sicily assault to the end of the war, there is a curious shortage of what may be called "tactical" amphibious operations. Despite the elaborate development of combined operations technique, there is a singular absence of confidence in using freedom of movement by sea to expedite the course of land fighting.

We have the immense, carefully planned landings in Sicily, Italy, and Normandy, and the smaller but still large-scale operations at Anzio and in the south of France. These took long periods of planning; in the case of Normandy, the time ran into years.

All these great operations were successful except Anzio, which fell far short of expectations. It is significant that the Anzio operation was the closest in concept to what I

Military Review, "The Sea Flank Was Open: Lost Opportunities of Amphibious Warfare," 32 (March 1953): 107–9. Reprinted by permission of *Navy International Magazine*.

have described as "tactical" amphibious operations. What is surprising is the absence of smaller landings, by which the sea flank is used to gain freedom for maneuver during the course of a land battle. Such operations do not call for the monumental planning of the major undertakings. It is essential that they should be mounted and executed quickly in order to take advantage of what may be a transient tactical opportunity. Although they demand less material, they require greater skill and confidence in the use of the sea than do the big shows.

The Italian campaign was fought in a narrow peninsula with long sea flanks manifestly vulnerable to amphibious action by the powers that dominated the sea. One might have expected an entire series of small-scale outflanking operations, using the sea as a way round the enemy's fortified lines. These need not have been expensive, ambitious efforts. They could have been within the scope of the troops available, the highly trained Royal Marine and Army Commandos.

Apart from Anzio there was only one such effort, the commando landings at Termoli, where a force seized this small Adriatic port to assist the Eighth Army to force the line of the Biferno River. The commandos used the sea flank to get behind the enemy, to take important road junctions and bridges in addition to the harbor, in conjunction with a frontal attack on the river line. This operation is a perfect example of a "tactical" amphibious operation. It was essentially subordinate to the land battle. The sea was used to gain room for an outflanking operation to pry the enemy out of a strong defensive position. It required only a small but highly specialized force and comparatively few craft. Moreover, it was successful.

The Anzio landings were a much more ambitious conception, but the boldness of the design was not matched by the execution. Nevertheless, this operation played a significant part in the grand strategic design by drawing in German reserves which could have been usefully employed elsewhere. The fact remains that once an amphibious operation exceeds small dimensions, a certain rigidity is imposed by the problems of supply which can only be overcome by the possession of a greater reserve of shipping than was ever available. This alone makes it more surprising that smaller attempts were not made.

Instead, the highly specialized commando troops were more often employed in the line of battle to perform the functions of infantry battalions which they were not properly equipped to carry out. Not until the close of the Italian campaign did the commandos have a further chance in something like their proper role, than on the inland waters of Lake Comacchio. This was a turning movement on a water-protected flank which was in many ways more difficult and dangerous than a seaborne operation. The lagoon waters of Comacchio were rich in mud and were infinitely harder to negotiate than any normal combination of beach and cliff. This awkward operation was successfully accomplished. The achievement makes even more mysterious the failure to use the sea at earlier stages to turn the Italian river lines.

When we turn from Italy to consider events subsequent to the Normandy assault in June 1944, once again one is faced by a similar failure to use the sea flank tactically. It is true that the heavily fortified coast line from Le Havre to the Zuider Zee presented a formidable deterrent to small-scale landings. It is equally true that the sea flank was exploited by the Allies with remarkable success by ingenious maintenance of the non-existent threat of a landing in force in the Pas de Calais. Thus, the enemy was totally deceived into the belief that the Normandy assault was a diversion, not the main effort. An entire German army was tied down uselessly behind the most massive defenses of the Atlantic Wall until the climax of the Normandy battle was reached. This enormous deception is a most remarkable tribute to the flexibility of amphibious power.

Nevertheless, neither this achievement nor the real strength of the Channel coast defenses are complete justification for totally abandoning the possibility of further amphibious attacks after the assault phase in Normandy was complete. Yet this was done. The highly trained commando brigades were committed to the land battle in which their special characteristics were largely wasted.

No doubt it was right to decide that a small-scale amphibious attack would be impossible by itself against the massive defenses between Le Havre and Antwerp. What was overlooked were the possibilities of amphibious attack in conjunction with attack from the land and within range of supporting artillery on the land. Immediately after the break-out in Normandy, such operations, in which seaborne attack could be closely integrated with land attack, became possible. Indeed, more than the opportunity, the necessity for them, arose.

It is evident now that a swiftly mounted landing operation close to Brest, timed to coincide with the rapid drive of General Patton's armored columns into Brittany could not only have been a justifiable risk but might have secured that important deep-water port at a time when it would have been of use. In fact, Brest was not available as a port until a time when it had become almost valueless to the Allied armies far away in Belgium and Alsace.

The greatest opportunity, however, was offered at Antwerp. On 4 September 1944, the great port of Antwerp, with its potential intake of 40,000 tons a day, fell intact before the dash and thrust of the British 11th Armored Division. Because the mined and fortified approaches up the Scheldt could not be cleared, the port was useless to the Allied armies until the end of November. It cost the Canadian army a long and bloody battle to clear the Breskens pocket south of the Scheldt Estuary. It required a formidable amphibious assault by the 4th Commando Brigade to destroy the great batteries on the island of Walcheren which dominated the estuary from the north. Only then could the minesweepers clear the channel up to Antwerp.

Yet Chester Wilmot, in his book *The Struggle for Europe*, gives this opinion:

> Immediately after the capture of Antwerp, while the disorganized Fifteenth German Army was struggling to escape from Flanders, an amphibious force could have been landed at the mouth of the Scheldt without great difficulty. The two German divisions which had been holding the sector of the Atlantic Wall, had been sent south to British advance leaving only a meager garrison in the coast defense. At SHAEF, however, no provision had been made for taking advantage of such an opportunity. All the planning had been based on the assumption that any ports or pockets of resistance on the Channel coast would be taken from landward and no amphibious reserve had been kept in mind to exploit the allied command of the sea.

In fact, the 4th Commando Brigade had to be withdrawn from the land battle to which it had been committed, reorganized, and retrained before the assault on Westkapelle dike in Walcheren could be carried out. This assault was completely successful and, considering the strength of the fortifications, by no means unduly costly. If it could have been executed early in September when the German morale was at its lowest, it could not have been more difficult than it proved two months later. Indeed, the risks must have been smaller. The landing on the dike was carried out in adverse weather. November in the Channel is no time for amphibious attacks. Conditions in September would have been infinitely more favorable. This chance was lost because the Allied command could not rid itself of the obsession that combined operations had to be huge setpieces, because the planners at no time were able to think in terms of the "tactical" use of the sea flank. If it had been taken, the war could have been ended in 1944 with all the economy of life and political advantage that would have flowed from the earlier victory.

ERA OF THE SUPERPOWERS

Inchon, 1950

By COLONEL ROBERT D. HEINL, JR., USMC (RET.)

A hundred and eighteen years before the Communists invaded South Korea, Clausewitz wrote, "A swift and vigorous transition to attack—the flashing sword of vengeance—is the most brilliant point of the defensive."

The landing at Inchon in September 1950 was one of the most dramatic such transitions from defense to attack in the annals of war. It is also a story of strategic prescience and unflinching nerve on the part of a high commander and of professional expertise in the forces which were his instrument. Above all, Inchon is a triumph which could only have been achieved by American maritime power.

One October afternoon in 1949, after paying compliments to colleagues of the naval services, the chairman of the Joint Chiefs of Staff (JCS) gave the House Armed Services Committee a forecast.

"I predict," said General of the Army Omar Nelson Bradley, "that large-scale amphibious operations will never occur again."

Within less than a year, the 1st Marine Division was fighting its way over the beaches and seawalls of Inchon, a Korean west coast port that few in Washington knew or cared about in 1949.

Our defense posture that year was less than brilliant. Demobilization had gutted the armed forces. "America fought the war like

Marine Corps Gazette, "The Nucleus for Victory at High Tide," 51 (September 1967): 20–28; and (October 1967): 45–50. Reprinted by permission. See also Malcolm W. Cagle, "Inchon—The Analysis of a Gamble," U.S. Naval Institute *Proceedings* (January 1954): 47–51.

a football game," said General Wedemeyer, "after which the winner leaves the field and celebrates." What remained was wracked by strategic controversy and interservice rivalry. The atom bomb, at the end of a conflict whose iron bombs had conspicuously failed to substantiate Douhet, Trenchard, and Mitchell, seemed to foreshadow an apocalypse in which future war—absolute and total—would be decided by aerial thunderbolts. In corollary, some said, sea power was through.

A sample of top thinking in the administration and Pentagon of those days can be found in a 1949 remark by Louis Johnson, then secretary of defense, to Admiral R. L. Conolly:

> Admiral, the Navy is on its way out. . . . There's no reason for having a Navy and Marine Corps. General Bradley tells me that amphibious operations are a thing of the past. We'll never have any more amphibious operations. That does away with the Marine Corps. And the Air Force can do anything the Navy can do nowadays, so that does away with the Navy.

Amphibious warfare, which General Bradley and many other senior officers decried, was a stepchild in the navy, too. The number of officers passed over while serving in amphibious billets was notorious. Op–343, amphibious warfare's front office in Chief of Naval Operations (CNO) was (as it still is today), headed only by a captain—in an organization containing 38 admirals and 335 other captains. Although the navy had 610 am-

Invasion of Inchon, Korea, 1950. Courtesy of the U.S. Navy Historical Center.

phibious ships in commission in 1945, only 91 were left four years later. In 1948 the navy scrapped 510 landing craft and built one. The Fleet Marine Force—thirty-five thousand strong in 1948, Forrestal's last year—had already been slashed by Louis Johnson to twenty-three thousand. For 1950 the Defense Department was programming an FMF of six infantry battalions and eleven aviation squadrons. Naval aviation's first postwar carrier, *United States*, had just been abruptly canceled by the defense secretary, and the Marine Corps, back to the wall, was fighting to avoid being abolished outright or transferred to the army.

In the Far East, thanks largely to Douglas MacArthur, the United States appeared strong. To be sure, China had fallen. And Korea, like Germany, was divided into two parts, one Communist, one free. Yet there was not much concern over Korea nor had there been since

1947, when the JCS red-banded a memorandum which read:

> The Joint Chiefs of Staff consider that, from the standpoint of military security, the United States has little strategic interest in maintaining the present troops and bases in Korea.

Even as this paper was being shuffled about, the *In Min Gun*, or North Korean Peoples Army—a well-armed Communist force of fourteen divisions—was proceeding with careful preparations to conquer South Korea.

The opening scenario of the Korean War is a familiar one. On 25 June 1950 the North Koreans—as MacArthur later said—"struck like a cobra." The South Koreans reeled back, and so did American troops hastily committed from Japan. By mid-August the forces thrown together by the United Nations for the defense of South Korea were penned in a small perimeter around Pusan.

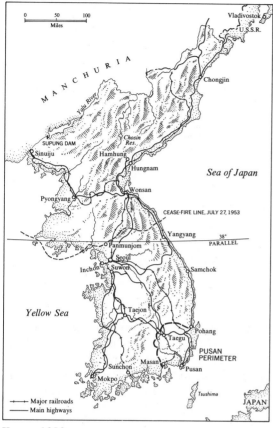

Korea, 1950.

and, as he was to repeat, "hammer and destroy the North Koreans." Anticipating his requirements, he had already radioed Washington for some amphibious engineer troops.

While MacArthur had no amphibious troops in July, he had an amphibious force. Early in 1950—alone among the army's senior commanders in his faith in amphibious warfare—MacArthur had borrowed from the Pacific Fleet a tiny training force, one each of an AGC, an APA, an AKA, and an LST and a fleet tug. Besides the ships he got a 67-man Marine team from TTUPac, a TacRon and, most important, the staff of Amphibious Group 1. The PhibGroup commander, Rear Admiral James H. Doyle, had been Kelly Turner's operations officer in the Pacific and was one of the few flag officers then in the navy with genuine enthusiasm for, and deep professional grasp of, landing operations. Doyle was conducting a training exercise in Tokyo Bay when the Communists attacked and of course became the Seventh Fleet's amphibious commander from that moment on. Doyle and his people and the marines were only a nucleus, but their skills gave MacArthur what he urgently needed. Only because of Doyle could MacArthur start planning an amphibious assault while the roof was still falling in.

Events moved too fast to land the 1st Cavalry Division at Inchon. Every single soldier was needed to slow up the Communists in central Korea. Nevertheless, although he kept an open mind as to possible landings elsewhere (Kunsan, particularly), MacArthur visualized his objective as Inchon, and he never deviated from that concept during the weeks of retreat and disaster that lay ahead.

The reasons MacArthur kept Inchon in mind are evident. Inchon is the seaport of Seoul, Korea's ancient capital and first city. The excellent railroads left by the Japanese fan north and south from Seoul, as do the less excellent highways. The national telephone and telegraph nets radiate from Seoul. Kimpo, Korea's largest and best airport, lies between Inchon and Seoul. Inchon, in effect, is to Seoul what Piraeus was to Athens.

Besieging this perimeter, the main Communist armies were heavily concentrated far south, intent on pushing the defenders into the sea. Because of the presence of the Seventh Fleet, enemy supply lines ran by land down the length of Korea, with Seoul the focal point of their communications. The Communist spearhead was sharp and strong, but their flanks and rear were totally exposed.

On 4 July 1950—no day for celebration in the Far East—when a weak infantry battalion was all we could field in Korea, General MacArthur had already decided how the Communists would be defeated. On that day he called a conference in Tokyo to consider a seaborne attack against the North Korean communications. What he had in mind was to land the 1st Cavalry Division at Inchon, seize Seoul, cut the enemy communications,

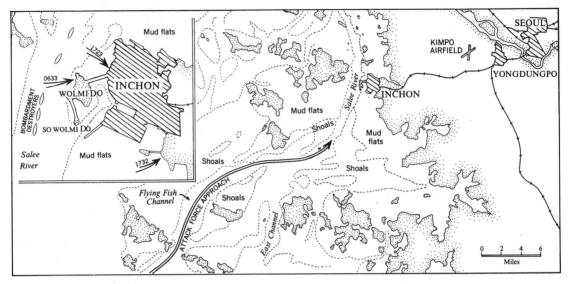

The approaches to Inchon, 1950.

If, as a strategic objective, Inchon was all advantage, from the tactical viewpoint it was exactly the reverse. The amphibious bible of those days was USF–6, predecessor of NWP–22A. USF–6 set out seven criteria for a landing area:

(1) ability of naval forces to support the assault and follow-up operations

(2) shelter from unfavorable sea and weather

(3) compatibility of beaches and their approaches to size, draft, maneuverability, and beaching characteristics of assault ships and landing craft

(4) offshore hydrography

(5) extent of minable waters

(6) conditions which may affect enemy ability to defeat mine-clearance efforts

(7) facilities for unloading, and how these may be improved.

How did MacArthur's chosen objective measure up to the above criteria? Inchon is a port of about the same size and general attractiveness of Jersey City. The tidal range at Inchon is 32 feet, a range only greatly exceeded in the Bay of Fundy. Tidal currents in the approach channels rarely drop below three knots and, in the main channel, reach 7 to 8 knots, close to the speed of an LCVP. Inchon's approach, the Salee River (scene of marine operations in 1871) is a tortuous dead-end street with no room for turning or maneuver. Here, one sunken or disabled ship could block the channel from below and pen in anything above. Despite the currents, Inchon's waters are eminently minable and are commanded by heights and islands well suited for batteries that could shoot minesweepers out of the water.

Of beaches, in the common use of the word, Inchon has none. In the Joint Dictionary's definition of *beach* ("that portion of the shoreline designated for landing of a tactical formation"), Inchon in 1950 had certain stretches of moles, breakwaters, and sea-walls which Admiral Doyle's planners considered least objectionable. Beach exits were mainly the go-downs, railroad yards, and factory alleys of a congested Oriental city.

Underwater gradients approaching these "beaches" demanded a tidal height of 23 feet to get LCVP and LCM ashore, while 29 feet would be needed for LST. Tidal heights of this magnitude prevail at Inchon only once each month, for about 3 or 4 days.

Later on, General Almond, of whom we shall hear more, said Inchon was "the worst possible place where we could bring in an amphibious assault." But, because it was the worst possible place, it was also, in a sense, the best possible. There is an ancient Chinese apothegm that "the wise general is one able to turn disadvantage to his own advantage."

Besides the physical obstacles to a landing at Inchon, there were two other obstacles which, if anything, might have seemed even more forbidding. One was to find the forces—landing forces and assault shipping—capable of executing such a near-impossible landing. The other was to convince an exalted body of doubters that an amphibious attack, even if practicable, was the correct counterblow to the invasion and that Inchon was the place. At this time, for example, a different strategy being urged on the JCS as well as any reporter who would listen, was that we should progressively bomb the communications and principal cities of North Korea and that, by the time this program reached the outskirts of Pyongyang, the Communists would sit down and negotiate.

Finding qualified amphibious troops presented difficulties because the only such we had were marines, and the last thing anybody in the Pentagon or White House of those days wanted to see was another exhibition of marine headline hunting, such as a victory. Besides, there weren't very many marines. Louis Johnson had seen to that.

From the outbreak of war, one officer in Washington had no illusions. In World War One he had commanded a platoon at Belleau Wood and a company in later actions. By the end of World War Two he had successively commanded (in combat) an infantry battalion, then a regiment, and finally a division. This officer—Clifton B. Cates—was commandant of the Marine Corps. To General Cates, the oddest thing about the outbreak of war in Korea was that nobody in the Defense Department, let alone Secretary of the Navy Matthews or Admiral Forrest Sherman, chief of naval operations, could find time to see the commandant of the Marine Corps. Some young planners on the Joint Staff were even suggesting that we could probably settle the Korean "emergency" without any marines at all. When General Cates finally did shoulder past the aides into Secretary Matthews's office on 30 June, the secretary remarked that the possibility of sending ma-rines to Korea just hadn't come up in any conference he could recall. But this subject, nevertheless, had arisen. On 29 June, after vainly seeking an interview for four days, General Cates ran into Admiral Sherman in a Pentagon hall.

Cates: "Things look pretty grim over there. Why doesn't MacArthur ask for Marines?"

Sherman: (after a pause) "What do you have?"

Cates: "I can give you an RCT and an air group from the West Coast."

Sherman: (another pause) "Leave it to me—I'll send a 'Blue Flag' to Joy." [Admiral C. T. Joy]

There was one more pause: as the situation worsened, Sherman waited two days—until after lunch on 1 July—before acting on Cate's offer.

The results of CNO's "Blue Flag," when at length sent to Admiral Joy in the Far East, were not long forthcoming. On 3 July, not to their unqualified satisfaction, the Joint Chiefs of Staff—General Bradley, chairman; General J. Lawton Collins, army chief of staff; General Hoyt Vandenberg of the air force; and Admiral Sherman—had before them a dispatch from General MacArthur, asking for immediate movement of a marine regimental combat team with supporting aviation, to the Far East. Another message they had before them (at least those who read the New York *Herald-Tribune* that morning) was from David Lawrence, the highly informed Washington columnist:

> General MacArthur . . . has no trained amphibious forces. The United States Marines at San Diego are all packed up and ready to sail, and will be invaluable as reinforcements for MacArthur's troops. . . . Ships must be gotten out of "mothballs" immediately, though no such orders have been given, up to today at least. It takes weeks—not days—to transport men and supplies across the Pacific.

To underscore Lawrence's point the chiefs had an uninvited guest in "the tank." When, by chance, General Cates learned that MacArthur's request for marines was on the agenda, he announced he would attend, and he did.

Although, for a variety of reasons, the Joint Chiefs of Staff had small stomach for the decision, their session had but one outcome: after clearing with the White House (where President Truman himself had to approve), the marines were ordered to mount out. To the last, General Vandenberg tried to strip the force of its aviation but July 1950 was no time for interservice politics.

Orders for the marines to send a brigade to the Far East were not a complete surprise. While General Cates was still in the dark as to what Admiral Sherman might be doing on what the latter later called his "Cates to Sherman/to Joy/to MacArthur/to JCS" play, the commandant had, on his own responsibility, sent a war alert to the 1st Marine Division. By "just playing a hunch," as Cates put it, he had gained more than a day's lead time for organization of the 1st Provisional Marine Brigade and its aviation, MAG–33.

Another officer who was taking time by the forelock was Lieutenant General L. C. Shepherd, Jr. En route to command Fleet Marine Force, Pacific (FMFPac) when the war exploded, General Shepherd cut short his fishing at Yellowstone, and reached Honolulu before breakfast on 2 July. Even before he could report in to Admiral Radford, the Pacific Fleet commander, his staff handed him the commandant's warning order and another (Sherman to Radford) alerting the commander-in-chief, Pacific (CinCPac) to prepare marine forces for Korean service.

Only taking time to call on Radford, an old friend, General Shepherd worked all day and into the night to organize the marine brigade for activation on 7 July. Brigadier General E. A. Craig, an officer of high reputation in World War Two, would be in command. When the brigade's orders were complete, General Shepherd, accompanied by his G–3, Colonel V. H. Krulak, set out for Japan. Their mission was to make arrangements with General MacArthur for the marines' employment.

On 9 July Shepherd and Krulak arrived in Tokyo. Next morning the marines were escorted by MacArthur's chief of staff (Major General Edward M. Almond) into the supreme commander's office. After complimenting the Marine Corps with the graciousness of which he was past master, MacArthur said, "I wish I had the entire 1st Marine Division under my command again as I have a job for them to do."

Rising, MacArthur pointed the stem of his corncob pipe at Inchon and continued, "I would land them here and cut the North Korean armies off from their logistic support and cause their withdrawal and annihilation."

Shepherd reacted immediately: "Why don't you ask for the 1st Marine Division, General?"

"That's the kind of talk I like to hear," said MacArthur. "Do you think I can get it?"

Surely, the marine responded, MacArthur could get the division if he were to ask the JCS. In his own capacity, as the division's higher commander, General Shepherd went on, he could if ordered have the unit (at full peace strength less brigade units already committed) ready by 1 September. Could Shepherd take this up with General Cates, asked MacArthur? No need, was the reply, he would assume responsibility. Good, said MacArthur, "You sit down and write me a dispatch to the JCS."

Looking at the general's king-size desk and chair and imagining the general's glance over his shoulder, General Shepherd decided he could do a better job elsewhere. Excusing himself he went into the office of General Almond, a fellow alumnus of the Virginia Military Institute, and drafted MacArthur's message. When he took it in, Krulak recalled, General MacArthur already seemed to be exuding "enthusiasm and resolute confidence."

The army reaction to MacArthur's proposal was conveyed in person since General Collins and his air force colleague Vandenberg were poised for a trip to Tokyo when the general's message arrived. Feeling he should remain in Washington, Admiral Sherman had asked Radford to go along from Pearl Harbor and represent him.

At Tokyo on 13 July, MacArthur confirmed that he intended to attack the enemy lines of communication on the west coast as soon as the *In Min Gun's* advance could be stopped. Inchon, he thought, was the best place, but he was also considering Haeju and Chinnampo. Then, and during staff talks next day, Collins was dubious as to the proposed amphibious counterthrust, especially when he learned the troop requirements. Still trying to divine whether the Russians would seize this convenient moment to march on the Rhine and points west, Collins told Mac-Arthur: "General, you are going to have to win the war out here with the troops available to you in Japan and Korea."

MacArthur smiled and shook his head. "Joe," he said, "you are going to have to change your mind."

Later, MacArthur turned to Radford (the two theater commanders were side by side) and, testing General Shepherd's offer, asked what he thought the marines might be able to contribute. Radford had the right answer: "A brigade rapidly; and probably in the fall, the rest of a division."

Later, before leaving, speaking at least for himself rather than the chiefs, Collins did change his mind: privately, he told Mac-Arthur, he thought a full marine division could be sent to the Far East. Thus encouraged, as soon as the visitors left, on 15 July, MacArthur sent his second request to the JCS for the 1st Marine Division and supporting aviation.

While these developments were in progress General Shepherd was on the West Coast. After briefing Radford ("I feel that there is a serious war in progress in Korea . . . for which Marines are trained and constituted," he said), Shepherd felt it imperative not only to see how the brigade was mounting out but, more important, to meet General Cates, there for the same purpose.

At Pendleton, General Shepherd disclosed MacArthur's plan. Cates, whose knowledge of the Korean situation and of the JCS deliberations was limited to what Admiral Sherman, a taciturn man, chose to disclose, was hesitant to commit a full division. An alluring offer was pending to assign marine forces to NATO. "Clifton, you cannot let me down on this," said Shepherd. "This is a hot war. We ought to be in it."

For a fighter like Cates, that clinched it. The two then conferred much of the afternoon and all evening on 12 July, and, when Cates took off for Washington, he knew what had to be done. At his immediate orders the staff at HQMC prepared plans for a war-strength division or, alternatively, to bring General Craig's brigade to war strength. The staff conclusions were quickly evident: to assemble a war-strength division from a corps numbering less than seventy thousand would require mobilization of the reserve. It would require transfer of practically all of FMFLant to the Pacific. It would require reactivation, organization, and mount-out—within days— of new regiments and new battalions made up of reservists, navy yard guards, and schools troops.

Nine days had elapsed since MacArthur's original request for a marine division, four days since his reiterated request, and still there was no reply. Learning that the brigade, however welcome, was nevertheless at peace strength, MacArthur on 19 July sent the chiefs still another message asking that the brigade be brought to war strength, and repeating for the third time that he needed a full marine division.

As General Cates knew by this time, approval of either, let alone both requests, would entail calling the reserve to the colors, and this information he quickly gave to the JCS when asked. With the *In Min Gun* in the very act of drubbing the 24th Infantry Division out of Taejon, the chiefs went to Blair House on 19 July and recommended mobilization of the marine reserve. Harry Truman nodded, signed the papers, and that afternoon warning orders alerted the ground reserve for active service.

While reservists packed seabags, a shabby tug of war was taking place to prevent mobilization of any of the Marine Corps's thirty reserve aviation squadrons.

Air Force Chief of Staff Hoyt Vandenberg

had been unalterably opposed to sending any marine aviation to Korea ("from a sensitive feeling here at the Pentagon," wrote David Lawrence, "that the Marines should not have their own aviation."). Now, for reasons not recorded, Admiral Sherman—never a marine enthusiast—joined Vandenberg and on 20 July curtly vetoed the commandant's urgent request that aviation units be included in the call-up for Korea. While it was clear to Cates—and equally to MacArthur, who had so reassured Shepherd and Craig—that aviation had to be an integral part of the marine air-ground team, this view was evidently not accepted in Washington.

On 23 July, under increasingly sharp prods from the press (two days earlier, Lawrence had charged Generals Collins and Vandenberg with "having combined to squelch the opportunity of the United States Marine aviation units to fight in the Far East"), Sherman told Cates he could order up six fighting and ground squadrons. A week later, following what the commandant described as "a plain, forceful, and harsh" session on 31 July, between Carl Vinson, House Armed Services Committee chairman, and Admiral Sherman and Secretary Matthews, the admiral announced that two more aviation squadrons would be mobilized and that the Corps would be built up to two war-strength divisions and eighteen squadrons. Shortly before this disclosure, General Bradley sought out General Cates and asked if he "couldn't do something to stop Lawrence's critical articles," as (in the chairman's words) Cates "was the only one that could do it." "I thanked him for the compliment," Cates drily recalled.

Now that the marines were mobilizing, the Joint Chiefs at length—it was 20 July, ten days since the general's initial request—gave MacArthur a reply: yes, he could have a war-strength marine division, but no sooner than November. This date represented HQMC's view of an "orderly" buildup but was far from meeting the imperatives of war, as MacArthur quickly underscored in his fourth message:

Most urgently request reconsideration of decision with reference to 1st Marine Division.

It is an absolutely vital requisite to accomplish a decisive stroke and if not made available will necessitate a much more costly and longer effort both in blood and expense. It is essential that the Marine division arrive by 10 September 1950. . . . There can be no demand for its potential use elsewhere that can equal the urgency of the immediate battle mission contemplated for it.

Under cumulative impact of four dispatches, the chiefs at least gave him a prompt reply. Within forty-eight hours they countered that he must provide more information on his plans for the period before 10 September, and, by way of encouragement, said orders had been issued to bring the marine brigade, and of course its aviation, to war strength.

In his response next day, MacArthur did not identify Inchon as his objective (though it had been unwaveringly in his mind from the beginning) but he said this:

Operation planned mid-September is amphibious landing of a two-division corps in rear of enemy lines for purpose of enveloping and destroying enemy forces in conjunction with attack from south by Eighth Army. I am firmly convinced early and strong effort behind his front will sever his main lines of communication and enable us to deliver a decisive and crushing blow. . . . The alternative is a frontal attack which can only result in a protracted and expensive campaign.

The general's *Reminiscences* recounts that this final message was greeted by "a silence of three weeks." This is not exactly true. On 25 July, the chiefs gave in. They ordered that the 1st Marine Division, commanded by Major General Oliver P. Smith, be brought to war strength (less one RCT) and mount out from San Diego between 10 and 15 August. Included in the JCS directive—another score for General Cates—was the phrase "with attached air" (actually only one-and-a-half more squadrons, but the precedent had been accepted). MacArthur's scheme now had its cutting edge.

Never the most pliant of Washington's subordinates, General MacArthur had not yet fully disclosed his concept of an assault on

Inchon. Troops were moving, ships were on the seas, and it was obvious the stakes were high, but the Joint Chiefs of Staff, military advisors to the president, did not yet know the name of the game.

"Frankly," General Collins later said, "we were somewhat in the dark."

Thus, on 20 August, General Collins, accompanied by Admiral Sherman, was sent to Tokyo, in Collins's words, "to find out exactly what the plans were." MacArthur, as he said in his *Reminiscences*, viewed the visit in a different light. "The actual purpose of their trip," he wrote, "was not so much to discuss as to dissuade."

Beside the JCS delegation, Admiral Radford and General Shepherd were both on their way to Tokyo; Admiral Doyle and staff were already there, aboard his flagship, *Mount McKinley*, and General O. P. Smith (en route by air from Camp Pendleton) would soon arrive. Alone among the key participants of the forthcoming operation, Vice Admiral A. D. Struble, soon to be designated as overall commander, was absent at sea, hammering the west coast of Korea.

There can be little doubt that General MacArthur looked on Admiral Sherman as the man he had to convince and therefore the key figure among the admirals and generals converging on Tokyo. The operation in MacArthur's mind was, above all, a naval operation; without the navy's ships and support, without the marines' amphibious troops, and without the professional knowhow of both navy and marines, the landing at Inchon—however brilliant a concept—could never become reality.

Moreover, General MacArthur already knew, there were serious reservations about the Inchon scheme, not only in his own staff but most certainly on the part of Admiral Doyle and his planners and generally among most senior navy and marine officers privy to the plan. In fact, the more the experts looked at Inchon, the more pessimistic they became.

For these reasons—and also because Sherman, at the height of his powers, was an officer of tenacious mind and purpose, profes-

sionally respected even by those who disliked him most—the admiral, short of MacArthur himself, was the dominant figure. And Sherman, in accordance with habit, was keeping his own counsel.

The panelled sixth-floor conference room in the Dai Ichi Building lay between the offices of Generals MacArthur and Almond. At 1730, 23 August, when the supreme commander entered the room, there were assembled Admiral Sherman and General Collins, representing the JCS; admirals Radford, Joy, and Doyle; generals Almond, Hickey, Ruffner, and Wright, all of MacArthur's staff; and a handful of key juniors. Curiously, neither marine general then in Tokyo (Shepherd and Smith) was invited, so the landing force interest was unrepresented save by a lieutenant colonel among Doyle's briefers.

A day or so before, concerned because MacArthur seemed oblivious of the enormous technical hazards posed by a landing at Inchon, Admiral Doyle had insisted to General Almond that MacArthur be briefed on exactly what the Inchon landing involved. Almond demurred, "The general is not interested in details." Doyle shot back: "He *must* be made aware of the details."

Now, following an introduction by General Wright, the operations officer, MacArthur puffed reflectively on his pipe for eighty minutes while nine officers of Amphibious Group I gave him nothing but details—details of intelligence, aerology, beaches, tides, currents, channels, communications, pontoonery, landing craft, boat waves, naval gunfire, and air strikes. After the last speaker uttered his last detail, Admiral Doyle rose and gave MacArthur the broad picture: "General, I have not been asked nor have I volunteered my opinion about this landing. If I were asked, however, the best I can say is that Inchon is not impossible." Then he sat down.

After a pause, MacArthur replied, "If we find that we can't make it, we will withdraw."

"No, General," said Doyle, "we don't know how to do that. Once we start ashore we'll keep going."

General Collins, who had "wanted to be darn sure just what these plans were," now knew and took the lead, "But not," he later said, "in any acrimonious way, as has sometimes been pictured." Why not Kunsan to the south? Or Posun-Myong, below Inchon? Sherman, said one account, was at first "lukewarm." However, when Doyle explained some of the dangers of the Inchon approaches, and mentioned the enemy shore batteries that could completely command the dead-end channel, Sherman sniffed, "I wouldn't hesitate to take a ship up there."

"Spoken like a Farragut!" exclaimed MacArthur.

History must regret that the conference room had no tape recorder. Thus we shall never know exactly what MacArthur said when the discussion had run its course. The several versions (including that in his *Reminiscences*) are at odds. But all who heard him that evening (dusk had fallen when he began to speak) agreed that his forty-five-minute reply, extemporaneous, without a note, was one of the compelling declarations of his career. Remembering that scene, Admiral Doyle said, "If MacArthur had gone on the stage, you never would have heard of John Barrymore."

The bulk of the enemy, MacArthur said, were committed against the Pusan perimeter. Frontal attack out of the perimeter would cost a hundred thousand casualties. The North Koreans were unprepared for an enveloping attack, least of all at such a place as Inchon. To land at Kunsan would be easier, to be sure, but the results would be "ineffective and indecisive." Nothing in war, he underscored, is more futile than short envelopments. With a deep cut across the Communists' lines of communications, they would soon be deprived of munitions and fighting power, and Inchon would become the anvil on which Eighth Army would smash the enemy from the south. "The amphibious landing is the most powerful tool we have. To employ it properly, we must strike hard and deep."

Adverting to what Wolfe's contemporaries in 1759 had disparaged as "a mad scheme,"

MacArthur likened the Inchon assault to Wolfe's surprise landing at the Anse du Foulon and his subsequent capture of Quebec. As for the navy's objections, he recognized their validity. They were not, however, insuperable. Perhaps he had more confidence in the navy than the navy had in itself. "The navy has never let me down in the past, and it will not let me down this time," he said.

"I realize," he concluded, "that Inchon is a 5,000 to 1 gamble, but I am used to such odds. . . ." Then his voice dropped so that the listeners strained to hear him: "We shall land at Inchon and I shall crush them!"

The effect was mesmeric. It might have been a minute before anyone spoke. Then Sherman said, "Thank you, a great voice in a great cause," and the meeting broke up. At dinner afterward, when all the navy and marine flag officers foregathered at Admiral Joy's, Sherman said to General Shepherd that MacArthur had been "spellbinding."

"I wish," the admiral remarked next day, "I had that man's optimism."

Once the spell wore off, some listeners had second thoughts. After sleeping on the matter, the admirals and generals Shepherd and Smith met in Joy's office for what O. P. Smith described as "an indignation meeting." The consensus was that army planners were giving insufficient, if any, weight to the naval problems that loomed so large to the eyes of experience and that a more feasible landing area must be found. As General Shepherd noted, however, "Nothing of a concrete nature developed."

Lack of developments in any situation frustrated General Shepherd, and an opportunity to press for such developments at the highest level arose that morning. Almond asked that Shepherd come to the Dai Ichi Building. MacArthur wished to see him.

Before the appointment, General Shepherd (accompanied by Colonel Krulak) had forty-five minutes with Almond. The first matter raised by the marine was to urge that the brigade, which had been heavily engaged in the perimeter, be withdrawn from action since Inchon's D-day was but three weeks ahead. Almond replied shortly that the marines wouldn't be withdrawn until just before D-day as Eighth Army's General Walker couldn't spare them.

General Shepherd then voiced the reservations he felt about Inchon and, as he had previously during this visit to Tokyo, urged that Posun-Myong be substituted. Almond then disclosed that the real objective of the Inchon assault was to take Seoul, "that Inchon was decided upon and that was where it would be." He added that he didn't believe there were any troops in Inchon, and dismissed the amphibious landing as "a simple mechanical operation."

At this moment, perhaps fortunately, MacArthur entered the room and took General Shepherd and Colonel Krulak into his office. There, grasping the nettle, Shepherd again urged another objective. Instead of cutting off discussion, MacArthur launched into an analysis of the importance of capturing Seoul which, he said, "would quickly end the war."

"For a $5.00 ante," he concluded, "I have an opportunity to win $50,000, and I have decided that is what I'm going to do."

Landing at Washington's National Airport, Sherman and Collins flashed brief smiles for the photographers while public information officers assured reporters there was "nothing extraordinary" about the trip. Then, with more pensive mien, the two told Bradley and Vandenberg, there to meet them, of MacArthur's plans and his unswerving determination to go through with them. On 28 August—there seemed nothing else to do—the chiefs sent a message of tepid approval to Tokyo:

> We concur in preparations for executing a turning movement by amphibious forces on the west coast of Korea, either at Inchon in the event the enemy defenses there prove ineffective, or at a favorable beach south of Inchon if one can be located. We further concur in preparations, if desired by you, for an envelopment by amphibious forces in vicinity of Kunsan. We understand that alternative plans are being prepared to best exploit situation as it develops.

Thus, the Joint Chiefs of Staff reluctantly approved MacArthur's plan (Operation Chromite) to land at Inchon and cut the communications of the North Korean armies attacking the defensive perimeter around Pusan in southern Korea. MacArthur was determined to strike as soon as possible. For MacArthur, "as soon as possible" meant 15 September. "One of MacArthur's greatest attributes," said Admiral A. D. Struble, soon to command the landings at Inchon, "was to get going *and to hit quick.*"

High tide at Inchon on 15 September would put maximum high water over the harbor's mud flats, a tidal height of 31.2 feet. Twelve days later, on the 27th, there would be 27 feet (2 feet short of what the LSTs needed). Not until 11 October would there again be even 30 feet of water. September 15th was, therefore, the best date. This left just twenty-three days between arrival in Tokyo of Major General O. P. Smith (commanding general 1st Marine Division and thus landing force commander), and MacArthur's target date. It left no time whatever for rehearsals and barely enough for final mount-out, when the seaborne elements of the division would reach Japan between 28 August and 3 September, some still in merchantmen, and—as in the case of Guadalcanal—would reembark and combat-load in assault shipping.

In this race against time and tide, things were humming at Pendleton. When the 1st Marine Brigade shipped out for Pusan on 14 July, an aching void was all they left behind. Although the marine unit at Camp Pendleton in June 1950 was called a division, Defense Secretary Louis Johnson's surgery had effectively pared it barely to the strength of a brigade. Moreover, while the depleted headquarters of the nominal 1st Marine Division stayed behind when the brigade left, even this was in caretaker hands. By an ironic coincidence only days before Korea exploded, Major General G. B. Erskine, the division's steely commander and one of the corps's most distinguished World War Two tacticians, had been dispatched on secret orders to find out for the State Department what was happening to the French in Indochina. Training and readiness were Erskine specialties and, although he had little to work with in 1948–49, what there was had been superbly prepared. Now, having fashioned a well-tempered weapon, it was Erskine's ill fortune not to wield it.

At war strength a marine division included 22,343 officers and men. The 3,386 people remaining when the 1st Brigade sailed in July represented fragments of the headquarters and service elements of a division, and little more.

On 25 July 1950, the morning General O. P. Smith, the new division commander, broke his flag, there remained but twenty-one days before his division must mount out. During these three weeks the 2nd Division at Lejeune would be stripped to the merest cadre by transfer and redesignation of East Coast units. From some ten thousand reservists who began flooding in on 31 July, ninety-one officers and twenty-eight hundred enlisted men were to be selected and absorbed. From over a hundred posts and stations, navy yard marines to the number of one hundred thirty officers and thirty-five hundred enlisted were to join. In fact during one frantic four-day period, 1–5 August, nine thousand officers and men reported for duty.

Amid this Niagara of people, the division staff had to plan movement to the Far East, receive war stocks of ammunition from depots as far away as New Jersey, and, not least, get units equipped. Fortunately there was Barstow to call on. Barstow reminded logisticians of a war surplus store. After World War Two, unlike others who left their gear where it stood, went home, and disbanded, the marines had cannily salvaged every weapon, every truck, every tank, every amtrac within reach (and without much nicety as to original ownership). This trove eventually reached Barstow where, from 1946 on, items had been patiently overhauled, mothballed, assigned serial numbers, and painted forest green when the olive drab or grey showed too conspicuously. "From this miser's lair at Barstow," recounted Andrew Geer in *The New Breed*,

> . . . came the trucks, DUKWs, jeeps, trailers, and amphibian tractors that were to go once more to war. There were more veterans of Iwo Jima and Okinawa among the vehicles than among the men who would drive them.

The day after General Smith took over his new command, General Shepherd arrived from Honolulu for a visit. While at Pendleton, he telephoned General Cates, the commandant, in Washington. During this call, General Shepherd made two important points: (1) that 1st Marine Aircraft Wing headquarters ought to go to Korea to assume command of air operations, and (2) that somehow the 1st Division *must* get its third infantry regiment, the 7th Marines.

The White House, the secretary of defense, and the JCS were not enthusiastic in mid-1950 about expansion of the Marine Corps. Thus, to obtain the 7th Marines, General Cates had first to convince the CNO, Admiral Sherman, and then fight it out with the JCS's Lieutenant General J. T. McNarney who (as Cates wrote) "personally checked every figure submitted and questioned many in detail." Fortunately, General MacArthur very much wanted a full marine division, and MacArthur's wishes could not lightly be flouted. Following a final confrontation with McNarney, Cates laconically jotted in his journal: "Can do. Few cadres left."

Few indeed. The 2nd Marine Division was so stripped that on 15 September 1950—D-day at Inchon—it had but 3,928 officers and men on board. The 2nd Wing had bodily transferred MAG–15 to El Toro; this, with 1,230 pilots and ground crews from the reserve, completed the tactical air command that would support Operation Chromite. To denude the East Coast and the Atlantic of their marines was a risk, but so, to say the least, was the impending operation.

Accumulation of intelligence for Operation Chromite should have proved no problem. Inchon had been used by the army as a port for years after World War Two, but much elementary information was lacking. Japanese and American tide tables differed appreciably and nobody could say which was correct. Would Inchon's mud flats support infantry or vehicles at low water? How high were the seawalls at various stages of the tide? And so on.

By dint of furious search the planners found a transportation corps warrant officer who had operated boats all around Inchon Harbor, and this invaluable man promptly joined Admiral Doyle's staff. Aerial photos were needed, but Far East Air Forces had no suitable photo planes. The only aircraft capable of taking the very low-altitude pictures which would reveal the characteristics of the seawalls were two marine F4Us and a photo detachment aboard one of the carriers. Flying up to thirteen sorties a day with only two airplanes, this detachment, commanded by Major Donald Bush, completed its assignment in four days and turned over the results to a photo-interpretation team flown to Japan from Dayton, Ohio. And plans were afoot to verify all information by the surest means of all—personal reconnaissance.

There was one item of intelligence that no one knew. In August, Naval Mine Depot, Vladivostok, had sent training teams and several trainloads of mines to Chinnampo and Wonsan. Four thousand mines were being distributed from Chinnampo to Inchon, Kunsan, Haeju, and Mokpo. Undertaken quickly enough, minelaying could take Inchon out of play completely. What the odds on this might be, nobody could calculate, but it meant that the sooner MacArthur could collect his forces and strike, the more favorable those odds would be.

Aside from mining Inchon out of the game, the Communists could heavily reinforce the Inchon-Seoul area. They could intensify fortification sufficiently to unbalance MacArthur's strategic equations. Russian aviation or submarines could intervene. With or without Russian support, Chinese ground forces could join in (if they did, however, MacArthur predicted that the air force would "turn the Yalu into the bloodiest stream in all history.").

While intelligence estimates somewhat underestimated the strength of the Inchon-Seoul forces at five thousand to ten thousand, Inchon itself was not strongly held, thus indicating that the North Korean G-2s tended to agree with General Almond's view of Inchon as "the worst possible place." The Inchon garrison comprised two battalions of infantry and two harbor-defense batteries of coast artillery, manning 76 mm and 106 mm guns. Engineers had plans for eventual fortification of Inchon, Russian land mines were already being laid, and, as mentioned, harbor-defense minefields were envisaged. (But there was one snag: although three hundred Russian pressure mines had reached Inchon on 29 August, they lacked cable harnesses. These the supply officer had on back-order.)

The tides dictated 15 September as D-day. That day, however, the tidal timing could hardly have been worse. Morning high tide came just forty-five minutes after sunrise. The next high tide would not crest until thirty-seven minutes after sunset. Morning tide would be many hours too soon for the underpowered, single-screw APAs and AKAs, in those days without modern navigational radar, to make a daylight approach up Flying Fish Channel to Inchon. On the other hand, thirty-seven minutes after sunset isn't ordinarily the best time for a landing, either. The nub of this problem was how to land a marine division on two separate tides, one so early that normal assault shipping couldn't make it up the approach channels, the other so late that landings would have to be conducted by twilight and darkness. Paradoxically, a third problem helped solve the other two.

The island of Wolmi Do in Inchon harbor is the tactical key to the city. Wolmi Do's peak commands both harbor and town. A landing at Inchon without control of Wolmi Do would be unthinkable.

General Smith's planners therefore concluded that Wolmi Do—which *had* to be secured initially—should be taken on the morning tide, and that the main landings at Inchon proper could then proceed in the evening. In this way, by solving the Wolmi Do problem separately, the main landings at Inchon could be simplified and streamlined.

But how could the Wolmi Do landing force—a battalion landing team (3/5)—get to its transport area in time for the morning flood just after sunrise? The usual shipping—APAs, AKAs, and LSTs—was out of the question. Admiral Doyle's chief of staff, Captain Norman Sears, proposed that the BLT be embarked in APDs and one LSD, all of which were adequately powered, maneuverable, and equipped with navigational gear suitable for the night approach. Then, to prove he had faith in his idea, Sears persuaded Admiral Doyle to let him command the Wolmi Do attack group.

After morning tide receded, the BLT on Wolmi Do would, although physically cut off, be on strong defensive ground and of course supported by the guns and aviation of the fleet. In late afternoon the remainder of the division would land over two widely separated beaches.

Besides the obstacles of intelligence collection, of the tides, of the approach and of the capture of Wolmi Do, certain others remained before the Inchon plan could be firmed up.

One-third of the marine division—what today we call a marine expeditionary brigade, built around the 5th Marines and MAG–33—was fighting in the Pusan perimeter. General Walker, commanding the Eighth Army, was, to say the least, unenthusiastic over losing his marines and had gone so far as to say he would not be responsible for the perimeter if the marines were withdrawn. General Almond—who knew little of landing operations—tried to persuade General Smith to go into Inchon without the 5th Marines. He even offered to provide a substitute army regiment (with no amphibious training, containing 40 percent recently drafted Korean civilian levies) and saw no reason why such a formation wouldn't do for an assault landing only two weeks ahead.

However, after a last-minute show-down with the naval commanders and Generals Smith and Shepherd, Almond and Walker yielded when General MacArthur ordered that the 5th Marines be released.

The plan for Operation Chromite contained the following missions:

- Seize the port of Inchon and capture a force beachhead line
- Advance rapidly and seize Kimpo airfield
- Cross the Han River
- Seize and occupy Seoul
- Occupy blocking positions north, northeast, and east of Seoul
- Using forces in the Inchon-Seoul area as an anvil, crush the Communists with a stroke from the south by Eighth Army.

To execute Chromite, General MacArthur, a unified commander, created a joint task force—Joint Task Force 7 (which was really a falseface for Seventh Fleet headquarters and its commander, Vice Admiral Struble). The troop component of JTF–7 ("expeditionary troops," it would have been entitled in the amphibious doctrine of the day) was to be a corps, since the assigned missions would require operations by two divisions.

The question of how to staff and organize the corps headquarters—and, most important, who would command it—went unsettled until mid-August. Early that month Admiral Sherman had suggested to MacArthur that General Shepherd be given the command. Such an assignment would have made sense not only because Shepherd, a lieutenant general (and thus of corps-command rank), was a veteran amphibious commander, but also because his headquarters (FMFPac) was organized for amphibious warfare, and, above all, was a going concern. General Wright, MacArthur's G-3, made these points in a memorandum of 7 August, urging that the marine headquarters be employed. General Hickey, MacArthur's deputy chief of staff, concurred emphatically and warned against ". . . the hasty throwing together of a provisional corps headquarters . . . at best only a half-baked affair." These recommendations stopped at the chief of staff's desk and rebounded with the obituary notation, "Return without action."

Three days later, when Wright again urged prompt formation of a corps headquarters, a provisional staff for this group was selected by General Almond, the chief of staff, from officers in MacArthur's headquarters. About that time, General Almond has related, he asked General MacArthur who was to command the corps, and was, he said, startled to hear the general reply, "It is you."

And so it happened that on 26 August, when Washington authorized activation of X Corps, an army organization, Major General Almond, who by dispensation remained as MacArthur's chief of staff, was named to command it.

But this corps headquarters for the first amphibious assault since World War Two had no amphibious qualifications. As Admiral Doyle later wrote, "The corps staff, with very few exceptions, had no amphibious training, experience, or basic understanding of amphibious operations." For this reason, X Corps could only enter the picture when the battle ceased to be amphibious. It was to embark in an MSTS transport without proper communications; its commander, Almond, would not even accompany Admiral Struble aboard the force flagship, *Rochester*.

To get around the amphibious impotence of X Corps, jointure of command did not take place until reaching the level of the attack force, under Admiral Doyle, and the landing force, under General Smith. Correspondingly, there was one further juncture of command below Doyle and Smith—that of Captain Sears's advance attack group with Lieutenant Colonel R. D. Taplett's 3rd Battalion, 5th Marines.

Considering the haste with which Struble had to organize it, the force was impressive: 71,339 officers and men in assault or followup landings; and two hundred thirty ships from seven navies, plus MSTS, and thirty Japanese LSTs, one commanded by a former battleship captain. Curiously, there was no air force participation in this joint task force. The inconvenient remoteness of shore bases from the objective area so curtailed air force time over target that air operations had to be left entirely to carriers positioned close by in the Yellow Sea.

The pre-D-day operations—settled only after heated debate—consisted of extensive diversionary strikes against Chinnampo, Ongjin, and Kunsan, and then two days of naval and air bombardment at Inchon, the latter especially planned, by exposing thin-skinned destroyers at short range, to tempt enemy shore batteries into opening fire. The principal points at issue were air force participation (strongly urged on MacArthur by Washington), and the duration of pre-D-day bombardment. Admiral Struble—whose experience had been in Europe and the Southwest Pacific—favored only one day of light bombardment, hoping for maximum surprise. Doyle and Smith, thinking in terms of the Central Pacific, wanted five days of everything that could shoot and fly. After considerable discussion, Admiral Struble decided on two days—a decision confirmed by events.

The landing plan called for seizure of Wolmi Do on the early morning tide, over Green Beach. Making the main effort in the late afternoon, the 5th Marines (Lieutenant Colonel R. L. Murray) would land in LCVPs over Red Beach and seize Observatory Hill, key terrain feature of Inchon town. Since the capacity of Red Beach was barely enough for one RLT, the 1st Marines (Colonel L. B. Puller) were to land in amtracs over Blue Beach. An added advantage of the Blue Beach landing was that it would put the 1st Regiment directly on the flank of any counterattack from Seoul and would also seal off Inchon from the South.

The limited duration of high water posed still another problem: the only time when LSTs could beach at Inchon would be amid early assault waves when front lines were but a block or so inland. Admiral Doyle nevertheless took the risk ("I had the utmost confidence in the Marines. In my book they could not fail," he later said) and accepted the major complication of bringing in eight rust-bucket LSTs (only one of whose skippers had previously beached or retracted) onto Red Beach at H + thirty minutes. Only if these ships—repossessed from the island trade, and aromatic with the fragrance of fishheads and urine—got in, to remain stranded overnight, could the landing force get the logistics needed to maintain it on the beach.

Fire-support would be provided by two heavy cruisers, two British light cruisers, eight destroyers, and four LSMR. Two marine F4U squadrons (VMF–214 and VMF–323, veterans of the fighting in the perimeter) would provide the bulk of the close air support, flying from CVEs. Navy ADs from the fast carriers would seal off the area and back up the marine squadrons. Although in the event this did not work out, planners hoped to get two light battalions of the 11th Marines into position on Wolmi Do to support the main landings.

As finally worked out and described here,

the arrangements for Operation Chromite sound tidy and almost matter-of-fact. Could General Almond have been right after all when he called the landing assault "a simple mechanical operation?" ("It looked simple," General Smith later remarked, "because it was done by experts.")

To work up such a plan—or any plan—in such a time frame was a virtuoso performance. Again resembling Guadalcanal, the subordinate echelons (attack force/landing force) instead of responding to directives from higher headquarters, anticipated and almost completely dominated the plans on higher levels. General Smith issued his Inchon order on 27 August, whereas the X Corps order (theoretically the starting directive for the landing force) didn't come out until three days later and then only when advance drafts of the marines's order had been sent to X Corps to help them along. The final version of Admiral Doyle's numerous drafts was promulgated on 3 September; that of commander, JTF–7 appeared the same day (Admiral Struble wasn't even aware of the forthcoming operation until 22 August and could not get to Tokyo with his staff until the 25th).

General Smith's staff never had a chance to assemble in one place at the same time until after the landing. Part functioned as the marine brigade staff in the perimeter and had to conduct unrelated, hard-fought operations while moonlighting on plans for Inchon. Another echelon (on whom the main planning burden fell) flew with the division commander directly to Japan, while the remainder of the staff had to accompany the seaborne main body from the West Coast (and most of these officers had to stay in Kobe to run loading and embarkation).

In the journal he faithfully kept throughout two wars, General Smith ended his entry for 15 September 1950 with one sentence: "Operations have gone about as planned."

Naturally, no battle really goes that smoothly (it was the elder Moltke who said, "No plan ever survives contact with the enemy") and Inchon was no exception. Generally, however, what Admiral Doyle and General Smith and their expert, highly professional staffs worked out, succeeded quite remarkably. D-day operations were completed on schedule with all objectives taken, at a cost of but 21 killed and 175 wounded. Twelve days later, after heavy fighting in and around Seoul, the Korean capital was reconquered, and—as MacArthur had predicted from beginning to end—the North Korean Peoples Army was destroyed. The *In Min Gun* had been hit so hard and so quickly, from the sea, that it was incapable of reaction or resistance until too late.

Down at Green Beach, on Wolmi Do, today stands the only monument erected by Americans to the Inchon landings. Each year on 15 September (for the Koreans do not forget) delegations visit the impressive concrete cenotaph with its bronze plaque to lay wreaths in memory of those who recaptured Inchon and liberated Seoul. The wording of the memorial plaque is simple. It says that here the landing elements of the 7th U.S. Infantry Division landed at Inchon in September (no date given) 1950. Inexplicably, the 3rd Battalion, 5th Marines, whose leading elements landed at this spot three days before the infantry division, at 0633, 15 September 1950, is neither mentioned nor memorialized.

The revisionism implicit in this monument quite aptly bespeaks the larger camouflage of revisionism with which history has draped Operation Chromite. It is curious that so dazzling and decisive a victory should already be near forgotten or remembered only in a haze of inaccuracy.

There has developed, for example, a tendency to downgrade the Inchon-Seoul campaign as a kind of freak—an operation that shouldn't have succeeded but did. Was Chromite somehow unworthy because closely calculated long odds paid off? Taking MacArthur's hyperbole of 23 August that the odds against success were 5,000 to 1, writers who should know better have used this figure of speech as a serious basis for saying that Inchon was a mere gamble and next to foolhardy at that. How much wiser, instead of meaningless quantifications like 5,000 to 1, to view the operation with Admiral Doyle's informed conservatism as "not impossible."

Speaking to somewhat the same point, O. P. Smith later said: "We had a break at Inchon, all right—we had the know-how."

Operation Chromite changed the entire course of the war. In immediate results alone, MacArthur's lightning campaign accomplished the following:

- It caused the disintegration of the North Korean perimeter about Pusan.
- By liberating Seoul and dislocating the Communist logistical system, it effected the destruction of the *In Min Gun*.
- It returned the United Nations to the 38th parallel and thus preserved the Republic of Korea.

Inchon must therefore by considered a masterpiece. Whether in virtuosity of execution, or—at the chill altitude of high command—as a Napoleonic example of nerve and acceptance of calculated risk, Inchon remains, in the words of David Rees, "a Twentieth-Century Cannae, ever to be studied."

More important than these military judgments, Inchon underscored in 1950 what America had nearly forgotten in the five years since its hour of greatest victory—what, indeed, it often forgets, save when it needs a victory—that America is a maritime power, that its weapon is the trident, and its strategy that of the oceans. Only through the sure and practiced exercise of sea power could this awkward war in a remote place have been turned upside down in a few days. As Thomas More Molyneux, author of one of the earliest complete works on amphibious warfare, wrote in 1759:

A Military, Naval Littoral War, when wifely prepared and discreetly conducted, is a terrible Sort of War. Happy for that People who are Sovereigns enough of the Sea to put it into Execution! For it comes like Thunder and lightning to some unprepared Part of the World.

The Fleet Marine Force in the Early 1950s

BY ROBERT B. ASPREY

Almost from the moment the first atomic bomb was dropped on Hiroshima, amphibious planners began searching for an improved concept of operations that simultaneously would eliminate troop concentration in the beach area and yet would retain maximum impact against, and maximum movement in, the target area.

The problem of achieving mass while practicing dispersion essentially rested on an improved means of troop mobility, and to gain this, Marine Corps leaders soon chose the helicopter. After eight years of the most intense planning including thousands of field tests run under an extensive variety of nuclear and nonnuclear tactical situations, a new doctrine of amphibious warfare was published in Landing Force Bulletin-17 of December 1955. Centered on the technique of vertical envelopment, this doctrine dictates a powerful two-pronged attack, one prong a surface assault across the beach by conventional but dispersed means, the other a vertical envelopment by assault troops in helicopters.

The sine qua non of the new doctrine is helicopter operations. The old operational concept of the amphibious task force working in conjunction with fast carrier and other naval forces remains, but certain conventional troop assault ships are to be replaced by helicopter-troop carriers from which as-

U.S. Naval Institute *Proceedings*, "New Fleet Marine Force," 85 (August 1959): 40–48. Reprinted by permission.

sault elements of the landing force can be lifted and carried ten or more miles inland. Initial penetrations as far as a hundred miles from the task force or fifty miles inland and extending over divisional frontages of as much as fifty miles are considered feasible. The long-term goal is an all-helicopter assault with immediate postassault elements coming in by aircraft.

To meet the present concept and to prepare for the future goal, the organization and structure of all Fleet Marine Force (FMF) units—three divisions, three air wings, and combat service elements (or force troops)—were rigorously reviewed from June to December 1956 by the "FMF Organization and Composition Board" headed by Major General (now Lieutenant General) Robert E. Hogaboom, USMC. The numerous and important recommendations of this group were approved by the commandant, General Randolph McC. Pate, who ordered phase implementation commencing early in 1957. Reorganization of all units was completed in September 1958.

The most vital changes in the FMF concerned the marine infantry division. The new division is completely air transportable with its assault elements completely helicopter transportable. Reduced in personnel from twenty-one thousand to just under nineteen thousand, the division has been stripped of much heavy equipment and some heavy weapons, yet by the incorporation of new but proven weapons and certain structural changes, it has actually increased in shock and fire-power capability. Among the major changes are the following:

- Command and staff personnel have been increased in order to maintain a division command post, an alternate command post, and an administrative command post. Regimental and battalion staffs have been reduced in size to meet the mobility requirement stemming from the regimental and battalion landing team concept of assault operations.
- Certain administrative and supply personnel have been transferred from regimental headquarters to division headquarters and certain weapons such as the 4.2-inch mortar and the tank have been removed from the regiment. The result is a tactical regimental headquarters with maximum mobility in the field. Administrative and supply lines now run directly from division to battalion.
- The weapons company in each battalion has been replaced by a fourth rifle company. Battalion weapons—a platoon of 106 mm recoilless rifles, a platoon of 81 mm mortars, a flamethrower section, and, for emergency purposes, eleven light machine guns and eight 3.5-inch rocket launchers— are now carried in the battalion headquarters and service (H&S) company.
- The division tank battalion has been transferred to force troops. It has been replaced with an antitank battalion equipped with forty-five Ontos vehicles, a tracked carrier holding six 106 mm recoilless rifles, each capable of killing any tank in existence or likely to be developed. The carrier itself is not helicopter transportable but can be lifted easily by aircraft. The 106 mm recoilless rifle detaches from the carrier and is easily lifted by helicopter for mounting on either the jeep or the new mechanical mule, an 800-pound, 27-inch-high vehicle that can carry a 1,000 to 1,500-pound payload up to 25 mph.
- The 155 mm howitzer has been eliminated from the division artillery regiment. The new artillery regiment consists of an intermediate support battalion armed with the 105 mm howitzer and three close support battalions armed with either the 105 mm howitzer or the heavy mortar, the former helicopter transportable by sectionalization, the latter as a single unit. Nuclear capability is furnished by close support aircraft, by heavy artillery support battalions, and by ships firing rocket projectiles.
- The division reconnaissance company has been increased to battalion strength.

The most controversial of these changes is perhaps that of removing tanks from the division. A number of marine officers hold that the dual role of the tank in the assault— that of providing close fire support for the infantry plus protection against enemy armor—should not be sacrificed to logistic expediency. The proponents of the change argue that other weapons, for example air-to-surface missile systems and helicopterborne close support artillery, will provide the necessary close support. As for protection against enemy armor, there are the 106 mm recoilless rifle effective at 1,000 yards and the 3.5-inch rocket effective at 200 yards. In addition, greatly improved antitank weapons are now being tested. Furthermore, the bulk of future operations will probably be undertaken in reduced visibility or darkness and tanks are not very effective under such conditions. Finally, when the tactical situation demands tanks, they can be supplied from force troops just as can other heavy weapon units. Interestingly enough, the decision to remove the tanks did not rest on a logistic factor, but once the decision was made it was discovered that so much weight was eliminated as to allow the thought of a completely air-transportable division.

The most significant tactical change in the division is the replacement of the weapons company in each infantry battalion with a fourth rifle company in order to provide the increase in reconnaissance capability and in shock power which modern warfare dictates to the infantry battalion, the basic tactical unit of a marine division. This battalion forms the core of the basic ground combat unit of the Marine Corps, the Battalion Landing Team

(BLT). In a recent test exercise described by Lieutenant Colonel W. A. Wood, USMC, one BLT consisted of an infantry battalion, a 4.2-inch heavy mortar battery, a pioneer platoon, an AT (Ontos) platoon, a naval gunfire detachment, and a medical detachment. This made a total of 61 officers and 1,390 enlisted men, with 116 vehicles and 108 radios—in other words a large and complex organization designed either for independent operations or for operations as part of a regimental landing team. Since nuclear warfare imposes the probable requirement of frequent independent or dispersed operations, the BLT commander must have sufficient forces to attack in strength while simultaneously protecting his exposed flanks and rear and also to meet casualty and fatigue attrition over prolonged periods of isolated employment. Although increasing the size of the battalion by only 1 marine officer, 58 marine enlisted men, and 11 navy enlisted men, the addition of the fourth rifle company, besides offering the tactical advantages derived from the quadrangular formation, offers the battalion commander 9 more reinforced rifle squads, or 27 more fire teams, or 108 more scouts on security and reconnaissance tasks than could the old triangular battalion.

Some of the same reasons that promoted the addition of a fourth rifle company to each battalion prompted the increase of division reconnaissance from company to battalion strength. Extended, dispersed, and extremely mobile warfare automatically increases the intelligence demand, both because of the increased vulnerability of semiisolated units to enemy action and because of the necessity of swift target acquisition to exploit the increased lethality of fire support weapons. The fivefold mission of the new reconnaissance battalion is to provide:

(1) helicopter and ground reconnaissance beyond the combat area but short of distant reconnaissance missions

(2) flank, separation, and rear area reconnaissance

(3) road reconnaissance

(4) battlefield surveillance by establish-

ment and displacement of helicopter-lifted observation posts

(5) counterreconnaissance.

The entire battalion is capable of being helicopter-lifted, and a helicopter reconnaissance squadron has been provided in each marine air wing for this purpose. Reconnaissance personnel are of course equally adept in conventional ground and amphibious reconnaissance techniques.

Extending division reconnaissance is the mission of a special reconnaissance company located in force troops. Consisting of an amphibious reconnaissance platoon, a parachute reconnaissance platoon, and a parachute pathfinder platoon, this company has a mission of preliminary operations in the assault area. Equipped for night operations in particular, the reconnaissance company is perfecting a number of new techniques that should satisfy the intelligence requirement peculiar to the vertical assault. In order to conduct deep reconnaissance, the parachute reconnaissance platoon is perfecting a technique of free-fall jumping whereby, to gain pinpoint landing accuracy, a paratrooper falls free a considerable distance before opening his chute. The amphibious reconnaissance platoon has come up with an unconventional and highly successful technique that involves the SCUBA underwater breathing apparatus. So equipped and trained, personnel can embark and disembark from a submerged submarine, a method which eliminates the former hazard inherent in a submarine surfacing in an enemy area. The parachute pathfinder platoon consists of highly trained teams that as little as fifteen minutes prior to a scheduled helicopter assault will drop into the target area where they will establish communication with inbound helicopters. After guiding them to the best landing sites, members of the team will then provide fire security during initial deployment.

The major change in the fire support system of the division is found in the artillery regiment. By substituting the heavy mortar for the 105 mm howitzer in the close support battalion for the vertical assault, and the 105 for the 155 mm howitzer in the intermediate support battalion, the regiment has lost its former long-range destruction capability. But this sacrifice, a necessary one if the artillery is to support infantry in the assault, is not without compensations. One is the development of a greatly improved close support weapon, presumably a howitzer type capable of single helicopterlift, that has been designed to replace the heavy mortar. Another has resulted from the organizational and tactical promotion of the artillery battery to the basic fire support unit capable of operating independently (a position formerly held by the artillery battalion). By providing its own observation, communications, supply, and maintenance and by preparing its own firing data, the new battery offers a self-sufficient unit which can readily and simply absorb heavier support units that may be attached to it. This task organization capability extends upward to battalion and regimental level and means, in effect, an increased capability of offering the infantry unit heavy artillery from force troops and, in conjunction with infantry fire support centers, more effective naval gunfire and close air support.

To exploit this tactical concept has meant a shift of emphasis in force artillery to give it the increased mobility and organizational flexibility necessary to permit rapid and smooth integration of its units into the division artillery regiment. Accordingly the battalion organization at force level has been dropped; all force artillery units are now organized as separate, independent batteries which will be either self-propelled or helicopter transportable and thus, once committed to the tactical area, able to go in and out of position in a matter of minutes. The potential here is tremendous. Both the Honest John and the Little John rocket batteries, the latter still under development, carry either nuclear or conventional warheads and are helicopter transportable. Although the heavier batteries must be brought in by sea lift, the self-propelled 8-inch howitzer has tremendous power at an 18,000-yard range as

does the self-propelled 155 mm gun at 25,000 yards (and a self-propelled 155 mm howitzer that *is* air transportable is scheduled for delivery in 1961). The ability of these units to integrate rapidly and smoothly into the division artillery task organization concept, whether at regiment, battalion, or battery level, means that the division has very great power on call without the logistic responsibility of such power.

A final compensation for the division's loss of the howitzers has resulted from an increase in the capability of close air support by the addition of a second forward air controller (FAC) to each battalion's tactical air control party (TACP), and by the addition of a third air support radar team (ASRT) to the marine air support squadron in the wing. The latter addition greatly increases the ability of the division to gain precise air delivery of nuclear weapons at any time and in any weather.

The service organization of the division has been streamlined by combining the old service regiment and the shore party battalion into one service battalion of 74 officers and 1,402 enlisted men which comprise an H&S company, three light support companies, one medium support company, and two landing support companies. The light support company—which, excepting ten 2½-ton trucks, is helicopter transportable—provides light supply and maintenance support to tactical elements of the division. The medium support company provides general support to the division as a whole and the two landing support companies assume the old shore party battalion function. The logistic capability of the battalion includes only those services habitually required by the division to initiate and sustain combat for the initial assault period. Extended division operations will require support from force service elements, a capability that has been increased by the new force service regiment which provides supply, maintenance, and essential services to a marine division-wing task force as well as to a number of force troop units.

Other service changes in the division include a redesignation of the engineer battalion as the pioneer battalion, whose three pioneer companies and one pioneer support company can be augmented from force service elements such as the force engineer battalion, fixed and floating bridge companies, and explosive ordnance disposal company. Because of the additional mobility provided by the helicopter, the division motor transport battalion has lost one truck company but, when necessary, it can be reinforced by the motor transport battalion in force troops. The medical battalion of the division has lost two hospital companies and gained one collecting and clearing company, the reason being that new helicopter and transport aircraft evacuation techniques have rendered obsolete a division hospitalization requirement. Standing behind this battalion at force level are separate surgical companies, hospital companies, dental companies, and the new mass evacuation company, a unit prepared to move immediately into any area that has received an atomic blast. This company provides the necessary personnel to control and direct operations at the site of the blast and a minimum of medical, monitoring, and decontamination personnel to perform essential tasks. A minimum force, it has been designed as an efficient core around which additional medical, damage control, and rescue teams can immediately build.

Reorganization of the marine air wing was not as drastic as that of the division. In strength the wing remains between eight thousand to ten thousand personnel with slightly less than four hundred operational aircraft that form six major operational groups: fighter (FJ–4 or Fury and F8U–1 or Crusader), attack (A4D or Skyhawk and FJ–4B or Fury), all-weather fighter (F4D or Skyray), fixed-wing transport, medium helicopter, light helicopter, and one helicopter composite reconnaissance squadron. Besides their conventional missions of preassault bombardment, air protection, and close air support of the landing force, the fighter and attack elements must now be concerned with tactics necessary to assault helicopter protection. Of predominant interest to the concept of vertical as-

sault is the helicopter and transport lift capability of the wing.

The Marine Corps is currently flying four types of helicopters: the HOK, a small machine primarily used for reconnaissance, the HRS which is being replaced by the HUS, machines primarily employed as assault vehicles, and the HR2S, a larger machine mainly used for heavy lift. Included in each air wing are two light helicopter transport squadrons (HUS and HRS) or a total of forty-eight machines, one composite reconnaissance squadron (twelve HOK and twelve HUS or HRS) or a total of twenty-four, and one medium helicopter transport squadron of fifteen HR2S machines. The HUS is capable of carrying twelve troops with full equipment or 3,000 pounds on a basis of a one hundred mile operating radius; the HR2S can haul twenty-six troops with full equipment or 5,800 pounds on a fifty mile operating basis or twenty troops with full equipment or 4,500 pounds on a one hundred mile operating radius.

Helicopter assault techniques continue to be improved on a converted escort carrier, the training ship, USS *Thetis Bay*. The first true helicopter-troop carrier or LPH, the USS *Iwo Jima*, has been designed to berth two thousand troops and carry more than 1,000 tons of cargo and approximately thirty HUS type helicopters—her keel was laid in March 1959. To plug the necessary operational time gap, the USS *Boxer* has been converted into an interim LPH and is in service with Atlantic Fleet units at this time; another carrier, the USS *Princeton*, has undergone limited conversion and is now serving with the Pacific Fleet. One other such carrier will probably be converted, but in any event the Fleet Marine Force now holds a two-battalion helicopter assault capability, a powerful weapon for any brushfire war that may involve this country. Complementing the LPH will be a new assault ship, the LPD.

Fixed-wing transport capability, now consisting of R4Q and R4D aircraft in the wing, will be greatly improved by the adoption of the C–130 aircraft which *inter alia* can carry ninety-two combat-loaded troops. Three squadrons of the C–130, each holding eighteen aircraft, are planned by the end of 1962 with the first squadron of an initial twelve aircraft being operational by the end of 1961. Each C–130 will be equipped with the marine inflight refueling system (MIRS), a package device installed for a fighter refueling mission and removed for a troop-carrying mission.

The difficult problem of supporting helicopter and aircraft operations from the ground has been partially resolved by the development of a bulk fuel handling system that is helicopter transportable and offers a fuel supply of 300,000 gallon capacity to the landing force. Tankers or smaller landing ship tanks (LSTs) converted to tankers will pump the fuel through a buoyant hose to the beach where a system of five 60,000-gallon tank farms will carry it up to fifteen miles inland. An attendant problem of construction needs in the target area may have been whipped by a sectionalization program designed to make the three basic machines of assault construction—the bulldozer, scraper, and grader—helicopter transportable. The Marine Corps now has prototypes of sectionalized pieces of these machines with no single piece weighing more than 6,000 pounds and thus capable of lift in the HR2S, though not for long distances. In a demonstration last year a sectionalized bulldozer weighing 36,000 pounds was lifted by helicopter to a target area and assembled in two hours and forty-five minutes by eight marines using hand tools.

These and other diverse problems are inherent in the doctrine of vertical envelopment just as problems are in any radical new operational concept. The pressing requirement for a better close support artillery weapon has been mentioned; improved helicopter protection is vital; a need for pinpoint accuracy of naval gunfire will exist so long as the conventional ship-to-shore landing phase is necessary; equally important is the development of equipment that will lighten the combat load of the individual marine who today carries an average ninety pounds which is much too restrictive for the mobile role demanded of him. Budgetary limitations have dictated certain severe shortages to the Fleet Marine Force, and until a sufficient number of LPHs and helicopters become available, the force is going to hold a limited helicopter assault capability. As Marine Corps planners point out, however, it was not long ago when the landing craft concept of the amphibious assault was developed without adequate landing craft, a difficulty that did not negate the validity of the concept. So in the last few years the Marine Corps has developed the concept of vertical assault despite material shortages. But, by the reorganization of its Fleet Marine Force units, by daily research and development of new weapons and equipment, by rotation of infantry battalions for operational training aboard the interim LPHs, the Marine Corps stands ready to exploit the necessary equipment upon its delivery.

Meanwhile the newly organized divisions, wings, and service elements are being tested in a variety of tactical situations. Minor changes are being made and another Organization and Composition Board will be convened in 1959 to review the present achievement. Although much remains to be accomplished, the recent reorganization, by fitting the Fleet Marine Force into the physical delimitations set by the vertical assault concept has increased enormously its readiness for modern warfare.

Riverine Warfare in the Indochina Conflict

BY MAJOR RICHARD M. MEYER, USA

Many river warfare studies have concluded that a river warfare capability is essential in order to support U.S. military doctrine. These studies, however, did not delineate which military service should be responsible for river warfare.

The only place where the United States is presently engaged in river warfare is the Mekong Delta area of South Vietnam. Because of the area's agricultural and fishing resources and its transportation and industrial facilities, it is important economically. And the military significance of the delta waterways is obvious. In a war where the great prize is the authority of the contending forces over the people, the control of these waterways, the vital arteries of the region, is the primary aim. It is no wonder, then, that the Communists' insurgency is most determined in the delta region.

The current conflict involving command of the vital Mekong River and the delta may be considered as a continuation of the Indochinese War fought by the French from 1946 to 1954. An examination of the French river operations during that period may suggest principles for U.S. river warfare doctrine.

In addition to controlling the coastal waters, one of the primary missions of the French navy during the Indochinese War was to clear and control the network of interior waterways. To accomplish this mission, the French

Military Review, "The Ground-Sea Team in River Warfare," 46 (September 1966): 54–63. Reprinted by permission.

organized several naval assault flotillas that in French naval technology were known as *dinassauts*. The French further established river districts, such as the Red River and Mekong River districts, and assigned one or more *dinassauts* to each.

Although the *dinassauts* varied in organization according to the area in which they operated, the average unit had about twelve ships. Included in each—during the last years of the Indochinese War—were an armored landing craft, infantry (LCI) or landing ship, infantry, large (LSIL) as flagship; two landing craft, mechanized (LCM) of the armored *Monitor* version to provide fire support; and nine or more landing craft, vehicle, personnel (LCVP) and LCMs for transport and fire support.

This force was usually augmented during critical operations by one landing ship, support, large (LSSL) for additional fire support and several landing craft, tank (LCT) for transporting troops and armored vehicles. By the end of the war, the average strength approached eight hundred men.

The *dinassauts* were equipped primarily with U.S.-built World War Two landing craft that had been modified for river operations. LCVPs, LCTs, LCIs, LSSLs, and LCMs were the mainstays in addition to a French, steel-hulled river gunboat. All of these craft had undergone initial modifications in armor and armament, and there were additional substantial changes as the war progressed.

The firepower of these vessels was greatly increased with the addition of 3-inch, 40 mm, 37 mm, or 20 mm guns, and .50 or .30 caliber

Riverine Operations, Vietnam. Courtesy of the U.S. Navy Historical Center.

machine guns. Many carried 81 mm mortars that provided fire support in depth for landing forces and also proved to be very useful in countering river ambushes.

By the formation of the *dinassauts*, the French believed that they had capitalized on the rich operational potential inherent in the intricate system of navigable waters and had thereby gained a new dimension in mobility. The boats of the *dinassauts* were not highly sophisticated weapon systems but rather craft modified to perform an immediate task. The tactics employed by the French river commanders were extremely flexible and proved essentially sound.

In coordinated operations with other arms of the French forces, river craft were used to resupply and reinforce areas where land lines of communication were vulnerable or nonexistent. *Dinassauts* were used in conducting independent raids deep into enemy territory where they supported offensive as well as defensive operations with their concentrated, mobile firepower and rapid landing of embarked troops at badly pressed points.

By patrol activity, the *dinassauts* were used to prevent Vietminh ground forces from crossing inland waterways. Such patrolling also ensured that the rivers and canals were not used as water lines of supply by the enemy.

Tactics for *dinassaut* forces had to take into account three major obstacles: river am-

bushes, river barricades, and remote-controlled mines. In a river ambush, the greatest danger to the force came from bazookas and recoilless rifles. To counter the Vietminh's increasingly deadly ambushes on the rivers, the French responded with air cover.

Few river barricades were encountered, because the Vietminh wanted to keep the rivers and canals open for their own use. The barricades that were used against the French were difficult to remove. Removal involved blowing up the barricades by direct fire from weapons mounted on the river boats, demolishing them with underwater-emplaced explosives, or dismantling them by towing away critical portions of the obstruction.

Although ambushes were considered the primary threat to the *dinassauts*, probably the greatest danger came from mines. Although most of these were fairly crude, they were exceedingly effective because they were sunk in the mud of the meandering streams and canals and thus almost defied sweeping. These mines were electrically detonated by individuals concealed in the dense vegetation along the canal banks. To detect these underwater mines or sever the electrical firing leads, the French tried sweeping the river bottoms with a heavy chain suspended between two LCVPs which preceded the main body of the *dinassauts*. To keep the chain from floating off the bottom, the craft had to advance very slowly, so this method was not recommended when speed was required. In those cases, the French used air reconnaissance to discover the position of the mine operator before the arrival of the *dinassauts*. Even the combination of these two methods was not considered adequate to locate and destroy this type of mine.

The tactics and techniques of the *dinassauts* can be compared to a land combat force. Out in front, to the rear, and on both flanks of any land army are the light, highly mobile scout units designed to detect, fix, and delay the enemy. In this manner, the French used small, lightly armored river gunboats.

When ambushed, these craft immediately returned the enemy's fire, while the main force—located within the protective screen of light craft—dispatched landing troops for a ground enveloping attack supported by fire from the mortars and cannon of the heavier ships. Thus, the tactics, at least for an ambush, are comparable to those of a land army, or as a *dinassaut* commander said, "The *dinassaut* was employed very much like a cavalry unit with the same type of speed and boldness."

Dinassauts were by no means invincible or a "final solution," but they did represent an imaginative adaptation by the French navy to the problems of applying seapower to an inland environment in an unconventional war. As Bernard B. Fall stated: "They may well have been one of the few worthwhile contributions of the Indochina War to military knowledge." The successes achieved by the *dinassauts* showed that amphibious raids into enemy territory were feasible and that the most dangerous part of many such raids, perhaps, was the return to base. The limitations of the *dinassauts* revolved around the necessity to modify World War Two landing craft for work never intended for them and to keep them in operation.

Anthony Harrigan, military consultant to the National Strategy Committee of the American Security Council, wrote, "The cardinal principle of river warfare is close cooperation with forces ashore. Troops and vessels acting in concert can accomplish military measures of great importance." The French adhered to this principle whenever possible, but the dense vegetation along the banks of the waterways sometimes made it difficult. Insufficient manpower and inadequate material prevented victory on the inland waterways just as it did farther inland, and the impact of the river war is still felt today. Ambassador Robert McClintock, charge d'affaires of the American embassy in Saigon in 1954, surmised this when he wrote, "The most important river-warfare since the operations of the Federal Navy against New Orleans and Vicksburg has been carried on during the past eight years in Indochina."

Immediately following the French defeat and withdrawal from Indochina, guerrilla warfare, led by a communist-dominated guerrilla organization, began in the newly created South Vietnam. These insurgents soon became known as the Viet Cong. The South Vietnamese government responded to Viet Cong activity by undertaking counterinsurgency operations. U.S. military and economic assistance, which began in 1954, was limited initially to military hardware, technical advisory teams, and economic aid. The Vietnamese navy was created in 1954 with U.S. aid and advice and has subsequently been organized, equipped, and trained to counter the Viet Cong. The river force of the Vietnamese navy conducts operations on the inland waterways. Included in the river force are seven river assault groups (RAGs).

Although the RAGs are essentially similar to the French *dinassauts*, there are two major differences. The French maintained a clear line of navy control over the actions of the *dinassauts*, whereas the RAGs have been operationally controlled by the Army of the Republic of Vietnam. The second major difference is the absence of a permanent landing force organic to any RAG. When required, Vietnamese army or marine units are assigned on a temporary basis to a RAG for assault missions. Each RAG is commanded by a Vietnamese navy lieutenant commander and usually consists of one LCM (*Commandament*), one LCM *Monitor*, five armored LCMs, six armored LCVPs, and six river gunboats. The LCM *Commandament*, primarily a command craft, is armed with two 20 mm guns and two .50 caliber machine guns.

The most heavily armed is the LCM *Monitor* which mounts one 40 mm cannon, one .50 caliber machine gun, two 20 mm guns, and one 81 mm mortar. The armored LCVPs are usually equipped with a 20 mm gun and three .30 caliber machine guns while the river gunboats carry a variety of machine guns. Thus, the organization and craft of the RAGs are almost identical to those of the French. As presently organized and equipped, each RAG has excellent capabilities for gunfire support with its organic weaponry. It can deliver effective supporting fire for ground attacks, harass enemy bases, illuminate targets during hours of darkness, and deliver interdictory fires on illicit canal and river traffic.

RAGs are used primarily to escort river convoys or perform resupply tasks and are occasionally used to conduct river patrols. The RAGs still confront, however, the three major problems once faced by the *dinassauts*—ambushes, barricaded waterways, and underwater mines. Tactics used by the RAGs to cope with these and other problems, although basically the same as those used by the French, are being modified and will undoubtedly produce some new techniques.

Although a particular U.S. military service has not been officially charged with the whole responsibility for the development of river warfare doctrine, a U.S. river force might, if formed, initially be similar to that used by the French and South Vietnamese. An immediate U.S. river warfare doctrine could be formulated by modifying present service responsibilities for amphibious warfare to include river warfare. Under such a modification, the U.S. Navy, in coordination with the other services, would be solely responsible for developing the doctrine, techniques, and equipment necessary. Also, under this modification, the U.S. Marine Corps would be charged with the specific task of developing the doctrine for the employment of river assault troops, and the army would be required to train certain combat units to function as river assault troops in accordance with the developed doctrines as is done today in amphibious training.

Even though the U.S. Navy does not presently have a river force, it has utilized them in the past. The U.S. Navy's gunboats played a prominent role during the American Civil War. In fact, they produced the first real victory of that war when river monitors compelled the Confederates to surrender Fort Henry on the Tennessee River. The river efforts of the U.S. Navy patrolling the Yangtze in China during the 1930s is another good example, and the navy's tremendous contribution in crossing the Rhine and other rivers during World War Two further illustrates the navy's concern with inland waterways. Therefore, under this modification, if the United States were actively committed to a river war campaign in the Mekong Delta, the U.S. Navy would be responsible for manning and equipping river units with the exception of embarked assault troops. Because of the terrain involved, all operations would be either joint or combined with ground and naval forces operating in mutually supporting roles—a true blend of ground and sea forces.

A U.S. river force would be faced with the dual tasks of waterway patrol and support of ground combat operations and thus contain both patrol and assault units. The labyrinth of canals necessitates the employment of river patrol units to block possible enemy routes of withdrawal whenever a river assault unit is used to attack an enemy position. The river patrol units would contain only navy equipment and personnel, and maximum coordination would exist with army and air force units operating in close proximity to river patrol routes. Patrol units would be primarily responsible for control of the major rivers, and some of their operational procedures would include twenty-four hour surveillance and inspection of all river traffic and the establishment of river control points. These operational procedures coupled with coordination with the sister services, would make it extremely difficult for the Viet Cong to operate successfully on or near the waterways. On the other hand, river assault units would carry the war directly to Viet Cong strongholds. Thus, the U.S. Navy would be responsible for providing fire support during initial assaults, disembarking troops, continuing fire support during the advance ashore, reinforcing previously committed troops, and reembarking troops after engagements.

This new role of the navy would create an urgent requirement for modern river craft. Harrigan has advocated a small shallow-draft boat with a 6- or 8-inch gun. He also believes that aerial bombing is tremendously useful, but that heavy artillery is the most devastating and effective of weapons to blast communist insurgents out of their river area strong points.

An experienced U.S. Marine Corps officer has proposed a floating mortar battery of four to eight 81 mm mortars or similar indirect fire weapons. He feels this would provide the substantial indirect fire needed. In other words, an armored river craft appropriately armed is required in sufficient quantity to provide the navy with an effective river fleet capability.

In addition, the doctrine must provide this river assault force with army- or marine-embarked assault troops. Based upon the experience of the French, the permanent assignment of troop units to each river assault unit might appear highly desirable, but this method does not provide for full utilization of the embarked troops. Assault troops should be obtained from U.S. Army and Marine Corps units as required and directed by the area commander.

Operational control of the river assault units should be flexible. For example, an operation in my opinion could evolve as follows: A river assault unit in an army corps area would be under the operational control of the commanding general of the corps. This control could be further decentralized to the most effective level of coordination. Thus, a marine landing party could be placed under the operational control of a river assault unit, commanded by a naval officer, which, in turn, could be under the tactical control of an army divisional commander.

Hence, organizational rigidity would be avoided with the major effort devoted to ensuring immediate and direct coordination between river unit commanders, close air support personnel, and tactical ground commanders. Joint operations with river assault units attacking from the river, coordinated with a land assault and helicopter-borne assault, would have the Viet Cong fighting in all directions at once. The problems inherent in this type of operation are numerous, but they can be solved with adequate prior planning.

No one should make the mistake of considering river warfare as just another aspect of amphibious operations. River warfare is distinct since it requires specialized craft, equipment, and techniques for its conduct. Modifying amphibious craft for river warfare, a necessary expedient in the past, has not produced satisfactory results in equipment or techniques. Now is the time to change. Thus, the overall approach to U.S. river warfare doctrine entails a navy river force containing both patrol and assault units with the assault troops furnished, as required, by the army and Marine Corps. Such a river force would not solve all the military problems in the Mekong Delta, but it would apply greater pressure to the enemy as well as increase the operational flexibility of U.S. forces.

Amphibious Warfare in Vietnam, 1972

BY MAJOR GENERAL E. J. MILLER, USMC,
AND REAR ADMIRAL W. D. TOOLE, JR., USN

On 1 April 1972, the armies of North Vietnam surged across Vietnam's demilitarized zone (DMZ). The magnitude and force of the North Vietnamese attack indicated that they had come to settle the war—once and for all. The North Vietnamese army (NVA) did not rely on new weaponry, but on surprise and overwhelming force. They were conventionally organized, equipped, and deployed, but with their in-depth strength of tanks, armored personnel carriers, artillery, and antiaircraft (AA) systems, they foreshadowed the type of threat that can be expected in future mid-intensity conflicts and, indeed, some of their tactical maneuvers were repeated a year later in the 1973 Arab-Israeli war.

This attack clearly indicated a decision by the leaders of North Vietnam to move into the final phase of the Communist strategy for revolutionary wars of national liberation. Emboldened now, they were finished with guerrilla war, through with hiding like fishes in the seas of farmers. They were ready to meet—head on—the duly constituted government forces of South Vietnam, in open conflict, with well-organized armies.

To achieve the goals of their invasion, the NVA followed Soviet-style tactics and patterns of attack and defense. Several divisions were employed with subordinate regiments in conventional two-up and one-back disposition. Attacks were made by troops equipped with the latest of Soviet-designed

small arms and supported by armored personnel carriers and tanks. Heavy volumes of precise indirect fire, delivered by a variety of weapons from 60 mm mortars up to the long-range 130 mm gun, supported all offensive and defensive operations. There was also an increase in antiaircraft gun defenses, both forward and in depth, which were supplemented by SA-7 heat-seeking missiles. Toward the rear, 57 mm AA guns, placed in successive lines, protected command points, lines of communications, and logistics support. The concentration and depth of enemy forces, the coverage of North Vietnamese artillery, and the intensity of antiaircraft defense suddenly had made the Vietnam War a whole new ball game.

Initially, the forces of South Vietnam reeled under the fierce NVA attack. The North Vietnamese rolled into Dong Ha and occupied the abandoned city of Quang Tri. All that blocked the NVA from an open road to Hue were the marines of South Vietnam (VNMC).

To help shore up the shattered defenses and allow time for regrouping and for civilians to flee to Hue, two brigades of South Vietnamese marines were ordered to fight a delaying action. The plan then called for the Vietnamese marines to fall back and hold at defensive positions along the My Chanh River Line. The marines executed the order brilliantly and although they were subjected to tremendous pressures from intensive artillery fire and tank and infantry attacks, their defensive lines held and were never broken. This respite, in an otherwise deteriorating

U.S. Naval Institute *Proceedings*, "Amphibious Forces: The Turning Point," 100 (November 1974): 26–32. Reprinted by permission.

Vietnamese marines disembarking from a CH-46 helicopter. Courtesy of the U.S. Marine Corps.

military situation, gave the South Vietnamese time to regroup and plan further actions.

The South Vietnamese Marine Division's area of operations, north of Hue, extended from the Gulf of Tonkin to the foothills eighteen kilometers to the west. The marines had stopped the NVA's advance on Hue from the north and were holding their assigned area. What was needed now, however, was some dramatic initiative to prove to the NVA and the world that the South Vietnamese still constituted a viable fighting force, capable of offensive action.

The Seventh Fleet's amphibious forces had been a dormant factor in the Vietnamese War since 1969. Constantly present, but essentially unused, they had contributed little more than the vague threat that is always implicit in a force in being. Still, because of the long inactivity of our amphibious forces, the North Vietnamese Army probably tended to discount any real threat from these ships and their embarked marines.

Within two days after the North Vietnamese invasion, more than three thousand U.S. Marines and twenty-six helicopters, embarked in seven amphibious ships, were on station off the DMZ ready to execute assigned contingency missions. While there was no immediate call for these forces, they continued to build all through April. By early May, the commander of Task Force Seventy-Six (PhibForSeventhFlt) embarked in the command ship *Blue Ridge* with a total of sixteen amphibious ships under his command and available for support operations. The embarked Fleet Marine Force consisted of Headquarters, 9th Marine Amphibious Brigade (9th MAB), two marine amphibious units (MAUs), and two battalion landing teams (BLTs). This was a formidable force in the type of war being fought but, even among the VNMC, there was doubt that the Seventh Fleet Amphibious Force would be allowed to participate actively in the fight.

The obvious objective was to project this available seapower ashore and strike the enemy behind his lines. Such action was clearly within the capability of the available units, inasmuch as the coast line was lightly defended and the enemy was well extended. The tactical advantage of such operations was clear, but political constraints precluded the reintroduction of U.S. Marine Corps troops

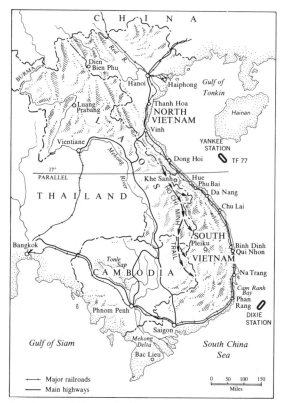

Southeast Asia, ca. 1968.

into South Vietnam in a land warfare role. Still, there were other alternatives to simply landing U.S. Marines.

These alternatives were examined and discussed by leaders of South Vietnamese and U.S. forces. In the plan that was finally approved by U.S. and South Vietnamese higher headquarters, South Vietnamese marines would be put ashore by U.S. marine helicopters and from landing craft based on U.S. amphibious ships. In effect, every facet of U.S. amphibious forces, except the U.S. marine, would be committed to action. It promised to be a textbook example of support for our allies under the Nixon Doctrine.

Acceptance of the basic objective, however, did not solve the immediate problems that faced the navy and Marine Corps amphibious planners in implementing this unique support concept. One complication was that other forces—afloat and ashore, American and Vietnamese—were already operating in the area, each with separate chains of command. It became apparent that methods had to be developed which would allow coordination of unit actions to provide a viable plan under the concept of supporting and supported forces in accordance with JCS Pub 2. Also, the methods used would have to provide for an overriding requirement that each operation must progress rapidly from plan to execution.

In developing such procedures, initial planning was greatly facilitated by the presence of the U.S. Marine Corps Advisory Detachment with the South Vietnamese Marine Division. Presentations concerning proposed operations normally were made by these advisors to the VNMC division, in conjunction with Vietnamese members of the division staff. These briefings would include timing, objectives, ground scheme of maneuver, assault forces, a concept for supporting arms fires, and enemy opposition. Such support factors were then compared with the number of 9th MAB helicopters and tracked landing vehicles (LVT) and the amphibious shipping available in order to establish immediately the feasibility of supporting an operation.

These initial planning sessions were relatively informal, but most effective in adjusting conflicting factors between requirements and available assets. With the initial concept plan developed, the next step was to work out the necessary refinements so that each participating command could develop a detailed supporting operation order. With the stage thus set and requirements defined, the supporting elements prepared and coordinated a definitive plan to provide the Vietnamese marines with their needs for specific objectives.

Each phase of the intended operation was briefed by the "duty-expert" in a particular area. The interaction of ideas, comments, recommendations, and suggestions among a small group of specialists, each geared toward providing the optimum plan, proved effective. For example, valuable current intelligence information was provided by the U.S. Army Air Cavalry representatives. This information, in consonance with predicted weather, assisted in defining helicopter approach headings, landing plans, and retirement routes. Representatives of the Seventh Fleet and of the Air and Naval Gunfire Liaison Company developed intensive naval gunfire plans to provide general support for an extended period of time prior to the assault. Corps Direct Air Support Center (I DASC) representatives responded by passing requests for B-52 "Arclight" support to the Seventh Air Force and assisted in preparing plans for landing zone preparation by tactical air. Forward air controllers, airborne, who would be directly involved, offered flight patterns, intended procedures and radio frequencies as input to the developing plan. U.S. Marine advisors, in conjunction with fire support coordination representatives from 9th MAB developed artillery fire plans in general and direct support of the assault force, coordinated to ensure a fire support plan geared to maximum destruction of enemy resistance. Air Cavalry representatives provided specific and detailed planning guidance for direct support of the assault helicopters into and around the intended landing zones. And, amphibious force representatives provided necessary plans for the positioning of the support shipping for development of take-off and recovery evolutions.

No one was specifically designated as *the* person responsible for the output of this conglomerate of planners; however, the commanding general, 9th MAB and Commander, Task Force 76 required assurance of the adequacy of the plans generated, as did the RVN Marine Division commander.

Colocation of CTF-76 and CG, 9th MAB and their respective staffs during this period of high tempo operations proved to be a necessity. The need to closely coordinate the employment of U.S. Navy and Marine forces and the reporting requirements to higher headquarters required the presence of the two commands and their staffs on the scene, embarked in the same flagship.

The opening round in the projected series of operations took place on the morning of 13 May 1972, when two battalions of Viet-

namese marines were landed by U.S. Marine helicopters behind enemy lines in a spoiling attack. This first South Vietnamese offensive action since the fall of Quang Tri, and the first such Navy/Marine amphibious operation since 1969, caught the enemy completely by surprise. More than two hundred forty enemy troops were killed at the cost of ten South Vietnamese. The operation was highly publicized in South Vietnam and visibly restored a sense of confidence in the defenders of Hue.

On 24 May, a second and even more ambitious operation was conducted. Within a forty-hour period, an operation was planned and executed which combined a helicopter assault by two battalions of Vietnamese marines with a landing by a battalion of Vietnamese marines in LVTs. The enemy, surprised by the bold action, lost over six hundred seventy men. The precision with which the U.S. and Vietnamese air, sea, and ground forces conducted the complex operation heralded the arrival of a new combat capability in Northern MR-I, an announcement that the NVA could not fail to heed.

The next operation came on 29 June as a part of the general offensive to recapture Quang Tri. This large helicopter assault involved almost fifteen hundred Vietnamese marines and required the helicopters and amphibious shipping of two MAUs in support. This operation, too, was a complete success and a rapid advance regained territory lost early in the offensive.

By July, the South Vietnamese offensive had slowed south of Quang Tri City. To regain momentum, on 11 July, one VNMC battalion was helilifted by twenty-eight helicopters of the 9th MAB in an attempt to break the impasse. The landing zones selected were located 2,000 meters directly north of Quang Tri City in an area known to be heavily defended by the NVA and considered a high-risk SAM area. In spite of extensive preparatory fires, the helicopters encountered heavy fire entering and leaving the zones. One CH-53 was lost to an SA-7 (Strella) missile. All of the assault helicopters were struck by ground fire. The assaulting South Vietnamese marines had to fight their way across two trench lines in order to secure a defensive perimeter and box themselves in with supporting arms fire. This heliborne assault succeeded in breaking the enemy's Quang Tri defenses and paved the way for the subsequent capture of the city.

The final U.S. Marine Corps- and Navy-supported heliborne operation of the Vietnam War was executed on 22 July. One VNMC battalion was landed along the coast ten kilometers northeast of Quang Tri City behind the NVA's front lines, interdicting their supply lines and causing the enemy to retain forces to the rear in anticipation of continued amphibious assaults.

Extensive use of supporting arms probably contributed most to the success of these operations. Fire support was built around L-hour, in the case of helicopter assaults, and H-hour plus L-hour when both surface and heliborne assaults were conducted. A general procedure of identifying fire support assets and then assigning targets based on capability and availability was followed. This resulted in a distribution of targets across the longest period of time to the artillery, with naval gunfire used almost as extensively. Tactical air support was used sparingly in the preparation until immediately prior to touchdown. This was done primarily to conserve air assets and provide flexibility for on-call air support to the RVN marines immediately upon their arrival at the LZ/Beach.

While the primary purpose of this article concerns the contributions of the amphibious forces, Seventh Fleet, and the 9th MAB, a discussion of amphibious operations would be incomplete without recognition of the considerable contributions of the tactical air element of the Marine Corps combined arms air/ground team.

Marine tactical air, by doctrine and training, is tailored for support of amphibious operations. Since the amphibious landing was not made immediately, however, marine tactical air could be employed effectively in support of other missions, while still ready to support a landing at the commander's option. Thus, while the navy/marine amphib-

ious force was off the DMZ in support of U.S. and allied operations, marine tactical air was providing combat support to the land campaign and TF-77.

Marine Corps tactical air response and readiness paralleled that of the sea-based marine forces. A marine all-weather attack squadron was conducting combat operations from a TF-77 carrier in the Gulf of Tonkin on 1 April. During the first week of April, two fighter-attack squadrons and one ECM detachment from the 1st Marine Aircraft Wing (MAW) in Japan were deployed to Danang AFB and NAS Cubi Pt., respectively.

On 10 April, a fighter-attack squadron was deployed from Hawaii to Danang. In mid-May, two 1st MAW light attack squadrons deployed to Bien Hoa AFB to bolster the close and direct air support capability in the southern region. Response time of the units based in Japan averaged less than nine hours from receipt of execute orders to arrival of the leading aircraft at the deployment base.

The diversity of the basing requirements and the combat support provided by marine tactical air in Southeast Asia are illustrated in Table 1 for the period 1 April through 31 July, 1972. Slightly over ten thousand combat and combat support sorties were provided from both land and sea bases during this period, with about fifty aircraft committed in the first few days of April, increasing to more than one hundred aircraft by mid-May.

Although marine tactical air was deployed and engaged in combat in support of the land battle and TF-77 operations independently of the naval amphibious force offshore, tactical air doctrine and aircrew training required in an amphibious operations environment proved combat capable, flexible, and responsive in the face of a variety of operational command requirements. This example of response and readiness of the elements of the marine air/ground team leaves little doubt as to the validity of the marine combined arms air/ground concept in the amphibious role—the primary role—and the flexibility to effectively support and participate in other missions as well.

Table 1. U.S. Marine Tactical Air Support in Southeast Asia, 1 April-31 July 1972

Base	Type Aircraft	Mission
USS *Coral Sea*	A–6A/B	Visual/all-weather attack
	KA–6D	Aerial refueling
Danang Air Force Base	F–4B/J	Fighter-attack
	TA–4F	Naval gunfire spot/observation
Cubi Point Naval Air Station	EA–6A	ECM support of TF–77
Bien Hoa Air Force Base	A–4E	Light-attack
Nam Phong, Thailand*	F–4B/J	Fighter-attack
	A–6A	Visual/all-weather attack
	KC–130	Aerial refueling
USS *America*	F–4J	Fighter

*Marine tactical air operations shifted from Danang to Nam Phong in mid-June.

Arclight strikes were planned for both the primary and alternate LZs and beaches. Timing of the landing was scheduled to take advantage of the neutralization effect of the B-52 strikes. Because of the predominance of U.S. fire support assets, except for field artillery, the weight of carrying out fire support coordination fell heavily on the U.S. personnel located at the VNMC brigade command posts. The principal coordinator was the brigade senior advisor, aided by his assistants and by the Air and Naval Gunfire Liaison Company (ANGLICO) representatives. A 9th MAB liaison officer was positioned with the assault brigade and, as operations became larger, another liaison officer was located at the division command post. At the battalion level, coordination was performed by U.S. advisors and ANGLICO personnel. Seventh Air Force provided the forward air controllers (airborne) supplemented by ANGLICO air spotters.

U.S. Marine helicopter support included troop lift, emergency medical evacuation, lo-gistic support, command and control, and visual reconnaissance. The helicopters of F Troop, U.S. Army Air Cavalry, assisted in helo route selection, medical evacuation, and last minute gun-ship support for the assault helos.

Marine helicopter squadrons assigned to the MAUs were trained for operating in a "conventional" (7.62 mm, 57 mm) AA environment. Consequently, changes to doctrine were implemented immediately when it was realized that the enemy possessed an extensive antiair capability not previously encountered. In addition to a quantitative increase in conventional AA weapons, the Strella missile provided the enemy with a weapon that could play havoc with slow-moving helicopters. Standard flight altitudes cited in current doctrines would have proven catastrophic in view of this new enemy capability. Thus, low altitude, high speed "nape of the earth" tactics became the standard method of operation. Sand dunes, shrubs, low tree lines, or other topographical features were used to shield against the Strella.

Additionally, the enemy could concentrate rapidly large volumes of heavy artillery and antiaircraft fire in and around landing zones to counter a heliborne assault. To blunt this threat, helicopter assaults were planned so as to maximize the number of assault troops that could be placed into a landing zone in a single insertion. This eliminated the "daisy chain" tactical procedure. To accomplish this type of operation successfully, both medium and heavy helicopter assault assets were used in one wave. CH-46 medium helos led the assault, followed closely by CH-53 heavy support. This tactic gave the Vietnamese marine commander the further advantage of having a good-sized landing force inserted in one wave. Average aircraft availability provided the ground commander with thirteen CH-46s and five CH-53s for single squadron operations and approximately twice that for dual squadron operations. Thus, approximately six hundred assault troops or about double that number could be landed in a single lift, depending on whether one or two squadrons were employed.

The concept of multideck operations made this single wave type of operations possible. Use of all the helicopter spots available on accompanying amphibious shipping, in addition to the LPH, provided the available decks and time to lift an entire battalion into an LZ in one lift. These single wave operations deprived the enemy of his capability to concentrate artillery and antiaircraft on successive helicopter assault waves and greatly improved the probability of successful helicopter operations in a highly hostile environment.

Of all the lessons learned in this series of operations, however, one of the most important was that the complexity of amphibious operations has not changed, even when used in a support role. The fact that an amphibious task force commander was not designated did not negate the effectiveness of the planning for, or direction of, the landings; rather, it increased the complexity of planning, required greater coordination and exposed clearly the variety of units that would

normally be placed under one guiding authority. For example, nine separate commands and organizations actively participated in one operation in May 1972. Yet, the planning approach to amphibious operations outlined in NWP 22B worked.

Without the ships and without the marine helicopters and LVTs more than five thousand Vietnamese marines could not have been put ashore where they were needed, when they were needed, to interdict and roll back the NVA forces. Had the same effort been expended on frontal assaults against the tenacious and sophisticated NVA forces, it is highly doubtful that South Vietnam would have regained control of territory as far north as Quang Tri City.

Undoubtedly, these operations marked a definite turning point in the war and accentuate the words of B. H. Liddell Hart: "Amphibious flexibility is the greatest strategic asset that a sea power possesses."

Airborne Operations and Amphibious Warfare, Cyprus, 1974

BY MAJOR PATRICK L. TOWNSEND, USMC

The U.S. Marine Corps is not the world's leading expert in vertical envelopment. Based on performance, Turkey is. On 20 July 1974, Turkey successfully invaded Cyprus using coordinated seaborne, helicopter-borne, and parachute-delivered attacks.

It is both dangerous and necessary to study the military aspects of the Cyprus crisis in isolation from the political, social, and historical factors. Dangerous because it implies that a purely military conflict can be waged separately from these other influences, but necessary if we are to draw any lessons for our own military training.

The population of Cyprus is composed of Greek Cypriots and Turkish Cypriots, with the former being the majority by better than five-to-one. In July 1974, Turkey believed it necessary to invade the island in order to wrest control of the Cyprus government from Greek-dominated forces that had seized it in a coup a short time before.

An overview is in order before laying out the details of the military operation. The main objective was to gain control of the road from the coastal city of Kyrenia to Nicosia, the capital city and communications center of Cyprus. Shortly after dawn, an amphibious assault force went ashore near Kyrenia while paratroopers descended on the Nicosia airport. Shortly thereafter, helicopters inserted troops about midway between the two previously landed forces. By nightfall, the road

U.S. Naval Institute *Proceedings*, "Vertical Assault: The Proof Is In the Doing," 103 (November 1977): 117–19. Reprinted by permission.

was under Turkish control. During the day, several diversions and local uprisings helped to hold the numerically superior Greek and Greek Cypriot forces in place, preventing them from taking part in the main effort to repulse the invaders.

That the Turks achieved tactical surprise is attributed to the Greek assumption that, as in previous crises, a diplomatic solution short of military confrontation would be found. Apparently, little importance was attached to the sailing of a fleet of approximately thirty-two ships from Turkish ports at 1100 on 19 July. After all, the Turks had sallied forth in 1967, only to be turned back by U.S. diplomatic efforts. The Cypriot National Guard, a pro-Greek organization, did man a number of antiaircraft batteries and heavy machine gun positions, but this effort did not match the Turkish Cypriot call-up of ten thousand reservists. The rather casual Greek Cypriot response is puzzling in view of the facts that Turkish papers carried the headline "Our Fleet Is Off Cyprus," and people were reported running through the streets of Nicosia shouting, "The Turks are coming!" Also, Turkey held "airport closing exercises" on the day and evening of 19 July.

The Turkish fleet appears to have been five warships (probably all destroyers), two large transports, twenty medium landing craft, and five small landing craft. While estimates vary, the amphibious landing force apparently consisted of about five thousand men. At 0630 on 20 July, Turkish Premier Bulent Ecevit announced that, "The Turkish Armed Forces have begun landing in Cyprus from the air and sea." At 0645, a Turkish language broadcast from Cyprus announced that five thousand Turkish troops had landed and that a Greek Cypriot boat had been sunk. The same broadcast gave the news that the "landing and air-dropping" of Turkish soldiers had begun. One report stated that just prior to the first Turkish paratroop drop, a helicopter, with fighter coverage, touched down briefly in a Turkish Cypriot enclave near the Nicosia airport. It is theorized that the helicopter deposited a paratroop command group which, by being placed on the ground prior to the drop, was able to give a high degree of organization to the landing forces. There were at least four waves of paratroopers inserted during the day, with their objectives being control of the Nicosia airport and the approaches to the airport and the city. In the afternoon, a Turkish Cypriot broadcast claimed that the paratroopers had taken control of the road to the airport. Earlier broadcasts in English and French had quoted "diplomatic sources" as saying the Turks controlled the airport.

The help of the Turkish Cypriots was invaluable. There were reports of paratroopers whose landings were off target getting rides in civilian cars to rejoin their units. Uprisings of Turkish Cypriots took place in several locations, with the largest being in Limassol. There were some reports of a second Turkish landing at Limassol, although these do not appear to be true. That the uprising was preplanned to coincide with the Turkish landings is, of course, a strong possibility. Although it ended in failure, with ten thousand Turkish Cypriots surrendering and being detained in a soccer stadium by nightfall, the action did drain off forces from the battle in Nicosia, only 20 miles away. Other landings were reported at the cities of Karavas, Kokkina, and Lapithos but again no further substantiation has appeared in the open press. These reports may have resulted from the three Turkish destroyers which cruised the coast, firing at a variety of targets following the initial landing.

On 20 July, the Greek navy made one attempt to resupply its forces in Cyprus. Near Paphos, the six supply ships, escorted by "warships," were turned back by Turkish ships. Three Greek supply ships were lost in the encounter.

Overlooking the Kyrenia-Nicosia road is a medieval fortress named St. Hilarion which was held by a small Turkish Cypriot garrison. Shortly before noon the first Turkish helicopter forces reinforced this unit and gave the Turks control of the middle stretch of the road. The helicopters then began carrying troops, vehicles, and equipment to a location near Nicosia to further bolster the paratroopers fighting there. By midafternoon, a "neutral military source" estimated "Turkey had so far landed some 6,000 men by air and sea and up to 40 tanks on the island since the invasion began at dawn." By this time the Greek Cypriots had gone to a total mobilization, even freeing and arming some recently imprisoned policemen. There were reports of some Greek Cypriot troops who evidently did not know how to use their weapons. By nightfall, Turkish tanks had traveled from Kyrenia to the Nicosia airport, demonstrating the Turkish control of the corridor that had been their objective less than fourteen hours before.

What can be learned from the Turkish military operation which quickly became secondary to the diplomatic efforts it precipitated? By expanding vertical envelopment and amphibious tactics to include paratroopers, the Turks gave depth to their area of operations, making it possible to have it coincide with their elongated objective. The apparent helicopter insertion of the paratroop command group was a major factor in executing one of the most organized and effective paratroop operations since humans first started jumping from aircraft. Use of indigenous disturbances and diversionary military operations, even on a small scale, was once again shown to have great potential for retarding the speed and strength of an enemy's reaction. And the fact that the Turks sailed in broad daylight, making no attempt to conceal their fleet's activities, and still achieved surprise proves that the adage, "know your enemy," applies. The Turks knew that the

Greeks would never believe that they would follow such a blatant operation with an invasion. The U.S. armed forces, in particular the Marine Corps, would be well advised to study in depth the Turkish invasion, the only full combat test of the twenty-five-year-old idea of combining vertical envelopment with amphibious assault.

Rescue of the SS *Mayaguez*, 1975

BY COLONEL J. M. JOHNSON, JR.,
LIEUTENANT COLONEL R. W. AUSTIN,
AND MAJOR D. A. QUINLAN, USMC

The SS *Mayaguez*'s Koh Tang Island operation was planned and successfully executed under conditions of uncertainty and, at times, extreme difficulty. This paper describes the assembly of a task group of marines from the III Marine Amphibious Force (III MAF) on extremely short notice at Utapao, Thailand, the planning of a major simultaneous assault and recovery operation in sixteen hours, and the operation itself as carried out over a fourteen-hour period.

The Seizure

The *Mayaguez* incident began for the U.S. armed forces at 1612 on 12 May 1975 (all times used in this article are local Gulf of Thailand times) when the National Military Command Center received a report from the American embassy Jakarta that a merchant ship, the SS *Mayaguez*, had been seized on the high seas. The ship had been fired on, boarded, and captured by Cambodian forces in international waters at about 1130 on 12 May while transiting a standard sea lane and trade route in the Gulf of Thailand. At the time of her seizure, *Mayaguez* was approximately 60 miles off the Cambodian coast.

During the early evening hours of 12 May a reconnaissance aircraft was launched from Utapao to begin coverage of the area. This was the first of a series of reconnaissance sorties which provided surveillance of *Maya-*

Marine Corps Gazette, "Individual Heroism Overcame Awkward Command Relationships, Confusion, and Bad Information off the Cambodian Coast," 61 (October 1977): 24–34. Reprinted by permission.

guez until the end of the operation. Throughout the first night of her captivity, *Mayaguez* was tracked as she moved from the vicinity of Poulo Wai Island to Koh Tang (*koh* is the Cambodian word for *island*) where she came to anchor about noon on the 13th of May.

Gathering the Forces

Mayaguez was seized just two weeks after the completion of Operation Frequent Wind, the evacuation of Saigon. The armada which had stood off the coast of Vietnam had been dispersed, the ships returning to their normal operating stations and areas. When *Mayaguez* was seized without warning there were only two U.S. Navy ships within twenty-four hours steaming time of the merchantman.

While the president was attempting diplomatic initiatives to secure the release of the ship and its forty-man crew, U.S. forces in the western Pacific area were placed on alert for possible employment in the event that military action was required.

During the early morning hours of 13 May, the escort destroyer *Holt*; the store ship *Vega*; the guided missile destroyer *Wilson*, conducting normal operations out of Subic Bay; and the *Coral Sea* carrier task group, en route to Australia, were directed to proceed to the waters off Kompong Som, Cambodia, from their various locations in the western Pacific. The amphibious ready groups which were in the process of returning marine units to Japan and Okinawa were ordered to put back to Subic Bay. At Subic Bay the attack carrier *Hancock* and the amphibious cargo ship *Mobile* would be able to proceed to the scene within twenty-four hours. The estimated time of arrival of these ships was 16 May 1975. For the third time in two months the naval forces in the western Pacific were "climbing back up on the step," this time, however, with no advance warning.

The commander-in-chief, Pacific, designated the commander, United States Support Activities Group/7th Air Force (USSAG/7th Air Force), Lieutenant General J. J. Burns, the on-scene commander and the central coordinating authority for the recovery operations.

General Burns ordered a task force under the command of Colonel L. J. Anders, the deputy commander for operations of the 56th Special Operations Wing to deploy to Utapao Air Force Base. All of the available heavy helicopter assets in the 7th Air Force were likewise ordered to Utapao. These aircraft were drawn from two squadrons, the 21st Special Operations Squadron (CH-53s), and the 40th Aerospace Rescue and Recovery Squadron (HH-53s). Additionally, a squadron of air force security police was moved from Nakhon Phanom Air Force Base to Utapao. One of the early recovery options was to insert security police aboard *Mayaguez*.

There were a total of fourteen CH-53 and HH-53 helicopters deployed to Utapao prior to 15 May. One crashed the night of 13 May while en route from Nakhon Phanom Air Base. Of the thirteen aircraft that arrived at Utapao, two were assigned as search and rescue aircraft. Therefore, the planners were looking to an available lift capability of eleven helicopters; of the total, six were HH-53s and five were CH-53s.

The HH-53, better known as the "Jolly Green Giant," carries more armor than the CH-53 and is capable of refueling inflight. The air force version of the CH-53, the "C" model, is equipped with external fuel tanks flush-fitted to the lower part of the fuselage on both sides of the aircraft. Each of these aircraft is capable of extended-range operations.

During the evening of 13 May, the commanding general of III MAF, Major General Carl W. Hoffman, was alerted to provide a command group, an air contingency battalion landing team, and other necessary forces to the commander, USSAG/7th Air Force, in support of the recovery of *Mayaguez*. The command group was composed of five officers from the III MAF staff under the command of Colonel John M. Johnson, Jr., who was designated as the commander of Task Group 79.9. In addition to the command element, the task group comprised two task units with Battalion Landing Team (BLT) 2/9, (TU 79.9.1) under the command of Lieutenant Colonel Randall W. Austin; and a unit from the 1st Battalion, 4th Marines, which comprised Company D(–) (reinforced) and a small command element, (TU 79.9.2) under the command of Major Raymond E. Porter. At that time, BLT 2/9 was located on Okinawa and 1/4 was located at the Marine Amphibious Unit Camp at Subic Bay, Republic of the Philippines.

At 2030 on the evening of 13 May when 2/9 received its movement orders, all four of its organic rifle companies were in the field, in the central training area of Okinawa, conducting normal unit training. Within three hours all units had returned to Camp Schwab which is the normal on-island home for the 9th Marines. During the next two hours the battalion prepared to move out to Kadena Air Force Base which would be its point of embarkation. Meanwhile, at various other marine camps on Okinawa, the units attached to 2/9 were also preparing to mount out. At this time the marines of BLT 2/9 could only speculate as to where they were bound. The news of the *Mayaguez* capture, however, had not escaped their notice.

At 0145 on the morning of 14 May the advance elements of the battalion departed Camp Schwab bound for Kadena. Other units of the BLT were likewise getting under way from other marine cantonments on Okinawa bound for Kadena. The movement order had set in motion a chain of activities within the 3rd Marine Division, commanded by Major General Kenneth J. Houghton, which would ensure that all of the elements of the BLT would arrive at Kadena in a rapid, orderly fashion. Since 1973, when Operation Eagle

Pull was first formulated, regularly scheduled loading exercises and joint airborne air transportability exercises had honed the division embarkation and movement control agencies to a fine edge of efficiency. The assembly of the BLT at Kadena was completed by 0545. The command element of Task Group 79.9 had closed on Kadena prior to the arrival of the BLT. The command element launched for Utapao, Thailand, at 0530, followed by the leading elements of BLT 2/9 which launched at 0615.

The task unit (79.9.2) from Subic had launched from Naval Air Station, Cubi Point, at 0115 on the 14th and arrived at Utapao at 0505. Accompanying the marines from 1/4 were six sailors from the *Duluth* and six civilian crewmen from the USNS *Greenville Victory* who had volunteered to board *Mayaguez* with the marines and sailors to get the ship under way. When the marines of 1/4 arrived at Utapao they were briefed by personnel from USSAG/7th Air Force on a plan to board *Mayaguez* directly from air force helicopters. The marines were put on thirty-minute stand-by to execute this plan. They were to remain in this posture until 0200 when the final plan for recapture was promulgated. In the interim, they set to the task of preparing detailed plans for boarding and recovery. Special equipment was fabricated at Utapao which would be necessary to execute the direct seizure of the ship. For example, the containers on the *Mayaguez* main deck were not strong enough to support the weight of a HH-53 helicopter. Therefore it became necessary to fashion rappelling gear for the drop from the hovering helicopters to the tops of the containers. Additionally, it was necessary to fashion portable platforms which would be used to bridge the gap between containers. By the time that Colonel Johnson arrived, the marines under Major Porter were well along in their preparations to board and recover *Mayaguez*.

Upon arrival at Utapao, Task Group 79.9 was assigned the mission of recovering *Mayaguez*. This mission was subsequently expanded to include the recovery of the crew. The final mission read, "... seize, occupy, and defend the island of Koh Tang, hold the island indefinitely (for a minimum of forty-eight hours) and to rescue any of the crew members of *Mayaguez* found on the island, simultaneously seize *Mayaguez* and remove the ship from its current location." (The ship was still anchored off Koh Tang, where it was believed that some of the crew were being held captive.)

Relocation of Crew

While the marine units were moving to the objective area, air force tactical aircraft had been directed to interdict any attempts on the part of the Cambodians to move the ship into the harbor of Kompong Som or to transport the crew to that location. In carrying out these orders on the morning of 14 May, the pilot of one air force aircraft, while attempting to stop a fishing boat from leaving Tang Island, noticed what appeared to be Caucasians on board. The pilot tried repeatedly to stop the craft with bursts of cannon fire across the bow and with riot control agents, but to no avail. It became apparent that the boat was not going to stop, and in the interest of safety of whatever *Mayaguez* crew members may have been on board, no attempts were made to disable the craft. Subsequently, we learned that the entire crew was on this boat. The vessel was a Thai fishing boat that had been commandeered by the Cambodians. Its captain had on several occasions, according to Captain Miller of *Mayaguez*, attempted to heed the warnings of the air force aircraft and turn about. He was dissuaded from this course at gunpoint by his captors. Air Force aircraft continued to track the fishing boat all the way to Kompong Som. This activity occurred during the morning of the 14th.

Planning the Operation

When the BLT command group arrived at Utapao at 0945 on the 14th, they were met and briefed by Colonel Johnson and his staff. (The remainder of the BLT continued to arrive via C-141, with the last elements arriving at 1400.) Following the initial orientation for the BLT staff, both staffs got down to the business of planning. At a 1300 meeting, the mission of seizing Koh Tang and rescuing the crew of *Mayaguez* was assigned to the BLT. Following this meeting a reconnaissance was arranged for the BLT staff.

Intelligence concerning Koh Tang island was extremely limited. All available Cambodian refugees in the Utapao area were located and queried for information which would be of benefit to the landing force. A former Cambodian naval officer, who allegedly had recently been on Koh Tang, was one source of information. He said that there would probably be no more than twenty to thirty people on the island and that the BLT could expect to find no organized regular units to contest their landing. The quest for information extended all the way to Washington. A former oil company employee who had spent some time on Koh Tang was interviewed to gain more information. The problem of very sketchy information upon which to build usable intelligence was compounded by the fact that there were no tactical maps of Koh Tang available. As Lieutenant Colonel Austin and selected members of his command took off in a U.S. Army U-21 aircraft to conduct a visual reconnaissance of the island there were very few "knowns." Essentially all that was known with certainty were the facts that the island was 195 nautical miles from Utapao, and that *Mayaguez* was anchored approximately one mile off the northeastern tip of the island. The exact location of all of the crew members was not known, although some of them were presumed to be still on the island.

The reconnaissance aircraft left Utapao at 1500 on the 14th. Aboard the aircraft were the BLT commander, his S-3, Major John B. Hendricks, the designated assault company commander, Captain James H. Davis, and the battalion forward air controllers, 1st Lieutenants John J. Martinoli and Terry Tonkin. The flight lasted approximately two and one-half hours. The aircraft was restricted from going below 6,000 feet over the island. This overflight determined that there were only two pieces of terrain that would pass as land-

ing zones. The capability to blast landing zones out of forested or foliated areas existed, but again in deference to the safety of the crew members of the *Mayaguez*, they decided not to use these weapons. The landing zones that were selected were located in the northern portion of the island, on opposite sides of a narrow neck leading up to the northern promontory. No signs of enemy activity were observed during the reconnaissance.

While the reconnaissance was being conducted, the frustrations of the task group commander were growing. His operations center was not equipped with secure voice communications, and the nearest secure point was several minutes away by vehicle. Throughout the afternoon and evening of the 14th, Colonel Johnson or members of his staff were continually being called away from the planning session to take incoming calls over the secure voice nets. The physical separation of Colonel Johnson from General Burns's headquarters (Nakhon Phanom) inhibited the operation.

At 1900 a final planning conference was held at Utapao. The participants were: CTG 79.9, USSAG representatives, CO, 56th SOW, CTU 79.9.1 (CO, BLT 2/9), and CTU 79.9.2 (OiC, Boarding Party). Several options were discussed. The final plan, based upon the requirement for simultaneous landings on the island and the ship, called for eight helicopters to insert approximately one hundred eighty members of BLT 2/9 on Koh Tang at 0542 on 15 May, while at the same time, three helicopters lowered sixty members of the boarding party onto *Mayaguez*. The boarding party would comprise forty-eight marines, six navy personnel, and the six Military Sealift Command personnel. Based upon the allocation of helicopters, Lieutenant Colonel Austin decided to organize his first wave as follows: the assault company, Company G (reinforced), under the command of Captain Davis would land with one platoon reinforced into the western landing zone and the remainder of the company into the eastern (larger) landing zone. A section of 81mm mortars and the BLT Command Group A would land in the eastern zone. The second wave would be composed of Company E (reinforced), under the command of Captain Myke E. Stahl. Subsequent waves would draw on the remainder of the BLT as required. For the second and subsequent waves, twelve helicopters were planned. A critical factor was the four and one-half hours turn-around time between waves. The consideration for the safety of the *Mayaguez* crew inhibited the plan for supporting fires. The frag order contained an "on-call" plan for continuous air and subsequent naval gunfire support units to be on station throughout the operation and to be under positive control of the landing force (the *Wilson* was expected to arrive off the island by mid-morning.) These requirements were transmitted to General Burns with the plan for his approval.

The necessary planning having been completed, the BLT commander issued his five paragraph order to an assemblage of all BLT officers and key personnel at approximately 2200. Following this meeting, final preparations for the assault began.

Shortly after midnight, General Burns, commander USSAG/7th Air Force, modified the operation plan as it concerned the boarding party. The boarding party would be inserted aboard the *Holt* and then, following the *Holt's* closure alongside the *Mayaguez*, it would board the *Mayaguez*. Additionally, General Burns's headquarters indicated that while the island assault and boarding operations were being conducted, navy tactical aircraft from the *Coral Sea* would interdict Cambodian naval and air bases on the mainland. All other parts of the plan formulated at the 1900 conference were approved as originally promulgated.

In the matter of command relationships and operational control of the landing/boarding forces, USSAG/7th Air Force opted for the procedure that had proven itself during operations Eagle Pull and Frequent Wind. Operational control of the marine forces and USAF TacAir would be exercised by USSAG through its airborne mission commander (AMC) located in the airborne battlefield command and control center (ABCCC), a

specially equipped C-130 orbiting approximately 90 miles from Koh Tang.

Because of the scarcity of helicopters, Colonel Johnson decided to hold his command group at Utapao during the first wave. This would permit Lieutenant Colonel Austin maximum space for the initial insertion. Being intimately familiar with USSAG command and control procedures by virtue of his liaison duty with USSAG during Frequent Wind, Colonel Johnson recognized that until he was inserted in a subsequent wave, he would be, in essence, "chopping" the landing force under the direct operational control of the AMC. He would, however, in the interim be able to advise USSAG directly from his COC at Utapao. It was an undesirable but necessary command relationship in view of the urgency of the mission and the scarcity of helicopters.

At 0230 on 15 May, the members of the landing force were assembled near their aircraft. At 0415 the first aircraft lifted off and departed for Koh Tang. The boarding party was embarked in three HH-53s and the assault elements of the BLT were aboard five CH-53s and three HH-53s.

Recovery of *Mayaguez*

The three HH-53 helicopters inserted the boarding party onto the *Holt* between 0550 and 0624. Each, in turn, came to a hover over the *Holt's* fantail helipad and discharged its heliteam. *Holt* on "helo operations station" at 0445 was approximately 12 miles northwest of Koh Tang. At 0710, a division of USAF A-7s laid riot control agents on *Mayaguez*. The *Holt* then proceeded alongside and the marines under Major Porter's command, in an action reminiscent of the eighteenth century, boarded *Mayaguez* at 0725. The team led by Corporal Carl R. Coker was the first aboard. Coker jumped to the deck of the container ship as the destroyer pulled alongside. He called for a line, and secured the two ships together, disregarding the possibility of being taken under fire by enemy forces who had been sighted on the ship prior to the boarding. The marines from D/1/4 swarmed aboard. Each of the boarding teams moved quickly to its objective area. Sergeant William J. Owens's squad was assigned the task of securing the engine room as quickly as possible before any damage could be done to the power plant. Owens led his men directly down the darkened ladderways into the gas-filled engine room. A thorough search of the ship revealed that the enemy forces had abandoned their prize and left no booby traps behind. The *Mayaguez* was declared secured at 0822.

At 0950, thirty-eight Marines and two corpsmen returned to the *Holt* for possible insertion as reinforcements on Koh Tang. The *Holt* took the *Mayaguez* under tow for international waters at 0958. At 1005, the *Mayaguez* crew, having been released separately, was aboard the *Wilson*, which had arrived four miles east of Koh Tang at 0718. The *Mayaguez* crew was transferred from the *Wilson* to the *Mayaguez* at 1300. The *Wilson* then closed on Koh Tang to provide naval gunfire support. The *Holt* cast off the towing rig at 1545. At 1615, the *Holt* was directed to join the *Wilson* off Koh Tang as soon as possible. At 1700, the *Mayaguez* was under way on her own power out of the area bound for Singapore.

Assault on Koh Tang

As the *Mayaguez* was being boarded, the first landing party approached the island at approximately 0615. It quickly became evident that the landing would be opposed. The first two helicopters to approach the eastern zone were shot down. As one of the helicopters neared its landing zone, it was hit by a hail of intense automatic weapons fire and rocket-propelled grenades. The port external fuel tank exploded. Another round of rocket-propelled grenades blew off most of the cockpit, killing the co-pilot. The aircraft crashed in the surf approximately 50 meters from the beach. Seven marines and two navy corpsmen perished in the helicopter. Three marines were cut down in the surf and killed by enemy fire as they attempted to rush into the tree line. With most of their weapons and equipment consumed in the raging inferno which had been made of their aircraft, the remaining ten marine and three air force survivors of

the crash opted to swim seaward. During the epic swim that followed several marines exhibited extraordinary initiative, perseverance, and courage. Among these was Private First Class Timothy W. Trebil, a fire team leader, who throughout the long swim continued to shout encouragement and provide assistance to the weaker swimmers until they were rescued. During the three and one-half hours that the survivors were in the water, from the time of the crash until they were picked up by *Wilson*, one of the battalion's forward air controllers, First Lieutenant Tonkin, was able to direct USAF attack aircraft making firing runs at enemy positions on the eastern shore. After his own UHF radios were destroyed in the crash, he was able to accomplish this feat by using an air force survival radio borrowed from one of the helicopter crewmen.

The other helicopter which was destroyed was able to land at the surf line. The heliteam immediately disembarked and established a defensive perimeter in the tree line at the water's edge. This team, composed of members of the 3rd Platoon, Company G, under the command of Second Lieutenant Michael A. Cicere, together with helicopter crewmen, was able to hold out all day from what became an isolated position. During the course of this action, one marine and one airman were wounded. The eastern zone was closed to prevent further loss of aircraft. All aircraft scheduled into this zone were diverted to the western zone.

Meanwhile on the western shore, the landings were also opposed. Of the first two scheduled helicopters into this zone only one was able to land and disembark its troops from Golf Company's 1st Platoon, under the command of Second Lieutenant James McDaniel. The other helicopter, with the assault company commander aboard, aborted its run in with one engine shot out and severe fuel leakage. It was able to limp back to the coast of Thailand where it was forced to put down because of fuel starvation some 50 miles from Utapao. The heliteam was picked up by USAF SAR helicopters and returned to Utapao. The other of these first two helicopters into the western zone crashed at sea shortly after lifting out of the zone. Three of the four crewmen were picked up by one of the helicopters diverted from the eastern side of the island. The fourth crewman went down with his airplane.

The four remaining helicopters in the first wave, three containing elements of the assault company, were able to land their troops in the western zone. Two of these aircraft made repeated attempts to get into the hot zone. One of these, with Second Lieutenant Richard H. Zales and members of his 3rd Platoon on board, finally made it into the zone on its sixth attempt at 0900. The final helicopter in the first wave, containing the BLT command group and a mortar section, was forced to land approximately 1,200 meters to the southwest of the zone on the shore of the island.

Elements of Company G, under the command of First Lieutenant James D. Keith, the company executive officer, were setting up and expanding their perimeter around the landing zone despite the fact that they were meeting with stubborn enemy resistance and were receiving intense incoming fire. The BLT command group with the mortar section firing in support was working its way up the coast, against resistance, toward the main body of Company G. The 3rd Platoon (−), under Lieutenant Cicere, had sustained two wounded and was defending its isolated enclave on the eastern shore. Of the 180 landing force personnel aboard the eight helicopters in the first wave, 109 were ashore in three separated locations. There were 29 with the command group, 20 with Lieutenant Cicere, and 60 under Keith's command in the western zone enclave. (Lieutenant Zales, with 21 other marines, landed to join Keith at approximately 0900.)

The most intense fire facing marines in the western zone came from the enemy positions south of the zone. Keith directed McDaniel to locate and destroy the position. McDaniel led a reinforced squad from his platoon against the enemy strong point to the immediate south of the landing zone. With the exception of the man-made cut, the vis-

ibility at ground level was approximately 5 to 15 feet. Before anyone was able to locate the automatic weapons which were enfilading the landing zone, McDaniel's patrol was hit in the flank by small arms fire and grenades from close range. The enemy's covering position was equally well concealed. In the initial exchange of fire McDaniel and four of his marines were wounded. Lance Corporal Ashton N. Looney was killed. During the ensuing engagement, McDaniel and his marines responded magnificently. Overcoming their initial surprise, the marines delivered a heavy volume of fire which neutralized the enemy. Although none of the patrol members had previously been exposed to combat, they individually and collectively displayed the aplomb of professionals. Lance Corporal Charles A. Gieselbreth, McDaniel's radio operator, although painfully wounded by fragments from the exploding grenade which destroyed the radio on his back, charged forward to a position from which he could better return fire upon the enemy. Private First Class Jerome N. Wemitt, despite severe leg wounds, crawled forward under enemy fire to render first aid to a more seriously wounded marine and assist him to safety. Staff Sergeant Seferino Bernal, Jr., McDaniel's platoon sergeant, responding to a call for assistance, dashed across thirty meters of fireswept terrain to administer lifesaving first aid to a wounded marine, and under a hail of enemy fire, carried the wounded marine to safety. Keith, concerned that the enemy might encircle McDaniel's patrol, ordered McDaniel to withdraw back to the landing zone perimeter. As McDaniel was disengaging, Staff Sergeant Bernal gathered a small force of marines from the perimeter and led them forward under enemy fire to a position from which they could cover the withdrawal of the patrol. McDaniel brought his patrol back in. Right on the heels of McDaniel's patrol, the Cambodians made their first major attack on the southern portion of the perimeter. McDaniel's marines drove them back.

At approximately 0900, Lieutenant Zales and his heliteam landed. Keith directed Zales to the heavily engaged southern portion of the perimeter. Ignoring the incoming enemy fire, Zales led his platoon to the hot spot and directed his men into positions from which they could deliver neutralizing fire on the Cambodian positions. Keith by this time had solid communications with the Air Force TAC(A) overhead who was tuned to the battalion tactical net. Keith personally directed the air force strikes onto the Cambodian strong points. Effective as these strikes were, they could not be brought in close enough to break the tenacious enemy who had closed to within a few meters of the marine positions. Throughout the remainder of the morning, combat in the western zone was sharp and at extremely close range. Grenade dueling was the rule rather than the exception. (In fact as the command group moved closer to the perimeter, Major John B. Hendricks, the battalion operations officer, noted what appeared to be a deadly tennis match with missiles going back and forth.) As the morning wore on, Keith kept looking for the helicopters to return with the second wave.

Of the eight helicopters in the wave (five CH-53s and three HH-53s), all but one was destroyed or had received some damage. This fact translated into five flyable helicopters available to lift the second and subsequent waves. These were: two of the three which had transported the boarding party to *Holt;* the one HH-53 which was in the first wave; an additional CH-53 which was down for repairs when the first wave launched, but which had since been declared "up"; and a sixth helicopter which had arrived at Utapao at 0720.

The helicopters in the second wave launched at various times between 0900 and 1000 carrying elements of Company E, under the command of Captain Stahl, and the command group of Captain Davis's Company G which had been returned to Utapao from its downed helicopter. There were a total of 127 landing force personnel on board the five helicopters.

At approximately 1000, Lieutenant Colonel Austin contacted the airborne battlefield command and control center to determine the status of his second scheduled wave. Under the circumstances, if he was to carry out the mission, he needed an additional rifle company. While the second wave was enroute to the island, the crew of the *Mayaguez* was recovered aboard the *Wilson* at approximately 1015. This fact was never relayed to Austin. With both of the major mission objectives accomplished, higher headquarters ordered the termination of assault operations against Koh Tang. This order was to cause some delay in the arrival of the second wave on the island. The five helicopters were ordered to return to base and headed back to Utapao. When it became clear that the battalion commander was insistent upon the second wave being landed, the helicopters were directed to reverse course once more and head for Koh Tang. As far as Austin was concerned his mission remained the same: secure the island and search for the crew.

While decisions were being made at higher headquarters with regard to what course of action to pursue, the link-up operations between Company G (−) and the BLT command group were proceeding. Keith and Austin worked out a plan over the radio whereby Keith would attack out from his perimeter with Zales's platoon through the Cambodian positions between the marines and physically link up with the command group to the south. Prior to Zales's attack the air force would be called upon to make preparatory air strikes on the Cambodian positions. Following the air strikes the 81 mm mortars with the command group would bring down explosive power on the enemy positions facing Company G. The delicate task of keeping the mortar fire to his side of the fire coordination line fell to Second Lieutenant Joseph J. McMenamin, the 81 mm mortar platoon leader who was with the battalion command group. McMenamin, acting as forward observer, positioned his guns with the main body of the command group. He then moved forward to the point of the command group where he estimated range and deflection to the Cambodian positions. Rather than risk a long round which would impact in the marine perimeter, McMenamin directed that a spotting round be fired to seaward. From the impact of this round, he relayed correction data to the gunners. A second spotting round was fired. It hit right on top of the enemy positions. The mortarmen had their fire-for-effect gun data. By the time that the two marine elements of the coordinated attack were ready, the third element was rolling in. And none too soon, since the Cambodians chose that time to make their second major thrust from the south. Again, the marine fire, supplemented by the air strikes, stopped the enemy in their tracks.

Keith and Captain Barry Cassidy, the air liaison officer with the battalion command group, demonstrated their resourcefulness in bringing the air support in close.

Utilizing the available VHF radios tuned to the battalion tactical net, Keith and Cassidy were able to coordinate the "hot" runs of USAF A-7s as the gap between the friendly forces diminished during the link-up operations. As was mentioned earlier the FAC party with the first wave had been aboard one of the helicopters which crashed off the eastern zone. All of the UHF radio equipment had been destroyed. The airborne mission commander was netted with the battalion tactical net as well as with the fixed-wing attack aircraft on station. When it became apparent that the battalion's UHF nets were inoperable, the airborne mission commander directed the A-7 pilots to tune to the battalion tactical net. Captain Cassidy had landed with both a UHF and a VHF radio. By this time the air force planes had switched to VHF so Cassidy's UHF, PRC-75 which had radio-checked "five-by-five" at Utapao, was tuned to a vacant net on Koh Tang. It should be noted that throughout this period there were numerous tactical aircraft on station over or near the island. On a rotational basis one of the pilots of these high performance aircraft would be designated the tactical air coordinator (airborne) (TACA). This fact brought about a problem, as successive flights of tactical aircraft did their utmost to bring air

support in close. As each new TACA took over, there came about a painstaking process of identifying the extent of friendly lines and the confirmation of the location of the BLT command group. For this reason Cassidy and Keith worked out their "wing-over" method of bringing ordnance down on the enemy between their respective groups of marines. As the aircraft made runs in a general west-to-east direction, Keith at the southern extremity of his perimeter and Cassidy at the northern point of the moving command group, would follow an aircraft through a dummy run. Adjustments, as required, were made on successive runs of the aircraft until the A-7 had bisected the gap between the marines, that is, a wing tip over each. The aircraft was then directed to make a "hot" run. As the last aircraft came off the target, McMenamin's mortars opened fire. McDaniel's troops laid down a base of fire for Zales's assault. Among the marines delivering this heavy volume of well-aimed suppressive fire on the enemy positions was Lance Corporal Gilbert C. Lutz, a machine gun squad leader attached to McDaniel's platoon. Earlier in the morning, Lutz and two members of one of his gun teams had been wounded. Lutz had refused evacuation and was himself keeping the gun in action.

Supported by the suppressing fires, Second Platoon jumped off in the attack with Zales, Second Lieutenant Daniel J. Hoffman, the weapons platoon commander, and First Sergeant Lawrence L. Funk leading the way. As Zales's troops closed on the Cambodian positions, McMenamin shifted his mortar fire to the exposed eastern flank of the attacking marines. As Second Platoon assaulted through the enemy strong point, a Cambodian squad was repositioning itself to get on the flank of the attacking marines. From their vantage point, McMenamin and the two marines with him, Lance Corporals Larry J. Branson and Robert L. Shelton, could clearly observe the Cambodian maneuver and foresee the threat to Zales and his people. McMenamin, Branson, and Sheldon charged forward across the 50 meters of fire-swept terrain lying between themselves and the enemy squad. Taken by surprise, the Cambodians fled into the jungle. The link-up of the main body of Company G with the command group took place at approximately 1245.

All morning, while attention was focused on the southern portion of the perimeter, a combined force of marines from the Second and Third Platoons of Company G, led by staff sergeants Fofo T. Tuitele and Francis L. Burnett, protected the northern sector of the perimeter. Initially, these marines overran two enemy bunkers close to the landing zone. They were thereby able to suppress by fire an additional enemy position from which an automatic weapon had been firing into the zone.

Meanwhile, the question of what to do with the second wave had been resolved at higher headquarters. They were going in. Four of the helicopters landed in the western zone, discharging their heliteams and picking up six wounded marines. The fifth helicopter, a CH-53, attempted to get into the eastern zone. As it was making its approach, it took such heavy fire that it aborted the run in. As the aircraft pulled out of its run, it was obvious that it had been badly damaged. The pilot was able to nurse his machine back to the Thai coast for an emergency landing. Therefore, of the 127 landing force personnel in the second wave, 100 were landing in the western zone. Subtracting the number of wounded which had been extracted, the landing force on the island numbered 225.

The remainder of the afternoon was spent consolidating the position, destroying captured enemy stores, and conducting air strikes against known enemy positions. The control of close air support had by this time been considerably facilitated with the arrival of USAF OV-10 aircraft, on station as TACA late in the afternoon and for the remainder of the operation.

While all of the activity was going on in and around Koh Tang, CTG 79.9 was forced to endure a communication relay which went via USSAG/7th AF headquarters and thence to the ABCCC and finally to the BLT. Lieutenant Colonel Austin, in order to communicate back to Colonel Johnson, had to use the same link in reverse. The wounded and aircrews returning from Koh Tang described a very serious situation on the island. Just how serious could not be determined quickly by the command group at Utapao. The communications were at best sporadic. The staff of CTG 79.9 resorted to every means available to them to obtain precise and timely information.

USSAG/7, through his ABCCC, was in direct operational control of the landing force and CTG 79.9 was relegated to an advisory capacity from a very disadvantageous geographic position.

During the afternoon of the 15th, the principal point of concern was the time of extraction of the landing force. The BLT commander was consulted by USSAG/7th AF via the ABCCC. There was little doubt that the forces in the western zone with appropriate resupply could more than hold their own if they were required to stay on the island overnight. There was considerable concern regarding the ability of the marines in the isolated pocket on the eastern side to hold out through the night. The decision was made by USSAG/7 AF to extract the entire landing force, providing the eastern zone could be evacuated first. Lieutenant Colonel Austin had stipulated that once begun, the entire extraction had to be completed in rapid sequence.

The Extraction

The first attempt to extract Lieutenant Cicere and his marines was made at approximately 1415, unbeknownst to the senior marine commanders. At that time there were two helicopters available at Koh Tang. This attempt was unsuccessful and resulted in battle damage to one HH-53. It flew to the *Coral Sea* where it was repaired by 1700. Three additional helicopters arrived from Utapao between 1725 and 1800. Successful extraction began at 1810 with one HH-53 extracting the personnel from the eastern zone. Four more extractions of 172 personnel from the western zone followed between 1845 and 2010. The specific extraction time had been relayed to neither Lieutenant Colonel Austin nor Colonel Johnson. The landing force was, however, prepared for such an eventuality. The wounded and support personnel had been grouped adjacent to the landing zone, and a plan to incrementally reduce the perimeter on the landing zone had been worked out. When the first helicopter arrived in the western zone unannounced, the marines were ready. The perimeter was progressively tightened as succeeding helicopters extracted more marines. At this time, the *Wilson* had an armed boat in the water, close inshore, which was laying suppressive fires on the Cambodian positions north of the marine perimeter. Earlier in the afternoon, in addition to taking enemy positions on the eastern shore under fire, the *Wilson* had engaged and sunk a Cambodian gunboat which was firing on U.S. aircraft. One among the many marines, who were conspicuous by their actions during the disengagement, was a squad leader from Company E, Lance Corporal John S. Standfast.

Standfast's squad was assigned the task of covering the remainder of his company as they withdrew to secondary positions to prepare for the final extraction from the island. Once the company was in its new positions, Standfast directed the final disengagement of his own squad. In the process, he advanced forward to the then-exposed and abandoned perimeter to ensure personally that all members of his squad had withdrawn. The final extraction of twenty-nine men occurred at 2010. Sunset had been at 1822, therefore the entire extraction on the western side of the island was accomplished in total darkness and required five attempts prior to the successful pickup. As the helicopters came into the zone they were met with increasing volumes of automatic weapons fire, as the Cambodians continued to close aggressively on the smaller marine perimeter. The OV-10, on station continuously, was marking muzzle flashes to give aiming points to an AC-130 gunship. When the final helicopter did make it in, it hovered at the water's edge with its nose pointing seaward. The last two marines to board the aircraft were Captain Davis and Gunnery Sergeant Lester A. McNemar, who had combed the beach area to ensure that there were no stragglers. All the marines extracted from the island were taken to the *Coral Sea*, *Wilson*, and *Holt*.

On the evening of the 15th, following the extraction, the order was passed to remove all marine forces from Thailand. This deployment was completed on the morning of 16 May 1975, again utilizing Military Airlift Command (MAC) C-141 aircraft. The landing force, embarked aboard the *Coral Sea*, *Wilson*, and *Holt* sailed for Subic Bay, arriving there on 20 May 1975. The marines from 1/4 were chopped back to their parent organization. The elements of BLT 2/9 who had landed on Koh Tang were flown back to Okinawa from Naval Air Station, Cubi Point, on the 21st. Task Group 79.9 was deactivated after the return of the last deployed marine forces to Okinawa.

The U.S. Navy's Clouded Amphibious Mission

BY VICE ADMIRAL ROBERT S. SALZER, USN (RET.)

The U.S. Navy's amphibious might came into being as an emergency response to the strategic imperatives of World War Two. Hugely successful though seagoing assault forces were, questions arose during the late 1940s as to the need for maintaining this unique capability in the postwar navy. Indeed, before the outbreak of hostilities in Korea, so distinguished a military figure as General Omar Bradley said that the day of the large-scale amphibious invasion had already passed.

These doubts were laid to rest by the stunning tactical success of the Inchon landing in September 1950. Subsequently, amphibious forces became an established part of the peacetime navy; and the size of the Marine Corps, which had been in jeopardy during Truman's presidency, was fixed by law at three marine amphibious forces (MAF).

Ascendancy of the Presence and Deterrence Mission

Over the ensuing decades, amphibious forces came to be primarily employed in quite a different way from the classic assault operations of World War Two and Korea. The disintegration of European colonial power in the 1950s and 1960s ushered in a period of geopolitical change and instability in much of Asia and Africa. American politicomilitary policy makers frequently found themselves confronted with situations in these areas which threatened to become inimical to Western interests—either as a result of

U.S. Naval Institute *Proceedings* 104 (February 1978): 24–33. Reprinted by permission.

Soviet activities or simply because of conflicts among newly independent nations. Moreover, America's ability to intervene effectively in these matters was increasingly subject to impairment by indigenous restrictions on, or outright termination of, the overseas bases granted to the United States by its allies in their former dependencies.

The seas, which bound so many of these trouble spots, provided an apt answer to this problem, for in the era of the three-mile limit, they were freely available to those with the capability to exercise control over them. The United States had emerged from World War Two supreme on the world's oceans. Small (four or five ship), forward-deployed amphibious ready groups (ARG), each with a marine amphibious unit (MAU) embarked, were developed to fill this "crisis control" mission in conjunction with naval air power.

For many years, ARG/MAUs proved to be most flexible and useful tools of power politics. Although vastly smaller than the scores of ships and thousands of troops required for even one of the more modest assaults of World War Two, the ARG/MAU was not an insignificant force in comparison with the ill-trained and poorly equipped ground units which were characteristic of many Third World countries during the earlier years of the postcolonial era. The marines' presence in troubled areas served as a constant reminder of U.S. capabilities to those who might have otherwise been tempted to harm our interests. Conversely, exercises on the beaches of friendly nations provided these allies with valuable training opportunities and afforded

Caribbean maneuvers, 1948.

tangible reassurance of U.S. readiness to commit ground troops—the ultimate arbiter of land battle—to assist them in time of need. And finally, if push came to shove, these forces could be committed to landing operations on very short notice in order to protect and evacuate endangered U.S. nationals or to stabilize a politically chaotic situation such as occurred in Lebanon in 1958.

Over time, the requirements of this peacekeeping mission—or gunboat diplomacy, if one prefers—became so important that they exercised a dominant influence on the size, composition, and characteristics of the navy's amphibious forces. This condition continues to the present day. The huge fleet of amphibious warfare ships with which the United States emerged from World War Two had been designed for maximum landing force mass and crushing supporting fire against enemy-held beach defenses. Troop habitability standards were virtually nonexistent, and severe water rationing was standard operating procedure. The ships were slow and of relatively modest size, for assault force speed was neither tactically nor strategically vital, and an opposed amphibious assault is not the kind of operation where a prudent person wants to put a great many eggs in a few baskets. These characteristics, however, were not well suited for the ARG/MAU task where troops might be kept embarked for the duration of a six- to nine-month deployment and fast ships were necessary for the rapid-reaction capability which is the hallmark of this concept.

Consequently, as the veterans of the World War Two amphibious warfare fleet were phased out because of age and obsolescence, they were succeeded by much larger and faster ships with far more commodious troop accommodations and other hotel services. A 20-knot capability became such unquestioned dogma that it was even applied to the *Newport* (LST-1179) class of tank landing ships—at no small cost to its beaching ability. Some type of helicopter-support feature was designed into every new class of amphibious warfare ship to enable each unit of an ARG to land and refuel these aircraft. Enough fully air-capable ships were added to the forces to permit sustained maintenance support of the assault helicopter squadrons which had become a vital part of landing force capabilities. Also, sophisticated command and control facilities were installed on sufficient ships to assure most adequate capabilities in each of the independently deployed groups.

The navy's readiness to carry out major opposed landings has long since been subordinated to ARG/MAU requirements. The new amphibious warfare ships are expensive; consequently, their numbers are so few that they are pressed to meet deployment schedules. Opportunities for larger-scale training are thus limited. It has been more than a decade since a division-size exercise (Steel Pike in 1964) has been conducted with more actual than constructive units. Indeed, this is a practical impossibility so long as mandatory ARG deployment commitments must be met. After allowing for ships in over-

Royal Marines, 41 Commando, during a NATO exercise, Sardinia, 1975. Courtesy of the U.K. Department of Defence

haul and unscheduled maintenance, the navy has sufficient amphibious lift for only one of the Marine Corps's three active MAFs. And this shipping is split between the Atlantic and Pacific fleets to meet deployment schedules to the Far East, the Mediterranean, and the Caribbean. The Washington planners' way around this problem is to provide, on paper, that in an emergency the Pacific amphibious forces would proceed to the Atlantic (and possibly vice versa). That evolution has not yet been performed for any purpose, and it is doubtful that it ever would be undertaken solely to accomplish necessary training in the complexities of division-size assaults.

The navy's capabilities to conduct large-scale assaults have attenuated in other respects as well during the continuing ARG/MAU era. Amphibious shipping carries only the assault elements of the landing force. The support forces and logistics, which are indispensable to the landing force's staying power, are necessarily transported in merchant shipping, with the ship-to-shore movement conducted by specialized naval amphibious units. However, it has been years since merchant ships have been made available to participate on more than a token scale in amphibious exercises.

The capability for massed naval gunfire,

which the navy learned at great cost to be essential in overcoming an enemy's beachhead defenses, has also largely passed into history. The inshore fire support craft, which once were an integral part of amphibious forces, have been phased out of the navy's inventory in the quest for economies in units not essential for the ARG/MAU task. Indeed, the only naval gunfire support assets left in the active forces are the 5-inch weapons of destroyers and frigates. And the majority of these ships are single-gun, single-screw vessels which were designed for open-ocean escort duty. They are considerably less than ideal for achieving close-in dominance over a hostile beach. And, in any case, our experience with the 5-inch gun in Vietnam amply demonstrated the limitations of that weapon against fortified positions. To be sure, the developmental 8-inch major caliber lightweight gun is programmed for eventual installation aboard the *Spruance-* (DD-963) class destroyers. However, the history of this interminable, low-priority developmental project is such as to make me less than optimistic about the eventual outcome.

The Need for Reappraisal

When a concept has been as unchallenged as the ARG/MAU over a protracted period of years, there is a tendency to regard it as sacrosanct. Nevertheless, changes in the technology of warfare and in the balance of global maritime power have been very significant over the past decade, and it is essential that naval planning take these realities into account. Amphibious forces consume significant resources. More than thirty thousand active navy personnel are committed to such ships and operational units, since virtually all of them must be kept fully manned to meet deployment commitments. Also, the continuing modernization of lift capabilities in support of the ARG/MAU concept has become exceedingly expensive. Nobody can be sure what the 40,000-ton *Tarawa* (LHA-1)-class vessels will really cost until the hundreds of millions of dollars of shipbuilder claims are finally adjudicated. The price tag could be in excess of $300 million per ship, and a significant part of the LHA's cost can be attributed to optimizing her design for protracted ARG/MAU deployments. Before making further investments of this magnitude, it is time to consider how important this concept continues to be to the pursuit of U.S. interests under present and foreseeable circumstances.

First, it is evident that the seas no longer afford a sure sanctuary for the projection of American amphibious power at will. The days when a lightly armed ready group, with little or no combatant escort, could loiter off a troubled shore with confidence that it was immune from effective sea or air retaliatory action *may* not yet be wholly past. But the areas of the world where this is possible are rapidly shrinking. Fast patrol craft, armed with antiship missiles, constitute a formidable threat to our large amphibious warfare ships. Such weapons have proliferated in the forces of even fourth- and fifth-rate powers. Similarly, military jets abound in the air forces of the Third World. They may be obsolete compared with the aircraft of the superpowers, but they can be quite effective against the guns of our current amphibious warfare ships. Also, it must be expected that the Soviet Union will employ its newly acquired global naval power to provide a countervailing presence to an ARG/MAU engaged in operations which are prejudicial to the Kremlin's interests. The credibility of this small group, as a presence or crisis-control force, has accordingly been impaired by the ability of other nations to pose a significant threat to its troop-laden ships at sea.

Conceptually, this problem could be overcome by providing the ARG with enough antimissile, antisubmarine, and antiair escorts to restore its aura of effectiveness. This is easier said than done, however, at current combatant force levels. Before one pays so heavy a price for continuing to ensure ARG/MAU viability at sea, it would be well to consider its deterrent and crisis control value as a landing force in today's world. The ground force capabilities of many Third World countries have improved even more dramatically than their sea and air power. Their weaponry

is modern, and they have a lot of it. The marine amphibious unit is a light force in comparison. Its handful of tanks and howitzers is not likely to overawe nations which possess hundreds of such weapons. And though the U.S. Marine remains the finest infantryman in the world, there are only four rifle companies in a MAU. Year by year, the number of countries where a force of this size can significantly influence events grows smaller. It is not that the MAU's capability has lessened but that the availability of opposing force has grown so greatly that the unspoken threat of the MAU's commitment ashore has lost credibility in much of the world—particularly where superpowers and their clients are actively competing for influence.

The contrast between the actions which this country found appropriate and feasible in the Lebanon crisis of 1958 and that of 1976 illustrates this point. In the former case, when the country was at the point of political disintegration into communal strife, the United States landed two battalion landing teams as the forward element of a peacekeeping force. After a tense hour or two, the Lebanese Army opted not to contest the landing, and the mission was successfully accomplished without combat. However, in 1976, with full-scale civil war in Lebanon, the ARG/MAU's intervention was cautiously confined to dispatching an unarmed landing craft to evacuate U.S. nationals from Beirut, after coordination with, and under the ostentatious protection of, the Palestine Liberation Organization's armed forces. This episode added little luster to the image of U.S. naval power. But it was clearly a prudent course. A repetition of the 1958 landings would have been most risky and probably unsuccessful. The array of potential armed opposition in Lebanon was of such magnitude that the United States had no reasonable choice but to maintain a low military profile when the only force we had available was one or two MAUs and perhaps some light army reinforcements from the U.S. European Command.

A third factor which has diminished the

credibility of the ARG/MAU is the psychological aftermath of the American failure in Vietnam. That lost cause is frequently proclaimed to be a closed chapter of U.S. history, but in international politics its effects will linger on for years to come. First, the fact that so small and underdeveloped a country as North Vietnam succeeded in holding its own against large-scale U.S. armed forces and ultimately wore out our will to continue the struggle, has tarnished in some degree the image of American military potency in the Third World. Neither friends nor adversaries in such nations are likely to attach as much weight to the possibility of U.S. intervention on their shores as they once did. Also, memories of the Vietnam War have seriously impaired the ability of U.S. decision makers to gain congressional or popular acquiescence, much less support, for *any* form of U.S. military intervention in troubled areas. The hornets' nest stirred up over Angola in Congress and the media cries of alarm over the shipment of programmed supplies to Zaire when it was invaded are indicative of how sensitive this issue continues to be. In essence then, the utility of the ARG/MAU as a presence or quick-reaction force has been seriously eroded by growth in the military and naval capabilities of other nations, psychological factors, and political inhibitions concerning its employment.

There remains a possible need to maintain such forward-deployed forces for the evacuation of U.S. nationals from "hot" areas. In fact, that has been the primary use of the amphibious ready group during the past few years. Besides Lebanon, additional examples are Cyprus, Phnom Penh, and Saigon. Evacuation has been an appropriate ancillary use of ARG/MAUs when they were forward-deployed for other useful purposes, but it seems questionable as a primary justification. No other nation finds it essential to keep so expensive a capability deployed against this contingency. If such services should still be deemed necessary by the State Department on occasion, they can be provided with much more efficiency than by deploying an ARG/

MAU. It has too little strength to prevail against opposition and much more than is needed for evacuation in a militarily permissive environment.

With the utility of such presence and crisis control capabilities so clearly on the wane, the case for maintaining sizable amphibious forces in the Navy has tended to focus on the postulated need for the United States to help its NATO or Far Eastern allies check massive continental aggression by rapid amphibious reinforcement or an Inchon-type thrust athwart the invader's land lines of communication. Whether such concepts are realistic in the light of hostile ground force order of battle is debatable. Without question, however, the growth of the Soviet Navy into a first-rate sea denial fleet has very sharply diminished the naval feasibility of such U.S. operations on NATO's flanks or in Northeastern Asia.

There is, in fact, little doubt that the United States will have to consider sea control to be the paramount mission of general-purpose naval forces during the early months of a conflict involving the modern Soviet Navy. Much more would hang on the outcome of such a struggle for domination of critical sea areas than solely the question of projecting amphibious power against a continental attack. The military effectiveness and very survival of U.S. forward-deployed divisions, our overseas alliances, and the import-dependent American economy itself would all be at stake.

Considering these circumstances, one school of thought holds that the resources now devoted to maintenance of amphibious capabilities should be realigned or reallocated to strengthen conventional sea control forces. For example, vessels of the LPH (amphibious assault ship) and LHA classes could be configured to support V/STOL (vertical or short takeoff and landing) aircraft and helicopters and to provide a needed supplement to the overcommitted carrier force in open ocean missions. Again, LPDs (amphibious transport docks) might be very useful as afloat helicopter support ships to ease the formidable air logistics problems which are likely to occur as small LAMPS (light airborne multipurpose system) helicopter detachments proliferate on board frigates. Conceivably, less versatile ships such as the LKA (amphibious cargo ship) or LST-1179 classes might be used for administrative, point-to-point shipping, or even inactivated, with the resources thus saved being used to improve the manning and equipment of what are perceived to be more important units for the sea control task.

The Amphibious Role in Control of the Seas

Unquestionably, it would be desirable to enhance the flexibility of selected amphibious warfare ships by equipping them and training their crews for participation in other operations. Moreover, some opportunities to do so could become available without undue detriment to amphibious training if the burden of the obsolescent ARG/MAU deployments were lifted. However, the reasoning which segregates the sea control and amphibious power projection missions into watertight compartments is flawed.

The amphibious capability of the Navy-Marine Corps team provides a vitally important means of establishing effective and continuing control over ocean areas in wartime. Task fleets and forces are essentially transient entities of naval power. Their mobility enables them to shift the locale of their operations rapidly in search of enemy concentrations. But once they have left an area, they cease to exercise significant military influence over it. On the other hand, the islands which abound in the Pacific and the less numerous archipelagos of the Atlantic and Indian oceans afford bases from which land-based air and other sea surveillance and attack systems can be employed to exercise control over sizable sea areas on a quasi-permanent basis. Some such bases are, of course, available to the United States now. But recent history has indicated how quickly such rights can be jeopardized when the political complexion of an ally or client state changes.

If such strategic ocean bases were to fall under the military control of a hostile major power, they could pose an intolerable threat to vital sea lines of communication.

In peacetime, it is most unlikely that the United States would resort to more than diplomatic pressure and the enticement of material aid to gain or retain such base rights. Indeed, in overseas areas, the Soviet Union itself has been unwontedly circumspect about the use of military power for such purposes. In the event of an ocean struggle between the U.S. and Soviet navies, however, the situation is likely to be quite different. Even the partisans on either side of the sterile and seemingly endless debate as to the "superiority" of one or the other of these fleets generally concede that their forces, though structurally dissimilar, are fairly closely matched. Under these circumstances, neither nation could afford to deny itself significant tactical advantage over its foe in the event of war. The task confronting the United States of exercising control over its indispensable sea lines of communication is inherently more difficult than would be the Soviet objective of denying us their safe use. To succeed, it is essential that the United States have the capability to hold, occupy, or, if need be, wrest from unfriendly hands the bases from which critical ocean areas could be dominated.

Future Amphibious Force Levels

A combat-ready amphibious capability is accordingly a key element in our readiness to carry out the sea control mission in the event of war. And rather than reducing force levels, it is time to consider seriously how the navy may be able to augment such capabilities within the constraints set by peacetime budgetary and manpower limitations. Opposed amphibious assaults are inherently chancy operations; they always have been. The odds against success go up sharply unless the landing force has substantial numerical and fire support superiority over the defenders; a three-to-one advantage is commonly used as a rule of thumb for planning purposes. The tactical consequences of sending too light a force ashore in such an environment are so drastic as to make the taking of "calculated risks" in this matter unwise. Thus, a division-size landing may be none too much to commit in the face of more than light opposition. The Marine Corps portion of the amphibious team maintains a capability in being for operations on such a scale in both the Atlantic and the Pacific. But as previously discussed, the navy's amphibious lift is far less.

Furthermore, the concept of "swinging" the amphibious forces of one fleet to the other in time of emergency does not provide a practical solution to the problems posed by this paucity of amphibious lift for division-scale operations. For one thing, it is a near certainty that the era of U.S. control over the Panama Canal Zone "as if it were sovereign" is drawing to a close. The new treaty negotiated with Panama necessarily includes provisos concerning freedom of transit through the canal for American naval forces under all circumstances. Otherwise, the chances of ratification would be nil. However, the history of similar accords in politically volatile areas warrants some skepticism as to the immutability of this paper guarantee once U.S. physical control over the Canal Zone is reduced or eliminated.

An even more important defect of the "swing" concept is that it is predicated on the assumption that the United States could afford to deprive either of its major fleets of its amphibious capabilities in time of emergency. It is naive to base plans for coping with a war at sea on the premise that a global navy such as the Soviet Union's would be so accommodating as to allow us to limit the struggle to a single ocean. Considering the importance of the North Atlantic sea lines of communication and the chronic nervousness of our NATO allies over any diminution of American concentration on the defense of Europe, a shift of East Coast-based amphibious forces to meet even a major emergency in the Pacific or Indian Ocean could be most unwise. Although less apparent, it would be equally dangerous to strip the Pacific Fleet

of this capability in order to bolster the Atlantic. The sealanes to Japan and Alaska and into the Indian Ocean are too important to national security to permit taking such a risk. Control over the island chains of the Northern Pacific could well play a major role in determining the outcome of a sea control campaign in this area.

For these reasons, it seems clear that the demands of the sea control tasks which could confront the United States require that the navy expand, as feasible, its amphibious lift capabilities, with the ultimate objective of providing each fleet with the means of mounting division-size amphibious operations. Moreover, the gaps which have developed in the navy's other capabilities to conduct amphibious landings against significant opposition require concurrent attention.

Amphibious Lift Forces of the Future

The stumbling block in the path of prompt realization of this strategic need is likely to be resource constraints. Certainly, over the past few years, efforts by the Marine Corps to generate support for an expansion of amphibious lift have foundered on this shoal. Advocates of amphibious forces have sometimes ascribed the navy's unwillingness to match Marine Corps capabilities to a parochial bias in favor of expending its available shipbuilding dollars on carriers and other "blue water" combatant ships.

There may be a little to this theory, but the primary blame for the inadequacy of lift forces lies more with the amphibious elements of the navy and the Marine Corps themselves. In their understandable desire to go "first class" and have all elements of the force fully capable of protracted ARG/MAU deployments, they have come perilously close to pricing the amphibious capability out of the range of reasonable attainability. The LHA fiasco should have been a lesson to everyone in the costs of superfluous sophistication. Yet for years, all planning for the replacement of the aging *Thomaston* (LSD-28)-class of dock landing ships was conducted on the basis of further "advances in the state of the art" without apparent serious cost constraints.

Only when the price for one of these proposed ships reached the $400 million range was an effective effort made to reverse the trend. Even now, however, the estimated cost for the proposed new class is in the neighborhood of a quarter of a billion dollars per ship. This cost must come down, or there will remain considerable doubt as to whether these replacement vessels ever will, or should, be built. And expansion toward a two-MAF lift capability will become a totally unattainable goal if the navy and the Marine Corps insist on it being composed of "gold platers."

Although opposed amphibious operations are extremely intricate evolutions requiring the best in modern weaponry for dominance of the objective area, success in the assault landing phase itself can effectively be achieved without dependence on sophisticated systems. Indeed, a case can be made that the complicated and expensive accessories—such as computer-based amphibious information systems—introduced over the recent past contribute only marginally to accomplishment of the assault mission, even on those rare occasions when they are working properly.

Designers of amphibious warfare ships would do well to take to heart Admiral of the Fleet of the Soviet Union Gorshkov's aphorism, "Better is the enemy of good enough." The critical characteristics of assault forces and systems are selective off-load configuration, rugged ship-to-shore subsystems, enough hulls for effective spread-loading, austere hotel services to sustain the landing force in combat trim over a two- to three-week transit, and simple, reliable auxiliary machinery. Fiscal realities dictate that the navy and Marine Corps concentrate on these key features in amphibious warfare ships of the future and ruthlessly dispense with the "nice-to-have" items they have become accustomed to regarding as essential. Austerity in requirements for manpower will also be mandatory. If ready group deployment requirements are relaxed, it should be practicable to man a larger number of these ships as naval reserve force assets, with only two-thirds of their crews being composed of active personnel. Experience with this concept has shown that such active duty contingents can both perform required maintenance and operate effectively for two- to three-day training periods at sea at times when the selected reserve portion of the crew is not available.

Some high-cost types will still be desirable in the amphibious lift mix. However, the existing force of relatively new and highly sophisticated ships should provide for such needs adequately, except with respect to air-capable units to support vertical assault. Conceivably, this need might be met without building new ships wholly dedicated to this task. When necessity so demanded for the evacuation of Saigon, an attack aircraft carrier was hurriedly reconfigured for the LPH task and performed acceptably (albeit reluctantly) in that role. In any case, before further new investment is made in sea support of vertical assault, the navy and Marine Corps should take a close look at the viability of this means of conducting landings in the face of modern antiaircraft opposition. Such mobile, hard-to-detect weapons as the one-man SA-7 surface-to-air missile could be devastating against the high-density landings required for rapid buildup by helicopter assault.

Merchant Marine Potential Capabilities

In their search for low-cost but effective lift capabilities, amphibious warfare planners should examine carefully the potential of modern ships in the U.S. Merchant Marine to serve as an element of the navy's assault landing capabilities. The design and configuration of such federally subsidized vessels can be modified to incorporate defense functions if the navy formulates its needs clearly and forcefully. In addition, certain of the existing commercial types, such as barge-carrying LASH and SEABEE ships, seem adaptable for use in the assault phase, with relatively minor modifications. It would be more economical in terms of both dollars and manpower to invest in the construction of landing craft and other ship-to-ship subsystems which would be compatible with the basic characteristics of LASH and SEABEE vessels than acquiring and manning new navy amphibious ships. Austere living and messing facilities could be provided for boat crews and vehicle maintenance men by embarking modular units such as are being developed from standard military containers by the Marine Corps. Such modules, embarked aboard containerships, may also prove a valuable supplement to the traditional techniques of emergency berthing in providing accommodations for larger numbers of troops.

There will be a multitude of control, loading, pre-H-hour transfer, training, and doctrinal difficulties to solve in adapting to so sharp a departure from current practices. None of these problems appear likely to be insuperable, however, unless the navy and the Marine Corps wish to make them so. Certainly, short shrift should be given to the argument that American merchant sailors cannot be relied on for carrying out such a mission in the face of the dangers of a combat environment. The annals of naval history are replete with proof to the contrary. If any modern-day refutation of this tired canard is necessary, it was amply furnished by the crews of the merchant ships on which the United States primarily relied to rescue the thousands of refugees who fled their country when the North Vietnamese finally triumphed. These merchant sailors acquitted themselves, under desperately difficult circumstances, in a manner which would do credit to any professional military oganization.

Regardless of whether such specialized commercial ships are used for the assault phase, there can be no question as to the essentiality of merchant vessels for the support of large-scale landings, commencing on D-day. As previously mentioned, this need has always been recognized in amphibious doctrine; however, its exercise has been neglected for a long time. Over this period, the composition and characteristics of the merchant marine have changed markedly. The break-bulk ships of the past are progressively giving way to containerships, and most of these are non-self-unloading because it is more economical to rely on port facilities for cargo

handling. The equipment which is currently available for unloading such ships offshore is, at best, marginal. Although research and development on this problem have been going on for years, it has proceeded at a snail's pace. Major technological breakthroughs are not required nearly so much as an adequately high priority and a sense of urgency.

Hand in hand with accelerated development of these off-load systems must go a buildup of the capabilities of the naval beach groups. Their amphibious Seabees, beachmasters, and landing craft crews are the core elements of the navy's assault forces. But the strength of these units has been so much reduced that it is now inadequate for the difficult task of delivering the logistic support carried by the "follow-on echelon" of shipping to the landing force. Development of such capabilities will not be cheap. Some offsetting savings may be made by a reordering of amphibious warfare spending priorities. The ability to utilize modern commercial ships is far more essential to successful accomplishment of the assault mission than some of the exotic equipments for which the navy always seems to find resources—for example, the development of an air-cushion landing craft on which scores of millions of dollars have been lavished.

Combat Support

Over the many years of the present mission and unopposed operations, the landing phase has come to dominate the navy's thinking about amphibious assaults. Such operations are regarded as the specialty of the "gator navy" and the Marine Corps.

Actually, however, the success of amphibious operations against serious opposition depends on the orchestrated application of virtually the entire array of naval power to establish domination over the air, ground, and sea space of the objective areas—antiair and missile defenses, antisubmarine warfare, close air support, defense against missile boats, naval gunfire support, and mine countermeasures. With the notable exception of the last two categories, the existing capabilities of combatant forces for open-ocean operations can be used to support amphibious assaults adequately. However, until regularly exercised for the purpose, these will remain no more than latent capabilities. The incredibly cluttered, shallow-water, land-background environment of the amphibious objective area presents special problems and challenges which can be surmounted only by training and familiarization. Rather than additional combat support forces, what is basically needed is genuine recognition that amphibious warfare is a mission for all naval surface and air forces. This must be reflected in training and operating schedules on a continuing basis.

There are, however, no quick or easy solutions to naval gunfire support and mine countermeasure deficiencies. Until new surface minesweepers can be built the navy will have to rely on the current helicopter mine countermeasure forces despite the hazards involved in their use to clear the approaches to defended beaches. Similarly, it will be necessary to accept the limited destructive power of the 5-inch gun until the navy's decade-long, slow-motion development of a lightweight 8-inch gun finally reaches fruition. However, the shortage of gunfire support might be alleviated in the near term by installing a 5-inch system to replace some of the 3-inch weapons which take up weight, space, and maintenance effort on board amphibious warfare ships for very little purpose. There is no reason why these vessels could not be used for close fire support of troops once they have completed their assault unloading.

In summary, the changes which have taken place in maritime power relationships have greatly diminished the effectiveness of the forward-deployed ARG/MAU as a means of presence and deterrence. The continuing commitment of our amphibious forces to this once valuable, but now outmoded, employment concept is wasteful. Moreover, its requirements operate to the detriment of the navy's ability to develop and maintain adequately trained, two-ocean amphibious forces in support of its wartime sea control function. The future of amphibious warfare lies in its contribution to the latter mission. The size, structure, doctrine, training, and employment of amphibious forces should all be focused on rebuilding a viable capability for the larger-scale landings associated with the sea control requirement. Readiness to accomplish such operations provides the only solid guarantee that the bases required for control of vital sea areas will be available to the United States in wartime. This need can only be met, within realistic fiscal constraints, by single-minded concentration of available resources on the essential functional requirements of assault landings in the design of future amphibious units. Full use should be made of the merchant marine's potential in order to minimize costs. Under all circumstances, the navy should eschew the expensive sophistication which has needlessly characterized amphibious construction programs of the recent past.

Where Do the Gators Go from Here?

BY VICE ADMIRAL FRANK W. VANNOY, USN (RET.)

My perceptions of the future of amphibious warfare in the U.S. Navy are not based on an operational analysis but rather on an amphibious background spanning the period between the invasion of Tarawa in 1943 and my retirement from command of the Amphibious Force, U.S. Atlantic Fleet in 1974. While I shall attempt to remain truly objective, a degree of bias is likely to appear on the side of the gator navy, for I am proud to be counted as one of that breed.

I take as a fact that an amphibious warfare capability has been of great importance to the United States. I also take as a fact that we enjoy significant amphibious capabilities not shared by the Soviets at this time (although their capabilities are improving). Our three active Marine Corps division/wing teams are superb fighting organizations. Our amphibious warfare ships are relatively new and are capable; they are being supplemented by major new ships now under construction, and others are programmed for later construction. In short, we now have an amphibious warfare capability that is time-tested and an important component of our military structure. Logic would dictate the continuation of this capability into the future.

Basics

The content of this section runs the risk of insulting the intelligence of those readers who understand amphibious warfare. Unfortunately, altogether too many naval officers do

U.S. Naval Institute *Proceedings* 104 (March 1978): 88–95. Reprinted by permission.

not have that understanding. While this is a condition which will be corrected to a degree by the relatively recent practice of splitting tours at the department head level between cruiser/destroyer types and amphibious/logistic types, the transfusion is not yet complete.

It needs to be recognized that amphibious warfare ships and some (but not all) of their problems are different from those of the rest of the surface navy. When most other navy ships are commissioned, manned, shaken down, and provisioned they are ready to carry out their assigned combat missions. The main battery is an integral part of the ship. Although amphibious warfare ships are able to train in seamanship and at-sea operations using ship's company, they cannot train in or carry out the primary functions for which they were designed without the presence of their "main batteries"—embarked marines. The combat troops, helicopters, and amphibious vehicles permit amphibious readiness to be achieved and assaults to be conducted. And, since our marines—whatever their many fine qualities—have little capability for walking on water, they are irrevocably tied to our seaborne amphibious forces. "The navy-marine amphibious team" is not a catch phrase, but rather a statement of fact. Neither part of the team can get along without the other. A case can be argued that this situation is little different from that of the aircraft carrier, which is impotent without her air wing on board. The point has merit. However, the carrier and air wing are controlled by a single type command. This is not the case with our amphibious warfare ships, which are a part of the Atlantic and Pacific Fleet Naval Surface Forces, and the Marine Corps elements, which are a part of the respective Fleet Marine Forces. Other than the names involved (the substitution of the Surface Forces for the now-disbanded Amphibious Forces), this situation is nothing new and is cited only as evidence that the amphibious warfare ships are truly without parallel within the navy.

The amphibious force commander has always been a parallel commander to the landing force commander during planning for an assault. The former has always been responsible for the conduct of the assault, and the latter has always been responsible for operations ashore. The command arrangements and interactions are admittedly complex and poorly understood by many. For instance, many naval officers may not know that a naval officer always commands the amphibious task force and is responsible for all operations in the amphibious objective area until responsibility is passed to the landing force commander after the assault is completed. Others, who understand the foregoing, may feel that the amphibious task force commander can or should direct the landing force in matters relating to its job ashore. This would be a major mistake. Since the navy and Marine Corps components have coordinate planning roles, the landing force commander will determine the landing area and the landing sequence which are optimum from his viewpoint. The amphibious force commander will judge his ability to support the optimum landing force plan from within his resources. Adjustments will be made as necessary to work out a mutually acceptable solution. If agreement cannot be reached, the problem will be passed to the common senior for resolution. These principles apply at all levels of amphibious warfare and validate the navy-Marine Corps team concept.

Tasks

It seems unlikely that future amphibious tasks will differ in significant degree from those existing today. They will include requirements to:

- *Provide a forward-deployed amphibious presence to add stability and to provide reassurance to an ally in an area of importance to the United States.* These amphibious forces are generally known as amphibious ready groups. They are usually quite small, consisting of perhaps five ships of varying types and a marine amphibious unit built around a reinforced battalion landing team and a mixed helicopter/Harrier aviation element. The advent of the 40,000-ton LHA—which is saddled with the impossible name of amphibious assault ship (general purpose)—will probably result in a lesser number of amphibious warfare ships in the "presence" group. These groups will continue to be deployed in the Mediterranean and Western Pacific and occasionally in the Caribbean. They are the only amphibious resources always immediately available for employment, and they have been frequently called upon.

- *Provide a cover force for evacuation of U.S. and perhaps allied citizens or, alternatively, conduct or assist in the evacuation.* The forward-deployed amphibious ready group would normally be used in this case, augmented as required and as time permits by other amphibious units. Since such operations would take place in a crisis, supporting aircraft and surface antisubmarine and antiair forces would be provided. Such contingencies would be unlikely to develop without some warning, thereby permitting enhanced readiness to be achieved. Vietnam and Cambodia evacuation operations involved participation by amphibious units.

- *Provide initial security of a logistic entry point (port or airhead) required for support of a friendly government threatened from within.* This presupposes a request for assistance from the friendly government under circumstances in which its own forces are committed elsewhere. The comments under the preceding task apply here as well.

- *Conduct assault landing to restore or sup-*

port a friendly government requesting assistance. This case would involve considerable preplanning and assembly of forces beyond those normally available in the forward-deployed amphibious ready groups. It also connotes a continuing commitment beyond that of the previous cases. The likelihood of significant opposition would also be higher than in the preceding instances.

- Conduct assault landings in support of alliances. This case is the upper limit of potential tasks. It would involve extensive preplanning and assembly of forces. The assault would have to be conducted in a more severe threat environment than that existing in other cases and would involve a heavy continuing commitment.

The foregoing tasks are ordered in general from the least to the most demanding as far as resources are concerned, although there is little to differentiate between the requirements likely to be necessary to carry out the second and third tasks. While the amphibious raid could be considered as a special task, it has been considered here as a subset of other tasks. The forces assigned to a specific task, and between specific tasks, will vary widely with circumstances. There is a common thread. Every organization conducting an amphibious warfare task has a naval officer acting as commander, amphibious task force (group/unit) and a Marine Corps officer acting as commander, landing force (group/unit). There is no reason that an army officer could not be the landing force commander in an amphibious assault. This was frequently the case in World War Two; however, army forces do not now train for this role.

Threat

Looking to the future, it appears very likely that the already severe maritime threat environment will worsen as more and better "smart" weapons come into the inventory. Of these weapons, the cruise missile, with its capability for air, surface, and subsurface launch, will continue to pose the most severe threat. Particularly in areas such as the Eastern Mediterranean and the Norwegian Sea—and to a lesser degree in other areas contiguous to the Eurasian landmass—the Soviets will increase their potential for multimedium attack against naval forces. Also, there is no reason to expect termination of a long-standing Soviet policy to provide relatively sophisticated weapons to client states. These states have, on occasion, displayed proficiency in the employment of such weapons. Although the threat will be less in waters contiguous to Third World countries than in waters contiguous to the U.S.S.R., it will still be significant. We cannot expect the benign maritime environment of Korea, Cuba, and Vietnam to continue in future crises.

Our amphibious warfare ships now have little to no capability for self-defense against submarine, surface, or air threats. The basic point defense missile system is now installed in some of the large ships, and there are plans for future installation of close-in weapon systems in all ships. These systems will provide some antiair and antimissile capability, as will upgraded passive defense systems; however, self-defense levels will remain low and will continue to require support from other sources. It has been suggested that embarked marine aviation resources could be used in antisubmarine warfare (ASW) and antiair warfare (AAW) roles, but the complexities of ASW helicopter operations would effectively negate the use of marine helicopters for anything other than visual detection. Also, the utility of marine V/STOL (vertical and short takeoff and landing) aircraft for AAW is marginal.

Thus, our amphibious ready groups are sitting ducks for a surprise attack until they have been reinforced. In a crisis, antisubmarine and antiaircraft ships and dedicated air support would have to be provided. Whether such action would suffice would depend largely upon the area of operations involved. The fact that our navy now has significant deficiencies in AAW and ASW is not encouraging (although ASW is showing progress). Even less encouraging is the current requirement to operate amphibious warfare ships close inshore, thus precluding effective use of those defensive systems which they do possess and the defensive systems of their supporting forces. In the projected threat environment, even the outmoded weapons of the superpowers would constitute an increasing threat in the hands of client states, for they would be more capable than the even older ones the clients now hold.

The foregoing is a reasonably bleak picture if taken in the context of a superpower confrontation, but much less so in other circumstances, which fortunately are also more likely. The first four amphibious tasks considered for the future would neither necessarily nor normally involve superpower confrontation. (The Eastern Mediterranean littoral is a special case. Any amphibious task other than the maintenance of a ready group risks confrontation in that area since superpower naval forces are continuously present there.) The fifth, the conduct of an amphibious assault in support of an alliance, might involve such confrontation and certainly would do so in the North Atlantic Treaty Organization (NATO) area. There is no question that severe problems will be encountered now and in the future in attempting amphibious assaults in areas in which multimedium major power forces can be brought to bear. Indeed, until such forces have been reduced to manageable proportions through attrition, an assault should not be attempted. There will normally be time for attrition to be accomplished during the time required to assemble, load, and transit the amphibious forces required for task five. Carrier task forces and attack submarines will have to implement the attrition task, which will be a difficult and potentially costly one. Success on the part of the carrier forces is likely to depend to a critical degree on significant improvement to existing capabilities to cope with the antiship missile.

At just what point the threat will have been reduced to manageable proportions for an amphibious assault is a judgment call which will be tempered by circumstances. Timing could be so critical that a higher-than-prudent threat level would be accepted. An excellent example of this was the Guad-alcanal operation of World War Two, which took place with major elements of the Japanese fleet in the area. That gamble paid off, although it was touch and go for a time. In any case, it would be naive to assume that any future amphibious assault would go unopposed afloat or ashore. It is therefore important that existing or anticipated problem areas be identified and remedied.

Resource Limitations

Perhaps the most critical problem area is one of resources. It is nearly impossible for anyone who did not participate in the campaigns in the Pacific late in World War Two to appreciate the sheer magnitude of the total effort. When Vice Admiral Harry Hill, for whom I worked, took over from Admiral Kelly Turner at Okinawa in the latter part of that campaign, he assumed responsibility for more than one thousand U.S. combatant and merchant ships of all kinds in the Okinawa area. Even that many ships did not constitute the major portion of the amphibious warfare resources available in the Pacific at that time. In the Pacific command, there were then six active marine divisions, together with marine fighter and attack aviation. There were three amphibious force commands, about fifteen amphibious group staffs, and lesser staffs and commands too numerous to mention. The strength of the Amphibious Force Pacific then was larger than the total navy is today. The point to all this is that neither the navy nor Marine Corps was then resource-limited (although on occasion we thought so). There were all sorts of gunfire and air support resources available, and many specialized ships and units were oriented solely to the amphibious missions. Good use was made of all these resources, and our naval warfare publications were written with all this abundance in mind. Now we continue to talk about multidivision/wing team amphibious operations at a time when navy resources are not available to do the job. In short, we haven't changed our pattern to accommodate the shrinkage of the navy cloth. We need to stop deluding ourselves in this regard and develop procedures commensurate with our real capabilities.

Today, there are three active Marine Corps division/wing teams, two in the Pacific, one in the Atlantic, and a fourth team in the reserve component. The navy has more than sixty amphibious warfare ships, split approximately evenly between the Atlantic and Pacific fleets. Each fleet keeps an amphibious ready group continually deployed; this is the "presence" unit of task one. The total capacity of all our amphibious warfare ships could embark the assault elements of about one and one-third marine division/wing teams. However, given ship overhauls and other considerations, the maximum Marine Corps unit which can be lifted in amphibious warfare shipping in either ocean without stripping the other ocean approximates the assault elements of one-half a division/wing team. This is an acceptable level for the first three amphibious tasks and perhaps for the assault elements required in the fourth task. The fifth task, however, will require more muscle. If amphibious lift is concentrated in one ocean, and if ships in overhaul or repair are buttoned up and used as practicable, something slightly in excess of the assault elements of one division/wing team can be lifted—a force that can make a very important impact even in a conflict situation involving major powers. However, the time to accomplish the assembly of forces and loading of ships would be measured in weeks, not days. Also, no provision is made for the other two active, highly trained, and ready division/wing teams. Because of existing and projected navy force levels, there is no possibility that the navy will or should support any significant increase in dedicated amphibious lift capability. Therefore, both to enhance more timely large-scale amphibious response and to permit effective early amphibious employment of something beyond one-third of the Marine Corps active force, merchant marine resources must be exploited. Containerships are being examined for this purpose and show promise. The idea of using merchant ships to supplement amphibious shipping is not new. For many years

the nonassault elements of the division/wing team have been planned for merchant lift. This has been practiced several times on a small scale— and on a relatively large scale on at least one occasion. Waterborne craft from amphibious warfare shipping were used for unloading. Containerization was not employed. What is new here is the idea of using merchant ships to lift a significant part of the assault elements of the landing force and to do so in containers. There are major operational problems associated with this approach which can be worked out only by testing. Three obvious ones:

- What equipment can be placed in containers without destroying the integrity of the landing plan?
- How can the containers be handled so as to make equipment available at the proper time and place?
- Recognizing that merchant ships have personnel accommodations for crew only, how are personnel associated with the containerized equipment to be provided for?

Also, it seems likely that some degree of container prepackaging will be necessary. If so, duplicate equipment will have to be procured for use in training. There is ample precedent for this in the case of army and air force elements earmarked for NATO, and the cost should be modest.

Elsewhere in the resource problem area is the matter of gunfire and air support. These resources are not available in the quantities that have been considered essential in the past. There are now no major-caliber guns in the active fleet, except for one lightweight 8-inch gun under evaluation in the USS *Hull* (DD-945). A number of these guns are planned for installation in the fleet after evaluation is completed, mostly in *Spruance* (DD-963)-class destroyers. The navy is also proceeding with a 5-inch and 8-inch guided-projectile program. Our best gunfire ships now come with only one or two guns, and many ships coming into the fleet have gun installations which cannot contribute effectively to amphibious gunfire support. Our aircraft assets have also been greatly reduced. It is obvious that alternatives to massive air and gunfire support must be developed around the improved conventional weapons which will be coming into our inventory. Also, the entire subject of preliminary air and naval gunfire preparation of the amphibious objective area needs to be reexamined in the context of tactical surprise considerations, which are discussed under the succeeding section.

Assault Procedures

For the purposes of this article, assault procedures encompass both those for preparation of the objective area and the ones spelled out in the ship-to-shore movement plan. This is the plan which takes the marines from the amphibious warfare ships in which they are embarked and delivers them to the spot desired by the landing force commander at the time he desires. The plan provides for both the heliborne troop elements which assault objectives behind the beach and the waterborne elements which assault beach objectives. The problem here is that the over-the-horizon capability of the heliborne forces—and their transit speed of more than 100 knots—is in no way matched by that of the waterborne elements. The waterborne landing force elements are led by amphibious tractors which have a water speed slightly greater than a tortoise going downhill and are not compatible with extended waterborne troop occupancy. This means that the ships carrying the tractors and their troops have to get close inshore to launch them. This is not a comforting thing to do if you have the prospect of heavy warhead missiles coming your way from the land. A true over-the-horizon launch capability for all elements of the assault force is badly needed, both to ease the problem of force defense against land-based weapons and to enhance the possibility of tactical surprise. This need has long been recognized and is being addressed. The navy has under development an amphibious assault landing craft (AALC)—a high-speed air-cushion vehicle capable of across-the-beach movement—and a waterborne landing craft with improved propulsion and speeds in the 25-knot range. The Marine Corps is working on a new amphib-

ious personnel carrier which it hopes will be capable of water speed significantly greater than 25 knots and can be launched much farther offshore than is now the case. The AALC is farther along in development than the other programs, but no procurement has yet been authorized.

There are many unresolved problems in regard to over-the-horizon launch other than the current lack of high-speed craft. Included are the location of our own ships and their objectives (that is, how do helicopters and landing craft launched from over the horizon get guidance to their landing area?). And, although not limited to over-the-horizon launch, how do you do the job without setting yourself up as a target for an antiradiation missile? There obviously are others, not the least of which are peacetime safety limitations on extended-range, fully-loaded, overwater helicopter flights without extensive search-and-rescue provisions. The navigational problems have been with us for years; technology is at hand to solve them and at reasonably low cost. Funding should be provided to get this job done.

A true over-the-horizon capability should permit tactical surprise as to the point of attack, but it would impose serious limitations on preliminary preparation of the objective area if that tactical surprise is to be exploited. This factor, taken in conjunction with the reduced air and naval gunfire assets cited earlier, leads to a dilemma. How can preparatory measures be compressed without jeopardizing the success of the operation? An optimum solution is to avoid enemy defenses altogether in selecting objectives, and certainly this will be attempted in over-the-horizon assaults. However, defense systems are increasingly mobile, and it would be unwise to assume a totally undefended objective. This leads to the conclusion that an intense but short prelanding preparation is needed, which leads to the further conclusion that high-shock conventional weapons should be applied to the objective area immediately prior to landing. We read of high-shock munitions being used against terrorists. Perhaps a much expanded version should be developed for amphibious applications.

Amphibious operations are notable for the number of radio frequencies employed and the nearly continuous nature of their employment. Since the amphibious operation is the most complex of all military operations, this is understandable. However, in the missile age, radiation is a target. There remains a requirement for the commander to be informed and to be able to command. If possible, it would be highly desirable to manage these requirements by means not associated with radiating ship systems. There have been tests of silent landings, but these have always been on a small scale. The problem needs further exploration.

Dedication

The Marine Corps exists to conduct amphibious operations—and other important but somewhat incidental operations. The navy exists to fight wars at sea—and other important but somewhat incidental operations. The Marine Corps, nearly two hundred thousand strong, is dedicated to amphibious warfare. The navy has no such dedication, at least in peacetime. The relatively modern amphibious warfare ships we now have are more an inheritance from the Robert S. McNamara regime as secretary of defense than the result of navy initiatives. The amphibious force command has ceased to exist at the fleet level, and the amphibious warfare organization in the office of the CNO is made up of four officers, buried within a subordinate office to the deputy CNO (Surface Warfare). Numerous excursions have been attempted over the years to establish an amphibious warfare flag billet in the office of the CNO; all have failed. The marines have had to pick up the ball on amphibious warfare, and they have done it well. However, the situation does little to encourage a naval officer to seek assignments in amphibious warfare. This is too bad, for the planning and operational challenges associated with assignment as an amphibious squadron commander are unmatched in the 1110 surface warfare community and thus constitute superb training for the flag responsibilities. Until and unless the 1110 community brings amphibious commanders into the top surface warfare command level, a bias against amphibious assignments by top performing captains will persist.

The Navy V/STOL Initiative

The reader may wonder how this subject becomes an amphibious warfare problem area. It is a potential future problem, tied to resource limitations. The amphibious assault ship (LPH) and the amphibious assault ship (general purpose) (LHA), have large flight decks and excellent aviation support facilities; the amphibious transport dock (LPD) has lesser but still significant capabilities. All will be experienced in V/STOL operations with the marine Harrier aircraft by the time navy V/STOL is off the drawing board. There will be a great incentive for the Navy to use these tested ships for navy V/STOL operations, with a consequent reduction in amphibious lift availability, and this will particularly be the case if the small carrier now planned is not available. There is also the likelihood that air-capable amphibious warfare ships would be used in a sea control role in early stages of a major conflict, and there is certainly nothing wrong with this concept. However, it would be well for the navy and Marine Corps to sit down before the event to work out jointly agreed policies and procedures within the navy family.

From the foregoing, there are no insuperable problems in carrying out the first three of the stated future amphibious tasks. The first two have demonstrated continuing utility over the years, and there is no evidence of reduction in importance. The last two require correction of some problem areas which will also make the first three tasks easier. There will be those who hold that the last two tasks are not realistic, that we will never become involved in "another Vietnam," and that a major war would end so quickly that amphibious capability would not be relevant. I do not agree that the future is subject to such precise definition. I participated in a meeting in Los Alamos shortly after the Soviets detonated their first nuclear weapon. Many of our most prominent nuclear physicists were there, and all were of the opinion that future amphibious operations would not be possible. Two weeks later came the Inchon operation. Many others followed in Vietnam. Even the best crystal ball becomes clouded when we look down the road to the next century. However, I remain convinced that an amphibious capability will be viable in the future and that it will continue to make a significant contribution to our security.

A New Look at an Old Mission

BY COLONEL J. J. GRACE, USMC (RET.)

The words *amphibious assault* conjure up an image of transports anchored a few miles offshore, disembarking their troops into landing craft and amphibian vehicles. These small craft form then into a series of assault waves and head toward a beach similar to that at Iwo Jima. At the water's edge the troops leave the craft and hurl themselves at an entrenched enemy who pours direct fire on the assault waves from positions seemingly impervious to the invaders' supporting arms.

Is there any connection between this notion of a bloody assault against a defended beach and the picture of an XM–1 tank easing down the bow ramp of a C–5A transport aircraft? Does the idea of a fuel truck being driven off a roll-on, roll-off merchant ship moored to a pier have anything to do with the scene of a cluttered beach in Normandy on 7 June 1944? Recent events near the Persian Gulf impel us to consider such questions, for they have made us vitally concerned with the ways by which we can project U.S. combat power overseas.

In last year's *Naval Review*, Bing West explained the Carter administration's Rapid Deployment Force (RDF) as follows: "this concept neither requires nor provides an assault capability on the part of our amphibious forces. Maritime prepositioning can be staged in commercial ships . . . for administrative landings at perhaps one-half the cost

U.S. Naval Institute *Proceedings*, "Land the Landing Force Where It Will Do the Most Good," 107 (May 1981): 114–31. Reprinted by permission.

of building assault ships of equal lift. . . . Assault shipping is intended for the recapture of territory or the outflanking of an enemy after war has begun. Maritime prepositioning is intended to prevent the loss of the territory and to deter the aggression in the first place. If forced by budgets to choose, maritime prepositioning should be developed, even at the expense of assault shipping."

In the same issue Bill Krulak argued that, rather than accepting the amphibious mission as its sole reason for existence, the Marine Corps should shift its focus to the RDF mission as a broader and more supportable basis for its institutional identity in the future. Both of these essays illustrate the long-standing expectation of many civilian commentators and managers within the Department of Defense (DoD) that the forces of the marketplace influence decisions on the efficient allocation of resources.

Amphibious warfare, which is on the margin between naval and land warfare, has almost always suffered from a lack of interest in both the army and the navy. And certainly the Air Force gives it little thought. One result of this neglect by the major services is that civilian policy makers who, at best, have a confused and incomplete picture of amphibious warfare, are inclined to dismiss the subject as an anachronism that survives only because it is the sole raison d'être of the Marine Corps, itself an organizational anomaly.

Conventional Wisdom

The Department of Defense has long assumed that the most demanding military task faced by the United States is the defense of Western Europe against an onslaught by Warsaw Pact forces. The principal role of naval forces in this scenario is the defense of shipping crossing the North Atlantic. These ships must sail safely, so the logic goes, in order for reinforcements to reach the land and air forces on the Continent if a conflict lasts longer than a few weeks without escalating to a general nuclear war. The scenario is reminiscent of the European campaign in 1944–45 except for the absence of any large-scale amphibious operations or, for that matter, major counteroffensives of any kind. But then, before Dunkirk, military planners in Europe anticipated no need for amphibious operations or, on the part of the Allies, for major offensive campaigns either.

As we know it, amphibious warfare was conceived and developed in response to the anticipated needs of our naval forces in a conflict with Japan across the Pacific. Given the location of areas of vital interest to the United States (the Philippines and the East Indies), and the capabilities of the ships and aircraft of the period, the success of a naval campaign (which in turn was a necessary precondition for any subsequent land or air campaigns) depended on the possession of advance bases. If such bases were held by the enemy, they had to be seized. If they did not exist, they had to be built. These geographic and operational aspects of the Pacific campaign had a significant effect on the tactics and logistics of amphibious warfare.

The ports and airfields needed to support the offensive across thousands of miles of open ocean were located on various small islands. Though the islands could be isolated from enemy reinforcements by naval operations, they offered few places for getting a landing force ashore. Once ashore the landing force had even fewer opportunities for maneuver. The rough, restricted terrain inland provided good defensive positions which the enemy fortified heavily. The inevitable tactical response to these conditions was a frontal assault by marine and army infantry.

Not only were the ports and airfields throughout the Pacific few in number but they were also underdeveloped for their intended use. This led to the creation within the fleet of an ability to construct expeditionary base facilities rapidly. The Seabees who did this became famous for their ability to improve airfields and clear ports while the fighting still raged ashore. And they built new facilities where before nothing had existed but palm trees and coral.

The combination of these advance naval bases and the fleet's mobile service forces provided the sustained support the carrier and amphibious striking forces needed to maintain their momentum from one island chain to the next. It was this expeditionary logistic capability, expanded to support land and air as well as naval forces, that played such a key role across the various European and Pacific beaches, in the strategic bombing campaign against Japan, and in the last battle for Okinawa.

Following the war, the Department of Defense was created, and in that department the experiences of all the armed forces were institutionalized. The new department specified the function of each of the uniformed services and delineated the relationships between them in what was to be the ideal "joint" environment. The navy and Marine Corps were chartered to provide forces to: "seek out and destroy enemy naval forces . . . suppress [the enemy's] commerce . . . gain and maintain . . . naval supremacy . . . control vital sea areas . . . protect . . . sea lines of communications . . . seize and defend advanced naval bases, and . . . conduct such land and air operations as may be essential to . . . a naval campaign." In addition, the Marine Corps was assigned "primary interest in the development of those landing force doctrines, tactics, and equipment . . . of common interest to the Army and the Marine Corps."

The *Dictionary of Military Terms* of the Joint Chiefs of Staff defines an amphibious operation as "an attack launched from the sea by naval and landing forces, embarked in ships or craft, involving a landing on a hostile shore." Joint doctrine on the subject tells us that "the salient requirement of the amphibious operation is the necessity of building up combat power ashore from an initial zero capability to full coordinated striking power as the attack drives toward the final objectives." These official statements invoke images of World War Two. But except for those few still in service who had first-hand experience in such operations thirty or more years ago (Inchon in 1950 was the last of this genre), officers can find these images now only in history books or old movies.

Many things have changed since Normandy and Okinawa. Because of nuclear weapons, tacticians of all kinds have had to find ways to reduce the vulnerability of military units while still retaining their capability to concentrate rapidly at a critical time and place. The solution seems to be to disperse the elements of a force while providing them with the tactical mobility they need to achieve combat power superior to the enemy's at the point of decision. Mechanized and air-mobile (helicopter) formations have much more of this capability than did the formations of World War Two. In Vietnam air-mobile tactics worked well against a guerrilla foe. But new weapons raise questions about the future viability of both helicopterborne and mechanized maneuver elements. Meantime, technology, as always, affects logistics as much as it does tactics.

With greater firepower, improved tactical mobility, and better command and control than any of their predecessors, today's ground and air forces also need much more logistic support in the form of supplies, maintenance, and transportation than their predecessors did. But then modern technology has improved the services' ability to provide themselves with this support. Most important, the ships and aircraft available to transport today's forces and the supplies they require are much bigger and faster than those of World War Two. Moreover, a revolutionary commercial development—containerized cargo handling—has greatly speeded the loading and unloading of ships and airplanes. Unfortunately, we have not yet been able to exploit this speed-up when we operate in an expeditionary environment. Once we do get

the material ashore, modern technology can aid in the rapid construction of facilities needed for personnel support and equipment maintenance. In order to realize the full potential of all these improvements, we must recognize logistic support for what it is—a necessary and integral part of any force's operational capability.

Table 1 lists the highlights of these trends in terms of both capability and share of available naval resources allocated. The ups and downs over the period reflect the changing priorities that have been assigned by strategists and programmers.

The Current Situation

Within the past year or two this country has been attempting to adjust to a new strategic situation. In the Indian Ocean and Persian Gulf, far from our shores or the borders of any of our traditional allies, some of the United States's vital interests are threatened. In the great distances between key locations, the need for advance bases, and the austere condition of most of the few manmade facilities that exist in the region, the Indian Ocean and Persian Gulf resemble World War Two's Pacific theater. But here, instead of being on a series of archipelagoes, all the potential tactical objectives of an amphibious force are on or near the coast of a continental landmass. Another important difference here is that inland the terrain generally is open. These facts affect both tactics and logistics.

The biggest problems arising from this situation are the strategic imponderables. Even if solutions can be found to the problems of deploying and supporting a sizable force in a hostile environment half a world away, what will be the military objectives of such a force? Will the strategy be purely defensive or will offensive operations be required to safeguard the nation's interests? Finally, these questions, and many others, must be answered under the shadow of the Soviet threat to the oil fields from the north.

Clearly, the strategic mobility planning and the means of implementation that may be appropriate in Europe are not suitable for the Persian Gulf. A strategic mobility planner

Table 1. Evolution Of U.S. Navy Amphibious Forces, 1940–80

Date	Active Ships	(% Fleet)	Ship Types	Lift (MAF Assault Echelon)	Resources	Remarks
1940	20	—	AP, AK, & APD	<1	Minimal	Ships were converted passenger liners, freighters, and destroyers
1945	1728	(.40)	APA, AKA, & LST	11	Mostly operations and maintenance dollars for active ships	Reliance on WWII residual ships activated from "mothball" fleet for Korea
1950	91	(.15)	APA, AKA, & LST	<1		
1955	242	(.21)	LSD–28 & LPH introduced	2		
1960	113	(.14)		1.75	$1.0B	FY 1961 budget request
1965	135	(.15)	LPD & 20 Knot LST added	2.0 (program objective)	$2.2B (26% of SCN)	Part of OSD's strategic mobility enhancement program
1969	162	(.17)		1.67 (p.o.)	$1.5B	Start of post-Vietnam "wind-down"
1970	118	(.14)		1.33 (p.o.)	$1.4B	LHAs cut from 9 to 5; high ship costs cited
1976	62	(.13)	First LHA added. Entire force 20 Knot	1.33 (p.o.)	$1.25B	
1979	65	(.14)		1.15 (p.o.)	$ .85B	Lowest ebb since pre-Korea
1980	60	(.13)	Last LHA delivered. LSD–41 programmed	1.15 (p.o.)	$1.3B (8% of SCN)	Includes $200M for Maritime Prepositioning Ships (Carter budget)

Sources: the pre-World War Two status of amphibious forces was gleaned from Isely and Crowl, *U.S. Marines and Amphibious War* (Princeton, 1951). Numbers of active ships, fleet size, lift capacity (in terms of life for the assault echelon of a marine amphibious force, or MAF), and the approximate dates of introduction of new ship types are from Lieutenant Commander Carl Douglas, USN, "Amphibious Deficiencies—The Navy's Ostrich Act'," *Marine Corps Gazette*, September 1980. The figures were cross-checked with the *Naval Review* issues of 1975 and 1980. Program objectives for amphibious lift and the resources allocated to achieve them are from annual secretary of defense reports to Congress and other DOD documents. All dollar figures are expressed in FY 1981 dollars of total obligational authority. Percentages of the Ship Construction, Navy (SCN) appropriation allocated to new amphibious ship construction are shown for two selected years to give an indication of how this percentage has varied over the past fifteen years (it was 0 percent in some of the intervening years).

looking at Europe knows that significant U.S. and allied forces will already be in place on the continent at the outbreak of hostilities. The requirement is to strengthen these forces rapidly. This can be done best by prepositioning equipment and airlifting people. Hence, we have placed large quantities of equipment and supplies in friendly base areas. The troops to use that equipment would be ferried from the United States by administrative airlift. After collecting their equipment, they would move overland to forward defensive positions.

In a Persian Gulf crisis there may be no

friendly forces ashore near the scene of potential conflict. There is no assurance that the terminals where the troops can meet their equipment and supplies will be in friendly hands when they are needed. Therefore, we must be able to move to the region, establish the necessary base facilities (if necessary by seizing them), and then conduct whatever combat operations may be required. As to the likelihood that local allies will do some of our work for us, it is well to remember that if we have to resort to military operations it will be to secure access to oil, not to prop up some weak local government. It is evident that amphibious assault equipment and tactics based on experience nearly forty years ago in other parts of the world are inadequate for the situations likely to be encountered east of Suez in the 1980s.

Because we cannot anticipate where we may have to land, the navy and Marine Corps should concentrate on developing and maintaining the most flexible capability possible to project landing forces ashore. This requires first mental flexibility in order to free planners from answers which were good solutions to problems we no longer have. Second, it requires the exploration and exploitation of new technology such as vertical/short take-off and load (V/STOL) aircraft, air-cushion landing craft, precision-guided weapons, and the whole range of equipment and tactics of electronic warfare as they might affect amphibious operations. Third, it requires adherence to the traditional bent of the naval service to "go in harm's way," in a thoughtful and innovative manner designed to make an opponent react to our actions rather than always having to react to its.

If the United States goes to Europe, it will most likely be going to the aid of reliable allies (or else why go?). There the tactical capability to force our way ashore probably will be less important than the expeditionary logistic capability to land without dependence on ports or airfields and to project ashore a tactically integrated, self-contained, air-ground force. For instance, the ability to support operations in extreme cold, as in Nor-

way, is more a logistical than a tactical problem.

Landings in the Caribbean or on the shores of the South China Sea will most likely face lower levels of opposition than we might expect in Europe. If we develop them properly, the mobility of amphibious and landing forces can be exploited in such circumstances to land at places and times most favorable to our side. As we have already seen in two wars over the past thirty years, helicopters (and potentially VSTOL aircraft) provide better tactical mobility ashore in such rough terrain as Korea's or the jungles of Southeast Asia than do ground vehicles. But in open terrain such as that in the Middle East, in Southwest Asia, and in Central Europe, it is probable that more mechanization will be needed than the marines have. At least, the experiences of the 1973 Arab-Israeli war point in that direction.

Because resources will always be limited, it is wrong to prepare solely for the "classical" amphibious assault landing when more often what will be needed is a landing across an uncontested beach or even through a friendly harbor. Indeed, sometimes the task will be not the landing of major combat elements but the evacuation of civilians in danger.

The establishment of a logical frame of reference for the examination of alternatives is the most important part of any review of strategy and forces. We need such a framework if we are to get even approximately right answers to such emotionally charged questions as:

- What is the proper relationship between airlift and sealift in the projection of conventional forces overseas?

- How do the Military Airlift Command (MAC) and the amphibious forces of the Atlantic and Pacific fleets complement each other in crisis management or combat operations?

- How do we relate the tactics and logistics of amphibious operations to the requirements of the land and air campaigns which may begin with them?

A New Look

Rear Admiral Henry Eccles has defined strategy as "the comprehensive direction of power to control situations and areas in order to attain objectives." Nowadays the overriding objective of military strategy is to deter potential enemies from taking actions harmful to one's own country and its interests. If deterrence fails, our leaders have said the United States will protect its interests, but at the lowest level and most restricted scope of violence possible. If we expect to be able both to limit the use of force and protect our interests we cannot always react defensively to an opponent's gambit. We must have an offensive capability at our disposal with which we can take the initiative in any part of the world where U.S. interests are threatened.

Consider the following hypothetical alternative to the scenario that unfolded recently. When the U.S. embassy in Tehran was overrun in February 1979, nine months before the hostages were seized, a combined diplomatic and military contingency plan could have been developed. Because Tehran is 345 nautical miles from the head of the Persian Gulf, an emergency evacuation like those conducted in Cambodia and Vietnam in 1975 would not have been feasible with the helicopters we have. So, let us imagine that arrangements were made to relocate the embassy staff to the U.S. consulate in Khorramshahr and that in the meantime an amphibious task group (ATG) was sailed to reinforce the navy's small Middle East Force.

All vital U.S. interests in Iran would have been consolidated in the southwestern corner of the country. Diplomatic relations could have been maintained with Iran as long as this was in our best interest but U.S. citizens would have been only 55 nautical miles from protection. While the ATG would be close to the scene, the aircraft carrier battle groups could be outside the Strait of Hormuz. This is more than 500 nautical miles away from Khorramshahr, no small distance, but under conceivable circumstances it would still have been possible to provide some air cover, if that were needed. In any event, this combination of amphibious force and carrier battle

group would have been more responsive than transport aircraft flying from sensitive foreign bases over a thousand miles away. The critical command and control link between Washington and officials on the scene would have been provided by secure communications facilities at the consulate or aboard the flagship of commander Middle East Force offshore. When it became obvious that the new government of Iran was unable or unwilling to protect American citizens the evacuation plan would have been implemented. Such "Monday morning quarterbacking" is intended only as an illustration of how a combination of initiative with a good set of operational capabilities can be useful in a crisis.

One needn't confine one's thoughts on this subject to small-unit deployments. As a crisis develops and the authorities in Washington deliberate, consult, and negotiate, as much amphibious shipping as necessary can be sailed to build up combat power offshore without automatically committing the United States to a conflict. That this can be done was demonstrated during the Cuban Missile Crisis in 1962, when a full marine division-wing team was embarked at ports on the East and West coasts, sailed to the waters off Cuba, maintained there for a month, and without ever being committed ashore, returned to its various ports of embarkation.

If Washington decides to land the landing force, the time and place can be chosen to exploit weaknesses in the enemy's dispositions and avoid his strong points. There are more than a thousand miles of continental coastline around the Persian Gulf alone, and most of them are usable by modern landing craft (helicopters and aircushion vehicles). But to realize the full potential of the mobility of an amphibious task force, the embarked landing force must have adequate tactical mobility once ashore and the whole force must have enough logistic support so that for a fairly long period it can be independent of established ports and airfields. (Keep in mind that the port of Cherbourg was not available to support the Allied landing forces until almost three months after D-day in

Normandy; until then the invading armies were supplied over the beach.) More will be said of these interrelated capabilities later.

Finally, amphibious forces of the fleet complement the much-publicized RDF in ways that can make the latter a force of real utility. If necessary, the airfields and ports needed to unload MAC transports and maritime prepositioning ships can be seized by amphibious operations. The landing force put ashore can secure the marshaling areas, which must be large enough for the tens of thousands of air-transported troops to find and make ready their heavy equipment and supplies and to reorganize themselves into tactical formations. And the amphibious force's ships, craft, and helicopters can help in the subsequent local transportation of units from wherever they join their equipment to wherever they are needed tactically. It is evident that the sea, air, and land forces of a balanced fleet with its own integrated command and control system meet the necessary—and may satisfy the sufficient—conditions needed to control a particular crisis. There is a good chance no additional force need be applied. If more force is needed, elements of the RDF deploying safely into the permissive environment created by landing forces already on the scene can reinforce the latter.

As much sense as this view of amphibious operations makes, and after nearly forty years of repeated demonstrations of their utility, amphibious forces still have difficulty getting 10 to 15 percent of the resources allocated to similar forces by the Defense Department. Only an institutional change can improve this situation. The solution can be found in the arrangements enjoyed by airlift within DoD, which have yielded great success in the continuing competition for resources. The commander of the Military Sealift Command (MSC) should be elevated to the status of a specified commander, coequal with commander-in-chief, Military Airlift Command (CinCMAC). With the rank and staff appropriate to the new status, that person would also be given the responsibility for planning and controlling the employment of all of our national sealift assets—

not only the U.S. naval ships currently operated by MSC, and chartered U.S.-flag merchantmen, but also all amphibious shipping. That officer would become the focal point of matters relating to the support and continued development of this national capability. What is good for one of our two means of projecting forces overseas should be good for the other.

The commander-in-chief, Military Sealift Command (CinCMSC) would still report to the chief of naval operations and the secretary of the navy, just as his counterpart, CinCMAC, answers to his service chief and department head. Active amphibious ships would continue to be assigned to the operational control of the Atlantic and Pacific fleets. Existing relations between the navy and Marine Corps within the Navy Department would not change. What would change would be the visibility of, and therefore the attention given to, this critical element of our strategic mobility. Effective, efficient solutions to a wide range of sealift problems could be pursued in a coordinated way without doing excessive violence to the amphibious warfare doctrine developed in World War Two. (To bring it up to date the old doctrine needs to suffer some violence. As long as we develop new ways and means of carrying out likely future amphibious missions, the violence will not be "excessive.") But most important, decision makers at the highest levels of government would have the benefit of a comprehensive and balanced exposition of the ways and means of projecting U.S. power overseas in support of national strategic objectives.

Results of New Look

Let us examine the ability of our amphibious forces to maintain a military presence where we have no troops ashore. Before the Vietnam War there were four amphibious task units deployed forward continuously—one in the Mediterranean, two in the Western Pacific, and one in the Caribbean. Because of our declining amphibious strength, the Caribbean deployment long ago became an "occasional" rather than a continuously maintained station. The current Arabian Sea deployment is carried out on a port-and-starboard basis, alternating the Mediterranean amphibious task unit (ATU) with the one in the Western Pacific that has the ability to conduct a vertical envelopment.

Considering both the uncertain future and our many years of successful crisis management (such as the landing in Lebanon in 1958, the Cuban Missile Crisis in 1962, and the recapture of the *Mayaguez* in 1975), it appears as if four forward-deployed amphibious task units is a prudent compromise between assuming the role of world policeman and abandoning the government's responsibility to protect its citizens overseas. The most likely missions of these units are to show the flag, to assist in the management of crises, and to evacuate U.S. nationals in emergencies. Their task organization should reflect the operational requirements of these missions. The ships should be reasonably habitable and should have good sea-keeping characteristics, for they will make long deployments. They should have secure communication links with headquarters around the world and adequate flag spaces so an embarked staff can work efficiently. And since the embarked landing force will depend primarily on helicopters or VSTOL aircraft for ship-to-shore movement in their most likely missions, these ships should be able to operate and support significant numbers of these types of aircraft.

To exploit the tactical mobility of the helicopter, the landing force units would necessarily be "light," just as they are now with, for mobility on the ground, a small number of helicopter-transportable vehicles, and, for fire support ashore, a few artillery pieces. If they are properly trained and equipped, such light, helicopterborne infantry units are most useful for limited-objective offensive and defensive missions such as the counterterrorist raids at Entebbe or Mogadiscio and the protection of embassies. In larger operations, such units are useful for deep reconnaissance and security missions. Currently, assuming the presence of the large CH-53D helicopter, which has a radius of 97 nautical miles, the

umbrella of protection offered by sea-based air-mobile units can be provided to about three quarters of the Americans living and working abroad. When the operating forces get aircraft like the VSTOL-A prototype, which has twice the speed of a CH-53D and a radius of 475 nautical miles, the umbrella can be extended to over 90 percent of the locations where American citizens can be found overseas.

The combined mission needs of the amphibious task unit and its embarked marine amphibious unit could be satisfied by a deployment unit, or DU, of two ships of modern design like the LHA and the LSD-41. Four such DUs of two ships each would add up to eight ships forward deployed at all times. This would provide better worldwide presence and responsiveness to crises than our current forward deployments of fourteen to sixteen ships out of a total force of about sixty-five amphibious ships (some of which are partly manned by naval reservists), and could be maintained by an amphibious force of thirty-two ships, or approximately one-half the size of our present force.

When the need arises to reinforce U.S. presence near the scene of a crisis, the surge capability of the amphibious force becomes important. The much smaller active force described above still has a significant surge capability provided it is composed of ships of modern design. Assuming that 15 percent of the force would be unavailable as a result of extended overhauls in progress, at least twenty ships would be immediately available to respond without drawing down on forward deployments outside the area of crisis. A force of this size could be assembled near a trouble spot in Southwest Asia within a few weeks and it could have embarked the combat power of a marine amphibious brigade, or MAB. The brigade could consist of as many as twenty thousand troops (a large number of whom would be aviation support specialists) and over three hundred aircraft. The aircraft complement could include both helicopters and tactical aircraft like the advanced Harrier, task organized for the mission at hand.

But even such a formidable force offshore could not be expected to "go it alone" if major combat operations were anticipated. First of all, any large-scale activities would most likely be joint-service affairs and the forces involved would have to be assured of adequate operating and support bases. Facilities at Diego Garcia would be used to the utmost but they are not all that large and they are more than 2,000 nautical miles from the Strait of Hormuz. Ports and airfields such as at Muscat, Oman (755 nautical miles to Khorramshahr, 200 to Bandar Abbas, by sea); Masirah Island (450 miles to Bandar Abbas by air); Berbera, Somalia (1,520 miles to Bandar Abbas by sea); and Mombasa, Kenya (2,520 miles to Bandar Abbas by sea) might be available in an emergency. But we must have more than last-minute approval to use existing facilities if we are to provide a large joint force with adequate logistic support. The concurrent combat operations of one hundred or more naval combatants, half as many amphibious ships and auxiliaries, more than six hundred land- and sea-based tactical aircraft, and up to three divisions, or more than one hundred fifty thousand troops, ashore would require a major logistic support effort.

The navy and marines are working now to improve the logistic support of tactical units in an expeditionary environment. The program, labeled Amphibious Logistic Support Ashore (ALSA), is intended to use modern technology, such as containers and rigid shelters, to provide support to a landing force until more nearly permanent facilities can be developed. By expanding and adapting this program to meet additional mission needs, the requirement for advance bases in the early phases of any joint operation can also be satisfied. The success or failure of this effort could have more impact on the outcome of a campaign than the results of any single, dramatic engagement between opposing tactical units.

ALSA consists of two complementary systems. The navy's contribution is the amphibious logistic system (ALS). It consists of both equipment and techniques for unloading containerized cargo, vehicles, and bulk fuel from modern merchantmen in the absence of port facilities, in harbors if possible, off unprotected beaches if necessary. The equipment includes such new items as a crane able to reach up to 150 feet while lifting 35 tons. This can be mounted on the deck of one ship to unload a non-self-sustaining container ship (CONT/N) alongside. (It is useful to think of a fully loaded 20-foot container as weighing about 22 tons and a 40-foot container as weighing about 33½ tons.) Also under development are self-propelled and elevatable causeways, and rubber bladders that can store 135,000 gallons of fuel afloat or ashore. By integrating new and existing equipment, ALS is designed to move dry and liquid cargo from ships offshore to the beach, where the other part of the program, the Marine Corps's field logistic system takes over.

Using specialized materials-handling equipment, a family of commercially designed vehicles, and the pipelines of the existing amphibious assault fuel system, the field logistic system moves cargo inland, to where it is needed. A variety of container inserts have been designed for the packaging of supplies in boxes, some of which can be handled easily by two persons. In addition to the transportation of supplies, the field logistic system provides shelters of various sizes for the performance of necessary personnel-support and equipment-maintenance functions. They are all dimensionally standardized so that the components of the largest shelters can be transported within the space occupied by 20-foot or 40-foot commercial containers.

Currently ALSA is being developed to support a marine amphibious force. This force, numbering about fifty thousand, consists of a reinforced division, about one hundred twenty tactical aircraft, and combat service support for up to thirty days of independent operations. The daily resupply requirements amount to some 1,500 short tons of dry cargo and 15,000 barrels (about 2,000 short tons) of bulk POL. If fresh water is added to the resupply requirements, as it certainly would be in most of Southwest Asia, as much as 50 gallons per person per day would have to be drilled, distilled, or transported. That is 2.5 million gallons, or 10,000 tons, daily.

To put these numbers in perspective it is worth noting that a single containership of the SL-7 design carries about 1,000 containers, or 22,000 tons. A 40,000-ton tanker carries about 300,000 barrels of POL products. A single elevated causeway can transfer 200 containers (each with a payload of 20 tons, or 4,000 tons total) per day, and the amphibious logistic system can move 24,000 barrels of bulk fuel to consumers ashore each day. These figures demonstrate that when developed, ALSA will have significant growth potential to support much larger forces in an expeditionary environment. Once logistically supportable courses of action are ensured by the existence of suitable advance bases, operational planners can consider their tactical options.

Modern technology assures us that future amphibious operations against a continental landmass will be very different from those of World War Two, whether in Europe or elsewhere. Especially where there are large, open, and lightly held areas behind the coastline, maneuver promises to play a bigger part if tactics than it did in the frontal assaults and battles of attrition that characterized the landings at Tarawa, Peleliu, Salerno, and Anzio. Inside of twenty-four hours, an amphibious task force steaming parallel to a hostile shore can cover a distance equal to that from Boston to Washington, D.C. Theater and fleet cover and deception operations can confuse the enemy as to the exact location of a landing until after the buildup ashore is well under way. The initial elements, consisting of reconnaissance and "light infantry" units, can be disembarked from amphibious ships while the latter are still under way and over the horizon from the selected landing site. Helicopters, VSTOL aircraft, and aircushion landing craft (LCAC), can deliver these troops to unoccupied or lightly held terrain deep inland. Provided they have adequate tactical mobility once on the ground, these forces can carry out the tasks once performed by the cavalry, screening the main force, acting as a covering force for the

landing, conducting raids and ambushes to unbalance the enemy, and performing reconnaissance, surveillance, and target-acquisition missions for long-range air and missile systems.

Though we still have no VSTOL transports, we will get some if and when the navy's VSTOL-A program gets off the ground. As we have seen, VSTOL aircraft generally have much longer ranges and higher speeds than helicopters do, even while carrying the same payloads. A tilt-rotor prototype such as the XV-15 would carry the same load as the present CH-46 and occupy no more deck area aboard ship. Such a VSTOL transport would be more expensive than current helicopters are because it involves new technology, and it would take ten to fifteen years to get a significant operational capability in the fleet. But since our current helicopters are reaching the end of their useful lives, the question is whether we should invest in new technology or old for their replacements.

Though we now have only two experimental air cushion landing craft (JEFF-A and JEFF-B), the Soviets have over forty such craft, some of them quite a bit larger than those we are considering. Table 2 compares the notional 88-foot LCAC the marines are using with conventional landing craft.

The LCACs would be launched from amphibious ships steaming some twenty-five miles or more from the landing sites. After crossing the coastline they would proceed inland along previously reconnoitered routes

Table 2. Comparisons of Landing Craft

	LCM–6	LCM–8	LCU	LCAC
Length	56'	74'	135'	88'
Beam	14'	21'	29'	47'
"Spotting factor"	1.0	1.98	5.0	5.3
Speed	9 kts.	9–12 kts.	11 kts.	35–50 kts.
Cargo area	37'×11'	45'×15'	124'×16'	67'×27'
Cargo capacity	34 tons	65 tons	188 tons	60–75 tons
Medium tank capacity	0	1	3	1

to near their initial objectives. Then the tanks and other combat vehicles would be disembarked. Obviously, the most efficient ship-to-shore force would be some mix of air and surface craft with the high performance, high cost elements kept to the minimum required to support the scheme of maneuver ashore. The balance of the lighterage requirement could be met by more economical conventional landing craft and LASH or Seabee barges. The optimum mix, of course, would depend on the conditions and circumstances of each individual operation. Consequently, what the services must try for are generally efficient solutions that can serve effectively over a range of missions and situations, rather than optimum solutions for a small number of narrowly conceived events.

It is because of these improved ship-to-shore capabilities and better means of reconnaissance that the first-wave maneuver elements can seize critically important objectives virtually unopposed before the defenders start to react to the landing. Then, as the enemy's armored columns move toward the landing area, long-range weapon systems guided by small, mobile target acquisition teams on the ground can delay, disorganize, and weaken them. In the time gained by tactical surprise and the depth of the initial landings, and while the enemy prepares to mount his counterattack, heavier combat and support units can be put ashore by conventional landing craft and by the lighters serving self-sustaining commercial containerships (CONT/S). This two-sided buildup of combat power in the vicinity of the beachhead thus becomes a race between the opposing forces. The advantage will likely go to that force that has gained the initiative, that is, the landing force, provided it can maintain its momentum.

The elements needed to implement this tactical concept are already to be found in our land and tactical air forces. Helicopter-borne forces are best suited for the development and defense of strong points in open terrain because of their limited tactical mobility once they are on the ground. When the terrain is too rough for armored warfare air-mobile infantry units can be used as maneuver elements, provided they can maintain tactical mobility superior to the enemy's. An example of such employment might be the use of helicopter-borne ski troops in Norway.

But for offensive operations in Southwest Asia, a landing force needs to be able to form mechanized, combined-arms task forces. These units can be carried by air cushion landing craft across any flat stretch of coastline, and moved inland along such avenues as rivers and salt flats. Carrying a 60-ton tank at 50 knots, the current JEFF-B has an endurance of four hours in sea state 2. If the technology of light armored vehicles is combined with this revolutionary landing craft even greater tactical advantages can be realized.

The aviation combat element of the landing force must also be specially configured if it is to be fully "mission capable." It should be seen for what it is—the landward extension of naval aviation. At times it will be the only tactical aviation available to support ground units. At other times it may be needed to support the operations of other fleet units in adjacent seas. Because of these diverse mission requirements, landing force aviation should possess the full range of air support capabilities, from antiair warfare to close air support of ground units. It should also be able to operate from the decks of amphibious ships and from expeditionary bases ashore. To achieve this flexibility and minimize its dependence on established air bases, VSTOL technology should be pushed to the utmost in the reequipping and modernization of landing force aviation.

All these proposed changes in equipment and doctrine will ultimately result in changes in amphibious lift and ship-to-shore movement requirements. Table 3 summarizes what our active amphibious force, including immediately available merchant ships, might look like in the year 2001 if the ideas that have been discussed so far are acted upon. The LHDX designation (called the LXA in some studies) is used as an example of something on the drawing boards that could be modified to support the concepts developed. The RO/RO and containership designs re-

Table 3. Amphibious Force Capabilities By The Year 2001

Ship	Number	Troops	Vehicles	Cargo	POL	Helos	Landing Craft	Remarks
Forward Deployment Unit (DU)								
LHA/LHDX	1	1,800	25Kft²	120Kft³	2,200bbls	38	26	4 DUs on station continuously worldwide
LSD–36/41	1	400	12K	12K	800	3	12	
Total	2	2,200	37Kft²	132Kft³	3,000bbls	41	38	
Surge Capability								
LHA/LHDX	9	16,200	225Kft²	1080Kft³	19,800bbls	342	234	Capability to mass at a single crisis location without drawdown of three other forward deployments
LSD–36/41/ LST	11	4,400	145K	90K	50,200	18	76	
Total	20	20,600	370Kft²	1170Kft³	70,000bbls	360	310	
Total MAF Lift								Based on retire/ replace plan shown in Table 4.
LHA/LHDX	14	25,200	350Kft²	1680Kft³	30.8Kbbls	532	364	
LSD–36/41	11	4,400	132K	120K	8.8K	33	132	
LST	6	2,400	90K	24K	56.4K	6	—	
RO/RO	9	—	1575K	—	—	—	—	
CONT/N/S	9	28,000	—	3400K	—	—	100	7 CONT/N Configured as AP, 4000 PAX each; 2 CONT/S with 50 lighters each;
AO	4	—	—	—	1,200K	—	—	Not part of amphib. ship plan
Total	53	60,000	2.15Mft²	5.2Mft³	1.3Mbbls	571	596	
% MAF		1.2	1.4	1.7	2.2	1.6	1.7	
(1 MAF)		(50,000)	(1.5 Mft²)	(3.0 Mft³)	(600Kbbls)	(350 CH–46)	(350 LCM–6)	Current norm, may change with changes in weapons, equipment and tactics

NOTE: Ship characteristics shown in this table are approximations taken from a variety of unclassified sources. The MAF defined in terms of its lift "footprint" is a notional task organization such as that used at the Marine Corps Education Center. The values of its dimensions are also approximations.

The roll-on, roll-off ships, containerships, and tankers shown under "Total MAF Lift" could be manned by civilian contract crews under the Military Sealift Command, by full regular navy crews, or by nucleus regular navy crews who could be augmented rapidly by personnel from shore stations or by naval reservists. In any major contingency, whether the action takes place in the Persian Gulf, Europe, or anywhere else, additional ships, taken from commercial use, would be needed.

ferred to are current commercial capabilities. They could be "navalized" for a modest cost and could be converted to different uses by the application of new technology (for example, containerized shelter technology combined with a 28,800-ton, 33-knot SL-7 equals an AP with a capacity of four thousand passengers). Table 3 represents only one of several possible combinations. Evolution in landing force weapons and tactics might lead to different results. Change is necessary, desirable, and inevitable. Will it also be rational and orderly?

In an attempt to demonstrate that the changes proposed could be accomplished in an orderly and deliberately planned way over the next twenty years, I have developed the amphibious ship retirement and replacement plan shown in Table 4. This plan is based on the anticipated retirement of our current ships as each reaches the end of thirty years' service. Its objective is to maintain our ability to lift and project combat forces ashore, and to do it at a reasonable cost. If the Defense Department and the Congress are convinced that the nation needs the kind of capabilities discussed in this essay, the comparisons show this can be done.

Conclusions

In the four centuries since Drake attacked the Spanish base at Santo Domingo, amphibious warfare has been both the ultimate offensive application of sea power and a useful operational capability with which to support a strategically defensive campaign. Over the past four decades it is apparent that World War Two experience has strongly influenced our impressions on the subject.

My aim has been to suggest a different way of looking at the need for and the problems of getting a landing force ashore—a way that would make more sense to civilian policy makers than the current rationale used in amphibious force planning. That rationale, to be able to lift a full marine amphibious force for a classical assault, has resulted over the years in amphibious lift dropping from enough to lift 2 MAFs to barely enough to lift only the assault echelon of 1.15 MAF. In

this age of deterrence, the maintenance and continued development of the ability to take a variety of military initiatives against an opponent is the modern equivalent of that traditional principle of war, the offensive. This is a different principle than that upon which the RDF is based, and the tactical and logistical capabilities of airlifted and sealifted projection forces clearly reflect this difference in principle.

While the RDF depends upon speed of movement to reception facilities under friendly control, so as to respond rapidly to a friendly government's invitation to intervene, amphibious forces are trained, organized, and equipped to seize control of and hold reception areas or any other facilities that may be needed in an objective area. For their responsiveness, the latter depend on early deployment to, and the ability to loiter near, a trouble spot. It is obvious that these qualities are complementary. By airlifting troops, we can move a light airborne division with about five days of supplies from the United States to Southwest Asia and do it in two weeks. At the end of those two weeks, the first troops to arrive will have had to be resupplied twice with food and water. If heavier units and fuel, ammunition, and water for combat operations are required, they will probably have to be transported by ship. Moreover, after the troops have gotten themselves sorted out and reconfigured into tactical organizations, they may depend on ships or landing craft to get them to where they are really needed. A seaborne force with thirty days of sustaining supplies can move to the same area in twice the time. (See Table 5.) Both forces would need the support of advance bases and secure shipping routes if they had to engage in combat. Because they are complementary, both projection capabilities should receive balanced consideration by strategists and programmers.

In a big bureaucracy such as DOD, however, the competition for limited resources often muddies the waters of rational decision making. To ensure that the consideration is balanced, related and complementary mission capabilities need advocates of com-

Table 4. Amphibious Ship Retirement And Replacement Plan (1982–2001)

Type	Number	82	83	84	85	86	87	88	89	90	91	92	93	94	95	96	97	98	99	00	01
LSD–28	8			−1	−3	−2	−2														
LPH	7									−1	−1	−1		−1	−1			−1	−1		
LPD	15										−1	−1	−1	−2	−1	−2		−2	−2	−3	
LSD–36	5																		−1		−2
LST	20																	−1	−7	−6	
LHA	5																				
Total	60																				
LSD–41	(New)			+1		+1		+1		+1		+1		+1		+1		+1		+1	
LHDX	(Constr.)				+1		+1		+1		+1		+1		+1		+1		+1		+1
RO/RO				+1		+1		+1		+1		+1		+1		+1		+1		+1	
CONT/N/S				+1		+1		+1		+1		+1		+1		+1		+1		+1	
Net:																					
DU	12	12	13	13	14	14	15	15	15	14	14	14	14	13	14	14	14	14	14	13	14
Ships	60			62	60	61	60	63	64	67	67	68	67	69	67	68	67	70	66	59	49

Resource Summary (FY 1981 Dollars)

SCN (Inc. investment for LCAC & ALS) = $720M/YR.   (12% of the total SCN appropriation)
(45% Sealift TOA compared to 1962–1981 Avg. of investment-to-TOA of 48% Airlift, 36% Sealift)

Sealift (Amphibs. + Merships) TOA = $1.6B/YR   (40% of the Mobility Forces TOA compared to 20 Yr Avg. of 34%)

Projection Forces TOA Mobility Forces = $4.0B/YR   (Compared to 20 yr. Avg. of $4.1B, FY 1981 Program of $3.6B, FY81–85 Estimate of $4.25B/YR)

M   = Millions
B   = Billions
SCN = Ship Construction, Navy
LCAC = Loading craft, air cushion

ALS = Amphibious logistic system
TOA = Total obligational authority
Avg = Average

NOTE: The schedule of ship retirements is that published by Headquarters Marine Corps. The proposed new construction schedule is designed to maintain between twelve and sixteen deployment units, keep the total force at least at its current strength, and accomplish both objectives at the level of resource allocation shown in the resource summary. Unit costs used to arrive at these estimates are: LSD–41–$350M, LHDX–$700M, RO/RO and CONT/N/S–$185M each. In the years that an LHDX is procured, $20M is available for investment in LCAC and ALS components. The two years that show no ship acquisitions (1982 and 1983) are left blank to allow for startup time, but the resources they represent (about $1.5B in investment) can be applied to programs like LCAC and ALS that are ready for quantity production now. Perfectly level funding profiles neither could nor should be maintained over twenty years, and other management actions would be necessary before we could achieve a ratio of sealift investment to operating expenses of .45-to-.55, but this is not a detailed procurement program ready for implementation. It is intended to stimulate informed discussion.

Neither LCCs nor LKAs are shown on this table.

The LCCs are already being used as fleet flagships. If we mount a major amphibious operation in either ocean area, at least one of these ships would probably be on the scene anyway. For lesser operations, the C³I requirements can probably be met by building equipment into the ships used for the regular sustained deployments. The same capabilities needed for crisis management can be designed to support amphibious operations.

Even now the LKAs, all of which are partly manned by reservists, are unavailable to us on short notice. Since essentially they are break-bulk cargo ships, they are less critical to the total amphibious capability than ships with a large vehicle square or aviation capacity. So long as the ALSA capability is developed, by the year 2001 the cargo requirements can be satisfied by containerships.

The numbers in the horizontal line, DU, show how many such deployment units we would have in each year of the transition period. The current number, twelve, is based on possession of seven LPH and five LHA, allowing one aviation-capable ship for each DU. There are enough other ships to satisfy the LSD requirement, which is also for one such ship in each DU. Over the years we never quite reach the number sixteen needed to support four DUs on station at the 4:1 ratio. We also never quite get down to the thirty-two-ship level (sixteen LHDX and sixteen LSD–41) because by 2001 we will still have two LSD–36 class and six LSTs in the force. The eighteen merchant ships (RO/RO and containerships) are intended to make up the balance of the sealift force in a more economical way than trying to replace our current amphibious ships, when they wear out, on a one-for-one basis.

Table 5. Using the Suez Canal

From	Closure Time in Days	Cumulative Force (DWT)
Mid-Mediterranean (1/9)	10	1/9
Okinawa (2/9)	18	3/9
Norfolk (3/9)	24	6/9
San Diego (3/9)	31	9/9
Not Using the Suez Canal		
Okinawa (2/9)	18	2/9
Mid-Mediterranean (1/9)	26	3/9
San Diego (3/9)	31	6/9
Norfolk (3/9)	32	9/9

NOTE: If we assume it takes four days to embark a MAB-size force at Norfolk, San Diego, or Okinawa, and if we assume an 18-knot speed of advance, a division-wing team can be placed at Al Basrah, Iraq, at the head of the Persian Gulf in thirty-one days using the Suez Canal. Without the use of the canal, the task would take thirty-two days.

parable stature and "clout" within the bureaucracy. This is why the commander, Military Sealift Command, should be a specified commander coequal with CinCMAC. He would act as the advocate of all our national sealift programs—amphibious, USNS, and privately owned U.S.-flag merchant shipping.

The mission is a naval mission—both traditional and newly urgent. If we let it slide, in twenty years our capability will dwindle to less than half of what it now is. But if we act with intelligence and vigor, we can have a powerful, versatile, and mobile force, all at a price far less than we will have to pay if we try to get by in some other way. The naval service owes it to the maritime nation it serves.

Amphibious Warfare: What Sort of Future?

BY COLONEL JOSEPH H. ALEXANDER, USMC

Amphibious operations are inherently risky. In particular, the waterborne ship-to-shore assault contains the greatest potential for disaster. This is well known. What is not as well known is the fact that the greatest risk may not be the initial unfavorable ratio of combat power between attacker and defender but instead our peacetime tendency to allow operational modernization to fall behind technological development. The amphibious assault, long stunted by the vulnerability of its surface component, is soon to receive a dramatic new capability with the advent of the landing craft aircushion (LCAC). Yet, without operational innovations at several levels, we may find ourselves increasingly vulnerable in amphibious warfare.

The basic ingredients of amphibious operations have changed little since World War Two. The major revolutionary input has been the helicopter, which greatly enhanced the range, flexibility, and nature of an assault from the sea. The amphibious task force commander thus has the option of conducting an assault by heliborne forces, by waterborne forces, or by a combination of the two. While the helicopters themselves are vulnerable to enemy fire, their speed and maneuverability can generally offset this threat.

It has been common practice in recent years for the landing force commander to use helicopters for two-thirds of his assault elements and surface craft for the remaining one-third. This practice, however, does involve a sec-

U.S. Naval Institute *Proceedings* 108 (February 1982): 62–68. Reprinted by permission.

ondary vulnerability. The limited lift capability of helicopters means that the heliborne forces are truly light infantry, lacking a great deal of combat punch against mechanized or fortified opponents. And while solutions to this problem are at hand—the new CH-53E helicopter, the M198 howitzer, and the forthcoming light assault vehicle (LAV)—there may be a "Catch-22" involved. With so much helicopter capacity now dedicated to external lift of assault vehicles, howitzers, and prime movers, the space available for troops will probably diminish. Similarly, the greater size of the CH-53E will reduce the number of smaller, troop-carrying CH-46s which the amphibious task force can accommodate. Helicopter operating spots on the decks of amphibious warfare ships will become a premium. The result will be greater reliance on the surface ship-to-shore movement to project the infantry ashore.

The surface assault is comprised of Marine Corps assault amphibious vehicles (commonly called LVTs) and navy landing craft and control boats. Tactics vary widely, but the typical surface ship-to-shore movement features several waves of LVTs containing infantry and light vehicles, closely followed by waves of landing craft (usually LCUs and LCMs) containing tanks and artillery. LVTs are lightly armored, provide a degree of protection to embarked troops, and are capable of crossing the beach to become, in effect, armored personnel carriers ashore. Landing craft are not amphibious (they cannot proceed past the water's edge) and provide little protection to embarked troops. Their lift ca-

Amphibious exercises, *ca.* 1970s.

pacity is a significant factor, however, and they provide the primary means of getting armor ashore during the assault phase. The current LCU, for example, can transport three M-60 main battle tanks from an underway amphibious warfare ship to the beach in a variety of sea and weather conditions. *Newport* (LST-1179)-class tank landing ships also have the capacity to deliver armored vehicles to the beach via bow ramp and causeway, but this is usually performed later on D-day, well after the assault.

Vulnerability in the surface ship-to-shore assault is currently a function of range and speed of the components, primarily the LVT. Naval landing craft can go farther at a somewhat faster speed, but they lack the capacity to fight their way ashore and are sometimes limited by hydrographic conditions offshore, such as those along the North Sea littoral.

The LVT, however, is the principal culprit. Like each of its predecessors, the current LVTP-7 has a tracked displacement hull which limits its waterborne speed to about eight knots. Habitability conditions in the troop compartment are grim. The combination of noise, motion, fumes, and heat limits the amount of time troops can endure in the waterborne mode to about thirty minutes. Hence, LVT launch distances are generally restricted to 4,000 yards from the beach. This factor vitiates the over-the-horizon advantage enjoyed by the amphibious task force commander with his heliborne assault. In-

stead, each of his surface assault launch and control ships is forced to operate within range of the full inventory of his opponent's weapons. The commander's optional use of surprise and deception is also severely restricted. It can thus be argued that if the surface assault is the "Achilles' heel" of an amphibious operation, then the sluggish LVT is the "inflammatory tendonitis" of that weak spot.

An improved landing craft and an improved infantry fighting vehicle (IFV) are easily within the state of the art—but not as a single entity. This is the dilemma of assault amphibian vehicles. The requirement for armored protection and cross-country mobility adds bulk and tracks to the design. Similarly, the requirement for surfing and deep water sea-keeping limits the LVT's capacity for heavier armor or a bigger weapon system. The result is an engineering compromise. The LVT by nature will thus be slower than a pure landing craft, less lethal than an IFV ashore. The LVT is nevertheless considered an integral component of Marine Corps combat arms. The commandant, General Robert H. Barrow, in fact, has publicly stated that he expects the LVTP-7 to be the "principal vehicle for amphibious assault and ground tactical mobility" throughout the 1980s.

The LCAC is coming to the fleet in the next five years, and it will be discussed below. In addition, the current LVTP-7 will undergo a service life extension program

(SLEP) to permit its employment with amphibious forces until the 1990s. The replacement vehicle at that time is expected to be the LVTX, another tracked displacement hull, although engineered for improved performance on the battlefield ashore with a bigger gun, lighter weight, and lower silhouette. Waterborne speed is expected to be only slightly better than that of the LVTP-7.

Two other amphibious designs, long prominent on the drawing boards in the 1970s, did not survive: the LCM-9 and the LVA. The former was an improved landing craft with a speed of 20 knots and a payload of either 250 troops or 2 tanks. (Now only the LCAC will replace the venerable LCUs and "Mike Boats.") The LVA (assault landing vehicle) would have broken the fifty-year LVT waterborne speed pattern by providing a tracked *planing* hull capable of 25 knots and a much greater range. The prototype was subject to the same engineering dilemma, however the capability to make such a heavy vehicle plane on top of the water could only be attained at the expense of other design requirements. The program was canceled in 1979.

As a result, the components of the surface assault during the mid-range period (1986–90) are expected to be the LVTP-7A1 and the LCAC, the tortoise and the hare.

How much are we willing to pay for technological means of reducing amphibious vulnerability? Given sufficient funds, our research and development facilities could most likely produce exotic devices to execute the ship-to-shore assault with speed, protection, and stealth. One possibility that comes to mind is a high-speed underwater craft that could convert to a tracked cross-country vehicle at the water's edge. Similarly, a squad-sized air-cushioned vehicle is envisioned that could convert to the use of wheels once ashore.

Such concepts contain elements of possibility, but as prospective solutions to the vulnerability problem, they are extravagant and lack grounding in political reality. Even in rare periods of unfettered defense spending, there will never be so high a priority on amphibious warfare that would permit such exotic long-range development. In addition

to affordability and political priority, technological solutions to vulnerability reduction must be framed with appreciation for long lead times in design, development, testing, and acquisition. The LCAC program, for example, is likely to wind up taking twenty years between inception and operational reality.

Let's now examine the LCAC. Will its introduction in 1986 be a milestone or a millstone for amphibious forces? Truly, its operational capabilities promise a breakthrough in amphibious assault almost as revolutionary as the helicopter. The production version is expected to be a shipborne, high-speed (50 knots), over-the-beach, ship-to-shore, amphibious landing craft with a 200-mile range and a 60-ton payload (75 tons at lesser range). The LCAC will be capable of operating in rough seas and high surf; ashore, it should be able to traverse mudflats, sand dunes, ditches, marshlands, and estuaries in order to offload assault forces in trafficable terrain near their inland objective. Moreover, the LCAC's coastal penetration capabilities will expose up to 70 percent of the world's beaches, rather than the 17 percent available to the current LCU/LCM craft.

The implications of these new capabilities are significant. With LCAC, the amphibious task force commander will finally be capable of conducting a true over-the-horizon launch. He will have the capability of conducting underway launches of both heliborne and surface assault forces from distances up to 50 miles at sea, thereby greatly increasing his security. Compared with present landing craft, the marines' LCAC's greater range, speed, and penetration—coupled with the tactical advantages of the helicopter—will give the commander new prospects of surprise, deception, and maneuverability that are downright exciting. Defense Department analysts have estimated that the LCAC will become such a "force multiplier" as to reduce enemy coastal defense effectiveness sixfold. The landing force commander also stands to benefit from the LCAC's ability to land his tanks and heavy artillery well inland early in the assault. If the measure of effectiveness of an amphibious operation is our force buildup rate vs. that of our opponent, then LCAC should provide us with a vast improvement.

This is all good. The problem will exist in viewing LCAC as the panacea for all the ills of amphibious assault. It will take more than LCAC to reduce amphibious vulnerability. Further, there are problems associated with LCAC employment that are potentially serious. Among them are the following:

- Cost. The projected price tag is $10.8 million per craft. This will likely increase by 1986.
- Quantity. There will rarely be enough LCACs for the landing force. The goal for 1986 is six. No more than sixty are expected to be operational in the fleet in 1992. A return to austere defense budgets at any time during the next ten years will critically affect even these totals.
- Relationship with LVTs. The Marine Corps intends to employ the LVT (successively, the LVTP-7, the LVTP-7A1, and the LVTX) throughout the remainder of the century. The LVT, if nothing else, provides armored protection for embarked troops. The LCAC does not. The over-the-horizon launch advantage of the LCAC is likely to prevail over the armored advantage of the LVT. What, then, should be the role of the LVT in the assault? One analyst has proposed that LVTs be transported ashore in LCACs—but then why retain LVTs when a less expensive, non-surfing, infantry-fighting vehicle would suffice? Again, the relatively scant number of LCACs has a bearing. A modified tactical role for LVTs in the surface assault needs to be developed.
- Payload. The LCAC can lift only one main battle tank. The initial six LCACs to become operational will thus be able, collectively, to land only one reinforced tank platoon at a time. The old LCU was better in this category.
- Amphibious Shipping. LCACs require well-decks and take up a good deal of space. An amphibious assault ship (LHA) can carry

one LCAC; a landing platform dock (LPD), two; the current dock landing ship (LSD), three; the new LSD-41, four or five. The navy has other requirements for well-deck space, including pusher boats and warping tugs for causeways and the assault bulk fuel system.

- Fragility. The LCAC will present a fast but large, noisy target with a characteristic "rooster tail" of spray or dust. Its component systems will resemble an aircraft more than a tank or a boat. It will be susceptible to aimed fire and, if damaged, will be difficult to extract. Maintenance could be prohibitive in terms of skills and facilities required.
- Command and Control. Historically, the navy's control of the ship-to-shore movement has terminated at the surf zone. With LCACs expected to penetrate several miles inland, what becomes the command relationship between the "pilot" and the landing force commander, especially in trips to the inland objective area after the initial assault?
- Inland Mobility. The LCAC should be able to far outperform the LVT under certain terrain conditions—mudflats, slippery river banks, wet snow, icy shorelines, for example. But the frequently heard claim that the LCAC wll be a "true amphibian" is euphoric and inaccurate. The LCAC will be essentially a flatland vehicle ashore. Its slope capacity of 11 percent hardly compares with the 60 percent capacity of most tanks and LVTs. Besides, the LCAC should not loiter ashore. Its primary value lies in the speed with which it can cycle heavy loads from distant ships to designated landing zones inland.
- Overcommitment. The only craft in the water in the 1990s are expected to be LCACs and LVTs. Which of these will provide the lighterage required for general offloading of amphibious ships after completion of the assault? LVTs are too small, and LCACs will forever be in demand by the landing force commander for subsequent tactical operations to expand the limits of the

beachhead along the littoral. LCACs will also be in heavy demand by the joint task force commander to augment his inadequate LOTS (logistics over the shore) capabilities after termination of the amphibious operation, especially in shallow waters such as those in the Persian Gulf region. Perhaps we have given up the LCU prematurely. Also, one of the greatest threats facing the amphibious task force commander is enemy mines. It is arguable that amphibious operations are not possible in a well-mined area. The LCAC propulsion system makes it less susceptible to mines than any other assault craft or vehicle. The naval officer commanding the task force may well decide that the interests of the amphibious task force will be best served by using his LCACs as an "airborne" mine countermeasure unit, towing Mark-5 sleds, rather than as landing craft. The decision would be his and not the commander's of the marine landing force.

These problems and questions are not unanswerable. They do point out the need to approach the goal of reducing amphibious vulnerability from separate directions. The LCAC will constitute part of the solution—a significant part—but other initiatives are required, too.

The biggest challenge in the field of applied tactics is to adapt existing doctrine to the LCAC's new capabilities. We should abandon the classic linear assault mode—a long line of vehicles struggling to keep abreast—in favor of staggered or irregular columns that do not pause at the high-water mark but continue across the beach at high speed. The LCAC particularly lends itself to application of maneuver warfare techniques recently espoused in professional journals and the Military Reform Caucus in Congress. The speed and versatility of the LCAC can provide the commander with the opportunity of operating easily within the reaction cycle of his opponent. Indeed, LCAC will enable the commander to terminate an unpromising or stalled landing attempt in one area and initiate a new one at a widely separated loca-

tion. Mobility and flexibility are the keys. LCACs and light-armored vehicles are primary ingredients in maneuver warfare in amphibious operations.

There are other useful tactical initiatives which can be employed to reduce amphibious vulnerability even without the advantage of operational LCACs. A much greater emphasis on tactical cover and deception is called for, as are more night operations and the employment of silent landing techniques. The use of preassault operations in which L-hour precedes H-hour to enable the heliborne forces to land and seize critical terrain to protect the subsequent surface assault has proven valuable in the fjords of Norway and in the Shetlands.

The high-speed launch of LVTs from underway amphibious warfare ships, a technique developed in the 1960s to reduce vulnerability in the surface assault, has proven to be disappointing for three reasons. First, the launching ships must still come to within 4,000 yards of the beach in order to accommodate the limited range of the LVTs. (It would be highly unlikely that an LHA, for example, would do this.) Second, most *Newport*-class LSTs are limited to launch speeds of about 5 knots because of structural problems with their stern gates. Third, while well-deck ships such as the LSD and LPD can launch dual columns of LVTs at speeds of 20 knots, their commanders are understandably concerned with the "squat effect" when conducting the launch in shallow water. A common concern with bottom-laid pressure mines also causes a significant reduction in launch speed. The underway launch remains superior to launching while at anchor, but the overall reduction of vulnerability has not been as significant as initially expected.

Another tactical means of reducing amphibious vulnerability is to increase the fire support of the initial assault waves. Yet naval gunfire capabilities continue to diminish, and now it appears that even the "born again" *Iowa* (BB-61)-class battleships may not be given an amphibious support mission. This is a grim prospect for amphibious forces, and they will have to take up some of the gunfire support slack by other means. Could a main battle tank embarked in an LCAC use its fine weapon system in a direct fire role to the front? Could we integrate this with a pair of AH-1T Cobra gunships flying alongside the LCAC at 50 feet as outriders? I like the prospects.

Listed below are some strategic and political initiatives which would have an indirect effect on reducing vulnerability in all aspects of amphibious warfare.

A decision is needed as to which role, if any, amphibious warfare is to play in our national security plan. Currently, there is a conflict within the defense establishment between those who advocate prepositioning/POMCUS (the U.S. Army's Prepositioning of Materiel Configured to Unit Sets program in Europe)/continental strategies and those who favor forcible entry/power projection/maritime strategies. The debate between these two schools of thought is likely to produce a combination of both approaches.

If amphibious warfare is still deemed an important element of national strategy, then several key questions should be asked, among them Sir Julian Corbett's "What will the war be about?" and, more specifically, "What should be the objective of U.S. amphibious forces?" The answers to these questions will provide critical guidance in preparing for amphibious warfare, including the vulnerability-reduction portion of amphibious planning.

A second political initiative which would indirectly ease the vulnerability of amphibious assaults is adherence to Bismarck's axiom regarding the conservation of enemies (A nation should fight one isolated enemy at a time: in Germany's case, this meant Denmark in 1864, Austria in 1866, and France in 1870). The proliferation of modern weaponry throughout the world is such that amphibious forces will have their hands full in taking on any single opponent at a time. If possible, the number of mortal enemies engaged at any given time should be held to a minimum.

A related initiative involves the fostering of good relations with those of our allies who are willing to fight alongside us. A number of countries in the free world have amphibious forces. We should encourage their training and development to avoid being the only nation with an amphibious capability when war comes. A protracted, coalition war is likely, and we'll need all the amphibious help we can enlist.

One strategic initiative which could greatly improve the viability of amphibious operations would be to reaffirm the principle of forward deployment and upgrade the composition of such forces to include periodic deployment of a marine amphibious brigade (MAB) in troubled waters. Deployment of a MAB-level amphibious task force early in a crisis can beat the eventual interdiction of choke points (such as the Red Sea), provide a heavyweight deterrent on the scene, and ease some of the monstrous problems of strategic lift involved in projecting power at the outer limits of U.S. political reach.

A corollary to forward deployment of significant amphibious forces in the initial stages of conflict is early decision making. Tough decisions made by national command authorities early in a developing crisis can give the forward-deployed amphibious task force commander a tremendous advantage in initiative, maneuverability, surprise, and shock—all ingredients for vulnerability reduction. The value of a preemptive amphibious strike, swiftly executed early in a crisis, may do more for deterrence or containment than a month of verbal saber-rattling.

Above all, amphibious vulnerability can best be reduced by a top-level willingness to develop imaginative new concepts for employment of the LCAC-equipped amphibious task force. We should encourage the forward deployment of sea-based, self-sufficient, expeditionary forces in international waters where our national interests are perceived to be in jeopardy. We should resurrect the fine art of amphibious raids to "put out the eyes" of enemy intelligence-gathering facilities; to seize lodgments along the enemy's sea lines of communication; to disrupt and distract his war efforts; or to seize terrain for quid pro quo in conflict termination negotiations. The historical model in this case should be Demosthenes at Pylos, not the British at Dieppe. We should also reconsider amphibious warfare possibilities in Corbett's "narrow seas"—the Danish Straits, the Dardanelles, Malacca, the various straits north of Japan. Amphibious assaults against urban port facilities should be examined as a new application of the art. The value of early seizure of a port and airfield complex by forward-deployed amphibious forces is directly related to administrative reinforcement by follow-on MPS brigades and rapid force buildup ashore. Similarly, we should develop doctrine for the difficult task of amphibious extraction—the recovery of embattled units under fire. Historical examples are abundant: Dunkirk, Odessa, Grant at Belmont in 1861, Sir John More at Corunna in 1809.

The strategic emphasis throughout all of these innovative measures should be on forward-deployed amphibious strike forces capable of conducting surprise landings by mobile forces in helicopters and LCACs against limited and disorganized opposition. These forces should be suited to a truly amphibious operation, fully supplied from the sea, with a concurrent ability for quick extraction, reconfiguration, and readiness to apply "armed suasion" at another location along the coastline.

The following specific measures will reduce vulnerability of all phases of amphibious operations:

- *Material Development*
  —Support and protect the acquisition cycle of LCAC
  —Establish a service life extension program for a proportion of our current LCUs to augment LCAC in lighterage operations (an alternative—resurrect the LCM-9 program)

- *Tactical Initiatives*
  —Develop operational concepts for LCAC
  —Define role of LVT vis-à-vis LCAC
  —Explore integrated LCAC/tank/Cobra fire support techniques in ship-to-shore assault

- *Strategic/Political Initiatives*
  —Reaffirm (or dismantle) amphibious forcible entry capability
  —Conserve enemies/support amphibiously capable friends
  —Forward deploy a marine amphibious brigade
  —Provide early decision making to forward-deployed forces
  —Employ new strategic concepts for amphibious forces, to include raids, lodgments, choke points, urban ports, and extractions

No aspect of an opposed amphibious assault is free of risk. A certain degree of damage by enemy action is to be expected. But losses can be minimized, and the overall potential for success enhanced, by applying an integrated approach to solving the problem of risk reduction. The figurative definition of an Achilles' heel is "a small but mortal weakness." A sensible application of the proposals discussed above can significantly lessen the historic "mortality" of the surface ship-to-shore assault.

The Soviet Naval Infantry

BY LIEUTENANT COLONEL DOMINIK G. NARGELE, USMC

Lessons learned by Soviet planners from World War Two have had a strong influence in the development of the naval infantry. In the beginning of the war, the Soviet government formed a dozen naval infantry units of battalion and brigade size totaling about 100,000 personnel. These were assigned to the Baltic, Northern, and Black Sea fleets, and to respective flotillas; later, more naval ground combat forces were created. Infantrymen and sailors were sent often as reinforcements to various fronts. After personnel totals were compiled at the end of World War Two, about 500,000 naval infantry and other naval troops were found to have served at many different fronts during large-scale fighting.

According to Admiral of the Fleet Sergei G. Gorshkov, the naval infantry conducted more than one hundred major amphibious operations during World War Two, and about three hundred thirty thousand troops participated in these landings. Gorshkov asserts that naval infantry operations in support of front actions were one of the main aspects of Soviet naval warfare. By 1945, forty various naval infantry and naval rifle brigades had been formed along with many separate battalions or detachments. Their contributions to the Soviet victory during World War Two were many.

Following the war the Soviet Naval Infantry was reduced in size and lost much of its importance. Reportedly, by 1947, it had been subordinated to the coastal defense forces.

During the early 1960s, however, a revival of the Soviet Naval Infantry as a separate branch of the navy took place. On 24 July 1964, reference was made to the naval infantry again in the open press. By the late 1960s, the organization had expanded to more than twenty thousand men and steady improvements have continued to the present.[1]

In keeping with Western precedents, the new Soviet amphibious force has participated in numerous small unit and large-scale exercises in recent times. In 1968, during exercise "Sever," naval infantry units of the Baltic Fleet conducted joint landings in East Germany with a Polish sea-landing division and East German Army motorized rifle troops. During "Okean-70," Soviet Naval Infantry deployed on a worldwide scale—simultaneously in the North, South, West, and East of the Soviet Union. "Okean-75" also used naval infantry extensively.[2]

According to the East German press, during exercise "Comradeship-In-Arms 1980," large-scale amphibious landings were conducted on the island of Usedom near Peenemunde on the Baltic coast, fom 4 to 12 September 1980. General Heinz Hoffman, East Germany's national defense minister, directed the exercise in which Soviet Naval Infantry, Polish sea-landing troops, and East German motorized rifle units again participated. The exercise allegedly demonstrated an increased level of operational training among the amphibious forces.[3]

During March 1981, exercise "Soyuz-81" again involved Soviet, East German, and Polish amphibious troops. Landings were conducted on the Baltic coast with aircushion

U.S. Naval Institute *Proceedings*, "Their Naval Infantry," 108 (October 1982): 152–59. Reprinted by permission.

vehicles and modern Mi-8 "Hip-C" helicopters. Later last year, Western newspapers reported a joint Soviet-Syrian amphibious exercise in the Mediterranean, in which naval infantry units of the Black Sea Fleet played an important part.

These demonstrations of naval power are designed to maintain Soviet influence in the world and keep amphibious forces ready to take advantage of opportunities for expansion as they may arise. The Soviets' quest for influence goes hand in hand with nationalism and the desire for a sense of superiority.[4] Their extension of power and influence is often not territorial but involves the projection of a high-seas navy with amphibious forces, nuclear weapons which can reach any corner of the globe, a growing merchant fleet, Aeroflot, and other government agencies. The naval infantry is an ideal instrument for the extension of Soviet power. It can add even more credibility to their military arsenal. Afghanistan has provided evidence for an "external function" of the Soviet armed forces, and Soviet authors have indicated a need for a mobile, well-trained, and well-equipped force to influence the "imperialists" and to counter local reactions. The Kremlin seems to be establishing its own global security system, in which the naval infantry will probably play an important role.[5]

Besides the Soviet Navy assault shipping, a large merchant fleet, transport aviation of the Soviet Air Force, and Aeroflot can all be rapidly pressed into service to move personnel and equipment. According to some sources, the Soviet Naval Infantry is the second largest marine force in the world with about twelve thousand personnel. But the estimate of the International Institute of Strategic Studies (IISS)—which claims that figure—is probably too low.

First, support for the numerous amphibious exercises which have been observed in the recent past can hardly be provided on a global scale by twelve thousand men. Second, the Soviet Navy does not reveal its true order of battle to the public and practices deception or disinformation to a great degree, often concealing units, training facilities, and installations. Third, additional units have been reported in the Soviet Union, which increase overall strength figures. Finally, large manpower reserves in the Soviet Union are often—and rapidly—called to active duty. Therefore, a figure of at least twenty thousand to thirty thousand active duty naval infantrymen is much more realistic.

Some ninety-three amphibious ships are also listed by the IISS. They include the large *Ivan Rogov* landing ship dock (LPD), which can carry a battalion of naval infantry, helicopters, armored personnel carriers, and aircushion vehicles. The current inventory of landing ship tank (LST) types includes fourteen "Alligator" and seventeen "Ropucha" amphibious ships. They also have forty-five "Polnocny" landing ship medium (LSM) types and six "MP-4" landing craft tank (LCT) vessels. An additional *Ivan Rogov*-class ship is fitting out and more will likely be provided to the Soviet Navy. In many exercises, the naval infantry uses aircushion vehicles or hovercraft, of which they have fifty-two. These consist of ten "Aist"-class, eleven "Lebed"-class, and thirty-three "Gus"-class aircushion vehicles. The "Aist"-class reportedly can carry two medium tanks, and the "Lebed"-class can carry one. The "Gus"-class is designed to land troops, and each can carry about thirty-five naval infantrymen.

The naval infantry organization reported by the Defense Intelligence Agency (DIA) includes one brigade apiece in the Northern and Baltic Sea fleets, and one regiment in the Black Sea Fleet, plus two deployed with the Pacific Fleet.

The modern naval infantry regiment, with a strength of about two thousand men, is believed to be organized similarly to a Soviet Army motorized rifle regiment. The internal structure can be called triadic since it has three battalions; each battalion has three companies; and each company has three platoons. In addition, each regiment has a tank battalion made up of three companies equipped with amphibious "PT-76" light tanks, and one company with medium tanks which use snorkels to drive through as much as 5.5 meters of water.[6] The organization presented by DIA leaves unanswered the relationship the two regiments of the Pacific Fleet have to each other. It is likely that they belong to a naval infantry division stationed with Soviet naval forces in the area, and that the overall strength figures are higher than estimated. It is also probable that naval infantry regiments in other parts of the world are actually brigades, with some supporting units which have not been identified.

A study of recent Soviet exercises, tactics, and equipment indicates that the naval infantry is not made up of merely a few ships and regiments unable to project power. Instead, it appears that it is a highly mobile, modern, and well-trained force which can be employed by the Kremlin effectively in the Baltic and Black seas, against the coast of China, and very probably against countries in the Third World. The Soviet Union no doubt is still discovering aspects of its superpower status. It is probing for opportunities to extend its influence. Soviet planners probably understand better than ever that amphibious forces can play a vital part in that regard. If the Kremlin is allowed a clear field in some parts of the world, it will be more likely to intervene, and resistance will probably decline. The United States is challenged in varied parts of the world, and its interventions are now made more dangerous by the availability of Soviet military forces. As Soviet confidence increases, U.S. diplomats may reject military options as unfeasible; the president may meet increasing opposition from Congress to any military solutions for difficulties abroad.

In the early 1960s, the Soviet Navy initiated an expansion in capabilities, equipment, and personnel which has continued for the last twenty years. The Soviet Union maintains the largest number of warships in the world—more than six hundred active major combatants; its air arm has about eleven hundred aircraft. The Soviet amphibious lift includes about one hundred active and preserved amphibious ships, along with about one hundred twenty short-haul landing craft for amphibious support. This capability can be augmented by ships of the merchant fleet. The actual number of naval infantry reservists is unknown but probably totals several hundred thousand.

In summary, Soviet military plans call for amphibious landings to be conducted by naval infantry transported in the amphibious assault ships of the Soviet Navy. In some cases, such operations would be supported by the merchant fleet, army, and air force. Ground forces are prepared to support and relieve naval infantry units after amphibious operations have been completed. The missions of the naval infantry involve amphibious landings against strategic targets and naval choke points. Of special priority in Soviet Naval Infantry targeting are the Straits of Denmark, the coast of Norway, and the entrances to the Black Sea and the Sea of Japan.

Amphibious landings can be conducted by the naval infantry either close to the Soviet borders in support of ground force operations or on distant shores anywhere in the world. The naval infantry can be used also in a commando role. Naval infantry commando platoons can parachute into target areas or be landed by helicopter, motor torpedo boat, or submarine.

It is sometimes asserted that an amphibious landing by the Soviets in the Third World is impossible, since it would require extensive air support, elaborate naval gunfire, and sea superiority. The history of the naval infantry, however, indicates that its doctrine is flexible and pragmatic. Naval Infantry men have landed before without the "necessary" support, and they probably can do it again. Although the Soviets' capabilities in this warfare area are not comparable to those of the U.S. Marine Corps, they are improving steadily and evolving into a potentially effective instrument of the Kremlin.

Notes

[1] L. N. Buffardi, *The Soviet Naval Infantry* (Washington, D.C.: Defense Intelligence Agency, 1980), pp. 1–2.

[2] P. E. Melnikov, *Soldaty Moria* (Moscow: DOSAAF, 1977), pp. 65–75.

[3] Dietmar Jammer, "Luftkissen Fahrzenge Und Sturmgruppen, *Nenes Deutschland* (Berlin: Deutsche Demokratische Republik, 11 September 1980), pp. 1–3.

[4] Richard Pipes, "Soviet Global Strategy," *Commentary*, April 1980: 32–38.

[5] Steven F. Kime, "A Soviet Navy for the Nuclear Age," *Parameters*, vol. X, no. 1: 58–70.

[6] Buffardi, *Soviet Naval Infantry*, p. 2.

The Falklands, 1982

BY EDGAR O'BALLANCE

Back in 1966, the British defense minister declared that British armed forces would never again have to face another opposed land, and never have to operate on their own. On 21 May 1982, they had to do just that when the 3 Commando Brigade, Royal Marines made an amphibious assault in the San Carlos area to regain possession of the Falkland Islands, which had been forcibly occupied by Argentine troops on 2 April. The British government had been caught completely by surprise, but the next day the first submarine of what became a 101-ship task force, commanded by Rear Admiral John Woodward, sailed southwards from the United Kingdom toward the South Atlantic.

The flagship of the task force was the carrier HMS *Hermes*. Aboard it and several other ships were the 40, 42, and 45 Royal Marine Commandos, each of about eight hundred men, and the 2d and 3d Battalions of the Parachute Regiment. Also embarked as part of the same 3 Commando Brigade, commanded by Brigadier Julian Thompson, were 59th Independent Squadron, Royal Engineers; 29th Commando Regiment, Royal Artillery, with its 105 mm howitzers and Rapier missiles; and two troops of The Blues and Royals (Cavalry Regiment) with sixteen light-armored Scorpion and Scimitar vehicles. The marines and paratroopers had mortars and Blowpipe antiaircraft missiles in addition to personal weapons.

The treeless Falkland Islands consist of an

Marine Corps Gazette, "The San Carlos Landing," 52 (October 1982): 36–45. Reprinted by permission.

area of about 4,250 square miles. There are two main islands, East and West Falkland, which are separated by the narrow Falkland Sound, and some two hundred small islets. The terrain consists of low hills, huge rocky outcrops, and bogland. About eighteen hundred people live on these islands, roughly half in the capital, Port Stanley, in the eastern part of East Falkland; the remainder are scattered in a dozen or so widely spaced hamlets, most of which have a grass landing strip. Sheep raising is the only occupation. There were only eight miles of surfaced, all-weather roadways around Port Stanley, and the tracks connecting some of the hamlets can only be used by Landrovers and tractors with difficulty, especially in winter. Communication with the main hamlets is mostly by coastal craft or light aircraft. The small international airport, 6 miles south of the capital, has a 4,000-feet runway.

The Argentine occupation force at first was fairly small, perhaps fewer than three thousand men, mainly marines, with two battalions of the 25th Infantry Regiment, three batteries of 155 mm and other field and antiaircraft guns. Initially, neither side thought the other would fight, but when it became apparent the British meant business, the Argentines began to hastily increase the size of their garrison, which was reinforced by the 3d and 9th Infantry Regiments (each of two battalions); more artillery, radar, supporting and logistic units and twelve Panhard armored cars. Maximum strength eventually reached more than fourteen thousand men. The British invasion force was just over

The landings at San Carlos, the Falklands, 1982. Courtesy of the Royal Navy

nine thousand strong. The headquarters and main body of the Argentine garrison was at, and around, Port Stanley. One battalion was at Goose Green on East Falkland, later reinforced by a second; another battalion at Port Howard and two at Fox Bay, both on West Falkland; and other small detachments were scattered around the coasts, and on certain islets, such as Pebble Island, for operating radar and observation.

Arrival of the Task Force

The Falkland Islands are some 8,000 miles from the United Kingdom. After calling at Ascension Island, which became the British midway base, the leading elements of the naval task force, led by two carriers, HMS *Hermes* and HMS *Invincible*, arrived near the Falkland Islands in mid-April, while the amphibious task group gathered at Ascension Island where troops trained ashore and continued planning for forthcoming operations. On 25 April, British marines recaptured South Georgia, which had also been occupied by the Argentines, and which was some 800 miles from the Falkland Islands.

The opening maritime shots at the Falklands proper were fired on 2 May, when the Argentine cruiser *General Belgrano* (with a crew of 1,042) was hit and sunk, with the loss of 368 lives, by a Tigerfish torpedo from a British nuclear-powered submarine, HMS *Conquerer*. This happened about 30 miles outside the declared British Total Exclusion

Zone (TEZ), of 200 miles around the Falkland Islands, on direct orders from the United Kingdom. Two escorting Argentine destroyers fled the scene, but returned later to pick up survivors. Orders to the submarine commander were not to sink them. After this, the Argentine Navy did not venture out again from the shelter of its 12-mile territorial waters limit.

On 4 May, the Argentines hit back, and sank the British destroyer, HMS *Sheffield*, with an Exocet (AM–39) air-to-sea missile, fired from a Super Extendard aircraft. The British task force was deficient in early airborne warning radar and conventional fighter cover. The *Sheffield*, which lost twenty men, for example, had only the Sea Dart missile, which has a 30-mile range (10 less than Exocet). The British had a good countermissile, the Sea Wolf, with almost twice the range of the Exocet, but it was fitted to only two ships, the destroyers HMS *Broadsword* and HMS *Brilliant*. The *Belgrano* did not have the naval Exocet (MM–38), but its two destroyer escorts did. Over eight ships in the task force were fitted with the naval Exocet.

Such technical considerations influenced British strategy. Instead of part of the task force basing itself on one carrier, and stationing itself between the Falkland Islands and the Argentine mainland, some 400 miles apart, to interdict Argentine ships and aircraft, major ships had to remain well to the east of the TEZ to be out of range of land-

The landing force is established ashore, San Carlos, the Falklands, 1982. Courtesy of the Royal Navy

based aircraft. The loss of a carrier, or troop-carrying ship, might have caused the whole operation to be aborted. Thus, the Argentine airborne Exocet missile, although it was thought they had less than half-a-dozen of the AM–39 type, clearly cast a shadow over the task force for the duration of the campaign.

On 15 May, a party of forty-four British Special Air Service (SAS) personnel landed on Pebble Island, at the northern end of the Falkland Sound, attacked the small garrison, destroying eleven aircraft on the landing strip, a radar post, and a small ammunition dump before withdrawing again. During this raid the Argentine positions were bombarded by

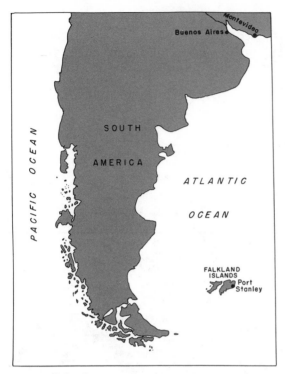

The Falklands.

Surprise was achieved by the British, who had persuaded their media to give the general impression that the three courses being considered by the task force commander were to launch a massive, head-on, Normandy D-day-type assault on Port Stanley; to be content with nibbling tactics like the raid on Pebble Island to destroy the defenders' morale; or just to tighten the naval blockade to starve the Argentines into surrender. On 21 May, in London, a government spokesman said "Our lads will sleep in their beds tonight."

The forked San Carlos Inlet penetrated the land mass eastwards from the Falkland Sound. The northern fork, known as San Carlos Bay, led to Port San Carlos, a hamlet of some thirty people. Along the northern side of San Carlos Bay, from Fanning Harbour eastwards for some 5 miles to Port San Carlos itself, were good landing beach sites, and above Fanning Harbour was the low hill ridge of Fanning Head, which was both a good observation point and site for Rapiers. The southern fork, a narrow fjordlike one, was known as San Carlos Water, with the hamlet of San Carlos, also of about thirty people, at its head. The southern flank of the San Carlos Inlet was covered by a low ridge of hills, known as the Sussex Mountains. An uncertain motorable track ran from Port San Carlos eastwards to Teal, Douglas, and other eastern settlements, and another from San Carlos south toward Darwin, Goose Green, and Port Stanley.

A Dawn Attack

D-day was 21 May. The assault troops were the whole of the 3 Commando Brigade, both marines and paratroops, who landed from the LPDs, LSLs, and the requisitioned passenger liner *Canberra*, which brought them into Falkland Sound to the mouth of the San Carlos Inlet by about 0300. Disembarking into small landing craft, assaulting troops moved quietly to four specified "beaches" on the north side of San Carlos Bay, and to three on San Carlos Water. All assault troops were ashore within four hours. As the days were

naval 4.5-inch guns. The SAS noticed that when they first attacked the positions, the soldiers, mainly conscripts, ran away, but were brought back again by their officers, only to run away again. Argentine officers became British targets in battle.

San Carlos

The place chosen for the assault landing was the San Carlos area on East Falkland, at the northern end of the Falkland Sound, where there was a forked inlet surrounded by low hills, which would afford some protection against attacking Argentine aircraft and would provide good positions for the Rapiers, a low-level (up to 10,000 feet) ground-to-air missile. Argentine pilots required a straight run of 2,000 yards to lock their Exocet missiles on to target. The narrow waters of the San Carlos Inlet, and indeed the narrow Falkland Sound, were ideal hiding places for ships particularly when there was mist and low cloud.

short with only about eight or nine hours of good daylight, the bulk of these forces were ashore before daybreak.

Tactical surprise was complete. There was no moon, but bright starlight silhouetted the surrounding hills. Conditions for an amphibious landing were ideal. As the leading waves of troops waded, or jumped, ashore, they felt the reality of the Antarctic cold for the first time, after being cramped on ships for several weeks. Save for one post of about forty men on Fanning Head, there were no defenders. The Fanning Hill position had been attacked by the Special Boat Section (SBS) prior to the main landings as part of advance force operations. Fourteen prisoners were taken during this action. For the main landings, there was no naval bombardment; silence was maintained as long as possible. Later in the day, however, the British lost two Gazelle helicopters to ground fire from the remnants of the Fanning Head post. In one case patrols of marines and paratroops, probing forward from their respective beaches, mistook each other for the enemy, and mortar bombs were fired, injuring one man.

The previous days had been cloudy and overcast, with mist obscuring visibility from the air, but the morning of D-day dawned bright and clear, giving excellent visibility to reveal the attacking armada, with several large ships, including the *Canberra*, crowded into the narrow Falkland Sound and other small ships and smaller craft packed into the forked San Carlos Inlet. Tactical success was achieved, and by 1030, some twenty-five hundred men were ashore. It was not until about 1000 that an Argentine Pucara aircraft appeared to see what was happening. It fired its rockets and disappeared again. Pucaras and other short-range aircraft operated from the grass landing strips. The Pucara is an Argentine plane specially developed for antiguerrilla operations.

Argentine Air Attacks

Early on D-day Port Stanley, Goose Green, and other targets had been attacked by British Sea Harriers, of which twenty were based on the two carriers. When news of the San Carlos landing reached the Argentine headquarters in Port Stanley, the British effort was thought to be a deliberate diversion. Aircraft apparently were dispatched from the mainland—the journey took up to two hours—but were not directed to the San Carlos area. The British had expected, and indeed hoped, to tempt the bulk of the Argentine combat aircraft that were capable of operating to the Falkland Islands into a massive air assault. When the Argentine air attacks did begin in San Carlos about 1030 on D + 1, they came in a continuous succession of waves.

The Argentine aircraft flew all day over the crowded, narrow waters, attacking from the east (not the expected west), having extra fuel tanks fitted to enable them to make the necessary detour, concentrating upon the combat ships, rather than the troop-carrying and smaller transports. Although some of the Rapiers were ashore they were not completely set up by the time these attacks began. The ships replied with missiles and antiaircraft fire. Most combat ships had the Sea Dart, which forced the pilots to fly low to avoid the missiles. At the end of D + 1, when air attacks ceased at dusk, the British claimed they had destroyed nine Mirages, five Skyhawks and three Pucaras, for the loss of one Sea Harrier, brought down by an enemy Blowpipe missile near Goose Green early that morning. The pilot ejected and was the only British prisoner to be taken in the whole campaign. Five British ships were hit, and the frigate HMS *Ardent* sank the next day. The Argentine air force did not operate at night in this campaign. Then followed a thirty-six-hour respite for the task force.

During this lull the British got the remainder of their assault troops, a few 105 mm howitzers, mortars, and more Rapiers ashore. On the ground the invasion force spread out to occupy the low hills surrounding the San Carlos Inlet, and to prepare for the expected counterattack, forming a bridgehead of some 10 miles square. No other contact had been made with the Argentines, whose nearest outpost was south at Shanty Ridge, about 15 miles away along the track to Goose Green. By the end of D + 1, the task force had more than four thousand men ashore, with sufficient food and ammunition for about four days but little heavy equipment.

More Air Attacks

Argentine aircraft resumed the attack about 1400 on D + 2 (23 May), another bright and clear day. Only two Skyhawks had appeared the previous day to drop their bombs harmlessly into the Sound. Small ships moved closer inshore to avoid the anticipated Exocet missiles, but became vulnerable to the Pucaras. All day successive waves of aircraft aimed primarily at the "gun line" of the combat ships in the Sound, that included three destroyers and five frigates. Skyhawks each carried two 1,000-pound bombs. One flew low enough to clip the radar antennae of the frigate HMS *Antelope* and to hit it with both bombs. One went through the bow and out, and the other fell through to the engine room to explode later when being defused. The *Antelope* sank three days later (26 May).

San Carlos Water became known as "Bomb Alley." Although Argentine pilots still concentrated on combat ships, other ships too were hit by bombs and rockets, and there were many near misses. The *Canberra*, for example, lying in the Sound, had twelve bombs dropped within a couple of hundred yards of it within four days. The troops ashore were often in danger of "wild missiles" that either missed their targets, went off course, or overshot their marks, to crash crazily into the hillsides. At the end of D + 2, the British claimed to have brought down six more Argentine planes and damaged two others. That evening, on direct orders from the United Kingdom, all combat and transport ships were directed to leave the San Carlos area and remain clear during daylight hours, only returning in darkness. This considerably slowed down the buildup of the bridgehead.

Many Argentine bombs—in fact, a high proportion of them—did not explode, and at first were thought to be "duds." The reason

for their not exploding reportedly was due to malfunctioning or misuse of bomb fuses. At least two British ships were hit by bombs that did not explode, but simply went in one side and out the other. The handicap of the eight-second fuse was kept secret by the British, and the Argentines did not really realize what was wrong, or correct it, until the very last day of the fighting. The following day, D + 3 (24 May), the Argentines admitted losing fifteen aircraft, but the British claimed to have brought down twenty-two, most being intercepted by Sea Harriers. That day the first Argentine plane was brought down by a British-fired Blowpipe.

Contrary to general expectations the slower Sea Harriers were beating the faster Mirages in dogfights, partly because the Mirages remained subsonic to conserve fuel (to be supersonic would double fuel consumption) and partly because the Sea Harriers were highly maneuverable and equipped with the very effective Sidewinder missiles.

Meanwhile on the ground there was still no counterattack or contact with the defenders at all. Trafficability was poor by any standards, but the Scorpions and Scimitars pushed forward on reconnaissance missions along the tracks eastwards and southwards. Their performance was considered one of the real success stories of the campaign.

Argentine National Day was 25 May (D + 4). The British expected heavy air attacks, and they were not disappointed, as over forty waves were launched against the San Carlos area. A Sea Harrier made its first "double-kill." In the morning Skyhawks attacked HMS *Coventry* inside the Sound. The destroyer brought down one plane with its Sea Dart missiles, but was in turn hit by four bombs. It sank with the loss of twenty-four men. Outside the Sound the Super Entendards made their first appearance since 4 May, and located the *Atlantic Conveyor*, a huge container cargo ship with a flat deck, which they sunk with an Exocet missile, nine men being lost. Three Chinook helicopters, nine hundred tents, and tons of other supplies went down with that ship. Controversy remains as to whether the Argentines mistook the *Atlan-*

tic Conveyor for the carrier *Hermes* which was nearby.

A few Argentine air attacks were made on the task force the following day, 26 May, but they were tailing off as the momentum had gone from their offensive. By this time Rapiers and Blowpipes, as well as naval missiles were taking their toll of aircraft, and the Argentines were feeling the loss of so many of their best pilots.

The buildup of the bridgehead was complete; the whole brigade was ashore, together with some 32,000 tons of ammunition and supplies. Although there was still no land contact with the defenders, nor any sign of the anticipated counterattack, the land force commander, Brigadier Julian Thompson, a marine officer, concentrated upon aggressive patrolling and keeping the perimeter well defended. He was waiting for the arrival of a second brigade, due in a few days time of the requisitioned luxury liner *Queen Elizabeth II*, a Rapier squadron of the Royal Air Force Regiment from Germany, and another twenty Harriers, before advancing toward Port Stanley. This extra formation was the 5th Infantry Brigade, consisting basically of a battalion each of the Scots, Welsh, and Gurkhas.

The Advance to Port Stanley

The waiting ended, however, when Brigadier Thompson's orders were suddenly changed. The British government anticipated there might be a United Nations Resolution passed imposing a ceasefire, which would leave the British ground forces in a distinctly disadvantageous position many miles from Port Stanley. Accordingly, it ordered the force to move at once. A two-pronged advance began on 26 May (D + 5). The southern prong, led by paratroops with 42 Commando in support, carrying all their equipment, crossed over the Sussex mountains to reach Camilla Creek on a narrow isthmus on 27 May. The loss of the Chinooks was felt. The next day, the paratroops moved to attack and take Darwin and Goose Green, where they captured some fourteen hundred Argentine prisoners. Another two hundred fifty Argentines had been killed, and about the same number

wounded. A company of marines were helicopter-lifted to support the paratroops while this battle was in progress. On 30-31 May, 42 Commando took Mount Kent. The northern prong of the advance, led by 45 Commando with the objective of Douglas Settlement and the 3d Parachute Battalion with the objective of Teal Inlet, seized its objectives on 28 May.

When the 5th Infantry Brigade, commanded by Brigadier Tony Wilson, and the new landing force commander, Major General Jeremy Moore, arrived, it was decided that elements of the 5th Brigade would make a landing about 15 miles short of Port Stanley at Bluff Cover and Fitzroy on the coast. Some of these elements were attacked by Argentine aircraft while still on the assault ship. They lost fifty killed and fifty-seven wounded. To maintain the momentum of the advance, two companies of marines from 40 Commando were brought in by landing craft, to remain with that formation and to trek with it through the battles for the low hills overlooking the capital. The 45 Commando and other marine elements accompanied the other, eastern prong of the pincer movement, having to "Yomp," that is march with their full kit, which weighed some 120 pounds, and weapons, across bogland and rocky outcrop, some 70 miles to reach and fight for the heights overlooking Port Stanley.

On 11 June 42 Commando, 45 Commando, and 3d Parachute Battalion launched a brigade night attack which secured Mount Harriet, the Two Sisters, and Mount Longdon. On 13 June the Scots Guards took Mount Tumbledown; the 2d Parachute Battalion, Wireless Ridge; and the Gurkhas, Mount William. On the afternoon of 14 June (D + 24) the Argentine defenders cracked and laid down their arms. The British the following day rounded up more than nine thousand prisoners. The Royal Marines lost twenty-six men killed in all these actions.

The Balance Sheet

The claims and counterclaims are still subject to an impartial accountant's audit, but some general figures are of interest. The British admit to 256 killed and 673 wounded, and 1 POW, a Harrier pilot; also to losing 5 ships sunk and 12 damaged; and to losing 1 Sea Harrier, 1 Sea King helicopter, and 2 Gazelle helicopters to the enemy (although they admit to losing other aircraft in accidents or for reasons other than combat). They claim to have destroyed more than 100 Argentine aircraft, to have captured 11,090 prisoners, killed probably more than 1,000, and wounded another 1,000.

Argentine admissions are sparse and partial. One official statement was that only 82 (of some 223) combat aircraft had been prepared for operations, of which 34 had been shot down. Some 11 percent of these had been lost in attacking the San Carlos area; 55 pilots had also been lost. Brigadier General Dozo, the Air Force commander, admitted that "261 aircraft sorties had been forced to turn back because of the effectiveness of the air and sea blockade." The Argentines admit they had 1,798 dead and wounded, and that "3,300 men were unaccounted for," but no mention was made of those taken prisoner. The Argentine armed forces on the Falkland Islands were remarkably well equipped, and huge quantities of weapons and equipment were collected by the British and are still being cataloged.

Comments

The Falkland Islands campaign came right out of the blue to confound world strategists, who were immersed in the East-West conflict, with China as a peripheral issue, but blind to the rest of the world. It smacked of a British nineteenth-century war, and also of British nineteenth-century attitudes, surprising for a country that had shed an empire that once covered one-quarter of the earth's surface. The key to success was political will and determination.

On the military side it was a textbook operation, with a little luck thrown in, conducted with an 8,000-mile logistic line across the ocean. The amphibious landing at San Carlos was also of textbook quality and can hardly be faulted. It overturned the entrenched assumption that complete surprise can no longer be obtained in this age of sophisticated surveillance aids. In battle much always depends upon the quality of the troops involved, their training, morale, and motivation. The British contingent was an all-volunteer one, well-trained, and keen to prove its skills, which was something of a vindication for the school that advocates small regular armed forces instead of large conscript ones. The Argentine garrison was a mixture. About half were conscripts, ill-trained, ill-cared for, and poorly motivated; the other half were either regulars or technicians and NCOs on short-term engagements. The Argentine officer-to-enlisted man relationship left much to be desired. Lastly, mobility was the key to the land battle, as the British troops were mobile on their feet, across terrain the Argentines thought was impassable, carrying over 120 pounds of kit on their backs. On the other side, the Argentines seemed to be completely immobile except in withdrawal from outposts.

Selected Bibliography

Abbreviations

AN   *American Neptune*
AQDJ   *Army Quarterly and Defence Journal*
JRUSIDS   *Journal of the Royal United Services Institute for Defense Studies*
MA   *Military Affairs*
MCG   *Marine Corps Gazette*
NWCR   *Naval War College Review*
USNIP   *U.S. Naval Institute Proceedings*

General References on Amphibious Warfare

Alaez, Octavio. "Evolucion Organica de la Infanteria de Marina [Organic Evolution of the Marine Corps]" *Review General de Marina* 186 (March 1974): 307–24. History of the Spanish Marines.

Bivans, Harold A. *An Annotated Bibliography of Naval Gunfire Support*. Washington, D.C.: HQMC, 1971.

Cresswell, John. *Generals and Admirals: The Story of Amphibious Command*. London: Longmans, 1952.

Daly, Robert. "The Soviet Naval Infantry." Paper delivered to the Marine Corps Command and Staff College, Quantico, VA in the 1970s; copy on file in Nimitz Library, U.S. Naval Academy, Annapolis, MD.

Dollen, Charles. *Bibliography of the United States Marine Corps*. New York: Scarecrow, 1963.

Duran Ros, Manuel M. "Prologo A Un Librio No Escrito [Prologue to an Unwritten Book]" *Review General de Marina* 194 (June 1978): 691–96. History of the Spanish Marines.

Isley, Jeter A., and Crowl, Philip A. *The U.S. Marines and Amphibious War*. Princeton: Princeton University Press, 1951; reprint ed., Quantico, VA: Marine Corps Association, 1979.

Lloyd, Christopher. *Atlas of Maritime History*. New York: Arco, 1975.

Merglen, Albert. *Surprise Warfare*. Tr. Kenneth Morgan. London: Allen and Unwin, 1969.

Millet, Allan R. *Semper Fidelis: the History of the United States Marine Corps*. New York and London: Macmillan, 1982.

Moran, John B. *Creating a Legend: The Complete Record of Writing about the United States Marine Corps*. Chicago: Moran/Andrews, 1973.

Moskin, J. Robert. *The U.S. Marine Corps Story*. New York: McGraw-Hill 1977.

Moulton, J. L. "The Marine as an Instrument of Sea Power." *USNIP* 101 (November 1975): 28–36.

————. *The Royal Marines*. London: Leo Cooper, 1972.

Reber, J. J. "The Evolution of Amphibious Communications." *MCG* 40 (9 November 1956): 38–43.

Reinhardt, G. C. "Who Said Impossible?" *MCG* 39 (January 1955): 1–16.

Richmond, Herbert W. *Amphibious Warfare in British History*. Exeter [England]: A. Wheaton, 1941.

Russell, William H. *Bibliography of Amphibious Warfare as Developed by [the] U.S. Marine Corps*. Microfilm reel no. 2, Gallipoli studies, Marine Corps Development and Education Command, Quantico, VA.

Schreier, Konrad F., Jr. "Whaleboats to Amtracs." *MCG* 53 (February 1969): 31–36.

Showalter, Dennis E. "Evolution of the U.S. Marine Corps as a Military Elite." *MCG* 63 (November 1979): 54–58.

Simmons, Edwin H. "The Marines: Survival and Accommodation." Paper presented to the George C. Marshall Foundation Conference. Lexington, VA, 25–26 March 1977.

————. *The United States Marines*. New York: Viking, 1976.

Vagts, Alfred. *Landing Operations.* Harrisburg, PA: Military Service Publishing, 1946.

Whitehouse, Arch. *Amphibious Operations.* Garden City, NY: Doubleday, 1963.

"Les Troupes de Marine de L'Origine au Lendemain de la Guerre de 1870–1871 [The Marines from their Origin to the Morrow of the War of 1870–71]" *Review Historique de l'Academy des Sciences d'Outre-mer* 26 (1970): 14–23.

Amphibious Warfare in the Age of Sail

Bellico, Russell. "The Great Penobscot Blunder." *American History Illustrated* 13 (December 1978): 4–9, 44–48.

Brown, Wilburt S. *The Amphibious Campaign for West Florida and Louisiana, 1814–1815.* University, AL: University of Alabama Press, 1969.

Cahill, Richard A. "The Significance of Aboukir Bay." *USNIP* (July 1967): 79–89.

Colby, Chester M. "The United States Marine in the Penobscot Bay Expedition." *MCG* 3 (December 1918): 281–92.

Cormack, J. N. "Anglo-Russian Combined Operations—An Attempt That Failed." *AQDJ* 105 (July 1975): 284–89.

Daly, Robert W. "Burnside's Amphibious Division." *MCG* 35 (December 1951): 30–38.

Donaldson, Gordon. *Battle for a Continent: Quebec, 1759.* Garden City, NY: Doubleday, 1973.

Duffy, Michael. "A Particular Service: The British Government and the Dunkirk Expedition of 1793." *English Historical Review* 91 (July 1976): 529–54.

Ingram, Edward. "A Scare of Seaborne Invasion: The Royal Navy at the Strait of Hormuz, 1807–1808." *MA* 46 (April 1982): 64–68.

King, Joseph E. "The Fort Fisher Compaigns, 1864–65." *USNIP* 77 (August 1951): 842–55.

Lawson, Don. *The Colonial Wars: Prelude to the American Revolution, 1689–1763.* New York: Abelard-Schuman, 1972.

Long, David A. "A Case for Intervention: Armstrong Foote and the Destruction of the Barrier Forts, Canton, China, 1856." In Craig L. Symonds, ed. *New Aspects of Naval History* (Annapolis: Naval Institute Press, 1981), pp. 220–37.

Luvaas, Jay. "The Fall of Fort Fisher." *Civil War Times Illustrated* 3 (August 1964): 31–35, 59.

Mackesy, Piers. "Problems of an Amphibious Power: Britain against France, 1793–1815." *NWCR* 30 (Spring 1978): 16–25.

Marder, Arthur J. "From Jimmu to Perry: Sea Power in Early Japanese History." *American Historical Review* 51 (October 1945): 1–34.

Marini, Alfred J. "Parliament and the Marine Regiments, 1739." *Mariner's Mirror* 62 (February 1976): 55–65.

McCawley, Charles L. "The Guantanamo Campaign of 1898." *MCG* 5 (September 1916): 221–42.

McClellan, Edwin N. "The Capture of Fort Fisher." *MCG* 5 (March 1920): 59–80.

McCormack, J. N. "Anglo-Russian Combined Operations—an Attempt that Failed." *AQDJ* 105 (July 1975): 284–89.

Montross, Lynn. "Amphibious Doubleheader." *MCG* 42 (April 1958): 36–44.

Nielson, Jon M. "Penobscot: From the Jaws of Victory: Our Navy's Worst Defeat." *AN* 37 (October 1977): 288–305.

Nihart, Brooke. "Our Pre-Colonial Experience." *MCG* 60 (July 1976): 29–34.

Polk, John Fleming. "Vera Cruz, 1847: A Lesson in Command." *MCG* 63 (September 1979): 61–66.

Ruge, Frederich. "Beachhead 1715." *USNIP* 92 (December 1966): 50–57.

Ryan, Brendan P. "Aboukir Bay, 1801." *MCG* 63 (July 1979): 47–51.

Smith, Charles R. *Marines in the American Revolution, 1775–1783.* Washington, D.C.: GPO, 1975.

Smith, Cornelius C., Jr. "Our First Amphibious Assault." *Military Review* 38 (February 1959): 18–28.

Sweetman, John. "Grim War Does Summon Me Hence: British Forces Invade the Crimea, September 1854." *AQDJ* 93 (October 1966): 99–110.

Symonds, Craig L. "The American Naval Expedition to Penobscot, 1779." *NWCR* 24 (April 1972): 64–71.

Syrett, David. "The Methodology of British Amphibious Operations during the Seven Years and American Wars." *Mariner's Mirror* 58 (August 1972): 269–80.

Amphibious Warfare in the Age of Mahan

Agnew, James B. "From Where Did Our Amphibious Doctrine Come?" *MCG* 63 (August 1979): 52–59.

Austin, Sir George Grey. *Letters on Amphibious Wars.* London: Murray, 1910.

Bald, Detlef. "Der Einsatz Der Marine Im Ostafrikanischen Austand 1905/06" [German Marines in the East African Insurrection of 1905/06]. *Marine Rundschau* 74 (January 1977): 21–24.

Bauer, K. Jack. "The Korean Expedition of 1871." *USNIP* 74 (February 1948): 197–203.

Baum, L. I. "Voennye Moriaki Latvii V Boiakh Za Vlast' Sovetov Na Daugave I Dnepre V 1919–1920 Godakh" [Latvian Marines in the Struggle for Soviet Power on the Western Dvina and Dnieper Rivers, 1919–20. *Latvijas PSR Zinatnu Akademijas Vestis* (1978): 38–51.

Bean, Charles E. *Gallipoli Mission.* Canberra, Australia: Australian War Memorial, 1948.

Bush, Eric W. *Gallipoli.* London: Allen and Unwin, 1975; New York: St. Martin's Press, 1975.

Cosmas, Graham A., and Shulimson, Jack. "The Culebra Maneuver and the Formation of the U.S Marine Corps' Advance Base Force, 1913–1914." Robert W. Love, Jr., ed. *Changing Interpretations and New Sources in Naval History* (New York and London: Garland Publishing, 1980), pp. 293–308.

Faust, Karl I., and Miller, Martin, Jr. "The Army's Navy." *By Valor and Arms* 2 (no. 4, 1976): 4–24.

Gibson, T. A. "Eyeless in Byzantium: The Tragedy of Ian Hamilton." *AQDJ* 91 (October 1965): 82–96.

Gillum, Donald E. "Gallipoli: Its Influence on Amphibious Doctrine." *MCG* (November 1967).

Hamilton, Sir Ian. *Gallipoli Diary.* London: Arnold, 1920; New York: Doran, 1920.

James, Robert R. *Gallipoli.* New York: Macmillan, 1965.

Kelly, Francis J. "Advance Base Problems." *MCG* 51 (November 1967): 47–49.

Keyes, Roger J. B. *Amphibious Warfare and Combined Operations.* New York: Macmillan, 1943.

Mackenzie, Compton. *Gallipoli Memories.* London: Cassell, 1929; Garden City, NY: Doran, 1930.

Miller, John G. "William Freeland Fullam's War with the Corps." *USNIP* 101 (November 1975): 37–45.

Montross, Lynn. "The Mystery of Pete Ellis." *MCG* 33 (July 1954): 30–33.

Morefield, John. *Gallipoli.* New York: Macmillan, 1916, 1925.

Mullen, John. "Zeebrugge—1918." *An Cosantoir* (June 1969): 184–85.

O'Connor, Raymond G. "The U.S. Marines in the 20th Century: Amphibious Warfare and Doctrinal Debates." *MA* 38 (September 1974): 97–103.

Painter, Dean E. "The Army and Amphibious Warfare." *Military Review* (August 1965): 36–40.

Reber, John J. "Huntington's Battalion Was the Forerunner of Today's FMF." *MCG* 63 (November 1979): 73–78.

Shulimson, Jack. "U.S. Marines in Panama, 1885." Paper presented at the Annual Meeting of the American Military Institute, April 1980, Washington, D.C.

Stokesbury, James L. *British Concepts and Practices of Amphibious Warfare, 1867–1916.* Durham, NC: Duke University Press, 1968.

Sweetman, Jack. *The Landing at Vera Cruz: 1914.* Annapolis, Naval Institute Press, 1968.

Tentative Manual of Landing Operations. Quantico, VA: Marine Corps Schools, 1934.

Wallach, Richard. "The War in the East." *USNIP* (September 1895): 692–740.

Wallin, Jeffrey D. *By Ships Alone: Churchill and the Dardanelles.* Durham, NC: Carolina Academic Press, 1981.

Amphibious Warfare in a Two-Ocean War

Ambrose, Stephen E. "Eisenhower's Greatest Decision." *American History Illustrated* 4 (May 1969): 4–11.

Ansel, Walter C. "Naval Gunfire in Support of a Landing." *MCG* 17 (May 1932): 23–26.

Assmann, K. "The Invasion of Norway." *Military Review* 32 (February 1953): 92–106.

Atschkassow, W. I. "Landing Operations of the Soviet Fleet during World War Two." *Militargeschichte* 16 (1977): 297–306.

Baldwin, Hanson W. "Amphibious Aspects of the Normandy Invasion." *MCG* 28 (December 1944): 34–40.

Balev, B. "The Soviet Landing at Novarossiisk, 1943." *Soviet Military Review* (July 1972): 40–42.

Ballendorf, Dirk A. "The Micronesian Ellis Mystery." *Guam Recorder* 5 (1975): 35–48.

Barclay, C. N. "Amphibious Assault on South Beveland, 1944." *MCG* 48 (March 1964): 20–24.

Bartley, Whitman S. *Iwo Jima: Amphibious Epic.* (Washington, D.C.: GPO, 1954).

Belous, N. "Example of Amphibious Preassault and Landing Operations." *Voyenno-Istoricheskiy Zhurnal* 20 (September 1978): 32–38.

Berenger, R. "Le Combat Naval De Koh-Chang, 17 Janvier 1941 [The Naval Battle of Koh-Chang, 17 January 1941]" *Ecrits de Paris* (1977): 72–79 no. 367.

Blumenson, Martin. *Anzio: The Gamble That Failed*. Philadelphia: Lippincott, 1963.

Bowser, Alpha L., Jr. "End Run in the Solomons." *MCG* 31 (November 1947): 24–32.

Broadbent, Ernest W. "The Fleet and the Marines." *USNIP* 57 (March 1931): 369–72.

Brown, John M. *The All Hands: An Amphibious Venture*. New York: McGraw-Hill, 1943.

Brown, Richard G. "Tarawa—Lest We Forget." *MCG* 64 (November 1980): 46–50.

Burton, Earl. *By Sea and By Land: The Story of Our Amphibious Forces*. New York: Whittlesey House, 1944.

Campbell, John P. "Marines, Aviators, and the Battleship Mentality, 1923–33." *JRUSIDS* 109 (February-November 1964): 45–50.

Coggins, Jack. *The Campaign for Guadalcanal*. Garden City, NY: Doubleday, 1972.

Cresswell, John. "Amphibious Commands in the Pacific, 1942–45." In John Cresswell, *Generals and Admirals: The Story of Amphibious Command*. London: Longmans, Green, 1952.

Crowl, Philip A. *Campaign in the Marianas*. Washington, D.C.: Center for Military History, 1960.

Crowl, Philip A., and Love, Edmund G. *Seizure of the Gilberts and Marshalls*. Washington, D.C.: Center for Military History, 1955.

Daly, H. "The Invasion of Crete, May 1941." *An Cosantoir* (February 1964): 184–85.

Davis, Frank. "Sealowe: The German Plan to Invade Britain, 1940." *Strategy and Tactics* 40 (1973): 20–33.

Dyer, George C. *The Amphibians Came to Conquer: The Story of Admiral Richmond Kelly Turner*, 2 vols. Washington, D.C.: GPO, 1971.

———. "Naval Amphibious Landmarks." *USNIP* 92 (August 1966): 51–60.

Evstigneev, E. "Na Novorossiiskom [On Course to Novorossiisk]" *Voenno-Istoricheskiy Zhurnal* 20 (1978): 120–25.

Falk, Stanley L. *Bloodiest Victory: Palaus*. New York: Ballantine, 1974.

Godson, Susan H. *Viking of Assault: Admiral John Leslie Hall, Jr., and Amphibious Warfare*. Washington, D.C.: University Press of America, 1982.

Hart, Thomas C. "Amphibious War Against Japan." *USNIP* 69 (February 1943): 267–72.

Heinl, Robert D., Jr. "D-Day, Roi-Namur." *MA* 12 (Fall 1948): 129–43.

———. "Naval Gunfire: Scourge of the Beaches." *USNIP* 71 (November 1945): 40–43.

———. "Target: Iwo." *USNIP* 89 (July 1963): 70–82.

———. "The U.S. Marine Corps: Author of Modern Amphibious War." *USNIP* 73 (November 1947): 1310–23.

Henderson, F. P. "NGF [Naval Gunfire] Support in the Solomons." *MCG* 30 (March 1956): 36–40 and (December 1956): 46–51.

Henri, Raymond. *Iwo Jima: Springboard to Final Victory*. New York: U.S. Camera, 1945.

Hewitt, Henry K. "Naval Aspects of the Sicilian Campaign: U.S. Naval Operations in the Northwestern African-Mediterranean Theater, March-August 1943." *USNIP* 79 (July 1953): 704–23.

History of Marine Corps Operations in World War Two. 5 vols. Washington, D.C.: GPO, 1958–68.

Hoffman, Carl W. *Saipan: The Beginning of the End*. Washington, D.C.: HQMC, 1950.

———. *The Seizure of Tinian*. Washington, D.C.: HQMC, 1951.

Hough, Frank O. *The Assault on Peleliu*. Washington, D.C.: HQMC, 1950.

———. *The Island War: The United States Marine Corps in the Pacific*. Philadelphia: Lippincott, 1947.

Hough, Frank O., and Crown, John A. *The Campaign on New Britain*. Washington, D.C.: HQMC, 1952.

Isby, David C. "Island War: The U.S. Amphibious Offensive against Imperial Japan, 1942 to 1945." *Strategy and Tactics* (September/October 1975): 21–36.

Isely, Jeter A. "Iwo Jima: Acme of Amphibious Assault." *USNIP* 77 (January 1951): 1–14.

Ivanov, S. "Crimean Landings." *Soviet Military Review* (November 1973): 57–59.

Ladd, J. D. *Assault from the Sea, 1939–45*. New York: Hippocrene Books, 1976.

Leckie, Robert. *Challenge for the Pacific: Guadalcanal, the Turning Point of the War*. Garden City, NY: Doubleday, 1965.

Lehman, Hans G. "Die Technik Japanische Landungsoperationen Im Zweiten Weltkrieg [Technique of Japanese Landing Operations during World War Two]" *Marine Rundschau* 68 (September 1971): 527–39.

Lodge, Orlan R. *The Recapture of Guam*. Washington, D.C.: HQMC, 1954.

Lowry, F. J. "The Naval Side of the Anzio Campaign." *USNIP* 80 (January 1954): 23–51.

Marshall, Samuel L. A. *Island Victory: The Battle of Kwajalein Atoll*. Washington, D.C.: Infantry Journal, 1944.

Maund, L. E. H. *Assault from the Sea.* London: Methuen, 1949.

McKiernan, Patrick. "Tarawa: The Tide That Failed." *USNIP* 88 (February 1962): 38–50.

McMillan, Ira E. "The Development of Naval Gunfire Support of Amphibious Operations." *USNIP* 74 (January 1948): 1–15.

Mennel, Rainer. "Die Geographischen Bedingungen Des Amphibienkrieges in Italien 1943–1945 [Geographical Conditions for Amphibious Warfare in Italy, 1943–1945]" *Marine Rundschau* 72 (April 1975): 211–23.

Merglen, Colonel. "Anzio 22–30 Janvier, 1944." *Revue Historique de l'Armee* 21 (February 1965): 83–88.

Miller, John, Jr. *Guadalcanal, the First Offensive—United States Army in World War II—the War in the Pacific.* Washington, D.C.: Center for Military History, 1949.

Morehouse, Clifford P. *The Iwo Jima Operation.* Washington, D.C.: HQMC, 1946.

Morton, Louis. "The Marianas." *Military Review* 47 (July 1967): 71–82.

Newcomb, Richard. *Iwo Jima.* New York: Holt, Rinehart and Winston, 1965.

Ramsey, Logan C. "The Aero-Amphibious Phase of the Present War." *USNIP* 69 (May 1943): 695–701.

Reber, John J. "Pete Ellis: Amphibious Warfare Prophet." *USNIP* 103 (November 1977): 53–64.

Rentz, John N. *Battle for Tarawa.* Washington, D.C.: HQMC, 1947.

Rothenberg, Gunther E. "From Gallipoli to Guadalcanal: The Development of U.S. Marine Corps Amphibious Assault Doctrine, 1915–1942." Paper presented at the Second International Colloquy on Military History, 12–15 August 1973, Stockholm, Sweden.

Schreiner, Charles W., Jr. "The Dieppe Raid—Its Origins, Aims, and Results." *NWCR* 25 (May-June 1973): 83–97.

Sendall, W. R. "The Sea Flank Was Open: Lost Opportunities of Amphibious Warfare." *Military Review* 32 (March 1953).

Sherrod, Robert. *On the Westward: War in the Central Pacific.* New York: Duell, Sloan, and Pearce, 1945.

———. *Tarawa.* Fredericksburg, TX: Admiral Nimitz Foundation, 1973.

Simmons, Edwin H. "The United States Marine Corps, 1941–1943." *MCG* 58 (August 1974): 39–46.

Sledge, Eugene B. "Peleliu: A Neglected Battle." *MCG* 63 (November 1979): 88–95.

Smith, Holland M. "Iwo Jima Cost Too Much." *Saturday Evening Post* 231 (20 November 1948): 32–33.

———. "Tarawa Was a Mistake." *Saturday Evening Post* 231 (6 November 1948): 15–17.

Smith, Julian C. "Tarawa." *USNIP* 79 (November 1953): 163–73.

Stewart, Raymond A. "Assault on Timor." *MCG* 58 (September 1974): 24–30.

Stockman, James R. *The Battle for Tarawa.* Washington, D.C.: HQMC, 1947.

Sufrin, Mark. "The Story of Earl Ellis." *Mankind* 2 (1970): 70–76.

Vasil'yev, V. "Defeat of the German Amphibious Landing at Hogland (Suusaari) Island in September 1944." *Voyenno-Istoricheskiy Zhurnal* (December 1978): 88–91.

Wagner, David H. "The Destiny of Pete Ellis." *MCG* 60 (June 1976): 50–55.

Weller, Donald M. "Salvo Splash! The Development of Naval Gunfire Support in World War Two." *USNIP* 80 (August 1954): 839–49 and (September 1954): 1011–21.

Willoughby, Malcolm F. "The Beach Pounders." *USNIP* 83 (August 1957): 818–27.

Amphibious Warfare in the Era of the Superpowers

Alexander, Joseph H. "An Amphibious Operation in Viet-Nam." *MCG* 50 (January 1966): 37–40.

———. "Amphibious Warfare: What Sort of Future?" *USNIP* 108 (February 1982): 62–68.

Asprey, Robert B. "New Fleet Marine Force." *USNIP* 85 (August 1959): 41–48.

Baker, John W., and Dickson, Lee C. "Army Forces in Riverine Operations." *Military Review* (August 1967): 64–74.

Bodron, Margaret. "U.S. Intervention in Lebanon—1958." *Military Review* 56 (February 1976): 66–76.

Brunsvold, K. T. "What the Future Holds for Assault Amphibians." *MCG* 64 (March 1980): 59–63.

Canzona, Nicholas A. "Is Amphibious Warfare Dead?" *USNIP* 81 (September 1955): 986–91.

Croizat, Victor J. "The Marines' Amphibian." *MCG* 37 (June 1953): 40–49.

Crossland, Roger L. "Rusty Hand of Steel: the

Naval Raid." *USNIP* 105 (December 1975): 60–66.

Gapp, Frank W. "The 'Capture' of Monterey in 1842." *USNIP* 105 (March 1979): 46–54.

Grace, J. J. "Land the Landing Force Where It Will Do the Most Good: A New Look at an Old Mission." *USNIP* 107 (November 1981): 114–31.

Heinl, Robert D., Jr. "The Nucleus for Victory at High Tide." *MCG* 51 (September 1967): 20–28 and (October 1967): 45–50.

Hittle, James D. "20th Century Amphibious Warfare." *MCG* 38 (January 1954): 14–21.

Hull, Andrew W. "Soviet Naval Infantry." *MCG* 64 (July 1980): 65–70.

Krulak, William M. "The U.S. Marine Corps: Strategy for the Future." *USNIP* 106 (May 1980): 94–105.

Johnson, J. M., Jr.; Austin, R. W.; and Quinlan, D. A. "Individual Heroism Overcame Awkward Command Relationships, Confusion and Bad Information Off the Cambodian Coast." *MCG* 61 (October 1977): 24–34.

Meyer, Richard M. "The Ground-Sea Team in River Warfare." *Military Review* 46 (September 1966): 54–61.

Miller, E. H., and Roule, W. D., Jr. "Amphibious Forces: The Turning Point." *USNIP* 100 (November 1974): 26–32.

Miller, John G. "Amphibious Warfare: The Decade of Decision." *USNIP* 107 (September 1981): 74–79.

Nargele, Dominik G. "Their Naval Infantry." *USNIP* 108 (October 1982): 152–59.

Norris, John S. "A New Strategy for NATO's Northern Flank." *Sea Power* 15 (November 1979): 12–17.

Pritchard, Charles G. "The Soviet Marines." *USNIP* 98 (March 1972): 19–30.

O'Ballance, Edgar. "The San Carlos Landing." *MCG* 52 (October 1982): 36–45.

Salzer, Robert S. "The U.S. Navy's Clouded Amphibious Mission." *USNIP* 104 (February 1978): 24–33.

Tomolinson, H. Pat. "Inchon: The General's Decision." *Military Review* (April 1967).

Townsend, Patrick L. "Vertical Assault: The Proof Is in the Doing." *USNIP* 103 (November 1977): 117–19.

Vannoy, F. W. "Where Do the Gators Go From Here?" *USNIP* 104 (March 1978): 88–95.

Wade, S. S. "Operation Bluebat." *MCG* 43 (July 1959): 10–23.

Index